Sociology Canada: Readings

Second Edition

Edited by *Christopher Beattie* and *Stewart Crysdale*

Butterworth and Co. (Canada) Ltd.
Toronto, Ontario

To John Porter
whose research on Canada
has helped to give
Canadian Sociology
a new beginning

Christopher Beattie
Associate Professor of Sociology
Atkinson College
York University
Toronto

Stewart Crysdale
Professor of Sociology
Atkinson College
York University
Toronto

Canada:
Butterworth & Co. (Canada) Ltd.
2265 Midland Avenue
Scarborough, Ont.
M1P 4S1

England:
Butterworth & Co. (Publishers) Ltd.
88 Kingsway
London, WC 2B 6AB

Australia:
Butterworth (Pty.) Ltd.
586 Pacific Highway
Chatsworth, N. & W. 2067
Australia

New Zealand:
Butterworths of New Zealand Ltd.
Law Society Building
26-28 Waring Taylor Street
Wellington 1, New Zealand

South Africa:
Butterworth & Co. (S.A.) (Pty.) Ltd.
152-154 Gale Street
Durban, Natal
South Africa

List of Contributors

Christopher Beattie	York University
John W. Bennett	Washington University
Reginald W. Bibby	University of Lethbridge
Raymond Breton	University of Toronto
Peter D. Chimbos	Mount St. Vincent University
Donald H. Clairmont	Dalhousie University
Stewart Crysdale	York University
James Curtis	University of Waterloo
Leo Davids	York University
Jacques Dofny	Université de Montréal
Frederick Elkin	York University
Frederick C. Engelmann	University of Chicago
Muriel Garon-Audy	Université de Montréal
Linda Grayson	University of Toronto
Paul Grayson	York University
Lee A. Guemple	University of Western Ontario
Hubert Guindon	Concordia University
Gad Horowitz	University of Toronto
John A. Hostetler	Temple University
Gertrude Enders Huntington	University of Michigan
Alan J.C. King	Queen's University
Seena Kohl	Washington University
Ronald D. Lambert	University of Waterloo
N.H. Lithwick	Carleton University
Isaiah A. Litvak	Carleton University
Rex. A. Lucas	University of Toronto
Dennis W. Magill	University of Toronto
W. E. Mann	York University

Patricia Marchak	University of British Columbia
Ralph Matthews	McMaster University
Christopher J. Maule	Carleton University
Craig D. McKie	University of Western Ontario
Donald L. Mills	University of Calgary
Colette Moreux	Université de Montréal
Judith Nagata	York University
Richard J. Ossenberg	University of Calgary
John Porter	Carleton University
Reginald A. Ripton	McMaster University
Pierre Roberge	York University
Guy Rocher	Université de Montréal
Edward and Jean H. Rogers	National Museum of Canada
Irving Rootman	University of Calgary
Abraham Rotstein	University of Toronto
Mildred A. Schwartz	University of Chicago
Robert Sévigny	Université de Montréal
Norman Shulman	McMaster University
Judy Torrance	York University
Tom Truman	McMaster University
Don Whiteside	National Indian Brotherhood of Canada
S.F. Wise	Carleton University

PART I

OVERVIEW OF CANADIAN SOCIETY

INTRODUCTION

The central unit of analysis in Part I is Canadian society as a whole. A number of scholars have noted that for the most part social scientists in this country have tended to focus on parts of the social system rather than on the whole (Vallee and Whyte 1968; Rocher 1970; Crysdale and Beattie 1977). But in order to comprehend the parts one must grasp also the overall context in which the parts have emerged. The articles in Part I treat major dimensions of Canadian society at a general or global level. They present the structural and cultural background of the vital themes that together account largely for the mounting Canadian consciousness – the widespread awareness of and commitment to the unique qualities of this society and its way of life.

John Porter discusses the ethnic composition of Canada. It is a familiar observation that Canada is a mosaic of ethnic groups rather than a melting-pot, but in this recent work Porter observes that each ethnic group tends to become concentrated at a certain level in the class system so that the current emphasis by the federal government and minority groups on multiculturalism and on strengthening ethnic cultures may lead to the perpetuation of economic differences between groups. Porter uses the sociological concept of social stratification, *the patterned inequality of positions in social systems in terms of possessions, prestige, privileges, and power, to show how ethnic groups become part of the national stratification system.*

Hubert Guindon pursues a theme similar to Porter's in examining relations between French and English, the two major ethno-cultural groups in Canada. Guindon notes how economic inequalities between the French and English in Quebec became an acute source of tension as the French went through the Quiet Revolution that modernized the educational, health, and welfare facilities of the province.

If French-English relations are the dominant conditioning factor in Canadian life, next would come Canadian-American relations. Although every aspect of Canadian society has been influenced by its great neighbour, in recent years it has been the effects on the economy which have provoked the most attention. The political economist Abraham Rotstein has been critical of the continentalism of recent Canadian policies, which have encouraged the American take-over of business and industry. In this article Rotstein argues that in recent years the American presence has promoted Canadian nationalism.

The remaining articles in Part I stress the way in which Canadian society differs fundamentally from the United States. Similarities are obvious and many social scientists think of differences in terms of degree. Tom Truman believes that there are important aspects of Canadian society and culture that differ in kind. He shows that the work of S.M. Lipset in comparing Canada, the United States, Australia and the United Kingdom is open to challenge on empirical as well as theoretical grounds. Truman produces evidence that in some respects Canada is more equalitarian than the United States and the other English-speaking democracies. Lipset's view that Canada is counter-revolutionary and elitist may have been true of the nineteenth and early twentieth centuries but since the Second World War she has taken giant strides towards equalitarianism and more open, democratic institutions.

Similarly, Gad Horowitz shows that the existence of a strong socialist party in Canada in contrast to the United States reveals basic differences in structures and values. The historical and cultural roots of each country are distinctive. The tendency of Liberalism in Canada to take a centrist position follows the European rather than American model and the resultant emergence of a pragmatic form of socialism discloses collectivist values which are widely legitimated and therefore dynamic.

The historian S.F. Wise also argues against the Hartz thesis that Canada, like the United States, is characterized by cultural fragments from its European sources which have hardened into relatively static forms. These are said to be French-Canadian feudalism and English-Canadian conservatism, in contrast to American democratic liberalism. This theory fails to take into account the interplay of diverse elements and events. Canadian complexity, Wise maintains, derives from local, regional, ethnic, and other variations as well as from the continued dialectic between muted conservatism and ambivalent liberalism.

Together these articles point to attributes of the emerging Canadian nationalism which amount to more than a negation of American republicanism and imperalism. Rather, the new nationalism encourages not uniformity but diversity in culture, language, religion, and ideology. This is the distinctive foundation upon which a many-sided Canadian entity is being built.

1

Ethnic Pluralism in Canadian Perspective*

John Porter

Canada, like the United States and many other societies around the world, has been experiencing a revival of ethnicity. The reasons for this world phenomenon are many and complex. In part it can be traced to the post-World War II decolonization which was so often bitterly fought over, as in Algeria, for example, where a heightened consciousness of racial and ethnic differences, beyond the visibility of color, was a part of the demand for independence and self-determination. In eastern Europe, socialist societies were allegedly suppressing the national cultures that lay within their borders, a situation which émigrés sought to counteract by enlisting their fellow countrymen and sometimes the descendants of previous generations in a national movement in exile. The escalation of the Vietnam war was interpreted in many parts of the world as the United States taking over from the retreating European powers the role of white domination through force in the affairs of the world.

In the United States a highly visible deprived minority was not sharing in the affluence that the society was supposed to have produced. In Canada, similarly, the French had been denied much of the opportunity and had carried a good deal of the cost in less education and lower paid jobs – lower, that is, than some immigrant groups that were coming in near the bottom – of Canada's take-off as an industrial society. The demand by some intellectuals in French Canada that something be done about this inequality led to the establishment in 1963 of the Royal Commission on Bilingualism and Biculturalism.

Canada was caught up in a global movement and although all the examples of the world-wide revival of ethnicity can best be understood within their own local and historical contexts, they have, through modern communications and common intellectual leadership, become mutually supportive. Fanon becomes widely read in Quebec and Wounded Knee takes on symbolic significance far beyond South Dakota.

One feature of this ethnic revival common to the two modern societies of North America is, then, the depressed status of a large minority group, but there are three important respects in which the Canadian situation differs from that in the United States. In Canada the deprived ethnic group that is large enough to have a political impact is white and hence ethnicity does not have the wide visibility that it has across the border. However, there is the barrier of language which can operate as effectively as color differences to reduce friendly interaction between groups. If people from two groups cannot communicate, as is the case in Canada where the

---

* Used in abridged form by permission of the author and publisher, from Daniel P. Moynihan and Nathan Glazer, eds. *Ethnicity.* Cambridge, Mass.: Harvard University Press, 1975. Chapter 9.

French and English have been effectively out of communication with each other, then the language division is as real as that of color.

The long-standing hostility of so many of the English in Canada to learning French is analogous to the hostility toward blackness that has marked black-white relations. In both cases the psychological elements are deep-layered, all the more so because Anglophones in Canada, like whites in the United States, are the dominant majority in both numbers and power. Occasionally the psychological tensions of color may be invoked by referring to the French as "les nègres blancs d'Amérique."[1]

Such symbolism, however dramatic, is scarcely appropriate because of the second major difference between these two plural societies of North America. That difference is that some French Canadians have enjoyed high status and power in collaboration with English-speaking Canadians and foreign investors, largely United States corporations. Canada has had three French prime ministers and two French governors-general as titular head of state. Moreover, in Quebec the French have power. There has never been an English *premier ministre* of Quebec. This seeming contradiction between being a large deprived minority within Canada and having representatives in the structure of power can be explained in terms of the class structure of French Canada which until recently has been premodern, with a narrow band of classically educated elites and members of the learned professions at the top, and a mass of poorly educated at the bottom who increasingly left a rural way of life for the industrialized cities. It was an American and an "adopted" Canadian, E. C. Hughes, who first drew attention to this phenomenon in his *French Canada in Transition*, or as its French title says, *Rencontre de deux modes.*[2]

By and large the French elites of church and state have been prepared to collaborate in the federal state, although in doing so they have exacted a price which has given a particular shape to Canadian federalism and has generally served the interests of the class from which they came rather than the interests of Quebec society as a whole. The strongest of the intellectual critics will argue that the French elites of Quebec have aided its colonization by English-speaking Canadians and Americans.[3] Whether or not one agrees with such strictures there is little to be said against the notion, whatever the behaviour of their elites, that French Canadians within the global context of Canadian society, until recently, were an "ethnic class" of deprived status.[4]

The third and perhaps the most important difference between Canada and the United States in the sphere of ethnicity is that French Canadians, concentrated as they are in Quebec where about 80 percent of them live, have territory or a homeland which was conquered, a historical and immensely symbolic fact which makes some sense and gives an impetus to a separatist movement for an eventual French-speaking state of Quebec as the visionary solution to the deprived status that the French as an ethnic class have experienced. It should be remembered also that the French are a large minority within Canadian society, comprising about three tenths of the population, a demographic fact that makes such a solution as the "equal partnership" recommendations by the Royal Commission on Bilingualism and Biculturalism a possible resolution of the current tensions. But the same demographic fact of numbers combined with the concentration in a "homeland" makes the separatist solution also possible.

French-English Relations: an Assessment

The wide-ranging examination from 1963 to 1968 of French-English relations by the Bilingualism Commission took place over the same period as official and unofficial inquiries were being made in the United States on the condition of non-white minorities and of increasing violence in interethnic relations. Even though in Canada violence has been minimal, the Royal Commission found the future of the society itself in question and suggested that with or without violence, Canada had a far greater problem in the solution of its interethnic tensions than had any other modern society.

In a preliminary report in 1965 the commission had said, "Canada, without being conscious of the fact, is passing through the greatest crisis in its history."[5] This view was reiterated in the first of several volumes of its *Report.* Canada was facing a national crisis, a time when, the commission said, "Decisions must be taken and developments must occur leading either to its break-up, or a new set of conditions for its future existence."[6] For all the violence in the United States, or to take another modern society, for all the suppression in South Africa, it is doubtful that similar commissions would come to such gloomy conclusions about the future of their societies.

It is not my intention exhaustively to review here the relations between the English and the French in Canada. They have involved varying degrees of hostility and cooperation since the English conquest of 1759 and have been the major preoccupation of Canadian history, politics, and sociological investigation for over two hundred years. With my rather optimistic observations about French-English relations since the Royal Commission's report and a brief discussion of Canada's non-English, non-French groups I intend rather to serve the more general purpose of critically examining the revival of ethnicity in modern societies.

In response to the recommendations of the Royal Commission for "equal partnership" and "institutional bilingualism," the federal government embarked on a series of policies to improve the position of the French and the French language in those agencies and institutions within its jurisdiction.[7] Bilingualism within the federal public service improved. The French became better represented than formerly within the higher levels of the bureaucracy. Ottawa began slowing taking on the aspect of a bilingual national capital.[8] Much money was spent on language training and grants were made to provincial governments to improve their provision of second language education. The federal government saw itself as constitutionally responsible for safeguarding the two official languages even though language, because it is the principal means of cultural expression, would normally be considered a provincial responsibility.

Since the Royal Commission's somber accounts it is becoming increasingly likely that an adaptive and flexible federal system can come about. Perhaps this is possible because on the matter of political and constitutional solutions concerning the French and Quebec within confederation, the Royal Commission literally gave up the ghost and failed to complete its job. The evolving Canadian federalism of the last few years is not without its problems for nation building, but neither is it confined to a rigid blueprint.

According to some Anglo-Canadians the concessions made to Quebec particularly in social welfare legislation appear to come close to providing a special status for that province. Somewhat the reverse has happened, however. As an outcome of ingenious diplomacy on the part of federal and provincial bureaucrats and politicians, all the other provinces are becoming more like Quebec, the final and ironic outcome of the insistence of the French that Quebec was not a province comme les autres. The lessening of federal power particularly in a wide range of social policy can be seen as a loss of the ability to establish national goals and as a process of decentralization.

Much of the change can be attributed to French political leaders and an intellectually strengthened provincial bureaucracy in Quebec who were determined to do something about the deprived status of the French. They were more conscious of the need for social and educational reforms than were earlier elites. Thus, as in the past, the French have continued to exercise great power in the shaping of Canadian federalism. Other provincial leaders and bureaucrats are enjoying the enhanced power that Quebec has won for the provinces as the federal government has become enfeebled in a wide range of important economic and social issues. The alternative of a special status for Quebec within the federal system is scarcely considered any more outside the context of complete separation. Special status is anathema to the present federal leadership under Mr. Pierre Trudeau, as indeed is separation.

The October 1973 provincial election in Quebec was an important test of the type of federalism that has been developing. The results indicate that a majority of those in Quebec favor *le fédéralisme rentable* combined with *la souveraineté culturelle,* slogans of the Liberal party which won 54 percent of the popular vote and 102 of the 110 seats in the National Assembly. However, in the same election the separatist *Parti Québécois* increased its proportion of the popular vote from 24 percent in 1970 to 30 percent in 1973.[9] Since the other parties running were all federalist – that is, wanting to work within confederation – the 30 percent for the *Parti Québécois* can be taken as a good measure of those who would like to create a separate French state. As yet no extensive analysis has appeared, but it is taken as self-evident that the separatist supporters were almost all French and heavily representative of the young. The less sanguine might, therefore, still consider the future of Canada in question. There are also some doubts about the legitimacy of an electoral system which gives a party 30 percent of the votes, but only 9 percent of the seats.*

Whatever directions "diplomatic" or "executive" federalism[10] and constitutional bargaining may take over the next decade, the future of French-English relations really lies within the provinces, particularly in Quebec where 19 percent of the polulation is non-French-speaking, in New Brunswick where 34 percent of the population speak French, and in Ontario where though overall only 6 percent are French-speaking, in some parts of northern Ontario almost half the population is French-speaking, and in some counties in the St. Lawrence–Ottawa River triangle the proportion that is French-speaking is over 80 percent. The absolute number of French-speaking people in Ontario is much greater than in any other province outside Quebec.[11]

It is not possible here to provide a province by province balance sheet on French-English relations. We might instead look at the country's two major and neighboring provinces, Quebec and Ontario. It is in the development within these provinces that the future of Canada may well be settled.

In Quebec it is clear that [present] English-speaking parents (and French for that matter) will always be able to have their children educated in English. Quebec will never become unilingual in education. No party seeks to remove this right from the English minority. However, one of the most seriously discussed issues in the 1973 and 1976 provincial elections was the existing legislation permitting immigrant parents to educate their children in either English or French. Immigrant parents, such as Italian and Portuguese, have shown a strong preference for having their children go to English-speaking schools because of the greater opportunities that an education in English provides in North America. The French, on the other hand, highly sensitive to their own falling fertility rates and substantially unable to recruit immigrants from the French-speaking world, foresee a gradual decreasing use of French in the province. In the 1973 election all political parties recognized this threat, and the reelected

---

* Since this article appeared the November 1976 election in Quebec returned a landslide victory for Parti Québécois. Surveys since the election, however, have shown only a minority in favour of separation. Whether the separatist cause can gain majority support in a forthcoming referendum is an open question. Editors.

Liberal government promised to review the legislation.

Among the most striking of the documentations of the Royal Commission on Bilingualism and Biculturalism was the use of the French language in the industries of Quebec, large segments of which are owned by American or Anglo-Canadian corporations. The pattern was familiar; French blue-collar workers, bilingual foremen, and a large over-representation of unilingual Anglophones in managerial and higher occupational levels of the private sector. French who did achieve these levels because of their professional education in fields such as law, accounting, and public relations were most often required to work in English. The upper levels of the work world were essentially English-speaking, imposing a requirement of written and oral bilingualism on the French, but not on the English Canadians or Americans. This condition was strongly resented by the younger French as they were being turned out in increasing numbers from a reformed educational system where their upward mobility in their home province might be blocked because their English was not adequate, and their own language was downgraded or never used by a "foreign" management.

The Royal Commission recommended that in private industry in Quebec the objective should be French as the language of work at all levels and that the Quebec government should set up a task force to discover means of achieving such an end.[12] The Quebec government did set up a special commission under the chairmanship of Jean-Denis Gendron. After four years of examining the problem the Gendron Commission recommended that French become the provincial *official language* and French and English be provincial *national languages.*[13] There is widespread recognition on the part of the government and political parties that French cannot be made the language of work at all levels by lightning legislation.*

By the end of 1973 there was still no official government policy on language of work. There was, however, a set of basic guidelines pressing firms in the direction of bilingualism. French should be the language in internal oral communication and all oral and written communication with customers, suppliers, and government agencies. Many firms have responded positively to this pressure and have set up French instruction programs for managerial personnel at all levels. The situation is complex, not only because of the ingrained habits of the past, but also because Quebec appeals to foreign investment and does not want to scare it away. That is why the tone of the language at work problem exemplified by the Gendron Commission is moderate, encouraging gradual change. Not all French nationalists are moderate, however. This is particularly true of Montreal where the proportion of French speakers (66 percent) is lower than in the rest of the province and the demographic forces of anglicization are most strong.[14]

With the democratization of education and an increased emphasis on science and technology in curricula, the prospects for the improvement in the occupational opportunities for the French are very good. Upward mobility and participation in an increasingly transnational and post-industrial world will, however, lead to a further erosion of traditional culture begun with the earlier industrialization of Quebec which transformed the rural *habitant* into an urban proletarian. The French face the dilemma of modernization or of maintaining a traditional culture. But there need not be a loss of language. If bilingualism can increase, and that requires a great effort on the part of the English, this distinctive dualism of Canada will remain, if not across the entire country, at least in Quebec, where French and English have lived long together. The undesirable relationship of elite collaboration and low occupational status for the

---

*Bill 1 of the new Parti Québécois government, however, proposed in March 1977, that French become the language of work in Quebec, with some exceptions to be negotiated. Editors.

majority of the French is becoming gradually transformed, not rapidly enough for some, but at least in the direction of a more equal partnership.

Ontario, the province which is the very heart of Anglo-Canadian traditions, pride, privilege, and power, has taken very positive steps, particularly in education, to improve the position of its large French-speaking minority in response to the Royal Commission's report, and to some militancy on the part of Franco-Ontarians. Until new legislation took effect in 1969, children from French-speaking families suffered a variety of handicaps in obtaining instruction in their own language. Educational attainment levels were low except for those whose families could afford to pay fees for private Catholic French-speaking schools. The legislation of 1969 transferred these fee-paying schools to the system of provincially supported local boards of education. The legislation also provided that when ten or more French-speaking parents submitted a written request to have French instruction for their children, local school boards were to provide it. Thus schools are English-speaking, bilingual, and French-speaking. The process of introducing bilingual schools had led to community conflicts but most of them have been successfully mediated.

Educational opportunity for Ontario's French in their own language is a major change. On the other hand extensive new programs to teach French to English-speaking students have been much less successful. French instruction is not compulsory. In 1972 the proportion of Ontario secondary school English students that were taking courses in French was only 37 percent.[15] It would seem, therefore, that much of the strong resistance to learning French on the part of English-speaking Canadians continues.

The teaching of French in Anglophone Canada has been described as a continuing catastrophe. If that is so the future of a bilingual Canada remains very much in question. What will probably happen is that enough bilingual Anglophones will be found to work with bilingual Francophones within federal institutions, and there will be a gradual movement toward more French spoken at work throughout Quebec. In the rest of the country bilingualism will decline the greater the distance from Quebec and Ottawa. An increase in bilingualism can make a workable system which might result in positive and beneficial French-English relations in Canada.

Canada's Other Ethnic Groups: A View From the Census

Interethnic relations in Canada are not confined to the French and English. Canada has always drawn and continues to draw its population from diverse sources. Some indication of this diversity can be seen from the following table. The first point to be noted is the decreasing proportion of those of British origin since the beginning of the present century. The second is the relatively stable proportion represented by the French. The drop to 28.7 percent in 1971 reflects the fact that the lowest fertility rates in Canada are now in Quebec, making for one of the most interesting reversals of reproductive behaviour to be found, a fact which many French Canadians view with alarm.[16]

The table also indicates that no other ethnic group comes close in size to the British or the French although in total they come to somewhere between one quarter and one third of the population of Canada. The ethnic categories shown in the table are those of the 1971 census. The 1961 census used twenty-eight categories, many of which are contained under "Other" in the table. These included in 1961, for example, Icelandic, Lithuanian, Roumanian, and Japanese, each with 0.2 percent of the population.[17] Thus the non-British, non-French component of the Canadian population is extremely diverse.

At this point it is important to note that all the distributions of ethnic origins shown in the table are artifacts of the census itself and result from the questions from which the data are derived. Ethnic "origin" has been asked for in a variety of ways in different censuses, and the instructions to census enumerators have also varied, adding a further artifactual element to the distributions.

In 1961 the question was "To what ethnic or cultural group did you or your ancestor (on the male side) belong on coming to this continent?" Two important facts are clear from the census treatment of ethnicity. One is that one's ethnic origin was to be patrilineally traced, and second, except for native Indians and Eskimo, there was no recognition in any census tabulations of Canadian or American ethnic origin. Thus for census purposes both those born in Canada and immigrants had to have a non-North American ethnicity. For the first time, in the 1951 census if all the techniques in their manuals failed them enumerators were allowed to write in "Canadian" or "American" if the person absolutely insisted. The same was also permitted in 1961. In that year according to an administrative report on the census only 118,185 persons reported their origin as "Canadian," 15,786 as "American," and 70,163 as "Unknown." These numbers combined make up slightly more than 1 percent of the population, about the same as in 1951.[18] These insistent and uncertain people were lost in the residual "Other" category in all census tabulations.

In 1971 the ethnic question was asked in the same way, but for the first time the census was self-enumerated. Neither Canadian nor American was among the response categories provided. The only possibility was "Other-Specify." The 1971 census form also included a question on citizenship, the main purpose of which was to enable those persons who wished to identify themselves as Canadian to do so, since Canadian was not a valid answer to questions on language or ethnicity. The conscientious self-enumerator, who would like to feel above all that he was Canadian, might have been satisfied by being able to say, two questions before he came to the ethnicity one, that he was a Canadian citizen.[19] His instruction booklet was clear on what the census officials wanted for the ethnic question. It read, "Ethnic or cultural group refers to descent (through the father's side) and should not be confused with citizenship. Canadians belong to many ethnic or cultural groups."[20,21] The patrilineal emphasis which has existed throughout becomes socio-

Ethnic Origin of the Canadian Population, 1901-1971[a]

Origin	1901	1921	1941	1961	1971
British	57.0	55.4	49.7	43.8	44.6
French	30.7	27.9	30.3	30.4	28.7
German	5.8	3.4	4.0	5.8	6.1
Italian	0.2	0.8	1.0	2.5	3.4
Dutch	0.6	1.3	1.9	2.4	1.9
Polish	0.1	0.6	1.5	1.8	1.4
Scandinavian	0.6	1.9	2.1	2.1	1.8
Ukrainian	0.1	1.2	2.7	2.6	2.2
Indian and Eskimo	2.4	1.3	1.1	1.2	1.3
Other	2.5	6.2	5.7	7.4	8.6
Total	100.0	100.0	100.0	100.0	100.0

Source: *Report of the Royal Commission on Bilingualism and Biculturalism,* book IV, 248

[a]Newfoundland was excluded from the Canadian census until 1951.

logically absurd where there have been exogamous marriages, because of the important role the mother plays in the socialization of children, and in language learning.

A trenchant critique of Canadian origin statistics was made by Norman Ryder in 1955.[22] He suggested that if the origin question were to have any sociological or cultural meaning it should be asked in terms of language. If the important socio-political question of assimilation to either French or English was to be reasonably answered, the question should be about the language first learned by the individual and by his parents. Two generations of English or French as mother tongue would give some indication of assimilation.

The 1971 census asked not only a mother tongue question but also one of the language most often spoken at home. The assimilation to English has been very marked. While the English-speaking ethnic origin constituted 45 percent of the population, English as the language most often spoken in the home was 65 percent. While the non-English, non-French enthnicities made up 28 percent of the population, only about 12 percent had the same mother tongue as their ethnic origin, and only about 6 percent spoke their ethnic origin language most often in the home. Thus if ethnicity and culture are based on language a considerable process of assimilation has gone on. The French ethnic origin showed a minor language loss, with 28 percent of the population reporting French ethnic origin and 25 percent as speaking French in the home.[23]

Despite the historical variations, the focus on patrilineal descent, nonrecognition of Canadian or American origin, and other inadequacies in the census statistics, it has proved impossible to eliminate the question or change its form, as indeed the federal government sought to do for the 1961 census, when John Diefenbaker was prime minister and spoke out strongly against hyphenated Canadians. The French were insistent on its retention because it provides them with some measure of their survival and their claims for co-charter group status within Canada, a status which can scarcely be denied. Organizations of the other ethnic groups have also demanded its retention because it gave grounds to their claim that Canada is a cultural mosaic rather than the so-called American melting pot.

A comparison of the history of the censuses in Canada and the United States would tell in a fascinating way how the two countries have attempted to treat ethnicity in the course of nation building. Melting pot and mosaic are almost stereotypical terms to describe the divergent ways in which these two new nations have tried to deal with ethnicity, but they do reflect the two opposed orientations, clearly to be seen in the policies and instructions surrounding the two censuses from the last century.[24] We know now that the lives of ethnic groups are not responsive to the intentions of the policy makers and the bureaucratic organizations that take the censuses. Melting pot and mosaic are not such extreme opposites as the terms would imply because in the United States, ethnicity, in the sense of awareness of European national origins of ancestors, is still very mcuh alive while in Canada many reject European ancestry and identify with the country where they were born.

Multiculturalism Within A Bilingual Framework

In October 1971 Mr. Trudeau, the prime minister, announced in the House of Commons a new policy which he called "multiculturalism within a bilingual framework" and which he considered "the most suitable means of assuring the cultural freedom of Canadians."[25] The government had already taken a number of steps mentioned earlier, such as the Official Languages Act of 1969, to make French and English equal as official languages within the federal jurisdiction, to promote the teaching of both the official languages, and to introduce bilingualism into the Public Service.

Canada was becoming caught up in the ethnic revival. The government was attempting to maintain a difficult balance between the hostility of many in Quebec to any formal recognition of the other groups and the electoral support that would be forthcoming from a program to promote multiculturalism. French critics of the new policy argued that it was an about-turn from the earlier position, on the basis of which the commission had been set up, that is, that Canada should be a truly bilingual and bicultural society based on the central ideas of two founding peoples, two societies, and two dominant cultures. Some argued that it was impossible to talk of multiculturalism without multilingualism because culture could not be detached from language. If that were true then the official bilingualism that was developing at the federal level, and in some provinces, would be endangered by demands that other languages be recognized. Moreover, multiculturalism in some provinces would be more likely to promote a bilingualism in the form Anglo-Ukrainian or Franco-Italian rather than English-French bilingualism which has basic sociological and historical links and which was so important for the future of Canada as a viable society.[26] Indeed, it has always been assumed that immigrants to Canada would assimilate to either the French or the English communities. If that was no longer to be so, French Canadians would interpret it as a threat to their own survival. As I mentioned earlier, lowering French fertility rates and English-speaking school attendance by immigrant children gave substance to these French fears.

The multicultural pronouncement has many critics also among English-speaking Canadians, particularly those who see the only hope for Canada to lie in a policy of biculturalism and bilingualism based on the two collectivities which they represent,[27] and seems to contradict the view of the commission which had written, "To the degree that the demands of certain ethnic groups make awareness of the fundamental duality of the country more difficult, to that extent they aggravate the state of crisis in Canada. Above all, they provide new arguments for the partisans of a 'One Canada.' "[28]

The Canadian government took quite the opposite view to the common sense one that strong ethnic loyalties, because they are little nationalisms, would be divisive. Mr. Trudeau, in fact, argued that multiculturalism would be integrative. He said Canada would become "a special place, and a stronger place as well. Each of the many fibres contributes its own qualities and Canada gains strength from the combination. We become less like others; we become less susceptible to cultural, social or political envelopment by others."[29]

All major political leaders outside of Quebec support some policy of multiculturalism. Robert Stanfield, the [former] federal leader of the Opposition, referring to the government's program as "grudging acceptance," went on to say, "If we really believe that Canadian pluralism should be encouraged, and not merely tolerated, government should work together with the various ethnic groups to help them survive, not simply as folklore, but as a living contributing element of the Canadian cultural mosaic."[30]

The official Canadian government policy of "multiculturalism within a bilingual framework" has as its goal the encouraging of non-British, non-French ethnic cultures. A multicultural program, established in the Citizenship Branch of the Department of the Secretary of State, was to study such aspects of multiculturalism as broadcasting in third languages, the role of the ethnic press, and language training in third languages. The most important part of the program, though, was the giving of grants to ethnic organizations to help them preserve their culture. Initially the program was modest. One and one half million dollars were allocated for grants in the first year, but by 1973 the budget had increased to 10 million dollars, and a cabinet minister was appointed whose exclusive responsibility was multiculturalism.

The "Guidelines for Submissions for Grants under the Multicultural Programme" emphasize the "multicultural" goal of the program in the Canadian context.[31] The criteria considered for granting funds to a specific project include whether it is "designed to share a cultural heritage with other Canadians," whether it will "promote an awareness of Canada's cultural diversity," and whether it will "assist immigrants to become full participants in Canadian society."

Non-English, non-French ethnicity, then, continues to be a salient feature of Canadian social structure. Whether it will eventually be integrative or divisive, in that the emphasis on Canada's multiethnicity will intensify French nationalism, must be left to time. For those who view the ethnic revival as something good because it represents something deep and primordial and genuinely human, Canada must appear as an attractive place to live.

Some Comments About the Revival of Ethnicity

In some respects the revival is regressive. Because it emphasizes descent group identification and endogamy, important principles of ethnic group survival, it runs the risk of believed-in biological differences becoming the basis of invidious judgments about groups of people (a matter to which we will return later). Moreover, where ethnicity is salient there is often an association between ethnic differences and social class and inequality. That is way much of the discussion of the relations between ethnic groups concerns equality, equality of legal rights, political rights, and in the more recent period, social rights such as education, jobs, good health, and equality of opportunity. Class inequality becomes obscured and more difficult to analyze where there is ethnic heterogeneity in the social structure. This many reflect some inadequacy in the sociological theories of class, almost all of which assume ethnic homogeneity.

Some scholars contest the views that when ethnic differentiation is an important organizing principle of social life it must also result in ethnic groups forming a hierarchy of inequality, creating what has come to be called ethnic stratification. One writer, Donald L. Noel, raises that question in developing a theory of the origins of ethnic stratifications and answers it in this way.[32] "Distinct ethnic groups can interact and form a stable pattern of relations without super-subordination." The "classical example" he gives is of the Tungus and Cossacks of northerwestern Siberia from an anthropological study of 1938. This at least suggests that ethnic differentiation without some hierarchical features is rare. Certainly the degree and strength of hierarchy depend upon many factors, and there have been many studies of the conditions under which super- and subordination exist in plural or multiethnic societies.[33]

I now return to the matter to which I referred earlier, that ethnic groups, because they are biological descent groups, are a regressive means of safeguarding and transmitting culture, a responsibility which many would assign to them. No doubt cultural survival can be most efficiently achieved through the biological descent group because when coupled with another principle firmly embedded in our values — that parents have the inalienable right through cultural transmission to make their children the vehicles of their values — recruits are always available. The use of the family for ethnocultural transmission requires that groups impress upon their members the value of marrying within their own group. If they do not they will lose the primordial link with tribe or nation and the exclusive ethnic claims on culture will be eroded. Endogamy is a process of exclusion. There was a time when lowering rates of endogamy could be taken as an index of lessening prejudice in a more liberal and open society. In the current return to ethnicity it seems a different judgment, that such lowering rates can be interpreted as a loss of ethnic communal strength, is being made. The metal of endogamy is more attractive because it is unmeltable.

When descent groups are the principal carriers of culture there are dangers of new forms of racism. If "races" have been evaluated as inferior and superior, so can cultures be. Racism and "culturism" stem from the fact that both are linked to the maintenance of descent group solidarity and endogamy. After all, if ethnicity is so important, if cultures are so different, then it is easy to extend the argument that those of different ethnic groups and cultures must also be different with respect to qualities which are thought important in different parts of the work world and for entrance to elite status. It may not take very long before that view becomes extended even further, to include the notion that qualitative cultural differences are inborn. When that point is reached we have come full circle and we begin to realize that those theories of race and ethnic differences which we thought destroyed or at least highly discredited by World War II have reappeared in a new guise with culture replacing race.

Along with the arguments supportive of the revival of ethnicity can be found also the view that cultures have a right to live and individuals and societies have an obligation to see that they survive, although surely history is as much the graveyard of cultures as it is of aristocracies. The desirability and responsibility of preserving culture through historical archaeological, and anthropological study, because we want to know how people lived at different times and places, is beyond question. Often, in discussions of the survival of culture, one gets the impression that the reference is to cultural artifacts such as dance, folklore, cuisine, music, crafts, and the like. Cultural artifacts always will survive, because people enjoy them, and that is good because they add variety. However, they do not require descent group identification to survive. Artifacts are unlike values, some of which when embedded in particular cultures are particularly inappropriate for modernity, for example, the low evalutation of education for girls.

If there are dangers of biological descent groups preserving cultures through living them, there are available associational ways of conserving culture. Some people find the culture of ancient Egypt fascinating and rewarding to study. But if the culture of ancient Egypt is of value the various groups that preserve it – archaeologists who get money to investigate it and amateur Egyptologists who make it a hobby – must recruit new members to carry on their interests. One way would be to require as a condition of membership that members marry within the Egyptology group, and, given the traditional role of the family as the unit of cultural transmission, ensure the survival of the culture of ancient Egypt through the generations. Alternatively, they can do as they always have done and that is to recruit members by persuading others that studying and keeping alive this particular culture is a good thing.

The obligation to conserve culture is different from the obligation to live it. In Canada, for example, it is at times suggested that the Eskimos should be left alone to live their traditional hunting and nomadic culture rather than be encouraged to modernism even though, for the individuals involved, life is more often than not nasty and brutish and seldom long, at least until modern government health services are delivered to even the most remote areas. Yet few would argue that medical attempts to control tuberculosis should be abandoned in favor of the more primitive harshness.

Not all cultures have equal claims on our moral support. Some cultures treat human beings in profoundly inhumane ways. As Conor Cruise O'Brien has said in a recent discussion of the rights of minorities in developing countries:

> The culture of a group may include systematic violations of basic human rights. When we are told to respect the cultures of groups we are being told to respect things which many include for example the Hindu caste system, the treatment of women in Islam and a number of other cultures, female circumcision in certain cultures, ostracism of twins, for example in others, and so on. [34]

So strongly are cultural rights advocated that people in modern nations, particularly those that make claims to being democracies, are reluctant to persuade developing countries to be either democratic or modern. Perhaps considering their histories of imperialism and aggression they do not speak with much moral authority. But our claim to the judgment of cultures is not put forward because we have created a perfect society, but because in the course of social evolution some principles of social life have emerged which are more morally supportable than others.

So far my emphasis has been on the costs of ethnic saliency in modern societies. Are there no benefits? One strong argument for ethnic pluralism, widely accepted to support the idea of multiculturalism in Canada, is that it creates diversity. A society with a number of different ethnic cultures in which the members of relatively exclusive groups behave alike, it is said, will be heterogeneous rather than uniform. Yet it could be that such diversity is more enjoyed by the beholder – whatever Olympus he might be viewing it from – than any of the actors within their enclaves. Moreover, modern societies are the most differentiated of all. Diversity is almost a defining attribute for them, but their diversity is one of choice rather than of descent. Indeed, the call to ethnic loyalty stems largely from the fear of the descent group that members will desert it for the diversity of an associational rather than a communal type.

A strong case can be made for the role of ethnic group affiliation in solving problems of personal identity in the modern world of bureaucracy and technology. There is no doubt that ethnic groupings can play this role, but, as I have argued, at the possible cost of perpetuating ethnic stratification. Identities and psychic shelters can be found in other forms of association and interest groups which are not based on descent, for it is this aspect of the ethnic group which is the source of irrational invidious comparison.

The psychic shelter function of ethnic affiliation has been and continues to be important in Canada and no doubt in other modern societies as well, in two special contexts. One is that of recently arrived immigrants, of which Canada continues to have large numbers in its population. The other is the positive function which ethnic afffiliation has for the raising of the self-concept of members of low status groups.

For the immigrant the transition to a new social environment can be fraught with psychic hazards, particularly if he comes from the Azores or the Abruzzi to metropolitan Toronto. The question from the point of view of general social goals is whether the useful staging camp role of the ethnic community becomes permanent, or whether some dispersion into the wider society of the various groups increases his chances of achievement and mobility in the receiving society.

Commitment to the receiving society on the part of immigrants may not be as strong now as it was sixty or seventy years ago. Immigrants come in modern jet aircraft, settle into enclaves in the receiving metropolis, and charter aircraft take them home for visits. What the jet aircraft does between Milano and Toronto, fast special trains do from Torino to Amsterdam. So the link with the society of origin is not as completely broken as it was in the time of the long steerage passage across the Atlantic, and with this shrinking of distance the social status of migrating labor will be ever more ambiguous in the societies to which it moves to work. The social status of permanent stranger is something new for modern societies. But where the status of citizenship can be acquired, as in the United States and Canada, social mobility and achievement almost imply a commitment to the values of modernism and a movement away from the ethnic community with each succeeding generation.

There remains the positive function that ethnic identification can play in raising the self-concept of members of low status groups. The enhancement of self-concept can serve contrary ends. One is to compensate for low status without doing anything about it, very much as evangelical religions do for lower classes in ethnically homogeneous societies or low status ethnic groups in ethnically heterogeneous societies. The other is to provide a firm base from which to achieve, although many cultures do not emphasize individual achievement, nor do they provide the appropriate skills for it. From the point of view of the Indians, does promoting their own culture help them toward equality in the postindustrial society?

If strong ethnic identification is to enchance the self-concept of an individual and thus provide a firm base from which to achieve, it is important to emphasize language rather than culture. Identification with and the use of their own language, particularly in school, may be important in providing opportunity for very low status groups. For example, the use of any immigrant language, say, Italian or Portuguese and certainly the language of native peoples in Canada, may help a child in overcoming learning impediments that arise from using one language at school and another at home. He acquires some self-confidence when his language is not despised. But such use of language is quite different from the goal of having ethnic communities become a permanent compensation for low status, or as psychic shelters in the urban-industrial world. We would hope for a society in which the compensatory role of the ethnic community is not necessary.

I have tried to argue what is an unpopular view, and that is that the saliency of ethnic differences is a retreat from the liberal notions of the unity of mankind. But I would be naive indeed – an inappropriate state for a professional sociologist – if I were not aware of the political realities in those modern societies where deprived minorities seek to redistribute social resources to redress grievances. Political realities are not principles although they are often confused with them, and hence, the question is whether interethnic conflicts can be solved in ways which are both ethically acceptable and sociologically possible.

It is my view that in Canada, in the emerging postindustrial phase, with its one culture of science and technology and its extensive transnational network, bilingualism can survive. But that phase can scarcely be bicultural, much less multicultural. If bilingualism is to be a part of Canada's future, we will require more exogamous marriages to offset falling fertility rates in Quebec. We will also require vastly improved language learning programs. Under such circumstances, there would be no need to rely on group exclusiveness and endogamy for Canada's two languages to survive.

What of cultures? Cultures are tradition bound. Anthropologists view culture as established ways of doing things, or of viewing the world, or as designs for living and survival passed from generation to generation, and, while for societies more simple organized than those of today, the role that cultures played and for many continue to play was important, they are less and less relevant for the post-industrial society because they emphasize yesterday rather than tomorrow. Can cultures of the past serve societies facing the coming of postindustrialism? The one recurring theme in many of the analyses of the next twenty-five years is the rapidity of change, of the shock of the future. One can almost speak of the end of culture, as some have written of the end of ideology. Many of the historic cultures are irrelevant to our futures. Opportunity will go to those individuals who are future oriented in an increasingly universalistic culture. Those oriented to the past are likely to lose out.

Notes

1. The title of a widely read book by Pierre Vallières, Editions Parti Pris, Montréal, 1968. Reprinted as *White Niggers of America* (Toronto, McClelland and Stewart, 1971).
2. Les éditions du boréal express, Montreal, 1972. The original is *French Canada in Transition* (Chicago, University of Chicago Press, 1943).
3. See, for example, Sheilagh Hodgins Milner and Henry Milner, *The Decolonization of Quebec* (Toronto, McClelland and Stewart, 1973).
4. The idea of French Canadians as an ethnic class was first discussed by Jacques Dofny and Marcel Rioux in a 1962 paper reprinted in Marcel Rioux and Yves Martin, *French-Canadian Society* (Toronto, McClelland and Stewart, 1964), as "Social Class in French Canada." There has been criticism, particularly from Marxist writers, of the "dubious metaphor" of an ethnic class. See Stanley B. Ryerson, "Quebec: Concepts of Class and Nation," in Gary Teeple, ed., *Capitalism and the National Question in Canada* (Toronto, University of Toronto Press, 1972). In the same volume see also Gilles Bourque and Nicole Laurin-Frenette, "Social Class and National Ideologies in Quebec."
5. *A Preliminary Report of the Royal Commission on Bilingualism and Biculturalism* (Ottawa, Queen's Printer, 1965), p. 13.
6. *Report of the Royal Commission on Bilingualism and Biculturalism,* Book I, *The Official Languages* (Ottawa, Queen's Printer, 1967), P. xvii.
7. The main instrument was the Official Languages Act of 1969, *Statutes of Canada,* 17–18 Elizabeth II, Chapter II.
8. One of the provisions of the Official Languages Act of 1969 was the appointment of a Commissioner of Official Languages whose task was to ensure compliance with the spirit and intent of the Act. On the whole his annual reports (Information Canada, Ottawa) have tended to be critical of the rate of progress toward the objectives of the act.
9. *La Presse,* Montréal, October 30, 1973.
10. "Diplomatic" and "executive" federalism are terms to describe the ways in which provincial and federal cabinet ministers and committees of federal and provincial bureaucrats bargain on a wide range of issues, like urban problems and higher education, and work out the responsibilities of the two levels of government. The federal Parliament and provincial legislatures become almost ratifiers, an unusual role for them in the traditional parliamentary system. See R. Simeon, *Federal-Provincial Diplomacy* (Toronto, University of Toronto Press, 1972), and Donald V. Smiley, *Canada in Question* (Toronto, McGraw-Hill, 1972).
11. Proportions based on mother tongue. There are bilinguals in both French-and-English-speaking groups. The 19 percent includes immigrants in Quebec whose mother tongue would be neither English nor French. *Census of Canada, 1971,* vol. I, pt. 3, Statistics Canada, Ottawa, 1973. If "ethnic origin," the definition of which is dealt with later in this paper, is used the proportions are non-French in Quebec, 21 percent; French in Ontario, 9.5 percent; and French in New Brunswick 39 percent. *Census of Canada, 1971*, Advance Bulletin, *Population by Ethnic Group* (Ottawa, Statistics Canada, 1973).
12. *Report of the Royal Commission on Bilingualism and Biculturalism*, Book III, *The Work World* (Ottawa, Queen's Printer, 1969), p. 559.
13. *Report of the Commission of Inquiry on the Position of the French Language and on Language Rights in Quebec* (Montréal, l'Editeur officiel du Québec, 1972).
14. For a series of interesting papers on contemporary Quebec see Dale C. Thomson, ed., *Quebec Society and Politics* (Toronto, McClelland and Stewart, 1973).

15. Norman Webster, "French Language Education: For Anglophone Bigots the Going Is Tough," *Globe and Mail*, Toronto, December 1, 1973.
16. *Vital Statistics* (Ottawa, Statistics Canada, 1973).
17. *Report of the Royal Commission on Bilingualism and Biculturalism*, Book IV, *The Cultural Contribution of the Other Ethnic Groups* (Ottawa, Queen's Printer, 1970), p. 32.
18. *Census of Canada, 1961*, Bull. 7.1–6. There is a brief history of the ethnic origin question in Warren E. Kalbach, *The Impact of Immigration on Canada's Population* (Ottawa, Statistics Canada, 1970), pp. 3–9.
19. *The 1971 Census of Population and Housing: Development of Subject Matter Content* (Ottawa, Statistics Canada, 1969), p. 13.
20. Instructions accompanying 1971 census self-enumeration forms (Ottawa, Statistics Canada, 1971).
21. Kalbach, *The Impact of Immigration*, p. v.
22. N.B. Ryder, "The Interpretation of Origin Statistics," *The Canadian Journal of Economics and Political Science*, 21.4 (1955), 466–479
23. *Census of Canada, 1971, Population by Language Most Often Spoken in the Home and by Official Language* (Ottawa, Statistics Canada, 1973).
24. Some comparison between the two censuses has been made by Joel Smith, "Melting Pot–Mosaic: Consideration for a Prognosis," in *Minorities North and South*, Proceedings of the Third Inter-Collegiate Conference on Canadian-American Relations, Michigan State University, 1968.
25. "Statement by the Prime Minister, House of Commons, October 8, 1971," Office of the Prime Minister, Ottawa.
26. Guy Rocher, "Les Ambiguités d'un Canada bilingue et multiculturel," paper presented to the 1972 Annual Meeting of the Canadian Sociology and Anthropology Association, mimeo, Départment de Sociologie, Université de Montréal.
27. See editorial in *Journal of Canadian Studies* (November 1971).
28. *A Preliminary Report of the Royal Commission on Bilingualism and Biculturalism* (Ottawa, Queen's Printer, 1965), p. 128.
29. "Notes for Remarks by the Prime Minister to the Ukrainian-Canadian Congress, Winnipeg, Manitoba, October 9, 1971, "Office of the Prime Minister, Ottawa.
30. *Globe and Mail*, Toronto, May 1, 1972.
31. Citizenship Branch, Department of the Secretary of State, Ottawa (undated).
32. Donald L. Noel, "A Theory of Ethnic Stratification," *Social Problems*, 16 (Fall 1968), 157-172.
33. See, for example, Tamotou Shibutani and Kian M. Kwan, *Ethnic Stratification: A Comparative Approach* (New York, Macmillan, 1965); Stanley Lieberson, "A Societal Theory of Race and Ethnic Relations," *American Sociological Review*, 36 (December 26, 1971), 902–910; Burton Benedict, "Stratification in Plural Societies," *American Anthropologist*, 64 (1962), 1235–1246; John Rex, *Race Relations in Sociological Theory* (New York, Schocken Books, 1970); R.A. Schermerhorn, *Comparative Ethnic Relations; A Framework for Theory and Research* (New York, Random House, 1970); M.G. Smith, *Stratification in Granada* (Berkeley, University of California Press, 1965). For two earlier statements see J.S. Furnival, *Colonial Policy and Practice* (Cambridge, Cambridge University Press, 1948), and Everett C. Hughes, "Queries Concerning Industry and Society Growing Out of Study of Ethnic Relations in Industry," *American Sociological Review*, 14.2 (April 1949), 211–220.
34. In *The Times*, London, reprinted as "In Secession a Case for the Individual," in the *Globe and Mail*, Toronto, January 27, 1973.

2

Two Cultures: Nationalism, Class, and Ethnic Tension*

Hubert Guindon

In highly industrialized societies, the increasing scale of economic organizations goes hand in hand with a corresponding degree of concentration of political power in the central governments. Canada, however, in the last decade has in a climate of political tension experimented in another direction; namely, an increase in the political and economic relevance of the provincial governments at the expense of the federal government. One of the factors bringing this unexpected turn of events has been in no small measure cultural dualism, within which the French-Canadian culture has been more aggressive and forceful. The question therefore becomes: What are the changes, the social forces, within French-Canadian society that brought about this development?

In this essay the social and cultural factors that seem to have been of paramount importance in producing change in French Canada--a new middle class and a resurgence of nationalism--are singled out and analyzed. There are three parts to this study. The first deals with neo-nationalism and traditional societies. Furthermore, elements of a conceptual model that could be useful in interpreting nationalist movements in a comparative fashion are described. The second section of the essay is an attempt to utilize the model in analyzing social and cultural changes in French-Canadian society. In a final section, the impact of the aforementioned cultural and social changes on ethnic accommodation is raised.

The Emergence of Nationalism in Traditional Societies

It is important to consider some of the structural features of contemporary or "current"nationalism. Paradoxical as it may seem, at the very time that the principle of nationality was reorganizing the political shape and foundations of Europe, the European powers were expanding, developing, and consolidating their imperial holdings over other parts of the globe. National groups of the imperial powers controlled the political apparatus of the colonies. These endeavours were carried on with the help of the army and the churches.[1]

In order to deal with local cultures, the imperial elite within the colonies would work with indigenous political structures of a tribal or feudal character or create such native political leadership. Administrative and political boundaries were carved with little or no regard for the ethnological homogeneity or heterogeneity of the indigenous populations.

The symbol of "legitimation" for the empire-building was the "spread of civilization". In providing this legitimation, the Christian churches were of paramount

---

*Abridged from Hubert Guindon in Richard H. Leach, ed., *Contemporary Canada* (Durham, N.C., Duke University Press, 1967). By permission of the author and publisher.

importance. The religious legitimation took the form of converting the indigenous populations to Christianity, thereby heeding the prescription of the Gospel. The "spread of civilization" involved the armies, to assure political stability; the capitalists, to spread the benefits of industralization; and the clergy, to bring them the Kingdom of God.

Colonial rule swiftly and deeply affected the local traditional cultures as well as the traditional social structure of the various indigenous groups. Not infrequently, the nature of traditional indigenous culture before the Western presence is clouded in mystery and is the object of historical speculation and of archeological investigation. The very success of the imperial ventures gave rise to an indigenous middle class recruited from the various indigenous groups, a middle class whose status, power, and prestige were derived from its formal though subordinate participation in the expanding institutions of the imperial regimes. While the newly acquired status of the middle class was honored by its co-nationals, it was bestowed upon them by the ruling aliens. The social mobility of the middle class was accompanied by a high degree of acculturation. The local clerically staffed schools gave its children their basic education and not infrequently the more promising would have some years in the metropolitan centres overseas.

Irrespective of the occupational dissimilarities, whether they were minor civil servants, teachers, industrial white-collar workers, or non-commissioned officers in the army, the members of this newly arisen middle class had many common characteristics: they were bureaucratically employed, they were culturally marginal to the traditionally local cultures, they had been shaped by the same school system, they had alien ethnic superiors, and social distance kept them from intimate social contact and integration with the Western elite. These common characteristics made them a status group with a distinctively characteristic style of life, with common class interests that led to class awareness, if not to the growth of political class consciousness.

Thus the growth and extension of colonial governments and administrations gave birth to a new indigenous middle class. It is within the ranks of this new indigenous middle class that nationalist movements were born.

Next, an analysis may be made of what may be called the structural dilemma of nationalist movements in traditional societies.[2]

Nationalist movements in traditional societies seldom, if ever, begin as revolutionary movements launching a full-fledged attack of the legitimations of the political structure of the state. The first phase is more aptly labeled a quest for social and political reform. This quest, which more often than not takes the form of a request from legitimate authorities, is voiced by the new indigenous middle class and very frequently in terms of its class interest. The symbolic basis for the requested changes invariably reflects the ideological acculturation of the native elite. For instance, in the British Empire it was based on the extension to the colonies of increased "home" rule, that is, increased and extended political participation of the citizenry. This, however, only reflected the colonists' acceptance of the political ideology that brought about such changes in Britain itself.

The second phase of nationalist movements begins when there is an effort to extend the social base of national claims and of the nationalist movement itself. The initial social base of nationalist movements as has been noted, is the native bureaucratic or liberal bourgeoisie. It is a social class of recent emergence and of relatively small size. As a class it possesses very little politcal leverage to bring about politcal reforms because of its restricted social base. In its search to extend its social base it faces what might be called a structural dilemma.

Two sets of structural constraints must be overcome by the nationalist movement to expand its social base. The first set of constraints stems from the nature of colonial rule and the local groups which have a vested interest in the persistence of the *status quo.* The constraint is that these groups, politically established or supported by the state, control the means of violence in the country. The other set of constraints stems from the pre-industrial character of the local culture and its traditionally commanding institutions. While they accommodate with the *status quo,* they are marginal to, if not resentful of, the ongoing social changes.

In order to overcome these structural constraints, the national movements must successfully launch a twofold symbolic attack: on the alien presence and control of the state on the one hand, and on the traditional culture and the social control of traditional institutions and traditional politcal leaders on the other.

This leads the nationalist movements to the third phase wherein they are transformed from reform to revolutionary social movements. They are revolutionary because they attack the very legitimacy of the exercise of power of the state as presently constituted; they are equally revolutionary because they attack the legitimacy of basic values legitimizing indigenous traditional social structures. As a class, the newly emerged native elites have an economic and political stake, not in arresting but in pursuing the socio-economic changes initiated by the colonial regimes. Thus not only their marginality and acculturation but their class interests compel them to pursue and accelerate socio-economic changes. The attack upon the legitimation of colonial rule as well as of the traditional social structure is centred on the positive acceptance of industrialization. It then focuses on the fact that the purpose of the colonial regime's political apparatus is to protect and assist the economic interests of the investing capitalist from the imperial centre, not to accelerate the economic development of the local people.[3]

The fourth and final phase of successful nationalist movements is to forge a new consensus in support of the new nation-state. This requires, to varying degrees, wresting the masses from the symbols of tradition, creating and celebrating a new kind of man, a product of the changing society, but initiating and controlling the formal and informal means of socialization — the schools, the public mass media, etc. — and finally, establishing a considerable degree of bureaucratic control and centralization over the whole territory to avoid the fractionalism of tribal or local cultures once the political dominance of the aliens has been removed.

Neo-nationalism, the Quiet Revolution, and the New Middle Class

From a consideration of the social basis of neo-nationalism in the traditional societies of the present, elements of a conceptual model that might prove useful in analyzing social changes in contemporary French-Canadian society have been developed. This model will now be used in assessing, in global terms, the direction of change in the ideologies and the social structure of French Canada.

The French Revolution was a social revolution designed to overthrow the feudal social order. The major social changes brought about in a violent fashion as a result of the French Revolution were an end to the dynastic exercise of power and to the political, fiscal, and economic privileges formerly held by the feudal lords and landed aristocracy, the accession to political ascendency of the liberal bourgeoisie, the abolition of the privileges of the estates, and changes in feudal ownership of land.

That no similar situation existed in French Canada is quite obvious. The feudal system of land tenure never had serious content within New France. Bush country was no major attraction for whatever feudal nobility emigrated to New France. In fact, agricultural settlement was marginal to the social organization of New France and did not keep pace with the agricultural settlements of the British colony to the south.[4] What feudal trappings there were in New France were an urban phenomenon and revolved closely around the political control of the administrative structure of the colony. The main economic drive was the development and exploitation of the fur trade industry, carried out by a metropolitan bourgeoisie, supported by the military and viewed with suspicion by the clergy. With the British conquest the traditional society collapsed. The military was recalled and what liberal bourgeoisie of any significance were left were supplanted quickly by their British counterpart from the south.[5]

The pattern of landownership, formally feudal in the political form of its distribution and allocation, was not so in social fact. It was neither politically oppressive, socially resented, nor economically burdensome. Under pressure to develop agricultural settlements in order to maintain ownership, the feudal landowners could manage to meet this requirement only by parcelling out ownership as an incentive or inducement to settlers to carve out arable land in bush country. This process had one major effect: it avoided the development of a class of indentured agricultural workers. The *colon* was never an indentured servant, although some of the *corvées* of the feudal agricultural system were implemented. Léon Gérin was therefore correct in stating that the French-Canadian rural society, which was left untouched by the conquest, consisted in a "juxtaposition of [landholding] families which are nearly all equal; nearly all engaged in farming; nearly all sufficient unto themselves".[6]

With the collapse of the political ties with France, the exodus of the entrepreneurial bourgeoisie, the absence of feudal landownership as an oppressive social structure, the withdrawal of the military and political elites, all this some thirty years before the revolution in France, it should not be a subject of amazement that the French Revolution, its ideology, its break with the past, and its new set of legitimations of the present, did not receive a sympathetic ear within the ruling elite of French-Canadian society— the clergy, the intelligentsia, or the habitants. The differences between metropolitan French and French-Canadian social structures were so great as to render meaningless in French Canada the revolutionary upheavals in France.

Nationalism did not feed therefore on a rejection of the past, of tradition, or of feudal social structure which did not exist, as it had in Continental Europe. Since Canadians were unattracted to French republicanism, because of the differences in social structure, the Crown, whether British or French, was not an object of resentment, and loyalty to the monarchy was not considered national treason. As a result, when the American Revolution or Rebellion, quite bourgeois in character and interest, occurred, the loyalty of the new British subjects of French descent, while crucial for the British Crown, could be easily pledged by the French-Canadian peasants and its clerical elite in exchange for political concessions assuring its cultural survival, namely, the right to stay French and Catholic. The tradition of political guarantees for cultural survival of the French Canadians as a community was thereby begun.

If French-Canadian national feelings were unaffected by the Continental context, the same is equally true of the British who moved into the newly acquired country. The British Canadians were not deprived of their military forces and their political elites. Rather than spurring a rejection of the British connection, the immigration of the United Empire Loyalists from the American colonies strengthened the emotional ties to the Crown and motherland. The effect of the American severance from Britain gave impetus to British-Canadian nationalism and its determination to forge a British North America. Furthermore, the political upheavals of Continental Europe had not had the same repercussions in England, where the accession of the liberal bourgeoisie to political dominance had been achieved without revolutionary upheavals.

French-Canadian society in the nineteenth century was a rural society. It consisted in a loosely integrated collection of rural parishes geographically expanding. As a social system it required an equilibrium between land and people.[7] Since the pattern of landholding was one of diffuse ownership among small farmers with large families, the stability of the system could only be maintained by handing down the family farm to one inheriting son. The equation between land and people could thus be kept intact. But this also meant that the system required an ever expanding geographical base in order to absorb the surplus population. As long as arable land remained plentiful there was no major problem. When it became scarce this social system became acutely vulnerable. It is within this context of geographically expanding parishes that a developing set of supraparochial institutions gave birth to an ethnic elite. Faced with a surplus population with no land to till, the traditional elite was in need of structural relief for its continued survival.[8]

Structural relief could only consist in industralization, which is the one thing the traditional elite could not deliver since it was not and had not been primarily an entrepreneurial bourgeoisie and therefore lacked capital. The vulnerability of the traditional elite set the stage for an easy introduction of industrialization even if it meant dependence on foreign capitalists. The capitalists transformed the French Canadians into urban dwellers. To service the needs of the recently urbanized masses, the traditional power elite had to transform its institutions into large-scale bureaucracies, giving birth in the process to the new middle classes of French-Canadian society. In French Canada, the new middle class was an outgrowth of traditional institutions, ethnically homogeneous in composition, in the process of urban transformation.

The new middle class equated its social role with progress and the growth of its institutions with modernization. Its cohesion was thus first achieved under the banner of modernization, not nationalism. This value of modernization was a product of the training and education of the new middle class. In the process of developing urban social bureaucracies, the need for functional specialization and training brought the new generation in contact with the various specialized social, human, biological, and economic sciences of industrialized societies. This new training was the basis of the internal status of that class within the developing hierarchies. This new competence had been achieved through cultural borrowing, and the new theories of organization welcomed within the developing bureaucracies were foreign to the traditional culture. Not only was this new knowledge the basis of status; it also became the yardstick by which traditional institutions were evaluated.

Marginal to traditional culture by training, the new middle class became politically restive by class interest. Because it settled mainly in bureaucracies that did not produce profits, it required outside financial resources, namely state funds, to expand its scope, develop its services, and perform its social role. Functionally indispensable in bringing about the institutional changes required in the urban setting, it became politically aroused and aggressive.

Its demands were directed toward the provincial government headed by the Union Nationale. By refusing to acquiesce quickly to its demands, the Union Nationale incurred its wrath and Duplessis, its leader, became its favourite scapegoat .

The Liberal party became the political expression of the new middle class, the champion of its interests and aspirations. It heralded a bureaucratic revolution under the banner of modernization and was spontaneously acclaimed internally and externally. Its election in 1960 publicly consecrated the political dominance of the new middle classes in French-Canadian society.[9]

The positive acceptance of modernization has been and still is the unifying ideology of the new middle class. The violent controversies manifest in the various segments of its intelligentsia do not centre on the desirability of this assumption, but rather on conflicting views on the methods of accelerating its historical implementation . . . In the bureaucratic institutions of health, education, welfare, and public service, the challenge to priestly rule or political appointees was not an attack on religion or on the older people, but on incompetence . . . What was necessary was that one should be professionally qualified. If he were not, he must forfeit the right to bureaucratic power. That scientific or technical competence should be the overriding concern in the selection, hiring, and promotion of bureaucratic personnel marked the claim to supremacy of bureaucratic leadership over traditional leadership.

Modernization, bureaucratic rationality, and personal qualification became the tools for the new middle class to assess the worth of not only the institutions but also the ideologies of the past. Ethnically homogenous, the new middle class was not initially ethnically conscious. In fact, nationalism was suspect during the first decade after World War II. Faced with the depression, the main stream of French-Canadian nationalism withdrew its support from capitalism. It could not endorse socialism, however, because of its atheistic materialism and its cultural matrix, which was Anglo-Saxon and Protestant and therefore foreign to the traditions and philosophical world view of a Latin and Catholic people. It endorsed instead corporatism as the ideal socio-political structure of the state.[10] The new middle class, at least those members of it who were trained outside the ethnic universities, did not take corporatism seriously. It had no sympathy for its political elitism and was fully aware of its economic sterility.

Not only did the new middle class of the period reject the political philosophy of the nationalism of the thirties and early forties but it remained skeptical about its indictment of American culture. Rather than fearing the assimilative effect of American culture, it admired the technological and scientific basis of that culture and found in American society the model for modernization it sought to establish in French Canada. The attempts by nationalist groups in the thirties and forties to make the French Canadian an ethnically conscious consumer had failed and were looked upon by this postwar-trained middle class as an indication of naive ignorance about the economics of the marketplace.

What is somewhat more surprising is that in the early postwar period the new middle class did not deeply share but rather remained skeptical of the nationalist suspicions toward the government and its encroaching jurisdiction within the network of French-Canadian institutions. While the Massey Report, one of whose authors was Father Levesque, founder of the Laval Faculté des Sciences Sociales, tended to legitimate centralization, and while it was castigated publicly and violently by the French-Canadian nationalist intelligentsia, it left the new middle class rather indifferent. Maurice Lamontagne's book on Canadian federalism [11] was an attempt to show how the modernization of French Canada could best be achieved within the context of a strong central government. It was strongly criticized by the same intelligentsia but was warmly received in academic and political circles, labour unions, and by the majority of the new middle class. Maurice Duplessis, in turning down federal aid to education, was not initially acclaimed by the new middle class for doing so but incurred its censure instead. Indeed, his action was applauded only by the Action Nationale and the nationalist wing of its intelligentsia.

Finally, to illustrate the little inclination toward nationalism of the new middle class from 1945 to 1955, one may refer to the celebrated asbestos strike, [12] which rallied the sympathy of the new intelligentsia for the workers and directed its attack on the provincial government for interfering in collective bargaining and supporting management and for its callous disregard for the workers' health. The strike was viewed as a class conflict, not an ethnic conflict; the government was attacked not for ethnic treason but for politicial interference with the rights of the workers.

If modernization was the initial claim to power of the new middle class, if at the beginning the middle class was rather hostile and suspicious of traditional nationalism, this is so obviously not the case in the sixties as to require some explanation for the change and shifts in the ideological positions of the middle class.

In the mid-fifties neo-nationalism as a force dissenting from traditional nationalism made its appearance. The main exponents of neo-nationalism were French-Canadian historians, Michel Brunet being the main spokesman of the new wave. Brunet made a celebrated attack on three tenets of traditional nationalism that were described as myths impeding modern development that could be cast aside. These myths were called: *l'agriculturisme,* or the glorification of the rural life; *le messianisme,* or the concept that French Canadians had a spiritual mission in the North American context, and *l'anti-étatisme*, or the conservative suspicion of the property of state-initiated social and economic activity. This declaration for modernization under the aegis of nationalism and the attack on traditional nationalist tenets heralded the emergence of the social power of nationalism within the new middle class. Traditional nationalism was offensive not because it opposed modernism and industrialization, which it did not, but because it subordinated them to what was felt to be a more basic, more important value, namely, religion.[13] Brunet did not disagree with the tenets of the thirties; he shared their suspicions of the central government.[14] Brunet's pessimism was based on what he perceived to be an inevitable fact — the incapacity of total social development for French Canada because it lacked statehood. He viewed the federal government as a political structure ethnical.y appropriated by English Canadians and as a tool of English-Canadian national interests and aspirations. This he stated as a sad yet inescapable fact which French Canadians must recognize and accept and which worked necessarily in the direction of depriving French Canada of a necessary tool to achieve modern development . . . The only solution lay in relying exclusively on the government of Quebec to transform its province into a national state and to use the full powers of its limited scope to achieve partial development.

For a decade the new middle class remained aloof from, if not hostile to, the tenets of nationalism since its emphasis subordinated modernization to traditional religious values. Nationalism became ideologically compatible when it became decisively modern, slaying as myths the traditional beliefs of agriculturism, messianism and antistatism. It became, in the last decade, increasingly nationalist in its effort to overcome the structural constraints to its growth. The constraints to the growth of the new middle class are a function of the specialized character and the smaller scale and size of the bureaucracies it staffs. The specialized character restricts the channels of mobility and the smaller scale and size restrict the level of mobility . . . This, indeed, is the most important structural clue to understanding the restive or restless character of the new middle class in French Canada and the various competing ideologies, the political attitudes, and the ideological agitation so rampant within its ranks in the last [few] years. To overcome the restricted social mobility of its small bureaucratic pyramids, it has adopted a twofold strategy: (1) a bureaucratic transformation of traditional institutions, and (2) a reaffirmation of linguistic identification, so that by expanding linguistic space and ethnic jurisdiction it can also increase job outlets.

The New Middle Class, Nationalism, and Ethnic Accommodation

Ever since 1760 the French and the English in Canada, for better or for wose, have had interlocking destinies and a shared fate. The pattern of ethnic interaction in the two centuries that have since elapsed can be roughly divided into three periods: (1) from conquest to Confederation, (2) from Confederation to 1950, and (3) from 1950 to the present.

The conquest, as it has been said, involved the takeover by the British of the political and economic institutions of New France. This was greatly facilitated by the massive exodus of the middle-class entrepreneurs and political administrators of New France. It was thus achieved swiftly, completely, and without conflict, for the French Canadians who remained were either farmers or priests. French Canada became a rural society with a clerical elite. Since French Canadians were concerned with ethnic and religious survival and were living in quasi-self-sufficient rural parishes, their interaction with the English political rulers and the economic elite was mediated by a clerically led ethnic elite. The *habitants* in the rural parishes could and did live out their lives in a French environment, with no direct contact with the ruling aliens.

While the French Canadians were rural dwellers, the English were urban, and the social and economic and ethnic division of labour was also to a large extent geographical. Nor did the rural French Canadian meet the English farmer, who was geographically concentrated in the Eastern Townships, so that even rural settlements were neatly divided along ethnic lines. The rural French, for the better part of a century busily involved in reproduction and parochial settlement, were not to meet the English. Contact with the English cam about with industralization, but even then its impact was cushioned by social distance — since the English were status superiors — and by informal interaction, since the linguistic environment of work, while formally English, was and still is informally French for the working class.

The second era in ethnic accommodation extends from Confederation to the postwar period. During this time two major sets of events affected the pattern of ethnic interaction. The first of these concerns the extension of Canadian sovereignty to the Pacific with the settling and development of the West. The second concerns the progressive industrialization of Quebec. Both of these affected the course of ethnic interaction between French and English in Canada: the first set of events affected the patterns of accommodation of the French minorities outside Quebec; the second set the stage for ethnic interaction within Quebec.

Minorities outside Quebec. The birth of Canadian nationalism coincides with Confederation, the political structure that facilitated the geographical extension of sovereignty from the Atlantic to the Pacific. Nationalism is often closely related to geographic expansion and conquest. The conquest and settling of land coordinates group activity, channels energies, provides a common vision and dreams, nurtures and develops nationalist sentiments.

The settling of the West set the stage for the pattern of ethnic conflicts in Canada. The national dilemma of the 1960s reflects the same basic strains in national consensus that arose in the 1870s. George Grant,[15] who laments the defeat of Canadian nationalism, nonetheless recognizes in Diefenbaker a true Canadian nationalist defeated by the concerted and coordinated efforts of the antinational ruling classes whose economic interests are tied to the continental economy and who did not respond to Diefenbaker's vision of the North.

A product of Prairie nationalism, Diefenbaker could not appeal to French Canadians because of his basically American conception of federalism. His emphasis on unhyphenated Canadianism, quite an acceptable doctrine as far as the rights of individuals were concerned, became a threat to the rights of French Canadians as a community. While Grant's diagnosis is correct, his contention that Prairie nationalism is a deviation from traditional nationalism is much more open to question.

The West was settled by the action of the central government, which financed, directly or indirectly, the system of transportation and facilitated immigrant settlement in the western enterprise. When ethnic conflict arose on the school question, Ottawa upheld legislation that curbed the possibility of the existence of French Canadians as communities. That this occurred not only in the West but also in New Brunswick and later in Ontario would indicate that unhyphenated Canadianism enjoyed a central rather than a marginal status in traditional Canadian nationalism. The consequence of the assimilationist impulse of traditional Canadian nationalism has been greater in Quebec than among the French minorities in other provinces. The latter, reduced to immigrant status as they moved out of the boundaries of Quebec, developed ethnic institutions as demographic density permitted, centred around the national parish. The greater impact, however, of these historical events took place in Quebec.

The French Canadian in Quebec. In Quebec the consequence of the assimilationist impulse was to restructure loyalty to and identification with land and institutions. Loyalty became more restricted in space and more selective in institutions. Loyalties of individuals and groups tend to take root and must find expression in space and time. They therefore are affected by proximity and daily interaction. That is why emotional ties to farm, town, and neighborhood need little conceptual elaboration and remain constant in times of stress, national fervour, or national indifference. These kinds of ties, basic to patriotism, are constant, irrespective of the direction of nationalist sentiment and feeling associated with larger social structures.

For the French minorities outside Quebec, the assimilationist pull from the civil and industrial society was counteracted by the norms of kinship and religion. The solution to the dilemma created by the contradictory pull of these opposing norms was and is perfect bilingualism . . . The French-Canadian could stay French only in Quebec, in public as well as in private, in official as well as in unofficial life. His linguistic environment within the confines of his province encompassed his school, his place of work and worship, his hospital, his town hall, and the public streets, and his loyalties could be more sharply differentiated.

Quebec: Industrialization and the pattern of self-segregated institutions. From Confederation to the postwar period the pattern of ethnic accommodation between French and English in Quebec developed within the context of rapid industralization, especially after the turn of the century. Historically, ethnic accomodation has been constructed successfully in Quebec on the basis of mutually desired self-segregated institutions.[16] In the fields of education, religion, welfare, leisure, and residence, institutional self-segregation has been total. The only two areas of societal living where inter-ethnic contact has been institutionalized are those of work and politics. The pattern of ethnic contact of work was established with the introduction of industrialization. Anglo-Saxon industry moved into a society faced with an acute population surplus, a distinctive political and religious elite, and a developing set of institutions anchored in the rural parish. This society, politically stable, economically conservative, and technically unskilled, provided ideal conditions for investing Anglo-Saxon capitalists. They could invest their capital, open industries, and be supplied with an abundant source of unskilled labour seeking employment. The managerial and technical levels were filled, with no protest, by the incoming group, who also brought along their own set of institutions servicing their own nationals. This social setting provided an easy introduction to industry. The French-Canadian elite was ideologically cooperative, protective only about its continued control over its demographic substructures. This led to a mutually satisfying pattern of self-segregated institutions. The English could live in Quebec as autonomous and separate communities, with their own churches, hospitals, schools, and ethnic neighbourhoods . . . This pattern of mutually self-satisfying, self-segregated institutions worked with no dissent up to and including World War II. The historical pattern is now being challenged by the recently emerged French-Canadian new middle class. The traditional ethnic division of labour is now under attack and the present climate of uncertainty has arisen as a result.

With the postwar emergence of the new middle class, a new era in ethnic interaction has set in, and a search for a new deal in ethnic accommodation is being sought by the French-Canadian new middle class under the impetus of reformist nationalism. As noted above, neo-natioalism in *traditional* societies is linked with social change in the direction of modernization. Reformist in outlook, the new middle class seeks to extend its scope, size, and mobility. It becomes revolutionary when it successfully enrolls the support of the peasants and working classes in taking over control of the state by successfully indicting colonialist rule. This situation is *not* paralleled in French Canada. Despite the inroads of separatism, separatist ideology has not succeeded in enlisting the support of the working classes or the rural people, and the colonialist indictment has been rejected. Historically, the exploitative view of the English presence is inaccurate and does not reflect the way it was initiated. Rather than rally to separatist unrest, the lower classes joined the Créditiste ranks in proclaiming the possibility of the middle-class dream for all.

The new middle class in French Canada, like its counterparts in traditional societies, however, has a stake in modernization. Having achieved political dominance, the provincial state to a large extent is seeking to meet its demands. In seeking to overcome the constraints to its growth and continued mobility, it is seeking a new social convention in ethnic accommodation and its institutional arrangements met the needs of incipient industrialization. At that time, the ethnic division of labour reflected the complementary needs of both ethnic groups, and ethnic competition did not take the form of occupational competition.

The new middle class, however, by training, outlook and culture increasingly similar to its ethnically alien counterpart, is also increasingly in competition with it. In its search to expand its channels of mobility and widen its areas of development it is examining the assumptions of institutional self-segregation. Now that it is politically in control, its views may be acted upon. Thus the traditional patterns of financing education, welfare, and health – wherein the pattern of institutional segregation has often meant better services, better facilities, and better salaries for the English involved in these areas within the confines of the province – are being questioned. The differentials in resources and income are not new, but the fact that these differntials are viewed as special privileges is recent and new. That in its search for resources to expand its bases the new middle class will seek to change traditional arrangements in these areas is a foregone conclusion. That such changes are upsetting to the English Quebecers is already apparent. Bred by the Church, having achieved control of the provincial state, the French-Canadian new middle class is not anxious to move from social to industrial bureaucracy. Bureaucratic state capitalism as well as linguistic expansion in the management of private industry are only assorted tools in its ongoing attempt to increase its social and occupational space.

Notes

1. Hans H. Gerth and C. Wright Mills, *Character and Social Structure: The Psyology of Social Institutions* (New York, 1964), 192 ff.

2. This whole development is to a great extent dependent on the model of collective behaviour given in Neil Smelser, *A Theory of Collective Behaviour* (New York, 1962), Ch. 3.

3. These themes are to be found abuntantly in the writings of C. Wright Mills, notably in his *Cause of World War III* (New York, 1958).

4. See Léon Gérin, *Aux sources de notre histoire* (Montreal, 1946), and also Hubert Guindon, "The Social Evolution of Quebec Reconsidered", *Canadian Journal of Economics and Political Science,* 26 (November, 1960), 533-551.

5. Michel Brunet, *Canadians et Canadiens* (Montreal, 1954).

6. Léon Gérin, *Le Type économique et social des Canadiens* (Montreal, 1938), as quoted in Everett C. Hughes, *French Canada in Transition* (Chicago, 1963), 4.

7. See Horace Miner, *St. Denis: A French-Canadian Parish* (Chicago, 1939), Ch.11.

8. Guindon, "The Social Evolution of Quebec Reconsidered", *op. cit.* 545-546.

9. Hubert Guindon, "Social Unrest, Social Class and Quebec's Bureaucratic Revolution", *Queen's Quarterly* 71 (Summer, 1964), 155.

10. Consult the works of Esdras Minville and especially those of François Albert Angers during the thirties and forties. See also the review *Action Nationale* during this period.

11. *La Fédéralisme Canadien* (Quebec, 1954).

12. P.E. Trudeau, *La Grève de l'amiante* (Montreal, 1956).

13. This is the striking difference between nationalist intellectuals like Minville, on the one hand, and Michel Brunet, on the other.

14. Brunet, *Canadians et Canadiens, op. cit.*

15. *Lament for a Nation* (Princeton, 1965).

16. Guindon, "Social Unrest, Social Class", *op. cit.* 155.

3

Canada: The New Nationalism*

Abraham Rotstein

For as long as most people can remember, a glance out of the corner of one's eye to the upper half of North America would bring warm reassurance that things were moving quietly and gracefully *somewhere* in the world. Alphonse and Gaston could invariably be heard out there bowing and scraping, and toasting their long undefended border. Today, official devotees of this stately two-step are still meeting and greeting, but few take the old shuffle at face value. Instead, private conversations in directors' board rooms, in expensive lunch clubs, in government cafeterias and in faculty lounges have a distinctly worried and wary undertone.

Bad consciences do exist about this overdeveloped and one-sided intimacy that has grown up between the two countries, but that, as everyone knows, is not the stuff of politics. It is not conscience and sentiment which are beginning to interfere with the work-a-day world of gas and oil and the purchase and sale of branch plants, but a new and distinct phase of Canadian nationalism.

This nationalism is still frail and, considering the circumstances, a belated arrival on the political scene. The editor of an eminent American publication put the crucial question in a recent visit. "Why," he wanted to know, "is there so *little* nationalism in Canada?" It was clear that he knew the background very well. On the economic side, 58 percent of the manufacturing sector is in foreign hands as are 61 of the largest 102 corporations in the manufacturing, resources and utility fields. Seventy-five percent of the capital employed in our oil and natural gas industry is foreign controlled and 52 percent of the trade union movement takes orders of one sort or another from American head offices.

On the cultural side the situation is no better. About half of the university professors in the humanities and social sciences are non-Canadian. Foreign magazines account for 85 percent of the total magazine circulation; foreign books (those not authorized by Canadians) form 83 percent of book sales, and 71 percent of the publishing industry in foreign-controlled; 96 percent of the films in Canadian cinemas are foreign, as are much of television, plays, art—and on and on it goes. In Canada, we may still own the cupboard, but little of the contents.

"Foreign," of course, means mainly American (about four-fifths) in every case. What one Canadian economist, Bruce Wilkinson, stated about Canada's intense trade concentration with the United States, can be applied to the economic and cultural situation as a whole: "Canada's position resembles more closely that of a less-developed nation than that of other developed countries."

---

* From *Foreign Affairs*, Vol. 55, No. 1 (October) 1976, 97–118, by permission of the author and publishers.

But statistics alone do not tell the story about the quality of everyday life. It would be a mistake to evoke the image of Canada as a seething colony struggling to break loose. Canada bears rather the signs of a successful lobotomy to which it has voluntarily assented. The routine of daily existence is comfortable, decent and sane. There is only the occasional disorientation of not really knowing what country you are living in. Saunter into a drugstore and there is hardly a Canadian paperback to be found anywhere, although an enormous number have been published. The 10,000 mass paperback outlets in Canada provide the American books read by the great majority of the population, while Canadian books have their home in the 400 proper bookstores. Stroll down the main street of your average city, the marquees alight with the titles and stars of the latest films, and hardly a Canadian film is available anywhere, although several hundred have been made in recent years. Turn on your TV set and the chances are two out of three that it will be an American network show on your television screen. Silent qualms surface now and then, but soon one is lulled into passive acceptance, with a fading sense of loss. Increasingly Americanized tastes in Canada acquire a priority of their own, while the very capacity to create and relay our own sense of self rapidly atrophies.

Occasionally there are surrealistic moments that break the numbness – untypical events that throw the "normal" situation into high relief. In the tangled skein of oil and gas negotiations between Canada and the United States, one of the landmark events occurred on September 29, 1970, when then Energy Minister Joe Greene announced that the Federal Cabinet had approved the largest gas export license in Canadian history – 6.3 trillion cubic feet, to be exported over a 15-to-20 year period. The National Energy Board had urged the Cabinet to approve the massive gas export to the United States on the basis of a set of reserve figures supplied by the Canadian Petroleum Association. (Despite its name, the Association consists largely of the major American oil companies which do over 90 percent of the production and refining.) On June 2, 1971, these reserve figures were made public by the Energy Minister when he stated: "At 1970 rates of production, these reserves represent 923 years supply for oil and 392 years for gas."

The rest is history. In April 1975, the same National Energy Board reported that Canada would have a natural gas shortage *within this decade* and oil production would decline to the point where Canada would become a net importer of oil. Canada is already in that position. Yet the American oil companies remain undaunted and are now pressing (with Canadian government support) for the Mackenzie Valley Pipeline to carry both the Delta and Alaska gas, *because* of the urgent and imminent gas shortage.

Data on energy reserves expand and contract like an accordion but even Canadian numbness and gullibility have their limits. The rising tide of popular skepticism begins to question all the oil companies' arguments, certainly questions the basis of all our oil and gas export agreements, and even begins to wonder wistfully why oil and gas production should not be in Canadian hands.

One further touch of the surreal in Canada will suffice to throw some light on the quality of everday existence. In recent years we have had a national university commission investigating the role (actually the absence) of Canadian courses in our universities. Its recent report, *To Know Ourselves,* recounts the testimony from some American sociologists who now predominate on the staff of Canadian universities. The report states that these sociologists "were even forthright enough to tell the commission that they would not hire Canadians for 'their' departments because 'once one hires a few then they will be pushing for more and more.[7]"

However bizarre these episodes, the American sociologists as well as the American oil companies are, in their own way, "right." Once the game warden has declared open season, everyone is quite entitled to look to his own catch.

As a nationalist and a dispirited critic of Canadian government policy, I had no immediate answer to the question: why indeed is there so little nationalism, so little concern with serious countermeasures that are crucial to hold the American tide in check and to sustain whatever is still possible of an autonomous national existence?

For the more articulate segments of the community, the press, the political commentators, the academics and so on, it required a sophisticated myopia to fail to notice the self-immolation of Canadian independence in the postwar period. Indeed, the great American takeover has been aided and encouraged by internal forces, what one author called in a summary theme, Canada's "silent surrender." These forces are as prevalent in government as in business. They exist in the trade unions as much as in the groves of academe. The transition to institutionalized dependence occurred with the greatest impetus in the last two decades at precisely the time when, in the rest of the world, the trend was in the opposite direction.

In a belated fashion, Canada is beginning to come awake, and beginning to explore and even to implement new policies. But the penetration of American society in Canada is now so great that there is no practical way to distinguish domestic and foreign policy. New domestic policies inevitably touch the huge American sector closely. Official Canadian foreign policy declarations, such as the "third option" (the move to somewhat lesser dependence on the United States), are little more than changing domestic policy seen in the rearview mirror. They are an effective guide to the past.

Thus, the future of the Canadian-American relationship must be sought on the domestic scene but not necessarily within the federal government. Its recent initiatives have, on the whole, been weak. The Foreign Investment Review Agency aims to achieve better terms for Canada on U.S. takeovers of Canadian business and on new ventures. But even the U.S. financial journal *Barron's* admitted: "It is difficult to imagine a legitimate business venture which would be impeded by the Foreign Investment Review Act . . . the only U.S. business which wouldn't be cordially welcomed to Canada is Murder, Inc."

As far as energy is concerned, the closing of the door on oil exports to the United States in 1982 will occur after the horse has gone. By 1985, net imports of oil to Canada will amount to 50 percent of Canadian requirements.

On the cultural front, the Canadians edition of *Time* has, after 15-year debate, been declared non grata because of the ease with which dumped U.S. copy would siphon off Canadian advertising dollars. Some additional cultural initiatives are pending.

Reassurances to Washington from the Department of External Affairs continue, but the rhetoric of officialdom in a federal state is bellied by unexpected eruptions at the periphery, somewhere in the disparate collection of regional loyalties and semi-autonomous institutional structures which constitute the kingdoms (in the plural) of Canada.

With little warning, gas export prices in British Columbia are hiked several times over; the province of Saskatchewan proposes to reclaim half of its potash industry now largely in American hands. Seemingly unfriendly gestures are being made by the autonomous Canadian Radio-Television and Telecommunications Commission to strip the cable TV commercials coming into Canada from U.S. border stations in order to provide a financial base for Canadian programming. The membership of "Canadian unions" is becoming much more restless under American control, and rapid moves toward autonomy are taking place among the teamsters, construction workers, railway workers and chemical workers.

Some other faint thunder is heard here and there in different parts of Canada, but does that really mean lightning is about to follow? Is the age of Canadian immobilism and benign somnolence coming to an end? Canadian nationalists might indeed wish this were so, but their aspirations are as premature as the darker American suspicions.

Everyone was looking for a toehold on the problem, including my visiting American, but none was immediately apparent. I told him that perhaps the answer to his question lay somewhere in the deeper recesses of the elusive Canadian psyche. Some sort of shifting internal deadlock in Canada suggested itself, but how could it ever be uncovered? It may take an unconventional imagination to probe the dynamics of Canadian-American relations at present. As with the ice floes of the Canadian north, th greater preponderance lies beneath the surface. My aim here is not to explore the merits of the immediate issues, nor to air the grievances on either side, but to probe th difficult substratum where the problems have their source. What is developing now is rooted in those antecedent dramas of history and those formative casts of mind that push periodically to center stage. To quote one of our better known Canadian poets and balladeers, Leonard Cohen, "let us compare mythologies."

II

In the year of the American Bicentennial, retrospective reflections are the order of the day. Among the most compelling is the work of the American historian Louis Hartz who, in *The Founding of New Societies,* explained how countries of the New World grew and developed within the matrix of that set of beliefs that existed at the moment of their birth. The "fragment" of the Old World that was planted in new soil was a seed carrying John Locke's philosophy of liberalism and freedom. "Born free," Americans must be allowed to become equal. The inner drive has a compelling hold, and, Hartz suggests, "cannot tolerate an accommodation of degree."

Much that was later to emerge as the ideology of American bourgeois society had its roots in that *forma mentis* or the pristine cast of mind of this liberalism. As U.S. history evolved, through Jacksonian democracy, the New Deal, and the Great Society, Hartz maintains that this ethos became "a moral absolute, a national essence, a veritable way of racial life." This ideological leaven pervaded the search for the solutions of ills such as the problem of blacks and poverty.

The very dragon that produced the ferocity of the American Civil War was reiterated in the moral brinkmanship of the cold war. The American liberal ethos, in Hartz' interpretation, proclaims that "the world is really one," and this ideology provides Americans "with a shield against the Saracen [and] the only imaginable moral way of dealing with the man outside the West."

A distinct economic ideology formed an integral part of American liberalism. Free exchange, freely arrived at, always and inherently evenhanded, became the filter through which economic life was viewed. If economic practice did not live up to this prescription, the function of national policy was to restructure the environment to appear to conform to the ideology, from fair trade practices to regulatory agencies and antitrust legislation.

In the 1960s—the coming of age of the multinational corporation—American economic liberalism acquired cosmic wings once more as the economic and moral elements fused. For Roy Ash, the former head of Litton Industries, the world corporation respresented a "transcendental unity," for "nothing can stop an idea whose time has come." This global vision pervaded the American view of much of what has transpired in Canada. Canadian concerns with the integrity of the nation-state, or the preservation of political and cultural autonomy, receive short shrift against this symphonic resonance of global progress ringing in American ears. Fair dealing, the justice inherent in the marketplace, the sancity of contracts that have been freely entered into by both parties—these serve as a moral shield against the seemingly outmoded objections that Canadians raise. Such an attitude deeply imbues the outlook of American officialdom as well as American business. The U.S. State Department, while sharing the traditional but limited American skepticism about its own corporations, takes a stand on opposing any Canadian legislation that appears to be either retroactive or discriminatory against American interests.

Thus Americans hold firmly to the implicit premise that all that has transpired to date in Canadian-American relations has, by and large, been evenhanded and mutually beneficial. There have, admittedly, been marginal problems in this vast web of interconnections, but a strong tradition of open lines of communication and administrative flexibility has been, and will be able, to resolve the difficulties.

The cumulative political effect with which we now have to contend in Canada appears as the result of unintended and unforeseen consequences; blind spots were at least as operative on the Canadian as on the American side. But the liberal ethos now provides the moral basis for downgrading and tuning out the difficult, unwieldly, and ultimately dangerous problem of the vast American presence. Those who uphold the code of square dealing and who expect their partners to do the same find that the frail Canadian nationalist rhetoric seems to saddle them with a bad conscience. But they tend to reassure themselves that they have played by the rules of the game and the rules carry no particular compensatory provisions for losers ("handicaps," in rare cases, must be specified at the outset). How, in any case, can there be "losers" in a game whose rules are always "even-steven"? When some understanding is forthcoming, it tends at the same time to echo Lyndon Johnson's first public reference to the Canadian-American relationship: "Canada is such a close neighbor and such a good neighbor that we always have plenty of problems there. They are kind of like problems in the hometown."

The latest expressions of American policy bear clearer marks of recognition of the Canadian situation, but are still not easily budged from the traditional stance. Richard Vine, a Deputy Assistant Secretary in the U.S. State Department, went over the ground recently before the House of Representatives Subcommittee on International Political and Military Affairs. While sympathizing with the "Canadian effort to promote expanded economic and cultural autonomy," he recognized the problems involved:

> National controls can rarely be expanded without some impact, usually adverse, on established interests in the area of control . . . The U.S. government has a responsibility to protect the American interests affected to the extent possible and appropriate.

Friendly personal relations, extensive consultation and administrative flexibility are desirable in themselves, but serve to disguise, even from Americans, the hidden rigidity of American policy. The friendly tone still continues with talk of "interdependance" and "mutual benefits" but it is entirely geared to the dubious objective of the preservation of the status quo. For Americans to insist on nondiscrimination in Canadian policies is tantamount to suggesting that we continue to play blindman's buff with the overwhelming American presence. For Americans to continue to insist on nonretroactive policies only is to abort from the outset any possibility of fundamental change. Together, the two pillars of U.S. State Department policy seem to some Canadians merely a license for cosmetic changes, a variant of Henry Ford's aphorism about black cars.

But on the other side, unpreparedness is just as great. Many Canadians greeted Nixon's declaration of the end of "the special relationship" with an inaudible but vast sigh of relief. But they were nevertheless still hard put to answer concretely and in some detail the increasingly truculent question, "What do Canadians want?"

III

> I'm struck by the clarity of the American sense of history: in the beginning, the Americans created America. And ever since, they've been consulting their beginning, the way fundamentalists consult the book of Genesis . . . Canadians don't have such a clear sense of when things began and ended.
> —*Northrop Frye*

What appears to many as the paralyzing deadlock of Canadian policy toward the United States, the substantial acquiescence by Canadians in their own takeover, stems from the effects of two different systems of belief that remain out of phase: Canadian liberalism, the credo of the dominant elite culture in Canada, and Canadian populism that grows out of a "homestead mentality." While elements of both systems may be present in the same individuals and in the same political parties and while we must ride roughshod over the fine points and exceptions, these two casts of mind are, so to speak, the two psychic horns of the English-speaking Canadian dilemma.

Canadian liberalism is a close cousin of the American variety. Their origins are common but the cadences and mode of development in Canada differ. The ingesting of nineteenth-century British liberalism was the inevitable consequence of the pride Canadians initially took in their colonial status. Philosophy, economics, politics and law had Oxbridge and Westminster as their respective models. Rhodes scholars and other cadres of the able and affluent went to England for many generations to pay homage to civilization at is apogee. They returned to slip into the waiting position in business, finance, the universities and the civil service. The global perspectives of nineteenth-century England became the official Canadian credo. Free trade (at least in theory if not in practice) and free markets, civil liberties and parliamentary government, would bring the latter-day millennium of the Enlightenment—English style. Oxford accents sometimes sat uneasily atop Canadian French and barely masked a native Ottawa Valley shrewdness, but the prerogatives of shouldering manfully the delegated responsibilities of the Empire were the order of the day.

The loosening of ties with Britain in the interwar period had no more dramatic consequences for national self-consciousness than that of a dutiful and dependent adolescent reluctantly home at last. The country's self-image never rose in stature above Mackenzie King's truculent ambivalence toward Britain and his seemingly cunning flirtation with the United States. Mackenzie King stated to the American Minister in Ottawa in 1935 that Canada was prepared to loosen its British ties and take "the American road," if a good trade agreement with the United States could be arranged.

The trade agreements were eventually forthcoming for reasons of their own, and the Second World War, in turn, brought a more substantial entente and integration between the two countries under King's direction. King became a good deal more suspicious of "the American road" toward the end of his life, but he had set a pattern followed in broad outline by successive Canadian prime ministers.

Lester Pearson's views heralded a transformation in Canadian opinion to "internationalism," leapfrogging the rather suspect and parochial elements of nationalism. This shining aura overlay the close ties being knotted together under the pressures of the cold war, the joint continental defense agreements, and the open-door policy to all things American. Few paused to wonder at the rather limited range of the "internationalism" we were, in fact, practising.

Among the most important new influences was the rise of mass education in the postwar period and the redirection of large numbers of Canadian university students from graduate study in Great Britain to the United States. The intellectual atmosphere and assumptions of the University of Chicago, MIT, Harvard and Columbia became the norms of expanding Canadian university staffs and of middle-rank and key civil servants.

In the area of economics, the drums began to beat once more for free trade, and by close analogy for free capital movement. When the institutional form of this capital increasingly became the highly visible hand of the multinational corporation, Canadian economists regilded this new phenomenon with the old paint of Adam Smith. Nothing really new was happening, they maintained, and a carte blanche welcome was to be the policy of the postwar decades. Whatever second thoughts arose in Ottawa were soon suppressed under the old mercantile wisdom of not looking gift horses in the mouth and genuine fears of unemployment. Political time-horizons were short and long-term consequences would look after themselves.

Among the more euphoric prophets of the liberal ethos, elegiac notions arose of Canada as an "international nation," bypassing all that embarrassing, chauvinistic talk of nationhood, which, as everyone knew, simply led to wars. (Whom would Canada attack?) This sentimental miasma produced a comprehensive integrated vision that legitimized the American tide—a vision liberal to its core. In brief summary its components were as follows: an international community seemingly without its constituent component—nations; national intellectual "excellence" without the "parochialism" of national traditions, a community of scholars without any special concern for those indigenous boundaries which shape the direction of national inquiry (the inquiry that *produces* knowledge rather than simply living off everyone else's insights); an economy without specificity—manufactured goods as well as resources are all "commodities," faceless units of exchange in both the domestic and international economy. As the gold rush developed for Canadian resources, the door was opened wider still by the conventional economic wisdom. It maintained that there can, by definition, be no overdevelopment in any sector, if "comparative advantage" is pursued under the aegis of the "market."

The Economic Council of Canada, the government's official advisory body, was under the full sway of this economic wisdom. It never deemed the problem of foreign investment in Canada worthy of a full and proper study, even though hundreds of other topics were closely scrutinized. The debate on foreign investment was launched instead by a tiny subculture of economists and politicians who refused to take liberal rhetoric and neoclassical economic theory at face value. The chief documents to emerge were the Gordon Commission Report (1958), the Watkins Report (1968), the Wahn Report (1970) and the Gray Report (1972).[1] They all tried to deal with the issues of Canadian independence in various ways that straddled economics and politics. A picture began to emerge of the "truncation" of Canadian industry — branch plants devoid of research and development facilities, dependent on marketing and purchasing decisions centralized in U.S. head offices—and an overdeveloped resource sector that provided relatively less employment than equivalent manufacturing activity.

The picture was of course mixed, for foreign capital did provide increased employment, paid taxes, and brought new technological and management techniques into the country. But foreign investment was clearly not foreign aid. The specific balance-of-payments effects of foreign investment were difficult to isolate, but one study may give a very rough indication of the magnitudes involved in the two-way flow. The short-term and long-term inflow of capital to Canada between 1950 and 1974 was around $20 billion. This was matched by an outflow of slightly over $40 billion in the same period ($7 billion in interest payments, $17 billion in dividends and $16 billion in "service charges," such as license and management fees).

The Science Council of Canada began to fill in the picture where the Economic Council feared to trend. Its 1972 study, *Innovation and the Structure of Canadian Industry,* by Pierre L. Bourgault, noted:

> We are the world's largest producer of nickel, but we are net importers of stainless steel and manufactured nickel products, including "cold climate" nickel-cadmium batteries; we are the world's second largest producer of aluminum, but we import it in its more sophisticated forms . . . We are the world's largest exporter of pulp and paper, but we import much of our fine paper and virtually all of the highly sophisticated paper, such as backing for photographic film and dielectric papers for use in electric components; we are one of the world's principal sources of platinum, but it is all exported for refining and processing and reimported in finished forms; we are large exporters of natural gas and petroleum, but we are net importers of petrochemicals; and, although we are the world's foremost exporter of raw asbestos fibres, we are net importers of manufactured asbestos products.

For a country with a higher than average unemployment problem, the low employment content of these resource exports should have meant something. The issue has now been recognized, but the inhibition on effective policy continues despite much talk in recent years about an "industrial strategy" to increase the manufacturing content of our exports.

Nothing was more emblematic of the whole mood of resignation to the incoming tide than the inability of the External Affairs Department to deal with the issue of the extension of American law to American subsidiaries located in Canada. Under the Foreign Assets Control Regulations (the Trading with the Enemy Act), the Sherman Act and Section 7 of the Clayton Act, the American government retains the primary jurisdiction in deciding which countries its foreign subsidiaries can or cannot trade with, when they might or might not discuss mergers, and so on. The divergence from Canadian policy in these matters was often marked, particularly in regard to the American embargo on trade with China, and up until very recently in regard to trade with Cuba.

The crux of the issue, however, lies neither in the value of potential exports to communist countries which have been foregone, nor in whether American antitrust law has had "good" or "bad" effects on the Canadian industrial structure. There may be legitimate debate about both these points, but the central question is the intrusion of American jurisdiction into a great segment of the Canadian economy through the insistence on the control of U.S. subsidiaries. An elaborate administrative apparatus encompassing several U.S. government departments is set up to try to ensure effective compliance with U.S. foreign economic policy and to impose severe penalties in case of violation. There are no "problems," of course, as long as the foreign economic policies of the two countries are congruent.

The records of the Joint Ministerial Committees of the two countries reveal much symbolic table-pounding, but the Canadians never produced a single workable proposal to implement Canadian sovereignty. The Americans, in turn, never budged an inch in principle, although they were prepared to grant case-by-case exemptions under Washington's total discretion.

Arnold Heeney was the top Canadian diplomat of the period and a living embodiment of the liberal vision. Along with the senior American diplomat Livingston Merchant, he produced the 1965 report entitled *Principles of Partnership,* which put forward the proposal that problems between the two countries be settled discreetly in the diplomatic corridors before they erupted as "public positions." But the report did contain the single blanket proposal that American extraterritorial law operating in Canada be unilaterally revoked by the United States. Paragraph 61 stated: "We strongly recommend that the two governments examine promptly the means, through issuance by the United States of a general license or adoption of other appropriate measures, by which this irritant may be removed . . . "

I was involved in a governmental task force at the time, studying the broad range of issues relating to foreign investment in Canada and was intrigued by the origins and fate of this proposal. In a July 1967 interview with Mr. Heeney, he expressed some belated uneasiness about the onrushing integration of Canada and the United States. But he confessed, somewhat shamefacedly, that the one original proposal of the report had come, to his own surprise, from Livingston Mercant, his American counterpart. He had not himself seen at any time how the problem could be solved.

I discovered later that the proposal had been blocked by the U.S. Treasury Department and never got anywhere. But the interview summed up for me the limits of Ottawa's liberal vision: the lurking regret and unwitting day-to-day participation in knotting together and smoothing out the strands of Canadian dependence; the excellence in soft-shoe tactics and the haplessness in strategy. After 1968, when legal proposals began to emerge for the first time from both the Watkins and Wahn Reports that showed how American extraterritorial jursidiction could be effectively blocked by firm action in Canada, the Canadian government ran true to form by deciding that the political costs of marring the American relationships in this way were too high. Nothing was done. In retrospect, it appears to have been an era of flatulent rhetoric and faceless floundering best exhibited by the two Ministers of External Affairs, Paul Martin and Mitchell Sharp.

While it may appear dubious to root concrete and massive economic and political dilemmas in Canada in the astigmatism of liberal theory, exactly that cast of mind, I believe, is the key to Canada's "silent surrender." Canadian liberalism was all of a piece: a sentimental internationalism, a pussyfooting "quiet diplomacy," and a procrustean view of multinational corporations as ever-friendly "market" phenomena.

As it happened, liberalism proclaimed, and indeed celebrated, the nation's nonexistence. Society was reduced by definition to a collection of self-seeking individuals; the state was merely the instrument of the protection of property and the enforcement of contract. The concept of the nation as such entered obtrusively only in awkward and negative ways: in its economic incarnation it was the progenitor of tariffs and other restrictions on the "natural" free flow of trade and capital. Such a natural flow would make, as everyone from Adam Smith to Milton Friedman knew, for grand global harmony.

The absence of a distinct and traumatic movement of self-creation in Canada gave great power and longevity to an imported British liberalism and its subsequent American version, despite the vital threat it posed to Canada's inner integrity as a nation. Missing as always from such colonial projection was the internally rooted sense of a national self, that is, an independent political culture with its accompanying symbols to evoke and protect Canadian nationhood.

What was thereby so effectively blotted out was the problem of power, particularly the locus of economic power. Thus when power began to shift out of the Canadian economy to Chicago, New York and Washington by virtue of the highly visible and active hand of the multinational corporation, and by virtue of our dependence on Washington's legal and economic policies, we were barely conscious that anything of importance had happened. All we could ask was whether the "market" was functioning properly and whether profits (somewhere, anywhere) were being "maximized."

But the nemesis of the twentieth century must come sooner or later to the adherents of nineteenth-century credos. So, too, this era moved to its grand moment of culmination when one event lit up the entire Canadian reality. On December 6, 1971, Prime Minister Trudeau visited President Nixon in Washington on a strange quest. He emerged from this meeting elated and euphoric, for the American President had granted Canada something quite "fantastic." Nothing less than a Canadian Declaration of Independence had emerged out of Washington. Presumably that is where it now had to be sought. However demeaning to Canadian sensibilities, a high degree of political realism was involved in this backhanded recognition of how far American control had extended. As Trudeau put the matter the following day to the Canadian Parliament: "He (the President) assured me that it was in the clear interests of the United States to have a Canadian neighbour, not only independent both politically and economically but also one which was confident that the decisions and policies in each of these sectors would be taken by Canadians in their own interests, in defence of their own values, and in pursuit of their own goals." *Noblesse oblige.* The event was "fantastic" in more ways than one: for Canadian liberalism, the head office is always elsewhere.

IV

But there is a backstage protagonist that has only sporadically appeared on the stage of Canadian-American relations. That protagonist is not, in the first instance, Canadian nationalism, but a more diffuse, unfocused and potentially very powerful force in Canadian politics—grass-roots populism. Its essential cast of mind is the homestead mentality and its articulation is through the politics of space.

In the inner recesses of the Canadian self-image there remains the indelible imprint of the pioneer struggle with the land—the vanquishing of hostile forest, stubborn rock and parched prairie. There is the lasting trauma of outliving bleak winters into a late spring, of existing on the precarious margin of a short Canadian agricultural season. This is the psychic crucible in which Canadian populism was shaped—in latent anxiety, in wariness and reticence and in a sense of ongoing silent siege.

But turning no-man's-land into one's own homestead carries with it ingrained or natural rights that accrue to the survivor. A political sense of earned jurisdiction over a vanquished space that was, at least in principle, inviolable and sacrosanct, became the nuclear element of political identity that arose in the Canadian psyche. Economic and political jurisdiction on the homestead should be untrammeled, and any trespass or political infringement would be resisted.

In the Canadian consciousness, as in Canadian history, the homestead precedes the establishment of the state. This mental landscape that harks back to the primal (even if recent) origins of the country provides the political footing from which the state itself in its various roles may be either substantially endorsed or roundly opposed. The specific political characteristics of the homestead mentality were, often enough, vague; without a strong ideological base and essentially anti-establishment in its orientation, it remained tied by a powerful navel cord to the land either in fact or in persistent imagination. The essential political framework was space rather than class.

Canadian populism is not unique but seems more firmly entrenched than American populism and more readily articulated in a federal system, particularly as the distance from Ottawa increases. Among its distinct features is the very high priority given to preserving social order over established territory. The national symbol in Canada is not the cowboy or the covered wagon—those self-reliant symbols of rough justice individually dispensed—but the opposite, the "Mountie," the lone representative and guarantor of central authority in barely policed areas who "always gets his man." Canadians are prepared to support a virtually unlimited role of the state in the preservation of social order and in the concomitant assertion of sovereignty over the "homestead writ large," the "Dominion from sea to sea." The evidence for such a deep-seated but widely pervasive cast of mind is necessarily impressionistic and scattered, only surfacing occasionally.

The primary concern is with the land. Thus it happened that from the apparently least nationalist part of the country, the Maritime Provinces, there emerged the most stringent legislation barring foreigners from owning land. This has been repeated in Saskatchewan, and has now become an active concern in virtually all provinces, and the federal government is prepared to follow their lead. On September 5, 1975, Prime Minister Trudeau sent a letter to the ten provincial premiers offering to introduce federal legislation granting the provinces the right to restrict foreign ownership of property.

The priority given to land, and the corresponding lethargy regarding industry and technology in the Canadian imagination, were never more dramatically illustrated than in an incident which occurred in 1969. At that time the Humble Oil Company, seeking a Northwest Passage to export Alaskan oil by ship, sent the American vessel *Manhattan* through the Arctic waters. This raised the specter of whether Canadian sovereignty in Arctic waters was being challenged or jeopardized (the legal issues of which we must bypass here). Recall that this was prior to the oil and gas boom in the Canadian north, so that what was at issue was the fate of the ice floes and glaciers in a virtually uninhabited part of the country. Suddenly, Canadian newspapers from coast to coast, most of which had traditionally welcomed the takeover of Canadian businesses, now wrote as many as two or three editorials a day in great alarm. "Fly the Canadian Flag" read the hysterical headline of the now-defunct Toronto *Telegram*, a newspaper that had viewed with complacency the passing of 70 percent of southern Ontario's industry to American control.

But this same consciousness underlies (quite apart from the economic issues) Canada's perennial concern with fishing zones, and more recently the 200-mile offshore limit, and its substantial initiative at the Conference on the Law of the Sea. It is also the homestead mentality that may account for the otherwise totally inexplicable Canadian preoccupation with water. Canada possesses something on the order of 20 to 50 percent of the world's supply of fresh water, and an enormous amount runs off annually into the sea, perhaps six percent of the world's runoff. (As usual, we have no exact statistics.) Yet one of the silent but absolute premises that unites Canadians from coast to coast is that not a single drop should be exported, no matter how great the surplus supply may be. As the former premier of British Columbia, W. A. C. Bennett, who had never hesitated to sell anything to the highest bidder, once stated: "Even to talk about selling water is ridiculous. Water is our heritage and you don't sell your heritage." This curious attitude was reflected in the Canadian response to the 1973 Point Roberts affair.[2]

Without wishing in any way here to advocate the export of water, or to minimize the enormous environmental issues involved, it seems clear from the data we do have that the potential export of a fraction of our surplus water might easily exceed in value any single item of Canadian exports. It is now completely wasted. My purpose, however, is to indicate one of the areas where the deep-seated homestead mentality has surfaced in the political arena and has held fast. The issue of water is as "self-evident" to Canadians at large, as it is puzzling to everyone else.

Land and water are the clues to the underlying attitudes in the new phase of Canadian nationalism which centers on resources, particularly energy resources. The important question in Canada is the extent to which the same cast of mind is now beginning to surface on these closely related issues. As the leading Canadian historian, Donald Creighton, a man of conservative bent, explained in 1970:

> Canadians instinctively regard their natural resources in a very special light. . . . . These natural resources are not looked upon as ordinary assets—things the Canadians have built or acquired themselves. They are regarded as part of the original endowment of nature, as the birthright of Canada. Many of them are not owned absolutely, as they would be in the United States, by private enterprises. They are properties in which the Crown retains a right, which it has sometimes converted into public ownership, for the beneficial interest of the people of Canada.

It appears that public opinion supports this position. A Gallup Poll of May 16, 1973, asked whether the "Canadian government should nationalize our energy resources, such as oil and gas." Of Canadians across the country 48 percent replied in the affirmative, while 36 percent were opposed. A positive plurality emerged in all three Canadian political parties. A similar Gallup Poll taken in the first week of November 1975 indicated a figure of 51 percent in favor of nationalizing oil and gas and 31 percent opposed.

Thus it would be a mistake to interpret the renewed call for reclaiming our oil and gas, as well as other resources such as potash, as a sudden spread of socialist ideology. The activation of the federal government's corporation, Petro-Canada, as well as similar corporations in provinces such as Alberta, Newfoundland and Saskatchewan, reflect an extension of this territorial ethic, not radical in its complexion but essentially conservative. It was a Conservative government that nationalized electricity in Ontario in 1910 and Conservative governments now operate in Alberta and Newfoundland while a social democratic government operates in Saskatchewan.

Thus, populist politics in Canada are indeed the politics of space. Canadian sensitivity to the extraterritorial extension of American law, referred to earlier, has been the chief basis for much unease over American investment. The traditional concern with the integrity of Canadian authority on the "homestead writ large" has far outweighed other considerations such as an unbalanced or truncated economic structure, overdependence on resource development for the U.S. market and a rapidly eroding technological capability.

But the politics of space does not make for a uniform endorsement of state intervention. An indirect legacy of this same cast of mind reinforces the existing struggle of both business and labor against various measures proposed by the federal government. The businessman who struggled to carve out his enterprise "against great odds" will barely tolerate any interference in his prerogative; hence the remarkable campaign mounted by the business community a few years ago against the tax reform proposals of the Carter Commission to fundamentally restructure the business "homestead." Economics was not at issue here (despite much rhetoric about free enterprise) but rather politics, the claim to untrammeled autonomy and jurisdiction of the institutional homestead.

Union leaders who carved out their "homestead," i.e., their union jurisdiction, in the difficult days of the early 1930s, will not tolerate limits on the collective bargaining process—their rightfully earned area of "total authority." In the debate over the government's anti-inflation program of wage and price controls, Canadian labor unions were militantly opposed as were unions in other countries. But a hidden dimension added a particular acrimony to this debate in Canada. Canadian unions were prepared to sink the whole anti-inflation program because it was an intrusion into their political space.

These are not primary but background features of the domestic political scene, and by no means unique to Canada. But in a federal state such as Canada, populism has held on longer and more forcefully, sheltered by the significant provincial enclaves of power. The implicit political game in Canada is somehow to tap this very powerful and widespread populist undercurrent. If successfully achieved on rare occasions, the political payoff can be enormous. This largely accounts, in my view, for the landslide Conservative victories by John Diefenbaker in 1958–59. Diefenbaker appeared as the living image of old-fashioned prairie populism. It also accounts, for quite different reasons—largely because of an image of popular irreverence and iconoclasm—for the substantial Liberal victory of Pierre Trudeau in 1968: the upper-class man in populist clothing.

Populists feel safest when they can have it both ways. While they retain a healthy skepticism of the liberal establishment—the moneyed, the educated and the bureaucracy—they are not prepared to trust their own leaders to govern except on rare occasions. (This syndrome is not unlike that of the British Labour Party's tendency to select its leaders from the graduates of the public school and from Oxbridge.) Populism is more often successful on the provincial rather than the federal scene where the risks of bungling by those without "class" or "experience" are less. In day-to-day politics, populism stands aside as a suspicious but vigilant monitor of potential state intrusions into the equivalent of the homestead, and as a militant guardian of social order and national sovereignty.

Thus at the time of the OPEC oil embargo, when Americans heard the crisp statements of Canadian intentions not to pool energy shortages with the United States, but instead to cut back on energy exports, they might have discerned several different notes in the chord. First, there was the reaction to the fiasco around the nonexistent reserves centered on the oil companies' misleading figures. Second, the underlying populist sentiment in Canada had now begun to come forward as an ongoing and overt political factor around the resources question. Third, the nationalist message itself had begun to penetrate the political process.

The linking of these latter two elements may be decisive and may become the dominant factor in future Canadian-American relations.

V

I have overdrawn somewhat the characteristics of the two major casts of mind in Canada. Their elements are often to be found in some combination within the same individual and within all three major political parties. How do they each relate to the new nationalism?

Modern Canadian nationalism is a relative latecomer to the political scene, barely two decades old. It cannot be understood as a movement, but as a countermovement to the astigmatism of the liberal position. Its aim is to protect the fabric of Canadian society against the autonomous and relentless forces running "free" in the North American market economy.

In their public image in Canada, nationalists stand in some awkward middle position between liberals and populists, somewhat suspect to both sides. Populists tend to regard nationalism as an elite heresy, the inverse image of the liberal ethic in which they have no direct stake, and have therefore largely stood aloof from a full nationalist program. Liberals, in turn, have tended to regard the nationalist position as a retrogressive, inward-looking throwback, vaguely populist, for which there is no clear place in the modern world.

Nevertheless, despite these suspicions, and because of the palpable force of circumstances, a limited form of nationalism has quietly spread to a wide segment of the population and has in its own way outrun the actual membership of nationalist organizations such as the Committee for an Independent Canada.

But there are no optimistic forecasts to be made any more for the recapturing by Canadians of their own economic and cultural autonomy—even though in the modern world, the issue can at best be only a matter of degree. Sometimes it seems to Canadian nationalists, from past experience, that if things can possibly go wrong, they will. Nevertheless, there are solid indications that the major battle in Canada has now begun over the question of resources. Here the populist consciousness may well become fully engaged in the reclaiming of the "homestead" along with nationalists whose concern has traditionally been the wider link between resources and industry. Liberals, in turn, now have cause to see all about them, late in the day as it is, the consequences of their beneficent sleepwalking and defer in a limited way to moderate nationalist arguments.

But none of this in itself necessarily makes for substantial policy changes in Canada. Change, rather, is being galvanized by economic factors: increases in heating and gasoline bills, the vast capital sums that will be needed for pipelines from the north and their attendant inflationary effects, and the major balance-of-payments problems that Canada may anticipate from mounting oil imports.

The nationalist program on energy exports now begins to make sense to many Canadians for it calls for a substantial further reduction in energy exports to the United States. While there is no unanimity on how much or how quickly, a further cut from the 1976 level of 460,000 barrels of oil a day would seem to be warranted, i.e., a more rapid implementation of existing policy.

In regard to natural gas, the Canadian government is following a standpat position, hoping to fulfill existing contracts with the United States—however fraudulent the information on which the 1970 export decision was based—and to meet the domestic shortage with a vastly expensive pipeline from the far north. Since Canadian discoveries of gas in the north are still inadequate to finance a pipeline (3.5 to 5 trillion cubic feet), the intention is to have the pipeline carry jointly Canadian and Alaskan gas, the latter destined for the United States. Total long term contracts call for the export of 14 trillion cubic feet of Canadian gas to the United States between 1974 and 1995. It is the commitment of these export contracts and the uncertainty about the rate of new discoveries in Alberta and their deliverability that prompts this pipeline policy. Meanwhile, the most easily accessible, high pressure gas field (Waterton B.H.K. and Kaybob South) are now under contract to California by the American-owned Alberta and Southern Gas Co. Approximately one trillion cubic feet of gas is exported annually from western Canada, equal to two-thirds of domestic Canadian consumption.

Most nationalists in Canada would argue for a drastic change in government policy. The Mackenzie Valley pipeline would cost some $10 billion to build. It would have substantial disruptive effects on northern ecology and on the native peoples, and would produce a serious inflationary impact on the Canadian economy. This could all be averted by a moratorium on the project contingent on a drastic reduction of gas exports to the United States.

Under sections 17(2) and 85 of the National Energy Board Act such reduction or elimination of licensed exports is legally possible if domestic supply conditions warrant it. The diversion of, say, 10 trillion cubic feet of gas, earmarked for export, to domestic use would add seven years to Canada's gas supply at 1975 consumption rates and would postpone the need for this expensive pipeline. While new discoveries were being sought in Alberta, American buyers might be given three year's notice of the rescinding of our export agreements and might then contract for whatever surplus gas they would discover that would begin to fulfill their overly sanguine 1970 reserve estimates.

Not to be neglected are the long-term political problems associated with moving Alaskan gas through a pipeline to the United States. The claims of native groups and environmentalists have hardly begun to be met and we can anticipate that political opposition in this whole area may be very great. Given the potential strategic importance of such a pipeline to the United States, the interests of the American military and intelligence establishments in the security of such a pipeline may tighten the American embrace on Canada even further, particularly since American financing and American gas would be centrally involved in the project. Canadians are not unmindful of the dangers of creating a land-based "Panama Canal" - type situation in their country. The contemplated pipeline treaty between the two countries may be reassuring, but cannot dissolve the political and strategic issues. Thus the pipeline carries with it substantial economic, ecological and political risks for Canada, risks that are too great, in my view, to warrant fulfillment of our American contracts. It is a precise case in point where Canada must, in its own interest, take action that is retroactive and discriminatory.

The populist response to such a program and to the larger question of a new resorce policy is not easily predictable. Populism is more at home as the unofficial opposition in day-to-day politics, and is more of an impulse than a movement. Much will depend on the political image the immediate issue assumes. If it comes up as an issue of social order cum sovereignty, one may expect widespread public support for greater Canadian control of our natural resources and great pressures on whatever government is in power. For example, a popular move would be for the government, through Petro-Canada, to buy out one of the major oil companies such as Imperial Oil.

The attempt to deal more forcefully with the high percentages of American control of the manufacturing industry is not on the immediate political agenda. This will have to await a further development of public consciousness around the issue of a national industrial strategy designed to integrate more directly our resource production and manufacturing activity. All that Canadian nationalists can hope for now is that the few initiatives will be sustained, that the screening and review process on foreign companies will be expanded and that resource nationalism will become the political base for expanded initiatives by Canadians to become masters in their own house.

VI

Such is the direction of the Canadian political endowment at the moment when the country is gathering its second wind. Hence the new American Ambassador to Canada, Thomas O. Enders, may have been somewhat premature in his maiden speech to the Canadian Club of Ottawa last March when he stated: "We are both conscious that the end of the 'special relationship' frees us both from historical hang-ups in pursuing our interests." In the traditional terms in which the Canadian-American relationship has been conducted, he was perfectly correct.

But a realignment of the old liberal credo, wearing its complementary faces in both countries, may not be the best preparation for what is to come. In Canada, an old set of "historical hang-ups" may just be coming into place. For example,

Saskatchewan's intention to acquire half the province's potash capacity (largely American-owned) may be better understood in the light of what we have been discussing. This prospect poses the dilemma that the province would then have control of one-third of the U.S. potash supply. "Although welcome," the Ambassador added, "statements that this power would be used benignly are not adequate reassurance."

The power question in all its new and interlocking dimensions goes to the heart of the matter in Canadian-American relations. The Ambassador did sympathize in his speech with "the assertion of Canadian national purpose" and did not contest the right of Canadians to expropriate "provided it is paid for fully, promptly, and effectively." But this expanded liberalism does not settle the question of power, and such an underlying and often hidden issue as potash may be the forerunner of similar problems yet to arise.

The power question—and there is none more important—is now on the agenda, and it is clear that the fundamental and long-standing lopsidedness of the distribution of power as it affects Canadian interests needs major correction. Canadians may be forgiven for a sense of déjà vu. Statements that American power in Canada, at so many different levels, "would be used benignly" have a remarkably familiar ring and are not, as the Ambassador states, "adequate reassurance."

It is on the resolution of this central item on our joint agenda that everything now turns.

Notes

1. The full titles of these government reports are respectively: *The Royal Commission of Canada's Economic Prospects; Report of the Task Force on the Structure of Canadian Industry; Report (11th) of the Committee Respecting Canada-U.S. Relations;* and *Foreign Direct Investment in Canada.*

2. In the relatively minor Point Roberts affair in 1973, the issue was the export of a miniscule amount of water from the lower British Columbia mainland to an adjacent five-square-mile resort area which was American territory. The Canadian verdict was a unanimous No. The sophisticated, and certainly non-nationalist Toronto *Globe and Mail,* "Canada's national newspaper," commented editorially that "To supply water to Point Roberts would set a most dangerous precedent" since "we do not have any accurate idea of what our future needs will be. We have many, many questions about water that are yet to be answered, and may have to wait for *future generations* to answer." And what was the *Globe's* own answer to the affair? Nothing less than "to make Point Roberts Canadian territory" (August 16, 1973, my italics).

4

A Critique of Lipset's Article on Value Differences Among The English-Speaking Democracies*

Tom Truman

This paper examines Seymour Martin Lipset's frequently cited article "Value Differences, Absolute or Relative: The English-Speaking Democracies" and attempts to evaluate the evidence he produces for ranking Canada, Australia, Britain, and the United States on his various dimensions, the ranking itself, and his dimensions of value patterns as analytic tools and bases of comparison.

Professor Lipset compares and scores the four countries according to the following value-dimension or pattern variables:

	United States	Australia	Canada	Great Britain
Equalitarianism-elitism	3	4	2	1
Achievement-ascription	4	2.5	2.5	1
Universalism-particularism	4	2	3	1
Specificity-diffuseness	4	2.5	2.5	1

Lipset explains his variables in these words:

According to the achievement-ascription distinction, a society's value sytem may emphasize individual ability or performance or it may emphasize ascribed or inherited qualities (such as race or high birth) in judging individuals and placing them in various roles. According to the universalism-particularism distinction, it may emphasize that all people shall be treated according to the same standard (e.g. equality before the law), or that individuals shall be treated differently according to their personal qualities of their particular membership in a class or group. Specificity-diffuseness refers to the difference between treating individuals in terms of the specific positions which they happen to occupy, rather than diffusely as individual members of the collectivity.[1]

The above dimensions are taken directly from Talcott Parsons. Lipset goes on to say:

I shall add the equalitarian-elitist distinction to the pattern-variables just outlined. According to this, a society's values may stress that all persons must be given respect simply because they are human beings, or it may stress the general superiority of those who hold positions of power and privilege. In an equalitarian society, the differences between low status and high status people are not stressed in social relation-

*Abridged from *The Canadian Journal of Political Science/Revue Canadienne de science politique,* IV, No. 4 (December/decembre, 1971), by permission of the author and publisher.

ships and do not convey to the high status person a general claim to social deference. In contrast, in an elitist society, those who hold high positions in any structure, whether it be in business, in intellectual activities, or in government, are thought to deserve,and are actually given, general respect and deference.[2]

Lipset adds the warning: "In actual fact, *no society is ever fully explicable by these analytic concepts, nor does the theory even contemplate the possible existence of such a society.* Every society incorporates some aspects of each polarity. We may, however, differentiate among social structures by the extent to which they emphasize one or another of these polarities."[3]

The polarities are developed by contrasting American and British societies. Lipset says that Tocqueville and Bagehot "accurately specified" the values and class relations around which these societies are integrated. "According to Tocqueville, American democratic society was equalitarian and competitive (achievement oriented); according to Bagehot, Britain was deferential (elitist) and ascriptive."[4] Australia and Canada are seen by Lipset as somewhere in-between--Australia being more like the United States and Canada more like Britain.

The numbers represent only Lipset's "tentative estimates of relative rankings"; and these estimates are based on his reading of the classics and a host of other diverse sources, from which he creates rankings which are *his* estimate of *their* estimate. He also cites certain statistics and other "quantitative indicators" in support of his rankings. It is to this evidence that I now turn.

Education Statistics as Evidence of Equality of Opportunity

Lipset argues that the equalitarian values of American and Australian societies are demonstrated by the higher proportion of the youth of these countries in institutions of higher learning compared with Britain and Canada. This is so, he says, because equalitarian values require "giving the means to take part in the 'race for success' to all those who are qualified." He cites the following figures of students enrolled in institutions of higher learning, as a percentage of age group 20 to 24, about 1956,[5] to prove his point:

United States	27.2
Australia	12.05
Canada	8.0
England and Wales	3.7

It is interesting to match Lipset's figures and conclusions with those of Robert Alford who compares the same countries, according to students in higher education per ten thousand population, about 1950.[6]

Britain	1.6
Australia	2.9
United States	17.8
Canada	5.4

The differences between these figures may be accounted for in part by the fact that they refer to different categories and a different time period. However, when Alford says "The greater opportunities for education in the United States and Canada than Britain and Australia suggest that the character of social mobility must be quite different in the former countries,"[7] his point is that education is the chief means of social

Table 1

Students in Post-Secondary Education*
Per One Hundred Thousand Population

	Australia	Canada	England and Wales+	United States
1950	441	593	242	1508
1955	485	565	239	1606
1960	785	793	300	1983
1963	1068	1034	321	---
1964	1101	1473	402	2577
1965	1159	1651	480	2840

* Post-secondary education includes students in universities and colleges, higher technical schools, teacher-training colleges, theological schools, etc., whether degree-granting or not.

+ The figures for England and Wales are for universities and teacher-training colleges only. There are, in addition, students taking advanced courses in institutions of further education. Of these there were 149,576 in 1965, or 374 per 100,000 inhabitants.

Source: UNESCO, *Statistical Yearbook, 1966* and *1967* (Paris, 1968 and 1969).

Table 2

Total Public Expenditure on Education as a Percentage of National Income

	Canada	United States	United Kingdom	Australia	New Zealand
1950	3.1			1.8	2.4
1951		3.1			
1952					
1953					
1954					3.5
1955		4.0			
1956	3.9			2.8	
1959		4.8			
1960	5.8			3.6	3.8
1961	6.1	5.3	5.3	3.8	3.9
1962	7.3	5.9	5.8	3.8	4.0
1963	7.2	6.3	5.9	3.8	4.0
1964	7.4	6.3	6.0	4.0	4.2
1965	8.5	6.5	6.4	4.3	4.4

Source: UNESCO, *Statistical Yearbook, 1967* (Paris, 1969).

mobility. It is thus clear that his conclusions respecting equality of educational opportunities in Australia and Canada are opposite to those of Lipset.

The conflict between Lipset and Alford over educational statistics, and their implications, has prompted me to look further into the matter and to present other statistics in Table 1. Judging from these figures Lipset is clearly wrong in deducing that Australia leads Canada in the number of students at this level. Canada comes next after the United States and well ahead of Australia.

If percentage of national income spent on education is an indication of the value a country attaches to providing equality of opportunity, then Canada is again ahead of Australia. Indeed, Canada even leads the United States (see Table 2).

In some countries there is a good deal of private expenditure on education, as in the United States. This practice could be construed as indicating elitist rather than equalitarian attitudes towards education. However, even when private expenditure is added to the figures Canada still leads the United States and Australia (see Table 3).

Lipset's contention that Australia's equalitarianism is borne out by educational opportunities receives a further setback from the inequalities which exist between the public schools with their poor facilities and overcrowding and the private schools to which the better-off send their children. Most people in the middle and upper ranges of income will try to send their children at least to a private secondary

Table 3

Public and Private Expenditure on Education as a Percentage of National Income

	Canada	United States	Australia
1950	3.2		
1955			
1959		6.1	
1960	5.8		
1961	6.3	6.7	4.5
1962	7.6	7.3	4.5
1963	7.4	7.4	4.5
1964	7.6	7.7	4.6
1965	8.7	8.0	5.0

Source: UNESCO, *Statistical Yearbook, 1967* (Paris, 1969).

school . . . But fees are about $1,800 per annum. However, it is not just the superior education which causes parents to make the financial sacrifice. As the *Sunday Times* story says: "in Australia the old school tie can be even more influential than in Britain, particularly in the traditional fields of law, stock-broking, accountancy and well-established business houses."

Anti-Communist Movements as Evidence of Equalitarianism

Lipset claims that another indicator of equalitarianism in both American and Australian societies is mass witch-hunting and heresy hunts. Implicit in these populist movements is the view that the opinions and values of masses should prevail to the extent of forcing conformity on dissidents and elites The evidence he gives for the similarity of Australia to the United States in this regard is that "both sustained large-scale, popularly based efforts to drive suspected communists out of key positions in unions and politics".[8]

Lipset is wrong as to the facts. In Australia there was no figure comparable to Senator Joseph McCarthy nor any great popular movement bent on purging the government, politics, or trade unions of communists or suspected communists, although there were several incidents on a much lesser scale involving popular hostility to communists.

The first of these anti-communist activities was the attempt made by the Liberal-Country party coalition government, led by Robert Gordon Menzies, to ban the communist party. However, the communists were never a significant force as a political party contesting elections. Only one communist candidate ever got elected to a seat in any Australian parliament, although communists were able to win office in a majority of the most powerful industrial unions in the country. Their efforts to create disruption to the economy of Australia as an ally of the United States and Britain in the cold war against the Soviet Union culminated in the great coal strike of 1949, providing the background to Menzies' Communist Party Dissolution Bill. However, the act was challenged in the High Court of Australia and declared unconstitutional. The prime minister then called an election, which took place in April 1951, with the proposed ban on the Communist party a prominent issue. But the government lost five seats in the House of Representatives to Labour. To get around the constitutional barrier set up by the High Court against banning the Communist party, the Menzies government decided to seek an amendment to the constitution. It was defeated. So there was no sign of the Australian electorate being carried away by anticommunist hysteria.

While this was going on, a more effective effort to eliminate communist influence from the trade unions was being pursued by the Australian Labour Party Industrial Group movement. In order to understand this development it is necessary to know that during the Second World War the communists were successful in taking over some of the most influential positions in the major industrial unions.
The groups most alarmed were, on the one hand, the leaders of Catholic Action and the bishops of the Catholic Church and, on the other, the ALP trade union and party officials whose jobs were threatened. The result was an alliance of these two groups to protect their mutual interest in the labour movement, and by about 1953 they had defeated in the main the communist drive for control of the labour movement. However, this was not a populist or even a popular movement. Although the ALP anti-communist groups had some general public approval, it was far from widespead or enthusiastic. They were not even well known outside the Labour movement.

The Royal Commission on Soviet Espionage in Australia, which took place during 1954, may also be examined to see whether it was a mass anti-communist movement or crusade. Three eminent judges were appointed by the Menzies government to examine the evidence of espionage, which consisted mostly of documents that Vladimir Petrov, a Russian Embassy official and spy who had defected, brought with him. These documents were found to be genuine by the commission, as were certain damaging allegations by Petrov concerning a number of Australian communists and leftwingers. But no witch hunt followed. There were two federal elections in the period, April 1954 and December 1955, but in neither was there much mention or much excitement about the affair.

In contrast, the royal commission set up in "elitist" Canada in 1946 following the revelation of Igor Gouzenko (a defecting Russian Embassy cypher clerk who turned over to the police documents concerning a network of espionage) was conducted by the authorities with a good deal less regard for the liberties of individuals. W.D.K. Kernaghan states that twenty-six persons implicated in the Embassy documents were arrested and held incommunicado, though no formal charges were presented against them, and they were examined *in camera.* In the interim report and the final report released by the commission, evidence of guilt of certain persons charged with espionage was published *before they were brought to trail.*[9]

In the depression years, under section 98 of the Canadian Criminal Code, the Communist party was declared unlawful and five of its leaders arrested.[10] The notorious Padlock Act, passed by unanimous vote in the Quebec Legislative Assembly on March 24, 1937, made unlawful the distribution of books and pamphlets which were favourable to communism. It also failed to define "communism" or "bolshevism" so that the attorney general had almost unlimited discretion in applying the act. The federal Liberal government did not disallow the act as it was empowered to do under the Canadian constitution. But it did, several months later, disallow three acts of the Social Credit government of Alberta which were to give effect to the unorthodox monetary measures which were part of the program it had put before the Alberta voters.[11]

Professor Kernaghan agrees with F.R. Scott that it is an invalid, even dangerous, assumption that Canada has inherited adequate guarantees to civil liberties from British traditions. There is in Canada, he maintains, less toleration of dissenting views and consequently a more willing disposition to restrict freedoms.[12] This viewpoint seems to be justified from the actions of the Canadian government in using the sweeping powers contained in the War Measures Act to deal with the threat to public order posed by the political kidnappings organized by the Front de Libération du Québec in October 1970; even more by the Quebec government's arrest of some 453 citizens on suspicion of their complicity in some sort of *FLQ* conspiracy to overthrow the elected government. These people were held, perhaps in a kind of preventive detention, for several weeks. Only a handful were charged (and all found not guilty of seditious conspiracy); most were released after a ten-minute interview with the police. The leading magazines of English-speaking Canada--*Canadian Forum, Canadian Dimension, Saturday Night,* and *Maclean's*--as well as two leading newspapers, the Toronto *Globe and Mail* and *Le Devoir* of Montreal--strongly protested the actions of the two governments as dangerous invasions of civil liberties.

This information about Canada is given not because it is intended to prove that Canada is a more illiberal country than Australia--it probably is not--but in order to show that Lipset's evidence for demonstrating that Canada is a more liberal country than Australia is faulty and inadequate.

The evidence concerning the state of public opinion on the communist issue in Australia during the fifties--especially the "no" vote in the referendum to ban the Communist party--may be contrasted with the state of American opinion in the same period. Of an American national sample of opinion examined by Samuel A. Stouffer in a 1954 survey, only 27 per cent were prepared to allow communists the right to make a speech in their community; 66 per cent were in favour of removing books by communists from the local library; 91 per cent said they would dismiss communist high school teachers; 68 per cent would terminate the employment of communist store clerks; 63 per cent would sack a communist radio singer; and 51 per cent would go as far as jailing admitted communists.[13] However, we must notice that the survey measured only attitudes. The Australian referendum, of course, measured actual voting behaviour. We cannot be certain, given the opportunity to vote on banning the Communist party, that the voting would have corresponded to Stouffer's figures. But from our experience of opinion polls as predictors of voting results we can say that attitudes at least roughly correspond to probable behaviour. This conclusion is strengthened by the extensive support given by Americans to the real heresy hunt and persecution of communists, suspected communists, and even dissidents and non-conformists, by Senator Joseph McCarthy and his followers from 1950 to 1955--evidence enough to indicate a climate of intolerance and fear .

Lawlessness as Evidence of Equalitarianism

Lipset argues that equalitarian America and Australia, with their anti-authoritarian traditions, have relatively negative attitudes towards authority and the law. Elitist Britain and Canada have much more respect for law and order. Acceptance of authority and informal social controls in Britain, he thinks, are based on deference to social superiors and traditional obligations to some extent mutual. New Equalitarian societies like the United States and Australia are said to have rebelled against social hierarchy and elitism and to have substituted the universalistic cash nexus as a basis of social hierarchy. Canada, in reaction to revolutionary and equalitarian America, clung to the elitist traditions of Britain and fostered respect for central political authority to prevent any weakening of the bonds between her people and the government that might encourage the United States to attempt an invasion and annexation. On the other hand, he says, lack of respect for the police and law enforcement, even "contempt for law", is typical of Australia and is traceable not only to equalitarianism but also the country's penal origins.[14]

With regard to this view I should like to quote from some comparisons between the crime rates of the United States, Canada, and Australia (see Table 4). Supplementary crime statistics as well as measures of levels of violence show "equalitarian" Australia to be more like "elitist" Britain and Canada than it is like "equalitarian" American in these matters. Indeed Canada is closer to the United States than Australia is. From this evidence we could conclude that Australia is not "equalitarian" but is "elitist" like Britain and Canada. However, there are some statistics which suggest that lawlessness is probably not related to equalitarianism, contrary to Lipset's claim. For example, the political violence index for South Africa is 158, Indonesia 190, United States 97, Canada 10, and Australia 4 (see Table 4 (b)). Table 5 shows the homicide rates in the United States to be far ahead of other western democracies but much further behind countries which are a good deal less democratic and equalitarian.

The Challenge of Crime in a Free Society: The Report of the President's Commission on Law Enforcement and the Administration of Justice (Washington, 1967) found that crime in the United States is mostly committed by young men in the age group 15 to 25, which is the fastest growing age group, living in city slums. Crime, they found, is related to parental neglect and family disharmony, to lack of adequate parental models for law-abiding lives. It is related to bad housing, poor recreation facilities, and to poverty in general. It is related to the restlessness and restiveness of youth, to family mobility, and social disorganization. It is related to affluent society, to the abundance of goods within easy reach and the opportunity to take them. It is related to the gap between society's promises and their fulfilment. These are the social aspects, but it is also related to the quality of justice and law enforcement.

The experts do not say anything about crime being related to equalitarianism-elitism, but they do mention the relationship to quality of the administration of justice and law enforcement, which relationship may provide one clue as to the reasons why crime rates are higher in the United States than in Britain, Canada, and Australia.

Table 4

Comparative Crime Figures for 1965*

Crime	Country	Total cases	Rate per 100,000 inhabitants
Criminal homicide	United States	9850	5.1
	Canada	243	1.21
	Australia	141	1.20
Rape	United States	22,740	11.6
	Canada	641	3.2
	Australia	257	3.2
Robbery	United States	118,920	61.4
	Canada	5576	27.88
	Australia	729	6.2
Aggravated assault (US)	United States	206,700	106.6
	Canada	no comparable figures	
Serious assault (Aus.)	Australia	1,895	16.1
Automobile theft	United States	486,600	251.0
	Canada	38,107	190.53
	Australia	12,772	108.7

*(a) The figures are from a paper delivered by Sir Reginald Sholl, an Australian judge, to a Conference of Chief Justices at the American Bar Association Meeting on August 3, 1968. His statistics are drawn from "Crime in the US", FBI Uniform Crime Reports (1965); Dominion Bureau of Statistics, *Crime Statistics (Canada)* (1965); *Australian Commonwealth Yearbook* (1967), 522 *et seq.* I have tried to get comparable statistics for England and Wales from the Home Secretary's *Report* for 1965 (comnd 3037, HM Stationery Office) but I have no confidence that I have managed to do so because I do not understand the way the offences are defined. Criminal homicide in Britain appears to be at the rate of 1.24 per 100,000, robbery 2.95, auto theft 2.95, violence against the person 31.0, and rape 1.2 per 100,000.

(b) Interpol *Reports (International Crime Statistics 1965-1966,* Paris) show that the level of criminality (total number of criminal offences reported to the police per 100,000 population) was for 1965: Australia 1984.88; United Kingdom 2373.96; and Canada 4352.1. Comparable figures for the US were not given, but the US National Commission on the Causes and Prevention of Violence states that for 1963-7 homicide in the United States was from 4 to 12 times more than in Canada and England, and the incidence of rape was twelve times more in the USA than in England and Wales and three times more in Canada. The United States rate of gun homicides is 40 times that of England and Wales, and of gun robbery 60 times. Political violence profiles of 84 countries, drawn from the same study, show the United States 71st with an index of 97. Canada has an index figure of 10, and Australia 4.

Table 5

Homicide Rates per 100,000 Population for Ten Countries Reporting

Country	Rate	Year reported
Columbia	36.5	1962
Mexico	31.9	1960
South Africa	21.8	1960
United States	4.8	1962
Japan	1.5	1962
France	1.5	1962
Canada	1.4	1962
Federal Republic of Germany	1.2	1962
England and Wales	0.7	1962

Source: *The Challenge of Crime in a Free Society,* Report of the President's Commission on Law Enforcement and Administration of Justice (Washington, 1967), 30.

The United States differs from the other English-speaking democracies in three respects which affect crime rates:

(1) The black ghettos of city slums.

(2) Greater societal pressure towards economic achievement and the greater public tolerance of "the notion that where money making is involved anything goes. Crime is caused by public tolerance of it".[15]

(3) A weaker tradition of pride in the quality of justice and the integrity and efficiency of the police than exists in Britain, Canada, and Australia; and, as a corollary, the greater extent of corruption of local officials, especially in urban government, in the lower courts of justice, and in the police. In regard to this last factor, the existence of a much more formidable, organized crime problem in the United States makes the point. "All available data", said the Katzenbach Commission, "indicate that organized crime flourishes only where it has corrupted local officials".[16]

The corruption of urban officials and the police in the United States is related to a distinctive feature of the United States--that is, domination of local government by grass roots political machines which derive from the American political culture and system. More will be said later on this score in seeking to explain the differences in political behaviour between the four countries which Lipset's equalitarianism-elitism dimension fails to do.

The Left (Equalitarian) National Identity of Australia

Making the distinction between "elitist" Canada and "equalitarian" Australia Lipset tells us that "Canadian unification in 1867 is associated with the Conservative Party, while the federating of Australia around the turn of the century was pressed by the Labour Party, which existed in most states".[17] He gives this as an instance of his general proposition that for Australia "the 'left' played the major role in defining political and social institutions in the periods in which national identity was established".[18] The "left" in the context seems to mean the Australian Labour party.

Lipset is plainly wrong about Labour being the main force promoting federation. In the three most populous colonies, and where Labour had its principal strength – that is, New South Wales, Victoria, and Queensland--the party opposed federation as inopportune and, in New South Wales particularly, they felt that federation jeopardized the gains in social legislation they had painfully won in the colonial legislature. Federation, the Labour party believed, by bringing in the more "backward" colonies would dilute the influence that Labour could bring to bear. According to Evatt, Labour men came to believe that "many Federationists were aiming at shutting the gate against social and economic reform".[19]

Labour had only one delegate elected in the federal convention elections of 1897 – Trenwith for Victoria – and he was repudiated by his own party. The people elected as delegates the most obviously eminent politicians of the day.[20] They were mainly "liberals", but there were some "conservatives" in the appelation of the times--in the contemporary British sense there were only radical liberals and conservative liberals, no ideological conservatives at all. The radical liberals on balance prevailed. These were the strong federationists, the nationalists among the federalists rather than the state-righters (only federalism was politically possible), the democrats rather than those who feared the popular vote, and those who thought the State had a duty to help the unfortunate and the underprivileged--section 51 which sets out the powers allotted to the federal parliament included the then very progressive clause (xxii) "Invalid and Old Age Pensions". The delegates were mainly middle-class people . . . Russell Ward has expressed the judgment of modern historical research on the federation movement in these words: "Generally speaking, Labour's political leaders actively opposed, or were at best lukewarm towards federation. Conservatives, whether Free Trade or Protectionist in complexion, were divided. Overwhelmingly the lead came from liberal middle-class politicians".[21]

While Lipset does not make explicit his causal model he does seem to be saying that equalitarian values cause a society to have: (i) a relatively large proportion of its youth in universities and other tertiary education institutions; (ii) populist-style heresy-hunting movements; and (iii) considerable lawlessness. Conversely he also seems to be saying that elitist values cause a society to have: (iv) a relatively small proportion of its youth in universities, etc.; (v) governments that protect the civil liberties of unpopular minorities and dissenters, like the communists; and (vi) relatively low rates of crime.

If Lipset is correct in assuming this causal relationship, then the data indicate that he has ranked the four countries wrongly on the equalitarian-elitist dimension. But the evidence could just as well be interpreted to show that equalitarian values are either, *not* the cause of (i), (ii), or (iii), are an *insufficient* cause of effects (i), (ii), and (iii), or again have some causal relationship to one or other and not the rest. Much more rigorous methods would have to be used to determine which of these alternatives is correct.

The Effects on Australia and Canada of the British Connection

One set of factors which Lipset has largely ignored and which may have a great deal of bearing on the differences of political and social behaviour between the four English-speaking democracies is the differences of political relationships between them. The close and cordial relationship of the governments and people of Australia and Canada to Britain, first in the British Empire, then in the British Commonwealth, and finally in the Commonwealth of Nations resulted in Australia and Canada being closer to Britain in some respects than either is to the United

States. It is difficult at this point to refine, define, and sort out the responsible factors which are obviously composed of a number of causal components or variables. The cabinet-parliamentary system definitely produces effects rather different from the presidential congressional system of government, to name only one of the major differences between Britain, Australia, and Canada on the one hand and America on the other. I shall content myself with discussing how British political institutions and British political culture may account for some of the differences of political and social behaviour Lipset discusses. The effects of these factors will be illustrated in three areas: (i) populistic heresy hunting; (ii) differences in the administration and policing of frontier areas reflecting different attitides towards law and order which persist down to the present time; (iii) differences in notions of equality which probably have bearing on differences in the party system.

There is evidence to indicate that amongst the four English-speaking democracies the United States is unique in the intensity and extent of populist style movements "wreaking their aggression against the structure of the polity",[22] in Lipset's words.

Australia, Canada, and Britain have all shown manifestations of nativism and intolerance of immigrants, but not on the scale of the Know-Nothing movement of the United States. Similarly, they experienced some popular hysteria about Bolshevism in the years following the First World War, but not comparable to the great Red Scare with the notorious Palmer Raids which landed many innocent people in jail. Ironically, it was "elitist" Canada rather than "equalitarian" Australia which came closest to American witch-hunting in the panicky reaction to the Winnipeg General Strike and strikes in other Canadian cities by the Tory government of Sir Robert Borden, the Liberal party opposition led by D.D. McKenzie, and the Canadian business community.[23] Of course, the Ku Klux Klan, which attacked not only Negroes, but also Jews, Catholics, and "cosmopolitan" Protestants in the prosperous twenties, was peculiar to the United States especially in its great popular support. It is not well known, however, that in the twenties it dominated political life in Maine, Indiana, Colorado, Oregon, California, Arkansas, and Oklahoma, apart from its great influence in the southern states of the union.[24] (There was a Canadian branch of the KKK. It was active in Saskatchewan in the late twenties and had some influence in the 1929 election in getting votes for the Conservative party. But J.T.M. Anderson, the Conservative leader, publicly dissociated himself from it and no politician wanted to admit any connection with it.)[25]

"Elitist" Britain came closest to the American Christian Front of Father Coughlin who preached Nazi racial doctrines in the thirties. But Sir Oswald Mosley's British Union of Fascists did not have anything like Coughlin's popular support.[26] Herbert Hyman, reporting on a study he made in Britain at the time of McCarthyism in the United States found that the British public, too, had intolerant feelings regarding leftist and dissidents, but they remained latent because of social restraints. He asks, "What insulates the elites and political structures from popular pressures (in Britain)? " His answer is that the British public accords more privacy and deference to the elites.[27] We have seen that his fellow socialogists, Lipset, also sees the explanation in terms of deference or "elitism". This may seem a plausible answer in the case of Britain. It is a good deal less convincing in the case of Canada, and hardly seems appropriate at all to Australia. It would seem more reasonable to conclude that a particularly influential factor that all three have in common is at work here.

What insulates the elites in the British Commonwealth countries is the political system. The cabinet-parliamentary type of government with its disciplined legislative parties, which fuse executive and legislative powers in the cabinet, makes for a governmental system strong enough to withstand very great public pressure.[28] All the conventions of cabinet government promote a cabinet-solidarity-loyalty to the government and its leader, and secrecy in relation to public opinion, and this is extended down through the ranks of the government party, which normally comprises a majority of the members of the legislature, by the twin spirits of partisanship and ambition. The latter seeks a normal outlet in rising to be a cabinet minister, and the path is very much easier for the *MP* who loyally supports his government. The discipline of legislative parties in the parliamentary system arises less from sanctions than from this spirit of partisanship which the system encourages by making the continuance of the government in office depend upon the loyal support of its parliamentary majority. So the government is a great deal more united than is the case in the United States and being more united is much stronger in relation to public opinion.

The political culture or traditions of British parliamentary government provide moral justification for a government exploiting these institutional fortifications since they insist on strong stable executive government, which, once it has made up its mind on what the public interest requires, should take the necessary action quickly and with determination to see it through to completion. "The duty of a government is to govern." [29] Frequently the cabinet will carry on with its program despite the fiercest opposition and despite the strongest pressures from public opinion and its back bench members will stand with the ministers. Compared to the British parliamentary system the American government at all levels—national, state, and local—appears to be divided against itself and very vulnerable to pressure because of the many openings in the loosely coordinated system. It is well known that at the national level the American system consists of separated institutions sharing powers and that these check and balance one another much as the founding fathers of the Constitution hoped they would. This tension is assisted by the separate election of president, house, and senate, and the division of congress into almost autonomous committees – and now we are informed by Neustadt that executive departments and agencies often behave as though they are independent of the president and responsible only to the interest groups who form their clientele.[30] The senators and congressmen, especially the latter, facing elections as they do every two years, are exposed to pressures from their electorates to a degree unknown to members of the British, Canadian, or Australian parliaments who are protected from much of the pressure of their constituents by the much greater pressure of party discipline. The amazing power of the National Riflemen's Association to defeat gun control legislation sponsored by President Johnson after the assassinations of President Kennedy, Martin Luther King, and Senator Robert Kennedy has no counterpart in the other three English-speaking democracies.

American political institutions and American politicians are clearly much more sensitive to public opinion in the constituencies and in the nation than are their British, Australian, and Canadian counterparts. The effect of the British parliamentary system is to damp down the waves of public agitation, whereas the tendency of the American institutions is to resonate to public opinion which increases the wildness of its swings. Nothing illustrates this better than the sudden rise to great power of Senator Joseph McCarthy and his equally sudden decline. Under their system, American politicians are more exposed and defenceless against those who can, like McCarthy, mobilize public opinion.

Another way of expressing the point that British, Australian, and Canadian political elites are better insulated from popular pressures through their political institutions than are their American counterparts is to say that citizens of the three countries with British political institutions are more firmly governed than are American citizens. This point is connected with the question of the effective maintenance of law and order—at which Britain, Australia, and Canada have been conspicuously more successful than the United States. The effects of traditions of the British system of the administration of justice and law enforcement followed by Canada and Australia must be added to the effects of the traditions of the British political system to explain the lower crime rates.

Lipset has noted the contrast between the frontier of settlement in the United States and Canada. In the United States frontier settements were both unprotected and autonomous whereas, he maintains, in Canada the long arm of the government in Ottawa in the shape of the North-West Mounted Police reached out to the remotest settlements because the government feared that they might be seduced by American democracy or taken over by American imperalism.[31]

Lipset makes too much of this fear of American expansionism in Canada,[32] and misses a significant and characteristic difference between the British and American attitudes towards law and order and local self-government. He seems to be unaware that the British in their colonies in sparsely settled lands, not only in Canada, but also in Australia (and in America, too, before they were expelled) followed the same general policy of trying to ensure that settlement did not outrun government and the provision of law and order. Law and order must be first established, because without them there would be no guarantee of personal liberty, of property, or safe conditions for Her Majesty's subjects. When these things were secure there could be negotiation with the settlers about local self-government. But not until then. The Americans, on the other hand, put the establishment of local self-government first and then proceeded to elect their own law officers. This order of proceeding was partly due to neglect on the part of the central government, but if the government had attempted to intervene the settlers would have resented and resisted it. Americans thought the British order of proceeding was uncomfortably paternalistic and authoritarian.

Nothing illustrates so well the contrast between the American and British values as the comparison of the government of mining camps in the gold rushes of the nineteenth century in the United States, Australia and Canada. In the United States the miners and settlers in California, the Rocky Mountains, and Alaska formed communities which were self-governing and made their own laws subject only to broad statutory limitations. They sometimes both made the laws and dispensed rough justice by public meeting. They elected their own officials, sheriffs, and justices who usually had no special education and training for their positions. Sometimes these democratic arrangements worked well enough, even if there was the inconvenience of the law varying from place to place, and they had the merit of being devised by people with local interest and local knowledge to guide them in making wise rules.[33] However, sometimes there was mob-rule and the tyranny and injustice of lynch law as at San Francisco and other Californian towns in the golden fifties. The news of these occurrences shocked Australians,[34] as much as it did Canadians.[35] Sometimes these American mining communities were dominated by crooked bosses who intimidated the citizens by the use of bands of hired thugs and gun-slingers.[36]

The Canadian Klondike rush and the mining town of Dawson were much more orderly and safe. When the rush began the North-West Mounted Police quickly moved in. It might have been expected that they would have had an almost impossible task in controlling a population mostly made up of fortune-hunters who came after the good gold-bearing areas were staked out, who were all armed with guns and knives and who, as about 90 per cent were Americans, might be expected to be resentful of authoritarian, if benevolent, rule. The testimony of observers was to the contrary. Tappan Adney, writing for American readers, was very critical of the lack of local self-government and the absurdity of laws made three thousand miles away in Ottawa; nevertheless he stated: "The police control of the country was as nearly perfect as one could expect. Thefts and misdemeanours were numerous and effectively dealt with, and one or two murder cases were tried. The saloons were closed on Sundays, nor was any labour permitted on that day . . . No city on the continent presented a more orderly appearance . . . The mounted police, both officers and men, in their capacity as preservers of order and as individuals, commanded the respect of every miner. Captain Constantine, upon his departure from Dawson, received a testimonial in the form of two thousand dollars' worth of nuggets . . . "[37] Americans too, apparently, appreciated law and order and personal safety even if the government was not democratic .

In contrast to the relatively good records of the British, Canadian, and Australian police those of the United States in general have a history and a reputation of poor performance. There have been many instances of police brutality and oppression. But the most common fault alleged against the American police has been political corruption and the subordination of police work to partisan political consideration.[38] The consequences were, and continue to be, low public regard. Lipset, reporting on a well-known study conducted in Oakland, California, states that the policemen saw their chief problem to be "lack of respect for the police" and they ranked the standing of their work with the public as "only fair" or "poor". The police are, according to Lipset, a "low-status out group". The vast majority "carry guns and enforce the law with less than five weeks' training".[39] "They are underpaid, undereducated and undertrained . . . They are regarded with fear and rancor by many in the underprivileged minority groups . . . "[40]

The relatively worse public image the police of America have compared with the police forces of Britain, Canada, and even Australia, where, it is alleged, the people with their working class equalitarian traditions are particularly hard on the police, is probably due to causes deriving from the nature of the democratic culture of the United States. One of these is surely the prevasiveness of partisan political influence in the judiciary and especially in the lower levels of justice and in the ranks of police commissioners and even the higher police officers.[41] This extensive party political influence seems to result from triple related causes. In the first place there is the American passion for local or grass roots control together with the overburdening of the people with elections, political decisions, and political responsibilities, which to discharge at all adequately would require of the majority of citizens a degree of knowledge of, interest in, zeal and capacity for politics that in fact are realized only by a tiny minority of activists. To this is added the complication of the separation of powers *and* division of the executive power which diffuse responsibilty and facilitate buckpassing. Combining with the understandable incapacity of the electorate (and serving to fuse informally powers that have been formally diffused and to give unified direction) is the local organization of the American political parties. The character of this organization was formed under the old spoils or patronage system which was more extensive and longer lasting than anything known in the three British countries. This party organization has always been run by "professionals" at the local level, who, being usually well down the educational and socio-economic ladder, escaped to a great extent socialization (or indoctrination) into the ideals of the sytem, having had rather too much exposure to the more sordid mechanics of the very pluralist political system. They imparted to the lower levels of the political, legal and police systems much of their "flexible" (or cynical) outlook to the detriment of impartial justice and the prestige of the police.

In contrast to the extremely decentralized American parties the British parliamentary system tends to produce much more centralized party organizations, although less in Canada and Australia, being federal countries, than in Britain. This centralized control of party organization seems to be a consequence of cabinet government and disciplined legislative parties and the corresponding habits of mind. Patronage tends to be rather less than in the United States' system and what there is tends to be dispensed at the centre where it is subject to controls that greater public attention brings. There are no professionals at the local level of party organization, which by American standards is weak, intermittent, and lacking in drive, initiative, and influence. Correspondingly, there is in the British systems rather more centralized supervision of police work. The effect of this more centralized and more bureaucratized control is greater impartiality and greater professionalization .

Conclusions

Is there not a sense in which Britain, Canada, and Australia are more equalitarian than the U.S.A. by reason of the existence of social democratic parties which are committed to a much more thorough-going notion of equality than is being promoted by any credible political force in America? But it is not only a matter of having viable social democratic parties; Britain, Canada, and Australia are more advanced than is the U.S.A. along the road to the welfare state to which progress, of course, the NDP-CCF and the labour parties have made a considerable contribution. Australia and New Zealand were pioneers in welfare measures (or social services). Nearly thirty years before the U.S.A. and Canada, and even before Britain, Australia had old age, invalid, and widow's pensions, workmen's compensation laws, and a basic or minimum wage. Trade unions enjoyed a stronger legal position and more legitimacy in Australia than they did in Canada or U.S.A., or even Britain, in the decade and a half before the First World War. Australia in those years certainly led all four countries in the number and variety of state enterprises which were set up either to provide services that private enterprise would not, or could not adequately, provide, or, to give the consumer cheaper or better service by competing with private enterprise in areas where it was operating profitably. But since the end of the Second World War Australia's rate of advance towards the welfare state has slowed down and Canada's has raced ahead. In some respects Canada is now more equalitarian.

Even if we confine ourselves to Lipset's narrow definition of equality, it is necessary to point out that Australian Liberal-Country party governments (but not Labour party governments) maintain the old tradition of the British Empire in respect of recommending to the British monarch twice a year long lists of citizens for knighthoods and other aristocratic honours. The practice of recommending these titles was allowed to fall into disuse in Canada in the twenties. It was renewed by the Bennett Conservative government in 1930 and 1935. It died out finally from the time the Mackenzie King Liberal government took office in 1935.[42]

Again, the private secondary schools modelled on the famous "public" schools of England, exist in Canada as they do in Australia, but the Australian upper and middle classes attach far greater importance to having their children educated in them than do Canadians of the same classes. Public not private school education in them Canada to be much more the rule for middle-class children than in Australia.

Second chambers of legislatures are usually thought of as brakes on democracy and as showing something less than enthusiasm for the unrestrained will of the majority. Only one of the Australian states (Queensland) has abolished its legislative upper house and in three of the six states (Tasmania, South Australia, and Western Australia) there are still property qualifications for voting and membership.[43] With the recent abolition of the Quebec Legislative Council not one of the ten provinces of Canada has more than one chamber to its legislature.

So, is Australia or Canada the more equalitarian? Lipset's criteria and methods of assessment do not allow us to decide this question satisfactorily. Lipset's view of

Canada as counter-revolutionary and elitist may have been true of the nineteenth century or even up to the Second World War. It is doubtful whether it is true of contemporary Canada. As Lipset points out, in the nineteenth century Canada had reason to fear military conquest and political annexation by the U.S.A. Canada reacted to this danger by clinging to the British connection and to a British identity. (The Australians, having much less fear of invasion, were more eager to assert their independence of the mother country and to establish their own nationhood.) The Canadian radicals and democrats could usually be routed by the conservatives appealing to the fervent loyalties of the Canadian people to Britain. In this way radicals could be made to look disloyal and democracy to appear a subversive Yankee notion.[44] So Canadian society was, in the nineteenth century, considerably less equalitarian and less democratic than the U.S.A. even lagging behind Britain in the matter of extending the franchise beyond the propertied classes to all adult citizens.[45] Still, English-speaking Canada, though elitist, was relatively liberal, but Quebec was under the sway of the authoritarian values of a Catholic and agrarian society. The new prairie provinces were more democratic than the older provinces, probably reflecting immigration patterns.

Since the end of the Second World War Canada as a whole has become decidedly more democratic and equalitarian. The Canadians, for the size of their population, mounted a tremendous war effort, and like the people of Britain, they were determined to have something to show for their great sacrifice of young Canadian lives and their war-time ordeal. They wanted a better life for the majority of people and this meant, politically, governments committed to giving the mass of people more say in the conditions under which they were to live and to bringing about improvements in their living standards by means of social services and welfare measures. Walter Young has claimed much of the credit for these reforms for the NDP. He states: "In 1942 (Prime Minister) King referred slightingly to the 'immature Radicalism' of the CCF, but in 1943 he saw the CCF as 'a serious threat on the national scene'." He was sufficiently disturbed by its growing strength to decide that the Liberal party had to counter-attack by placing more emphasis on postwar policy and by "keeping in touch with the working classes and farmers." The radicalism of the postwar reforms proposed was the result of the CCF "presence".[46]

Then, too, the Quiet Revolution in Quebec--the title must surely be ironical--while clamorously challenging the dominance of the English-speaking, is also in another aspect a social revolution set in train by industralization and tending to make Quebec liberal, democratic, secular, and middle class in values. Paradoxically, emphasizing their difference from the English-speaking Canadians, the Québécois have become much more like them.

The Britishness of Canada has diminished a good deal since the end of the Second World War. This has been brought about partly by the natural maturing of Canadian nationhood, partly by Britain's tendency, as it declined as a world power, to draw back to Europe, and partly because the postwar federal Liberal governments have deliberately hastened both processes by phasing out such symbols as the old British red ensign flag of Canada, the British national anthem, and the British monarchy. They have done this partly to conciliate the Frenchness of Quebec nationalism and partly to foster an independent Canadian national identity to hold together a country of diverse national origins and strong regional loyalties.

But Canada was never simply British. It was British North America, with an enclave of conquered French North America. As it has become more North American it has become more like the Americans of the United States. This process is aided by Canada's subordinate role in the alliance, by American ownership of Canadian industry, by the penetration of American mass culture, and by the relationship between two people who are in so many respects alike. Conversely, if Canadians want to defend their national identity against Americans it would seem that the sensible thing to do would be to strengthen their ties with Britain, France, and other European nations whence they originated, not on the former filial or colonial basis, but as an independent nation dealing with other nations and not, as Lipset sees us, embracing elitist imperial Britain to escape revolutionary America, but joining with other small and middle power nations, each to save his own modest revolution from imperial America.

Notes

1. Seymour M. Lipset, *The First New Nation: The United States in Historical and Comparative Perspective* (Garden City, N.Y., 1967), 240-2, 284-5.

2. *Ibid.*

3. *Ibid.*, 242-3.

4. *Ibid.*, 244.

5. *Ibid.*, 297.

6. Robert Alford, *Party and Society* (Chicago, 1965), 117.

7. *Ibid.*, 116.

8. Lipset, *The First New Nation*, 299.

9. Kenneth Kernaghan, "Civil Liberties and Constitutional Bill of Rights", in F. Vaughan, J.P. Kyba, and O.P. Dwivedi, *Contemporary Issues in Canadian Politics* (Toronto, 1970), 74-5.

10. Arthur M. Lower, *Colony to Nation: A History of Canada,* 4th. ed. (Toronto, 1964), 516.

11. Vaughan *et al., Comtemporary Issues in Canadian Politics,* 71-2.

12. *Ibid.*, 69.

13. Samuel A. Stouffer, *Communism, Conformity and Civil Liberties* (Garden City, 1955), 35-46.

14. Lipset, *The First New Nation,* 262-6.

15. *The Challenge of Crime in a Free Society,* Task Force report, "Crime and Its Impact", 1.

16. *Ibid.*, 191.

17. Lipset, *The First New Nation,* 292, n. 17.

18. *Ibid.*

19. H.V. Evatt, *Australian Labour Leader* (Sydney, 1945), 97.

20. R.S. Parker, "The People and the Constitution", in G. Sawer *et al.*, *Federalism in Australia* (Melbourne, 1949), 141.

21. Russell Ward, *Australia* (Englewood Cliffs, 1965), 91.

22. Lipset, *The First New Nation,* 299.

23. Lower, *Colony to Nation,* 503-5, and William Rodney, *Soldiers of the International* (Toronto, 1968), 23-7.

24. Seymour M. Lipset, "The Sources of the Radical Right", in Daniel Bell, ed., *The Radical Right* (Garden City, 1964), 311-13.

25. Peter C. Newman, *Renegade in Power: The Diefenbaker Years,* 2nd paperback edn. (Toronto, 1968.)

26. Bell, ed., *The Radical Right,* 374-446.

27. *Ibid.*, 281.

28. *The Economist* of July 19-25, 1969 thought that Reginald Maudling, the Chancellor of the Exchequer in the previous Conservative government, was right when he said, "Ours is a system of dictatorship by majority party."

29. Harry Eckstein, "The Sources of Leadership and Democracy in Britain, in Samuel H. Beer and Adam B. Ulam, ed., *Patterns of Government* (New York, 1966), 74-7.

30. Richard E. Neustadt, *Presidential Power* (New York, 1964).

31. Lipset, *The First New Nation,* 287.

32. For a discussion of the motivations of the Canadian government in forming the North West Mounted Police and its relations with the Americans, see Sir Cecil E. Denny, *The Law Marches West* (London, 1939).

33. See Charles M. Shinn, *Mining Camps* (New York, 1965), Chaps. 12,13,16, and

34. The Australian respectable classes, that is, Australians on the California gold-fields had a bad reputation as robbers and thieves. They seemed to have included a large proportion of exconvicts.

35. See Jay Monaghan, *Australians and the Gold Rush* (Berkeley, 1966), 135-6, 183-93.

36. See Pierre Berton, *Klondike* (Toronto, 1963), 333-65.

37. Tappan Adney, *The Klondike Stampede* (New York, 1900), 440-3.

38. *The Challenge of Crime in a Free Society,* Task Force report, "The Police", 202-12.

39. Seymour M. Lipset, "Why Cops Hate Liberals and Vice Versa", *The Atlantic* Monthly, *special supplement: "The Police and the Rest of Us" (Mar*ch, 1969), 76-83.

40. Editorial comment, *ibid.*, 75.

41. See Richard Dougherty, ex-deputy police commissioner of New York, "Requiem for the Center Street Mafia", *Atlantic Monthly* (March, 1969), 110.

42. Lower, *Colony to Nation,* 524.

43. R.D. Lumb, *The Constitutions of the Australian States* (Brisbane, 1963),

44. Lower, *Colony to Nation,* 243.

45. *Ibid.*, 404, 469.

46. *Anatomy of a Party,* 8.

5

Conservatism, Liberalism, and Socialism in Canada*

Gad Horowitz

1. Introduction: the Hartzian Approach

In the United States, organized socialism is dead; in Canada, socialism, though far from national power, is a significant political force. Why this striking difference in the fortunes of socialism in two very similar societies?

Any attempt to account for the difference must be grounded in a general comparative study of the English-Canadian and American societies. It will be shown that the relative strength of socialism in Canada is related to the relative strength of toryism, and to the different position and character of liberalism in the two countries.

In North America, Canada is unique. Yet there is a tendency in Canadian historical and political studies to explain Canadian phenomena not by contrasting them with American phenomena but by identifying them as variations on a basic North American theme. I grant that Canada and the United States are similar, and that the similarities should be pointed out. But the pan-North American approach, since it searches out and concentrates on similarities, cannot help us to understand Canadian uniqueness. When this approach is applied to the study of English-Canadian socialism, it discovers, first, that like the American variety it is weak, and second, that it is weak for much the same reasons. These discoveries perhaps explain why Canadian socialism is weak in comparison to European socialism; they do not explain why Canadian socialism is so much stronger than American socialism.

The explanatory technique used in this study is that developed by Louis Hartz in *The Liberal Tradition in America*[1] and *The Founding of New Societies.*[2] It is applied to Canada in a mildly pan-North American way by Kenneth McRae in "The Structure of Canadian History", a contribution to the latter book.

The Hartzian approach is to study the new societies founded by Europeans (the United States, English Canada, French Canada, Latin America, Dutch South Africa, Australia) as "fragments" thrown off from Europe. The key to the understanding of ideological development in a new society is its "point of departure" from Europe: the ideologists borne by the founders of the new society are not representative of the historic ideological spectrum of the mother country. The settlers represent only a fragment of that spectrum. The complete ideological spectrum ranges — in chronological order and from right to left — from feudal or tory through liberal whig to liberal democrat to socialist. French Canada and Latin America are "feudal fragments". They were founded by bearers of the feudal or tory values of the organic, corporate, hierarchical community; their point of departure from Europe is before the liberal

---

*Abridged from *The Canadian Journal of Economics and Political Science*, XXXII, 2 (May, 1966). By permission of the author and publisher.

revolution. The United States, English Canada, and Dutch Africa are "bourgeois fragments", founded by bearers of liberal individualism who have left the tory end of the spectrum behind them. Australia is the one "radical fragment", founded by bearers of the working class ideologies of mid-nineteenth-century Britain.

The significance of the fragmentation process is that the new society, having been thrown from Europe, "loses the stimulus to change the whole provides".[3] The full ideological spectrum of Europe develops only out of the continued confrontation and interaction of its four elements; they are related to one another, not only as enemies, but as parents and children. A new society which leaves part of the past behind it cannot develop the future ideologies which need the continued presence of the past in order to come into being. In escaping the past, the fragment escapes the future, for "the very seeds of the later ideas are contained in the parts of the old world that have been left behind".[4] The ideology of the founders is thus frozen, congealed at the point of origin.

Socialism is an ideology which combines the corporate-organic-collectivist ideas of toryism with the rationalist-egalitarian ideas of liberalism . . . The corporate-organic-collectivist component of socialism is present in the feudal fragment--it is part of the feudal ethos--but the radical rationalist-egalitarian component of socialism is missing.

In the bourgeois fragment, the situation is the reverse; the radical rationalist-egalitarian component of socialism is present, but the corporate-organic-collective component is missing, because toryism has been left behind. In the bourgeois fragments "Marx dies because there is no sense of class, no yearning for the corporate past".[5] The absence of socialism is related to the absence of toryism.

It is *because* socialists have a conception of society as more than an agglomeration of competing individuals – a conception close to the tory view of society as an organic community–that they find the liberal idea of equality (equality of opportunity) inadequate. Socialists disagree with liberals about the essential meaning of equality because socialists have a tory conception of society.

In a liberal bourgeois society which has never known toryism the demand for equality will express itself as left-wing or democratic liberalism. The left will point out that all are not equal in the competitive pursuit of individual happiness. The government will be required to assure greater equality of opportunity . . .

In a society which thinks of itself as a community of classes rather than an aggregation of individuals, the demand for equality will take a socialist form: for equality of condition rather than mere equality of opportunity; for co-operation rather than competition; for a community that does more than provide a context within which individuals can pursue happiness in a purely self-regarding way. At its most "extreme", socialism is a demand for the *abolition* of classes so that the good of the community can truly be realized. This is a demand which cannot be made by people who can hardly see class and community: the individual fills their eyes.

2. The Application to Canada

It is a simple matter to apply the Hartzian approach to English Canada in a pan-North American way. English Canada can be viewed as a fragment of the American liberal society, lacking a feudal or tory heritage and therefore lacking the socialist ideology which grows out of it. Canadian domestic struggles, from this point of view, are a northern version of the American struggle between big-propertied liberals on the right and *petit bourgeois* and working-class liberals on the left; the struggle goes on within a broad liberal consensus, and the voice of the tory or the socialist is not heard in the land. The pan-North American approach, with important qualifications, is adopted by Hartz and McRae . . . .

But Hartz notes that the liberal society of English Canada has a "tory touch", that it is "etched with a tory streak coming out of the American revolution".[6] The general process of bourgeois fragmentation is at work in both English Canada and the United States, but there are differences between the two fragments which Hartz described as "delicate contrasts",[7] McRae as "subtle" and "minor".[8] Put in the most general way, the difference is that while the United States is the perfect bourgeois fragment, English Canada is a bourgeois fragment marred by non-liberal "imperfections" – a tory "touch", and therefore a socialist "touch". The way Hartz and McRae would put it is that English Canada and the United States are "essentially" alike; differences are to be found but they are not "basic". Surely, however, whether one describes the differences as delicate, subtle, and minor or as basic, significant, and important depends on one's perspective, on what one is looking for, on what one wishes to stress . . . . If one shifts one's perspective and considers English Canada from within the world of bourgeois fragments, the differences suddenly expand. If one's concern is to understand English-Canadian society in its uniqueness, that is, in contrast to American society, the differences become not "delicate" but of absolutely crucial importance.

. . . McRae's pan-North Americanism, however, is not merely a matter of perspective, for he seems to consider English Canada's un-American characteristics to be absolutely "minor". For McRae, they are minor not only from the world perspective, but from the narrower perspective which considers the bourgeois fragments alone.

Take as an example the central concern of this study – the differing weights of Canadian and American socialism. From the world perspective, the difference is perhaps "insignificant". As Hartz says, "there may be a Tory touch in English Canada, but the fragment, despite the CCF of recent times, has not yielded a major socialist movement".[9] From the narrower perspective, however, the presence of a socialist movement in English Canada is remarkable. The danger of a pan-North American approach is that it tends either to ignore the relative strength of Canadian socialism or to dismiss it as a freak. It explains away, rather than explains, the strength of Canadian socialism. This is the approach adopted by McRae . . . . McRae's stress on English-Canadian-American similarity is so strong, however, that it is no longer a question of perspective but of error, for he attempts to boil a *minor* socialist movement away into *nothing,* and thence to conclude that there is no "basic" difference between the two bourgeois fragments.

The first step in his argument is to point out that socialism was "successful" only among Saskatchewan farmers, that it "failed" in the industrial areas. The CCF was therefore "basically" a movement of agrarian protest similar to American farmers' protests; its failure in urban Canada is parallel with the failure of socialism as a working class movement in the United States.[10] But words like "success" and failure" are dangerous because they hide degrees of success and failure. The CCF failed to become a majority party in urban Canada, but it succeeded in becoming a significant minor party--a success denied to the American socialists. This is a difference, not a similarity. Furthermore, McRae ignores the fact that in one urban Canadian province – British Columbia – the CCF *did* succeed in becoming a major party. (Editor's Note: In 1972 the New Democratic Party, successor to the CCF, won an overwhelming majority in British Columbia and formed the third provincial socialist government in Canada, the earlier two being Saskatchewan and Manitoba.) And he ignores the ties between the Canadian labour movement and the CCF-NDP (surely a phenomenon worthy of explanation) by identifying the Canadian labour movement "in broad terms" with the American, as one "not significantly attracted to socialism".[11]

In the second step of the argument, the success of the CCF in Saskatchewan is just another American agrarian protest. This is also an error, because unlike the American movements the Saskatchewn CCF was *socialist*. Confronting this hard fact, McRae attempts to explain it by noting that the Canadian prairies were "generously sprinkled with Britain immigrants already familiar with Fabian socialism".[12] But is it not *significant* that immigrants who brought socialist ideas to the American liberal society had to abondon them in the process of Americanization, while those who brought these ideas to Canada built a major (provincial) party with them?

McRae's *coup de grace* to Canadian socialism is the observation that "with the formation of the NDP . . . the last half- realized elements of socialism . . . seem to have been absorbed into the liberal tradition".[13] The error here is to ascribe the moderation or liberalization of "doctrinaire" socialism in Canada to a special Canadian circumstance – the (overestimated) power of liberalism – when it is in fact a part of a general process of liberalization of socialism which is going on in every country of the West . . . .

The most important un-American characteristics of English Canada, all related to the presence of toryism, are: (i) the presence of tory ideology in the founding of English Canada by the Loyalists, and its continuing influence on English-Canadian political culture; (ii) the persistent power of right-wing liberalism in Canada (the Family Compacts) as contrasted with the rapid and easy victory of liberal democracy (Jefferson, Jackson) in the United States; (iii) the ambivalent centrist character of left-wing liberalism in Canada as contrasted with the unambiguously leftist position of left-wing liberalism in the United States; (iv) the presence of an influential and legitimate socialist movement in English Canada as contrasted with the illegitimacy and early death of American socialism; (v) the failure of English-Canadian liberalism to develop into the one true myth, the nationalist cult, and the parallel failure to exclude toryism and socialism as "un-Canadian"; in other words, the legitimacy of ideological diversity in English Canada . . . .

3. The Presence of Toryism and its Consequences

Many students have noted that English-Canadian society has been powerfully shaped by tory values that are "alien" to the American mind. The latest of these is Seymour Martin Lipset, who stresses the relative strength in Canada of the tory values of "ascription" and "elitism" (the tendency of defer to authority) and the relative weakness of the liberal values of "achievement" and "equalitarianism".[14] He points to suh well-known features of Canadian history as the absence of a lawless, individualistic-equalitarian American frontier, the preference for Britain rather than the United States as a social model, and generally, the weaker emphasis on social equality, the greater acceptance by individuals of the facts of economic inequality, social stratification, and hierarchy. One tory touch in English Canada which is not noted by Lipset, but has been noted by many others (including McRae), is the far greater willingness of English-Canadian political and business elites to use the power of the state for the purpose of developing and controlling the economy.

Lipset accepts the notion, common among Canadian historians, that the Loyalist emigrés from the American revolution were a genuine tory element; that their expulsion from the United States to Canada accounts for the development of the United States in a liberal direction and of English Canada in a conservative direction. English Canada's "point of departure", in this view, is not liberal but conservative. The idea is that English Canada was founded by British tories whose purpose was to build a society which would be not liberal like the American but conservative like the British.

McRae correctly finds this notion to be an exaggeration of the difference between the Loyalists and the revolutionaries, between English Canada and the United States.[15] The picture of English Canada as a feudal fragment rather than a bourgeois fragment (which is what is implied by the Loyalist myth) is indeed a false one. McRae argues correctly that the Loyalists and the Family Compacts did not represent British toryism, but pre-revolutionary American right-wing liberalism with a "tory touch". But he errs in underestimating the significance of the "touch". He notes several factors differentiating the Loyalists, and subsequently English Canadians in general, from the revolutionary Americans: belief in monarchy and empire unity, greater stress on "law and order", revulsion against American populistic excesses, different frontier experiences, and so on. But he notes them only to dismiss them. "Basically, the Loyalist, and therefore the English Canadian, *is* the American liberal".[16] He is not "exactly" like the American,[17] McRae adds, but nevertheless he is the American. This is going too far. It is legitimate to point out that Canada is not a feudal (tory) fragment but a bourgeois (liberal) fragment touched with toryism. It is not legitimate to boil the tory touch away to nothing. If the tory touch was strong enough to produce all the un-American characteristics we are considering, it becomes misleading to identify the English Canadian with the American liberal . . . .

The next step in tracing the development of the English-Canadian political culture must be to take account of the tremendous waves of British immigration which soon engulfed the original American Loyalist fragment. Here McRae's concern is to argue that the liberal ideology of the Loyalist fragment had already "frozen, congealed at the point of origin"; that the national ethos had already been fully formed (an American liberalism not "exactly" like American liberalism); that the later waves of immigration played no part in the formation of English-Canadian political culture; that they found an established culture, and were impelled to acclimatize to it.[18] It is important for McRae to prove this point, for while there is room for the argument that the Loyalists were American whigs with a tory touch, the later British immigrants had undoubtedly been heavily infected with non-liberal ideas, and these ideas were undoubtedly in their heads as they settled in Canada. The political culture of a new nation is not necessarily fixed at the point of origin or departure; the founding of a new nation can go on for generations. If the later waves of immigration arrived before the *point of congealment* of the political culture, they must have participated actively in the process of culture formation. If this be so, the picture of English Canada as an almost exactly American liberal society becomes very difficult to defend . . .

Between 1815 and 1850 almost one million Britons emigrated to Canada. The population of English Canada doubled in twenty years and quadrupled in forty. The population of Ontario increased tenfold in the same period — from about 95,000 in 1814 to about 950,000 in 1851.[19] McRae himself admits that "it would be inaccurate to say that this wave of migration was absorbed into the original fragment: an influx of these proportions does not permit of simple assimilation."[20] Nevertheless, he concluded that "despite the flood tide of immigration . . . the original liberal inheritance of English Canada survived and dominated."[21] According to McRae, the universal urge to own property and the classlessness of North American society had such a powerful impact on the immigrants that they simply "forgot their old notions of social hierarchy" and became American liberals.[22] Surely this argument is an instance of stretching the facts in order to fit a theory! Do people simply "forget" their old notions so quickly and so completely? Is it not possible that the immigrants, while they were no doubt considerably liberalized by their new environment, also brought to it non-liberal ideas which entered into the political culture mix, and which perhaps even reinforced the non-liberal elements present in the original fragment? If the million immigrants had come from the United States rather than Britain, would English Canada not be "significantly" different today?

The difficulty in applying the Hartzian approach to English Canada is that although the point of departure is reasonably clear, it is difficult to put one's finger on the point of congealment. Perhaps it was the Loyalist period; perhaps it was close to the mid-century mark, there are grounds for arguing that it was in the more recent past. But the important point is this: no matter where the point of congealment is located in time, the tory streak is present before the solidification of the political culture, and it is strong *enough* to produce *significant* "imperfections", or non-liberal, un-American attributes of English-Canadian society . . . .

Canadian liberals cannot be expected to wax enthusiastic about the non-liberal traits of their country. They are likely to condem the tory touch as anachronistic, stifling, undemocratic, out of tune with the essentially American ("free", "classless") spirit of English Canada. They dismiss the socialist touch as an "old-fashioned" protest, no longer necessary (if it ever was) in this best (liberal) of all possible worlds in which the "end of ideology" has been achieved. The secret dream of the Canadian liberal is the removal of English Canada's "imperfections" – in other words, the total assimilation of English Canada into the larger North American culture. But there is a flaw in this dream which might give pause even to the liberal. Hartz places special emphasis on one very unappetizing characteristic of the new societies – intolerance – which is strikingly absent in English Canada. Because the new societies other than Canada are unfamiliar with legitimate ideological diversity, they are unable to accept it and deal with it in a rational manner, either internally or on the level of international relations . . . .

To be an American is to be a bourgeois liberal. To be a French Canadian is to be a pre-Enlightenment Catholic; to be an Australian is to be a prisoner of the radical myth of "mateship"; to be a Boer is to be a pre-Enlightenment bourgeois Calvinist. The fragments escape the need for philosophy, for thought about values, for "where perspectives shrink to a single value, and that value becomes the universe, how can value itself be considered?"[23] The fragment demands solidarity. Ideologies which diverge from the national myth make no impact; they are not understood, and their proponents are not granted legitimacy. They are denounced as aliens, and treated as aliens, because they *are aliens* . . . .

The specific weakness of the United States is its "inability to understand the appeal of socialism" to the third world.[24] Because the United States has "buried" the memory of the organic medieval community "beneath new liberal absolutisms and nationalisms"[25] it cannot understand that the appeal of socialism to nations with a predominantly non-liberal past (including French Canada) consists precisely in the promise of "continuing the corporate ethos in the very process" of modernization.[26] . . .

English Canada, because it is the most "imperfect" of the fragments, is not a one-myth culture. In English Canada ideological diversity has not been buried beneath an absolutist liberal nationalism . . . The result is that English Canada does not direct an uncomprehending intolerance at heterodoxy, either within its borders or beyond them. (What is "backlash" Parti-Pris or PSQ-type separatists would be getting if Quebec were in the United States!) In English Canada it has been possible to consider values without arousing the all-silencing cry of treason. Hartz observes that "if history had chosen English Canada for the American role" of directing the Western response to the world revolution, "the international scene would probably have witnessed less McCarthyite hysteria, less Wilsonian messianism."[27] . . .

My argument is essentially that non-liberal British elements have entered into English-Canadian society *together* with American liberal elements at the foundations. The fact is that Canada has been greatly influenced by both the United States and Britain. This is not to deny that liberalism is the dominant element in the English-

Canadian political culture; it is to stress that it is not the sole element, that it is accompanied by vital and legitimate streams of toryism and socialism which have as close a relation to English Canada's "essence" or "foundations" as does liberalism . . . .

4. Un-American Aspects of Canadian Conservatism

So far, I have been discussing the presence of toryism in Canada without referring to the Conservative party. This party can be seen as a party of right-wing or business liberalism, but such an interpretation would be far from the whole truth . . . . If there is a touch of toryism in English Canada, its primary carrier has been the Conservative party. It would not be correct to say that toryism is *the* ideology of the party, or even that some Conservatives are tories. These statements would not be true even of the British Conservative party. The primary component of the ideology of business-oriented parties is liberalism; but there are powerful traces of the old pre-liberal outlook in the British Conservative party,[28] and less powerful but still perceptible traces of it in the Canadian party . . . .

If it is true that the Canadian Conservatives can be seen from some angles as right-wing liberals; it is also true that figures such as R.B. Bennett, Arthur Meighen, and George Drew cannot be understood simply as Canadian versions of William McKinley, Herbert Hoover, and Robert Taft. Canadian Conservatives have something British about them that American Republicians do not. It is not simply their emphasis on loyalty to the crown and to the British connection, but a touch of the authentic tory aura — traditionalism, elitism, the strong state, and so on. The Canadian Conservatives lack the American aura of rugged individualism.[29]

It is possible to perceive in Canadian conservatism not only the elements of business liberalism and orthodox toryism, but also an element of "tory democracy" — the paternalistic concern for the "condition of the people", and the emphasis on the tory party as their champion . . . John A. Macdonald's approach to the emergent Canadian working class was in some respects similar to that of Disraeli. Later Conservatives acquired the image of arch reactionaries and arch enemies of the workers, but let us not forget that "Iron Heel" Bennett was also the Bennett of the Canadian New Deal.

The question arises: why is it that in Canada the *Conservative* leader proposes a New Deal? Why is it that the Canadian counterpart of Hoover apes *Roosevelt?* This phenomenon is usually interpreted as sheer historical accident, a product of Bennett's desperation and opportunism. But the answer may be that Bennett was not Hoover. Even in his "orthodox" days Bennett's views on the state's role in the economy were far from similar to Hoover's: Bennett's attitude was that of Canadian, not American, conservatism. Once this is recognized, it is possible to entertain the suggestion that Bennett's sudden radicalism, his sudden concern for the people, may not have been mere opportunism. It may have been a manifestation, a sudden activation under pressure, of a latent tory-democratic streak . . . .

The Bennett New Deal is only the most extreme instance of what is usually considered to be an accident or an aberration—the occasional manifestation of "radicalism" or "leftism" by otherwise orthodox Conservative leaders in the face of opposition from their "followers" in the business community. Meighen, for example, was constantly embroiled with the "Montreal interests" who objected to his railway policies . . . . Meighen is far easier to understand from a British than from an American perspective, for he combined, in different proportions at different times, attitudes deriving from all three Conservative ideological streams: right-wing liberalism, orthodox toryism, and tory democracy.

When Western or agrarian Conservatives of the contemporary period, John Diefenbaker and Alvin Hamilton, who are usually dismissed as "prairie radicals" of the American type, might represent not only anti-Bay Street agrarianism but *also* the same type of tory democracy which was expressed before their time by orthodox business-sponsored Conservatives like Meighen and Bennett. The populism (anti-elitism) of Diefenbaker and Hamilton is a genuinely foreign element in Canadian conservatism, but their stress on the Tory party as champion of the people and their advocacy of welfare state policies are in the tory democratic tradition. Their attitudes to the monarchy, the British connection, and the danger of American domination are entirely orthodox Conservative attitudes. Diefenbaker Conservatism is therefore to be understood not simply as a Western populist phenomenon, but as an odd *combination* of Conservative views with attitudes absorbed from the Western Progressive tradition.

Another aberration which may be worthy of investigation is the Canadian phenomenon of the red tory. At the simplest level, he is a Conservative who prefers the CCF-NDP to the Liberals, or a Socialist who prefers the Conservatives to the Liberals, without really knowing why. At a higher level, he is a conscious ideological Conservative with some "odd" socialist notions (W.L. Morton) or a conscious ideological socialist with some "odd" tory notions (Eugene Forsey). The very suggestion that such affinities might exist between Republicans and Socialists in the United States is ludicrous enough to make some kind of a point.

Red toryism is, of course, one of the results of the relationship between toryism and socialism which has already been elucidated. The tory and socialist minds have some crucial assumptions, orientations, and values in common, so that from certain angles they may appear not as enemies, but as two different expressions of the same basic ideological outlook. Thus, at the very highest level, the red tory is a philosopher who combines elements of socialism and toryism so thoroughly in a single integrated *Weltanschauung* that it is impossible to say that he is a proponent of either one as *against* the other. Such a red tory is George Grant, who has associations with both the Conservative party and the NDP, and who has published a book which defends Diefenbaker, laments the death of "true" British conservatism in Canada, attacks the Liberals as individualists and Americanizers, and defines socialism as a variant of conservatism (each "protects the public good against private freedom").[30]

5. The Character of Canadian Socialism

Canadian socialism is un-American in two distinct ways. It is un-American in the sense that it is a significant and legitimate political force in Canada, insignificant and alien in the United States. But Canadian socialism is also un-American in the sense that it does not speak the same language as American socialism. In Canada, socialism is British, non-Marxist, and worldly; in the United States it is German, Marxist, and other-worldly.

I have argued that the socialist ideas of British immigrants to Canada were not sloughed off because they "fit" with a political culture which already contained non-liberal components, and probably also because they were introduced into the political culture mix before the point of congealment. Thus socialism was not alien here. But it was not alien in yet another way; it was not borne by foreigners. The personnel and the ideology of the Canadian labour and socialist movements have been primarily British. Many of those who built these movements were British immigrants with past experience in the British labour movement; many others were Canadian-born children of such immigrants.

When socialism was brought to the United States, it found itself in an ideological environment in which it could not survive because Lockean individualism had long since achieved the status of a national religion; the political culture had already congealed, and socialism did not fit. American socialism was alien not only in this ideological sense, but in the ethnic sense as well; it was borne by foreigners from Germany and other continental European countries. These foreigners sloughed off their socialist ideas not simply because such ideas did not " fit" ideologically, but because as foreigners they were going through a general process of Americanization; socialism was only one of many ethnically alien characteristics which had to be abandoned. . . .

A British socialist immigrant to Canada had a far different experience. The British immigrant was not an alient in British North America. The English-Canadian culture not only granted legitimacy to his political ideas and absorbed them into its wholeness; it absorbed him as a person into the English-Canadian community, with relatively little strain, without demanding that he change his entire way of life before being granted full citizenship. He was acceptable to begin with, by virtue of being British .... The prevalence of doctrinaire Marxism helps to explain the sectarianism of the American Socialist party. The distinctive quality of a sect is its "other-worldiness". It rejects the existing scheme of things entirely; its energies are directed not to devising stratagems with which to lure the electorate, but to elaborating its utopian theory. Daniel Bell describes the American Socialist party as one "whose main preoccupation has been the refinementof 'theory' at the cost, even, of interminable factional divisions".[31] ... For Bell, the failure of American socialism is its failure to make the transition from sect to party, to concern itself with popular issues rather than theoretical disputes.

The CCF has not been without its otherworldly tendencies; there have been doctrinal disagreements, and the party has always had a left wing interested more in "socialist education" than in practical political work. . . . The party has expelled individuals and small groups — mostly Communists and Trotskyites — but it has never split. Its life has never been threatened by disagreement over doctrinal matters.

6. Canadian Liberalism: the Triumphant Centre

Canadian Conservatives are not American Republicans; Canadian socialists are not American socialists; Canadian Liberals are not American liberal Democrats.

The un-American elements in English Canada's political culture are most evident in Canadian conservatism and socialism. But Canadian liberalism has a British colour too. The liberalism of Canada's Liberal party should not be identified with the liberalism of the American Democratic party. In many respects they stand in sharp contrast to one another.

The three components of the English-Canadian political culture have not developed in isolation from one another; each has developed in interaction with the others. Our toryism and our socialism have been moderated by liberalism. But by the same token, our liberalism has been rendered "impure", in American terms, through its contacts with toryism and socialism. If English-Canadian liberalism is less individualistic, less ardently populistic-democratic, more inclined to state intervention in the economy, and more tolerant of "feudal survivals" such as monarchy, this is due to the uninterrupted influence of toryism upon liberalism, an influence wielded in and through the conflict between the two. If English-Canadian liberalism has tended since the depression to merge at its leftist edge with the democratic socialism of the CCF-NDP, this is due to the influence which socialism has exerted upon liberalism, in and through the conflict between them. The key to understanding the Liberal party in Canada is to see it as a *centre* party, with *influential* enemies on both right and left . . .

Mackenzie King had to face the socialist challenge. He did so in the manner of European Liberal Reform. No need to worry about abandoning individualism; Locke was not Canada's national god; like European liberalism, Canadian liberalism has been revised. The similarity of socialism and Liberal Reform could be acknowledged; indeed it could be emphasized and used to attract the socialist vote. At the same time, King had to answer the arguments of socialism, and in doing so he had to spell out his liberalism. He had to stop short of socialism openly.[32] Social reform, yes; extension of public ownership, yes; the welfare state, yes; increased state control of the economy, yes; but not too much. Not socialism. The result was that King, like the European liberals, could not go as far as Roosevelt . . .

"In America, instead of being a champion of property, Roosevelt became the big antagonist of it; his liberalism was blocked by his radicalism."[33] In Canada, since King had to worry not only about Bennett and Meighen and Drew, but also about Woodsworth and Coldwell and Douglas, King had to embark upon a defence of private property. *He* was no traitor to his class. Instead of becoming the antagonist of property, he became its champion; his radicalism was blocked by his liberalism. . . .

The Liberal party has continued to speak the language of King: ambiguous and ambivalent, presenting first its radical face and then its conservative face, urging reform and warning against hasty, ill-considered change, calling for increased state responsibility but stopping short of socialism openly, speaking for the common people but preaching the solidarity of classes.[34] . . .

In the United States, the liberal Democrats are the party of organized labour. The new men of power, the labour leaders, have arrived politically; their vehicle is the Democratic party. In English Canada, if the labour leaders have arrived politically, they have done so in the CCF-NDP. They are nowhere to be found in the Liberal party. The rank and file, in the United States, are predominantly Democrats; in Canada at least a quarter are New Democrats, and the remainder show only a relatively slight, and by no means consistent, preference for the Liberals as against the Conservatives.

In the United States, left-wing "liberalism", as opposed to right wing "liberalism", has always meant opposition to the domination of American life by big business, and has expressed itself in and through the Democratic party; the party of business is the Republican party. In Canada, business is close to both the Conservatives and the Liberals. The business community donates to the campaign funds of both and is represented in the leadership circles of both.

Policy Approach

The policy approach of a left party is to introduce innovations on behalf of the lower strata. The Liberals, unlike the liberal Democrats, have not been a party of innovation. As a centre party, they have allowed the CCF-NDP to introduce innovations; they have then waited for signs of substantial acceptance by all strata of the population, and for signs of reassurance against possible electoral reprisals, before actually proceeding to implement the innovation. By this time, of course, they are strictly speaking no longer innovations. The centre party recoils from the fight for controversial measures; it loves to implement a consensus .

The bare facts are these: In August, 1943, the CCF became the official opposition in Ontario. In September, 1943, the CCF overtook the Liberals in the Gallup poll (Canada: CCF 29%, Liberals 28%; Ontario: CCF 32%, Liberals 26%; The West: CCF 41%, Liberals 23%).[35] . . . . Almost immediately after the release of the September Gallup Poll, the Advisory Council of the National Liberal Federation, meeting at King's request, adopted fourteen resolutions "constituting a program of reform . . . of far reaching consequences".[36] King wrote in his diary: "I have succeeded in making declarations which will improve the lot of . . . farmers and working people . . . . I think I have cut the ground in large part from under the CCF . . . . "[37] "The great numbers of people will see that I have been true to them."[38]

The Liberal slogan in the Campaign of 1945 was "A New Social Order for Canada". The election of June 11 returned King to power with a drastically reduced majority. The CCF vote rose from 8.5 per cent to 15.6 per cent, and its representation in the Commons from 8 to 29. But King's swing to the left had defeated the CCF's bid for major party status . . . .

Electoral Support

There is a dearth of information about the influence of class on voting behaviour in Canada, but there are strong indications that the higher strata are more likely than the lower to vote Conservative, the lower strata are more likely than the higher to vote

	Union families	Non-union families
Conservative	26%	40%
Liberal	38%	48%
NDP	22%	8%

Source: R. Alford, "The Social Bases of Political Cleavage in 1962", in J. Meisel, ed., *Papers on the 1962 Election* (Toronto, 1964), 211.

CCF-NDP, and that both groups are about *equally* attracted to the Liberals.
The left-centre-right character of NDP, Liberals, and Conservatives appears very clearly in the distribution of the trade union vote among the three parties in the election of 1962.
This would, of course, confirm the picture of Conservatives as the right, NDP as the left, and Liberals as the "classless" centre. This is in sharp contrast to the situation in the United States, where the lower strata prefer the Democrats, the higher prefer the Republicans, and there is no centre party.

Although this picture of the relationship between class and voting is broadly true, it is also true that class voting is as high as in the United States or higher. Nevertheless, in Canada *considered as a whole* class voting is lower than in the United States; non-class motivations appear to be very strong.[39] Peter Regenstrief suggests that one factor accounting for this is the persistent cultivation by the Liberal party of its classless image, its "abhorrence of anything remotely associated with class politcs",[40] its refusal to appeal to any class *against* any other class.

What this points to again is the unique character of English Canada as the only society in which the centre triumphs over left and right. In Europe the classless appeal of Liberal Reform does not work; the centre is decimated by the defection of high-status adherents to the right and of low-status adherents to the left. In Canada, the classless appeal of King centrism is the winning strategy, drawing lower-class support to the Liberals away from the left parties, and higher-class support away from the right parties. This forces the left and right parties themselves to emulate (to a certain extent) the Liberals' classless strategy. The Conservatives transform themselves into Progressive Conservatives. The CCF transforms itself from a "farmer-labour" party into an NDP calling for the support of "all liberally minded Canadians". The Liberal refusal to appear as a class party forces both right and left to mitigate their class appeals and to become themselves, in a sense, centre parties .

F.H. Underhill believes that *if* the Liberal party becomes a left party, organized labour and other leftist elements will join it. But the Liberal party will not become a left party *unless* these elements join it. What makes this vicious circle possible is the existence in Canada of an alternative which does not exist in the United States – a socialist party which is strong enough to play an important role in national politics. As long as a socialist party is alive and as long as the left has this alternative to a Liberal party interlocked with the business community, the Liberal party will continue to be centrist in the European way rather than "truly liberal" (leftist) in the American way; and as long as it continues to be centrist, the left will continue to support the socialist party. The "antagonistic symbiosis" of Canadian liberalism and socialism probably cannot be ended even by the magic of a charismatic leader.

Notes

1. (New York: Harcourt, Brace; and Toronto: Longmans, 1955), hereafter cited as *Liberal Tradition.*

2. (New York: Harcourt, Brace and World; and Toronto: Longmans, 1964), hereafter cited as *New Societies.*

3. Hartz, *New Societies,* 3.

4. *Ibid.*, 25.

5. *Ibid.*,7.

6. *Ibid.*, 34.

7. *Ibid.*, 71.

8. Kenneth McRae, "The Structure of Canadian History", in *ibid.*, 239.

9. *Ibid.*

10. *Ibid.*, 269-70.

11. *Ibid.*, 269.

12. *Ibid.*

13. *Ibid.*, 273.

14. In *The First New Nation* (New York, 1963), esp. Chap. 71.

15. *New Societies,* 235-40.

16. *Ibid.*, 234.

17. *Ibid.*, 238.

18. *New Societies.* 244-7.

19. *Ibid.*, 245.

20. *Ibid.*, 248.

21. *Ibid.*, 247.

22. *Ibid.*, 246.

23. Hartz, *New Societies,* 23.

24. *Ibid.*, 119.

25. *Ibid.*, 35.

26. *Ibid.*, 119.

27. *Ibid.*, 120.

28. See Samuel Beer, *British Politics in the Collectivist Age* (New York, 1965), esp. Chaps. 3 and 9-13.

29. Historic toryism finds expression today in the writings of Conservatives like W.L. Morton, who describes America as a liberal society integrated from below, by a *covenant* of brothers, and Canada as a monarchial society held together at the top, integrated by *loyalty* to the Crown. (*The Canadian Identity,* Toronto, 1961, 99-114.) In another of his writings Morton stresses the tory belief in personal leadership, in loyalty to leaders, and readiness to let them govern. ("Canadian Conservatism Now", in Paul Fox, ed., *Politics: Canada,* Toronto, 1962, 287.) He takes an organic view of society, stresses the values of authority and tradition, rejects the liberal values of individualism and egalitarianism. He calls for the rejection of the "dangerous and improper idea of the electoral mandate" (*ibid.*, 289). He calls for the "creation of a Canadian system of honors" (*ibid.*, 290). And he exhorts Canadian Conservatives frankly and loyally to accept the welfare state, since "laissez faire and rugged individualism" are foreign to "conservative principles" (*ibid.*, 289). Canadian and British tories are able to rationalize their parties' grudging acceptance of the welfare state by recalling their precapitalist collectivist traditions. Can one conceive of a respected spokesman of traditional Republicanism denouncing "rugged individualism" as un-Republician?

30. George Grant, *Lament for a Nation* (Toronto, 1965), 71. See Gad Horowitz, "Tories, Socialists and the Demise of Canada", *Canadian Dimension* (May-June, 1965), 12-15.

31. "The Background and Development of Marxian Socialism in the United States", in D. Egbert and S. Persons, ed., *Socialism in American Life* (Princeton, 1952), 401.

32. Speaking in the Commons on February 27, 1933, King assured the socialists that their objectives were not alien to the spirit of Liberalism. His objection was to their "implied method of reform through dictatorship". Norman McL. Rogers, *Mackenzie King* (Toronto, 1935), 186.

33. *Ibid.*, 267.

34. "The Canadian voter is in favour of progress *and* against social experimentation" (my emphasis). (*The Liberal Party of Canada, Ottawa,* National Liberal Federation, 1957, 15.) "Liberalism accepts social security but rejects socialism; it accepts free enterprise but rejects economic anarchy; it accepts humanitarianism but rejects paternalism". (Lester Pearson, Introduction to J.W. Pickergill, *The Liberal Party,* Toronto, 1962,x.) "Liberalism insists that the government must not stand by helpless in the face of . . . human suffering . . . Liberals, however, do not believe in socialism, with its veneration of the powerful state; with its emphasis on bureaucracy; with its class consciousness". (Pickergill, *The Liberal Party,* 115.)

35. *Globe and Mail,* September 29, 1943.

36. National Liberal Federation, *The Liberal Party,* 53.

37. J.W. Pickersgill, *The Mackenzie King Record* (Toronto, 1960), 601.

38. *Ibid.*, 635.

39. R. Alford, *Party and Society* (Chicago, 1963), Chap. 9.

40. "Group Perceptions and the Vote", in Meisel, ed., *Papers on the 1962 Election,* 249.

6

Liberal Consensus or Ideological Battleground: Some Reflections on the Hartz Thesis*

S.F. Wise

In the last few years it has become clear that Canadian historiography has entered a new phase, and that most Canadian historians are interested in questions which concern narrower horizons than those which attracted their predecessors. The point is an obvious one; the awakening or revival of interest in such areas as urban and labour history, land holding and land use patterns, family history and collective biography, or the study of particular groups has been remarkable. Regional history has become a major preoccupation, accompanied by the appearance of excellent journals. Canadian historians, moreover, have begun to group themselves with varying degrees of formality into regional or area study associations.

It is easy enough to trace the origins and development of this movement in historiography. For a considerable time it has been evident that the interpretative sweep of the Laurentian thesis, a brilliant explanation of the nation-building process, has been found less satisfactory as an account of other aspects of our life. As long ago as 1946, W. L. Morton launched a series of important critiques of the thesis, drawing attention to its centralist and nationalist bias. Since then, others have challenged its division of the Canadian population into winners and losers, heroes and villains, depending upon where they stood with respect to the national dream. Thus J.M.S. Careless, observing that "the nation-building approach to Canadian history neglects and obscures even while it explains and illuminates," suggested an approach in terms of the "limited identities of region, culture and class." Alan Smith subsequently traced the historical content of the idea of the mosaic, and concluded that "the national preoccupation came to be . . . with creating a nation out of culturally disparate groups, not with establishing cultural uniformity".[1]

Perhaps the deep divisions laid bare by the politics of the last decade or more have induced historians to seek explanations through more restricted and specialized studies. Perhaps English-speaking historians have become somewhat envious of the distinctiveness and coherence, if not the concord, that marks the historiography of French Canada, and are searching for a comparable uniqueness in the complexities of the rest of the country, if only to demonstrate that English Canada, too, has both a special past and destiny. Historians are no more immune than other groups to the resonances of their times. Quite apart from these considerations, however, it is perfectly clear that much has been overlooked of our past, and that the content of Canadian history positively invites more specialized approaches.

It will be some years before a new synthesis emerges; before historians can

---

*From *Historical Papers, 1974,* with the permission of the author and the Canadian Historical Association.

speak with more confidence both to each other and to a larger public. When such a synthesis forms, it will inevitably be a richer and more complex explanation of the life of the Canadian people than we now have. The Laurentian thesis is not a sufficient explanation; too much is left out of account. The idea of limited identities is a perception, not a thesis; it identifies an historical reality, but offers no illuminating hypothesis for it. Among other explanations of the manner in which our society has developed, by far the most interesting and stimulating is the Hartzian fragment thesis. Even though it, too, is an oversimplification, it is filled with provocative insights and has the decided merit of positively inviting fruitful challenge from many angles.

The fragment thesis deals with the problem of limited identities by denying the importance of such variations in the society-building process. When this lunar perspective is applied to the history of the English-speaking colonies of British North America, significant detail recedes, angularities are softened and rounded, mountains are made low and rough places plain. Yet the more conscientiously the formula is applied, the more anomalies swim upwards into view. The view from space has a blurred symmetry, yet one that we who are earthbound scarcely recognize as our own landscape.

But if it is assumed that discordance and complexity are at least as significant as correspondence and similarity, then, in answer to the fragment thesis, a counter-hypothesis comes to mind. Ideological clash, a possibility specifically excluded by the Hartz analysis, can help to explain the persistence of limited identities and can offer a less deterministic explanation of the society-building process.

Every historian of the pre-Confederation period must take cognizance of Louis Hartz's *The Founding of New Societies*, for, as "a general theory of five societies created by European migration in modern times," it grapples with the very problems they are attacking. To Hartz, English Canada is a liberal bourgeois fragment of the Old World, and therefore, despite certain "Tory touches", it has been "governed by the ultimate experience of the American liberal tradition." His approach has achieved a measure of influence. J.M.S. Careless, for example, accepted the hypothesis of the formative power of transferred cultural fragments, but contended that the traditions of English Canada were shaped, not by the weak remnants of the eighteenth century American empire, but by "the swamping force of earlier nineteenth century British immigration" and by "the organic, pragmatic Victorian liberalism" these immigrants brought with them.[2]

When distilled from the persuasive witchery of his language, his wealth of allusion, and his almost endless flow of insight and perception, Hartz's argument reduces to a few main points. All the societies considered by his collaborators and himself are fragments "struck off", "hurled outwards", "extricated" from Europe into new lands. According to differences in time and place of detachment, the fragments are feudal, liberal, or radical. Whatever its type, the fragment is transformed in a fashion that creates the cultural co-ordinates of the new society. That transformation is described as a "purely mechanistic" process, resting upon Hartz's quasi-Hegelian perception of the European historical process. His great ideologies—feudalism, bourgeois liberalism, radicalism and radical socialism—are the inexorable results of the clash of opposites. Since Europe "locks them together in a seething whole," none has the freedom to evolve according to its own inner logic.[3]

The dictates of the European historical process do not apply to the fragment. Freed from the strangling effect of the ideological jungle of the Old World, the fragment's development pursues a strange new course. "All sorts of magic inevitably takes place." The first piece of magic is the traditionalizing or conservatizing effect. The fragment freezes culturally; the United States, for example, has had "over three hundred years of liberal immobility," In the American case, the liberal fragment escaped not merely its enemy, the feudal and authoritarian past, but because of that very fact, it escaped the European future as well—"Marx fades because of the fading of Laud." So, with both past and future removed, and disturbing emanations from Europe cut off, the fragment, like a time capsule, is cocooned within its new environment.[4]

Out of the cocoon rapidly emerges a "rich interior development", faithful to the ideological nature of the fragment, but free to flourish in a manner impossible in the Old World. For the fragments are Cinderallas; "the story here is marvellous," Hartz declares; "Bossuet, Locke and Cobbett, miserable men abroad, all wake up to find worlds finer than they have known." What transpires is the swift emergence of fragment nationalism. The ideology of the fragment becomes a universal, "sinking below the level of thought to the level of an assumption." Then, "almost instantly", it re-emerges as nationalism. "Feudalism comes back at us as the French-Canadian spirit, liberalism as the American way of life, radicalism as the Australian legend." Since the fragment, by definition, cannot contain its enemies, its nationalist ideology has a peculiarly conformist quality. Europe is rejected as decadent, sinful and alien. The immigrant becomes the object of utmost suspicion, either to be rebuffed, as by the French Canadians or the Afrikaners, or to be subjected to a conscious process of assimilation to the ideological norms of the new nation.[5]

Canada is unusual, though not unique, in that it is a two-fragment situation, containing competing ideologies of feudalism and liberalism. (It should be observed incidentally that Hartz has little or nothing to say about the possibility that this conjunction may have started the Hegelian engines humming once more.) Adopting A.R.M. Lower's primary antithesis, he states that "it is to be corporate and Catholic to be French in Canada; to be Protestant and liberal to be English". Since English Canada, by definition, could contain no genuine conservative element, its political tensions resolve themselves in struggles between Whigs, the elite wing of the liberal spectrum, and liberal democrats, the counterpart of the petit bourgeois Jacobins of Europe. Thus we are presented with the picture of that great Jacobin, George Brown, refusing to "knuckle under the Whigs of Kingston".[6]

We are told by Hartz that the fragment process is "as simple, as intelligible as an historical process we normally take for granted." Moreover, if one is disposed to reject the mechanistic determinism of the hypothesis, and to argue that English-speaking Canadians in the past did make choices about their future, even though the context in which such choices were made was not so variegated as that of the world left behind, then one becomes part of that "bottomless subjectivity" of the fragment that is its fate as the memory of Europe recedes. So much for Hartz.[7]

II

Now with all this there are serious difficulties. The first and most obvious is the identification of the fragment itself, that potent leaven. In American history, the liberal movement is precisely that when the first Puritans set foot on the soil of New England. What group or collectivity is the liberal cultural bearer, the fundamental moulder of English Canada's cultural tradition, the Canadian Cinderella? It would be unfair to suggest that it was that group which first settled within the geographic bounds of English Canada — but the very presence, and survival, of the Acadians introduces a first unsettling complexity. Though Hartz himself does not particularize, his followers seem to have settled upon the Loyalists as the founding group, and we might perhaps assist them by addinq the pre-Loyalist Yankees of Nova Scotia and the thousands of American settlers who poured into Upper Canada in response to Simcoe's open door policy. Somewhat anomalously, these groups are all sub-fragments of a fragment. Passing for the moment over that complication, we must nevertheless ask ourselves whether the American components of the English Canadian fragment were liberal brethren to the Scottish Presbyterian of Nova Scotia and their Upper Canadian compatriots, to the mélange of foreign Protestants at Lunenburg, to the Ulstermen of the Moncton region or to the Yorkshiremen of Chignecto. If they were, then in what relationship did they stand to such groups as the Highland Catholics of Cape Breton, Prince Edward Island and the eastern counties of Upper Canada?

A second difficulty has to do with the timing of the liberal moment. Though Hartz tells us that the coming of democracy in English Canada was "delayed by a Tory touch, by imperial arrangements, or the presence of the French feudal fragment" – it is somehow characteristic of his argument that it does not really matter which – he nowhere reveals just when the liberal ideology became co-terminous with the fragment, just when homogenization occurred, just when that ideology, having been sublimated, was reborn as nationalism, and just when immigrants were consciously assimilated to it.[8] The problem is, of course, that imperial arrangements, geography and communications divided colonial societies from each other in a manner far more isolating than the pre-Revolutionary American colonies. All of them had separate existences for appreciable lengths of time: Upper Canada and New Brunswick for three-quarters of a century, Prince Edward Island for about a hundred years, Nova Scotia for a century and a half, and Newfoundland for at least three hundred years. The Hartzian scholar may be forced either to defer the timing of the magical liberal moment, or to face the possibility that he is examining, not the founding of one but of several new societies in British Canada.

Part of the problem is the level of abstraction upon which Hartz is writing. It is not men, women and children who migrate, on crowded decks, or packed in holds and steerages, it is ideas and symbolic figures; it is not peoples who evolve, but ideoligical-cultural entities. One of the strengths of his argument is his emphasis upon the significance of the European heritage, but the very generality of his categories makes them difficult to apply to the awkward facts of Canadian history. The Acadians, perhaps, were feudal, but since they lacked most of the hierarchy implied by the category, the identification itself is useless. Were the Newfoundland Irish feudal, or liberal with tribal touches? Does it help to identify the Chignecto Yorkshiremen as liberal, or is it more important fo know that they were Methodist, or that in Yorkshire they had been small tenant farmers and landless labourers? The work of the Annales School in France, or that of the modern English social historians – or, for that matter, that of the historians of colonial America – shows that it matters very much indeed, in terms of cultural norms, whether an immigrant came from Nantes, Dieppe, or Marseilles, and whether a man had farmed in Devon, Yorkshire or Fife. At this level of analysis the fragment thesis is of no utility, for it overrides variation and assumes the very points we have yet to investigate. By the same token, Canadian historians can no longer be content with their own crude categories of Scots, Irish, English, French or even Loyalist and American: European and American scholarship is now making available the kind of evidence that will permit a more precise and therefore a more complex appreciation of the variety of the European cultural legacy.

III

A crucial part of the fragment thesis is the contention that, once freed from the inhibiting effect of the European context, the fragment flowered untrammelled, in a Platonic fashion, towards its Ideal Form. There is a major objection to this contention. British North America was never isolated from Europe; it was never free to develop fully according to its own inner impulsions. It was not simply the continuing fact of the imperial presence, an imposing force in itself in the relatively small and weak colonial societies. Even more important was the continuing transmission to British North America of the political and social ideas of the Old World. The vehicles, human and literary, official and unofficial, for the transmission of British ideas, beliefs and assumptions to the several colonies need not concern us here; it is, after all, the familiar metropolitan story.

Admittedly, the inflow of the metropolitan culture was not uniformly spread throughout each colonial society. Its centres of dissemination were urban, and the degree to which it touched and influenced the mentality of the bulk of the population through the intricate internal network of communication each colony possessed has yet to be sufficiently explored. But the impact of what may be called the official culture upon those actively participating in the political life of the colonies was substantial. It determined the roles, set the standards and established the norms of those whose business it was to conduct the colonial institutional apparatus, it affected the attitudes and behaviour of those who aspired to a place in the structure, and it defined the limits even for many of those who found themselves in positions of political opposition.

There is an important contrast here with American colonial history. The presence of the metropolis and the diffusion of ideas from it were never so powerful and pervasive in the American colonies as in British North America. In colonial America, political power had devolved in considerable measure to such institutions as the town meeting and the parish vestry. In British North America, until the reforms of the era immediately before Confederation, each colony was a mirror of the Blackstonian principle that sovereignty (the qualified colonial version of it) was located at the centre. There decisions were made; the administration of them was left to the bureaucracy and to a chosen few in the localities. In a situation of power and no power (except for the periodic flurry of assembly elections), the socializing effect of political participation was far weaker than in colonial America. The lack of local representative institutions, a relatively low participation rate in assembly elections despite a quasi-democratic franchise, and the fact that most of the time politics was the concern of the few, seems to have acted to preserve local variations and to stratify values.

There is another important point in contrast with the American colonial experience. In all the British North American colonies with the exception of Newfoundland, imperial authority coincided with the arrival of settlers. In colonial America the very legitimacy of existing governments was from time to time called into question; in British North America immigrants of all origins were confronted by a constitutional structure, laws, rules and principles that seemed beyond challenge. Whether the American colonies were "born" liberal, as in the Hartzian conception, or, as seems more likely, they arrived at that happy state by the slow permeation through the culture of the implications of the early covenants and compacts, local government institutions or Lockean ideas by way of his Radical Whig popularizers, it is beyond question that by the Revolutionary era the root idea had taken hold that what legitimized government was the consent of the governed.[9] This idea, fundamental to the liberal ethos, got short shift in British North America. A brief attempt to institute the town meeting and local proprietorial control in Nova Scotia was cut off at birth in the 1760s. The Maugerville rebels, who mimicked Congress in composing their declaration of independence in 1776, were swiftly overawed by armed force, then inundated by New Brunswick's Loyalist influx.

This brings us to the knotty question of the ideological content of Loyalism. According to the fragment formula, since America was liberal by definition, Loyalists could not possibly be conservatives. The American fragment, containing no feudal element, could not produce conservatism, since (again by definition) conservatism was the by-blow of the onslaught of the European liberal bourgoisie upon feudalism. Loyalism, therefore, was simply the defeated wing of American liberalism; the Loyalists were nothing more than anti-Americans, Old Whigs, in the current scholarly vocabulary.

K,D. McRae, Professor Hartz's Canadian collaborator, has added some glosses to this picture. He has suggested, for example, that the high proportion of the European-born among the Loyalists is of little consequence. "That these recent immigrants," he observes, "were willing to pioneer a second time under similar conditions indicates an acceptance of the liberal ethos." This conclusion strains the evidence to meet the exigencies of the thesis and ignores W.H. Nelson's depiction of Loyalism as "congeries of conservative minorities resisting Americanization."[10] To be sure, McRae notes that the principle of selection involved in the Loyalist exodus "has served to differentiate the English Canadian tradition from the American in certain subtle, minor ways." It all depends on the perspective. Others examining the content of Loyalist beliefs may conclude that "subtle" and "minor" were "major" and "significant."

It is undeniable that within the Loyalist spectrum Lockean ideas existed, though much depends upon whether Joseph Galloway, say, is taken as representing Loyalist thought and not, for example, Thomas Hutchinson, Daniel Leonard, Jonathan Boucher, or Mather Byles. More important, perhaps, is the fact that among the Loyalists who came to British North America, a distinctively American attitude towards government and authority was common. In Nova Scotia, a Loyalist-led Assembly impeached judges in the 1780s; in New Brunswick, in the sharp division between elite and rank and file which occured at the inception of the colony, the rhetoric of the popular cause contained strong American accents. In Upper Canada, an individual like David MacGregor Rogers plainly represents the liberal vein in Loyalist thought. Accused as early as 1796 as being connected with a "republican and enemy of government" by a brother Loyalist, Nicholas Hagerman, by 1808, from his seat in the Assembly, Rogers bitterly attacked the forming network of power and patronage in the colony. "Upon any vacancy do we not see persons running, writing and using every means in their power to influence some powerful person in Europe . . . An American can have but little chance, let his abilities be what they may . . . Can it be any wonder that they should not feel such a warm attachment to the Government or constitution of the Country? " Rogers specifically objected to the freedom from popular control permitted the local government through its independent source of revenue from customs. Privately he reflected that the American Revolution was "a natural consequence of their arriving at a state of Opulence and Popularity;" the unstated future of Upper Canada seems plain enough.[12]

Though the persistence of the liberal democratic element among Loyalists is a matter of record, it is equally certain that among the bulk of the Loyalists who inclined to the government side, the liberal strain was rapidly subordinated to the values of the official political culture. Those values were conservative even in Hartzian terms; the only justification for calling them Whig could be the identification of Edmund Burke as a Whig when he wrote *Reflections on the French Revolution.* A careful examination of the rhetoric of the Upper Canadian elite and its substantial followings discloses little that is Lockeian; only among some of the moderate conservative assemblymen are there occasionally such shadings. The most frequently cited political philosopher, at least among the conservatives of Upper Canada, was neither Locke nor Burke, but Sir William Blackstone. Blackstone has customarily been considered a Whig, but in the context of resurgent aristocratic and anti-democratic thought, he was a conservative, as R.R. Palmer has pointed out. As selectively used by Upper Canadian conservatives, Blackstone provided an eloquent evocation of the glories of the British constitution, a justification for aristocracy, and a specific rejection upon legal and historical grounds of popular sovereignty, of the Lockeian compact and of the right of revolution. During the Revolutionary and Napoleonic Wars, it was not Blackstone and Burke alone but the whole floodtide of counter-revolutionary British conservatism that surged though the arteries of British North America and permeated the mentality of its ruling groups. Europe has returned to North America. The fragment was not a fragment, but the seat of clashing ideologies, a dialectical battleground.

It seems a curious anomaly to charge the Hartzian school with neglect of the European dimension of British North American values, yet that seems to be the case. The conservatism of the colonies was the product of a fusion of the values of British conservatism, Loyalist hostilities, and the survival ethos of the leadership of other groups within each colony, for of course the Loyalists were by no means the only or even the chief component of the oligarchies in most of these societies. Just how such an intermeshing of values occurred, and how it varied from colony to colony, must await further investigation. In Upper Canada, for demographic, historic and geographic reasons, conservatism was most intense, the line between it and North American liberalism most sharply drawn, and the struggle between the two most embittered.[13]

IV

An understanding of the fundamental beliefs of any era, and the intensity with which they were held, is unlikely to be reached when one reasons solely from a set of postulates about the nature of the world historical process. It is necessary, still, to engage in the laborious analysis of the surviving written record of a period, to crack its linguistic code, as it were, in order to identify the values and beliefs actually held, and their relationship to each other. The employment, no matter how dazzlingly, of such evocative names as Locke and Cobbett—or Blackstone—or even of such broadly inclusive terms as liberalism and conservatism, is to short-circuit the task of the historian.

Even a limited acquaintance with the literary record of early nineteenth century British North America is sufficient to indicate that a condition of ideological clash, not liberal consensus, existed. But it is not enough to pursue ideas through the literary records; they must be related to the cultural and material environment within which they were held. The fate of the idea of aristocracy will illustrate the point. Its reception in liberal North America has been counted as absurdity, and it is true that its enunciation in European terms scarcely survived the 1790s, though W.W. Baldwin for one can be found in its praise at a much later date. The idea itself did not die but was modulated and transformed (though in no magical way) until by the 1820s it had been reformulated as a rationale for the leadership of the best however determined. This modulation had occured in response to a complex set of variables which included both the shifting constellation of beliefs and the changing social and economic institutions of the society. The idea, and the operative strategy that was connected to it, has had a long life in Canada. John Porter's *Vertical Mosaic* needs to be given historical underpinnings. How fascinating it would be to trace the mentalities, the behaviour patterns, the institutional folkways that have enabled the descendants of supposedly superseded elites—Cartwrights, Symonses, Robinsons, Richardsons and many others—to find places of honour and status for themselves, generation unto generation.

It is the persistence of culturally diverse societies that raises the greatest difficulty about the applicability of the fragment hypothesis to British North America. Liberal values, especially egalitarianism and individualism, ought to have been solvents of distinctions, eating away at differences stemming from other lands, and converting peoples into the People. To explain why this did not occur remains a challenge to pre-Confederation scholarship, and returns us to the theme of limited identities. How did the many groups of the Atlantic Provinces and Upper Canada first establish separate identities? Were their numbers reinforced, and their identities thereby sustained, by accretions from further immigration or through natural increase? To what extent did economic and geographic factors contribute to the forming pattern of particularism? To what degree did various groups and collectivities conform to broader norms in provincial societies, and to what degree were their values threatened by those of the dominant groups in society? How far, in each province, was a condition of stable pluralism achieved, and how was it brought about? Answers to questions such as these require a complex historical scholarship, drawing upon the whole range of methods available, and employing the materials of what was once scornfully thought of as parish pump history.

It would be rash to venture at this point any covering statement to encompass such questions. What might be suggested is that a hypothesis that argues for the dominance of a conservative outlook among the directing groups of British North America may offer a readier explanation for the fact of pluralism, and some approaches to the manner in which it was articulated, than does the hypothesis of the liberal fragment.

What seems to have happened as a result of the immigration experience was not the flowering of a fragment but the efflorescence of group myths. Some of them are sectarian—the powerful consciousness of being a people set apart—although there may well be ethnic and economic dimensions of this phenomenon. Some myths fasten upon the migration experience itself, like that of the Pictou Scots and the coming of the *Hector*. Some are myths of a Golden Age overlaid by tragedy, as with the Acadians and the Loyalists. All sustain separate identity, all are exclusive in character.

The alien question in Upper Canada in the 1820s centred around the issue of whether or not post-Loyalist Americans should be accorded full civil rights as British subjects. Underlying the issue was a conflict between an exclusive and an assimilative myth. Here is the voice of the Loyalist:

> I am an old man, but I have not forgotten the scenes of my youth—the house wherein I was born—the garden where I play, and the fields where my hands first leaned to labour. Well can I remember how I was driven from them, and from the spot where my father fell, fighting for his king against rebels. By whom was I robbed of my patrimony? Even by such as (Barnabas Bidwell) who now claims equal privileges with the best of us . . . . (He) now comes forward after a lapse of a few years, to enjoy one of your highest prerogatives, to amend and make your laws, to sit, cheek by jowl, with your honourable men. What are you about, ye sons of Loyalists? Will ye suffer these things? [14]

Speaking for the Americans, John Rolph said of them:

> Upon their arrival they received grants of land; for they did not emigrate here to settle as squatters in the woods—not to spend the flower of their youth in hunting muskrats and destroying wolves—not to waste their strength in clearing

> the forest without the honour of owning an acre of it that the mosquitoes might the less disturb the dignified repose of those who sent the invitation—not to linger in the wilderness without a title to clear an acre, pluck a mushroom, or strip a slippery elm bark to prepare even a dish of Indian soup—by no means. They came at this Imperial invitation not to be degraded—they came from a free country, elated with the assurance that they would enjoy freedom here.[15]

Here history speaks against the homogenizing force of the common pioneering experience.

Colonial conservatism did not act to break down such myths. Rather, in a variety of ways, it tended to sustain them. Since conservatives were disposed to think in terms of collectivities, not of individuals, their tendency was to identify individuals with reference to the groups to which they belonged. Conservatism, at least in Upper Canada, was a coalition both of interests and or particularisms, whether religious, ethnic or both. It made no high assimilative demands beyond its insistence upon adherence to vital survival values—loyalty, order, stability—values that coincided with the interests and outlooks of many of the groups and collectivities that made up colonial society. The remarkable convergence of attitudes held towards the United States, its political system and its social tendencies by a wide variety of disparate groups in British North America is not accidental. It can be interpreted as an expression of the success of long-dominant conservatism in imposing its outlook; it is just as likely that to each group, in different ways and from different perspectives, American civilization was perceived as threatening. Though the language of hostility towards the United States had a high degree of uniformity, its subjective content or inner meaning might be quite different for each group. For the most part, conservatism dealt with leaders, not followers. Elitist politics, though assimilating group chieftains to the values of the directing elites, made less impression upon their adherents.

This is not to claim any special virtue for early conservatism. Many of its spokesmen would have preferred more uniform and organic societies, and some of its leaders were prepared, like John Strachan, to use drastic methods to build such societies.[16] But it does suggest that the prevalence of conservative beliefs is a factor to be taken into account when explaining the phenomenon of limited identities. Professor Careless, in referring to the swamping effect of British immigration and of the liberalism it purportedly brought with it, proposes to stand the Hartz thesis on its head. The arrival of the fragment is delayed until the 1830s or 1840s; the fate of the already existing people of British North America was to be assimilated to it and its values. This seems too George Brown-centred a view. I would suggest that there *was* a continuity in the society-building process of British North America. Though the shape and content of the early societies was certainly modified by massive immigration, to an extent yet to be explored, later comers took on some of the values and patterns of the long-established societies. In other words, perhaps George Brown did knuckle under to those Whigs of Kingston.

For the pattern of English Canadian complexity derives not only from local, regional, ethnic and other variations, but also from the continued workings of a liberal-conservative dialectic. How far were the two sides of the dialectic reinforced by importation from abroad? When did a synthesis of values occur, and what forms did it take? It is probably right to look for its beginnings in the generation immediately before Confederation, but we have scarcely begun to trace its nature. The English Canadian style and character is not to be understood in terms of the consensus of a triumphant liberalism, but, out of its contradictory heritage, in terms of muted conservatism and ambivalent liberalism, of contradiction, paradox and complexity.

Notes

1. W.L. Morton, "Clio in Canada: the interpretation of Canadian history", *University of Toronto Quarterly,* XV (3), April, 1946; J.M.S. Careless, "Limited identities in Canada", *Canadian Historical Review,* L(1), March, 1969, pp.2-3; Allan Smith, "Metaphor and nationality in North America", *ibid.*, LI(3), September.

2. Louis Hartz, *The founding of new societies: studies in the history of the United States, Latin America, South Africa, Canada and Australia,* (New York, 1964), vil. p.4, p.33; Careless, "Limited identities", p.4.

3. Hartz, *Founding of new societies,* p.3, p.6, p.24.

4. *Ibid.,* pp.4-6.

5. *Ibid.,* pp. 4-5, pp. 13-14.

6. *Ibid.,* pp.15-16n, pp. 35-6.

7. *Ibid.,* p.9, pp.24-5.

8. *Ibid.,* p.40.

9. On the quest for legitimacy in the American colonies, see Michael Kammen, *People of Paradox: An Inquiry Concerning the Origins of American Civilization,* (New York,1973), 31ff.

10. W.H. Nelson, *The American Tory,* (New York 1961); Hartz, *Founding of new societies,* p.236, pp. 238-9.

11. See especially Bernard Bailyn, *The Ordeal of Thomas Hutchinson,* (Cambridge, Mass. 1974), and A.Y. Zimmer and A.H. Kelly, "Jonathan Boucher: Constitutional Conservative", *Journal of American History,* LVIII (4), March, 1972, pp. 897-922.

12. Public Archives of Ontario, D.M. Rogers Papers, D.M. Rogers to James Rogers, 29 July 1795; Memoranda on speeches and proceedings of the U.C. Assembly on the school bill, 5 March (1808).

13. S.F. Wise, "Conservatism and Political Development: The Canadian Case", *South Atlantic Quarterly,* LXIX (2), Spring, 1970, pp. 226-43.

14. Kingston *Chronicle*, "Address to the freeholders of Lennox and Addington", 1 February 1822.

15. *Canadian Freeman*, 8 February 1827.

16. Periods of high immigration and rapid social change frequently evoked the latent conservative urge to impose uniformity. Thus in the 1850s Egerton Ryerson called on all groups to forget differences born of national origin and religion and to "unite in one noble feeling of *Canadianism*—regarding Canada as their country, their *Home*—the home and hope of their children, and its highest advancement their highest earthly interest and glory." Yet even Ryerson had to repress such urges. *Dr. Ryerson's letters in reply to the attacks of foreign ecclesiatics against the schools and municipalities of Upper Canada,* (Toronto, 1857), p.100.

PART II

THE LIFE CYCLE AND PERSONAL IDENTITY

INTRODUCTION

The life of man in society is a series of transitions. By examining the major stages in the life of a typical individual we come to understand society as a whole. Two types of transition are of special interest: biological-birth, puberty, parenthood, and death, and social-beginning and advancing in an occupation, migrating from one area to another, or immigrating to a new country. Papers in this part of the Reader deal with both types of transition.

Few perspectives in the study of social phenomena are as meaningful as the life cycle. Each person advances from complete dependence on others through increasing levels of autonomy; from limited to increasing knowledge, range of feelings and self-awareness; from the performance of few roles to the performance of many.

A "Canadian life cycle" may be distinguished by components which derive from the status of being Canadian. But what is this status and what is its source? Is it geography, climate, politics, culture, or a question of self-definition? However one may define its elements and dimensions, its base varies considerably. This follows from the complexity or mosaic of cultures in Canada and from variations by region, origin, history, and placement in the social structure.

We begin with anthropological overviews by Edward S. and Jean H. Rogers of an Indian culture and by John A. Hostetler and Gertrude E. Huntingdon of socialization in a Hutterite community. World-view of each society leads to unique methods of socialization. With these outlines of life cycles in relatively traditional societies as a baseline, we can compare structures and processes in other Canadian settings.

In a section on the family group, Colette Moreaux studies baptism in a Quebec parish, Seena Kohl and John W. Bennett deal with Prairie youth, and Leo Davids with the future of the family.

The adult world presents its own problems of entrance and mobility. In an ethnographic report, Judith Nagata considers the problems of Greek immigrants in a large metropolitan Canadian centre. Patricia Marchak studies the discrimination women experience at work in British Columbia. The motives of anglophones and francophones who work for the federal public services, the nation's largest employers, are analyzed by Christopher Beattie. Rootman and Mills contrast the professional behaviour of American and Canadian chiropractors.

The final articles in Part II touch on the latter years of life. Lee A. Guemple shows us that old age and death, even in the relatively simple social world of the Inuit, are complex and stressful. Rex Lucas takes us directly into the critical anxieties of men trapped in the coal mines of Nova Scotia.

Here we sample the wide variety of problems Canadians in different subcultures face in the course of their lives. We see as well the range of research approaches and methods which help us to understand how people adapt as they grow older.

Part II Section A

INFANCY TO DEATH IN TWO SOCIETIES

7

The Individual in Mistassini Society From Birth to Death*

Edward S. Rogers and Jean H. Rogers

From July 1953 until August 1954 the authors carried out ethnographic research among the Mistassini Indians of south-central Quebec. The purpose of the present paper is to record those observations and informants' statements regarding the life cycle of the individual. An attempt is made to trace the changes which an individual undergoes from birth to death and to record the socialization process.

The Mistassini consider age as important factor, and on the basis of it they recognize four stages in the life of a person. A very small child is *AwAsIs;* an unmarried boy and girl are *napesIs* and *IskwesIs,* respectively; an adult man and woman are *napew* and *Iskwew,* respectively; and an old person is *cIsenIw,* regardless of sex. These stages are not sharply differentiated except possibly in the case of unmarried boys versus men. In general, the transition from stage to stage is gradual and in a sense continuous.

For convenience of presentation, several stages, not always comparable to the preceding, have been selected more or less arbitrarily. The first is infancy, starting at birth and ending with the "Infants' Rite" at the age of two or three. The rite does not, however, mark any change in the status of the child. Childhood for boys can be considered terminated when the "First Kill Rite" is given; for girls, when the "Puberty Rite" is performed. In the former case, this occurs at approximately ten years of age. For neither sex is life basically altered. Marriage generally marks the transition from adolescence to adulthood and the use of the terms *napew* and *Iskwew*, at which time the individual assumes new responsibilities. We found nothing that could be taken as marking the commencement of old age. This scheme can be thought of as only an approximation. In the old days, girls sometimes married before menarche, but they did not thereupon assume the status of adult women. It was still necessary for them to

---

* Abridged from *Contributions to Anthropology, 1960, Part II,* Bulletin 190, 14-26 Ottawa: Department of Northern Affairs and National Resources, 1963, with the permission of Information Canada.

undergo the Puberty Rite.

Socialization continues practically throughout the life of an individual. Only in old age can a person feel free of the guidance offered by the elders. Training is gradual and varies somewhat, depending upon circumstances. During the first few years of life, frustrations are few, and a child is allowed a good deal of freedom. This is not meant to imply that there are no social controls. By the age of five or six, children tend to be rather aggressive and independent, except with strangers. Beginning at this age, pressures are slowly brought to bear to make the child conform. The emphasis on conformance is gradually increased so that by the time a child reaches adolescence, he or she is completely under the domination of the senior members of the group. At this age, a breach of conduct is not tolerated as it is for very young children.

By the end of adolescence, the individual is a fully participating member of the society, as far as practical tasks are concerned, and basic economic roles have been established.

On entering adulthood, the man can aspire to several optional roles, such as leadership of a hunting group or shamanism. Nevertheless, as age still counts, these positions cannot be attained for a number of years. Old people hold a position of great respect and always receive deference. While they generally can no longer contribute materially to the maintenance of the group, especially the men, their wisdom is valued. Old men have a leading position in religious affairs, which are considered essential for the welfare of the group.

Infancy

In presenting the material dealing with infancy, pregnancy and birth are first discussed. These are not circumscribed by innumerable restrictions and prescriptions. Granted there are some—standard methods of dealing with the situation—but in general they are dealt with naturally and, in a way, casually.

Children are desired, and in the past this was one reason for polygyny. An old man sometimes acquired a second wife after his first has passed the child-bearing age. Today, although no longer polygynous, the old men usually marry young women rather than elderly widows when their wives die, so that they may continue to have children.

No elaborate preparations are made prior to the birth of a child. No clothes are made for the expected infant, but if a birth is due in the winter, a quantity of sphagnum moss is gathered and brought inside the lodge to thaw and dry. As the time for the birth approaches, the husband remains near camp. If he goes on hunting trips, he generally returns by evening.

Births take place in the family or communal lodge. The woman is assisted by her husband and another woman. The latter may be a sister, mother, sister-in-law, or a non-relative. If, as it sometimes happens, a daughter is the only available female, she serves. If the husband is absent, a woman substitutes for him, as apparently no other male is permitted to be present. Younger children are usually sent to another tent during parturition, although an informant stated that there is no rigid exclusion practised, at least of girls.

As soon as the delivery is accomplished, the mother and child cared for and the afterbirth disposed of, the woman's other children, if they have been excluded, may then return. Female relatives and friends are now allowed to visit the mother, but all men except the husband are excluded for several days.

Attention is lavished on babies by people of all ages. The degree to which an infant is cared for exclusively by its mother varies with circumstances, such as the number and ages of other children in the family and the health of the mother.

At the request of the mother, a female relative or friend, a day or two after birth, performs the service at which the child receives its name. It is fairly common for at least one child in a family to be named for a grandparent. Boys are often named for their fathers. The person who suggests the name is expected to give the child a present. Nowadays, English Christian names are almost variably used, and the surname is generally Indian or a translation of an Indian name. It is also customary for children to be formally baptized at the church when the group returns in the summer.

Children usually have the surname of their fathers, but it sometimes happens that a son may have a different one, although other children in the same family have their father's. If the new surname is passed on, the sibling relationship becomes obscure, and a new surname may thus appear without one new family immigrating into the area. For example, William, a son of Sandy Shecapio, was given a nickname which became Scharles. He is now known as William Scharles, and the Shecapio surname has disappeared from his direct descendants.

Children are very commonly given nicknames, usually in reference to some pecularity. These nicknames are somethimes used throughout life but are usually dropped as the child grows older. Examples of nicknames include *slklmew,* "mosquito" (with phomenic change), used for a child who was always covered with mosquito bites; *ka piclskwet*, "one who gossips"; *mAclskwesls,* "ugly-girl"; *ka wAcAskoplslt,* "muskrat-eyes", *nAmes emlhkon,* "fish spoon."

As stated previously, for the first few days after birth the infant is cared for by another woman, mostly likely the attendant at the birth. During this time the child is not nursed by the mother, her colostrum not being used. Formerly, the new baby was given "fish liquor," water in which fish has been boiled. Today, infants are given powdered milk, if available, mixed with water and sugar.

Supplementary foods are not introduced until the child is about two months old. He is then given such foods as rice, oatmeal, and bannock softened in tea. Small pieces of fish are given early, but it was stated by one informant that meat would probably not be given before the child was a year old. The infant is fed whenever it cries.

Weaning, which is accomplished gradually, takes place when the child is at least a year old. And though the mother does not force the child, she tries constantly to interest him in solid foods and offers the breast only if the baby is very fretful or ill.

Toilet training is a gradual process. When a baby is old enough to walk, he may be taken outside by an older sibling. A baby between the ages of one and a half and two years may announce his need, at which time an older sibling is immediately told to take him outside. All those present show interest in the older sibling's report, expressing pleased surprise if the infant has been successful. There is no reprimand at this age for failure. With older children, the case is different. A child of four was sharply scolded for defecating in her clothing.

There is no disgust for the products of elimination. Small children playing outdoors defecate wherever they are at the time. Urination is a very casual matter, and slips on the part of the four-year-old may be cause for amusement to children and adults alike.

By the time children are beginning to walk, they are given commands and sent on errands by their elders, children or adults. There is apparently little expectation that the baby will carry out the order, but the older person usually waits a short time and, if the infant is successful, rewards hime with a smile. A baby of a year and a half may be told to fetch something, to throw something away, or even to put wood in the stove. He may also try to help his older siblings at various tasks, such as bringing stove wood into the lodge or carrying water in a small kettle.

There is little attempt to discipline a baby. If he persistently bothers his mother while she is engaged in some delicate task, she may slap his hand and then ignore his tears. Generally, however, a mother resorts to attempts to distract a baby's attention to some other occupation. Certain actions that are discouraged in older children are encouraged in infants. A toddler may be greeted with general applause for chasing a dog with a stick, but children beyond the age of three or four are generally told not to tease the animals. Small children are often encouraged to be demonstrative and to act before the group. For example, clowning and attempts at dancing were met with approbation and laughter. But in later years children grow submissive and reserved.

Infant's Rite

When a child first leaves the lodge unaided, the "Infants' Rite" is performed and is followed by a feast. There is a tendency to keep an eye on a baby who is learning to walk, with a view to preventing this occurence until a time when big game is available for the feast. If a baby who had not even learned to walk crawled out of the lodge unobserved, the rite would have to be given immediately, even though bannock and fish were the only available foods. Such a situation is remembered and laughed about for a long time.

The essence of the baby's rite is the symbolization of the child's future role as an adult. A boy "kills," brings the kill to camp, and distributes the meat; a girl carries in firewood and boughs. Only one such rite was observed. Given for three boys and two girls at the same time, it occured at the village of Mistassini during the summer of 1953. All the children appeared to be between the ages of about a year and a half and two years. They wore new clothing, and each boy had new embroidered moccasins, a small shot pouch, a small hunting bag, and a tumpline. The boys were gently pushed out of the lodge first. Two of them were led by two men (fathers?) holding twenty-two caliber rifles, which they were attempting to place in the boys' hands. The third boy had a toy gun. After the boys were outside the tent, the two girls came out and sat on the "porch" steps. Each girl carried on her back a tiny load of firewood and balsam boughs tied with a small tumpline. One girl carried a toy axe.

The head of a freshly killed moose had been placed in front of the tent. A *nimapan* or ceremonial carrying string was attached to each antler, and another was tied through one nostril.

One of the men took a gun and helped each small boy, in turn, to shoot it, while the spectators backed away laughing. Next, the boys were made to walk toward the door of the tent, each with a *nimapan* in one hand. The men followed them into the tent, carrying the moose head, which was placed in the middle of the floor. The little girls then entered, and finally as many spectators as possible crowded into the tent. The boys' hunting bags were spread out, and each boy was made to offer food to those present. Each person thanked the child and left when he received his share. The food distributed consisted of small pieces of bannock, doughnuts, and crackers. After the hunting bags were emptied, they were folded by the woman whose tent it was and, with the shot pouches and *nimapan,* hung on a nail at the back of the tent. The girls' bundles had been arranged on either side of the moose head. These were now untied. The small pieces of firewood were put in the stove, and the boughs were arranged in the flooring. The girls' tumplines were rolled up and hung on another nail at the rear of the lodge. The rite took place in the morning, requiring about an hour. That evening, a feast was given.

Childhood

Following the "Infants' Rite" is the period of childhood, lasting until the "First Kill Rite" for boys and the "Puberty Rite" for girls. As far as the child is concerned, however, nothing is radically changed by the transition. During this period, the child is taught to conform, and thus the basis is laid for adulthood.

As the child matures, he or she spends more and more time working and less and less playing. When girls reach approximately ten years of age and boys thirteen, they work the full day during the spring and autumn travel periods and the winter hunt. No outward signs of rebellion against socialization were observed, except in young children about four years old. In both sexes, tantrums were witnessed at this age, which may have been a reaction to the commencement of disciplinary action.

Children are cared for by their elders and learn from the,. usually within the context of the immediate family. Occasionally, permanent or temporary adoption occurs for several reasons. But the parents are generally responsible for the care and training of their children. The mother cares for the very young children, although the father renders whatever help he can. A hurt or frightened child is quite likely to go to the mother for comfort, although occasionally he may go to the father.

Older siblings are teachers and guardians almost as often as parents are, administering punishment and rewards. Among children, protective behaviour on the part of an older sibling for a young one is very noticeable. This begins by the time the older one reaches the age of four, and the younger one, two. There is, on the other hand, a tendency for the older ones to bully the younger. This situation is not a matter of great concern to adults if it is not carried too far. If an older child causes one younger than himself to cry, the mother may comfort the child, but she generally does not repimand the older one. Quarrelling or fighting among children, however, is immediately stopped by any older person present.

Besides parents and siblings, other people enter the individual's life during childhood as teachers and occasionally as guardians. When a child is placed with another family, he is directly under their authority. At other times, the child has contacts with his uncles and aunts. Only when the latter are older than the child do they have any control, and then only on certain occasions; e.g., when the hunting group lives in a communal lodge. A child may visit his relatives in another part of the lodge while his parents remain in their own area. The relatives will then control the actions of the child, even though its parents are within earshot. But if the parents are also visiting, they control the child.

As mentioned previously, great affection is shown toward very small children, and this continues for a number of years. As the child grows older, outward acts of affection are suppressed. The father tends to suppress his emotions at an earlier date than does the mother. A mother will hold and comfort the child of ten whether it is a boy or a girl. Grandparents show affection and concern for their grandchildren in many ways. One case was reported of a man composing a song for his granddaughter after she had been badly bitten by black flies.

A child gradually learns the proper behaviour and duties. It is generally considered that too much should not be expected of children, especially when they are too young to understand the reasoning behind an order. It is said that, later, when they are older, they will understand. Most misbehaviour and non-co-operation are spoken of in terms of understanding. As the child is not old enough to behave sensibly, he is therefore not considered wilfully bad.

There is a tendency for tasks, graded in difficulty, to be assigned to children on the basis of their age and capabilities. Adults compare the abilities of different children. This results in a definite recognition of individual variation, which is expressed in terms of differing rates of development rather than differences in innate ability or intelligence. Usually this is of no great concern to the parents. One child may be unable to perform certain tasks that another of similar age can do. For the most part, however, no great emphasis is laid upon the differences. It is thought that with time these variations will disappear. But, when a child reaches adolescence, considerable concern is often shown for retardation.

During childhood, training is begun in earnest, and discipline is administered for the first time with the avowed intention of making the child conform. During this period, the child gradually learns to obey without question. This is first brought about by means of repeated verbal commands. No commands that cannot be backed by practical reasons, whether to initiate or stop an action, are given. With young children, if any order is not carried out, nothing is done. Later, a command will be repeated until the action is performed. Sometimes an order is rescinded. Generally, if a child cries persistently for something, he is indulged. There are times when the parent will not indulge the child. If, during the winter, a child rushes outside in a fit of temper, he is allowed to remain for a few minutes. Then he is carried bodily inside, whether he wishes it or not, becuase of the fear of frost bite. Furthermore, a child's reluctance to perform chores about camp is rarely, if ever, tolerated.

Corporal punishment, which is rare, is applied only to young children. It is resorted to when the mother's repeated commands are of no avail. The punishment is administered by switching the child's legs with a bough from the flooring or by striking it several times on the buttocks with a stick. The child immediately bursts into tears. Generally all that is necessary is for the older person to pick up a spruce bough from the floor. Children exhibit considerable fortitude in the face of physical discomfort or pain incurred in an accident, but little in the face of violence on the part of another person.

Threats are occasionally used. These generally invoke the fear of harm from supernaturals and strangers. The most common sanctions used in training children besides repetitive commands are laughter, ridicule, and, as a last resort, ostracism. Good-natured laughter is frequently effective, and the child is taught to laugh at his own clumsiness. Yet children are not allowed to jeer at one another. Ridicule may be resorted to but is generally stopped if it is resented. A form of ostracism occurs, whereby all other members of the group, children and adults alike, ignore the recalcitrant. This is very rarely necessary but is always effective when used, since, during the winter at least, the recalcitrant has no other recourse but to co-operate.

Children are trained in practical tasks through conscious instruction and observation. In addition, they imitate the actions of adults, much if not all of which can be considered play. Girls work with older girls, especially their sisters, and learn from them and from older women, generally their mothers. A boy spends considerable time with his mother and sisters until he approaches puberty, by which time he has developed the strength and stamina to work with the men away from camp. First, at the age of nine or ten, he accompanies his father on short trips; later, on longer ones. The boy is usually with the men when they are working in camp.

A four-year-old girl is given cloth, scissors, and a threaded needle to amuse herself while her mother sews. By the time a girl is nine or ten she is capable of mending clothes quite efficiently and will amuse herself by sewing small items of clothing and equipment, such as shot pouches for her younger brothers. During childhood, girls are coached in cooking and in preparing game. By ten, they know a considerable amount about cooking generally and can make a passable bannock.

Children of both sexes accompany their mothers on expeditions to gather boughs and firewood, to examine snares and traps, or to hunt ptarmigan. Sawing logs into stove lengths is primarily children's work. Although children of all ages play with axes and make attempts to split wood, they are not expected to accomplish much in this respect until they reach adolescence.

Children's play is based mainly on imitation of adult behaviour. Most toys are miniature replicas of adult equipment. The Mistassini recognize this imitative play and say that children learn from it. A few normal games are indulged in, such as the stick-and-bundle game and string figures.

For boys, the "First Kill Rite" can be thought of as marking the transition from childhood to adolescence. In actuality, this is not a real "rite of passage" since there is no radical change in the boy's life or status.

As a boy approaches puberty, he makes more and more short hunting trips about the neighbourhood of the camp, usually accompanied by an older person. If alone, he never journeys far from camp. Eventually he makes his first kill unaided. For this occasion, a feast is given at which the meat is distributed. This constitutes the "First Kill Rite."

A girl's transition to adolescence is marked by the "Puberty Rite."[1] At menarche, she is isolated from her family group. A tent is erected for her by the women, usually a small trapping tent, out of sight of the main camp. The distance varies depending upon the local terrain and the denseness of the woods. She gathers her own firewood and cooks her own food, using her own cooking utensils. If there is another young girl in camp, she may sleep with the menstruating girl, but no men or boys are allowed to see even the menstrual tent. Formerly, the period in isolation lasted about a week, according to one informant; nowadays, it is two or three days. As this is not an occasion for public celebration, no feast is given.

Adolescence

The transition from childhood to adolescence is not an abrupt one and involves the gradual ascription of more and more responsibility for competence and the performance of all types of work. This change occurs for girls at a younger age than for boys.

Once having reached adolescence, boys and girls undergo an intensive training in all the tasks for which they will be responsible in their adulthood. During the winter they work full days, with very little time for play. In summer, boys have more freedom than girls, whose tasks continue regardless of the season.

At this stage in life a real sex dichotomy takes place. A brother and sister, who as children slept under one blanket, are now rigidly separated when sleeping. There is, however, no other form of avoidance between siblings of opposite sex.

When a boy acquires the necessary stamina and strength, he spends all his time working for his father—hunting, trapping, and learning the manufacture of various items of equipment. A girl works with her mother and performs the greater part of the less skilled tasks, such as drawing water, mending, cooking, and laundering. At the same time, she is trained in the more skilled tasks, such as lacing snowshoes.

The sanctions invoked by adults on adolescents are generally the same as those for children, although corporal punishment is not administered. Verbal commands are still the most frequent form of sanction, but laughter and ridicule are also readily employed. In their dealings with adults, adolescents of both sexes appear to be more subdued than children. Their parents exercise a real control over them.

Young people of opposite sex are not supposed to associate without supervision. During summer, practically no privacy is possible near the encampment, and a girl would soon be missed if she disappeared for any length of time. A similar situation maintains during the winter months.

Love affairs do develop as a result of the young people's associating at the public dances. Such innocent affairs are public property and, if the parents approve, may lead to marriage. Clandestine affairs also occur, although apparently they are not frequent. An unmarried girl who becomes pregnant is criticized. In such cases there is an attempt on the part of the girl's family to arrange a marriage for her as soon as possible. No stigma is attached to the illegitimate child.

Adulthood

Marriage, which is considered a desirable state, marks the commencement of adult status for both sexes. Monogamy is the rule, although in the past polygyny was practised to a limited extent.

Formerly, girls married young in life, even occasionally before puberty. More recently they marry during the latter half of their teens, although sometimes marriage is delayed until the early twenties. At the time of our field work there was only one spinster over thirty, and she was a hunchback. Boys are usually married in their early twenties. Most individuals marry at least twice during a lifetime, not because of divorce but because of the death of a spouse.

The basis for the selection of a mate appears to be eminently practical. The capabilities of the prospective spouse in everyday tasks are considered carefully. A proficient girl is sought as a wife. There is apparently no feeling that some women, being basically unattractive, will never marry. Besides economic considerations, kinship and geographic proximity appear to enter into the choice of a mate.

Cross-cousin marriage was and still is practised. Although the evidence is not conclusive, this is apparently a preferred type of marriage. One informant told of a friend of hers who used to laugh and say that if so-and-so, her cross-cousin, had been a man, she would have married "him" because "he" would be the "right" one to marry.

The sororate, which is strongly criticized, is almost never practised as it is considered definitely improper. This is undoubtedly the result of the teaching of the Anglican Church, which until about forty years ago banned marriage with a deceased wife's sister.[2]

There is a tendency for marriages to occur between families whose hunting territories are in close proximity to each other. Marriages are contracted with lesser frequency as the distance between the two families increases. Marriages with whites sometimes take place, and there is no evidence that this is considered either desirable or undesirable.

Marriages are arranged by the parents of the young couple or, if they are not living, by other older relatives. Usually the boy's parents ask the girl's; only rarely do the parents of the girl initiate the contract. A boy generally expresses his preference to his father, who, if his wife also approves, broaches the subject to the girl's parents. Occasionally, the parents of one or the other may interfere with a marriage desired by the young couple on the grounds that one of them is lazy or otherwise unsuitable. On the other hand, if the boy's parents were to arrange a marriage that he did not approve of, he might refuse to marry the chosen girl. In such a case, the matter would be dropped. Similarly, a girl who found the projected marriage highly distasteful might refuse to comply. She would be criticized for being headstrong, but if she is obstinate enough, she can sometimes thwart the desires of her parents. One informant stated that today the young people, disregarding the wishes of their parents, become headstrong and arrange their own marriages. This may or may not be a true picture of the situation.

There is no recollection of a marriage ceremony or feast in the days before church weddings. Today, all marriages take place during the summer, two to four couples usually being married at the same time by the native deacon or visiting minister. No preparations, such as making wedding clothes or cooking for the feast, are made until the day of the wedding. If these things were done ahead of time, the marriage might not take place or other bad luck might ensue. The marriage ceremony is always followed by a feast and almost invariably by a dance to which everyone goes. The newlyweds dance first. Directly after marriage, the couple usually spends the first night or two in the lodge of the boy's parents. After this, they erect their own home wherever they wish, though generally it is near that of the boy's parents.

The place of residence during the winter often varies. Ideally, a man remains with his father, except for one winter which he spends with his father-in-law. This occurs within his first three years of marriage. Often it is not possible to follow this ideal, and a man may go with his father-in-law permanently, his father's brother, his own brother, or his brother-in-law. During most of the year, the couple occupy their own lodge, but occasionally during the winter the individual families of a hunting group all live in one communal lodge.

At the time of marriage, the newlyweds have not only to adjust to each other but to their affinal relatives. No evidence was acquired of any avoidance between the couple and their parents-in-law. Deference is shown the latter, but this appears to be due more to the age factor than to anything else. No special relationships were observed to take place between siblings-in-law.

Marriages are generally stable, although occasionally discord arises. Usually, couples appear to be quite happy. Quarrelling does not take place between husband and wife, and mutual affection is frequently expressed. With time, a strong marital bond develops. The emotional ties binding the family together are firmer than those binding the member families of a hunting group.

The nuclear family is the most permanent unit within the society, disrupted only by the death of the parents, the marriage of the children, or by separation. Separation is extremely rare, and only one case was recorded. A woman left her husband to live with his brother, an action which was universally condemned. Nothing was done, however, and the woman bore ten children by her brother-in-law. At first, the situation caused trouble between the brothers, but eventually the husband forgave them, and the two men associated freely, looking at fish nets together and co-operating in other work. The woman lived with her brother-in-law until he died, and then she returned to her husband. She survived him also and is still living. All her children died, and the community considered that this was her punishment. There is no divorce. This fact and the low incidence of separation may be the result of church influence.

The nuclear family forms a unit of primary importance in the life of the Mistassini Indians. It is an economic unit which rivals the hunting group in prominence and co-operates throughout the year to provide for maintenance and welfare of its members. The husband hunts and traps; the wife tends the camp chores. The younger boys and girls help their mother, and the older boys aid their father. There are joint undertakings to gather berries and tend fish nets. Parents are the guardians, providers, and disciplinarians of their children. The mother has more direct contact with the young children than the father has. The older children aid their parents in these responsibilities.

Each member is recognized as contributing his or her share to the common good of the family. This is true to such an extent that traps are set on behalf of even the small children. The animals captured, which include those whose fur is restricted to home consumption, such as rabbits, and a few whose fur is saleable, are considered theirs. In the latter case, the furs are of small value; no instance, for example, has been recorded of a child securing a beaver pelt. The saleable furs are placed in account with the Hudson's Bay Company for the children.

The husband is recognized as the official leader, although his wife may exert a considerable amount of actual control. The degree to which one dominates the other varies with personality factors. When minor disagreements occur, little attempt is made to force one to conform to the other's point of view. Ideally, there is a respect for individuals regardless of sex.

After marriage, and this is perhaps more especially true of the men, they continue to perfect themselves in the fundamentals of their culture. In addition, they may seek further advances, such as becoming a shaman or chief.

By adulthood an individual's basic role has been established. While there is a habitual division of economic tasks between the sexes, there are times when these overlap. In many cases each sex is able to perform the task of the opposite sex, although not so proficiently. There is no stigma attached to performing work usually reserved for the opposite sex. On the contrary, it is usual for a man to help his wife if she is sick or in the advanced stages of pregnancy. There are no specialized craftsmen in Mistassini society. Each man or woman is capable of producing whatever items he or she needs, apart from purchased items of European manufacture.

The economic role of the men is primarily that of hunter and trapper, and they are often away from the camp for a day or more engaged in arduous hunting and trapping trips. They butcher the game and transport it to camp. The women help the men prepare the large hides, and, on occasion, men dress smaller game and stretch the pelts. The men set fish nets under the ice during the winter, but a man and his wife often tend the net together. Summer nets are often set and tended by a man and his wife, and set lines are placed and tended by either sex.

The heavy work of moving supplies during summer and winter is done by the men. They erect the tents or lodges and set up the stoves. Almost invariably the men run the outboard motors and repair them. Men do most of the work required in the manufacture of wooden articles such as snowshoe frames, toboggans, sleds, snowshovels, grease ladles and fish spoons, axe handles, and skin stretchers. Moreover, they may, while they are in camp, collect firewood and boughs. Nowadays, a certain amount of wage work is available to the men. A number of them have worked at Oskelaneo for several years. In addition, limited opportunities for work exist about Mistassini, such as in mining camps, for the government, and as guides for tourists.

Man are pre-eminent in religious affairs. Nevertheless, their role is difficult to define in certain respects because of the part which may be played by the women. The shaking tent rite, the sweat lodge, the drumming, and, from the available evidence, many, if not all, of the lesser divinatory practices are conducted solely by the men. Although most of the religious practices are performed by the men, the women are rarely excluded from witnessing them. The "beaver-tailbone" divination was the only rite for which there was an explicit statement that women were excluded—and then the men merely waited until the women and children were asleep.

After a man is married, he drums, generally for the first time. At least, no occasion was witnessed of an unmarried man drumming. During adulthood a man continually increases his knowledge regarding the super-natural. Some men are capable of acquiring power in excess of the average individual. With this power, such men could act as shamans.

Today, Christianity offers a new religious position for men, that of resident deacon in the Anglican Church. During the winter the leader of the hunting group conducts any joint Christian services for the group as well as family prayers and hymn singing. The latter, however, is often an individual matter.

As mentioned previously, when a man marries he is in official charge of his wife and later their children, and possibly younger dependants, such as unmarried brothers and sisters. During the early years of marriage and occasionally throughout a man's life, his authority is confined to his immediate family. Depending upon circumstances and a man's personality, he may widen his sphere of influence and become the leader of a hunting group. If the older male members of the group die, he is automatically assigned the role of leader. This generally does not take place before a man reaches forty, and sometimes much later. Furthermore, a very young man is practically debarred from the position because of his lack of experience and wisdom. Formerly, this was apparently more often the case, since many of the important aboriginal religious practices were in the hands of the old men, practices which, if they can be judged correctly, were considered fundamental to existence. The personality factor enters into the situation most sharply when several of the older males are approximately the same age. In such cases the man with the most powerful personality assumes the leadership and wins the support of those with a less aggressive nature. Those refusing to support the new leader split from the group.

The transition of the position of leader is not marked by rites. Leadership is entirely informal, and the leader, though recognized as such by his followers, has little real control over the actions of the member families. Policies are discussed jointly, but the leader's initiative is followed. The members of the group are generally content to allow decisions affecting the whole group to be made by him. There are times, however, when the leader relinquishes his role. This occurs whenever one of the other males kills any large game animal. The hunter is then in charge of transporting the game to camp; the others, including the leader, wait for him to decide when and how it should be done. In addition, the leader occasionally gives a younger brother full authority and places him in charge of a day's activities. Whenever the leader is away, the eldest male member, so long as he is an adult, remains nominally in charge of the camp. Finally, plans made by the leader may later be changed, if so directed by the dream experience of any adult male of the group, although he may choose not to follow these revelations.

The pattern of leadership among the men of the group has little or no tendency to alter their companionship under usual conditions. At all times, laughter and sociability among adults are the most noticeable characteristics of social relations.

Today, besides the position of leader of the hunting group, a man can aspire to become a chief or councillor. The position is attained by "free" elections. In the past, only men voted, but since a woman is now Queen of the Commonwealth, some Mistassini Indians feel that women should also vote. Although these positions carry no real authority, middle-aged men generally hold them because young men are considered too immature.

The role of women in Mistassini society has been briefly mentioned at various points in the preceding material. Their economic role is primarily restricted to those tasks performed in and about camp, although they may earn money for their own use by making such items as moccasins and mittens for sale. In the neighbourhood of the camp, the women gather boughs and firewood, saw and split the wood, catch fish with set lines, set traps, and hunt. The last activity cannot be too greatly stressed. On frequent occasions, a woman hunts grouse and feeds her family with them during lean periods when her husband is away from camp trapping or in search of big game. Sometimes, during the season of open water, women set and tend gill nets.

In addition to outdoor tasks, the women perform innumerable duties in the home, which include placing new boughs on the floor several times a week, laundering, cooking, mending, making and repairing moccasins and mittens, lacing snowshoes, skinning furbearers, and preparing the pelts. In these tasks, she is aided by teenage daughters and female dependants if any are present. Also, the small children have to be cared for, although at times older children assume much of this responsibility.

The status of women is comparatively high, and, as a group, they are respected. Although their authority does not extend outside the family, they do have control over younger children and unmarried girls within the family circle, a control which may even extend to a teenage sister or sister-in-law living with them. On the death of a husband, the wife becomes the head of the family until she remarries. If she is old, a grown son is expected to care for her.

From the available evidence, women apparently do not participate to any great extent in aboriginal religious activities. Women were said to "dream," and there is no reason to doubt this assertion. In addition, they may perform some of the lesser divinatory practices.

Social control of adults is entirely informal and takes forms similar to the sanctions brought to bear in the socialization of children. Ridicule and gossip are used with varying effectiveness. A determined transgressor can ignore them. Physical coercion is never resorted to. Quarrelling is rare, occuring most frequently between men who hunt together. Where mutual dislike exists, the individuals avoid each other whenever possible. Ostracism of deviants is not usually applied outside the hunting group. This is consistent with the lack of collective action in the total group.

Old Age

Perhaps one of the strongest deterrents to socially disapproved actions is the respect for age. Age is all important in Mistassini society. There is no attempt on the part of the younger members to excel their elders. The emphasis on age was apparent in many cultural situations—the oldest male is leader of the hunting group; the old men acquire the greatest amount of religious lore; the older siblings are in charge of their younger siblings; the elders must be cared for; old people must receive game, even though there is not enough for distribution to younger members of the group. This emphasis on age is also reflected in the kinship terminology, where, for example, special terms are employed for older brother and older sister, in contrast to the single term for younger siblings, regardless of sex. As a child grows up, he develops great respect for his elders, especially his parents.

Accordingly, old people enjoy a position of affection and respect. In general, this is true of all old people, not only of an individual's relatives. An old person's advice is requested and usually followed. Several respected adults and even young people not yet married stated that they consciously strove for the wisdom attributed to the old people. This wisdom was most apparent in their esoteric knowledge regarding beliefs and practices.

Nevertheless, no thorough-going gerontocracy exists. According to some informants, there are some old people who are not wise. Tales are told of the mistakes of some old men, which cause a mixture of surprise and amusement. No one is exempt from ridicule purely on the basis of age, although no cases were recorded of an old person being ridiculed in his presence. Furthermore, each family is more or less autonomous except for those restrictions imposed on it as a member family of a hunting group. There is little, if any, interference by the elders of other families.

The relatives of the elders provide their economic needs, even to the point of assigning a child as permanent helper to his grandparents. A son is expected to care for his elderly mother if her husband dies. The economic situation is eased today with governmental old age pensions.

Death

Death creates a situation of tension and anxiety, affecting not only the immediate relatives but the community as a whole. When a death occurs, a separate tent is erected and the body is placed inside. The next day the coffin is constructed, and the body is consigned to it. The deceased is fully dressed, and his head rests on a small pillow. Next, a grave is dug. At the summer encampment the body is interred in a cemetery, but when death occurs away from the post, a sandy area that is well drained is selected. The coffin is carried to the grave and lowered into it, the body oriented with the head toward the west and the feet toward the east. The coffin is then opened, and all those present pray. After prayers have been said, the lid is closed and the grave is filled. A picket fence is erected about the grave, and a small wooden cross is placed at the head.

When a man dies, his possessions are stored for one year, and it is taboo to disturb them during this period. At the end of this time, the belongings are disposed of. His clothing is presented to an old person who is not a member of the family. Most of his other possessions, however, are kept within the family. On occasion, one or more of his guns, or a motor, may be sold.

The name of the dead man, especially if he was old and respected, is rarely mentioned and then only with great reluctance.

Sometimes a feast is given in honour of the deceased. One was observed in February, 1954. It was held for the father of Alfie Matoush, who had died two years before. The day following the feast, a visit was made to his grave and also to the grave of his wife and an infant daughter. The man and his wife were buried, side by side, in separate graves, the woman having died twenty years previously. Several trees in the vicinity had been blazed to mark the location of the graves. On reaching the foot of the rise to the grave, everyone proceeded in single file. The leader of the hunting group, son of the deceased, led the way. Just before reaching the graves, each person picked a small black spruce twig. They then proceeded first to the man's grave and then to the woman's, stopping at the head of each and placing a spruce twig by the cross. They continued around the woman's grave and back to the head of the man's. The leader then took out a package containing a little tobacco and handed it to his eldest half-brother, who added more tobacco to it. The leader then placed a small package (contents?) on top of the spruce twigs. On top of this package, the lower jaws of a beaver were placed, and on top of these, the package of tobacco. Everyone now removed his or her head-covering and bowed his head while the leader recited a prayer. They then replaced their head-coverings, and the leader distributed tobacco and cigarettes to the group. After smoking, all left the graves. The package of tobacco was removed and tied to the branch of a tree near by.

One informant claimed that a widow might remarry at any time after the lapse of one year, but to do so sooner would be improper. If a widow violates this injunction, she is considered "wild and not smart" and "didn't care for her husband." Another informant claimed that they would wait three, sometimes six years, before remarrying. This extended period may have been the aboriginal pattern.[3]

Notes

1. This custom is not now so consistently adhered to as in the past.

2. Robert H. Lowie, *Social Organization* (New York, 1953), p. 183.

3. Thwaites, Reuban Gold, ed., 1896–1901, *The Jesuit Relations and Allied Documents,* XVI, pp. 203–05.

8

Communal Socialization Patterns in Hutterite Society*

John A. Hostetler and Gertrude Enders Huntington

Most attempts at cummunal living in North America have not been successful. Only four of 130 communal societies survived for a century or more (Williams 1939, 15), and three of these four are now extinct: the Seventh-Day Baptists of Ephrata (173 years), the Shakers (162 years), and the Harmonists (100 years). The Hutterian Brethren or Hutterites, who originated in South Tyrol and Moravia in 1528 and immigrated to the United States in 1874, is the only group that has survived and flourished. Since their original settlement in the Dakota territory, the Hutterite colonies have grown from three to more than 170, and from 443 colonists (Eaton and Mayer 1954, 6) to a population of about 18,000 in 1968.

The Hutterites' notable ability to train their young for adult responsibility and for living within the confines of their communal society was the impetus for a research project on socialization in Hutterite society.[1] Research effort was directed toward investigating personality development and motivations in a society where the goals were communally rather than individualistically oriented.

An important issue involved selecting units for observation. It was decided to observe a small number of people intensively in order to gain a detailed knowledge of interpersonal relations. Many colonies were visited, but only three were selected for intensive study on the basis of such criteria as size, age, social and economic practices, residents' willingness to cooperate, and affiliation. One colony was selected from each of the three *Leut* or kinship groups--Schmiedeleut, Dariusleut, and Lehrerleut. In this report these sample colonies are designated Schmiedehof, Dariushof, and Lehrerhof. One of the colonies was located in the United States and two in Canada, and the three were separated from one another by more than 500 miles. One was newly formed, one was of average size, and the third was a large colony. Population breakdowns are presented in Table 1. The data, which were gathered by both male and female field workers, were derived from direct observation and from conversations with members of the colony.

Goals and Concepts Unique to the Culture

The Hutterites, who originated during the Protestant Reformation in the sixteenth century, are one of three surviving Anabaptist groups, the other two being the Mennonites (Smith 1957) and the Swiss Anabaptists including the Amish (Hostetler 1963). These Anabaptist groups all practise adult baptism, pacifism, and "noncon-

---

* Abridged by permission of the authors and the publisher from *Ethnology,* Vol. 7 (October) 1968, 331-355.

formity to the world", but only the Hutterites have continuously and successfully taught and practised communal living. Maintenance of communal living is equated with the will of God, requiring diligent nurture of all ages, since "no man is free from the tendency to serve his carnal inclinations" (Riedeman 1950, 57). Those who "submit and surrender" to God are His children. Obedience to God is evidenced by forsaking natural carnality, subordinating self-will to the will of the colony, renouncing private property, and sharing with the "community of the poor".

Human nature is believed to be evil, fallen, and displeasing to God. Children are believed to be born in sin with a tendency toward carnal rather than spiritual desires. Their carnal tendency can be mitigated and the spiritual nature restored by vigorous and proper teaching, by accepting God's word as interpreted in Hutterite sermons, by repentance of sin, and by continuous surrender of self through proper communal living. Baptism is not practised until the threshold of adulthood, when the full implications of denial of private property and acceptance of "the narrow path" are understood.

The Hutterites regard themselves as Christian believers maintaining the divinely ordained pattern of social relationships, and not as a rational experiment in utopia.

Relatively few Hutterites have abandoned colony life since migrating to America. According to Eaton and Weil (1955, 146), 258 men and eleven women left the colonies from 1880 to 1951, but more than half of these returned. No hope of salvation is entertained for the 106 men and eight women who defected permanently.

Role of the Family and Age-Sets

The Hutterite nuclear family, consisting of a man and wife and all their unmarried children, lives together in an apartment in one of the long houses. Newly-weds are given a room and if possible an entrance of their own; they are given additional rooms as their family increases. There are virtually no limits to the number of children a couple may have, except those set by nature. The median age at marriage, reported by Eaton and Mayer (1954), is approximately 22 years for women and 23.5 for men. The median size of a completed family is 10.4 children.

Hutterite socialization is a consistent, continous process toward two peaks in the individual's life. The period of childhood is one of preparation for initiation into adult life, one of training the child to identify with society. Socialization during adult life reinforces this identification and prepares the individual for death. The pattern of socialization is remarkably consistent from one colony to another, from one family to another, and from one individual to another. The function of the nuclear family is to produce new souls and to care for them until the colony assumes the greater responsibility. At all points in the socialization activity the family supports the colony.

Since the Hutterite world view requires "a right order" for every activity, the "proper" ordering of social relationships is determined by both age-grading and sex. The human life span is divided into a series of relatively distinct age-sets which serve as an impartial and definitive means for establishing order in the process of becoming an adult. Age determines both the group to which an individual belongs and generally his place within the group. Cultural conceptions of the human life cycle are thus imposed upon the natural biological rhythm. The significant socialization experiences in each of these functionally derived age-stages form the basis of this report. Although the age-sets discussed in the following pages are distinct in the life cycle, one concept may overlap several stages. For example, a child is considered a baby until he hits back, until the next is born, until he enters kingergarten, and until he enters German school. A person becomes an adult through a series of stages; when he begins eating

Table 1

Population of Three Hutterite Colonies by Stages of Life, Age, and Sex, 1965

Age Group	Schmiedehof			Lehrerhof			Dariushof		
	M	F	Total	M	F	Total	M	F	Total
Over 55	2	3(1)	5	1(4)	0	1	1	1	2
Adults, 33-35	8	6	14	7	8(5)	15	2	3	5
Married to 35	6	8	14	5	5	10	5	4	9
Baptized-unmarried	1	1	2	1	4(6)	5	1	2	3
Youth, 15 to baptism age	9(2)	4	13	10	7	17(7)	4	3	7
School, 6-15	16	23	39	17	16	33	11	7	18
Kingergarten, 3-5	12	13	25(3)	4	7	11	3	0	3
House Children, 0-2	7	5	12	3	6	9	5	3	8
Totals	61	63	124	48	53	101	32	23	55
Married couples			18			12			8

Notes: (1) One widow.
(2) Includes one single male over 30 mentally retarded.
(3) Includes 17 "runabouts" (Schulela group) ages 5-6: 7 boys, 10 girls.
(4) Widower.
(5) One widow.
(6) One single girl who will likely not marry.
(7) In this colony "youth" begins at 14 years.

with the adults, at age 15, when he is baptized, when he is married, when he grows a beard, and when his first child is born.

House Children: Birth to Three Years

The Hutterites are strongly opposed to any means of birth control and regard children as gifts from God. There is no institutional recognition of pregnancy, nor is there any notable modification in the work program of the pregnant woman.

In contrast to the lack of emphasis on pregnancy and the actual birth, the mother is given considerable attention during the postpartum period. At the same time that the new mother attends to her new baby, she herself is cared for, typically by her own mother. During this period the colony members and relatives from neighboring colonies visit the mother and the new baby. The length of this period of complete care and dependency varies, but the mother's caretaker usually leaves when the infant is four weeks old. For two more weeks the mother is relieved of colony work. Although she usually eats in the colony dining room and resumes her other family responsibilities, she still has extra time to devote to the baby. As she re-enters the colony work program more fully, the pattern of the baby's life meshes more closely with that of the colony. The colony schedule determines when he will be fed, played with, left alone, and put to sleep.

The extensive care provided for the new mother is not only part of her continuing socialization, but it also affects the early socialization of the baby. During his first four weeks of life, his mother is able to devote herself exclusively to his care. The Hutterities consider the neonate, who has in no way adjusted to societal dictates, extremely demanding, but the mother enjoys nurturing the completely dependent infant.

The baby is traditionally swaddled; this is believed to make him easy to handle and play with (that is, less easily injured). A red ribbon is tied on the baby, which is thought to make him less vulnerable to various evils and illnesses. Both swaddling and the red ribbon are usually abandoned by the time the mother returns to full colony participation. Hutterite mothers accept nursing in a matter-of-fact manner. Nursing periods rarely last longer than ten minutes, and pacifiers are widely used. Most babies nurse for about a year or until the mother becomes pregnant again, but occasionally babies are not weaned until they enter kindergarten. Toilet training frequently begins as early as three months, and always by the time the child can sit alone. Many children do not wear diapers after they are six months old, even though many are not fully trained until they enter kindergarten.

Religious training begins with the introduction of solid foods into the baby's diet (at some time between three weeks and three months of age). His mother folds his hands in hers and prays with him before and after feeding him. Already religion is a ritual, a formal activity, and a social activity for him and is intimately associated with food. A hungry infant will often clasp his hands in the prayer position when he catches sight of food. A prayer is recited aloud by the parent when the child is laid in his crib for the night. This recitation is invariable, regardless of whether the baby is awake or already asleep.

Hutterites of all ages love babies. Both boys and girls vie for the privilege of holding or caring for a tiny infant, and adults hold any available baby whenever THEY are not working. Adult colony members and visitors pay a great deal of active attention to very young children. However, when it is time for church or for the adult meal, the baby is placed in his crib and left. Thus, from the time he is seven weeks old, he alternates between a socially stimulating environment and one of lying completely unattended in his crib.

A "good" baby is one whose behaviour does not disrupt the colony time schedule and who accepts the attention af all colony members. A child is believed to be completely innocent until he hits back or tries to comb his hair, at which time his level of conprension is believed to be sufficiently developed for the application of discipline. Some very young children will hit each other and immediately hug and kiss to avoid adult displeasure at their disagreement. Discipline is more varied for the older house child, who may be strapped for refusing to go to someone other than his parents, for refusing to share food, or for being noisy and disturbing adults. He may be slapped for putting garbage in the wrong receptacle, flicked on the head or pinched for getting in the way of an older child or an adult. Sometimes there is an attempt, usually unsuccessful, to frighten him into good behaviour. Although he is disciplined quickly and frequently, the child is considered entertaining and is petted, played with, and enjoyed.

Hutterite mothers almost never take their house children with them while doing colony work. During the winter the younger house children are left alone in the apartment. If colony work is pressing at a time when the house children are not napping, they may be looked after by an older child or by the father if his colony work permits. During the summer the older toddlers, especially the boys, play near the place where the men are working and are watched by the youngest school boys. There is a united effort on the part of the colony, an effort in which the parents actively cooperate, to wean the house child from his parents and incorporate him into the group.

During his first three years of life the child grows from complete dependency on his family to a degree of independence. By the time he is ready to enter kindergarten he has learned, first of all, that the colony takes precedence over the individual; when the bell rings, his mother leaves him. Second, he has learned that the individual has little control over his environment. Punishment is usually physical, arbitrary, inconsistent, and, from the child's point of view, often unpredictable. Third, he has discovered that although physical insults are unpredictable, the pattern of living is invariable. Fourth, he has learned to respond positively to every Hutterite person and does not complain when he is handed from one caretaker to another. He is happy to be with people.

Kindergarten: Three to Five Years

Parents look forward to the child's entrance into kindergarten, or *Klein-Schul.* Although *Klein-Schul* is translated into English as kindergarten, it is not synonymous with this educational concept in the American educational system. It is more akin to the concept of "pre-school," used in this country to encompass the nursery school and kindergarten classes. The Hutterite child-rearing institutions evolved during the second quarter of the sixteenth century and have remained almost unaffected since then.

Hutterites consider the pre-school child to be willful and useless, that is, unable to contribute any labour to the colony. Such willfullness is somewhat threatening to a rigidly controlled people, and because the uselessness is no longer combined with complete dependency, it cannot be enjoyed by nurturant caretakers. The kindergarten delineates for the child his place within the entire colony, as well as within his nuclear family. It also teaches that the colony position takes precedence over the family position, and that colony traditions and regulations supersede the individual wishes of family members.

The child undergoes his first major change in status when he reaches kindergarten age. He plummets from a relatively desirable postion to a very low one, within both his family and the colony. The kindergarten child is expected to be more obedient and quieter than a house child. Adults rarely spend time with a kindergarten child, and visitors from other colonies do not exchange greetings with him.

The largest number of threats are levied against children of this age, since they are old enough to understand them but do not yet realize that the threats are empty. Threats used most frequently outside the kindergarten hours fall into two categories: those that teach that exclusion from the group is unpleasant, and those that teach that danger lurks beyond the established boundaries.

The kindergarten mothers alternate, each woman taking responsibility for one full day. If one is ill, she generally obtains a substitute from among her relatives. A school-age child supervises the kindergarten on Sunday so that the adults may attend church services.

The kindergarten children arrive before breakfast; led by the teacher, they recite prayers before and after breakfast. Gradually these prayers are memorized. During their kindergarten years children learn numerous prayers and hymns by rote, although little or no effort is made at the kindergarten level to explain the meaning of what is memorized. Despite variation in schedule among the three *Leut*, it is obvious that one major function of the kindergarten is to free the mothers for colony work.

The outdoor play, which is vigorous, is barely supervised; the children may be taken on walks which are not seen as educational experiences but as enjoyable pastimes or as a convenience for the kindergarten mother.

Social misbehaviour is quickly punished with scolding, switching, or threats. The children may not quarrel, hit, call names, or disobey the person in charge. The kindergarten mother does not take any aspects of the children's misbehaviour personally, nor does she inflict punishment vindictively. Rather, she regards the children almost as her own and believes that they need punishment to help them learn correct behaviour. She also uses encouragement, praise, and rewards to modify their behaviour.

There are certain factors that greatly facilitate the child's entrance into kindergarten: he has been visiting the kindergarten since he was a toddler, he knows all the other children intimately, and he has been familiar with the kindergarten mothers all his life. Nevertheless, kindergarten requires some important adjustments for the child. For one thing, he must remain there for the full day, under the supervision of an adult who is not his parent. Children's initial dislike of kindergarten is considered natural and is hardly noticed. Hutterites feel that children of this age have stubborn wills that must be broken, an end that the kindergarten helps to attain.

The primary functions of the kindergarten are the following: (1) It helps wean the child from his family and to some extent wean them from him. (2) It introduces the child to his peer group and teaches him how to function WITHIN this group. This function is particularly important, since the boys remain in the peer group throughout their lives, and the girls until adulthood. At an age when the child in North American society is expressing his emerging individuality and developing concept of self, the Hutterite child is placed in a setting that minimizes his individuality and maximizes his identity as a member of the group. (3) The kindergarten teaches the child to respect the authority of the colony, in addition to that of his parents and babysitters. (4) The kindergarten teaches the child to tolerate a limited, restricted environment, and rewards him for cooperative, docile, passive responses to correction and frustration.

The colony's impact on the individual is maximal during his kindergarten years, for these are the most restricted and regimented, and have the least variation in program. This intensive socialization occurs at a psychologically important point in the child's development. Concomitant with his entrance into kindergarten, his parents and other adult colony members cease to tolerate behaviours they allowed while he was still considered a baby. The child might easily interpret such changes as rejection. Having fallen to the lowest position within the colony, he must now begin the steady climb toward full colony membership.

School Children: Six to Fifteen Years

All children are taught German before English. At about age five children enter the *Gross-Schul,* or German school, and from age six to fifteen they attend the public or English school. German school is taught by a married man selected by the church. His role is defined by tradition, and his work is supervised by the council members and noted by all the members of the church. The position is equal in importance to any other department leadership position. Often, but not always, the German teacher is a member of the colony council. The German school mother is either the teacher's wife or an older woman appointed by the council. She helps supervise the children's meals, both serving and teaching manners. She has no responsibility for teaching any religious material, nor does she give permission, assign jobs, or punish. Her function is to assist the German teacher and to instruct the girls in their female work roles, training them in patterns of work rotation that will organize their colony work for the remainder of their lives.

Every morning all the school children assemble in the dining room for prayers and breakfast. From the moment they assemble until after supper they are either under the German teacher's direction or are technically released by him to do specific chores or to attend English school. Children over six meet before and after English school and on Saturday to practise writing in German script, to read German, and to recite their memory verses from Hutterite hymns and the Bible. During these meetings the German teacher admonishes them about their beliefs and their bahaviour. He announces new rules to the children and punishes those who have misbehaved. He teaches the children to accept punishment without resistance or anger. Usually three straps on the palm of the hand are given for a first offense or for a minor infringement. If a child lies about his misbehaviour, two more are added. A more serious transgression warrants being turned over the bench. During the long winters the children wear so many layers of flannel that when a switch is used it is the disgrace rather than the physical pain that constitutes the punishment. These and milder punishment (e.g., being scolded or sent to stand in the corner) function primarily by removing the child from the group and shaming him in front of his peers. Praise is used to encourage all children, even the slowest.

Work is never used as a punishment, for no colony work is categorized as unpleasant, and everyone must be willing to do his share of any assigned job. Privileges are not withheld from a naughty child, nor is he punished by being deprived of food. Misbehaviour is punished as soon as possible after it occurs. Immediately after a child is strapped by his father he is comforted by his mother or even by his father if his mother is absent, for it is believed that the punishment erases the misbehaviour, and that no further atonement is necessary. Occasionally a father who is considered to be overly lax may be asked by the colony to punish the child at home or in the presence of the council.

The German school also teaches children to work together. Often the German teacher is the gardener, a convenient arrangement since school children regularly work in the garden after English school has closed in the summer. When the children have worked especially hard or well the entire group is rewarded. In addition to contributing some labour to the colony, school children can perform certain other functions such as babysitting. Usually only girls are assigned to a specific family, but boys babysit informally and within their nuclear families, and may be assigned if needed.

German school is "ungraded" in the modern sense, and children progress at their own speeds. Material is assigned in terms of a child's ability. Instead of grades or formal levels, there is an accepted sequence of material to be learned. Children learn to read and write medieval German script. Throughout their school years they practise handwriting and memorize prayers, hymns, Bible stories, the catechism, and episodes of Hutterite history. They also learn the directions of the compass, measurement equivalents and how to write to ten thousand. Children are taught to work efficiently, but they are never given an opportunity to ask why something is learned.

Within the system there is no room for doubt. The primary function of the German school is not the intellectual content of the curriculum but rather to teach Hutterite children the ritual of life. This ritual applies essentially to two areas. The first is the class of ritual that insures the smooth social functioning of the group in all details of everyday interaction. The second reduces the fear of death and physical injury. The German school emphasizes the first type of ritual, although the second is not neglected. Psychological studies of Hutterite adolescents show they are not frightened by threats to their bodily integrity. Although there are in fact many instances of physical injury, these are not anticipated nor do they constitute a source of worry.

Children learn the verbal content of their religion within the larger context of ritual and internalize the theological and moral content when they seek baptism. At this early stage in the child's development religious material is learned in order to avoid punishment from supervising adults. Children memorize the material because they must be obedient; only at a later age are they expected to understand the concepts they are reciting.

School children learn a great deal about the authority structure of their society and how to live comfortably with it. Although they have internalized the Hutterite hierarchy that gives precedence to age, they have also learned that each individual's authority is limited. The child knows when and whom he must obey and what orders can be safely ignored. Children disturbing the young pigs pay little attention to a reproving adult, but they will immediately leave at the command of the "pig boss".

Boys and girls are taught to play differently. In some colonies sisters in each family have an assigned playhouse where they spend hours playing with each other and with girls from other families. Usually the girls play house or occasionally pretend that they are "English" women who wear funny clothes and strut about talking loudly. On the very rare occasions when one of the girl's brothers is allowed into the playhouse the children may play "doctor", drawing realistic incisions complete with sutures on one another's arms.

The oldest sister in each family keeps the key to the playhouse, and children are free to exclude whatever other children they wish. Boys are customarily excluded; the play groups among the girls themselves constantly shift and divide into temporary cliques. The girls demand detailed conformity within the clique, and dissenters are excluded. Only by adjusting completely to the play group may a girl remain a member. Most of the girls' play is carried on near the long houses and the centre of the colony whereas the boys range much further in their play. Boys are more individualistic and often work or play alone or with only one other boy.

Much of the children's play is physically vigorous, often rough, and sometimes even dangerous. Adults ignore this dangerous play, considering the children to be the German teacher's responsibility. School children play many games that are exercises in discomfort and endurance. Free play reinforces community values: the physical nature of their play teaches them to ignore physical discomfort and fear of injury and to minimize the importance of the body; the changing play groups teach the unpleasantness of being excluded.

During the school years the children identify closely with their peer group. Everyone in the group is rewarded for a successful group endeavour and everyone is scolded when most of the group members misbehave. Transgression may go unnoticed if no one in the group reports it. However, the child learns that his own peer group can punish him even more severely than adult authority. Colony rules can sometimes be circumvented; family rules more often can be overlooked; but one's peers cannot be ignored.

All school-age children attend the English school on the colony grounds. The colony usually supplies the school buildings and heating and maintenance costs, and the public school board selects and pays the teacher's salary. In many of the more isolated colonies the teacher and his family live on the colony in a separate house, a "teacherage", and the colony makes an effort not to interfere with the living pattern of the teacher and his family. In many colonies the school is also used for church services every evening and on Sundays. In addition to their desire for children to obtain a good knowledge of arithmetic, reading, and writing, Hutterite leaders insist that discipline be maintained in the English school. A colony generally accepts the English school complex but restrains its influence to serve colony ends. The English school remains emotionally distinct from the colony. German is the first language the child learns to speak and write, and German school is more important than English school in a child's day. The English school is clearly encapsulated within the colony pattern, and its influence serves colony ends.

It is believed that it is a child's nature to misbehave when he is unwatched, but these same children are expected to grow into responsible colony members. Misbehaviour during childhood neither endangers the child's future reputation nor presages an unsuccessful adulthood. It is expected that the child will develop into an increasingly more responsible and more highly socialized person. The school child must accept his place in the colony's social structure, respecting older members and caring for those younger than himself. It is not his responsibility to care for himself nor to exercise self-discipline.

During the brief periods each day when the school children are completely free from authoritarian direction, they can function as a self-contained peer group and work out relationships that will last into adulthood. During the school years children learn to function within both the sibling group and the peer group. They learn to adjust their dual membership as the two groups overlap, interact, and supplement one another. The two configurations persist, with traditional modification until the peer group embraces the entire colony.

The school-age child is taught unquestioning obedience to Hutterite authority: to the authority of his parents, his teachers, his colony, to any Hutterite older than himself, and to Hutterite traditions and teachings. Self-discipline is not taught, but rather obedience to those in authority who will supervise and punish and protect him. If in the weakness of childhood he fails to obey, he is taught to accept punishment meekly. The Hutterite child does not develop a strong sense of guilt. Because it is considered natural for a child to sin, he does not internalize the responsibility for his misbehaviour. His actions must be directed through the praise and punishment of those in authority positions.

The school child masters the basic ritual of Hutterite life. Although he learns the verbal expression of the belief system by rote, he is not expected to internalize the more difficult aspects of these beliefs until adulthood. He learns to adjust to his designated position in the society, to accept many frustrations passively, to interpret teasing as attention, to enjoy hard physical labour, to begin to appreciate a life uncluttered by material objects, and to accept with a kind of pleasure the cleansing process of pain and punishment.

Childhood comes to an end with the fifteenth birthday. The young Hutterite leaves the children's dining room and is said to be *bie die Leut* with the people. The *mandle* (little man) becomes a *buah* (boy); the *dindla* becomes a *die-en.*

The Casual Years: Age Fifteen to Baptism

The Hutterite young person is in a transitional stage between childhood and adulthood. The colony recognizes both aspects of his personality. The young person is considered to be physically an adult who is capable of hard work with other adults. Religiously he is viewed as a child who must attend Sunday school and memorize his weekly verses. Emotionally he vacillates, and this period is sometimes called "the in-between years" or "the casual years", meaning that the individual's loyalties have not completely crystallized. Some disregard of colony mores is expected during this period, but moodiness or poor work performance is not tolerated.

At some point after his fifteenth birthday, he is given various gifts, items that reflect his change of status and that are needed in his new role. Both boys and girls are given a wooden chest with a lock in which to keep their personal belongings. They are also given cloth for suits and dresses, a catechism, and several Hutterite books for personal use. Boys are given tools which they must keep in good working condition. Girls receive such items as a scrub pail, a paint brush, a hoe, kitchen knives, a broom, knitting needles, and in some colonies a rolling pin and until recently a spinning wheel.

For two years the young person is in an apprentice position. He is not given responsibility for an expensive machine such as a tractor, or for work that would cause a great deal of inconvenience or loss of money if improperly done. Boys and girls of the in-between years constitute a mobile labour force which is utilized throughout the colony as needed (in jobs suitable to their sex) or which may be sent to other colonies to help during times of need or crisis. Boys in this age group supply most of the hard labour and enjoy the opportunity to demonstrate their strength and stamina.

The young person is subject to the control and influence of the colony, his family, and his peer group. However, the influences exerted by these three groups are less well integrated than at any earlier period. Because the areas of control are more diversified, the young person has slightly more freedom than at an earlier age. His work is under the control of the colony, although there may be some tendency to let a son work with his father and a girl with her mother or a sister. In areas of religious development and moral and social behaviour the young person is primarily the responsibility of the German teacher or the preacher, depending on the colony.

The colony permits dating among young people, although a specific family may forbid it. If a young person dates someone of whom the colony disapproves, for instance, a first cousin or the English school teacher, the German teacher or preacher speaks to him about it. If he is dating someone whom his family dislikes, the family must resolve it and the colony is not involved. Parents have almost complete veto power over a child's choice of a marriage partner, and they begin early to express interest in the heterosexual aspects of his life. The colony and the family expect a certain amount of deviant behaviour among the young people, much of which takes place within the peer group in the form of such forbidden activities as singing English songs and playing mouth organs. However, the peer group will tolerate only certain activities, and the individual who deviates too radically is ostracized even by his peers.

Dating generally begins when the child becomes a young person. Occasionally and surreptitiously it may begin earlier in colonies where there are children more distantly related than first cousins. There is considerable individual variation among young people with respect to the number and length of dating relationships. It is not unusual for courtships to last five or six years. Frequently, there is no one in his home colony whom a young person can date because all those his own age are his first cousins. Whether or not a young person is dating, he is included in the mixed peer group activity and remains absolutely loyal to this group.

The young person is no longer grouped with the school children in the family constellation. Relationships in the family are still completely hierarchical, but now that the German teacher is no longer responsible for virtually all the child's waking hours, the parents take more interest in their child's free time.

Siblings support one another in various ways. A girl may sew clothes for her brother that deviate slightly from the accepted pattern, or iron his clothes just the way he likes them. Boys have some opportunities to earn extra money which they may lend or give to their sisters or a girl friend. Brothers from one family frequently date sisters from another family, and it is not uncommon to find marriages where several brothers have wives who are sisters. The cooperative patterns learned in the nuclear family influence the courtship pattern. Colonies that visit frequently, exchange work and produce, and from whom marriage partners are chosen, are usually ones that are related fairly closely by family ties.

Although the young person no longer attends the German or English school, his formal religious education continues. Young people are required to attend Sunday school, which reinforces the Sunday morning sermon and disciplines the young people to listen to the sermon. Although all the German school children also attend and participate, the Sunday school program places particular emphasis on the young people who have not yet been baptized. The Sunday school as representative of colony authority functions to direct and if necessary punish a young person for moral or social transgression. The offender is admonished in the presence of his peers or made to stand during Sunday school. The Sunday school physically groups the young people with the children and continues their ritualistic participation with the school children for religious training. Thus those who are not yet baptized are constantly reminded that spiritually they are still children who must memorize and recite their lessons correctly at their teacher's bidding. The push of society is toward adulthood even while recognizing and tolerating residual childish elements.

Boys and girls work with and under the direction of older colony members, but they also work in peer groups. For example, all the young men make hay together, and all the young girls paint as a group. Work and social life intermingle, for young people talk as they work together, especially when adults are beyond earshot. It is considered a privilege to go to other colonies to work, since in these settings the young people also work with their peers and establish new friendships. After supper the peer group expands to include both sexes and visitors of the same age group from other colonies.

The peer group is of supreme importance, for it encompasses virtually all the young person's social life, and many of his working hours are spent with his same-sex peer group. The group demands absolute loyalty, and anyone who does not support the group or who talks about his own activities or plans is completely ostracized. Exclusive cliques may develop in large colonies or among the young people of neighbouring colonies, but they present a united front to all those who are not included in their age-set. Adults conveniently overlook mild transgressions and the young people enjoy the excitement of semi-forbidden behaviour and escape from adult surveillance.

The "casual years" are a time for testing boundaries. The young person eventually rejects the world and chooses the colony way of life, but during these years there is some flirtation with the world, some investigation of that which will be rejected. Most young people have their photographs taken, although no one is permitted to make a graven image; many have their own cameras and wrist watches. Some boys own transistor radios on which they listen to western songs; some trap during the winter or "moonlight" to earn extra money; occasionally boys smoke secretly. Girls may use coloured polish on their toenails, which are hidden by their heavy shoes. They buy perfume, dime-store jewelry, and sometimes fancy underwear. The in-between years are a period of limited self-realization. In extreme cases a young man may temporarily leave the colony, knowing he will return to marry and raise his family.

Girls in particular may create a secret world. As long as this make-believe does not interfere with work, it is tacitly accepted by adults. The secret world may be confined to a locked wooden chest or to a corner of the attic where bits of the temporal world are kept—photographs, sheet music, suntan lotion, souvenirs. These artifacts represent, however meagerly, what the young person is free to pursue or renounce. They represent the world outside the colony; they represent the self in its indulgent, vanity-pleasing aspects. The young person continually measures these trinkets and indulgences against the full life in which he is involved. As he participates more completely in this very real and active life, he generally finds that the satisfactions received from participation in colony affairs far outweigh those of self-development. The self-image requires colony identification.

During much of this transitional period the young person measures himself first as a member of his peer group and then as a colony member. He is usually extremely interested in the outside world, an interest that eventually provides him with fuller understanding of what it means to be a Hutterite. His status within his nuclear family is quite high during this period. During the later years as a young person he is expected to demonstrate by his daily behaviour his ability to adhere to the colony rules. When he has displayed by his actions that emotionally and intellectually he is no longer an irresponsible child, he willingly and humbly requests baptism in order to become a full member of the colony. At this point the goal of the Hutterite child-rearing system has been achieved.

Baptism

From babyhood on the Hutterite is socialized to believe that the collective unit is more important than the separate individuals who comprise it. Starting at seven weeks of age he learns to fit into the group pattern and is treated as a member of the group rather than as an individual. He first identifies with his nuclear family, then with his peer group in school, and finally with his post-school work group. With each stage in growth the number of people above him in status decreases and the number below him increases. He is taught to serve and obey those above him, to care for and direct those below him. Although there is some competition within his peer group (primarily in work performance), the group is cohesive and provides strong support, especially in the face of threats from the outside. When the Hutterite voluntarily requests baptism, the whole colony becomes in effect his peer group.

Hutterite ritual prepares the individual for two important rites of passage: baptism and death. Baptism is essential to the adult's participation in the ritual of daily life; death leads the true Hutterite into life everlasting. Both rites of passage stress dying as an essential step to life. Baptism requires that the natural man must die so that the "spiritual man" may be born. Similarly, the human body must die so that the spiritual man may be released into eternal life.

Every Hutterite has by birthright a place in his colony that insures his constant care. Should he die during childhood, before reaching the age of discretion, he is assured a place in heaven. As an adult he is initiated into church membership, which he retains until death unless some major transgression against the rules of the community causes the church to exclude him either temporarily or permanently.

The goal of Hutterite child-rearing is the individual's voluntary decision to submit himself to the church. Baptism is equated with this submission and also signifies one's voluntary acceptance of responsibility for the actions of everyone in the colony. It signifies the internalization of Hutterite values. All the child's life has in effect been a preparation for this major rite of passage. Girls are about 19 and boys are between 20 and 26 years of age when baptized. In all colonies baptism is requested in a highly stylized form and generally has the support of the peer group. The colony decides months or even a year in advance to have baptism. Baptism is held every year in *Schmiedehof*, but many colonies baptize once every two to five years. If there is only one person who needs baptism, he may receive instruction with a group of applicants from a neighbouring colony. The baptismal service usually takes place on Palm Sunday, or occasionally at Pentecost.

Everyone in the colony generally knows who will request baptism and who will wait. If there is a question about any candidate, all aspects are discussed so that the colony is in agreement; often a young person is advised to postpone his request for baptism. During the six to eight week instruction period, the group of candidates is admonished for about three hours every Sunday afternoon. Hutterites place greater emphasis on correct acting than on correct thinking. Wrong thinking is bad, but wrong behaviour is considered sin. The entire colony cooperates in admonishing, punishing, and forgiving its members. During the period of instruction for baptism, applicants must demonstrate that they have humbled themselves, are void of self-will, and are completely obedient to the community. During the course of instruction in one colony applicants formally request baptism 36 times. Each applicant must know that he is ready to make the greatest commitment of his life.

The baptismal ceremony has two parts: on Saturday afternoon the candidates are examined about their belief, and on Sunday afternoon the preacher baptizes the candidates by laying on of hands and sprinkling with pure water while he prays that they may be preserved in piety and faith until death. After baptism men are given voting privileges and become eligible for more responsible work assignments, but there is no change in the work status of young women. Both men and women who have been baptized customarily attend weddings and funerals in other colonies.

Baptism is considered a first step to marriage, since one's commitment to God takes precedence over one's commitment to a spouse. Ideally the interval between baptism and marriage is not long, especially for a young man. In fact, often a young man is not baptized until he is contemplating marriage. The baptized but as yet unmarried person participates only marginally in the young people's social life. He has made his choice and has to a considerable extent lost interest in the material baubles of a rejected way of life. He prefers to use his energies in the interest of his colony.

Baptism produces a closer relationship between parents and child. Parents now treat their child as a colony member as well as an offspring. With the help of God and the colony they have accomplished their task of raising this child "in the nurture and admonition of the Lord". Children become their parents' spiritual brothers and sisters, and as a result they work together almost as peers and identify much more closely with one another. The child remains emotionally dependent on his parents, but the earlier sharp division between them is gone. Within the colony's hierarchical power structure, sons tend to cooperate closely with fathers and with biological brothers. In a highly integrated colony these patterns are extended to include all the baptized men.

Marriage and Adulthood

The degree of secretiveness maintained in courtship, as well as the number of opportunities to visit each other, varies from couple to couple. Sometimes everyone knows that a particular couple is going together, while other couples may tell no one except their families until a few weeks before they actually marry.

Marriages may not take place immediately before Christmas nor in the period from just before Easter until after Pentecost. A wedding provides an occasion for the gathering of relatives and friends. Former acquaintanceships are renewed, relatives visit one another, and young people court. Since a wedding entails considerable work and expense for the colony, double or triple weddings are encouraged, and often as many as five couples are married at the same time. Multiple weddings also enhance the festivities of the day; many more guests attend, and the crowd is larger and gayer. The wedding formalizes the marriage, makes explicit the relationship between the two colonies involved, brings relatives together, and strengthens intercolony ties by pleasant visitation.

In the individual's socialization, the wedding is a rite of passage to a new stage of life. In contrast to the long, rigorous preparation for baptism, preparation for marriage is incidental. The groom must make only minimal adjustments. Often he retains his former room in or adjoining his parents' apartment; his brothers move out, and his bride moves in. His pattern of work does not change, except that he becomes eligible for a more responsible position. Emotionally, the husband is in a strong position. He maintains all his primary ties and in addition acquires a wife. He is completely familiar with all aspects of colony life and with every colony member.

Marriage involves a considerable adjustment for the bride. Usually she moves to a new colony, sometimes one she has never visited. She must leave her parents, her siblings, her peer group, and come under the direction of her mother-in-law. Her work patterns are altered because of her married status and also because things are done in slightly different ways in the new colony. However, the bedroom is referred to as hers and becomes her niche. The bedroom belongs to the wife and mother, the colony to the husband. Compared to her husband, a new wife is in a vulnerable postion. Her husband is her only source of support and information. The Hutterite marriage patterns function to maintain the husband in his dominant position and to emphasize the dependency of the wife.

Education for pregnancy and childbirth is even more rudimentary than formal preparation for marriage. These topics are rarely discussed among Hutterite women and never in the presence of girls. The young wife is generally living in another colony when she becomes pregnant, and her mother does not come to care for her until after the baby has been born. Most young women know almost nothing about the details of labour. However, they have grown up in a society that has a high birth rate and a positive attitude toward babies. They have been taught to ignore discomfort, to accept their lot without complaint. The attitude toward pregnancy and childbirth is apparently either one of passive acceptance or mild annoyance when there are already many children.

The adult Hutterite receives constant social reinforcement. Virtually all his activities are carried on within the age-set hierarchy, and he participates primarily in his same-sex group. The Sunday and daily religious services are part of his continuous formal socialization. These group ceremonials function both to teach the young and to reinforce beliefs which the adults have internalized. All adults must set a good example at all times. In work situations both men and women constantly participate in patterns of decision-making that enable the group to reach consensus. An individual does not try to persuade the group; rather, a subject is discussed by most group members, and the final decision is indeed a product of the group.

The youngest adult men may still have onerous labour assignments; those who are a bit older occupy leadership positions such as departmental heads of various economic enterprises. The men with greatest seniority tend to hold executive positions, that is, as council members. Although there may be muted intra-group competition for various positions and fairly obvious competition among the different positions to demonstrate maximum efficiency in their particular operations, the individual generally progresses to higher status positions as he grows older. Within the well integrated colony there are no contests for place (which is determined by age and sex), or for office (which is determined by vote of the church). Hutterites do not seek the satisfaction that may accompany a position of dominance. They have been well socialized against self-assertion. Power, authority, and influence are expressed as group action.

Biological brothers cooperate closely among themselves and with their father in all areas of life, but this is not necessarily disruptive to the colony as a whole. These men have learned to handle feelings of jealousy and competition and to work smoothly together, depending on one another's strengths and compensating for one another's weaknesses. Early identification and constant interaction with the peer group have also taught Hutterite men to work well with their spiritual brothers. One's emotions toward a spiritual brother are somewhat less intense than toward a biological brother and therefore easier to control. Brother groups are functional in making colony decisions. News spreads informally among biological brothers and they freely argue the relative merits of various alternatives. One set of brothers may discuss the problem further with another set, each individual knowing that he has some support in the group. A decision can often be reached rapidly. The men have been socialized against stubbornness. They have also been taught that when a colony issue reaches the voting stage, church members must vote as spiritual rather than as biological brothers. Biological brothers thus function as a closely cooperating subgroup within the larger cooperative.

Both formal and informal types of social control are based primarily on the individual's fear of rejection. The adult Hutterite has identified with the group, and his self-esteem requires full group acceptance. Admonishment by a brother represents the simplest form of social control. An individual who is disturbed by the conduct of another should speak to that person about his behaviour. If this approach is not effective, the preacher will speak privately to the erring member. If his misconduct persists, he may be approached privately by one or more council members, or asked to come before the council and the church. In the case of continued transgression, for example persistent drunkenness, the ban may be applied. A banned person may not eat with others, and he is deprived of his church membership. Most individuals soon reunite with the church, but a few remain under the ban and eventually leave the colony. Other than the shedding of blood, which the church cannot forgive, desertion of the colony is the worst possible offense. There is no hope of heaven for anyone who dies outside the church.

A successfully socialized adult Hutterite gets along well with others, is submissive and obedient to the rules and regulations of the colony, and is a hard-working responsible individual. An adult Hutterite must never display anger nor precipitate quarrels. Intensity and imagination are not admired; rather, quiet willingness coupled with hard work are considered desirable qualities. The constant pruning which adapts each individual to the group results in a minimizing of differences and a muting of emotional expression. The elimination of extremes and the imposition of a strict order enable members to find satisfaction in the "narrow way" that leads to salvation.

The Aged

The formal aspect of Hutterite culture requires the aged be respected by all younger persons. The pressure to move upward in the age-set is invariably present from kindergarten through the final rite of passage, death. Older people are believed to deserve "rest", and work is optional for them. They may spend more time traveling, going to town, and talking with neighbours and visitors.

There is no arbitrarily predetermined age of retirement. Women between 45 and 50 are usually relieved of their rotating colony jobs, although women who hold the positions of head cook or kingergarten mother continue in these functions until they are too old to fulfill their responsibilities. The first jobs women give up are milking and hoeing, and usually cooking and baking. Most older women continue to help with food preparation, for they prefer working to being alone in their apartment. When an older person loses a spouse he often moves in with one of his children. A grandchild is assigned to run errands or even to sleep with the older person, and the latter's meals are brought to him when he becomes too infirm to go to the dining room.

Retirement is more difficult for a man than for a woman to accept. An elderly man is frequently removed from a foreman position and simultaneously elected to a position on the council. By this means his conservative influence is used constructively, and the economic development that requires constant change is put into the hands of a younger man. Once elected, a man remains on the council indefinitely. Often the most difficult person to relieve of responsibility is the householder. Conservatism is a disadvantage in the householder, for the colony rests on its willingness to risk capital and remain dynamic in its economic practices. Several years may be required to change householders. Gentle persuasion rather than coercion is the rule.

Older people who are ill consult physicians in nearby towns. The Hutterites emphasize good health, but utilization of medical help is influenced by the view that the body is only important because it houses the eternal soul. Hutterites go to great lengths and expense to obtain special treatment for chronically ill members, but the best physicians are often unavailable to them because of their relative geographical isolation. Their famed sixteenth century tradition of healing, bathing, and surgery (Friedmann 1961, 126) has been greatly altered, but their own contemporary practitioners still include midwives, masseurs, and bone-setters.

The psychology of aging and preparation for death is unique and consistent with the culture. Old people are not forced to exert themselves, nor are they denied active participation. They can reduce their work load without fear of losing status or being excluded from the policy-forming group. An old man's contribution to the colony is limited economically, but his strong identity with colony tradition and the respect he is accorded by younger members exert a stabilizing influence. Intergenerational communication is maintained and provides older persons with a means of keeping abreast with changing times. Old age is not a period of loneliness and isolation or of economic deprivation. Occasionally the oldest active man is given the honourable position of *Brotschneider* (bread cutter), and cuts the fresh loaves and keeps every table in the communal dining hall supplied with bread. In this capacity the father-figure as provider is symbolically activated in community life.

Death

Death represents to the Hutterite the termination of the earthly struggle and the beginning of paradise for those who have lived faithfully. Life is seen as preparation for death. An adult explained that Hutterites prefer slow to sudden deaths "even if it involves pain, so that we are sure to have plenty of time to consider eternity and to confess and make everything right." Adults envy children who die, since they have been spared the temptations and the lifelong struggles of self-denial.

Throughout life there is little speculation about heaven or the kinds of enjoyment or activity anticipated. Preparation through submission to the divine and right order is considered most important. Heaven is seen as a place of more perfect communal living. The communal emphasis is inculcated through vigorous teaching from a young age and is reinforced by visions of the dying. The emotional acceptance of death is supported by many aspects of the culture, specifically by the lack of sentiment attached to property and by adequate provision for the families of the deceased. The beliefs and practices so consistently taught during life provide meaning and fulfillment for the final rite of passage.

Summary and Conclusions

This research is based upon participant observation of Hutterite colony life. Although the major characteristics of each age-set have been summarized in the previous sections, several conclusions can be drawn to relate Hutterite socialization practices to the culture as a whole.

Hutterite child rearing and socialization practices at all ages are remarkably successful in preparing the individual for communal life. From early childhood to adulthood there is continual indoctrination within culturally defined age and sex groupings. Every Hutterite is subservient to the colony at every stage of his life, and the goals for each stage are attainable by virtually all members. Individuals are thoroughly trained to meet clearly defined roles, and each member is rewarded by the awareness that his contribution is essential to the colony. There is minimal interaction with and dependency upon outsiders. The individual identifies ideologically and emotionally with the colony system.

Socialization patterns in Hutterite society have the following unique characteristics:

1. All socialization is characterized by a supernaturally oriented source of authority and an absolutism which determines the proper ordering of social relationship, including the ordering of functionally derived age stages.
2. The individual is socialized to be obedient, submissive, and dependent upon human support and contact within a spatial and temporal context that includes all the social institutions, activities, and resources he will need to achieve the societal goals. Self-development is de-emphasized, and individuality is subordinated to colony ends.
3. According to the Hutterite conception of human nature, the individual requires constant nurture as well as supernatural aid to change his "carnal nature" into a spiritual one, a necessary condition for salvation. This appraisal of human nature is functional in the colony system. "Good" behaviour in a child means that he relinquishes individual wishes and conforms voluntarily to the will of the colony. A child

who transgresses is punished not because of his inherent "bad" nature, but because he must suffer the consequences of his carnal nature. The colony expects the youngster's misbehaviour to be supplanted by voluntary responsibility as he matures.

4. The Hutterite culture permits some informal deviancy, mostly within the peer subgroup where its noxious effects are kept within manageable proportions. Absolute conformity by the individual is not required, nor is it ever achieved. The Hutterite position maintains simply that the individual is not perfect and cannot attain perfection without the aid of his brothers. The result of this viewpoint is an emphasis on rehabilitation of the deviant individual with a minimum of condemnation.

5. Dependency patterns are firmly established in infancy so that aloneness is seen as unpleasant. As the individual matures and participates in communal activities, he experiences gradual acknowledgement of his individuality in socially approved ways.

6. School-age children receive limited companionship from their parents. They also learn to accept pain and punishment with mild pleasure and to enjoy hard physical labour. The individual acquires by experience a knowledge of how his peer group can both protect and punish him.

7. The transition from childhood to adulthood is pronounced, and is rewarded by appropriate changes in status, work, participation in social life, use of property, and greater companionship and acceptance within the family.

8. Personal security is attained by conforming to the interest of the colony: its schedule, its reinforcing rituals, and its definitions of social situations. Personal goals for living encompass an eternal one through submission of individual will to the colony, a temporal one through the realization of a successful colony, and a social one through the perpetuation of colony life. The successfully socialized Hutterite knows why he is alive, how he should live, and subjectively he feels capable of meeting the behavioural standards set by his culture.

Notes

1. The project was entitled "Education and Marginality in the Communal Society of the Hutterites", No. 1683 of the Co-operative Research Branch of the United States Office of Education. The senior author was the principal investigator, and the junior author the principal field worker. Principal consultants to the project were Bert Kaplan (psychology), Laura Thompson (anthropology), Joseph H. Britton (human development), and Calvin Redekop (sociology of religion). The period of study extended from June 1, 1962 to September 30, 1965. Assistance rendered by Abbie C. Enders, David Huntington, and Abigail Huntington in the field research is gratefully acknowledged.

References

Eaton, J.W.
1964 "The Art of Aging and Dying". *The Gerontologist* 4:94-101.

Eaton, J.W. and A. Mayer
1954 "Man's Capacity to Reproduce: The Demography of a Unique Population". *Human Biology* 25:206-264.

Eaton, J.W. and R.J. Weil
1955 *Culture and Mental Disorders,* Glencoe, Illinois.

Friedmann, R.
1961 *Hutterite Studies,* Goshen, Indiana.

Hofer, P.
1955 *The Hutterian Brethren and Their Beliefs,* Starbuck, Manitoba.

Hostetler, J.A.
1963 *Amish Society*, Baltimore.

Hostetler, J.A. and G.E. Huntington
1967 *The Hutterites in North America,* New York.

Riedeman, P.
1950 *Account of Our Religion, Doctrine and Faith,* trans, by K. Hasenberg from the German edition of 1565. Bungay, Suffolk.

Smith, C.H.
1957 *The Story of the Mennonites.* Newton, Kansas.

Williams, J.E.
1939 "An Analytical Tabulation of the North American Utopian Communities by Type, Longevity, and Location". M.A. Thesis, University of South Dakota.

Part II Section B

THE FAMILY GROUP

9

Baptism in a Quebec Parish*

Colette Moreux

Certain rites, marking a minimal adherence to Catholic religion, are unanimously observed by the French-Canadian population of the village. Indeed, it is difficult to conceive of how any French Canadian could be "without any religion" since each one must necessarily be declared to the presbytery and be baptized in order to have a legal recognition of existence, must receive the nuptial benediction to be considered married, and must be buried following Catholic rites to officially die.

The unanimous respect for these rites and the absolute social obligation to submit to them do not allow us to use such signs of adherence as indices of the degree of religiosity of the parish and its population. Their automatic obervance does not reflect the will of the individuals or families to go or not to go through the church at the important moments of life. In some cases, however, the individual does exercise his free will regarding religious rites not with the intention of detachment from or faithfulness to the Church but for reasons apparently irrelevant to religion; that is, economic, familial and social reasons take precedence over the strict adherence to the laws of the Church or to the traditions following from them. Indeed, the priority of motives of a temporal nature often leads to slight forms of disobedience or indifference towards religious prescriptions which were unknown in the Province some ten years ago. In other cases religious orthodoxy is totally preserved but we note some detachment regarding the social customs tied to these religious acts which, through the centuries, have themselves received a sacred aura. Does not their transgression also indicate an evolution of the notion of the sacred? From this perspective, we report on the changing practices of Baptism.

All French-Canadian residents of Saint-Pierre are baptized and, generally, the baptism respects the law of *Quam Primum* which prescribes that it be as near as possible to birth. It is profitable to study the actual margin of time between the date of birth and that of baptism.

B. Favreau[1] shows that from 1801 to 1921 only one or two days passed between birth and baptism of the children of Saint-Pierre, except during the anti-clerical troubles of 1870-1875 which gave rise to delays. After 1941, Favreau reports the gap grew considerably, reaching a duration in 1961 of sixteen days.

---

*Translated by Louise Gervaise-Barker and abridged with the permission of the author and publisher from Colette Moreux, *Fin d'une religion? Monographie d'une paroisse canadienne-française.* Montréal: Les Presses de L'Université de Montréal, 1969, Part II, Chapter II, 163-175.

We may go back for more precision to four test periods[2] – 1917-20, 1932-35, 1947-50, and 1962-65 (see Table 1). In the parish, in the sixties, we find a great rise in the tendency to lengthen the time between baptisms and births. Also during this time the majority of children were born in medical clinics and not at home as had been the practice until then. Between November 1, 1962 and November 1, 1965, of 225 births, only five took place at home. Further, for reasons of hygiene and administrative convenience, the child could not be baptized at the hospital anymore except when in danger of death. Only the mother and medical personnel had contact with the baby. Thus it was usually recommended that the child's baptism take place in his parents' parish.

Table 1

Period	Number of Baptisms*	Mean Age at Baptism (in days)	Baptisms held the same day as the birth or the next day	Baptism held between the 2nd and 7th day after birth	Baptisms held during the 2nd week or later
1917-20	882	1.8	75	5	2
1932-35	112	2.91	30	78	3
1947-50	168	5.9	53	93	10
1962-65	225	17.9	1	40	142+

*Any differences between the number of baptisms by period and total sums derive from a lack of information in the civil registers.
+Among these, 46 baptisms were held more than three weeks after birth.

In general, it is on the sixth day that the child returns home and he could be baptized on that day. Ordinarily, on Sundays as well as on weekdays, it is sufficient to notify the priest in the morning of the day desired for the baptism. However, for external reasons, the parents may extend the waiting period; it is not as if they are deliberately transgressing the customs of early baptism. At first, they might wait for the next Sunday. However, if it were too near the birth, the mother might not be well enough and the ceremony would he held on the following Sunday: "I wanted to be able to drink champagne and eat well," admits Mrs. Beaudin. "I wanted to carry the child," says Mrs. Berthier.

The social and worldly aspects of baptism do not stand out as much as those of marriage and burial, but the wish for a family reunion and the display of wealth can also delay the baptism. The parents may wait for the guests to be available and sometimes for the bi-monthly pay cheques. The custom of collective baptisms does not exist in Saint Peirre; each family insists on having its own ceremony, its officiating priest, and the ringing of bells. Thus, if many baptisms have already been booked for the chosen Sunday, the ceremony may again de delayed. In several cases the baptism of a later child was delayed longer than that of the first-born.

Because of the reduced risk of death at birth and the hygiene and administrative complexities, the religious doubts of the parents are now calmed; a certain slackness affects their behaviour with regard to a precept held to be absolute until the Second World War.

A custom still very much respected in Quebec consists of giving the newborn the first names of Mary or Joseph. These names serve very rarely to name the child and they do not appear in the later officials acts, but are an evident sign of attachment to the Holy Family. On the one hand, we note an increase of cases where the newborn is not named Mary or Joseph and, on the other hand, a correlation exists between the delay of baptism and a neutral first name. This shows that this choice does not come by chance but from a more or less conscious decision of the parents (see Table 2).

Table 2				
	1st period	2nd period	3rd period	4th period
Number of cases where the child was not named Mary or Joseph	2	1	6	25
Number of cases where the child was baptized after a delay and was not named Mary or Joseph	2 of 2 delays of more than 2 weeks	0 of 3 delays of more than 2 weeks	2 of 10 delays of more than 2 weeks	11 of 46 delays of more than 2 weeks

Finally, among the customs related to birth and baptism there are two, without any apparent relationship to religion, which deserve mention--one dealing with godparents, the other with place of birth. Both seem to go in the same direction and, like the more properly religious aspects we have discussed, reinforce the impression of a change of attitude of one part of the population towards the socio-religious complex surrounding birth and the social integration of a new parishioner.

Tradition demands that the godfather and godmother be chosen from among members of the family: for the first-born, it will be the paternal grandparents for a boy and the maternal grandparents for a girl;[3] then, following the parents' preferences and the obligations or acquired rights of complicated familial relationships, the brothers and sisters of the child's parents and their spouses follow as godfathers and godmothers. The list of "my aunts"[4] and "my uncles" being quite long, a child, whatever the number of his older brothers and sisters, can therefore always have a godfather and a godmother among his uncles and aunts. Until the fifties, omitting those cases where records did not indicate the family ties between godchildren and godparents, the rules of choice were never transgressed. However, in the years 1962-1965, of 225 baptisms, the choise fell fifteen times on the brothers, sisters or cousins of the child and eleven times on friends of the family. This choice of friends, not members of the family, was done precisely on request by the younger parents for whom the existence of friendships is so much more common than among the older population.

The other fact we want to emphasize is the almost unanimous abandonment of giving birth at home. The choice of hospital is not an indifferent matter: some women always give birth at Saint Alexandre, others, not less regularly, give birth in Montreal. In the first case, the reasons have a positive character: "Saint-Alexandre is near . . . We are used to going there . . . We know some nuns or nurses there." In the second case the alleged reasons not to go to Saint-Alexandre are: "It is dirty . . . There are no individual rooms and, like my sister, I could meet an Italian woman with all her sausages." In neither case are any questions raised on the quality of the medical care received. For the period 1947-1950, thirteen children were born in Montreal and twenty-nine at Saint-Alexandre: all others were born in Saint-Pierre; from 1962 to 1965, 79 were born in Montreal, 110 in Saint-Alexandre, 5 in Saint-Pierre and 10 in

Table 3
Changes in Characteristics of Baptism During the Four Test Periods

	1st Period				2nd Period				3rd Period				4th Period				
Occupation of Fathers of Baptized Children	Total Number of Baptisms	Number of Baptisms on Day of Birth	Baptized After Two Weeks	Baptized Children Not Named Mary or Joseph	Total Number of Baptisms	Number of Baptisms on Day of Birth	Baptized After Two Weeks	Baptized Children Not Named Mary or Joseph	Number of Baptisms on Day of Birth	Baptized After Two Weeks	Total Number of Baptisms**	Baptized Children Not Named Mary or Joseph	Total Number of Baptisms**	Number of Baptisms During The First Week	Baptized at Three of More Weeks	Baptized Children Not Named Mary or Joseph	Grandparents or Uncles and Aunts not chosen as Godparents
A	2	0	1	1	3	0	1		18	1	4	2	48	4	14	17	7
B	6				7	4		1	57	6	3	1	72	10	6	2	7
C	11				10	1	1		25		1		44	7	9	3	5
D	53		1	1	70	23			35	8	1		11	4	1	1	0
E	7				8	2			21	5	0	3	16	4	3	0	2
F	3				5	0			9	2	1		23	5	7	2	5
G	0				0				3				3	1	0	0	0
Total	82	75	2	2	103	30	2	1	168	22	10	6	217	35	40	25	26

*A - Professionals, skilled technicians, artists; B - Workers-Craftsmen; C - Commerce-Services; D - Farmers-Stock Breeders; E - Laborers; F - Employees-Civil Servants; G - Industrial Owners.

**The totals do not correspond to previous numbers: here we have only included the baptisms for which the father's occupation was shown in the registers. (e.g., 2nd period: 103 known occupations of 112 registered baptisms.

various places but always at a hospital; the other cases are not specified in the registers.

Our evidence suggests that the choice of the various alternatives results from a very clear desire to conform to certain models which socially situate the newborn and his family. Table 3 shows the types of behaviour with respect to the four characteristics mentioned and the occupation of the father of the baptized child, the only information about the parents given by the parish registers. It shows that often it is the same children who are concentrated in the ranks of non-conformism and that the majority come from quite well-defined levels in the population.

An analysis of Tables 5 and 6 shows that the growth of professionals in the population is correlated with the increase of exceptional cases in the various choices permitted in baptism. Using only the occupational categories in which the numbers are sufficient or present significant variations, we find the increases in each category from the first to the last test period to be:

A. professionals, skilled technicians, artists: from 2 to 48
B. workers-craftsmen: from 6 to 72
C. commerce-services: from 11 to 44
D. farmers-gardeners: from 53 to 11
F. employees-civil servants: from 3 to 23

For each of these occupational groups, the figures in Table 4 indicate the changing proportions of cases of early baptism and of anomalies.[5]

Table 4

	1st Period		2nd Period		3rd Period		4th Period	
	% early baptisms	% anomalies	% early baptisms	% anomalies	% early baptisms	% anomalies	% early baptisms	% anomalies
A	0	100	0	33	5	33	8	79
B	100	100	57	14	10	7	13	20
C	100	0	10	10	0	4	15	38
D	100	4	33	0	23	3	36	18
F	100	0	0	0	21	11	21	60

Although the small number of cases might raise doubts about the rates, it is evident that the farmers remain the most attached to the traditional forms of baptism and that the professionals have always been the farthest away, while the other categories oscillate between the two. Only the category F of employees and civil servants shows a striking increase in the number of anomalies stemming from changes in the origins of the group.

If we compare Tables 5 and 6 which show the numbers of baptisms following births in Montreal and Saint-Alexandre, we obtain further details about the differences between occupational groups.

First we note that three-fourths of the children of professionals are born in Montreal compared to one-quarter of the children of workers-craftsmen and one sixth of the children of labourers. Generally, the baptisms following the births taking place at Saint-Alexandre offer fewer exceptions (29%) than those of the children born in Montreal (45%). The professionals and the office and commerce employees especially, when their children are born in Montreal,[6] have more exceptional cases than the workers, the labourers, or merchants.

Finally, certain occupations are more often characterized by certain types of exceptions: the commerce and office employees and the managerial staff of commerce

Table 5

Children whose Baptism Presents Exceptions to the General Rule (1962-1965)

Children Born in Montreal						Children Born at Saint-Alexandre				
Children Born in Montreal: 79 Number of Exceptional Cases: 36 Average Age at Baptism: 32 days						Children Born at Saint-Alexandre: 110 Number of Exceptional Cases: 32 Average Age at Baptism: 32 days				
Age at Baptism (expressed in days)	Unusual Godfathers and Godmothers	First Names other than Mary and Joseph	Occupation of Father	Occupational Category*		Age at Baptism (expressed in days)	Unusual Godfathers and Godmothers	First Names other than Mary and Joseph	Occupation of Father	Occupational Category*
35	X	X	Pharmacist	A		34	X		Bus Driver	B
73	X	X	Pharmacist	A		22	X		Foreman	B
21	X		Office Employee	F		85	X		Storekeeper	F
21	X		Salesman	C		21	X		Inspector	C
210	X		Office Employee	F		74		X	Commercial Director	C
24	X		Commerce Employee	F		10	X	X	Mechanic	B
25	X		Merchant	C		8		X	Silk-Screen Process Worker	B
100	X		Surgeon	A		7		X	Garage Manager	C
40		X	Producer (Radio Canada)	A		5		X	Milkman	C
32		X	Office Manager	F		4	X		Labourer	E

23		X	Clerk	F		20	X		Labourer	E
25		X	Producer (TV)	A		3	X		Office Employee	F
26		X	Pharmacist	A		9	X		Electrician	B
25		X	Stock-Breeder	D		19	X		Merchant	C
23		X	Biologist	A		19	X		Worker	B
17	X	X	Teacher	A		7	X		Cabinet-Maker	B
17	X		Publicist	A		17	X		Male-Nurse	C
14	X		Publicist	A		16	X		Worker	B
14	X		Industrial Designer	A		233			Artist Publicist	A
17		X	Teacher	A		38			Unknown Occupation on	
9		X	Technician	A		68			Technician (TC)	A
3		X	Appraiser	A		27			Technician	A
13		X	Veterinarian	A		27			Federal Civil Servant	F
1		X	Teacher	A		22			Electrician	B
14		X	Accountant	A		23			Manager	C
14		X	Sculptor	A		23			Worker	B
16		X	Engineer	A		40			Plumber	B
17		X	Appraiser	A		48			Worker	B
17		X	Appraiser	A		27			Deliveryman	C
21			Accountant	A		27			Deliveryman	A
60			Company Inspector	C		21			Labourer	E
30			Engineer	A		21			Labourer	E
30			Engineer	A						
53			Labourer	C						
51			Superintendent	F						
22			Representative	C						

*See lengend, Table 3

Table 6

Baptisms Presenting Exceptions to the General Rule and Occupation of Fathers of Baptized Children (1962-1965 - Parish Registers)

Occupation of Father*	Children Born in Montreal		Children Born at Saint-Alexandre		Total of Occupations Represented For The 225 Baptisms
	Number of Represented Occupations	Number of Baptisms Presenting Exceptions	Number of Represented Occupations	Number of Baptisms Presenting Exceptions	
A	33	24	11	3	48
B	14	0	50	12	72
C	16	4	20	9	44
D	2	1	6	0	11
E	2	1	13	4	16
F	11	6	9	3	23
G	1	0	1	0	3
Total	79	36	110	31	217 Known

*See legend, Table 3

and industry more frequently choose the godparents for their children outside the family; undoubtedly, they are in daily workaday contact with many persons outside the family group and they easily become friends. The influence of the Anglo-Saxon patterns (importance of social relationships, independence from the family) may be combined here with types of behaviour characteristic or urbanized groups. In contrast, the representatives of the professions are more tempted by irregularities at the level of the first name. The typical choice of Mary and Joseph is considered rather obsolete and is mixed with the snobbish desire to have a child answering solely to a neutral first name. This kind of exception is much more frequent among the newborn of Montreal.

Although we can see a link between occupations, birth in Montreal, and social and religious deviances in baptisms, we realize, from this brief report, that belonging to one or another level of society does not automatically determine, or even allow us to predict with any precision, the religious adherence of individuals. In the same way, the behaviour of a person of a given occupation with respect to a particular aspect of catholicism does not reveal his broad religious attitude; thus, the delay of baptism seems to be characteristic of people with modest occupations but, as we shall see, these very people are the most attached to the catholicism of the parish.

We saw before that there is no consciousness in the parish of belonging to a certain social level. The idea of stratification by occupation is only weakly experienced by the representatives of the professions and the managerial staff of industry and commerce. Therefore, no one sees or lives his religion in relation to his status in the group. We cannot expect individuals to recognize their social determinism, but the fact that most rarely know any other ties that those of kinship and any dissimilarities except the ones separating the new from the old, reduces the consciousness of differentiation of social and religious patterns based on occupational differences. An opposition can evidently exist outside this consciousness, but as long as it is not defined or crystallized into an institutionalized ideology, it remains apart and latent and becomes actualized only in personal behaviour. For example, regarding baptism, it could be said that a number of parents, many fewer than those represented by the number of anomalous cases, have adopted a certain independence towards the Church; if we include here only the cumulative cases of anomalies, we would have 20 of 68 cases of baptisms offering deviations in a total of 225 baptisms. Among these, the representatives of professions, artists, and office employees belonging to the new population are surely predominant, but with so many exceptions that no clear tendency is yet apparent.

Notes and References

1. Bernard Favreau, *Monographie de la paroisse de Saint-X. Etude de la natalité et de la mortalité à partir des registres de la paroisse et de la desserte et interprétation sociologique des changements survenus,* M.A. Thesis, Montréal, Université de Montréal, 1965, 59, graph no.5.

2. Since the baptisms of Catholic anglophone children are recorded in English in the civil registers, we can be certain by language alone that we have taken into account only the francophone children. And since non-French-Canadian francophones in Saint-Pierre are rare, we may assume that our sample is all French Canadian.

3. The custom of selecting a child's grandparents to be his godfather and godmother is accompanied by the custom of giving him their first names. This custom recalls the widely held belief in the primitive world that the grandson is the rein-

carnation of the grandfather and therefore his namesake.

4. In the terminology of the family, everyone uses terms which express the relationships with the children. Thus, a mother, when speaking of her own sister to her children will say "my aunt"; the married couple at times will call themselves "her father" and "her mother". These expressions are specific and invariant.

5. One "abnormal" baptism can evidently involve many anomalies. Thus 79 anomalies may derive from a total 100 baptisms of which many fewer than 79 are "abnormal".

6. The professional whose children are born at Saint-Alexandre may well belong to the more traditionalist, older population. Two contrary influences are then at work: the professional and the traditonal, which leads to a reduced rate of exceptional cases.

10

Succession to Family Enterprises and the Migration of Young People in an Agricltural Community*

Seena Kohl and John W. Bennett

Introduction

The population of most rural regions of nations with market agrarian economics is controlled mainly by migration. The classic process involves a constant flow of people from rural areas to the cities in search of occupational and career opportunities. This out-migration in North America has created a static or, in recent decades, a declining overall rural population. That rural out-migration is controlled by factors other than the attraction of urban jobs is indicated by the fact that the rate of migration remains high even in periods of economic recession. Among the factors involved in the migration process are economic and resource availabilities in the rural areas, and interpersonal relationships in families and kin groups. Over a long period of time, therefore, it is to be expected that rural social systems have adapted to a fairly regular flow of population out of the communities.

This paper presents some of the findings of a longitudinal study (conducted 1962-1972) of the relationships of succession to family enterprises and migration of the sons and daughters of agricultural operators in a region we call "Jasper", after the pseudonym for its principal service-centre town.[1] This region is in the Saskatchewn section of the northern Great Plains. In this region succession to the enterprise or marriage to local men are the alternatives to emigration for the young men and women respectively. However, we have found that kinship and family structure play quite different roles in emigration for men and women.

The geneological patterns of kinship in Jasper and its terminological features do not differ significantly from those described by various writers for Anglo-American society in general.[2] This is also the case with respect to kinship functions, which display the flexibility and the variability noted by observers for Anglo-American groups. Since Anglo-American kinship is lacking in specific rules governing inheritance association of kin, and the choice of occupations, considerable variability in the role of kinship in such processes is found from case to case. Moreover, we find that kinship can be "opted" according to the demands of particular situations .

We find in Jasper that kinship serves routinely as a means to enter the agricultural occupation. The "development cycle"[3] of the nuclear family and its associated enterprise involves the takeover of the enterprise by the son from his father, and the eventual retirement of the father and mother. The successor then prepares his own

---

*Abridged from an article in K. Ishwaran, ed., *The Canadian Family,* Toronto: Holt, Rinehart and Winston, 1976 based on the paper "Kinship, Succession and the Migration of Young People in a Canadian Agricultural Community", *International Journal of Comparative Sociology 6* (March, 1965), 95-116. By permission of the editor.

son for a similar succession.

Entrance into agriculture in Jasper is possible primarily through this cyclical transition from family of orientation to family of procreation,[4] or in cases where succession is not possible, with the financial help of the family in buying an enterprise. Thus, in one way or another, the young man who desires to enter agriculture is placed in a position of economic dependence on his family.

As Jasper farms and ranches increase in value the son is required to pay a proportionately larger amount to the father, which means an increasing debt for the young man starting out. Given the land prices prevailing in 1963-64, a viable ranch in the Jasper region cost anywhere from $150,000 to $600,000; a farm cost from $35,000 to $150,000. These prices had increased by 15 percent to 20 percent in the early 1970's. Few young men were able to accumulate the necessary capital for purchase, and all looked to the retiring generation for financial aid. If the son was unwilling to accept his dependent role, then his opportunities were severely limited. Ranch labour was one possibility, with the remote chance of eventually buying the "place" if there were no heir.

The Jasper social system is adjusted to the fact that economic support is required for entrance into agriculture. Thus Jasperites did not usually criticize young men for entering into dependent relationships with fathers or employers. However, after marriage and the initiation of a family and serving a number of years of apprenticeship to an older man, the young man ideally was expected to assume control. If this did not take place in reasonable time, the young man could be accused of excessive submissiveness, or the old man could be accused of excessive stinginess. While there were similarities between ranch and farm practices, the amount of capital necessary to establish or refinance a ranch is far greater than that for a farm, and this established conditions for the succession of ranch sons requiring greater economic and social dependency. However for both ranch and farm sons, the nuclear family ties were a means to keep them within the Jasper region.

The daughter's situation was quite different: while her affective ties with the family of orientation were strong, entrance into adult status by marriage or an occupation did not depend on aid given to her by parents. Since women did not, except in rare cases, succeed to the family enterprise, there was agreement on the part of both mother and father that she had to find training and a career elsewhere. Thus she was encouraged to emigrate.

Migration of young people from rural areas into urban centres is increasing thoughout the province of Saskatchewan, in keeping with a similar trend throughout North Ameica and most of the world. However, in Jasper the out-migration of young people has not been so great as to result in an absolute reduction of numbers over the past generation. Emigration of women is greater than men, and during the past fifteen years emigration by sons has actually decreased, creating additional pressure on the land (see Table 1).

The reasons for relatively low out-migration in the Jasper region are to be found in its relative current prosperity,[5] its devotion to a cultural tradition emphasizing local history and the continuity of the family enterprise, and to the limited opportunities for rewarding occupations in the larger region or inadequate educational preparation for the few opportunities offering suitable rewards.

In studying intimate forms of social organization in modern rural communities it is always necessary to remember that the people are members of the larger community of the nation and of the world. The residents of Jasper speak the Midwestern variety of English; they possess the familiar traditions and myths of Ango-American society; they look at the same television programs as city people, and have learned the value, or the lack of value, of the almighty dollar. At the same time they possess a local social

Table 1
Permanent Emigration of Young Men and Women*

	Total No. Women Born in Region		Women Emigrants				Total No. Men Born in Region		Men Emigrants			
	Ranch	Farm	Ranch		Farm		Ranch	Farm	Ranch		Farm	
			No.	%	No.	%			No.	%	No.	%
1900-1915	14	–	7	50	–	–	13	–	6	33	–	–
1916-1930	25	11	14	56	6	55	21	12	9	43	4	33
1931-1945	30	33	20	67	21	66	28	47	13	46	30	64
1946-1961	30	32	25	83	17	56	25	49	4	16	25	32

*This table was compiled by tracing the migration patterns of the siblings of the contemporary generation and the siblings of their parents. Thus this sample includes only those ranch and farm families who were studied in depth – 26 ranch enterprises and 38 farm enterprises.

system of considerable solidarity and kinship connectedness, with its own folklore and historical mythology. In many North American rural communities the external pull of the national culture is extremely strong, stronger than local attractions.[6] However, the local social system in this community has been strong enough to encourage ranch sons, and to a lesser extent farm sons, to view city life with considerable disdain. Our task was to determine the role that kinship plays in maintaining this solidarity and ideology, as it simultaneously afforded possibilities for establishing ties with the outside world if they were desired.

Setting

This research on family and enterprise is one part of a regional study featuring an ecological approach to settlement and socio-economic change.[7] The region is part of the semi-arid northern Great Plains, subject to extremely variable climate and soil, adaptation to which entailed hardships and concomitant changes in technology and way of life on the part of the settlers who came from a humid environment. Within the region there is wide variation in habitat which has resulted in the juxtaposition of various forms of farming and livestock production. Some of these possess cultural styles of relative distinctiveness. This paper deals with the ranching and farming popultion.[8]

Settlement

The agricultural settlement of the region began in the 1870s with the movement of sheep and cattle ranches mainly from the United States. Following these came single young men from eastern Canada and the British Isles who drifted west with the frontier. Many of them arrived with the Royal Northwest Mounted Police and stayed to establish a cattle enterprise. The completion of the railroad in 1883 opened the area to migrants from eastern Canada and the U.S., and by 1900 the ranching community was well established. Jasperites distinguished carefully between those families who arrived before 1900 and those who arrived later. The pre-1900 arrivals, mostly ranchers, are "old timers", and this term denotes respect, admiration, and nostalgia for the "real" pioneer.[9]

Encouraged by the active settlement policy of the Canadian Pacific Railroad and the Canadian government, most Jasper farmers arrived between the years 1904 and 1916, especially in 1910. The farming population designates as pioneers those farm families who came as part of the 1910 tide of homesteaders.[10] However, the ranchers designate as pioneer farmers those farmers who came prior to the 1910 homesteader group. Many of the pre-1910 farm settlers were as much rancher as farmer, and there was less distinction between the two occupational cultures than exists today.

With the arrival of increasing numbers of farmers as competitors for land and the closing of the open range, a sharper distinction arose between ranch and farm both as economics and cultures. After 1905 the influx of farmers and the new legislation led to the establishment of fenced agricultural properties, and from this time on differences in life style, traditions, and attitudes between ranchers and farmers became important. These differences have persisted, reinforced by the mass media and commercial exploitation.

The region is sparsely populated (1.7 persons per square mile in both 1960 and 1970 census data).[11] Often one must drive from one to seven miles in from the main road to get to the ranch house. The topography is varied, the vistas endless: rolling hills and plains, cut through by small creeks along which the ranchers settled. The famers, who arrived later in time, homesteaded in the flat plains north and south of the range of forested hills which constitute the region's most prominent natural feature. The town of Jasper, population 2,500 in 1962, and 2,290 in 1970, is a few miles off the major east-west highway and is the chief trading centre and railhead for the region, although not its geographic centre.

Kinship and Household

Kinship Connections

The majority of agricultural households in the Jasper region were related by blood or marriage. However, since ranches were few and far apart and farms bunched in particular districts, the kin ties of the ranchers were dispersed throughout the region, whereas farmer kinship networks were much more localized.

The most numerous marriage connections were found between families who were early settlers and who were able to keep their sons in the region. This is a direct result of the fact that they were able to provide land for their sons, a fact that in itself is a consequence of early settlement.

In the past marriage was frequently a result of propinquity, and several local nuclei of intermarrying kin groups in the first generation of settlement have been mapped. In the 1960s and 1970s the brides came from a wider geographic area, although almost three-fourths of the marriages were between regional residents.

The husband's family of orientation served as an initial determinant of status in the community for the new family of orientation. Thus, in those few instances where ranch daughters married farm operators, the girl retained family ties, but as a wife of a farm operator, she was tied to the social activities of farm rather than ranch wives, and her children were to a much greater extent incorporated into farming activities. Similarly, those farm daughters who married ranch sons become incorporated into the ranching world, and often dropped their social contacts with farming society.

Household Composition

Although in both ranch and farm populations the nuclear family served routinely as a means to enter the occupation, there were differences in the process of transference of resources and the accompanying changes in household composition and residential patterns. The ideal is to have one's own "place" independent from one's family. However it is an accepted practice for a newly-married couple to live with the young man's family, with the implicit or explicit aim of taking over the enterprise when the parents retire.[12] As a consequence, despite the strong nuclear kinship ideology, this creates a *de facto* form of the extended family. Although the major residential unit consists of the nuclear family, parents and unmarried children, 54 per cent of all the contemporary operators have been at one time or another residents of multiple household enterprises.

Although the dominant residence pattern for the ranch and farm population is patrilocal and is supported by the value placed on the continuity of the enterprise from father to son, where it is economically advantageous sons-in-law will move to their wife's parents' place. During the decade of observation there were two cases of succession to a ranch by a farm son-in-law, and one case where a ranch son moved to his father-in-law's enterprise.

Residence Patterns and the Role of the Paternal Grandfather

The emphasis on and relatively high frequency of patrilocal residence inevitably means greater involvement by the paternal line in the lives of the young couple. Where ranch sons married ranch daughters such affinal ties strengthened past bonds between ranchers. In the instances of ranch-son farm-daughter marriages, there was in most cases no tendency toward less contact with the maternal than with the paternal kin.

Aged ranchers typically prolong their control over the enterpise and their succeeding sons, even when they are physically unable to perform many routine tasks.[13] The type of father who refuses to retire has become a figure of folklore in Jasper, judging by the many anecdotes told about such men. The prolongation of control, in contrast to the farmers, who retire earlier and more willingly, or who are less inhibited by tradition and are ready to sell the farm outright, is due not only to the father's desire to guard the family establishment, but also to the fact that ranchers dislike town life. Farmers are much more inclined to retire to the local towns or distant urban centres. The ranchers display a genuine attachment to the country and an abhorrence of crowds, cramped spaces, and close social interactions.

The reciprocal of this continuity of parental control was the aid given to the new family of procreation. The most common form of succession is purchase of the ranch in installments by the son, and the terms are usually arranged so as to make it relatively easy for him to do so. In the light of the steadily increasing value of land, acquisition of a ranch is usually impossible or very difficult without this type of arrangement. The "bound-dependent" features associated with the takeover, as described above, are viewed locally as the price one must pay in order to obtain a ranch, and the young couple is expected to cope with it and not to complain too much. As one young wife put it, "Sure, I get mad at my father-and mother-in-law, but what can I do? After all, without their help we could never be where we are."

Succession and Emigration

In the introductory statement we noted that in contrast with many rural regions of North America, out-migration of the young men from the Jasper ranching community was minimal; that the majority of ranches remained in the hands of their founding families: 67.8 percent of all sons who came of age during the decade of research succeeded to the parental enterprise by 1972. The basic reasons for this relative stability of population can be found in the profitable status of livestock production, and in the existence of few acceptable occupational alternatives.

With few exceptions, ranch sons were more likely than farm sons to remain on the parental enterprise. However, in the late 1960s son succession to diversified enterprises tended to increase as a result of increased affluence and availability of government subsidies, particularly loans of various types.

In the earlier version of this paper, in the discussion of the different rates of succession for ranches and farms, we emphasized the role of the ranching tradition as a factor.

We suggested that one consequence of this ranching ideology which stressed self-reliance and initiative was an ambivalence on the part of the rancher toward formal education, and that this ambivalence operated toward supressing education accomplishment. However, we have found subsequently that the succession to farm enterprises has also involved many sons with low educational levels. We conclude currently that it is the decision to take over an enterprise which depresses educational goals,[14] not the presence or absence of particular ranching traditions.

However, ranching traditions do play a role in setting occupational goals for sons. Ranching remains the preferred occupational goal of the sons of ranchers.[15] It is considered a prestigious occupation, as well as romantic, and as such is supported by the community as well as family traditions. In the 1960s, the majority of ranches in Jasper were succeeded to by sons or close relatives in cases where there were no sons; a minority were sold to nonrelatives. When an old ranching family sold the place to an outsider or to a local farmer bent upon expansion, the ranching community regarded it as a shame; that is, the separation of the enterprise from the family name was considered a break with tradition. However, in the 1970s this was changing; traditions were giving way to the logic of high prices and more ranches without son successors were being sold to outsiders.

Farmer fathers were not so insistent that agriculture is the only possible career for their sons, and they are willing to help them explore alternatives. They were universally favourable toward higher education, and encouraged their sons and daughters to go to college even if it meant permanent loss of contact with agriculture and the community. Farming is not bound up with the special traditions of the frontier, and it is not a profession with automatic connotations of prestige. It is simply a way of earning a living, "a good, honest way, mind you", but not the only way. On our Regional Schedule very few farmers stated that they would never consider any other occupation.[16] Almost all ranchers, or at least all men representing the second or third ranching generation, did say so.

Succession of the Ranch Son

For both Jasper ranch and farm families apprenticeship is the preferred means of introducing the neophyte to the occupation.[17] It starts early in childhood when the child, at the age of two and a half to three years, rides in the truck with his father to put out salt for the cattle, or to town for the mail or to get machinery fixed. Apprenticeship is particularly vital for the rancher for basic ecological reasons; successful management and development of a particular ranch property requires the most intimate possible knowledge of the terrain and its resources, and this knowledge can be acquired only by lengthy experience. There is a genuine question as to whether agricultural college is of any great value in training a future rancher, although business school might well benefit him. In any case, the need and the fact of apprenticeship, plus the factor of attachment to the locality and the "place" and, of course, the high cost of starting out, all combine to keep the ranch son or at least one of the siblings at home. This paves the way for an inevitable succession.

"Starting out" usually involves working for the father in the position of hired hand, then gradually investing the wages in cattle, working toward a joint leaseholding, and gradually accumulating equity. By the time of the father's death the ranch could be transferred by inheritance. In some cases, especially where conflict between the fathers and sons and between the sons makes succession ambiguous, the property is left to the widow, who then gets one of the sons to operate it until her death. In such cases the operator might well be into his thirties before he is sole manager and proprietor.

Succession of the Farm Son

The transition of the farm son to independent status from his father is not as difficult as that for a ranch son, although in most cases he must assume a greater amount of indebtedness. With a few exceptions of marginal ranches, the retiring rancher was able to accumulate cash, and he did not have to place the same demands for cash payment on his son as does the farm father who had not been able to accumulate cash over the years. Thus where the ranch father was satisfied with the son's ability and was willing to step down, a ranch son could succeed to say, a $600,000 enterprise with less indebtedness than a farm son who took over a $50,000 enterprise and had to provide for the support of his retiring parents.

The economic and ecological demands for farming require less capital outlay than for ranching. The young man who works with his father, sharing equipment and labour, could rent or buy the farm through crop shares which eliminates the problem of a large capital outlay. He also had available various means for credit through government loans, or private sources. A half-section (320 acres) was inadequate to support a single family during the period of research, so expansion was necessary. Until this could be done, for example by taking over the father's land, the son could supplement his income through casual labour with road crews, on irrigation projects, or on local farms or ranches. If married, the farm son would establish a separate household. This was reflected in a comparison of the household compositions of the comtemporary ranch and farm populations, which show higher neolocal residence frequency for the latter. However, although the economic and social dependence of the farm son upon his family was less than that of the ranch son, he was still economically dependent.

There was no established rules which simplified the transfer of property. Jasperites viewed the choice of a son for succession as subject to idiosyncratic factors and historical accidents. The flexible inheritance pattern, frequent disputes between parents and sons, and the vicissitudes of the economy influenced succession so as to prevent strong tendencies for primogeniture or any other fixed form.

There was a slight tendency toward *de facto* ultimogeniture due largely to the age and physical health of the father at the time his son reached maturity and the need for labour in the enterprise. Thus we found youngest sons inheriting long after their older brothers had left . The usual explanation was given in words to this effect: "There was no one else to take over and Dad couldn't work it himself."

However, age of father at the time of son's maturity was not the only factor involved in succession practices. Also important was the son's willingness to accept the father's authority and control. Willingness to accept control occurs in cases where he happens to be the right age at the time of the father's retirement, that is, not too young, but not too old to have established himself on another place. An additional factor may be that as a father ages, he becomes more dependent upon his son as a source of labour. The increased dependence of the father gives the son more control.

Alternatives to Succession

We may consider the question of alternatives for the sons who wished to stay in the region but where the enterprise was large enough for only one to succeed. One possibility is for the father to attempt to build up the ranch or farm by improving pasture and water resources to permit the support of more than one family. Another is an attempt to buy land for the same purpose, a course of action which will involve him in competitive relationships over a scarce commodity with his neighbours, also in general, with other Jasper ranchers.[18] These situations also have their ramifications in practices followed by the land bureau of the provincial government. The bureau permits the nuclear family members, that is, father and son, to pasture each other's cattle on respective leases, but it forbids others relatives, for example, uncles and nephew, to do so. The bureau encourages what it calls "natural succession" (father-son) and the "primary family" (nuclear family). Thus the nuclear kin role in maintaining tradition and in cementing the succession system is reinforced by the role of the government bureau in administering a vital resource, grazing land.

In many cases the procedure noted above could not be followed, and the surplus sons would have to leave the ranch. If their education had stopped before the twelfth grade, as it did for a large number, their choices were very limited. Ranch labour was one possibility, with the remote chance of buying the place if there was no heir. Another was to migrate further west into upper British Columbia and Alberta, where pioneer ranches were still available. Those ranch sons who left Jasper did so primarily because it was the only way they could enter the occupation of rancher elsewhere. In contrast no farm sons migrated from Jasper with the intention of establishing a new agricultural enterprise. Farm sons made use of their agricuultural skills and took jobs with experimental agricultural stations or with projects of the Prairie Farm Rehabilitation Act, but none established their own enterprise. Those who desired to farm did not leave.

A common practice is for ranch sons to leave, try their hands at various semi-skilled urban trades, and then return to take over the ranch or buy another with help, in an effort to resume the satisfying identify of "rancher". Often they are unsuccessful and leave after the period of work on the home place or elsewhere in the region.

That most of the enterprises were in the hands of second-generation successors indicated that there was a close connection between the expectation of lineal succession and actual behaviour. This close connection was due in part to the fact that no alternatives other than ranching are presented to the ranch son. Ranchers do not usually regard cities as offering much in the way of excitement or interest except for short stays. The "good life" is the ranching life, and while a son might wish to escape from his father's control, permanent departure from the region was not perceived as a desirable solution.

The Emigration of Young Women

The expectations held by family and community for the ranch or farm daughter virtually assure emigration if the young girl does not marry within the region (see Table 1).

The emigration pattern of young women has been consistent since early settlement. Ranching or farming is a man's occupation and a daughter knows from early childhood that women do not become ranchers or farmers.[19] Women can participate fully in ranch and farm activities, and their participation is economically important, particularly in families without sons. However, women are not considered fit to operate the enterprises. Marriage is regarded as the ideal feminine career, although not necessarily within the region. In fact, some mothers' objective for their daughter is marrriage to a professional or business man, which of course means departure from Jasper. They see no conflict in desiring the emigration of their daughters and the succession of their sons .

The fact that expectations for the daughter's career are not bound up with the development of the enterprise, and that her labour is less highly valued, makes it easier for her to leave. It is through this departure, ostensibly to learn a skill, that a young girl is accorded new status and independence of action. However, marriage remains the ideal means for the girl's entrance into adult status within the community. The large number of farm daughters who remain in Jasper is a consequence of their more frequent marriage to the young farm men in the region. Those few young girls who are not married soon after the twelfth grade choose migration and training in one of the serving skills, teaching, nursing, or secretarial work, but retain the eventual goal of marriage.

There are higher educational expectations for daughters than for sons, as well as differential rates in fulfillment of these expectations. Daughters of ranch and farm families do better in school than the sons. In the period 1950-1961, 65.5 percent of the farm girls and 66.5 percent of the ranch girls finished twelfth grade or more, as compared with 41.8 percent of farm sons and 27.1 percent of the ranch sons.[20] In the period 1962-1973, there was an increase in the completion of twelfth grade for all daughters and for farm sons, but ranch sons remained the same.

The daughter recognizes that she must finish high school if she wishes to enter her chosen vocation. Those girls who find school too difficult choose vocations which do not require graduation from the twelfth grade. However, even these occupational skills necessitate leaving the Jasper region and taking specialized training in urban centres.

Parents, particularly mothers, project into the girl urban middle-class ideals of what is proper in terms of achievement and decorum. By high school age the young ranch or farm girl is virtually indistinguishable from her urban counterpart. With few exceptions, the ranch or farm women would find little that is different in the world of urban or suburban women. The women's primary concerns of children, home, and husband are similar in rural or urban settings; the man's base of primary concerns, his occupational experiences, are, however, far different. It is this basic uniformity in the woman's roles and the experiences that mothers transmit to their daughters which enable the ranch or farm daughter to prepare much more successfully than her brother for life in urban settings.[21]

Notes

1. Data used in this paper were obtained in several seasons of continuing work in southern portions of the province of Saskatchewan. The research has been supported primarily by the National Science Foundation and the National Institute of Mental Health of the U.S. Government. Since we feature the out-migration of young people,

we do not consider emigration of adults due, for example, to drought or economic failure.

2. Talcott Parsons, "The Kinships System of the Contemporary United States", 22-38; and Raymond Firth, ed., *Two Studies of Kinship in London.*

3. Meyer Fortes, "Introduction", in Jack Goody, ed., *The Developmental Cycle of Domestic Groups.*

4. For a conceptualization of the "family farm cycle" on Canadian farms and ranches see J.C.Gilson, *Family Farm Business Arrangements.*

5. See the Saskatchewan Royal Commission on Agriculture and Rural Life, Report No. 10 (1956), 81, where prosperity of the agricultural enterprise is seen to be closely related to family-enterprise continuity.

6. This "pull" is almost universally assumed by rural sociologists (for example, Saskatchewan Royal Commission, Report No. 7 (1956), 123).

7. See John W. Bennett, *Northern Plainsmen,* and *Hutterian Brethren*, Chapter 1, for a description of the approach. Also see Seena B. Kohl,"Working Together: Women and Family in Southwestern Saskatchewan."

8. Due to the distances between ranches, and as one result of the "Code of the West", the interviewing pattern usually included dinner or supper. This gave the interviewers the opportunity to put notebook aside and "just visit" while washing dishes or peeling potatoes, or in the case of the men, just sitting and talking. Needless to say, these occasions afforded the greatest insight into the community and permitted observation of the entire family group in a relaxed situation. Fathers always came home for dinner (the noon meal), and where there were hired hands, they were present too. Often neighbours (male) would be present; either they were on their way to town and has stopped to visit, or were helping out. If they were present at the dinner hour, they were also fed. Often visiting continued past the dinner hour since the men had no time clock to punch, and enjoyed the opportunity to socialize with the investigators.

The history of each family was obtained by writing the family genealogy, beginning with the entrance of the first member into the region. We collected the history of the family's movements into and out of the community for two, and in some cases, three generations as well as information about the informant's attitudes towards and knowledge of his family members. This permitted the interviewer to get information about the values the informants held toward occupational choices other than ranching, as well as the informants' attitudes toward the outside community and toward other family members in the region.

9. The frontier isolation of the region should not be overstressed. This part of Canada has been called the "last best West", which means that it was settled a generation or more later than comparable portions of the U.S. northern plains. Its settlement, except for a brief period in the 1870s, was created by the railroad, and rail contacts with eastern Canada were available from the beginning. However, in comparison with the situation today, the early years were lived out in relative isolation and frontier individualism (Paul Sharp, "The American Farmer and the Last Best West", 18-20).

10. Arthur S. Morton, *History of Prairie Settlement;* and Sharp, *op. cit.*

11. The density for the ranching district is even less, about one person per square mile.

12. This pactice occurs more commonly among ranch successors than among farm successors. It is possible for a young man who desires to farm to do so by renting or purchasing, with some financial help from his father, one half section of land (1 section = 1 square mile). A ranch operation requires much more land and a much larger capital outlay. In the majority of cases of farm sons starting out, the young man would rent an additional one half section or one full section of land and work with his father, sharing labour and equipment. If he is married, he will establish a separate household on his own or rented land. Such opportunities are not commonly available for the ranch son, and those young couples who plan to ranch expect to live with the husband's parents during their first years of marriage, hoping to gain independence when the older couple will retire. The difficulties in terms of access to resources and capital make family help desirable in the eyes of most sons, despite the emphasis in the culture on individualistic achievement.

13. For comparative cases from Norway and Ireland, see George Park, "Sons and Lovers", and Conrad Arensberg, *The Irish Countryman.*

14. Also see Glen H. Elder, Jr., "Achievement Orientation and Career Patterns of Rural Youth," *Sociology of Education,* 37 (Fall 1963), 30-58.

15. As in most parts of the North American West the term "ranching" has a dual meaning: economic and cultural. In the former sense if refers to the raising of commerical beef cattle on extensive tracts of land. All or nearly all of the income of a particular enterprise is obtained from the sale of cattle. In the second, or cultural sense, ranching is a particular style of life, involving a certain type of clothing, attitudes and hobbies. In the community studies here all the families were ranchers in a cultural sense, and nearly all of them were likewise in an economic sense. Only two enterprises derived more than 15 percent of their income from the sale of crops and forage.

16. This is a lengthy questionnaire containing items on all aspects of the research administered to a sample of farmers and ranchers stratified by income and type of enterprise.

17. For comparative data dealing with the issue of succession see Jack Goody, *Succession to High Office.*

18. Some farmers have access to a relatively new type of facility: the cooperative grazing organization, which can drain off competitive rivalries for grazing land. This partial solution is unacceptable to the ranchers. Incidentally, nearly all grazing land in the region is leased from the government. Each lease has a small owned piece which, when bought, transfers the lease with it, providing the land bureau approves.

19. In the early 1960s there were three women in the area who had run ranches. Two were regarded as examples of "what happens to a woman who tries to do a man's job", that is, masculine in manner, or in violation of the norms by living with the hired man. The third was able to run her ranch "only because she is lucky

enough to have a special kind of hired help", that is, a man who accepted the direction of a woman and did not demand sexual satisfaction. In these three cases, the women had undertaken the ranches since there were no male heirs. In the early 1970s there were two additional women who took over the opertion of an enterprise. One case involved a widow who was helped by her adult sons who had their own enterprises. In the other case the male heir had rejected returning to the enterprise and his sister took it over. See Seena B. Kohl,"Working Together: Woman and Family in Southwestern Saskatchewan" for further analysis of the woman's roles.

20. Hall and McFarland find a similar situation. They conclude that "the school world of Paulend and Croyden (pseudonyms) turns out to be, fundamentally, a feminine world. It provides an academic atmosphere in which the girls thrive and the boys fail. Moreover the school is feminine in the vocational sense. The skills they learn are immediately transferable to the job world. Especially is this true for those who continue to university, those who prepare for school teaching and nursing, and those who enter clerical occupations. The graduate of a stenography course can start work immediately as a full-fledged stenographer. The graduate of a four-year course in mechanics starts as an apprentice. (Oswald Hall and Bruce McFarland, "Transition from School to Work", 65).

21. James Deetz uses the concept of "female culture" to explain the similarity of implements used by women (grinders, scrapers, etc.), in contrast with the greater differentiation of the implements used by men (fishhooks, projectile points, etc.). He suggests that the technological demands make for greater similarity in the women's implements (James Deetz, "Dynamics of Stylistic Change in Arikara").

11

The Future of Parenthood*

Leo Davids

Canadians are well aware that family life is changing, but where is it heading? There is a growing literature on the future of marriage, but not enough attention has been given to the probable future evolution of parenthood and child rearing. Let us look ahead about one generation, to see what may be in store for urban Canadians as their family roles and relationships continue to change with increasing speed.

Various scholarly observers of the social scene today have found that most fathers and mothers, isolated in the big-city nuclear family, are in sober fact ill equipped to achieve the development of such young people as will be required in modern, postindustrial society.[1] The Vanier Institute's booklet on day care contains the clear suggestion by a number of writers that motherhood in its present form is just not doing the job traditionally accomplished by mothers, and they join the growing chorus of demands for a system of day care that would be available not to a tiny minority of Canadian children but to the great majority of them.[2]

Others have gone further and proposed the professionalization of parents. As social critic Mary Van Stolk puts it:

> Not all woman are fit to bear children, not all men are fit to sire children. Not all woman are emotionally fit to tend children, although they may be physically fit to conceive, carry and deliver them. Not all men are emotionally fit to raise or be around children . . . . The raising of children must be considered a profession, one for which a person works in order to qualify . . . . Women can and are encouraged to receive degrees in home economics so that they may keep the house better for their husbands, cook better for their husbands, and handle their husband's money in the wisest manner. There are no expensive buildings or degrees available for the science of raising children. Plant science, pig science, if you like, but no child science.[3]

More and more Canadian mothers appear to prefer taking up paid jobs outside the home and using day-care arrangements so that even preschool children are, in effect, a shared responsibility between parents and other adults. The tax laws now made provision for this as a legitimate expense to be deducted from working mothers' incomes.[4]

What should we expect Canadian parenthood to be like, in the closing years of this century? Although our expectations are derived from speculative models based on extrapolations from, or critique of, what we know today, one is led to think that such predictions have some validity by the very fact that numerous independent writings, cited below, are concurring with regard to certain major trends. They are all

---

*From the author's article in S. Parvez Wakil, ed., 1976, *Marriage, Family, and Society.* Toronto: Butterworths.

attempting to predict the consequences of today's declining birth rates, rising abortion, divorce, venereal disease, geographic mobility, and so on.

We may expect a very fundamental change in our general view or understanding of what parenthood means. Whereas today the decision to have children and to determine aspects of their care and rearing (except formal education) is a private matter which is only affected by people outside the family in extreme cases of neglect or other distress, it is predicted by many authors that parenthood is going to be a much more public, professional and consequently, quality-oriented role than it has been. In other words, there appears to be a growing consensus that mothers and fathers in (urban) Canada are not private actors entitled to freely build a life which pleases them and which happens to include small children, but that insofar as they are producing society's future members they are actually discharging a community responsibility of the highest order, so that the consequences of this "stewardship" on behalf of society have to be drawn and acted upon. As Mary Van Stolk puts it:

> The belief that we should do nothing to diminish the authority of parents lends support to those parents who perpetrate acts of brutality upon children. In view of the fact that parents are among the major killers and maimers of North American children, it becomes imperative to recognize that we must not continue to allow parents to have this almost unlimited authority over children.[5]

Similarly, the professionalization of child rearing is being predicted very widely. Professionalization here means that, since child rearing will be understood as important work that must be kept under some kind of direct control by society, parents will have to be prepared for discharging those responsibilities related to it in an effective manner. This means that fathers and mothers will not be permitted to continue acting on impulse and emotion, with occasional guidance from the newspaper-columnist "expert" or a social worker (after trouble has caused some agency to be called in), but that all parents will have to acquire the knowledge and skills they require by training which precedes or accompanies their fulfillment of these responsibilities. Thus, education for parenthood is expected to become a standard part of the process preceding one's assumption of a mother or father role, so that some of what has been learned by scientists about childhood can be transferred from the pages of professional journals and monographs into the actual behaviour of adults who are responsible for raising children. Larson agrees with many American authors in predicting that training for child rearing is going to be required in future, instead of society's having to face the effects of bad parenting after the fact.[6]

This changed idea of parenthood as a representation of the community under the control of society may well mean not only that parents are prepared so as to be capable of doing the right thing for children, but also that the environment for all children will be supervised and assessed by the public authorities. The problems of the battered child have led some to think about changing the law in the direction of a more direct access to what is happening to children by agents of the state, and Davids has spoken about licensing for parenthood in the near future.[7] Since it is obvious that ecology—even in land-rich Canada—will eventually force us to limit population growth and therefore restrict the number of children reared by any given couple, it is most likely that future "mother of the year" contenders will be assessed not in terms of the quantity of their offspring, but by the quality of maternal performance as a child rearer, measured by the success of children according to the standards set by their community.

It is thus anticipated that homes will be "opened" to agencies and institutions in the community for participation in child care to a greater degree than at present.

The currect practice is that children who are not yet of school age are taken care of only by their parents, or by those directly appointed by the parents. It is only when the children are of school age that their care and socialization is shared by agents of society. In future, however, the privateness of child rearing is likely to diminish a great deal, and massive sharing by others in child rearing will begin at a much earlier age and affect many more children than at present.[8] Most notably, there have been repeated proposals that day care for children should not be an occasional or custodial measure (in cases where working mothers or early deprivation of children makes it necessary), but should be more and more a normal and accepted part of the child-rearing scene. There have been considerable discussions in the literature about professional day care as a positive force in the preschool development of Canadian children, which would be at least as adequate as traditional mother's care rather than being seen as a poor substitute used where child rearing by the mother alone is not possible.[9] Alternatively, some have suggested that formal education start earlier—at age two or three, say, rather than at five.[10]

This realization that old-style motherhood may be not at all the best thing for many children is reflected not only in proposals by such "angries" as Van Stolk, but in a self-help organization like Mothers Anonymous, which has been described in the mass media. Such groups indicated that values have changed sufficiently, in many places, that the old notions of privacy and parental exclusiveness—which prevented people from sharing their child-rearing difficultires with others—are now becoming a thing of the past, so that a major part of the Canadian population may soon be mentally ready for a situation in which parenthood is a communal, rather than a solo, speciality.[11]

Action in keeping with this new thinking has already appeared on the Canadian scene. Ryan reports on the programme of the Family Revitalization Experiment North District (FREND) which was set in motion by the family service agency of Hamilton, Ontario, a few years ago. An assessment of this programme, which included parent education and special enrichment programmes for preschool children, indicated that "the mothers in the programme seemed to achieve greater confidence in their roles as parents; the mothers appeared to become more sensitive to interaction patterns with their children; programme participation resulted in more optimistic attitudes about the neighbourhood's effect on children."[12] Thus, research begins to suggest that a programme that departs from the conventional thinking that parents should "do their own thing", and provides a considerable professional and community input, will provide real benefits for the families and the community.

In a similar vein, but taking a "far-out" stand, Whitehurst endorses radical children's liberation, and establishing new rights for children which could be exercised against their parents in ways heretofore unheard of. He writes:

> As a longer term goal, the establishment of an ombudsman for each child as an outside-family supervisor is a desirable goal. This would add some impetus to the child to begin to feel a sense of control over his own life earlier, and the feelings of entrapment involving child abuse, neglect and physical punishment could be rationally controlled by this outside influence. In some cases, children should be given the right of temporary or permanent separation or divorce from parents, in the same way that parents can legally use these separation techniques now. The gist of all this is to give the child back to himself.[13]

In regard to children's liberation (which is not very likely to progress in the way that Whitehurst suggests) we may predict considerable differences between more traditional, conservatively inclined eastern Canada and the rest of English-speaking North America. In Quebec and the Maritimes, which appear (from the vital statistics) not to change their culture and family habits as rapidly as Ontario or British Columbia,[14] respect for parents and age-prestige stratification in general may be more deeply ingrained in the ordinary citizen and more strongly upheld as a central value which must be adhered to for the sake of society. If this is so, then parental supervision and control will remain significant there longer than in the rest of Canada, which is more affluent, modern and anti-authoritarian. Such differences would be most noticeable, probably, in the case of early adolescents; there is great variation now in the degree to which twelve-to fifteen-year-olds are allowed to make their own decisions. These differences may gradually tend to become regional norms, with more guidance by parents in the rural and conservative parts of the country and more freedom for adolescents in other areas.

Conclusion

This paper has attempted to predict certain consequences of such major developments as the smaller number of children in Canadian families in the last quarter of this century, and various liberation trends that have opened up the traditional roles of women and children, thus permitting unprecedented variations to emerge. Patriarchal domination is disappearing and the traditional structure of intergenerational relationships in the Canadian family is soon likely to be replaced. Increasing supervision or penetration of parental functioning by public agencies has been predicted, which could include earlier schooling for children and rational controls over access to parenting roles. This has led us to serious thoughts about training for parenthood, as well as licensing. These speculations gain credibility by the fact that a number of independent sources have apparently converged in the belief that such developments are coming.

Greater freedom for young people living at home has also been predicted, although brevity has prevented our considering certain negative implications that are touched upon in the literature. In other words, many authors have simply accepted the idea that the old dependent roles of married women and children are going to fade away, without considering anomie, alienation and resultant conflict. We have also noted that there are enduring differences between various parts of Canada, in that the more conservative regions are likely to continue to exhibit more traditional forms of parental relationships than we would find in the areas with more rapid social and cultural change.

Notes

1. See E.E. LeMasters, *Parents in Modern America* (Homewood, Illinois: Dorsey Press, 1970), pp. 10-11; also Derek Miller's remarks in K. Elliott, *The Family and Its Future* (London: Longman Group, 1970), pp. 25 and 29-30.

2. Roslyn Burshtyn, ed., *Day Care – A Resource for the Contemporary Family* (Ottawa: Vanier Institute of the Family, 1970).

3. Mary Van Stolk, *Man and Woman* (Toronto: McClelland and Steward, 1968), pp. 134-135.

4. See *Tax Reform and You: Child Care Expenses* (Canada-National Revenue, Taxation Department, 1972). For one of the many reviews of women's paid employment, see *Report of the Royal Commission on the Status of Women in Canada* (Ottawa: Information Canada, 1970), pp. 52-60.

5. Mary Van Stolk, *The Battered Child in Canada* (Toronto: McClelland and Stewart, 1972), p. 100. See also R.N. Whitehurst "Families: Some Revolutionary Potentials and Radical Proposals" (paper presented to the Ohio Valley Sociological Society at London, Ontario, 19 May 1972)p. 12; and L. Davids, "North American Marriage: 1990", *the Futurists,* vol. 5, no. 5 (October 1971), pp. 190-194.

6. Lyle W. Larson, "The Family in Contemporary Society and Emerging Family Patterns", in *Day Care,* ed. R. Burshtyn, pp. 37-38.

7. Davids, "North American Marriage: 1990", p. 193.

8. This is in keeping with the prediction in that Canadians will be faced with a sharply rising "invasion of privacy through data banks and monitoring devices". See Harold J. Dyck, *Social Futures Alberta 1970-2005* (Edmonton: Human Resources Research Council of Alberta, 1970), p. 46.

9. Thomas J. Ryan, ed., *Poverty and the Child* (Toronto: McGraw-Hill Ryerson, 1972), pp. 237-238.

10. Farson, Richard E. et al., *The Future of the Family* (New York: Family Service Association of America, 1969), pp. 34 and 119. Also, see Larry Shorter, "Early Childhood Education", *Education Canada,* vol. 13, no. 2 (June 1973), pp. 5-9.

11. Lisa Hobbs, "Mothers Anonymous", *Chatelaine*, vol. 45, no. 10 (October 1972), p. 66. Some exploration of the "privacy" issue can be found on pp. 95-98 of Farson et al., *The Future of the Family.*

12. Thomas J. Ryan, "Canadian Intervention Programmes", in *Poverty and the Child,* chapter X, p.205.

13. Robert N. Whitehurst, "Families: Some Revolutionary Potentials and Radical Proposals". See similar thoughts in Marvin A. Zuker and June Callwood, *Canadian Women and the Law* (Toronto: Copp Clark, 1971), p.45. They also propose a guaranteed annual income for children, separate from that of parents.

14. Eastern Canada has consistently lower abortion and divorce rates, for instance, than the North and West. There are very large statistical differences between Newfoundland and British Columbia in most of the relevant data series, including birth rate or suicide as well as abortion and divorce. See *Preliminary Annual Report - Vital Statistics: 1971,* catalogue no. 84-201 (Ottawa: Information Canada, 1973), table 2, p.8.

Part II Section C

ADULTHOOD AND THE WORK WORLD

12

Greek Working-Class Immigrants in Toronto*

Judith A. Nagata

Early in the course of research it became clear that recent Greek immigrants of the working class are typically involved in relatively small social networks, hence are socially isolated and fragmented. Not only are their linkages with the wider host society limited but even their ties with other Greeks and with Greek ethnic institutions are minimal. Characteristic of this segment of the Greek population, too, is their inadequate command of the English language, an apparently high degree of cultural conservatism, and considerable residential segregation in the East End of the city, which has resulted in a certain institutional, cultural, and linguistic self-sufficiency in that area. Approximately 50 per cent of the new immigrants fall into the category of unskilled labour.

It is my intention in the present paper, first, to describe the general social organization of the Toronto Greeks as a whole, and the place of the new working-class migrants in that organization. I shall then examine more closely the social circumstances in which the newcomers find themselves and the nature of their adaptation to these conditions.

Greek immigration to Canada began early in the present century, although it did not gather momentum until the years following World War II.[1] From approximately the middle of the 1950s the rate has shown a consistent annual increase and continues to do so.

Before 1910 there were only about 200 Greeks in the entire city of Toronto while by 1942, there were estimated to be approximately 1200. By 1958 the figure of 12,500 Greek residents in Toronto indicates that the intensive wave of migration from Greece had begun. The Greek settlement in Toronto today might be between 35,000 and 40,000.

An overwhelming majority of Greeks entering Canada (about 97 per cent) may be designated as working class, including both unskilled and semi-skilled categories in approximately equal ratios. The remaining migrants comprise a variety of professional and business occupations which provide immediate access to the middle ranks

---

* Abridged from *International Migration Review,* No. 4 (Fall, 1969). By permission of the publisher. The author expresses her appreciation to Marilyn Salutin, her research assistant, and acknowledges the receipt of a grant from the Citizenship Branch, Department of the Provincial Secretary and Citizenship, Ontario.

of both Greek and Canadian society. Of the working class segment, most are of exclusively rural background, the exceptions having generally migrated from Athens.

Almost without exception, the ability to speak English by Greek immigrants on their arrival in Canada is very low. Definicency in the English language is in part related to complete lack of education beyond the six years elementary schooling whch is all that is available in the rural areas of Greece.

For purposes of the present paper the assumption will be made that the recent Greek immigrants (i.e., within the last ten years or so) may be equated with the working class, and that in general the second (and third) generation of Greeks may be considered members of the middle or upper-middle class.

Institutional Structures of the Greek Settlement

In no sense can the aggregate of Greeks who have come to settle in Toronto be referred to as a "community". No all-embracing pattern of organization provides the basis for integration or for the frequent and close interaction necessary for a community in the sociological sense. Nor are there clearly demarcated boundaries. Only in the most general respect can there be said to exist a collective consciousness or identity of Greekness, and this rarely finds any form of overall institutional expression.

In reality, the heterogeneity of the Canadian Greeks, both along lines of class and of place of origin within Greece, tends to be pervasive and effectively obstructs any overall unity of the settlement. Not only does internal stratification create horizontal lines of cleavage, but a futher division cleaves the settlement along vertical lines, that is, cross-cutting socio-economic distinctions. This is the Macedonian-Southern Greek division. Macedonia, the northern part of Greece, also bears a somewhat different linguistic and cultural heritage from the rest of the country, and despite nominal political unity with the south, has largely retained its separate identity. Migration from Macedonia has always been heavy, for both economic and political reasons. While no census or other official figures are available, it is estimated by Macedonian informants that at least 55 per cent of the "Greeks" entering Toronto are in fact, Macedonian.

Notwithstanding the lack of social and cultural homogeneity among the Greeks as a whole, an attempt is made by the Greek Orthodox Church to perpetuate the concept of the "spiritual community" *(Kinotis)* which is used to designate any body of Greeks, whether in their homeland or an enclave overseas. This is a peculiarly Greek concept whereby all members of a Greek settlement and the congregation of its Church are ideally synonymous. In ideal, the Church would provide the overall structure required to integrate the settlement into one sacred community. In this spiritual community the main life crises, social activities, and enterprises of its members would receive religious sanction and priestly blessing. Only in theory, however, does this spiritual meaning of the community live on. In most modern urban Greek settlements, Toronto included, the term has taken on a more specialized connotation. Today, the *Kinotis* refers more narrowly to those Greeks who have paid their annual dues of $26 per person for formal membership in the Church. Out of the total complement of the 40,000 Greeks estimated to be resident in the city, a scant 1200 individuals, or approximately 3.3 per cent, are fully paid members of the Orthodox congregation. This congregation has the privilege of electing from its membership a highly elite committee of twenty-five members, also known loosely as the *Kinotis* or "Community". The committee consists entirely of laymen who conduct and administer the "non-spiritual" affairs of the Church, namely, the finances, social activities, and Greek language classes. As may be readily perceived, this arrangement places considerable power in the hands of the committee, even to the extent that they can steer the "official" policies of the priest and Church along the lines they most favour.

The council of twenty-five, or the *Kinotis* of the narrowest range, is composed exclusively of second and third generation individuals of Greek origin, who are also clearly of the middle and upper-middle class, prosperous, and successful by the standards of the wider Canadian society. Further, the evidence points to a continual rotation of committee offices between the same small clique of prominent Greeks from year to year. Ties between some of these families are cemented by intermarriage, between others by professional and business interests. Undoubtedly this small group of laymen has been effective in establishing and entrenching its power within its own domain.

The actual power of the Church committee derives from the members' financial and organizational skills. The Greek Orthodox Church overseas is little more than just another ethnic institution which, like all other institutions, requires funds. Divorced from the sources of financial support that traditionally fed the Church in its homeland, new sources must be tapped, and success in this domain lies largely in maintaining the loyalties of all Greeks to their faith and to their culture. Consequently, the overseas Church has acquired a reputation both as a Greek culture-preserving force and as a financially demanding institution.

Political skills are also applied to this task of fund-raising by the committee, particularly through their administration of a number of ethnic associations. A large variety of voluntary associations, representing regional, Church, professional, business, and philanthropic interests, have arisen in Toronto, some as branches of organizations founded in other cities of the United States and Canada. Some of these associations are explicitly, by their membership requirement, [2] designed for the elites. Among these would be the various business and fraternal men's organizations. The rest, however, are formally open to membership by all Greeks. Regional associations in particular would seem to have a potential appeal for all emigrants from the same area of Greece, but, in practice, few of the newcomers actually join. Partly this is due to the fund-raising functions of the regional clubs, partly because of their domination by the same small body of prominent individuals who control the Church. Indeed, most of the associations are directly sponsored by the Church, use its facilities, and contribute to its coffers.

It may be said, by way of summary of the formal organizations of the Toronto Greeks, that the ethnic institutions tend to be both culturally conservative and monopolized by a core of families who play multiple leadership roles in many of them. Few of the recently arrived, working-class immigrants, however, participate in the activities of the formal ethnic organizations. Contrary to the claims of the "leaders" themselves, therefore, they are not representative of the Greeks as a whole, and are frequently totally unknown to the working-class population whom they are supposed to "lead".

Social and Cultural Adaptation of Recent Immigrants

In view of the rather sharp social disjunctions created by the patterns of stratification sketched above, and in view of the fact that little material assistance or social orientation is forthcoming to the newcomers within their own ethnic group, how do new immigrants establish themselves? More specifically, how do the newcomers accommodate to the requirements of life in Canada, and in what sense can they be said to be "integrated" into Canadian society? It is suggested that, in the initial stages at least, structural or objective integration is greater than the subjective, and that public behaviour is very different from that in the private sector of life. Considerable compartmentalization of the two sectors emerges at this stage.

This distinction is fequently tempered, however, by the demands made upon the private sector by the public: the impingements of employment on traditional family patterns, of education on linguistic integrity. What apparently emerges is not so much a "unilinear" model of acculturation, whereby individuals become progressively "less Greek" or more "Canadian", and from which no reversal is possible, but a "situational" process in which sometimes Greekness prevails, sometimes Canadianness. The norms and behaviours that prevail on any particular occasion depend as much on expediency as on loyalties to either culture.

The applicability of this oscillating model of acculturation will now be examined in the light of the data on recent Greek immigrants.[3] From the total social networks of the migrants studied illustrations will be given as to the degree of participation and apparent commitment to Greek and Canadian institutions respectively. I shall then attempt to indicate the extent to which accomodations seem to occur between the public and private sectors of life, and in what situations.

The Private Domain

The Family

At the core of the social network of most Greek immigrants is the family. Within the extended family which may extend as far as the first collateral line or first cousins, the family is customarily both close-knit and male-dominated. It is also the realm in which Greek culture probably persists most tenaciously, particularly those customs pertaining to sex, courting and marriage preferences, language, food habits, patterns of authority, and recreational pursuits. The family is also the group within which sponsorship operates, and the most frequent visiting takes place.

For some of the families interviewed, the limits of the extended family (whether or not co-resident) also provides the boundaries of their informal social network. Some respondents claimed to be acquainted with no other family save immediate kin, and the average number of families known to those in my sample was as low as ten. It appears to be the exceptional immigrant who has more than twenty or thirty acquaintances, and these generally arise as a result of participation in a trade or an ethnic association. Further, unless they live very close to one another, even kin visiting is infrequent, and may be restricted to major ceremonial occasions, that is, a few times a year. Friendships with non-kin rarely cross ethnic lines, and do not even seem to extend to neighbours of another ethnic group.

The strongest forces for Greek cultural conservatism within the family are often exerted by aged relatives, such as grandparents, who never join the labour force, rarely go out unaccompanied, and never need to learn English. These are the individuals who often bring pressures to bear on the Canadian-born children in the family, particularly in matters of linguistic and friendship behaviours.

Membership in Greek Associations

It has already been noted that both formal Church and associational memberships on the part of new immigrants tend to be low. A mere 18 per cent of my sample had ever attended any association gathering, mostly as non-member guests at open activities. Only 10 per cent of those who had attended knew the name of the club president or could describe the main goals and activities of the group. Two individuals alone had ever been paid association members, and in each case had dropped their memberships through disillusionment. The formal organizations represent a Greek cultural domain, therefore, in which the newcomers seem to participate but peripherally. While all respondents without exception claimed to be subscribers to the Greek Orthodox faith, attendance at church was generally poor and sporadic. By contrast, attendance at church by those Greeks of the higher socio-economic levels, who are also prominent in the ethnic institutional structure, appeared to be much more frequent.

The Greek Orthodox Church is remarkable for its qualities as a culture-preserving institution. It attempts to maintain Greek loyalties by providing essential social services, by its Greek language classes, its stress on ties with the homeland, and by its patronage of the ethnic associations. In his Sunday sermons too, the priest is not notable for encouraging integration into Canadian life or the learning of English among his congregation. Most of the emphasis, rather, lies in encouragement of contributions to Greek charities and organizations, of attendance at Greek classes and of Greek "civilization". The sentiment of Greekness exists independently of the church, however, in the light of the low esteem for the overseas church held by most immigrants and of their minimal participation in its activities.

Restrictions on more active participation emerge on two fronts. The first is the highly stratified nature of the Greek organizations which inhibit extensive lower-class participation. The second restriction is probably imposed as a direct result of the conditions of employment in Canada. Erratic working hours, night shifts, working wives, and fatigue all deprive the migrants of the opportunity for enjoying activities within their own ethnic group, and this tends to be reinforced by a general attitude of delaying gratification which pervades so much of immigrant life in the early years in this country.

Language and Culture

In the linguistic sphere Greeks of both sexes, of first and second generation and of all socio-economic strata, manifest considerable conservatism. All the new immigrants recognize the inevitability of their children's learning English in this country, but out of a total of 76 parents to whom the question of the linguistic training of children applied, only one of the fathers expressed the desire for his offspring to be monolingual English speakers. The remainder were unanimous in their support of bilingualism (either Greek and English or Macedonian and English), and despite their indifference or hostility to the Greek Orthodox Church in this country, many parents would have liked to be able to send their children to the Greek language classes offered by the church. Most, however, were unable to afford the cost of $40 per month, while the hours of class (5 to 7 p.m.) were prohibitive to those mothers who were working. Most of the recently arrived Greek children therefore must learn their mother tongue from other relatives at home, but may never learn Katharevousa[4] nor how to write the language correctly. The students in the church-run Greek classes are almost without exception children of second and third generation Greeks, who appear to remain very conscious of their heritage.[5]

All the immigrants, however, admit the need to increase their competence in English. All are willing to learn, although their rate of improvement is often agonizingly slow. It must be recognized, however, that the slowness of many Greek immigrants in learning English is not entirely due to cultural conservatism. Other factors intervene. One of these is that employment of new-comers is frequently obtaned in a non-English-speaking environment: either employer and co-workers are also Greek, or they may speak Italian or Yiddish or some other tongue. Even where English language classes are available at night school or the International Institute, shift work, overtime, and general fatigue are usually sufficient to prohibit consistent attendance and study. In one case where an opportunity for learning English together with nursery facilities was provided for immigrant women, it was admitted by most students that attendance was only provisional until such time as a suitable job would be available. In some respects, therefore, greater structural integration through participation in the economy of the wider society may jeopardize the acculturation of the immigrants in other domains.

National Identity

Greeks of all backgrounds generally exhibit a strong interest in politics. Their interest, however, even in the second generation, appears to remain with the political fortunes of their homeland. Some of the deepest cleavages in the settlement today follow political lines, and seem to fall into three major categories: pro-royalist, pro-junta, and supporters of the Committee for the Restoration of Democracy. The majority of the latter come from the working class, while the projunta line tends to be the "official" line of the Church, that is, of the *Kinotis* committee, and thus it reinforces the stratification patterns. None of the recent immigrants showed any knowledge of the Canadian political scene despite the fact that it was a national election year, and, unlike the Italians, the Greeks have no "ethnic" representative.

As far as commitment to Canada as a nation is concerned, it emerged that very few of the newer immigrants had ever thought very deeply about nationality. The highly personal little world in which most of them live does not encourage such conceptual abstractions, and few have thought further than immediate needs of jobs and families, sponsoring relatives from Greece, and buying a home. The immigrants I came to know invariably referred to themselves as "Greeks", never as "Canadians", nor even as "Greek-Canadians". In the initial stages, most immigrants are firmly convinced that their stay will be a temporary one, during which they will amass their fortune, educate their children, then return to Greece. It is usually only a matter of a few years, however, before the new arrivals have realized that Canada has become their permanent home, and plans for buying a house in the city are underway. For many, the fortune cannot be amassed as swiftly as anticipated, and many more realize that they are in better circumstances here than they could ever be in Greece.

Although much of the evidence points in the direction of strong preferences for Greek culture and behaviour, particularly in the more private social domains, closer examination indicates that this is not necessarily from inertia or conservatism alone. Numerous external pressures, stemming from initial lack of certain skills, lack of opportunity, ignorance, and financial exigency all play their part in contributing to a considerable degree of encapsulation within the ethnic group and in reducing the immigrants' potential for participating in a wider social network.

Social Network

Maintenance of a restricted range of social ties within the ethnic group also appears to be characteristic of the use of special services by the average working-class Greek. Utilization of professional services (e.g., those of lawyers, doctors, real estate dealers) of Greek origin tends to exceed the patronage of their English-Canadian counterparts. It would seem that the reasons may be sought, however, less in ethnic loyalties or cultural preference than in linguistic expediency.

It is worthy of note that special services, such as explanation of tax forms and union contracts, are available through the somewhat unlikely medium of the Greek travel agencies who regularly provide such information for a fee. The priests likewise will furnish letters of reference to employers, insurance companies, and the Immigration Department at a standard fee of $20 per letter. In these latter cases, it must be recognized that Greek immigrants seek out services from within their own ethnic group, not through any strong sense of cultural commitment or ethnic loyalty, but merely from force of circumstance by which either no alternatives are available or are not known to be available.

The Public Domain

I turn now to the involvement of Greek migrants in the wider "host" society, and to their participation in Canadian institutions. I will try to assess to what extent their public behaviour appears to reflect a change in reference group (i.e., adoption of Canadian norms and their internalization), and how far observable changes may be considered the result of severe external constraints, and only temporary.

Employment

By far the most extensive involvement of the Greek immigrants with the wider society is through the medium of employment, and to the extent that employment is with non-Greek agencies it represents a major form of structural integration. Direct participation in Canadian economic institutions is probably greater among present-day immigrants than was the case one or two generations ago, partly because fewer of the new arrivals are self-employed. Before World War II it was characteristic of Greek (and Macedonian) immigrants that they created occupations rather than entering into jobs in existence. Prominent among the occupations created were restaurants, food importing businesses, tailoring and fur-making establishments. Today, however, possibly because fewer economic niches of this variety are available, and also in view of the relatively larger amounts of capital necessary for such enterprises, few immigrants move into these service industries. Only 5 per cent of the working family heads among my interviewees were self-employed (one tailor, one furrier, and one shoe repair shop owner) while the overwhelming majority were in labouring and manual occupations. Approximately 50 percent of these were unskilled, and employed as factory workers, dry cleaners, waiters, cooks, and floor sweepers. In the semi-skilled category, those most commonly found included electricians, carpenters, mechanics, bookkeepers, and welders. Most of the unskilled workers expressed satisfaction with their jobs, and felt that they were more prosperous and secure in Canada than in Greece. Among their more skilled counterparts, however, some dissatisfaction was voiced. Several of them claimed to be unable to obtain jobs commensurate with their skills, either because their Greek diplomas were not recognized in Canada, due to "lack of Canadian experience", or through the unavailability of suitable jobs. Consequently, these men felt they had suffered downward mobility since their emigration from Greece.

Most immigrants come to Canada with the avowed aim of improving their economic status, at least in the future if not immediately, particularly in the interests of their offspring. As a result, most are willing to work excessively long hours, and under substandard conditions if necessary, in order to save. Moonlighting is common, as is work on unpopular shifts (as many as 40 per cent of my respondents worked in the late evening or at night) which seriously disrupts the ideal Greek family patterns. Some men are reduced to baby-sitting functions while their wives work during the daytime, an occupation that in Greece would be regarded as insulting to their masculinity. Such work patterns also curtail very effectively the extent to which recreational pursuits and convivial visiting can be enjoyed. This may be an important factor, therefore, contributing to the small size of the social network of the average Greek newcomer.

Traditional Greek family patterns are further modified by the exigencies of employment. An extremely high incidence of working Greek women runs in diametric opposition to the situation in the homeland, where even women with such trades as hairdressing and dressmaking are employed within the home. In Toronto, where many unskilled jobs are available for women, as many as 86 per cent of my sample were employed, full- or part-time, despite the fact that most are also mothers of small children. This has a number of implications. First, it alters the ideal patterns of authority within the family, since her job responsibilities and economic contribution provide the working wife with somewhat more autonomy than she would otherwise enjoy. This is reinforced by the necessary baby-sitting tasks of some husbands who correspondingly lose status. Second, it has resulted in a growing acceptance of the idea of special babysitting service or day care. Several Greek women now have established for themselves a full-time job in caring for the off-spring of other working mothers (for a daily fee). That the whole idea of leaving one's children with non-kin is still not fully accepted, however, is made clear by the fact that some families prefer to sponsor dependent aged kin (mothers, mothers-in-law, grandparents) to fulfil this function and enable the wives to work.

Although attempts are made to rationalize the entry of their womenfolk into the labour force by Greek males--for example, by claiming that the fruits of their labour merely represent a substitute for the dowry *(prika)* that would have accrued to them in more traditional circumstances--there is little doubt that most of the men find the custom difficult to accept.[6] Financial necessity, however, usually prevails over traditional Greek values, hence adherence to Greek culture is in this case latent.

Female employment also enjoins the other forms of forced accommodation that affect the male worker: limitations in social contacts with recreational activities and the constant stress on delayed gradification. All interest and reward lies in the future, often only in the future of the children. Somewhat paradoxically, however, the almost constant involvement of both parents in their jobs may be seen to be detrimental to the children. Little time is available for parents to take an active interest in the education of the latter, to attend PTA meetings or even to take them to the Greek language classes. In fact, few working-class Greek parents seem to regard eduction beyond the lower grades as potentially important in the upward mobility of their own offspring.

Other Social Linkages

Other activities that bring Greeks into contact with Canadian instutions do not appear to require the degree of social and cultural accommodation that work conditions entail. Most Greeks shop at English-Canadian stores, mainly for reasons of price, and only patronize Greek establishments for ethnic specialties. None of my respondents shopped exclusively at Greek stores. Peripheral contact only is made with such Canadian institutions as banks and post offices, and may be mediated for non-English speakers through bilingual friends. Many activities, of course, including travel and shopping, can be accomplished without the exchange of words. Use of government services, such as Manpower and welfare offices, legal aid or the police, again tends to be low, largely due to ignorance of their availability. Significantly, the one most frequently used is the Department of Manpower, for employment.

In general it may be said that, aside from the employment factor, Canadian institutional involvement is low, and insofar as it occurs, does not entail the major modifications in traditional custom or language required by conditions of work. A fairly full life (within the above-mentioned limitations) can be lived in a Greek institutional and cultural framework, and there is little doubt that a considerable amount of cultural conservatism encourages this pattern.

Conclusions

Most of the evidence from the life styles of recent Greek immigrants of the working class does reveal a certain compartmentalization between two broad spheres of activity. These may provisionally be designated the public and private sectors of life. Attempts are made, as far as possible, to retain Greek language and culture in family, recreational, and religious domains, and to segregate these from obligatory involvements with external institutions or the public domain--for example, work and education. On the other hand, it is clear that the Greek and Canadian sectors of life overlap and interact with one another resulting in mutual accommodations which may vary with the individual occasion.

The position of the recently arrived, working-class Greek immigrant may be conceptualized as one of precarious marginality in which two social networks must be managed and a narrow course steered between the demands of two cultures. It is not so much a question of permanently discarding one culture or parts thereof in favour of the other, nor yet as a unilinear process in one direction or the other. Frequently, observed behaviours that are classified as more or less Greek or Canadian respectively are generated as a result of local circumstance or individual situation, and are not best interpreted as manifestations of "degrees of acculturation". In practice, however, the demands of structural or institutional ties may cause Greek values to be suppressed, and even rationalized away (e.g., the "dowry" interpretation of working woman).

One additional variable in the general pattern of situational selection of behaviour is undoubtedly that of the internal organization of the Greek settlement itself. The conservative forces exercised by the formal ethnic institutions (church and associations) are only effective insofar as the newcomers participate in their activities and subscribe to their beliefs. Since most newcomers are alienated from these organizations, however, they are relatively immune from their conservative influence, and in the case of religion at least individuals may be driven to attend other churches outside the Greek domain.

If we may for the moment extrapolate from the experiences of the present second generation of Greeks, now largely of the higher social strata, it is suggested that the new immigrants will follow substantially similar avenues of upward mobility once travelled by their predecessors. This appears to be characterized by an all-out effort, in the course of which many Greek values must temporarily be set aside. Family and recreational life may suffer as a result, and Greek cultural interests appear to be threatened on all fronts. That this is only a temporary expedient, however, an example of situational selection, may be inferred from the fact that once social and economic security is attained, by the standards of the wider society, the individual will then frequently begin to take part in the associational and other institutional life of the Greek settlement.

In summary then, it is suggested that one possible approach to the study of that complex process variously known as "integration" and "acculturation" is by means of a situational method, in which two sets of cultural norms may co-exist and alternately re-assert themselves in the appropriate context.

Notes

1. George D. Vlassis, *The Greeks in Canada* (Ottawa, 1953).

2. Some associations require, as a condition of membership, fluency in English, Canadian citizenship, and a sponsor within the organization.

3. Most intensive interviews were obtained from a sample of 44 families, consisting of 22 students at the language school and 22 controls. Additional open-ended and structured interviews were held with many other recent, working-class immigrants, however, bringing the total number of respondents to almost 100. The percentages cited in the text apply only to the basic sample of 44.

4. In modern Greek greater distinctions exist between the literary form of the language, *Katharevousa,* and the popular form, or *Demotiki*, than in English. *Demotiki* is normally spoken in the home by the working and rural classes, while *Katharevousa* is taught in the schools.

5. The same appears to be true of second and third generation Greeks in the United States. See, for example, E. Vlachos, "The Assimilation of Greeks in the United States: With Special Reference to the Greek Community of Anderson, Indiana", Ph.D. Thesis, University of Indiana, 1964. Similar conclusions are reached by R. Theodoratus, in "The Influence of the Homeland on the Social Organization of a Greek Community in America", Ph.D. Thesis, University of Washington, 1961.

6. Women likewise may find it difficult to adapt to this custom. On several occasions women tried to disguise from me the fact that they were working, and they apparently regularly withhold this information from the school authorities when registering their children. My only interpretation is that to them it causes some shame or embarrassment.

13

Women Workers and White-Collar Unions*

Patricia Marchak

Three salient features of Canada's labour force, according to the 1961 census, were the ratio favouring white-collar to manual workers (39 to 35 per cent of the total); the increasing proportion of working women (29.5 per cent of all women, 50 per cent of whom were married); and the high proportion of working women who occupy white-collar jobs (57 per cent of all working women and 41 per cent of all white-collar workers) (Canada, Department of Labour, 1968: Tables 4, 5, and Chart 1).

These features, which have emerged since the mid-1950s, are critical to the continued strength of trade unionism. Union membership in Canada rose fairly steadily from the 1920s to the late 1950s. Since 1959, however, the percentage of union members in the non-agricultural labour force has levelled off, even declining slightly during the mid-1960s (Canada, Department of Labour, 1968: Table 1). In British Columbia, which has had a higher proportion of its labour force organized than Canada as a whole, the same trend has become apparent. After a steady climb to 1958, the proportion of workers who were organized declined during the mid-1960s and appear to have levelled off over the past several years. Unions have drawn their membership and strength in a male-dominated manual labour force. They have never been successful in recruiting substantial portions of white-collar workers. One of the reasons frequently cited for this failure is the high proportion of women in that sector. Women, it is claimed, are less committed to the labour force and are therefore less interested in unions. Their lack of commitment is assumed to be due to their temporary involvement with jobs, prior to and following the raising of a family (Blum et al, 1971: 34, 63, 76; Sturmthal, 1966: 356, 375). If the present trend toward a predominantly white-collar labour force with a high proportion of women workers continues, then we might expect a decline in union membership. However, it is apparent that increasing numbers of women are permanently involved in the labour force, and that raising a family is no longer as extreme a barrier to participation as it has been in the past. In addition, the general level of education for women, as well as for men, has steadily risen, and this factor may motivate women to seek careers, or at least to exercise skills and talents encouraged in the education process (Ostry, 1970). Lack of commitment to work may, therefore, no longer be either an explanation for women's lack of interest in unions (which has been assumed, rather than demonstrated), nor a reason for the failure of unions to organize white-collar workers.

The predisposing factors toward union membership are not clear. Although North American unions have been directed alomost exclusively toward material issues, fluctuations in recruitment have not been as closely associated with economic trends as anticipated by earlier theories (Commons, 1958; Wolmar, 1936).

The most consistent theoretical rationale has explained membership in terms of bargaining strength. Workers with low job security, low upward mobility, low control over work processes, and easy replaceability are in weak bargaining positions. Their incomes are, therefore, low. It is these who have the highest union potential (Marx, 1867; Webb, 1965; Perlman, 1928; Hoxie, 1928; Barbash, 1948).

---

*Abridged from the *Canadian Review of Sociology and Anthropology* 10:2, 1973, with the permission of the author and the Canadian Sociology and Anthropology Association.

It is assumed by those who wish to explain the failure of white-collar workers to join unions that these workers have not suffered these conditions in sufficient numbers to give rise to strong unions. In addition, some theorists have argued that the failure to organize white-collar workers lies with their tendency to identify with management, and to consider unions as "blue-collar" associations (Mills, 1951).

Women in the white-collar labour force, however, do experience these conditions. With the possible exception of job security, their work is characterised by all the factors associated with weak bargaining positions. If, then, these factors are the source of union membership, white-collar women should have high union potential.

Sample Selection

A survey of white-collar workers in British Columbia was undertaken in the summer of 1969 to learn the attitudes of these workers toward unions, and the correlation between attitudes and the various factors cited above. The respondents were selected in the following way: first, all firms having white-collar workers covered by union contracts were listed. Lists of firms in corresponding size, location, and product areas without union coverage were then compiled, and a random sampling of the second lists was made. The union list could not be sampled, since the total number of entries was limited. A total of 153 firms were contacted by letter and telephone, requesting interviews with employees. Of these 111 refused. Of the 42 remaining firms, 20 were unionised. Between 5 and 25 employees were interviewed in each firm, depending on the total number of white-collar workers employed. The interviewees where chosen by the surveyers from lists of employees provided by employers. Workers were chosen in as wide a variety of occupations as possible, with a rough rule of thumb to maintain over-all proportions similar to those of the 1961 census distributions. Of the sample of 307 persons, 47 per cent were union members; 49 per cent were clerical workers, 28 per cent were professional or technical workers, 5 per cent were administrative (non-managerial level) workers, 12 per cent were in saleswork, and 6 per cent were in marginal white-collar service jobs. Forty-nine per cent were women.

Job Characteristics

Percentage differences between the sexes were computed with respect to job descriptions, job control levels, employment plans, expectations of promotions, estimates of job security and replaceability, income, personal assessments of income levels, and beliefs about the importance of sex in promotions. Income data were obtained from employers and personnel records. Job description data were obtained from extensive and detailed descriptions provided both by respondents and employers, and were rated by two coders (with cross-checks for comparability) for skills and for personal discretion or control of work processes on ordinal scales. The scales reported below are short forms of these codes. For example, the "Machine-Work" code has as its "machine-controlled" level: "works constantly with machines, machines determine the work-load and pace; worker tends the machines, but does not initiate or choose timing of use." The second level involves constant work with machines but with some options open to the operator; the third level involves much work with machines, but with many options for timing, pacing, etc.; and the fourth level involves no work or very little work with machines and the worker is not tied to or programmed for machine work.

Differences Between Union and Non-Union Workers

The same inequalities between the sexes were found for both the non-union and union samples. Women enjoyed less control over their jobs, received lower incomes, and had fewer hopes for promotion, especially into management positions, than did men in the same sector of the labour force. These inequalities remained when educational levels were held constant. Income inequalities remained also when levels of job control were held constant.

Some differences in job control and income distributions were found within the sex groupings by union status. A lower proportion of union women than of non-union women exercised high job control, and this difference persisted when educational levels were held constant. Differences in job control among men by union status were relatively small and not consistent.

Table I

Job Descriptions (Percentage at each level*)

	Male	Female		Male	Female
Machine work			**Decisions involving materials**		
machine-controlled	7	20	none	15	44
op. some control	6	17	little	31	44
op. controls	22	30	fair amount	36	9
no machine work	65	33	great deal	18	3
Verbal skills required			**Idea generation, discussions on ideas**		
not at all	20	42	not at all	45	80
not very much	41	46	not very much	37	11
fair amount	27	8	fair amount	8	6
much	12	5	great deal	10	3
Task complexity			**Extend to which worker completes own product/process**		
simple procedures	21	48	not at all	41	66
some complex tasks	32	35	little	7	17
fairly complex	39	14	fair amount	21	8
very complex	8	3	great deal	31	10
Extent to which knowledge of particular company important			**Extent to which job integrated in main production process of firm**		
not at all	27	36	not at all	21	54
little	25	29	little	23	12
some, fair amount	32	9	some	32	22
great deal	16	7	great deal	24	14

* In some instances, percentages do not add to 100 due to rounding errors.

Table II

Job Control

Dimension	Degree	Per cent		Dimension	Degree	Per cent	
		Men	Women			Men	Women
Choice on task content	none	19	47	Choice on task sequencing	none	17	46
	little	27	25		little	29	30
	fair amt.	41	24		fair amt.	43	23
	great deal	13	3*		great deal	11	1
Choice on task pacing	none	26	51	Amt. of supervision (direct)	none	32	13
	little	17	23		little	28	27
	fair amt.	45	25		fair amt.	24	32
	great deal	12	1		great deal	16	28
Control over quality of product	none	23	58	Control over quantity of work	none	22	54
	little	43	28		little	33	33
	fair amt.	27	13		fair amt.	40	12
	great deal	7	1		great deal	5	1
Choice on time allocation (stops, starts, breaks)	none	38	64	Choice on space for work, variation of space use	none	29	59
	little	33	28		little	33	30
	fair amt.	22	7		fair amt.	28	10
	great deal	7	1		great deal	10	1

*Does not add to 100 due to rounding errors.

A higher proportion of union than of non-union workers were at the lowest levels of the income scales and this was more marked for women than for men. However, three-quarters of all women earned $450 a month or less regardless of union status. Ninety-four per cent of non-union men and 64 per cent of union men with high school diplomas earned the higher income; 24 per cent of non-union women and 9 per cent of union women did likewise. Over-all, 79 per cent of all men and 18 per cent of all women with high school education earned over $450 per month. When educational levels were held constant, a much higher proportion of non-union than of union workers earned incomes over $450 per month, yet the differences between the sexes in both subsamples was greater than that by union status. Slightly higher proportions of union than of non-union workers with high job control earned $450 or more, yet the differences in proportions in that income group between the sexes in unions was 52 per cent, and outside the unions, was 46 per cent. Low control women workers fared no better: there was a 68 per cent difference between the proportion of union women and than of union men who earned $450 or more, a 32 per cent difference between non-union women and non-union men.

Table III

Income Distribution Cumulative Percentages

Amount	Total sample	Men			Women		
		all	non-union	union	all	non-union	union
$300 or less	8	1	0	1	12	18	9
$350 or less	17	1	1	1	34	29	40
$400 or less	37	7	6	11	65	61	71
$450 or less	48	21	14	27	77	76	78
$500 or less	57	28	22	34	87	89	87
$550 or less	71	49	40	58	94	94	96
$600 or less	78	59	57	61	96	96	97
$650 or less	83	70	64	76	97	97	99
$700 or less	87	77	68	85	98	99	99
$750 or less	90	82	74	93	98	99	99
$800 or less	92	86	81	93	98	99	99
100 percent =	298	151	77	74	147	79	68
Income data unavailable	9	4	4		5	4	1

Of particular interest, the income of union men was congruent with job control levels, with high income associated with high control, low income associated with low control. Non-union men had considerably less-consistent associations between income and control. Union status did not confer consistent incomes at control levels for women, who, like non-union women, were mainly found in the low income brackets.

In short, regardless of comparability in other relevant respects (education and job control), and regardless of status with respect to unions, women in the white-collar labour force earned considerably less than men in the same work areas.

Commitment

Sixty-eight per cent of the women as compared to 58 per cent of the men planned to stay with their present jobs, and the slight differences between the sexes in intended future involvement in the labour force was in favour of women (84 to 81 per cent). The reasons of those who proposed to withdraw differed by sex, but for every woman who planned to rear a family, there was a man who planned further education, travel, or retirement. A question regarding past involvement in the labour force showed that 67 per cent of the men and 49 per cent of the women had been continuously employed since taking their first jobs; and 27 per cent of the women had interrupted their work to rear families, but had since returned to work.

Replaceability

Responses regarding job security showed that the majority of respondents of both sexes felt secure in their jobs and anticipated no difficulty in finding other jobs if the need arose. However, 81 per cent of the women as compared to 68 per cent of the men felt that they could be very easily replaced by employers if they left their jobs.

Promotion and Identification with Management

When asked about their chances for promotion, 32 per cent of the men and 5 per cent of the women expected management jobs in the future; 21 per cent of the men and 30 per cent of the women thought they had little or no chance of any promotions. Management officials' estimates of likelihood of promotions held that for 6 per cent of the men and 21 per cent of the women no promotions were likely, but that for 43 per cent of the men and 26 per cent of the women, the employees "could go to the very top." Managers also said that in the previous year 45 per cent of the men and 60 per cent of the women had experienced no promotions of any kind.

The question "in general, do you feel that you are more like management or more like industrial workers? " elicited the choices of "management" from 63 per cent of the non-union men and 42 per cent of the non-union women, and "workers", from 25 per cent of the non-union men and 39 per cent of the non-union women. These responses were clearly associated with job control levels – the low job control workers choosing "workers" – but were not associated in any systematic way with several "job satisfaction" measures. Union workers more frequently chose "workers," with 53 per cent of the men and 41 per cent of the women making this choice. Differences by control levels were less marked for union members.

Responses on Union

Non-Union Sample

In the straight breakdown of responses by sex, the non-union women were clearly more favourable to unions than were the non-union men. Thirty-six per cent of the women, compared to 28 per cent of the men believed that in general, workers like themselves should belong to unions; 35 per cent of the women compared to 26 per cent of the men said they were willing to join a union themselves; and 41 per cent of the women compared to 36 per cent of the men said their wages would improve if they were unionised.

In comparative breakdowns of responses by job control levels, income and education, the sexes were similar in direction though different in proportions, with in each case a higher percentage at the lower levels preferring unions (Table 4). Job control levels were not predictive of men's willingness to join, though they were associated with the more general attitude favouring unions. Income levels were much more effective predictors. For women, job control and income were equally good predictors. Education levels were less consistently related to attitudes. The differences in union sympathies by promotion expectations showed that those most supportive of unions were those with some expectation of promotion short of a management position. Further analyses showed that promotion expectations were not related to job control levels of income.

Identification with management provided a weak predictor of union sympathies for men, but did not clearly differentiate between women. Since identity for non-union workers was associated with job control levels, and since the differences in union sympathies by that variable were significantly greater, job control level would appear to be the better predictor.

Union Sample

Union men were more favourable to union membership than were union women – the reversal of the non-union pattern. Seventy-seven per cent of the men, and 64 per cent of the women favoured membership for white-collar workers. Twice as many men as women held or had held union offices. The breakdown by job control, education, and income showed a contrast to the non-union distribution in that it was the men most advantaged in control and income who favoured the union. The response distribution for women showed inconsistencies: high control women favoured the union less than low control women, but high income women favoured it more. Education provided no consistent correlation with union attitudes. Promotion expectations again showed the most supportive members to be those with some expectations short of management positions. Again, these were not related to job control levels.

Contrary to the non-union findings, the identity measure was a strong predictor of attitudes for women, and was less so for men. Eighty-six per cent of those women who chose workers, contrasted to 52 per cent of those who chose management, favoured the union.

Discussion

The union potential in the unorganized sector of the white-collar labour force, as indicated by this survey, is fairly high. Approximately a third of the workers are potential members. Support for unions is correlated with weak bargaining positions – easy replaceability, low control, low mobility, and low rewards. The same factors that create weak bargaining positions are associated with a shift from identification with management to that with other workers. The trends are the same for both sexes, but the conditions of work are not the same. The higher union potential among women is directly related to their much weaker bargaining position and chronically low income. Where men find themselves in the same position, they also support unions – but fewer white-collar men are hampered by low income, low control, low mobility, and easy replaceability.

A majority vote is required in a firm before it can be unionised. On the basis of the evidence here, it seems reasonably to conclude that firms having a high proportion of low control and low income persons in their employ are those most likely to host

Table IV

Percentage Willing to Join a Union (non union sample)

Criteria	Level	Men		Women	
		Percentage	(N = 100 per cent)	Percentage	(N = 100 per cent)
Job control (content)	low	25	(36)	45	(56)
	high	27	(45)	15	(27)
Education	less than high school graduation	46	(13)	42	(19)
	high school graduation	19	(36)	33	(52)
	more than high school graduation	19	(27)	33	(12)
Income	$450 or less	64	(11)	42	(60)
	$451 or over	20	(66)	16	(19)
Promotion expectations	no promotions likely	21	(18)	14	(36)
	within skill group or related work	33	(24)	48	(27)
	supervisory or management levels	21	(29)	43	(14)
	(remainder unsure)	20	(10)	17	(06)
Identity	with workers	35	(20)	40	(32)
	with management	20	(51)	31	(35)
	(remainder unsure)	20	(10)	31	(16)
Total willing to join		26	(81)*	35	83*

*Total is not the same for each breakdown because of missing information (education and income).

white-collar unions in the future. As long as women continue to be employed at low control levels in large numbers, information on the proportion of women employed by a firm would alone provide an index of that firm's union potential. The failure of white-collar unions so far to organize these workers may be due more to union organizers' beliefs about women in the labour force than to any real disinclination of women to join. The bargaining agents for all of the unions representing the union workers in this sample were men, and informal discussions with several of them provided exactly the same sentiment heard from male employers: that women are not committed to work and would therefore not join.

It is suggested that the explanation for the reversal in enthusiasm between men and women in unions is located in the income distributions together with the job market in which there is a large supply of women who have interchangeable skills and who are therefore easily replaced. The over-all effect of union membership for men is to create greater consistency between job control levels and income levels. Those with high control are more likely to receive high incomes, and those with low control are more likely to receive low incomes if they are in unions. The consistency is readily understood as the logical outcome of the extensive and systematic job evaluations that precede union negotiations. Non-union shops are not obliged to undertake such systematic evaluations with their workers, nor are they are hampered in dealing with individuals on an individual bargaining basis. Thus their income distributions are less consistently related to job control. These systematic evaluations have the effect of reinforcing existing inequalities among workers. Since more men have high control jobs, unions actually benefit men more than women, and benefit high control men most of all.

In addition to this effect of union negotiation procedures, union women must operate in the same job market and against the same presumptions about women workers as non-union women. The income distributions shown indicate that the negotiations provide consistency for men (which provides most men with an advantage) but the same low rewards for women whether they have high or low control over their jobs.

Men's attitudes toward unions reflect their economic advantage, even though it may have been the same high control men who least needed and who least favoured union membership prior to unionisation.

Men were the more active members of unions, but the percentage of women who indicated willingness to take office was much higher than that of women who said they had actually done so. Their inactivity was not, therefore, necessarily due to apathy.

A recent study of male union members' attitudes toward women workers, done for the Royal Commission on the Status of Women, showed strong evidence of men's opposition to female equality (Geoffroy and Sainte-Marie, 1971). In the course of this investigation, we read union contracts that openly discriminated against women by inserting different pay scales for the sexes. The attitude, together with the income discrimination, is a deterrent to the belief that women will be well served by present white-collar unions. However, unions of women only, designated to bargain not only with employers but also with male workers and male-dominated unions, have not yet appeared. Given the high union potential of these women, such unions could well be not only the solution for women workers, but also the surest way that the union movement could re-establish its strength in a white-collar labour force.

References

Barbash, Jack
1948 *Labour Unions in Action.* New York: Harper and Brothers.

Blum, Albert A., et al.
1971 *White-Collar Workers.* New York: Random House.

Canada, Dominion Bureau of Statistics
1961 *Census.* Ottawa: Queen's Printer. Volume 111–1.

Canada, Department of Labour, Economic and Research Branch
1968 *Labour Organizations in Canada.* 57th ed. Ottawa: Queen's Printer.

Commons, John R., et al. (eds.)
1958 *A Documentary History of American Industrial Society.* New York: Russell and Russell.

Geoffroy, Renee and Paule Sainte-Maire.
1971 *Attitude of Union Workers to Women in Industry.* Royal Commission on the Status of Women in Canada. No. 9. Ottawa: Queen's Printer.

Hoxie, R.F.
1928 *Trade Unionism in the United States.* New York: D. Appleton and Co.

Marx, Karl
1867 *Capital.* Edited by Frederick Engels. 1967 ed. New York: International Publishers, Volume 1.

Mills, C. Wright
1951 *White Collar.* New York: Oxford University Press.

Ostry, Sylvia
1970 "Labour Force Participation and Childbearing Status," *Demography and Educational Planning.* Toronto: Ontario Institute for Studies in Education.

Perlman, Selig
1928 *History of Trade Unionism in the United States.* New York: Macmillan.

Sturmthal, Adolf
1966 *White-Collar Trade Unions: Contemporary Developments in Industralized Societies.* Urbana: University of Illinois Press.

Webb, Sydney and Beatrice
1965 *History of Trade Unionism.* New York: A.M. Kelley.

Wolmar, Leo
1936 *Ebb and Flow in Trade Unionism.* New York: National Bureau of Economic Research Inc.

14

Why People Work: Middle-Level Men at Mid-Career in the Federal Public Service*

Christopher Beattie

What draws persons to a particular sector in the economy or type of work and motivates them to keep working once they have started? This is a general question that this research report seeks to answer. Although the present enquiry has to do with Anglophones and Francophones at the middle level of Canada's public service, the findings might well apply in other work settings.

Method

Findings are drawn from a study of five government departments in the Canadian federal administration: the Departments of Finance, National Revenue (Taxation Division), Agriculture, Public Works, and the Secretary of State. They were chosen to provide a cross section of departmental structures and corporate functions in the federal public service.

The Department of Finance is one of the central, powerful, policy-advising agencies in the federal administration. Its officers are responsible for the study and development of Canada's financial policies. There are fewer than 100 officers (middle level and above) manning the core of the department. The Department of National Revenue is responsible for the collection of income and other taxes, as well as customs and excise charges, through a network of regional offices. I studied only one of its two main divisions, the Taxation Division, which has about 6,600 employees. The Department of Agriculture has a large staff of scientists doing basic research as well as a service organization that safeguards the quality of produce on the market and provides advice to the farming community. It is the seventh largest department among the twenty-three departments which make up the public service and has a staff of about 8,000 across Canada. The Department of Public Works is also a large one (8,800 persons) and is charged with the construction and maintenance of federal buildings, roads, bridges, wharves, and other properties. Like National Revenue (Taxation), it maintains a string of regional offices. The Department of the Secretary of State has three quite autonomous sectors, each concerned with the protection or

---

* An original paper prepared for this volume. It is an expanded version of Chapter 7 of Christopher Beattie, Jacques Désy, and Stephen Longstaff, 1972, *Bureaucratic Careers: Anglophone and Francophone in the Canadian Public Service,* Royal Commission on Bilingualism and Biculturalism (Ottawa: Information Canada). Drawn from Christopher Beattie's doctoral thesis, University of California at Berkeley, 1970.

extension of Canadian culture: the National Museum, the Translation Bureau, and the Patent Office. The units ranged in size from about 400 in the Patent Office and the Translation Bureau to 165 in the National Museum. Nearly all the staff of these three units is located in the Capital area.

My focus was on officers (middle-level men) at mid-career working at headquarters in the national capital. I concentrated on persons who have several years of their worklife behind them, either outside or inside government service, and now face the prospect of a life-time career in the federal administration. To insure that only persons of officer status were included, anyone earning less than $6,200 a year (in 1965) was eliminated. As no upper limit on salary was set, the sample included some who had professional or technical expertise or responsible administrative posts.

A second consideration was the stage of the career. To eliminate those not likely to be settled on a career choice the lower age limit chosen was 25 years. And to exclude those who had likely reached the limits of their capacities or were too old to receive major promotions, the upper limit was set at 45 years.

To treat ethnolinguistic factors, I divided each department into the minority "Francophones" and the dominant "Anglophones". This terminology indicates attachment to one of the two major ethnolinguistic traditions in Canada. They are terms which can be applied to all Canadians depending on whether they are oriented to and identify with the mass media, voluntary associations, economic units, or political affairs of either the French or English sector.

When the population was divided in Francophone and Anglophone segments, I found that the small number of Francophones satisfying our age and salary conditions in four of the five departments demanded a 100 per cent sample. Otherwise, simple random sampling was used. Table 1 shows the size of the Francophone and Anglophone population falling within the established age and salary boundaries in each department and the size of the sample selected for interviewing. Only one man refused to be interviewed. Altogether a total of 168 Anglophones and 128 Francophones were interviewed.

Main Concepts and Analytic Categories

What attracts men to bureaucratic careers? In the interview they were asked to give their main reasons for joining the federal public service. The following are the most prominent:

(1) Career Opportunities: the work appeared attractive and the chances for promotion, for assuming a position of responsibility, or for making a higher salary looked good.

(2) Unique Field: the federal administration was the only place or one of the few places in which to pursue a specialized interest.

(3) Training Experience: the job provided an opportunity to learn new skills that would be useful in the future, often in a career outside the public sector.

(4) Public Service: a desire to do valuable and important work and serve the "public good" could be fulfilled.

(5) Security: the federal service offered job security, a steady income, good working hours, or low pressure.

(6) Ottawa-Hull Attraction: the federal government was the main employer in the Capital Region and the person wanted to stay in or come to the area.

(7) Only Job: the federal administration made the only acceptable offer at a time when immediate employment was a necessity.

(8) Language: a few Francophones either wanted to work in French in a unit where

Table 1

Ethnolinguistic Composition of Canadian Public Servants in National Capital Area, 25-45 Years of Age, Earning $6,200 or More per Annum in 1965. Population and Sample Size in Selected Departments

Departments	Anglophones		Francophones		
	Population	Chosen for Interview	Population	Chosen for Interview	Total Population
Finance	48	28	6	6	54
Agriculture	279	37	28	8	307
National Revenue (Taxation Division)	154	33	33	33	187
Public Works	173	32(33)*	28	28	201
Secretary of State	114	38	57	33	171
Total	768	168(169*	152	128	920

*There was one nonrespondent in Public Works.

that language predominated or saw government employment as an opportunity to learn English.

The above categories were developed in the course of interviewing, and later, reviewing responses to the questions about entering the federal administration. In addition, the categories were shaped by the theory of work motivation. A fundamental distinction appears in the theoretical and empirical literature. Some workers mainly emphasize the nature of the work itself, the presence or absence of opportunities for applying their knowledge or learning new skills; others are chiefly concerned with security, or other factors not instrinsic in the work. The latter mainly revolve about the benefits provided by the employing organization. Entry motivations of the former type—represented by reasons (1) to (4) above—where termed *work* factors; the latter, as seen in reasons (5) to (8) were called *benefit* factors.

The distinction between work and benefit factors, or to put it in a more general way, between factors related to the *content* of the work and those bearing on the *context* in which work is done, has appeared in several guises in the sociological literature. In a study of a federal agency in the United States, Dwaine Marvick (1954) distinguished between "task" and "benefit" factors. Employees concerned with task factors gave special emphasis to opportunities for learning new skills, trying out ideas, or making full use of their abilities. The focus was on job content and the possibilities of enjoyment offered by the work. Concern with benefit factors meant an emphasis on the by-products of working in the organization: security, salary, advancement, and prestige in the community. Marvick compared the civil and military administrators, "institutionalists", with "specialists". He found that specialists were more likely to value task factors while institutionalists emphasized benefit factors.

Herzberg and colleagues (1957) reviewed the literature on job satisfaction and other job attitudes published through 1954. With this background, the Herzberg group (1959) conducted a seminal piece of research, *The Motivation to Work.* The main focus was on 203 engineers and accountants in nine companies in Pittsburgh. The respondents were asked to provide stories about times that they felt either exceptionally good or exceptionally bad about their work. Factors which made people happy with their work were different from those that made people unhappy with their work (Herzberg 1959, 113):

> When our respondents reported feeling happy with their jobs, they most frequently described factors related to their tasks, to events that indicated to them that they were successful in the performance of their work, and to the possibility of professional growth. Conversely, when feelings of unhappiness were reported, they were not associated with the job itself but with conditions that surround the doing of the job.

Company policy, administrative procedures, and the quality of supervision appeared to be the chief sources of dissatisfaction. In short, employees dintinguished between factors associated with the content of the work (intrinsic) and factors in the work setting (extrinsic). The degree of satisfaction with work was an outcome of weighing these two sets of factors.

Similar results for managers are reported in a survey carried out by Lyman W. Porter (1962). Satisfaction of the need for security was roughly equal across all levels of management, but the satisfaction of needs for esteem, autonomy, and self-actualization increased at each higher management level . . . . The main finding was the sharp distinction between a security-benefit syndrome and a work content syndrome.

In another study of scientists and engineers Friedlander and Walton (1964) found that decisions to leave an organization and expressions of dissatisfaction resulted mainly from problems in the work environment, while high satisfaction and decisions to stay on a job were related to opportunities for self-development . . . . The report by Robert Blauner (1964) about levels of alienation among workers in four industries adds weight to this contention. Friedlander (1965), however, found evidence that self-development and other such work factors may be important to professional and managerial people but not to those in blue-collar jobs. Occupational level, therefore, is an important determinant of whether one chiefly values features of the work itself or aspects of the setting in which work is done.

Variations in Reasons for Joining

Anglophone personnel in our civil service sample are generally more oriented toward their work and creative aspects of it than are Francophones (Table 2). Fifty-two per cent of Anglophones join for work reasons as aginst 33 per cent among the Francophones. In particular, relatively more Anglophones are attracted by the career opportunities available and the possibilities of doing specialized work.

Table 3 verifies that it is the professional and scientific workers in both linguistic groups who most desire creative work. Within all career types, however, larger proportion of Anglophones than Francophones join the public service because of the attraction of the work. The difference is especially strong among those in technical and semi-professional careers. Here, the Anglophones are almost as strongly motivated by their work as are their fellows in professional-scientific fields. More than half the Anglophones name work factors, but only 29 per cent of the Francophones do so. Among administrators the linguistic difference is considerably less sharply drawn.

Table 4 lists careers according to the proportion of persons who join the government chiefly because of work rather than benefit orientation. The same ordering per-

Table 2

Percentages, Main Reason for Joining the Federal Public Service, by Francophones and Anglophones at the Middle Level, 1965.

Main Reason for Joining	Linguistic Group				Total	
	Francophones		Anglophones			
Career Opportunities	17		23		22	
Unique Field	9		20		18	
Training Experience	6		7		6	
Public Service	1		2		2	
Total Work Factors		33		52		48
Security	19		23		22	
Ottawa-Hull Attraction	12		8		8	
Only Job	22		9		11	
Language	2		0		0	
Total Benefit Factors		55		40		41
Other Reasons or Not Determined	13		9		10	
	100 (N:128)		101 (N:168)		99 (N:296)	

tains in both linguistic groups. Scientists and senior policy-makers are most likely to enter government service for work factors. They are followed in order by semi-professionals, engineers, technicians, and last of all lower administrators. The position of the engineers is anomalous; as a professional group it would be expected that they would be high in their desire for creative work. Instead, they stand below semi-professionals. It appears then that government engineers are especially prone to view their employment as offering security. The extreme examples of this, however, are the Francophone technicians and lower administrators, among whom approximately eight in ten enter the federal administration mainly for the fringe benefits it affords.

In addition to the influence of language and career, organizational ethos is related to job motivation. In four out of five departments there is a similar orientation to work expressed by members of the two linguistic groups, as Table 5 reveals. Fringe benefits are highly and equally relevant to both language groups in Public Works, National Revenue, and the Secretary of State. This reveals much about the essential character of these departments. Since they perform routine service functions, few opportunities for deriving satisfaction from the nature of the work are available, whatever the language background of the employee. On the other hand, in the Department of Finance both the Anglophones and Francophones (few as there are) are excited by the policy-planning and fact-finding that transpire.

Table 3

Percentages, Main Reason for Joining the Federal Public Service, by Francophones and Anglophones at the Middle Level, 1965, and by Career Type.

Career Type and Linguistic Group	Main Reason for Joining			
	Work Factor	Benefit Factor	Other Reason or Not Determined	N*
Professional and Scientific				
Anglophones	56	36	8	84
Francophones	40	49	12	43
Technical and Semi-Professional				
Anglophones	52	38	10	42
Francophones	29	61	10	31
Administrative				
Anglophones	38	52	14	42
Francophones	32	55	13	54
Total Middle-Level				
Anglophones	51	40	9	168
Francophones	34	54	13	128

* These are the bases on which the percentages joining for specified reasons are calculated.

Table 4

Percentages, Main Reason for Joining the Federal Public Service, by Francophones and Anglophones at the Middle Level, 1965, and by Career Category.

Career Category and Linguistic Group	Work Factor	Benefit Factor	Other Reason or Not Determined	N*
Scientists				
Anglophones	83	11	6	35
Francophones	57	36	7	14
Senior Policy-makers				
Anglophones	72	28	0	25
Francophones	53	35	12	17
Semi-Professionals				
Anglophones	43	54	4	28
Francophones	39	47	14	51
Engineers				
Anglophones	35	53	13	40
Francophones	17	58	25	12
Technicians				
Anglophones	33	52	14	21
Francophones	11	78	11	18
Lower Administrators				
Anglophones	26	53		19
Francophones	13	81		16
Total Middle-level				
Anglophones	51	40		168
Francophones	34	54		128

*These are the bases on which the percentages joining for specified reasons are calculated.

Table 5

Percentages, Main Reason for Joining the Federal Public Service, by Francophones and Anglophones at the Middle Level, 1965, and by Department

Department and Linguistic Group	Work Factor	Benefit Factor	Other or Not Determined	N*
Secretary of State				
Anglophones	28	56	16	38
Francophones	21	57	22	33
Finance				
Anglophones	68	29	4	28
Francophones	**	**	**	6
Agriculture				
Anglophones	73	22	6	37
Francophones	29	64	7	28
Public Works				
Anglophones	49	42	11	32
Francophones	47	43	9	28
National Revenue (Taxation Division)				
Anglophones	36	55	9	33
Francophones	27	58	15	33
All Departments				
Anglophones	51	40	9	168
Francophones	34	54	12	128

* These are the bases on which percentages are calculated.
** Too few cases to estimate.

Agricultural appears to be a deviant case; only here does a gap between language groups exist. However, this may be seen to support the thesis about the importance of a departmental ethos.[1] The Francophones are a great deal more isolated from the mainstream of this department than is the case elsewhere. In particular, the Francophone researchers have a somewhat different style of work and do not embrace some of the intellectual concerns which dominate the department and which Francophones consider "English".

Anglophone personnel were most likely to state that it was a desire for more security and few job pressures which drew them to the public service. This is especially true of those Anglophones whose mother tongue was not English. While 36 per cent of these persons sought security, only 21 per cent of the Anglophones of English mother tongue did so. Many security-seekers had had adverse experiences in private industry or had recently arrived from abroad. The federal public service was felt to be a fair employer. Salaries might not be as high as in private industry, but regular raises and promotions were regarded as more likely.

Among the Francophones who cited benefit factors, what is striking is the large proportion who admitted that they entered the public service mainly because they cold not find suitable employment elsewhere and it offered the only job position at the time. More than one in five (22 per cent) of the entire Francophone sample entered the public service under these extreme circumstances. This makes comprehensible their strong feelings about the benefit aspects of their employment. There are, of course, Anglophones who value security, but few—about 10 per cent – who recounted the sort of difficult job-hunting undergone by Francophones.

Francophones at all seniority levels mention the benefits derived from government employment, while it is mainly the Anglophones with long-term service who feel this way (Table 6). These Anglophones entered government service in the 1940s and early 1950s, generally with inferior professional or technical training. They are usually grateful that they have been able to go as far despite their lack of education. Here is how a draftsman with twenty years service and a few technical courses beyond high school phrased his answer:

> Round about the end of the war, you're young and you've had big ideas, but then the war ends, and you have to get a job. And there are hundreds of servicemen looking for jobs. Suddenly, security, whether you like it or not, becomes important. You get security-conscious.

The younger Anglophones who have recently joined are much more likely to view the federal administration as an exciting workplace than are the older generation. Six in ten of the Anglophones with short-term service joined for work reasons. Of course, these younger men are also more likely to have university degrees and to move directly into work areas where individual responsibility and creativity are called for.

The benefits attached to government employment are markedly more important to those from certain geographic areas than from others. On the Anglophone side, it is those raised in Quebec Province (excluding Hull) or the Atlantic Provinces who are most attracted by employment benefits. Among the Francophones, those who grew up in the Capital Region seek out benefits more than their compatriots from the Province of Quebec (excluding Hull). In fact, the Quebec Francophones are remarkably similar to the Anglophones in the reasons they give for entering government service. In both groups, about 40 per cent cite benefit factors as their main reason for federal employment. This figure is much lower than that for the Francophone group as a whole (54 per cent) and substantially lower than that of the Francophones from the Ottawa-Hull area (64 per cent). Thus, it is primarily the corps from Ottawa-Hull that makes the Franchophones appear more concerned than the Anglophones about

Table 6

Per Cent Joining the Federal Public Service for "Benefit" Reasons among Francophones and Anglophones at the Middle Level, 1965, by Years of Government Service

Francophones		Anglophones	
Years of Service	Per Cent Giving Benefit Reasons	Years of Service	Per Cent Giving Benefit Reasons
5 years or less (N:36)	56	5 years or less (N:60)	30
6 to 14 years (N:63)	51	6 to 14 years (N:73)	41
15 years or more (N:29)	59	15 years or more (N:35)	57
Total (N:128)	55	Total (N:168)	40

benefit factors. The Ottawa-Hull public servants of French background appear to be out of tune not only with the Anglophones but also with their fellow Francophones from other parts of Quebec.

It is chiefly those raised in the Ottawa-Hull area who give as their reason for entering the government a desire to be in that region. A fifth of the native Anglophones and nearly a quarter (24 per cent) of the Francophones from the region give a wish to be in their "hometown" as their main motive for seeking a job here. The overall greater preference for Ottawa-Hull among Francophones is not surprising when it is pointed out that some 43 per cent of them spent their teenage years in the Ottawa-Hull region.

It is the rare person raised elsewhere in Canada who is specially attracted to the Capital area as a place to work. In particular, few Anglophones from Western Canada or Francophones from Quebec (excluding Hull) ever state that it figures as a main motive for taking up federal employment. For these people it is the character of the work going on there that counts most. Above all it is the Anglophones from Western Canada and the Québecois who are attracted by the work of the government rather than by its benefits. More than six in ten of these Anglophones and 47 per cent of these Francophones mention that the work itself drew them in.

It is the level and type of education which is most clearly the genesis of a concern for creative work. First, there is a direct relationship between level of education and joining the government for work reasons (Table 7). In both linguistic groups, those with higher university degrees are most likely to be in the federal administration because of the challenging work there. Second, it is those with university training in the arts or humanities, rather than science or engineering, and commerce or law, who

Table 7

Per Cent Joining the Federal Public Service for "Work" Reasons Among the Francophones and Anglophones at the Middle Level, 1965, and by Level of Education.

Level of Education	Per Cent Joining for "Work" Reasons			
	Francophones	N*	Anglophones	N*
Some University or Less	22	46	30	44
First University Degree	30	47	48	78
Postgraduate University Degree	54	35	74	46
Total	33	128	52	168

* These are the bases on which percentages are calculated.

talk most often of pursuing a government career because of the interesting work. Those persons with a "generalist" education seem to be more desirous of getting a job with intellectual appeal than those with specialist training. This finding somewhat contradicts Marvick's results reported earlier.[2]

After leaving full-time education, the experience of job-changing and switching in one's employment outside the federal administration has a differing impact on the two linguistic groups. Although only a small proportion of Francophones had a chaotic work history, those who had were unlikely to join for work reasons (Table 8). The experience of holding a series of jobs that were unrelated or that came to an abrupt end made workers yearn for more security. The same experience had the opposite effect on Anglophones. The Anglophones with disorderly work histories are more likely to be attracted by the work itself than are other Anglophones. After switching among jobs and work areas they seem to regard the public service as just another employer with an interesting job offer. One reason for the difference between linguistic groups is the scope of the opportunities available to each. For Francophones without a job there is a considerably narrower range of possiblities than there is for Anglophones. The Anglophones have access to the whole of North American industry. In contrast, particularly if they wish to work in French to avoid work settings that are totally English, Francophones must select within a limited framework and their search is more desperate as a consequence. They need the steady job and income offered by the government; Anglophones know that if the work is not interesting they can easily leave for something else.

There are two further themes that are fairly prominent among those who join for work reasons. First, there are those who find government work attractive because of the unique research or training opportunities it provides. For some of them it is one of the only agencies in the country doing important work in their field; for others it offers experience that can be gained nowhere else and which is crucial for a later career in private industry. The scientists in the Department of Agriculture illustrate one type of careerist who feels this way about federal employment. These men are strongly concerned about scientific accomplishment and gaining recognition in the scientific community. In certain areas of agricultural research the federal

Table 8

Per Cent Joining the Federal Public Service for "Work" Reasons Among Francophones and Anglophones at the Middle Level, 1965, by Work Histories Outside the Federal Administration

Nature of Work History Outside Federal Administration	Per Cent Joining for "Work" Reasons			
	Francophones	N*	Anglophones	N*
Direct Entry -- No Work History	39	52	45	40
Orderly Work History -- No or Few Job Changes	32	60	51	96
Disorderly Work History -- A Great Deal of Job-Switching	25	16	56	32
Total	33	128	52	168

* These are the bases on which percentages are computed.

government is the main employer. Here are several accounts of the reasons these scientists give for joining the federal service:

> At the time (1948-49) the Research Branch of the department (Agriculture) contained at least 95 per cent of the entomologists employed in Canada. It was an exciting time in entomology in the Civil Service then, too . . . . That influenced me away from private industry or teaching. So, I suppose the main reason was that if you wanted to do entomology you automatically went into the civil service in those days. It might be different now.

> Je n'ai aucun sentiment envers le government fédéral; c'est pas que j'aime ca ici, la fonction publique. Mais c'est que je peux y faire de la recherche fondamentale.

> Well, I don't think it was a case of joining the civil service so much as having a chance to work in this lab. It had top people and a top reputation. I have a good opportunity to gain experience in research work, and to build up a reputation of my own. It was the quality of the research that attracted me.

The scientific orientation of these men is strong; their organizational attachment is weak. The guiding theme of their worklives is to do good research and it happens that the federal government offers this opportunity.

The federal government offers a special training experience to others. A stint in government work may be a virtual necessity for moving into certain careers in the private sector. Such is the case, for example, among those who work for private firms that draw up patent applications or law firms that go to court on behalf of businesses involved in a tax suit with the government. Here is how one of these men describes his sojourn in government service:

Right now I represent the government in tax litigation. Before, while I was with the law firm in Vancouver, I had a good amount of work in this field. I became really interested in it and decided I should get out and see the other side of the operation. I came here for the experience, you might say. Most lawyers in this field go through the department (National Revenue) at some time.

Like the research scientists, these men also take a rather opportunistic view of federal employment. As long as they are learning and doing advanced work they will stay on; when it appears that they have picked up enough skills or that their upward career movement has slowed they will leave. These scientists and professionals, in short, are "discipline-oriented" and "cosmopolitan" in outlook, not firmly tied to a single organization.[3]

Contrast with this, men who sound the second important theme:

Je voulais venir à Ottawa pour contribuer, via la politique fédérale, au relèvement du niveau de vie et des conditions économiques des Acadiens d l'Ile du Prince-Edouard.

At university I became interested in social and economic problems. I decided then I wanted to tackle the world's problems by working in the public sector, not for industry. Some professors steered me into economics but an athletic coach was the person who started my interest in community work.

That is not a common motive--it is expressed by only 1 or 2 per cent of Anglophones and Francophones--but it is one that figures importantly in certain work settings that are training grounds for the upper-level of the public service, for example, Department of Finance, Treasury Board, and the Department of External Affairs. Indeed, this sort of attitude seems to be assumed of those officers whose careers are leading to upper-level positions. Paradoxically, even though such attitudes are assumed, it is often difficult for public servants to be articulate about them. Most felt somewhat modest about voicing what could appear as overly selfless and public-spirited sentiments. Nevertheless, the theme of "public service" is an important part of the ethos of the federal administration, and it especially underlies the efforts of many of its senior personnel.

The foregoing discussion of the "discipline" and "public-service" orientations covers the two themes which are most prominent in the dynamic and creative work settings of the federal administration. In these and other work settings, a specialist with advanced training or with a desire to acquire new knowledge will often set aside other motives for employment in exchange for work experiences that allow for the application or expansion of specialized knowledge. Also, in both the public and private sectors some persons will regard it as important to serve some larger purpose than that of seeking security or greater personal wealth. Duty to country or company does move some rare individuals to take up a new work assignment and carry it through.

Summary and Conclusions

There is a strong emphasis among these middle-level employees on work as a means to security or some other benefit rather than an end in itself with its own intrinsic interest. They were mainly attracted by the extrinsic factors attached to a job. On the other hand, sizeable proportions (from one-third to one-half in different samples) did view work as offering intrinsic satisfactions and were drawn into employment by the prospects of challenging and creative experiences.

There is variation between persons in different careers or with different levels of education as to what draws them to a job and keeps them at it. Scientists and professionals are especially likely to seek opportunities for interesting tasks. Semi-professionals, technicians, and lower-administrators express less concern about the content of the work and more concern about the benefits provided by the work context. A similar finding is that the higher a person's level of education the greater the concern with obtaining a post that offers interesting work. This is especially so among those with an educational training in the arts or humanities. In short, those with higher education and particularly those with "generalist" training are more concerned about the appeal of the work than about the benefits it may provide.

Persons with a short term of employment, who are also likely to be younger, are likely to seek work that provides a source of personal growth (the tendency is less strong among Francophones). Persons with long years of service, who are also likely to be older, had a greater concern for organizational benefits at the time they were seeking a post. This may reflect a difference in generations between those who entered the labour force in recent years and those who sought out their first job in the 1930s, 40s, or 50s.

A desire to stay in one's "hometown" appears to be a strong motive propelling many persons (one-quarter to one-fifth in this study) to look for and stay with a particular post. It appears that many persons will go to the major employer in an area and take a job, almost any job, to enable them to maintain ties with kin and friends.

Some persons work in order to expand their repertoire of intellectual skills often with an eye to using these new skills in a different employment setting later in their careers. Here, the work is approached in an opportunistic way, as an activity worth doing so long as personal intellectual growth is experienced.

A few persons feel that it is their public duty to do certain jobs while, in the private sector, some persons likely feel that loyalty to their company requires them to stay on or to take a new work assignment.

Many Francophone Canadians and many Anglophone Canadians whose mother tongue is not English express a need for the income and personal sense of security which a job provides, particularly because they have found it difficult to locate and hold a suitable post.

Organizations attract different types of persons: the routine, service organizations are havens for the benefit-minded, while persons joining research and policy settings are attracted to the work going on there.

The major general conclusion is that work is a double-edged activity. For many it is chiefly a means to security with little intrinsic interest. For others, to work is to do something interesting that offers personal challenge and valued learning experiences. Working likely offers both aspects to every employee but in widely differing amounts.

Notes

1. The examination of a "deviant case" to aid in clarifying a general explanation of the relationship between factors is a usual procedure in sociological analysis. An excellent example of this technique is the clarification of Michels' "iron law of oligarchy" derived from the study of a democratic trade union. See Seymour Martin Lipset, *et al* (1956).

2. That these "generalists", or "institutionalists" to use Marvick's term, are more interested in work factors may be a by-product of the fact that many of the Canadian

generalists were doing exciting policy and personnel work while Marvick's institutionalists seemed to be chiefly routine administrators and career-minded military men.

3. The distinction between "cosmopolitans" and "locals" or "organizationals" derives from Robert K. Merton (1955) and Alvin W. Gouldner (1957 and 1958). A similar distinction is developed in a study of staff experts in labour unions by Harold L. Wilensky (1956).

References

Beattie, Christopher
1970 *Minority Men in a Majority Setting: Middle-Level Francophones at Mid-Career in the Anglophone Public Service of Canada.* Unpublished doctoral dissertation. Department of Sociology, University of California (Berkeley).

Beattie, Christopher, Jacques Désy, and Stephen Longstaff
1972 *Bureaucratic Careers: Anglophones and Francophones in the Canadian Public Service.* Ottawa: Information Canada.

Blauner, Robert
1964 *Alienation and Freedom,The Factory Worker and His Industry.* Chicago: University of Chicago Press.

Friedlander, Frank
1965 *"Comparative Work Value Systems", Personal Psychology* 18, (Spring): 1-20.

Friedlander, Frank and Eugene Walton
1964 "Positive and Negative Motivations Toward Work". *Administrative Science Quarterly* 9 (September): 194-207.

Gouldner, Alvin W.
1957 "Cosmopolitans and Locals: Toward an Analysis of Latent Social Roles--I". *Administrative Science Quarterly* 2 281-306.

1958 "Cosmopolitans and Locals: Toward an Analysis of Latent Social Roles--II". *Administrative Science Quarterly* 2 444-480.

Herzberg, Frederick, *et al.*
1957 *Job Attitudes: Review of Research and Opinion.* Pittsburgh: Psychological Services.

1959 *The Motivation to Work.* New York: John Wiley and Sons.

Lipset, Seymour Martin, *et al.*
1956 *Union Democracy: The Internal Politics of the International Typographical Union.* Glencoe, Ill.: Free Press.

Marvick, Dwaine
1954 *Career Perspectives in a Bureaucratic Setting.* Ann Arbor: University of Michigan Press.

Merton, Robert K.
1955 *Social Theory and Social Structure.* New York: Macmillan.

Porter, Lyman W.
1962 "Job Attitudes in Management: I Perceived Deficiencies in Need Fulfilment as a Function of Job Level". *Journal of Applied Psychology* 46 (December): 375-384.

Wilensky, Harold L.
1956 *Intellectuals in Labour Unions: Organizational Pressures on Professional Roles.* Glencoe, Ill.: Free Press.

15

Professional Behaviour of American and Canadian Chiropractors*

Irving Rootman and Donald L. Mills

In the context of research on "limited, marginal and quasi-practioners," including chiropractors, W.E. Wardwell (1963: 235–6) suggested that "topics deserving investigation center on the social forces producing changes over time in the status or development of these professions." Thus he urged the ". . . comparative study of these professions in other societies for the light which cross-cultural investigation can shed on the forces and factors operative on the American scene." As a step in the latter direction, we have attempted to compare American and Canadian chiropractors in terms of their professional behaviour.

Even though there have been numerous references to the universality of the professional model of work (e.g., Whitehead, 1956: 77), there appear to be few systematic intersocietal comparisons of professional behaviour. Perhaps more intriguing, though, is that a review of over 9,000 titles in a bibliography on the sociology of work indicates that there have been relatively few attempts at systematic study of professional behaviour, per se, even in the context of a single society or a more limited social setting (e.g., Barber, 1967: 17–19).

Professional behaviour in the present instance refers to the extent to which role performance of occupational incumbents corresponds to the behavioural prescriptions and expectations associated with the professional role (Gross et al., 1958). Allport devised means for "defining, observing and describing behaviour . . . to study the relation of human behaviour to human roles" (1938: 693), but he and his associates described and categorized specific "units, or acts, or behaviour" of bank tellers, grocery-store clerks, machine workers, and ten-cent store clerks. Gross, Mason, and McEachern (1958) undertook an impressively designed, skillfully executed, and thoughtfully analyzed study of more than 100 U.S. school superintendents. Among other things, using 12 items, they examined "the degree to which role behaviour conforms to or deviates from expectations that role definers (superintendents) apply to position incumbents (school boards – specifically) the isolation of factors differentiating position incumbents who conform to (professional) expectations from those who do not" (Gross et al., 1958: 222). A small-scale application of Gross, et al. in the research of Bible and McComas on "Role Consensus and Teacher Effectiveness" used a few overt behaviour indicators of "teacher effectiveness," e.g., "professional improvement" and "participation in community affairs and public relations," but the main interest was in "job satisfaction" rather than role conformity (Bible and McComas, 1963: 228). "Professional-

*Abridged from *Journal of Health & Social Behaviour* 15 (March), 1974 with the permission of the authors and the American Sociological Association.

ism and the Poor—Structural Effects and Professional Behaviour" by Walsh and Elling (1968) was limited to samples of American nurses, physicians, and sanitarians, and the behaviour in question was restricted to an intraprofessional striving dimension in relation to client orientations. The study of "militant professionalism" among American teachers by Corwin (1970) focused on intra-occupational conflict as manifested in complaints, impersonal competition, and overt incidents about discipline, classrooms, policy, and students, and is non-comparative. Although Form's "Occupational and Social Integration of Automobile Workers in Four Countries: A Comparative Study" (1969) does afford American, Argentine, Indian, and Italian comparisons among craftsmen, machine tenders, and unskilled occupations, the comparisons are largely concerned with attitudes about work rather than work behaviour as such.

In their study, *Lawyers and their Work,* Johnstone and Hopson (1967) examined the legal profession in England and the United States, but with the exception of the formal substance of laws, rules, regulations, codes, orders, and directives, this comparison is relatively general and unsystematic and there are few direct comparisons of occupational behaviour. George Baron and Asher Tropp in their consideration of teachers in England and America (1961: 545-557) observed that: "Ideally, comparison should await the results of similar research carried out with similar methods in the two countries." Similar limitations may be seen in the comparisons by Robert Platt (1963) of physicians in Britain and the U.S.A., by Michael Banton (1964) of policemen in Scotland and the United States, by Jeremy Tunstall (1964) of advertising men in England and the United States, and by John Fry (1970) of physicians in the U.K., U.S.A. and the U.S.S.R.

In the tradition of Carr-Saunders and Wilson (1933) and Hughes (1958), the present investigation employs a comparative approach; it also builds on recent extensions of this approach on professionalism (Vollmer and Mills, 1966; Mills, 1966) as well as on professional behaviour (Gross, et al., 1958; Sussman, 1966). Sussman indicated this " . . . approach assumes . . . that some individuals behave more professionally than others. The objective for certain types of occupational problems is to tap these professionals by analyzing their behaviour, an empirical approach." This in turn involves an ideal typical formulation of "the core characteristics of a profession," which for Sussman are:

> . . . service orientation and a body of theoretical knowledge, with autonomy of the work group as a by-product of the two. A service orientation has two components: the first refers to professional roles performed by motivations of community ("other") rather than self interest; the second is concerned with the community's definition of service. The community defines the need for the service and accords it varying prestige, status, and power; and the practitioner responds with criteria of performance in reference to public expectations.
>
> The body of theoretical knowledge is abstract, not merely technical, largely based on the canons of science, the codification of practical experience, and rooted in a humanistic tradition; its mastery requires a prolonged period of time.
>
> Autonomy comprises control of functions in the work situation and substitution of self-regulation for control by the society (client or state). To the extent that the society has confidence in the occupation's service orientation and recognizes the rarity of occupational knowledge, it will grant autonomy in defining tasks and practices as borth safe and necessary. (Sussman, 1966: 190).

Through the collective efforts of an occupational association "the profession . . . determines standards of training and education for tasks and professional roles. The intended outcome is rededication and reinforcement of the service orientation, mastery of new knowledge for maintaining professional competence over time, and further division of labour which supports the rationale for autonomy" (Sussman, 1966: 184). Given these characteristics of a profession, it follows that:

> Professional behaviour involves technical and social skills based on a high degree of knowledge learned by incumbents in the profession. It presupposes practical application of this knowledge to achieve work goals. It also presumes an understanding of behaviour which is to be controlled in achieving these goals. Social control to ensure a high level of professional performance is partially a product of self-regulation through internalized ethical codes and ingroup activities of professional collectivities (Sussman, 1966: 185).

Thus the Sussman formulation provides a composite approach in assessing behavioural conformity to occupational role expectations that encompasses variant role definitions from the several constituents of the occupational role set.

In keeping with this formulation, a number of indicators of a "service orientation" and a "body of theoretical knowledge" (and the several attributes these imply) are used in this analysis to compare the professional behaviour of American and Canadian chiropractors. Given an interest in the systematic measurement of overt professional behaviour in a comparative context, this approach is intended to circumvent some of the limitations in earlier studies noted above.

Method

Samples. This study was based on a secondary analysis of two sets of data collected for purposes other than that of the present paper. The first group of data was obtained by Stanford Research Institute using personal interviews (Stanford Research Institute, 1960: 51–69) and employed a geographically-stratified random sample of the estimated 2,500 chiropractors practising in California in 1958. The total number of cases was 517, which constituted about one-fifth of the chiropractor population. Seven per cent of the sample refused to be interviewed (Stanford Research Institute, 1960: Appendix II and III).

The second set of data was collected by Mills (1966) in connection with the Royal Commission on Health Services research in Canada using a self-administered questionnaire mailed to all chiropractors known to be practising in Canada in 1962. A total of 914 chiropractors comprising 85 per cent of the estimated 1073, practising Canadian chiropractors, returned the questionnaire (Mills, 1966: 69-74).

For the purposes of this study, consideration is given only to those chiropractors practising in provinces with the same kind of chiropractic legislation as existed in California in 1958. The reason for eliminating Canadian chiropractors in other legislative jurisdictions is that in an earlier study the authors found a marked relationship between political/legal context and professional behaviour (Mills and Rootman, 1968). It was thus decided that it would be important to hold legal context constant in any comparison of the professional behaviour of chiropractors.

Accordingly, the Canadian sample consisted of 307 chiropractors from the five provinces (British Columbia, Alberta, Saskatchewan, Manitoba, and New Brunswick) with "Chiropractic Acts" in 1962. This constituted about 84 per cent of the practising chiropractors in these provinces (Mills, 1966: 69–74).

The American sample had a higher proportion of female practitioners than the Canadian (9 per cent vs. 4 per cent); was older (44 per cent of the Americans were over 50 compared to 23 per cent of the Canadian); were more likely to be born in their country of practice (90 per cent American vs. 85 per cent Canadian); were more likely to have had some college education in addition to their chiropractic training

Table 1
Comparison of American and Canadian Chiropractors in Terms of "Service Orientation"

Service Orientation	American Chiropractors		Canadian Chiropractors			
	f	%	f	%	x^2	$p \leq$
Overhead costs						
Under $200 per month	210	42.9	73	24.8	....	....
$200 or more per month	280	57.1	221	75.2	25.85	.001
Make house calls?						
No	100	19.6	18	5.9	....	
Yes	411	80.4	286	94.1	28.65	.001
Average fee for office visit						
Less than $5	264	52.0	293	96.1	....	....
$5 or more	244	48.0	12	3.9	171.64	.001
Use of collection agency						
No	321	62.1	92	30.0	....	....
Yes	196	37.9	215	70.0	79.65	.001
Use of prepaid plan						
No	379	74.0	223	81.4	....	....
Yes	133	26.0	51	18.6	5.36	.05
Use of telephone directory announcements						
No	254	49.1	287	95.3	....	....
Yes	263	50.9	14	4.7	181.88	.001
Use of newspaper announcements						
No	417	80.7	212	69.3	....	....
Yes	100	19.3	94	30.7	13.85	.001
Use of radio or T.V.						
No	506	97.9	300	99.3	....	....
Yes	11	2.1	2	0.7	2.63	.200

(54 per cent American vs. 45 per cent Canadian); and more American chiropractors first seriously considered chiropractic as a career after the age of 24 (52 per cent of the Americans compared to 29 per cent of the Canadians).

Analysis. The questions and categories used in the two studies were examined carefully to determine which items were sufficiently similar to allow legitimate comparisons (Stanford Research Institute, 1960: Appendix III-C; and Mills, 1966: Appendix II). This procedure yielded about 30 comparable items, 13 of which were taken to be measures of "professional behaviour." The analysis reported here deals only with the latter items. Chi-square was used to measure sampling variation.

Findings

The 13 "professional behaviour" items are subsumed under two of Sussman's (1966: 184) core characteristics of a profession—"service orientation" and "theoretical knowledge."

Service Orientation. The following items measure the "service orientation" of chiropractors: overhead costs; making house calls; average fees for office visits; use of collection agency to collect unpaid fees; use of a prepaid course-of-treatments plan; use of telephone directory announcements; use of newspaper announcements; and use of radio or television.

Overhead costs were used to measure the availability of adequate facilities and assistance for diagnosis and treatment. American chiropractors were more likely than Canadians to score low on this indicator of "service orientation." About 43 per cent of the Americans as compared to 25 per cent of the Canadians claimed overhead costs of less than $200 per month (see Table 1).

Whether or not a practitioner is willing to make house calls indicated "service orientation" in that such willingness suggests that a practitioner places the interests of the patient before his own. In this case, the Canadians were more likely to do so — 94 per cent of them compared to 80 per cent of the Americans reported that they made such calls (see Table 1).

Average fees are indicative of a "service orientation" because practitioners who charge high fees are more likely than those who charge low ones to have their own interests at heart rather than those of their patients. Once again, the American chiropractors were more likely than their Canadian counterparts to charge higher fees. About 48 per cent of the Americans charged five dollars or more for an office visit during regular office hours compared to only about 4 per cent of the Canadians (see Table 1).

Similarly, use of a collection agency indicated a lack of "service orientation" because it also suggests that the practitioner puts his own interest before that of the patient. In this case, the Canadians were more likely than the Americans to use such agencies to collect outstanding fees (70 per cent compared to about 38 per cent of the Americans). (See Table 1.)

The remaining four items measure "service orientation" because they all represent attempts to increase practice size through solicitation or public information, and such activities suggest a pecuniary orientation, among other things. The Americans were more likely than the Canadians to use a prepaid course-of-treatment plan, to use telephone directory announcements, and to use radio or television. For the remaining indicator, use of newspaper announcements, the differences were reversed (see Table 1); it should be noted, however, that with this last item Canadian chiropractors were paralleling the common practice of Canadian medical physicians.

In summary, of the eight items selected to measure "service orientation," all but one (use of radio or television) differentiate the two samples in a statistically significant manner (at the .05 level). In addition, on six indicators the Americans were less likely than the Canadians to behave "professionally."

Theoretical Knowledge. The following indicate "theoretical knowledge" of chiropractors: length of training, use of X-ray routinely, specialization, subscription to professional journals, and membership in professional associations. An individual who has received formal training in his discipline for a great length of time is presumed to have a more extensive and intensive knowledge and understanding of its concepts and theories. It was found that the Americans were less likely than the Canadians to have trained as chiropractors for three or more years—about 67 per cent compared to about 77 per cent of the Canadians (see Table 2).

Use of X-ray on a routine basis was thought to indicate an application of "theoretical knowledge" because of the heavy emphasis on such training in most modern chiropractic schools. (It can also be argued that use of X-ray for diagnosis is indicative of a "service orientation" in that it protects the patient from possible injury by manipulation.) Again, the American chiropractors were less likely than the Canadian to make routine use of X-ray in diagnosis—only 33 per cent of the Americans compared to 96 per cent of the Canadians used X-ray on a routine basis (see Table 2).

Specialization is suggestive of "theoretical knowledge" because it implies that the practioner has great depth of theoretical knowledge in one area. Again, the Americans were less likely than the Canadians to claim that they specialized in some particular aspect of chiropratic—25 per cent vs. 30 per cent (see Table 2).

Subscription to professional journals may indicate "theoretical knowledge" because reading such journals is one means by which a practioner can keep informed of the new theoretical developments in his field. Once again, the Americans were less likely to score high on this indicator of "theoretical knowledge"—77 per cent subscribed to one or more professional journals compared to 91 per cent of the Canadians (see Table 2).

Table 2.
Comparison of American and Canadian Chiropractors
in Terms of "Theoretical Knowledge"

Theoretical Orientation	American Chiropractors		Canadian Chiropractors			
	f	%	f	%	x^2	$p \leq$
Length of training						
One or two years	168	32.6	68	22.6	9.06	.001
Three or more years	348	67.4	232	77.3	....	......
Use of X-ray routinely						
No	345	66.7	13	4.3	....	......
Yes	172	33.3	291	95.7	303.84	.001
Specialization						
No	384	74.6	214	69.7	....	......
Yes	131	25.4	93	30.3	2.27	.200
Subscription to professional journals						
No	118	22.8	28	9.1	....	......
Yes	399	77.2	279	90.9	24.82	.001
Membership in professional associations						
No	175	33.8	13	4.2	....	......
Yes	342	66.2	294	95.8	95.80	.001

Belonging to a professional association measures "theoretical knowledge" because it too is a method for a practitioner to keep abreast of new developments in his field and to exchange ideas with a wide spectrum of colleagues. Americans were also less likely than Canadians to score high on this indicator, as only 66 per cent belonged to one or more professional associations compared to 96 per cent of the Canadians (see Table 2).

To summarize the findings on "theoretical knowledge": there were statistically significant differences between the two samples on four out of five indicators of such knowledge. In all cases, the Americans were less likely than the Canadians to score high, suggesting, once again, that American chiropractors were less likely than Canadians to behave "professionally."

From both the findings of "service orientation" and "theoretical knowledge" base, it is suggested that the Canadian chiropractors tended to be more professionally oriented—even though not all the indicators pointed in this direction. We must now consider possible explanations for these differences.

Discussion

There is always the possibility that differences are not real but merely reflect *methodological artifacts.* For example, they could be due to the different techniques of data collection employed, that is, interviews with the American sample and self-administered questionnaires with the Canadian. An examination of the findings, however, suggests that in most cases the California chiropractors interviewed were not as likely as Canadian chiropractors to give "socially desirable responses" which Selltiz, et al. (1960: 240) have argued are more characteristic of interview research. Another potential methodological problem is that the sample designs differ and that therefore differences between the two samples may not represent real differences between chiropractors in the two countries. Yet a very large majority of chiropractors in the samples were interviewed or returned questionnaires and it is believed that in both cases the samples are representative of their respective populations and that differences between the samples indicate differences between the two populations. A further explanation to be considered is that the American data were collected four years earlier than the Canadian; it is possible that data collected at the same time would have shown less difference in professional behaviour. But it seems implausible that major non-legislative changes could have occurred in as short a time period as the four years in question.

Perhaps the behavioural differences can be explained by the compositions of the two samples—that is, the overall differences between the samples may be due to the fact that the California sample is older and less well educated than the Canadian one. To examine this possibility, differences between the two samples were calculated holding age and extent of preprofessional education constant for all indicators of professional behaviour. Doing so changed the pattern of the differences for only one category of one indicator. In addition, on those 11 variables where there were overall statistically significant differences, these differences remained significant in about 90 per cent of the control categories. Thus, it seems reasonable to conclude that, on the whole, the differences in professional behaviour between the Canadian and American samples are probably not a result of compositional differences.

Another possible explanation involves the state of the profession in the two jurisdictions at the time of the studies. According to the Canadian researchers, a realistic possibility was "the general continued decline of chiropractic in its present form" in California (Stanford Research Institute, 1960:9), whereas the Canadian Royal Commission found chiropractic to be in a state of expansion in Canada (Mills, 1966). Perhaps as a consequence, Canadian chiropractors in 1962 were more optimistic about their profession than California chiropractors in 1958 and thus were more likely to behave "professionally." (It was found that 23 per cent of the California chiropractors compared to only 4 per cent of the Canadian chiropractors would "offer discouraging comments to relatives who might propose entering chiropractic.")

It also might be argued that the particular state from which the American sample was selected is atypical. California, particularly in the southern part, is composed of a very mobile population and as such there may be a greater tolerance for deviant behaviour there than in other states with more stable populations. As a result, chiropractors may be allowed greater behavioural latitude and consequently may exhibit more "deviant" or "unprofessional" behaviour than would be typical elsewhere in the United States.

A final possible explanation entails the part played by major social values (cf. Rueschemeyer, 1964). One obvious difference between the two groups of chiropractors is that they experienced different cultural influences. Empirical evidence for the part played by cultural differences may be seen in the interesting comparison by Whitehill (1961) of American and Japanese blue collar workers' motivational levels and loyalty to the workplace. Melvin Kohn and associates' large-scale survey compared Americans' and Italians' inter-related values, social class, and, among other things, "the occupational conditions thought to be determinative of the exercise of self-direction in work" (Kohn, 1969: xi). They concluded that "nationality, in fact, matters more than social class" (Kohn, 1969: x).

In his studies of industrial relations, Stuart Jamieson noted that " . . . there appears to be a certain lack of self-confidence among Canadians. It is expressed in an attitude of dependence upon the approbation and support of others, a need to be identified with something larger than themselves and to judge their own level of performance in various fields in terms of criteria used by others . . . " (Jamieson. 1957: 10). Interpreting this in the present instance, Canadian chiropractors may carry out the professional role more carefully because they perceive colleague social pressure more keenly than do their American counterparts.

Like Jamieson (1957), Lipset (1964: 178) suggests that Canada is more collectivity-oriented—a value essential for the effective operation of intraprofessional controls. Comparing the two countries in terms of pattern variables, Lipset (1963: 521) cites many kinds of evidence to show that Americans and Canadians differ in equalitarian values as well; the former are seen as more willing "to tolerate lawlessness" perhaps because "the absence of traditional mechanisms of social control . . . has weakened the pressure to conform with coercion" (Lipset, 1968: 490): ergo, Canadian chiropractors may be expected to adhere more closely to their occupational role.

With respect to impact of differences in national values, Vallee and Whyte observe that "the evidence points to comparatively low rates of deviance . . . and the absence of raw conflict in Canada" (Blishen et al., 1968: 839). This may be seen with the behavioural adaptions of American and Canadian chiropractors because the former more typically have experienced a relationship of keen competition and legal conflict with the medical profession, whereas the Canadian relationship has been one of avoidance and accommodation (Mills, 1966). Jamieson shows a counterpart with industrial relations in Canada and the United States wherein: "Personal or group antagonisms are likely to be expressed in forms of the 'cold shoulder' or the 'brush-off' rather then overt hostility" (1957: 9). Research on American chiropractors (Wardwell, 1955: Stanford Research Institute, 1960) indicates extreme reactions to the medical profession, taking the form of professionally questionable practices with patients and public—something less in evidence on the Canadian scene (Mills, 1966: 41–50).

Thus we conclude that differences between Canadian and American society may be crucial in explaining differences in professional behaviour. But additional work [on] behaviour data about professionals [is] needed to document the effects of societal value and contextual variables on professional behaviour. We also conclude that Wardwell's suggestion about the comparative study of occupations is noteworthy: we were surprised by the many marked differences in the way American and Canadian chiropractors carried out their occupational lives when much of their training backgrounds and practice circumstances were quite similar.

References

Allport, F.H.
1938 "Occupational and societal roles studied with relation to the human behaviour pattern." *Psychological Bulletin* 35 (November): 693–694.

Banton, Michael.
1964 *The Policeman in the Community.* New York: Basic Books.

Barber, Bernard.
1967 "Some problems in the sociology of the professions." In K.S. Lynn (ed.), *The Professions in America.* Boston: Beacon Press.

Baron, George, and Asher Tropp.
1961 "Teachers in England and America." In A.H. Halsey, et al. (eds.), *Education, Economy, and Society,* New York: Free Press.

Bible, Bond L., and James D. McComas.
1963 "Role consensus and teacher effectiveness." *Social Forces* 42 (December): 225–233.

Carr-Saunders, A.M., and P.A. Wilson.
1933 *The Professions.* Oxford: Clarendon Press.

Corwin, Ronald G.
1970 *Militant Professionalism.* New York: Appleton-Century-Crofts.

Form, William H.
1969 "Occupational and social integration of automobile workers in four countries: A comparative study." In N.F. Duffy (ed.), *The Sociology of the Blue-Collar Worker.* Leiden: E.J. Brill.

Fry, John
1970 *Medicine in Three Societies: A Comparison of Medical Care in the USSR, USA and UK.* New York: American Elsevier.

Gross, Neal, W.S. Mason and A.W. McEachern.
1958 *Explorations in Role Analysis: Studies of the School Superintendency Role.* New York: John Wiley.

Hughes, Everett C.
1958 *Men and Their Work.* Glencoe: Free Press.

Jamieson, Stuart.
1957 *Industrial Relations in Canada.* Ithaca: Cornell University Press; Toronto: Macmillan of Canada.

Johnstone, Quinton, and Daniel Hopson.
1967 *Lawyers and their Work.* Indianapolis: Bobbs-Merrill.

Kohn, Melvin L.
1969 *Class and Conformity – A Study in Values.* Homewood, Illinois: Dorsey Press.

Lipset, Seymour M.
1964 "Canada and the United States: A comparative view." *The Canadian Review of Sociology and Anthropology* 1 (November): 173–192.

1968 "Value differences absolute or relative: The English-speaking democracies." "In B.R. Blishen, et al., *Canadian Society-Sociological Perspectives.* Toronto: Macmillan of Canada.

Mills, Donald L.
1966 *Study of Chiropractors, Naturopaths and Osteopaths in Canada.* Ottawa: Queen's Printer.

Mills, Donald L., and Irving Rootman.
1968 "Law and professional behaviour: The case of the Canadian chiropractor." *Univeristy of Toronto Law Journal,* XVIII (2): 170–178.

Montague, Joel B., Jr.
1966 "Professionalism among American, Australian and English physicians." *Journal of Health and Human Behavior* 7 (Winter): 284–89.

1970 "Reported advantages of medical practice in three national health service systems." A paper presented to the International Sociological Association Meetings, Varna, Bulgaria.

Platt, Robert
1963 *Doctor and Patient: Ethics, Morale, Government,* New York: Atherton.

Selltiz, C., M. Johoda, M. Deutsch and S.W. Cook.
1960 *Research Methods in Social Relations.* Revised edition. New York: Henry Holt.

Stanford Research Institute.
1960 *Chiropractic in California.* Los Angeles: The Haynes Foundation.

Sussman, Marvin B.
1966 "Occupational sociology and rehabilitation." In M.B. Sussman (ed), *Sociology and Rehabilitation.* Washington: American Sociological Association.

Tunstall, Jeremy.
1964 *The Advertising Man in London Avertising Agencies.* London: Chapman and Hall.

Vollmer, Howard M., and Donald L. Mills.
1966 *Professionalization.* Englewood Cliffs: Prentice-Hall.

Walsh, James Leo, and R.H. Elling.
1968 "Professionalism and the poor—structural effect and professional behaviour." *Journal of Health and Social Behaviour* 9 (March): 16–29.

Wardwell, Walter I.
1955 "The reduction of strain in a marginal social role." *American Journal of Sociology* 61 (July): 16–25.

1963 "Limited, marginal and quasi-practitioners." Pp. 213–239 in H.F. Freeman, et al. (eds.), *Handbook of Medical Sociology.* Englewood Cliffs: Prentice-Hall.

Whitehead, A.N.
1956 *Adventures in Ideas.* New York: Macmillan.

Whitehill, Arthur M., Jr.
1961 "The Japanese worker." *California Management Review* 3 (Winter): 32–38.

Part II Section D

OLD AGE AND DEATH

16

The Dilemma of the Aging Eskimo*

Lee Guemple

This essay is concerned with the social position of old people in Eskimo society. More specifically, it views old people as a kind of exploitable resource which has value to those who run Eskimo society, the adults. We examine briefly the utilization of the human resource for the benefit of the community. Old age is also seen to be a kind of crisis which adults inevitably face, and an attempt is made to show how the aged cope with the crisis when classification as old becomes inevitable. Perhaps the most interesting fact of aging in Eskimo society is the institutionalized ways Eskimo have of delaying being classified as old people. We examine these usages, isolating "delaying tactics" and "renewal activities". In the summary and conclusions we explore some parallels between the Eskimo treatment of the old and certain features of Euro-North American practice in an effort to gain insight into the North American situation and to see how it compares with the Eskimo's.

Eskimo are not all alike. They are similar in language and in many technological aspects of their culture, but the range of variation in social life is substantial, and so we must be careful to distinguish those subgroups to whom our discussion applies. In this paper we speak in particular of the Qiqiktamiut Eskimo of the Belcher Islands in the south-east corner of Hudson Bay. In a more general way, our discussion is relevant to all Inupiaq-speaking Eskimo (Dumont 1965) of the Canadian Arctic, Greenland, and northern Alaska, but is probably not relevant to the Upiaq Eskimo who inhabit the southern part of Alaska, the coastal islands, and the Siberian coast.

Eskimo have no blanket term for "old people" or "the aged". Old people and adults are always identified by terms which differentiate by sex. A mature adult male is called simply *angutik*, "man", while an adult female is called *arngnak*, "women".[1] When a man becomes old, the term *angutik* is dropped and an individual is characterized by the term *ituk*, "old man", and the term for a woman is similarly changed to *ningiu*, "old woman". In address, names or kinship terms are commonly applied to people. Terms denoting age-grade status are ordinarily used only when referring to old people. These terms are occasionally extended. Thus, the term *ituk* is sometimes used to refer to the leader of a camp, just as in Canadian society the

---

*Revised and abridged from *Sociological Symposium*, 2 (Spring 1969), 59-74. By permission of the author.

boss of the company may somethimes be called "the old man". Both *ituk* and *ningiu* are applied to children under certain circumstances. All these are special applications, however. Ordinarily, the terms are understood to apply only to old people.

The absolute age at which Eskimo identify themselves as "old" is difficult to determine, both because the Eskimo do not calculate age in years and because no outside birth records were kept by authorities in the Canadian Arctic before the 1940s. The result is that age can be based only on rough estimates.[2] Using such figures as the estimates afford, it can be said that both men and women are reckoned by Eskimo to be on the threshold of old age by 47 years, and will be called "old" without exception by age 55. A good dividing line between adulthood and old age is thus approximately 50 years of age.

Eskimo classify an individual as an "adult" when he or she marries, but they have no explicit formula for determining precisely when a person is to be classified as "old". Gubser (1965, 120-122) writes that the North Alaskan Eskimo identify a person as old when he or she begins to show signs of physiological aging, but this does not appear to be a common method of classifying them among the Central Eskimo and is not used by the Qiqiktamiut Eskimo. Numerous Qiqiktamiut are physically old without being classified as such, and several who are physiologically youthful are called old by most Belcher Islanders.

Qiqiktamiut use two methods to determine when a person is old. One is based on the birth cycle, the second on physical capability (not physical appearance). Eskimo reckon that a person is old when he has grandchildren, and most call an individual "old" by the time that person's grandchildren are of an age when they begin to learn basic work skills in earnest, in other words by age 8 years.

The second method is probably the most important, however, and is based on the individual's work status. Work is very demanding in the Arctic in terms of strength and endurance, and there is a relatively rapid reduction in the efficiency of adults after they reach a peak at about 30 years of age. The division of labour in Eskimo society is based primarily on sex, with the result that there is no major work area in the task structure that is specifically allocated to old people; the old people are expected to do the work of any normal adult. Men of any age are expected to hunt if they are able, and the women are required to pursue routine household work for as long as they are capable. Both men and women receive help in work in the later years as their families mature, and they can eventually look forward to a time when most arduous work and all outdoor work will be performed by younger people. Thus, a man can rely on his sons and sons-in-law to hunt with him in his later years. As the father becomes senile, the sons can be expected to hunt for him. The woman relies on her mature daughters and daughters-in-law to fetch water, chop wood, scrape skins, and perform all the arduous tasks in the household, while she does the more sedentary tasks such as sewing, preparing sinew thread, softening skins, cooking, and the other tasks which do not take her far from the sleeping platform at the back of the igloo. These are normal expectations.

Men and women alike are identified as old when their working status becomes marginal, in other words, when they can no longer do the work of fully efficient adults. A man is "old" when he can no longer hunt regularly. Spring and summer hunting is not particularly demanding, and it is not beyond the capability of a man of even 60 years to hunt seal in a kayak in open water season. When a man cannot hunt in mid-winter, when the work is most rigorous, and when the need for food is most pressing, then he will be called "old" by his fellows. Old age comes to a man suddenly; the transformation can take place in a single year.

The transformation of a women to *ningiu* is more subtle. Because women's work is less demanding and is ordinarily performed collectively, the decreasing physical capability of a woman does not appear so obviously or so dramatically as it does in man's work. Women, then, are not labelled "old" until they are well beyond the ability to do a full round of work.

The application of the old age label is hastened by debilitating and crippling diseases and by incapacitating injuries. Typical diseases are arthritis, causing loss of agility, and trachoma, causing loss of sight. Both sexes appear to be equally prone to arthritis, but the women suffer more from trachoma. In the total population of 168 Belcher Islanders, the four who are seriously affected by trachoma are women. Men suffer more from crippling accidents such as loss of digits or limbs while hunting, or impairment of functioning due to freezing or gun shot wounds, which occur at the rate of one or two yearly in many communities. A major cause of incapacity in the modern era is tuberculosis, which necessitates an operation. These impairments result in a loss of efficiency, and if a person is prematurely incapacitated he will be designated "old" at a comparatively early age.

Eskimo are extremely practical. They highly esteem those who make the greatest contribution to the welfare of the family and community. This is true for the old and young as well as the adults. Sentiment is not absent in Eskimo life. Although they are not demonstrative, Eskimo do feel very strongly about family and relatives, and will go to great lengths to be hospitable even to a stranger. But the margin for sentiment in the Arctic is very narrow; the pragmatic business of making a living takes precedence over sentiment. People, then, are judged in terms of their worth as producers. If we are to evaluate the position of the old in Eskimo society, it is best to consider them as do the Eskimo themselves, namely, as a special kind of resource. Viewed in this light, the old make two important contributions: (1) a source of extra labour for the camp, and (2) a source of knowledge and wisdom essential for order and continuity in the society.

The typical domestic unit in Eskimo society consists of a nuclear family, that is, the man, his wife, and their unmarried offspring (Murdock 1949). The family is founded at marriage when the couple go to live with the wife's family until the first child is born. They are then free to establish their own household neolocally or independent of others. There they raise their children. Eventually, the children mature, marry, and move away, leaving only the aged parents alone in the household.

Old people without children to care for and without hunting obligations have considerable spare time on their hands; thus, they are available to help others with their routine work. There are numerous occasions when their help is needed. The routine chores of the woman in the household are suspended during the birth of a child, sickness, or an emergency sewing job such as repairing a kayak. At such a time, old women are called in to supply the needed labour. During the making of an *umiak* (whale boat) or a kayak, special tasks are sometimes assigned to old women. For the men, it is much the same. Old men can assist in the building of a sled or in butchering. Occasionally there is special remuneration for this work,[3] but ordinarily it is enough that they receive the customary share of food when game is distributed after the hunt.

More than for their labour, old people are respected for their knowledge and experience. Societies without a literate tradition usually assign a special role to their old people. The old provide continuity by acting as repositories of conventional knowledge. Thus, an old man will be called on to advise on the making of some item of equipment, to judge the effect of weather and ice conditions on hunting prospects for the day, to instruct on the proper method of building a snow house, or to decide when it is time to erect tents in the spring. The advice of the old is also sought on questions of customary behaviour or on the remedy for an ailment. More often than not, the advice of the old is well-received, since there is no one else who can provide any answers or suggest a better course. The old man is thus respected, even revered, for providing knowledge which the society requires in order to carry on the business of life.

Women play a humbler if no less indispensable role. They advise on sewing and the proper way of curing, preparing, cutting, and sewing skins. Since the women are generally more familiar with the social relationships in Eskimo society, it is the old women who provide information to those inquiring or puzzled about kinship connections. Women provide what knowledge of medicine the Eskimo possess. they instruct on child care, food preparation, and so forth.

Both the old men and women play an important role in the maintenance of social control and in reinforcing concepts of ideal behaviour. It is the old people who are permitted to comment publicly on the social impropriety of members, and they do not hesitate to do so. Making such comments is not permissible for adults. Old people are the keepers of the sacred and secular lore of the society, and so play a crucial role in maintaining the traditional models of appropriate conduct. Oral tradition in the form of folk tale and myth provides for the Eskimo the only models for normative action. The old people are the story-tellers. They play the key role in maintaining and perpetuating the models which serve as ideal guides to socially approved behaviour.

Eskimo cannot easily express their feelings about old people. Adults sometimes say they indulge their children as a form of old-age insurance, that their children will treat them well when they as parents have grown old. It is not unusual for a child to point out that this is the reason he is so attached to his parents. Apart from this indirect statement of sentiment, the Eskimo find no words to express their views on the treatment of the aged.

It is not difficult to find indices of respect paid the old people, however. The imperative form of address, for example, is a command adults use when addressing children and, good naturedly, and sometimes angrily, when addressing other adults. Men especially address younger people and women in this manner, and women often address younger girls and children using this mode of speech. Use of the imperative form of address, then, is evidence of a rough status hierarchy, a pecking order, in which men stand above women and women about the young. Hardly ever is the form used in addressing old people, which suggests they stand at the head of the hierarchy in esteem if not in authority.

The aged do not want for attention in other respects as well. Children leave the natal household at marriage, but kinship is the sole basis for social affiliation. Kinship exercises a more profound influence on the relations between parents and children when the latter have married. In the ideal situation, parents raise a house full of children to maturity and marriage, and then "retire" in their old age to be supported by the children. The ideal is best exemplified where several married children set up households in the same locality of their parents and thus become the basic nucleus of a localized hunting camp. Organized into a series of joint households focussing on the aging parents, the family will consist of parents and married children, their spouses and offspring, occasional collateral relatives and their families, and even affinally-connected families, adopted children, and strangers. The camp will thus consist of a collection of relatives linked together (Bohannan 1963, 126-129), and centred on the old couple. The aged parents in such a situation will never want for food or other necessities and their household will continually be filled with children and relatives who come to visit, learn the news of the camp, and listen to the old stories which the parents tell with great delight and skill.

These old people will have social ties of another sort which stretch throughout the community. Successful Eskimo begin to accumulate ritual relations of various kinds when they are quite young (Guemple 1966a). At first, these involve obligations they incur toward others for economic and ritual support and for intimate social interaction. In old age, the direction of the relationships is reversed, and the young people have special obligations to the old people in caring for them and in providing them with necessities and luxuries. The man or woman who has been successful in life may have a dozen or more such connections with members of his own camp or other camps in the community. In times of need, these persons can be relied on for help. The old people are not wanting for close, intimate connections and economic support.

Because old people are thought to be "near death", they enjoy an unusual ritual status. Eskimo believe that when a person dies, part of his soul returns to the underworld to reside in the land of the dead. When a child is born the soul returns to the community to take up residence in the body of the child.[4] Adults, anxious to please the soul and assure its return to inhabit a new body, will be respectful of the old people.

This same belief helps to rationalize death to old people. As one Eskimo put it: "Life is like an endless string that goes on and on without beginning or end." Believing that the old can be reborn in the young, they have no real fear of dying. There is an aura of serenity about old people, then, even as they await death.

We have presented an ideal image of old age at its best in Eskimo society. This is the image Eskimo themselves like to stress in discussing the situation of the old walrus hunter and his aged, toothless wife. Yet adult men and women invariably resist becoming old. Reasons for this spring in part from the situation of old people in the status system and in part from negative elements in the treatment of the old.

In practice, the elderly suffer a reduction of status. The concept of social cynosure (La Barre 1956) helps to show why this is so. The idea of a social cynosure encompasses the notion that in every society specific social roles are considered prestigeful and thereby hold the focus of social attention. Almost everyone in the role position becomes an object of prestige and honour. In Chinese society, for example, it is the patriarch and his aged wife who occupy the most prestigious positions both within the family and the society at large. A Chinese looks forward eagerly to his later years as the best time of his life. It is during old age when he receives the most attention and is most admired, respected, and cared for. In Canadian society the young nubile female occupies centre stage; one important motif governing the Canadian's social life is the virtue of "youth" and "being young". Adulthood signifies that the best stage of life is passed. The rest of life is anti-climatic.[5] In Eskimo society the cynosure is the adult, particularly the adult male. The powerful hunter is the focus of attention. It is the man who receives most attention, is most admired, is most readily accepted. To be old is to step out of the most prestigeful position; hence both men and women resist being identified as old.

There are also many negative elements in the treatment afforded the old by the adults. First, the old people maintain their positive position, as we have described it, only so long as they are productive. They suffer a marked reduction in both respect and affection when they are no longer able to make a useful contribution. As they grow older and are increasingly immobilized by age and disease they become dependents without influence and without consideration.

The loss in status may take the form of indifference or cruel hazing. Children will taunt an old man because he can no longer hunt but only eat. Girls will make cruel remark to an old women because her gait is slow and her limbs are crippled. At first, adults control the sharp tongues of the children but after a while the adults no longer bother and may themselves becomes disrespectful of the elderly. Impatient treatment of the non-productive members is not reserved for the old. All unproductive persons, be it a lazy girl or a crippled adult male, are targets for a continual barrage of criticism and jokes. But the elderly are most often the object of ridicule because they are most uniformly unproductive.

An economic squeeze is also put on the old people by virtue of the prevailing value system. The ethic is that "Eskimo share everything", and the fact mirrors the conviction in most cases. Even so, there are two elements of unequal treatment afforded the old. The Eskimo ideal specifies that each family is to receive an equal share of the traditional goods, but shares vary in quality. The shoulder of the seal is preferred to the hind flipper, for example. The rules of sharing dictate that if a person receives a poor cut of meat one time, he is entitled to a choice cut the next but, in fact, the old people always receive the poorer cuts. The reason is that they make little contribution to the subsistence base.

The most difficult economic hardship has to do with trade goods. Traditional goods are viewed as essentials and are shared as a matter of right. Trade goods, on the other hand, are viewed as luxuries and for these one must fend for himself. The main source of these goods is the trading post where they can be obtained for barter or cash. The chief source of income in the Arctic has always been derived from fur trapping. This being a form of winter hunting, it is obviously an activity in which the old no longer engage. Old age creates a crisis because it deprives people of money income. They have no means, therefore, to obtain even relatively essential trade goods like tea, tobacco, thread, needles, weapons, ammunition, and especially the ingredients for baking bannock, a fried bread that constitutes their main food staple. In order to procure these items, the old people are reduced to begging money from relatives and friends. Unable to repay the lender, the elderly must ask for charity.[6]

In spite of the fact that the kinship network provides protection for the aged, Arctic living conditions make this kind of insurance extremely unreliable at times. Should one parent die, the other is forced to give up the household and move in with one of the married children. Friction often develops between the parent and the son- or daughter-in-law. Parents in this situation are frequently overworked and undercompensated. More critical is the predicament in which both parents survive their children and close relatives. They are accorded respectful treatment as long as they are productive to some degree; otherwise, they are subject to increasing isolation. Though they need not fear starvation, they may be reduced to poverty and isolation. The most pitiable situation occurs when only the one parent survives children and close relatives. The survivor is forced to seek shelter in the household of some relative. Occasionally, one finds an aged Eskimo more than a hundred miles from his natal community, living in the household of a virtual stranger. The plight of the aged in these circumstances compares with the plight of the orphan. Occupying a very low status, he remains outside the circle of kinship. Such persons are accorded no respect and are assigned the most odious work tasks in the household. They occupy the lowest status in the society.

The ritual status enjoyed by old people can also be a source of tension. The belief that the aged, especially the women, possess special powers can have positive good, as is the case in the treatment of a sick child by an elderly women or the selection of a compatible name for a child by the elderly man.[7] But these powers can also be viewed as potentially dangerous (Gubser 1965: 122; Spencer 1959: 251-252). Strange events are attributed to the secret activities of some old woman. This witchcraft-like attribution sometimes protects old people against the cruelty at the hands of adults. More often, however, it becomes a source of hostility and suspicion leading to social isolation, estrangement, and sometimes violence.

It is little wonder, then, that mature men and women resist being tagged "old".

They search for ways to postpone "retirement". The two main strategies are: (1) economic participation in the community, and (2) manipulation of social relations.

An old man attempts to delay retirement by masking his inadequacy. To compensate for his inability to hunt in winter, for example, he may increase production during the latter part of winter and early spring or during mid-winter days when the weather permits. In the spring the aging hunter will launch a flurry of hunting activity, struggling to out-produce the younger men by skill or sheer exertion. Further, he takes pains to liberally distribute his kill in the form of gifts even when food is not needed. At other times, he offers gifts of seal skin, sinew thread, or handmade tools to remind the community that he is still productive.

Another delaying tactic is to exploit others. The old man may assiduously control productive output and see to a careful distribution of it. He may struggle to keep his daughters and their husbands closely tied to the house to utilize their labour. He attempts to control his sons and their wives as well. He may even collect distant relatives, orphans, or strangers to maintain a labour force.

The other strategy is renewal through social transformation. An old person may establish a relationship with a young person so that they share the same activity. Similar activity expresses symbolically the restoration of youth. Notably, an old man may "renew" himself by taking a young wife. A man approaching old age with family of mature or nearly mature children has need of additional labour in his household. This need is usually met by a young woman or an older orphaned girl. She is introduced into the household as an "adopted daughter" and may replace the wife in performing the household chores. On occasion, she may replace the wife in sexual obligations as well and thus become a second wife to the household head. This marriage has the effect or realigning the husband generationally with the younger members of the society. The husband's involvement in the activities and concerns of the maturing children, the concerns of courtship, marriage, and childbearing, provides him with a sense of renewal and restoration of youth.

For the older women there is no opportunity for delaying old age through intensified economic activity. No work that women customarily perform is counted so important that increased activity will enhance her social position. A woman may manipulate the value system by being generous with gifts and by helping with the work in other households. But these methods have limited usefulness as delaying tactics. Remarriage to a younger man is improbable because old age makes the woman sexually unattractive. A more effective strategy to demonstrate continual productivity is the adoption of children.

The prevailing pattern of adoption is for the child to pass from its parents to its parent's siblings (Dunning 1962). Another adoption pattern gives the child to a grandparent or great aunt. Old women adopt grandchildren because "it makes one feel young again to have a child to care for". Adoption has the dual effect of placing the grandparent on the generational level of her own children and of restoring the grandparent's usefulness to the community in rearing a potential producer. The old women readily recognize the significance of this, for it is said that "when an old woman has no child to care for, she feels old and useless and comes close to death". Generally, male children are preferred.[8]

Sooner or later the old become too incapacitated to perform adult duties. An old woman becomes so infirm she can no longer care for her adopted child. The parents reassert their rights and reclaim the child. An old man can no longer obviate the attentions of a younger hunter paid to his young wife. She will soon be appropriated by the younger man. The old man must shift for himself. The position of the aged becomes desperate; they are abadoned and their uselessness is exposed.

Until recently when the elderly became a drain on the resources of the community, the practical bent of the Eskimo asserted itself. To alleviate the burden of infirmity, the old people were done away with. As Hawkes (1916, 117) points out, this was done when life had become a burden but the act was usually in accordance with the wishes of the persons concerned and thought to be a proof of the devotion of the children.

The matter could be initiated by either party. The children might take the initiative by abandoning the aged parent on the trail. They might break camp, load the sled, and send the aged parent back to the snow house to fetch an item supposedly left behind. The family would then drive off, leaving the old one to his fate. More often it was the parent who initiated the process. During a storm or when the family was busily occupied, the aged parent would quietly slip off into the tundra to die from exhaustion and exposure.

There are major differences between Eskimo and Southern Canadians in handling the problem of old age. But old age is a universal phenomenon, so that many problems and remedies encountered by the Eskimo have analogies in our way of life.

Our comparison concerns the use of the aged as economic and social resources. Eskimo have a very practical attitude toward old people. They are valued according to their productive contribution to the community. They are respected for their labour and knowledge. Southern Canadians also have a practical bent in their evaluation of the social contribution of persons, but little value is placed on the aged as such. Little importance is attached to their labour potential or output and less to their conventional wisdom. Advanced technology and labour specialization make the labour of the aged superfluous. Advanced and specialized media serve as information and knowledge purveyers in place of the oral tradition of wise old men and women. Scientific and technological advances leave the old people far behind.

An important difference exists in the treatment of old people. Eskimo maximize the potentialities of the aged; Southern Canadians view their aged as obsolete and consign them to compulsory retirement. The Canadian tragedy should not be judged in terms of the waste in labour alone, but in terms also of the social and sentimental waste of old people.

A second point of comparison between Eskimo and Euro-Canadian societies concerns the role of the family in maintaining the social position of old people. The structure of the family (nuclear) and the pattern of residence (neolocal) is the same for both societies. In the articulation of old people in the family, however, the societies are different. Eskimo continue to support their old parents socially and economically after the children have grown, married, and set up new domestic units. This support is binding on both the immediate family and the wider range of relatives. Sometimes old people in Eskimo society are isolated from relatives because of the vagaries of the environment, but the old are rarely completely cut off from close kinsmen. In Euro-Canadian society, when children marry and establish their own domiciles, they usually do so at the expense of kinship relations. After marriage there is a tendency to establish social ties without references to the family of origin. The most significant social connections generally flow from occupational contacts and non-kinship associations. When the family matures, parents are socially separated from their children; at retirement parents lose most occupationally related social connections. The old are gradually cut off from the mainstream of social life (Cavan 1962).

A final point of comparison relates to renewal activity. Eskimo renew themselves through the institutionalized forms of marriage and adoption to maintain intimate contact and involvement with young people. There is evidence of this type of activity in Southern Canadian society. Women attempt to renew themselves by means of cosmetics, weight-control programs, and other "maintenance" activities. Older men marry young women. Persons in middle years have become increasingly active in "youth" activities . . . . The marriage of two aged persons has become more common now that the barriers to such unions in the social security laws have been eliminated.

Other forms of restorative activity include new careers in retirement and travel. Renewed interest in education is probably the single best evidence of restorative activity on the part of many old people, and one that best exemplifies the symbolic aspect of renewal activity.

Eskimo are rapidly becoming acculturated and the position of the Eskimo aged may soon approximate that of Southern Canada. It would be ironical if, while attempting to resolve the problem of the aged in Southern society through recourse to Eskimo social patterns, we were to impose our dilemma upon the Eskimo hunting culture, eradicating those patterns.

Notes

1. An individual becomes an adult at marriage, so it is little wonder that these terms also carry the meaning of "husband" and "wife", at least in the eastern Arctic.

2. Robert Flaherty visited the Belcher Islands in 1917 to become the second white man ever to land there, and the first to make any lasting impression on the people. Most adults reckon their births from his arrival, so that their absolute ages can be calculated with some accuracy.

3. Thus when women aid in childbirth, it is customary to give them a small gift (Jenness 1922: 165-167) and men and women receive a gift of tobacco when they help in recovering a kayak (Guemple 1966a: 18).

4. This is one reason why children are sometimes called "old man" or "old woman" as mentioned above. See Carpenter (1954), and Guemple (1965).

5. The reticence of young people to go into "business" and have families may be related to the cynosure, where going to work means accepting adult status and thus "growing old".

6. In the modern era an increase in various transfer payments such as old age pensions has somewhat alleviated this burden. But modernization has also meant that fewer men hunt regularly. Recently, old couples have suffered more for want of traditional food because of a shortage of hunters and this shortage can only partly be relieved through purchases at the store.

7. The object of name-choosing is to find the appropriate name of the soul that inhabits the child. If the child then becomes ill, it is assumed either that the wrong name has been chosen or that the soul is incompatible with the body of the child. In both cases, a new name is selected and the change is accomplished in a ritual.

8. Eskimo traditionally practiced female infanticide in order to reduce the population size and alleviate the burden of feeding the community. Male offspring were always kept even when they were not particularly wanted for they would become hunters and producers.

References

Bohannan, Paul

1963 *Social Anthropology.* New York: Holt, Rinehart and Winston.

Carpenter, E.S.

1954 "Eternal Life and Self-Definition Among the Aivilik Eskimos". *American Journal of Psychiatry* 60: 840-843.

Cavan, Ruth

1962 "Self and Role in Adjustment in Old Age", in Arnold M. Rose, ed., *Human Behaviour and Social Processes.* Boston: Houghton Mifflin. 526-535.

Dumont, D.

1965 "Eskaleutian Linguistics, Archaeology and Pre-history". *American Anthropologist* 67: 1231-1267.

Dunning, R.W.

1962 "A Note on Adoption Among the Southampton Island Eskimo". *Man* 259: 163-167.

Gubser, Nicholas

1965 *The Nunamiut Eskimo: Hunters of Caribou.* New Haven: Yale University Press.

Guemple, Lee

1966a "The Pacalik Kayak of the Belcher Islands". *National Museum of Canada Bulletin* 204: 152-218.

1966b *Kinship Reckoning of the Belcher Island Eskimo.* Ph.D. dissertation, University of Chicago.

Hawkes, Ernest

1916 *The Labrador Eskimo.* Geological Survey of Canada, Memoir No. 91 (Anthropological Series No. 14).

Jenness, Diamond

1922 *The Life of the Copper Eskimos.* Report of the Canadian Arctic Expedition, 1913-1918, Vol. 12.

LaBarre, Weston

1956 "Social Cynosure and Social Structure", in Douglas G. Haring, ed., *Personal Character and Culture Milieu.* Syracuse: Syracuse University Press. 535-546.

Spencer, Robert, F.

1959 *The North Alaskan Eskimo.* Bureau of American Enthnology, Bulletin No. 171. Washington, D.C.: Smithsonian Institute.

17

Social Implications of the Immediacy of Death*

Rex A. Lucas

Our knowledge of the psychological and social processes surrounding death is limited because of lack of data. Accounts of the experience written immediately before death are suspect because they are written for loved ones or a general public. What is more, the sedation used in comtemporary hospital care usually keeps the seriously ill patient in a state of neutrality or euphoria. Because of these facts, most of our rather hazy notions about the prelude to death probably come to us through fiction and film. The bulk of the non-fictional literature on death is philosophical or theological in nature, although recently there have been articles on death as seen by the physician, nurse, clergyman, and the social scientist.[1]

Death is an experience faced but once by each individual; yet dying, like living, is a social role, and it is in this sense that death is considered here. Doubtless, individuals die with no foreknowledge of death, but many--perhaps most--know that death is approaching and this becomes part of their role and the roles of their associates. Just as avoidance of the immediacy of death is crucial to everyday roles, recognition of the immediacy of death would be expected to call for social and role adjustments. Thus, although each death is unique, it is also social.

Individuals, groups, and societies have developed social patterns to cope with the social aftermath of death, so that the bereaved maintain some integrated social roles, "reinvest their emotional capital", and yet have some legitimate expression of their feelings.[2] The social patterns appropriate to those who are dying are far less clear.

The data used in this article were drawn from intensive interviews of survivors of a coal mine disaster.[3] An underground upheaval trapped six men in a limited space for eight and a half days; in another part of the mine twelve men were trapped for six and a half days. For the first three days of their entrapment the uninjured men in both groups explored, dug, and tunnelled ceaselessly in their futile attempts to work through tons of rock and debris. When the batteries of their miners lights were exhausted, darkness altered their relationships to the environment. The men abruptly changed from active attempts to escape to conserving their energy, waiting either for death or rescue. Without food or water, with no certainty that they could be rescued in time, the men in each of the two separate groups considered the immediacy of their own deaths.[4]

---

* Abridged from *The Canadian Review of Sociology and Anthropology* 5:1, 1968, 1-16. By permission of the author and the Canadian Sociology and Anthropology Association.

Implications of the Avoidance of Death

Death is a phenomenon common to many orders, for at death "the system has passed a one-way boundary through which it can never return under its own dynamic."[5] Death is common to all members of all societies and although the finality and inevitability of death are accepted by individuals, "death stands before us, not like fate that will strike at a certain moment, but, prior to that moment, exists only as an idea of prophecy, as fear or hope and without interfering with the reality of this life."[6] Death, the one inevitability, is relegated to an unconsidered limbo for great stretches of time and the pretense that life is unlimited permits us to carry over unfinished business from hour to hour, day to day, and even year to year. The denial of the immediacy of death permits the delay of decisions and actions because each day's business does not have to be completed as though it were the last one. Long-term plans, deferred gratifications, careers, and even immediate social action make sense only if it is assumed that death will not interfere.

The effect of the immediacy of death on the patient is a concern of the physician. The medical doctor has to decide if and when a terminally ill person is told that he is about to die. The decision depends not so much upon the patient's being able to accept the information as the effect of the knowledge upon the patient's behaviour: "Hope must never die too far ahead of the patient; either hope of getting better or hope of enjoyment of conversations tomorrow."[7] In much the same way, in face of deprivations and the immediacy of death, some definition of hope and with it faith in a future was crucial to the trapped miners.

Although these underground workers had witnessed death and injury in the course of their day-to-day work, prior to entrapment, they had managed to avoid the discussion of death and it remained a remote and distant prophecy. Few of the miners thought of death on a moment-to-moment basis. In much the same way, the miners considered the death of companions in the disaster which trapped them alive in quite a different way than they ultimately came to view their own impending deaths. We will first consider the ways in which the miners considered the deaths of their companions.

The Death of Others

The entrapped miners could not avoid the reality of the deaths of their close companions. When the underground unheaval struck the mine, the quake moved in waves, literally burying every other man working at the coal face; each man found a heap of debris beside him instead of a vital work companion. Later, during their persistent attempts to escape, the men had to crawl around and across dead bodies of former companions. They handled corpses to remove lamps and batteries. One miner, some distance from one of the groups, was given up for dead; another miner, pinned in the debris, died a few feet from his companions after several days of delirium. Despite all of these close associations, however, the detailed accounts of the men showed little preoccupation with the death of these companions.

One persistent tendency running through the accounts of the miners was to define live men as dead. Consider the following evidence: "We seen the dead men--they were breathing of course." "We knowed there was three dead because I went down below the pack and there was one fellow laying across the pans. Then there was another fellow laying right on top. He was breathing when I went down. I took the lamp off him."

A number of miners defined other men as dead when they were not physiologically dead at the time, and the deadest one (the isolated man) never did die. But in all cases these men were socially dead, regardless of breathing or pulse beat. So far as the miners were concerned if the man was "unconscious" or "not himself" or unable to interact or "couldn't talk", he was dead.[8]

The second persistent tendency was not to experience emotion on the loss of work mates at the time of the upheaval. Friends were buried under tons of rock and coal, dead and dying men had been alive vital people a few moments before, and yet all the accounts are matter of fact. Even the death of the pinned miner within a few feet of one group of miners was not considered as stressful: "It didn't bother me too much." "The pinned miner dying didn't bother me one bit. It didn't bother me a particle. I set right there."

It is difficult to account for this lack of emotion without introducing *ad hoc* psychiatric or pseudo-psychiatric explanations. The evidence suggests four social factors which may have influenced the behaviour of the men. In the first place, the survivors were preoccupied with their own lives, rather than with the deaths of others. As a result, the first three days, for instance, were filled with intensive physical activity as they attempted to escape to safety. Second, within this frame of reference a corpse was seen as a possible source of an extra miner's lamp and battery or of extra drinking water rather than as a body of a dead friend. Thus it is no wonder that the distinction between social and physiological death was made. Third, the miners' norms incorporated general emotional restraint in all matters concerning danger and distressing stimuli. Fourth, this normative pattern, an important part of the miners' subculture, was deeply internalized as part of each miner's self-conception. Each miner felt that a "real" man does not betray emotion.

Generally, the men were protected from omnipresence of death by the darkness. Even during escape operations the men were unable to avoid distasteful stimuli by directing the beam of light from their miner's lamps away from the object. The importance of the darkness may be judged from this abridged comment on seeing in the rescuers' lights what had been covered by darkness for a week:
"The worst thing I seen was that body—when I seen him that morning (of rescue), I'm telling you, it was terrible, and I think if I had seen him like that during the time we was there, it would have bothered me; but we couldn't see him, see. But that morning when the men (rescuers) come up and I saw him when they put the light on him—he was an awful looking sight. This is the first time I ever seen anything like that."

For the most part, then, the miners were able to remain shielded from the dead bodies, so that the only direct contacts with the dead were utilitarian when obtaining light batteries or water pails or accidental while exploring in the dark.

After the fifth day of entrapment, the men began to contemplate their own deaths. We will consider this in terms first of the physiological nature of death, and then of the social implications of death in terms of unfinished business, vacant social roles, and accounting of achievement.

The Physiological Nature of Death

The sketchy research that exists suggests that many people fear other things much more than death. College students reported more fear of snakes, cancer, and death of others than of their own death.[9] Children do not fear death greatly; in some cultures old people welcome death,[10] and in some, such as Japan, death by one's own hand is desirable in certain circumstances.

There are some forms of death which are feared more than others.[11] Of the many forms of death, four were mentioned by the men--death by starvation, thirst, lack of oxygen, and deadly gas. Although there were no persistent patterns, individuals discussed marked preferences for certain types of death: "We figured if the gas was going to get us we would just lay down and go to sleep."

Diggory and Rothman suggest that the physiological aspects of dying might include the experience of pain.[12] It is usually assumed that some deaths are more painful than others. The miners speculated on this physical nature of death and demonstrated a strong tendency to mitigate the connection with suffering:[13] "I just said to myself, 'Well, I'll likely not know much about it because I'll keep getting weaker all the time.' The way I figured it, we would just keep getting weaker and weaker all the time and *go to sleep* and that would be the end of it."

These comments indicate little expressed fear of physical death; curiosity is more characteristic than fear. Many were able to persuade themselves that dying was "going to sleep", "more like a dream than anything", "we would never know what happened". The few who were not convinced that death was "going to sleep" were content to "wonder" about the nature of death. Sleep is familiar and usually implies a state of pleasant social neutrality and, as such, is a commonly used euphemism for death.

Although life ends when it crosses a death boundary, it is commonly held that it may reform itself in afterlife. The eighteen miners included Protestants and Roman Catholics, church attenders and nominal adherents, but only one mentioned afterlife. Most supernatural references were in terms of the present--the relationship of God to prayer and aid and comfort in the present rather than the future. Prayer was most important in order to sustain hope, to delay death, but it was not used to influence afterlife. The one direct reference to afterlife expressed curiosity rather than a declaration of faith: "I always thought all my life that if we die and when we die, if we meet again . . . I thought about that and I though to myself—it is not going to be too long before I'm going to find out for myself. I said to myself—I'll soon find out now, whether we see one another when we died."

Social Implications of Death

It has been suggested that fear of death may be associated with the loss of utility of the self.[14] This means that death is a different phenomenon when seen through the eyes of people of different ages, religions, marital states, classes, and sexes. The time dimension of death has been noted in terms of temporal orientation,[15] age,[16] premature death,[17] and social loss.[18]

1. Unfinished Business

There are three aspects of this temporal aspect of death which are pertinent here. First, "premature" death cuts through ongoing activity leaving short-term unfinished business. These unfinished activities were brought to the attention of the miners by the prospects of immediate death. Despite the fact that they had worked daily in a dangerous occupation the men had been able to work as if there was no undue threat to themselves. When faced with the immediacy of death they thought about incomplete short term activities: "Funny thing, I got a couple a pieces of hose to put on the heater of the car, and I—as a rule when I do anything like that, the boys at the auto shop, I know them real well—I often take little things like that. It was $1.40, and I didn't pay them and I didn't leave a note for my wife to see that I owed them this $1.40 and I worried about them not getting their pay."

"I had just bought my son a .303 rifle, and I never even had a shot out of it." . . . "I thought a lot about that hunting trip we had planned for our week-end." "I happened to mail three letters on my way to work and I thought about them."

2. *Vacant Social Roles*

The second aspect of death was seen as more important than immediate short-run and sometimes peripheral concerns. Premature death creates a number of vacant roles; this phenomenon has also been called social loss. Social characteristics such as age, education, occupation, family status, social class, and accomplishments influence the total value which the dying individual embodies; they indicate the social loss to family, occupation, and society at death. Aged people, for instance, have made their major contributions to family, occupation, and society. Their loss, while felt by the bereaved, is considered less than if they were younger. The aged often have a far greater sense of completeness of roles than younger people, for social loss or vacant roles derive much of their meaning from the length of the anticipated future.

The youngest miner was 22, the oldest 58; all but two had children. The miners' main preoccupation was with vacant roles. Their basic concern was not with the physical facts of death, but with the social implications of their death. Among young and middle-aged males, care for dependents, the desire to have experiences and to complete plans and projects, are at the high end of the fear scale rather than fate in afterlife, fate of the body after death. or possible pain while dying.[19]

If the dying person is a young male with a family, one social loss is his financial contribution to his dependents. The maintenance of children and a home usually strains family budgets during the early stages of marriage, so precautionary financial measures are often deferred on the assumption that the death of a young breadwinner is not imminent. Often financial security is maintained in the form of life insurance; the cost of this security rests upon the balance of security and chance in the different phases of peoples' lives.[20]

In this single-industry mining community characterized by a high fatality rate, where death and serious injury are commonplace and anticipated, elaborate provisions for death had become an integral part of the social structure in the form of funds for widows and voluntary pay deductions for pre-paid church support, municipal taxes, and medical and hospital benefits. Despite these assurances--"I figured my wife would get compensation"--several of the trapped men considered the financial implications of their death: "Well, I'd just bought an insurance policy about three months before this, and I went up a couple of weeks before this, and I paid the insurance premium. It was paid up and if I was killed it was six thousand dollars. I was kind of easy minded because I knew that would do the wife for a little while."

The men indicated, however, that the financial aspects were not so important as the social aspects of their roles of husband, father, son, and brother: "I began to think of my wife and daughter. I have a lovely daughter. I thought what my poor wife would do." "I wondered if they would be all right." "I thought of my family. I thought of them all. I figured my wife could get compensation. I hoped and prayed she would stay home with the little girl."

While the men were contemplating their own death in terms of the social loss incurred by the bereaved, they were assessing their own worth. This sense of worth was discussed by the men in terms of the size of the social loss that death would bring about. Four men entered into a competition about their relative worth: "Tom said to me 'Oh, if I could only go home and see my little Mary,' I said, 'Look, Tom, there is nobody would like to see their wife more than I would.' "

The speaker assured Tom that "there is nobody (who) would like to see (my) wife more (than I would)," and went on to explain that his worth (loss) was much greater. Then the man with the largest family joined in, "My wife will be well provided for, but it is so hard to bring up a *large* family alone." In the meantime, the only unmarried man in the group noted, "I was single myself, but all the rest of the fellows were talking about how they would like to get home to their wives, and I just talked about how I would like to get home too, you know." The unmarried man then introduced the assertion that he would like to return to his girl friend. He was announcing that he too hada sense of worth (as sons and boyfried) even without a wife.

The preoccupation with role vacancies, the sudden finality led thoughts back to bygone days. The men remembered things long forgotten or fondly recollected: "I thought about all the good times I had had." "And there is a brook down there--my wife and I used to go down in the summertime." "I thought a lot about old friends and a lot of my childhood memories came back to me."

They could not convince themselves that they were dying a hero's death, for all past anxiety and sense of foreboding connected with their dangerous occupation as well as the objections of their wives were justified. It was too late to do anything about it.

3. Accounting of Achievement

The third temporal aspect of death is the final accounting of life's achievement. This is closely related to the notion of social loss or social worth. The men realized that they were socially if not yet physiologically dead. Socially they had died, for in their role-playing beyond the mine, there was no tomorrow, no going back, and, most frustrating, although they were physiologically alive, there was no way of making amends. Social activity in the family, groups, the community, and society irrevocably terminated, each miner turned to an evaluation of his completed life span. The evaluation was difficult because the miners had been cut off from ongoing activities; this in our society is treated as "premature" and thus undesirable.

The miners' conversation indicates that most sought a feeling of self-worth and reassurance that they had creditable achievements. The men could be said to have used an apologia as a form of self-justification. Goffman notes that in asylums, "given the stage that any person has reached in a career, one typically finds that he constructs an image of his life course--past, present, and future--which selects, abstracts and distorts in such a way as to provide him with a view of himself that he can usefully expound in the current situation."[21] In the mine, the men could only talk of the present, for they had no future, but the miners reviewed their lives, pleased with the successes, disturbed by failures and omissions. One summed up the process with Biblical simplicity: "We started thinking about the things we should have done and we didn't do, (at) home. You know what I mean? "

The miners did not use identical values as the basis of their judgments of their own accomplishments: certainly all miners did not come to similar conclusions about their accomplishments, as the following excerpts illustrate: "I had no regrets in that respect because I had enjoyed myself while I was around; me and mine individually, and I had gone according to my means and I figured that I had enjoyed life." "I've got a bathtub out there. I got a sink in there, and everything all ready to hook up; I never even got it hooked up yet. I had just bought it; it is still brand new, still in the bathroom. My home is not too nice, I built it myself, and I'm paying for it now, but the furniture, you know, we just let it go. I figured that after a while we would get a new chesterfield." "I thought of all I had done and everything that went on in my life."

These statements and the conversation of the men indicate that the miners were seeking reaffirmation that their achievements were creditable. In some cases, the men were literally asking their companions to redefine the situation so as to provide them with maximum credit. This exchange, however, necessitated enough interaction space for each individual to talk about his accomplishments to an uninvolved listener.

Death and Bereavement as Social Patterns

In reviewing these data, it is obvious that facing immediate death poses problems similar to those faced by the other actors in the drama—the bereaved. Both the bereaved and those about to die have similar concerns about the physical aspects of death)"he did not know a thing about it, but passed peacefully in his sleep") and incomplete activities ("he had intended to finish this next week"). There is a similar preoccupation with vacant roles; in both cases, the bereaved and those to die are worried about the people left to reorganize their activities. Anyone familiar with bereavement has noted the nostalgia, the urge to discuss pleasant incidents from the past, and the tendency to evaluate the life just completed. At the time of bereavement, the social worth of the deceased is accentuated, for his faults are forgiven. Consideration for the dead is greater than for the living.

The bereaved, like the dying, faced with finality, take stock of creditable achievements. These achievements are judged upon the extent to which the bereaved had cooperated with, assured, and supported the deceased during his lifetime. Often the bereaved wishes for a second chance so that things could be done differently. Both bereaved and the dying come to the end of the system unexpectedly with things left undone and unsaid with no second chance.

An old person, or one with chronic illness, has less difficulty as he has had enough "time" (conscious realization that the end is not many indefinite years away) to put his affairs in order. He tends to finish up each day's business, so that there is little or no work caught midway to completion. In addition he is able to talk to various role partners (the future bereaved) and evaluate their relationship, and if desirable, redefine these roles in assuring terms. Under these circumstances, death takes on a different connotation for the bereaved, death "has taken him from us", but it is "a blessing" or "a blessed release".

This similarity between the individual facing imminent death and the bereaved survivor provides some clues about the social requirements of the person facing death. The kin and friends congregate to allow the bereaved to give vent to emotional behaviour and "talk it out" or "cry it out". . . . Among other things, an occasion is provided for the regulated expression of strong emotions and the reinforcement of these reactions which are most favourable to the continued solidarity of the social group.[22]

In addition to legitimately encouraging and structuring emotional behaviour, the bereaved are given emotional support and the opportunity to talk at length about things done and undone, and are given assurance that the bereaved contributed to the happiness and success of the deceased. This is all done through the protocols of paying respects to the dead—and to the living—whether in the form of a wake or some other arrangement. The role of friends, acquintances, and kin is to listen, and assist the bereaved through a series of adjustments. In large part assistance consists of assuring the bereaved that both the bereaved and the deceased have brought about creditable achievements.

It would be surprising if men who were socially dead but physiologically alive would require any less outlet for their strong emotions. It turned out that the group of six men, particularly, lacked this very outlet. This was partly because of the normative emotional restraint associated with the miner's male role and partly because of the peculiar social situation in which they found themselves. The men wished to talk about things done and left undone in their life and to derive assurance and support. In order to accomplish this, each miner sought sympathetic listeners; they were not easy to find. Even if it had been possible to ration the time span evenly among the speakers in the confined space, each miner would have had to spend one-sixth of this time speaking and five-sixths listening. The confined space restricted the formation of subgroups which might have accommodated simultaneous conversations.

The quality of the interaction was a concomitant factor in the quantity of interactional space. The situation was such that there were no interested sympathetic and understanding listeners in the role-set. No uninvolved listener was phychologically free to give the speaker full attention or full reassurance because each miner sought similar support.

These data have relevance to a number of observations which have been made about death. Parsons, for instance, in accounting for the reluctance to face death suggests that death, along with personal financial affairs, religious convictions, and sex life, is to a large degree in an area of "privatization"--an area not casually probed.[23] That this is so in our society generally, there may be little argument. Whether this privatization is appropriate to the role of the dying and the bereaved is another matter. The accounts of the miners support the contention of Quint and Strauss[24] that the nurse and the doctor have an obligation to discuss death with a terminal patient. "They can be told that one of their tasks is to help people die and die gracefully."[25] That this is not easy only substantiates Parsons' thesis, "Death is a delicate subject in our society and is seldom discussed openly by laymen.[26] Closely related to this is the problem raised by Feifel, about the research ethics of discussing death with individuals facing death. He reports that the vast majority of respondents showed no untoward reactions. "Information that you are to die in the near future does not necessarily constitute an extreme stress situation for specific individuals.[27] In the case of the miners, the general conclusion is that more opportunity to discuss their deaths would have been welcomed rather than resented.

The control of expressive behaviour in the face of death is a general expectation in our society. Although premature death is not approved, it must be faced, and if foreseeable, people are still exhorted to endure the sufferings to which they are subjected.[28] One must "take it like a man", or in the words of one miner, "It is pretty hard, but we will have to do our best." Under the circumstances, we would expect each miner to try to die "like a man", with little expressive outcry, but with stoic determination. Dying is part of his role, and, perhaps more important, the final interaction. Although there are recorded deaths filled with shouted protest and indignation, the peaceful stoic death seems to be a widespread expectation which applies as much to the little old lady, or the prisoner at the gallows, as to the miner. Tolstoi writes, "Propriety does not permit Ivan to shriek. . . . It would be offensive for him to admit that he is dying."[29] Within a North American hospital situation, Aronson notes the desire of people to die within role, "How often the patient murmurs even toward the end, 'I don't want to make a fuss.' He wants to be a human, to play a role consistent with his identity, his individuality. I think no man is different from the martyrs who died according to a code of ethics, with an inbuilt script still rolling out."[30]

Notes

1. Particularly useful are: *The American Behavioral Scientist, VI,* No. 9 (May, 1963); H. Feifel, ed., *The Meaning of Death* (New York, 1959); A.L. Strauss, *Awareness of Dying* (Chicago, 1965). Other recent books include: R. Fulton, ed., *Death and Identity* (New York, 1965); S. Standard and H. Nathan, *Should the Patient Know the Truth?* (New York, 1955); M. Field, *Patients are People* (New York, 1953); D. Sudnow, *Passing On: The Social Organization of Dying* (Englewood Cliffs, New Jersey, 1967). Articles related to the subject include: J.C. Diggory and D.Z. Rothman, "Values Destroyed by Death", *Journal of Abnormal and Social Psychology,* LXIII, No. 1 (1961), 205-210; M.H. Means, "Fears of One Thousand College Students", *Journal of Abnormal and Social Psychology,* XXXI (1963), 291-311; P. Schilder and D. Wechsler, "The Attitudes of Children Toward Death", *Journal of Genetic Psychology,* XLV (1934) 446-451; W.A. Faunce and R.L. Fulton, "The Sociology of Death: A Neglected Area of Research", *Social Forces,* XXXVI (1953) 205-209.

2. E.J. Jackson "Grief and Religion", in H. Feifel, ed., *Attitudes Toward Death* (New York, 1959), 218-233.

3. The project was supported by the Disaster Research group, National Academy of Sciences—National Researces Council, Washington, D.C. The interdisciplinary research team was made up of H.D. Beach, L. Denton (Psychology), R.J. Weil, P.N. Murphy (Psychiatry), Nellen Armstrong, R.A. Lucas (Sociology). Other aspects of the situation have been reported: H.D. Beach and R.A. Lucas, eds., *Individual and Group Behavior in a Coal Mine Disaster,* Disaster Study Number 13 (Washington, D.C., 1960); R.A. Lucas, "The Influence of Kinship Upon Perception of an Ambiguous Stimulus", *American Sociological Review,* XXXI, No. 2 (April, 1966), 227-236.

4. Sudnow, *Passing On: The Social Organization of Dying, op. cit.* Chap. 4.

5. K. Boulding, "A Pure Theory of Death: Dilemmas of Defense Policy in a World of Conditional Viability", in G.W. Baker and L.S. Cottrel Jr., eds., *Behavioral Science and Civil Defense,* Disaster Study No. 16 (1962), 53.

6. G. Simmel, *The Sociology of George Simmel,* K.H. Wolff, ed. (New York, 1950), 124.

7. C.J. Aronson, "Treatment of the Dying Person", in H. Feifel, ed., *The Meaning of Death* (New York, 1959), 253.

8. B. Glaser and A.L. Strauss, *op. cit.,* 669 *passim.*

9. Means, "Fears of One Thousand College Students", *op. cit.* 291-311.

10. P. Challaye, "Psychologie génétique et ethnique", in G. Dumas, ed., *Traite de Psychologie,* II (1924), 725-726.

11. Means, "Fears of One Thousand College Students" *op. cit;* Diggory and Rothman, *op. cit.* "Values Destroyed by Death", 205-210.

12. Diggory and Rothman, "Values Destroyed by Death" *op. cit.* This study and the present discussion exclude one form of death—suicide. None of the eighteen miners mentioned suicide.

13. T. Parsons, "Death in American Society—A Brief Working Paper", *The American Behavioral Scientist,* VI, No. 9 (May, 1963), 61-65.

14. Diggory and Rothman, "Values Destroyed by Death", *op. cit.* 205.

15. Faunce and Fulton, "The Sociology of Death: A Neglected Area of Research", *op. cit.* 208.

16. Parsons, "Death in American Society—A Brief Working Paper", *op. cit. 63.*

17. W.E. Moore, "Time the Ultimate Scarcity", *The American Behavioral Scientist,* VI, No. 9 (May, 1963) 60.

18. Glaser and Strauss, "The Social Loss of Dying Patients", *op. cit.*

19. Diggory and Rothman, "Values Destroyed by Death", *op. cit.,* 209-210.

20. W.J. Goode, "Perspectives on Family Research and Life Insurance", *The American Behavioral Scientist*, VI, No. 9 (May, 1963), 58.

21. E. Goffman, *Asylums* (Garden City, New York, 1961), 150.

22. Parsons, *Essays in Sociological Theory, Pure and Applied, op. cit.* 59.

23. Parsons, "Death in American Society—A Brief Working Paper", *op. cit.* 65.

24. Quint and Strauss, "Nursing Students, Assignments and Dying Patients", *op. cit.*

25. Strauss, Glaser, and Quint, "The Non-Accountability of Terminal Care", *op. cit.*

26. Quint and Strauss, "Nursing Students, Assignments and Dying Patients", *op. cit.*

27. H. Feifel, "The Taboo on Death", *The American Behavioral Scientist,* VI, No. 9 (May, 1963), 85.

28. Parsons, "Death in American Society—A Brief Working Paper", *op. cit.* 62.

29. The Works of Lyof N. Tolstoi (New York, 1904), Vol. 14

30. G.J. Aronson, "Treatment of the Dying Person", in H. Feifel, ed., *The Meaning of Death, op. cit.* 252.

PART III

MAJOR SYSTEMS AND PROCESSES

INTRODUCTION

We learned in Part II that how one participates in social settings varies considerably through the life cycle. In Part III we deal with those settings in large scale: the major systems and processes of Canadian society. The economy, which governs the production, distribution and consumption of necessary goods and services, is being constantly altered. Politics attempt to keep in order the machinery of government and balance the use of power by conflicting interests. Education prepares or socializes the young to take their place in the adult world. Control systems define and enforce the rules of normal behaviour and punish those who deviate from them. The modern city prescribes for nearly everyone today where and how they shall live. Religion, through which a society helps its members deal with life's breaking points—injustice, uncertainty, and death—by reference to the grounds of ultimate reality, also faces the challenges of change.

It is evident that this introductory volume cannot treat these major systems and processes adequately. The articles chosen, however, deal with most of the key issues from the viewpoint of social science. The authors, we will see, usually begin their analysis by defining major concepts, or sets of ideas, around which issues revolve.

The concepts, processes and theories related to institutions are at the same time specific and more complex than those connected with change through the individual's life cycle. They are more specific because they deal with particular and easily recognized practices and organizations, such as corporations, political parties, governments, schools, reform establishments, urban bodies and churches. But they are also more complex because they assume that institutions will function smoothly in advanced societies by being well integrated with other major institutions. Beneath the surface there is an incredibly complicated network of communication between each specialized part as it continually adapts to the pressures of other parts.

The dynamism of Canada's major institutions is reflected in these articles. Several aspects of the economy are examined. Litvak and Maule study multinational corporations directed from Canada. Craig McKie reveals the nature and spread of gargantuan corporatism in Canadian society. Frederick Elkin analyzes the advertizing business in Quebec to show how it responds to the pressures of French-Canadian nationalism. Jacques Dofny and Muriel Garon-Audy compare occupational mobility in Quebec over ten years to show how the values of equality and autonomy affect the economy. And the factors which create and sustain poverty are weighed by Clairmont and Magill.

Under the subheading of politics and conflict, Engelmann and Schwartz discuss the factors which affect support of various parties. Pierre Roberge studies language conflict in Quebec and the manner in which it generates intergroup differences. Don

Whiteside traces the persistence with which institutions of established power have for generations blanketed the Indian people.

Similar patterns emerge in education. Raymond Breton, in a large national study of career decisions among secondary school students, discloses that hopes and expectations for advancement in schooling and in jobs are lower among children of low-income families and low-income regions, regardless of tests of intelligence. Alan King and Reginald Ripton find that the ideals of education are subverted for lesser goals by the needs of teachers to improve their own careers and the willingness of students to settle for less than the optimum learning experience. In a study of school history textbooks, Judith Torrance shows how the historians communicate an image of Canada as a "peaceable Kingdom."

Turning to the underside of society, in the section on control and deviance W.E. Mann interviewed inmates of a medium-security prison to learn that an informal power system effectively controls socialization so that it is frequently at odds with the official system. In a study of bar behaviour during the Calgary Stampede, Richard Ossenberg observed the persistence of social class differences among patrons. Peter Chimbos in a paper on murder reveals that the act is more common within the bosom of the family than in dark alleyways.

Urbanism may be thought of as a social process in the sense that it is a means of providing accommodation, work, transport, and a wide variety of cultural experiences, and it has a persistent, coercive influence on the life style of residents. Norman Shulman reveals the patterns of friendship and support within an urban centre in the Ottawa area. In a paper on Small Harbour, Newfoundland, Ralph Matthews shows that fishermen prefer village life to a government plan to relocate them in a larger centre. N.H. Lithwick discusses optional policies for the urban future.

Finally, the characteristics and functions of religion are considered. Stewart Crysdale reviews the problematic but persistent place of religion in secular society and Reginald Bibby presents findings of the first national survey of religiosity in Canada. Robert Sévigny traces the increasing individualism of belief among Quebec college students. Paul and Linda Grayson show how religious and political movements emerge within changing society.

The articles in Part III suggest both the diversity and integration of recent work in sociology with regard to major institutions and processes. They also illustrate, along with articles in Parts I and II, the rich variety of methods social scientists use. Whereas in Part I historical and comparative methods prevail and in Part II most researchers use participant observation for the investigation of minority groups, many of the studies in Part III gather data by sample surveys. The latter include Beattie, Breton, King and Ripton, Shulman, Bibby, and Sévigny. However, Dofny and Garon-Audy examine public records for their data; Chimbos and Mann interview key informants; Matthews and Ossenberg gather observations by participation; Whiteside and Roberge examine historical materials; Torrance employs content analysis; and Crysdale and Lithwick use a variety of methods.

Part III Section A

THE ECONOMY AND INDUSTRALIZATION

18

Canadian Multinationals in the Western Hemisphere*

Isaiah A. Litvak and Christopher J. Maule

Canadian direct investment abroad runs at about one-fifth of direct investment in Canada. Since much of this inward investment is U.S. controlled, Canadian attention has been focussed largely on the behaviour and operations of U.S. multinational representatives. Their numbers and size have been increasing in recent years. Canadian direct investment abroad (CDIA) doubled from \$2.5 billion in 1960 and \$6.5 billion in 1971, at which time it represented about half of Canadian total long term investment abroad, which includes portfolio and other investments.[1] The purpose of this article is to examine the factors which have motivated Canadian controlled firms to internationalize their operations, with special reference to the Western Hemisphere, where approximately three-quarters of CDIA is located. The term "Canadian multinational" will be used to include firms which operate subsidiaries in at least two foreign countries; however, in the majority of cases discussed, the firms will easily satisfy the more commonly accepted definition of having subsidiaries in six or more countries. The article will also highlight some of the characteristics which distinguish Canadian multinationals from their U.S. counterparts.

Internationalizing The Domestic Operation

Why do Canadian firms invest abroad? In a recent interview with executives of Canadian Packers Limited, the following reasons were offered:

1. *Growth* – The Canadian market is small, and its growth potential is limited relative to the rest of the world whose standard of living is rapidly increasing.
2. *Tariff and Non-Tariff Barriers*—Specifically, trading blocs such as the European Economic Community tend to limit the scope for direct exporting

---

*Abridged from *The Business Quarterly,* Autumn, 1975, with the permission of the publisher.

through quotas and health regulations.

3. *Sources of Supply* – Canada alone does not have a large enough surplus of lamb and beef to allow the firm to capitalize on the many profitable opportunities that are identifiable in the global market place.
4. *Defensive Marketing* – Establishing overseas subsidiaries not only provides access to new markets, but, in addition such action may dissuade a local firm from exporting to Canada.
5. *Transportation* – Distant and affluent markets can often be more profitably serviced from overseas affiliates, e.g., exporting to the Japanese market from the Australian affiliate.

Canada Packers produces a full line of packing house products and by-products The company also handles other farm products, in addition to canning certain foods and processing leather. Canada Packers ranked (by sales) 99 in the 1973 Fortune Directory of the 300 Largest Industrial Corporations outside the United States. Its consolidated sales approximated $1.5 billion, and less than 10% of this total was realized through its overseas operations which include wholly and partially owned subsidiaries in the United States, United Kingdon, Australia, Germany and Mexico. In addition, the company maintains marketing subsidiaries and trading agencies in the major geographical markets of the world.

Canadian Packers exhibits certain corporate characteristics common to many of the largest Canadian-owned firms which have "gone international" but have yet to achieve a "multinational" status. These characteristics include the following: corporate sales and assets are largely concentrated in the North American market; the companies are recent entrants in the field of "global" investment and business as distinct from North American business; there is usually a structural division between domestic and international business activities, with the latter divided between exporting and operating subsidiaries. Exporting may be handled through a trading division or company, and the foreign subsidiaries may report either to a senior vice-president, or, depending upon the importance of their operations, directly to the president. This typology with certain variations would characterize a number of the 17 Canadian-owned firms which made the Fortune list of 300 (see Table 1).

Most of the firms in Table 1 are undergoing various degrees of internationalization. The experiences of some of these firms, particularly the ones which have achieved a multinational status, will now be examined in the context of the key motivational factors which promote the growth of multinational business.[2]

Need For Command Over Vital Resources

Companies in the extractive industries may find themselves pressured to become multinational because the major ore deposits are not to be found in Canada, or because of insufficient domestic supplies. The growth and operations of Alcan Aluminum Limited, Canada's largest multinational enterprise, is one such example. In international terms, Canada ranks among the major world producers in 16 of 17 key minerals. The notable exception is bauxite, the basic aluminum ore, which is absent in Canada. This fact is all the more significant since Canada is the world's fourth largest producer of primary aluminum, and Alcan is one of the world's leading manufacturers of primary aluminum and its related products.

Alcan's operations involve the mining and processing of bauxite, the production of alumina from bauxite, the reduction of alumina to aluminum, and fabrication of aluminum alloys into semi-finished and finished products. In 1974 Alcan's assets were

Table 1

The "Fortune 17" Largest Canadian Companies

(Ranked by Sales)

Rank 1973	Company	Industry	Sales ($000)	Assets ($000)	Net Income ($000)	Employees
74	Alcan Aluminum	Aluminum Products	1,871,746	2,448,967	82,647	62,600
98	Massey-Ferguson	Farm, Indus. & Bldg. machinery, engines	1,506,234	1,249,044	58,213	51,267
99	Canada Packers	Food Products	1,503,384	277,273	19,186	15,000
117	MacMillan Bloedel	Lumber, Paper Products	1,214,911	1,020,152	81,734	24,478
122	International Nickel	Nickel, Copper	1,172,814	2,248,832	226,859	31,311
154	Steel Co. of Canada	Iron and Steel	937,446	1,147,855	87,664	22,580
176	Noranda Mines	Mining	848,350	1,358,997	121,366	18,500
197	Distillers Corp.-Seagrams	Alcoholic Beverages	776,705*	1,568,346	68,068	17,500
224	Domtar	Pulp, Paper, Chemicals, Bldg. Materials	655,693	573,736	50,550	18,017
234	Northern Electric	Telecommunications Equipment	612,680	494,222	32,023	23,455
243	Moore	Business Forms, Packaging, Machinery	587,078	485,703	55,760	17,742
270	Burns Foods	Food Products	543,053	107,321	5,047	5,250
279	Dominion Foundries and Steel	Iron and Steel	519,439	670,503	52,529	10,600
283	Cominco	Mining, Smelting, Chemicals, Fertilizers	513,868	675,919	42,825	11,129
285	Genstar	Bldg. materials, Cement, Chemicals, Fertilizers	509,472	503,305	25,023	10,040
288	Molson Companies	Alcholic Beverages, Construction Products, Furniture	502,131*	354,986	22,020	10,928
292	Consolidated-Bathurst	Pulp and Paper Products, Packaging, Glass	497,559	537,125	18,966	19,100

*Fortune estimate
Source: *Fortune*, August 1974, pp. 174-183.

worth about $2.5 billion. Alcan's subsidiary and related companies have bauxite holdings in seven countries, produce alumina in six, smelt primary aluminum in ten, fabricate aluminum in thirty-four, and have sales outlets in over one hundred.

Unlike Canada Packers, Alcan is heavily dependent on its overseas operations, measured in capital employed and sales in aluminum. In 1974 45% of the company's fixed capital was outside of Canada, and 85% of sales were realized in foreign markets. In addition, more than two-thirds of the approximately 63,000 Alcan employees work outside of Canada.

The constituent companies of Alcan are integrated from the basic raw materials to the finished product. During the past twenty years, the company has considerably increased its fabricating activities to achieve a near-balance between the three main phases of its integrated operations – raw materials, smelting and fabricating. At the same time, the company in terms of assets, sales and employment has become much more "international". On January 1, 1968, Nathaniel Davis, the President of Alcan, announced a company reorganization, pointing to factors of absolute size, geographical diversity, and increased vertical integration as the prime considerations.

The company saw the need for reoganization as a result of internal and external pressures:

> Not only had the company itself changed – from essentially a basic metal manufacturer to increasingly a leading producer of semi-fabricated and finished products –but so had the world in which it lived. Communications were faster, markets were different, competition was intensified.

Though significant, the move was by no means path-breaking, nor were the circumstances leading to it unique to Alcan. As a Harvard University study points out, of a surveyed 170 U.S. multinational companies, by 1968 only eight had not made this or similar moves.[3] The basic characteristic of reorganization was to move from a highly centralized staff-functional to a more decentralized product-line structure.

Table 2

Geographical Distribution of Capital Employed and Sales of Aluminum in all Forms - 1974

Region	Working Capital	%	Fixed Capital	%	Sales	%
	(millions $ U.S.)		(millions $ U.S.)		(000's tons)	
Canada	311	49	1,519	55	248	15
United States	110	17	218	8	452	27
South America and Caribbean	67	10	329	12	–	–
United Kingdom	65	10	302	11	287	17
Continental Europe	52	8	132	5	207	12
All Other	36	6	250	9	468	28
	$641	100	$2,750	100	$1,662	100

Access To Foreign Markets

Canadian based multinationals stress that to remain competitive in most export markets will usually oblige them to consider investing in local manufacturing and sales operations. The reasons offered are two-fold: first, at the macro level, most foreign governments, like Canada, pursue a myriad of import substitution and export promotion policies designed to foster local manufacturing activity. When such activity is apparent, other market barriers are usually introduced to favor the local manufacturer over foreign suppliers. Elements of such policies usually include tariffs, fiscal incentives, and non-tariff barriers including government procurement guidelines which tend to discriminate against foreign suppliers.

At the micro level, the successful Canadian exporter may decide to establish an overseas operation because of inreasing competition faced from domestic (local) manufacturers, including the prospect of another foreign supplier establishing an affiliate in that market. Transportation costs, problems of servicing local customers, and the opportunities of pursuing product differentiation strategies, unique to the export market, are some of the other factors which may influence the decision to invest abroad.

An excellent example of a Canadian multinational enterprise which has responded to, as well as having initiated, pressures for internationalizing its manufacturing and marketing operations is Massey-Ferguson Limited. In 1974 Massey-Ferguson's net sales approximated $1.8 billion, its assets were $1.6 billion and it employed some 61,000 persons. The 1974 geographical distribution of assets employed and net sales were as follows:

Table 3

Asset and Sales of Massey-Ferguson

	Net Sales		Assets Employed	
	(millions $ U.S.)	(% of Total)	(millions $ U.S.)	(% of Total)
North America				
Canada	142.4	8.0	–	–
U.S.	471.6	26.4	–	–
TOTAL	614.0	34.4	589.4	36.5
Latin America	316.1	17.7	221.1	13.7
Europe	566.8	31.8	688.6	42.7
Africa	127.0	7.1	40.2	2.5
Australasia	92.4	5.2	74.1	4.6
Asia	68.3	3.8	0.6	–
TOTAL	1784.6	100.0	1614.0	100.0

Massey-Ferguson's manufacturing and marketing operations are highly integrated. It ranks among the world's largest manufacturers of farm machinery, industrial and construction machinery and diesel engines. In 1974 the company had seventy factories in twenty-six countries, half of which are developing countries. One of the interesting features of Massey-Ferguson's corporate strategy is its international production strategy which promotes a policy of maximum interchangeability of component parts, especially for tractors and combines. This policy appears to reduce the costs of production by having factories situated in different countries specializing in different models at differing levels of production.[4]

The fact that almost every country in the world constitutes a potential market for Massey-Ferguson products means that corporate management must make decisions on a world-wide basis. This is particularly so since Massey-Ferguson has major investment commitments abroad, a product line that can be merchandised in a series of markets, and because of the product line's interchangeable parts which can be supplied from several production bases. A major benefit of the foregoing strategy is that management can shift sources of supply for a given market from one country to another, in response to differing governmental and non-governmental policies and pressures, such as dividend restrictions or work stoppages caused by militant union elements in a particular country.

Massey-Ferguson has also pioneered in the area of joint east-west industrial co-operation. For example, in September 1974 Massey-Ferguson entered into an agreement with a Polish enterprise to assist in the expansion and modernization of the Polish tractor industry. Under this agreement, Poland will acquire Massey-Ferguson technology leading to the production of 75,000 Massey-Ferguson tractors and 90,000 Perkin engines annually. Initially, Massey-Fergusion will export a substantial volume of parts and engines to produce these products, with the long run objective of utilizing certain Polish manufactured components in its own manufacturing operations, as well as in marketing Polish-made goods through its distribution channels. The joint East-West Co-operation Agreement is but another way of achieving access to foreign markets where legislation may prevent foreign companies from establishing their own operations, without sacrificing the advantages of international specialization of labor, and the attendant benefits in the areas of production and sales.

Market Saturation and The Drive For Growth

The Canadian market is a small one relative to the United States, the European Economic Community and Japan. Expanding the size of its market has been a major factor underlying the growth of the multinational enterprise. The larger and more successful Canadian firms have found it necessary to expand overseas in order to achieve both plant and firm economies of scale. These firms also contend that market size and share are pre-requisite conditions for supporting a managerial and technological capability to allow them to compete against foreign multinationals in Canada and abroad. An oft heard statement from the management of these firms is that investing in foreign market development provides a higher return than the one realized from achieving a marginal improvement in the Canadian market. This statement is most apparent where the Canadian firm enjoys a substantial portion of the Canadian market. Attributing the foreign investment decision to the fear of drawing the attention of the anti-combines authorities appears to be of secondary importance.

One of the unique features of prominent Canadian multinationals is that the domestic market declines rapidly in importance as the firm internationalizes its operations. This fact may be measured in terms of sales, assets, and employment. For example, in terms of sales for 1974, the following figures are illustrative:

Table 4

Sales of Selected Firms, by Region

(In percentages)

Company	Total	Canadian	U.S.	Other
Alcan	100	13	27	60
Massey-Ferguson	100	8	26	66
MacMillan Bloedel	100	21	39	40
International Nickel	100	15	37	48
Moore (1973)	100	11	86	3

A number of observations concerning the operations of these Canadian multinationals may be drawn from the foregoing figures. The Canadian market as a percentage of total corporate sales is considerably less important than the U.S. market. The U.S. market usually accounts for more than twice the Canadian sales, and at least one-quarter of total corporate sales.

Many large Canadian firms with overseas investments tend to depend on the U.S. market for their survival and success. In fact, their new product diversification programs are often predicated on their anticipated ability to achieve market success in the United States.

Canadian firms which go international often establish their first foreign subsidiary in the U.S., not unlike many U.S. multinationals which have incorporated their first foreign affiliate in Canada; however, the similarity stops at this point. The Canadian market seldom occupies a position of critical importance to the U.S. firm. To take an extreme example, Moore Corporation Limited was formed in Toronto in 1882 and established its first foreign affiliate in Niagara Falls, N.Y. in 1884. By 1973, the U.S. market account for 86% of total corporate sales, and both the research and marketing divisions of the corporation are based in New York.

The heavy dependence on the U.S. market has a profound effect on the Canadian company's corporate strategy and structure. The geographical proximity between the Canadian head-office and the U.S. subsidiary, and the similarity in language and management philosophy promote ease of communication between the two parts of the corporation. The same phenomenon holds true between the head-office organization of a U.S. firm and its subsidiary in Canada. In the case of the latter example, the Canadian division is sometimes viewed as an appendage of the U.S. organization or as a division in the North American geographical region, largely dependent on the U.S. corporate infrastructure. The situation is different when the head office is located in Canada. The similarities between the two countries, coupled with the size of the U.S. market promotes a situation where market forces suggest that the U.S. subsidiary should enjoy far greater power vis à vis the parent, to the point that critical parts of the corporate infrastructure are based in the U.S., servicing both the U.S. divisions as well as the Canadian part of the operation.

Relative Scarcity of Production Factors

The factors of production include land (including raw materials), labor, capital, and intermediate products. In the case of capital one includes financial and human capital. The latter component may involve skilled labor, managerial talent and entrepreneurship. Countries possess different proportions of factors of production, and the company is faced with the need to judge the relative costs associated with establishing the unit of production in different locations. The "scarcities" of the different factors are continuously being altered as a result of inflationary forces, tariffs, changes in tax, wage agreements, and other forms of government intervention.

The U.S.-Canadian situation is a good example of the foregoing point. At present, the comparative labor cost advantage enjoyed by Canada over the U.S. is being gradually eliminated. A comparison of unit labor costs shows that in the United States, the recent rate of increase has been lower than in Canada.

Table 5

Average Annual Percent Change in Unit Labor Cost in Manufacturing Industry, 1960 - 1973[5]

(Calculated in U.S. dollar value)

Country	1960-73	1970-73	1971	1972	1973
U.S.	1.9	1.3	-- 0.2	1.0	3.1
Canada	2.2	4.7	5.6	4.9	3.5

Since labor costs in the manufacturing industry are supposed to approximate 70% of the final costs, this comparison acquires added significance for the Canadian firm in deciding, for example, whether to expand its Canadian operation or to invest in the establishment, or expansion, of an American base of operation.

Tax and Other Financial Advantages

Governments, especially those in developing countries, pursue policies aimed at encouraging multinationals to establish overseas manufacturing operations in their countries. These policies usually consist of tax holidays, customs exemptions, financial subsidies, loans, or special tariff treatment. In some instances, the governments of certain developed countries such as Canada offer incentives of their own to encourage their firms to establish overseas operations in the third world. In short, the Canadian firm may find an initially unattractive investment to be commercially profitable, by virtue of tax and other financial advantages offered by both the parent (Canadian) government and the prospective host government. A good case in point involves Reliable Toy Company Limited of Toronto.

This company received financial assistance from the Canadian International Development Agency (CIDA) when it first explored the feasibility of establishing an overseas subsidiary in the Caribbean. One of CIDA's goals is to promote Canadian investment in developing countries. It does this by providing a $2500 grant for a "starter" study which is designed to assist the Canadian investor to make an "on the spot" assessment, to be followed with an up to $25,000 grant for a feasibility study on a shared cost basis (50/50) with the potential investor. Apparently, this incentive spurred Reliable Toy to investigate the potential market opportunity in Jamaica. The net result of this study was the establishment of a joint-venture arrangement in 1973 between Reliable Toy and a local Jamaican firm, split 60/40 in favor of Reliable. This joint venture received a tax holiday for five years from the Jamaican government, it was permitted to import the necessary machinery duty-free, and it can import some of the critical materials such as resins at a preferred rate of duty. Moreover, the joint-venture receives a rebate on customs duty on toys exported to Canada.

Not all incentives need be initiated by governments. As companies internationalize their operations and increase intracorporate trade, the technique of transfer pricing offers attractive opportunities for pricing the movement of goods and services between different countries in ways which take advantage of different tax jurisdictions. The most common example is to have the low tax affiliate sell high and buy low in non-arms length transactions. Pricing management and research services at unrealistic rates is another way of repatriating funds between jurisdictions whose level of taxation may differ. Tax havens in such countries as Switzerland, Lichtenstein, Monaco, Bermuda and the Bahamas simply help to promote and perpetuate "dummy" trading companies and subsidiary/head office configurations which have little resemblance to the actual economic activities of these operations. Canadian multinationals are not unique in employing tax havens and other fiscal arrangements to their advantage.

Notes

1. *Statistics Canada Daily,* Catalogue No. 11-001E, Ottawa, April 3, 1975, p. 4.

2. Information about these companies was obtained through interviews, corporate financial reports, and press releases.

3. R. Vernon, *Sovereignty at Bay,* New York, Basic Books, Inc., 1971, p. 119.

4. E.P. Neufeld, *A Global Corporation,* Toronto, University of Toronto Press, 1969, p. 390.

5. S. Webley, *Foreign Investment in the United States: Opportunities and Impediments,* London, United Kingdom, British North American Committee, 1974, p. 29.

19

Some Views on Canadian Corporatism*

Craig McKie

Recent studies of Canadian economic and social development have underlined the transformation in the structure both of capital and of private enterprises. With the introduction of the modern limited liability company and the progressive, inexorable concentration of capital, the modalities of personal wealth, the patterns of recruitment and paths to upward mobility and the authority relationships between managers and workers have all changed to accommodate emergent capital structures. Some social types, for instance the lone entrepreneur, have virtually died out in the process. The ideology of *laissez-faire* has declined as emphasis on production and investment planning within the context of the giant corporate organization has heightened, and the state control apparatus has swollen.

Drawing heavily on the insights of Harold Innis (1930), contemporary scholars seek to portray this process as a systematic transformation of the structure of capital. Naylor (1972, 1975), Clement (1974, 1975), and others (Gonick 1975) see the development of private enterprise in Canada in terms of historical periods. In each of the historical periods, there is a modal structure of capital. Briefly stated, these periods are (1) pre-Confederation state-sponsored monopoly enterprise; and post-Confederation; (2) enterpreneurial mercantile enterprise, (3) portfolio investment enterprise, and (4) direct investment enterprise.

As well as entailing a modal structure of enterprise, each period has sustained a dominant form of political integration of private interests. For, as Nelles (1974) has recently pointed out, close coordination between private and public interests in Canada developed progressively throughout the nineteenth and twentieth centuries. Thus, to understand the current political integration of private interests in Canada it is necessary to understand also the changing shape of private and public relationships.

Private Interests and Public Policy

The attention paid to the changing modes of capital accumulation in Canada in the last 150 years has diverted attention from other contemporaneous developments, of which the relationship between public and private interests is an example. An oversimplified portrayal of the relationship between private capital and the state has been one result.

Teeple, for instance, has written that "the role of government in a capitalist

---

* Revised and abridged from a paper presented at the annual meeting of the Canadian Sociology and Anthropology Association, April, 1976, at Quebec City.

country is to regulate social relations in the interests of capital accumulation" (1972:x). Another, more familiar, treatment of the same point of view lies in the aphorism that "the state is the executive committee of the bourgeoisie". This over-simplified view necessarily implies that officials are totally responsive to their political masters and indeed cannot be logically separated from them, a suggestion which flies in the face of bureaucratic realities. Contemporary studies by Vernon (1974) and Wilkins (1974), for example, show in contrast just how complex the politician/state/private enterprise relationship has become. Further, there is considerable evidence, particularly in Wilkins (1974), that this is not a recent development. Naylor's accounts of bonus schemes in early twentieth century Canada (1975) strongly suggest that the relationship has been growing more complex for decades.

Therefore, it is proper to conclude that just as the structure of capital has changed to the present time, so too has the morphology of corporate enterprises, and their mechanisms for interacting with governments. The sum and substance of the change has been what John Crispo has recently termed the "consolidation of the power structure" (Osler, 1976). In this view, countervailing forces, notably those of an autonomous public sector and an autonomous private sector, have lost their arm's-length relationship in the interests of coordination of activities and priorities. In outward aspect, this relationship appears, as Robert Presthus (1973, 1974) has suggested, to closely approximate the corporatist model.

Corporatist theory

From nineteenth century corporatist theory, which enjoyed wide appeal in European nations, the notion developed of the desirability of institutionalizing the private/public relationship in joint policy-making bodies. From it, too, the more sinister fascist variants of social organization developed. Their common features lie in the mistrust of individual endeavour and the importance placed on coordinated, vertically and horizontally integrated corporate loci of policy determination. Drawing on the works of sociologists, Le Play, Saint-Simon, Comte, and especially Emile Durkheim, turn of the century corporatists stressed the necessity of creating intermediary institutions which "were to stand as a barrier between the individual and the state" (Elbow 1966:15).

Of particular interest are the works of the most prominent of the nineteenth century corporatists, Rene de la Tour du Pin. In the words of Matthew Elbow (1966: 63-4):

> La Tour described individualism as an abnormal state of mind -- 'abnormal and against nature because the nature of man is essentially social' -- which was increasingly prevalent and which was characterized by systematic contempt for social ties and duties. It betrayed a spirit of materialism and lust for gain inherited from the Reformation and the tendency to perpetuate the 'rupture of historical continuity' accomplished by the French Revolution.

Rejecting the doctrine of liberalism in its entirety, a sort of cooperative federation of all public and private interests was offered in its stead. As Elbow puts it, "the very kernel of corporatism was the doctrine of social peace, of solidarity between classes" (1966:102).

In western countries, such an *outcome* has been to a considerable extent realized, *not so much out of a desire to suppress liberal freedoms, but more as a result of the necessity of coordinating public and private decision-making, which is in turn a direct result of transformations in the structure of capital.*

Writing about British society for instances, S.H. Beer (1957:627) speaks of 'quasi-corporatism'.

Canadian Corporatism

Presthus applies the corporatist model in his analysis of Canadian interest groups. Their leaders, he says, "assume a critical role in formulating the claims of their various constituencies and hammering out an accommodation among such claims with political elites" (1973:8).

As the bargaining power of private interests increases with the progressive concentration of control of capital, the power of the unorganized citizenry decreases. The representatives of private interests come to play, in Presthus' words, "direct, continuous and active roles in the Canadian political apparatus" (1973:9) and to provide coordinated management of the resources of the society for the benefit of members of organized and articulate groups.

In this context, "group influence is enlarged by anything which restricts the influence on policy-making of anything else" (Eckstein 1960:155). The lack of articulate defenders of the public (as opposed to statist) interests, or the lack of an independent press thus automatically increases the influence of organized private interests.

As the previously mentioned transformations of capital structure have occurred in Canada, public/private relations have moved toward the corporatist model of full political integration with the government policy-making apparatus precisely because of the concentration of capital. Fewer, larger firms have been able to organize more effectively to put their case before governments. As their capacities for coordinated action have increased, the form in which representations are put has changed as well.

In the initial period, where state monopoly was the norm of capital structure, state and private interests were essentially indivisible. With the emergence of the private company, however, (and of the owner-operator as a social type) a realistic division between these interests emerged. The securing of state subsidies, bonuses, and favourable legislation became a major concern of important economic interests. The legislative committee became the forum for accommodation of interests.

Naylor, for example, writes that "the parliamentary railway committee was openly the tool of the railway (the Canadian Pacific) ... " (1975:II-29). He also cites the recollections of George Hague, then general manager of the Bank of Toronto, on the occasion of the framing of the first Bank Act in 1871 (Naylor 1975: 11-74). Hague writes:

> We sat in one of the committee rooms of the House and discussed the bill with a considerable sense of responsibility, being well aware not only that our conclusions would affect the whole banking interest of the country, but every other interest, commercial, manufacturing, and industrial not to speak of the interest of the government itself . . . . Many of the directors of the banks and several of their presidents were members of Parliament, some in the Senate, some in the House of Commons. These, *of course,* sat with us from time to time, so that, though not formally constituted as such, we were really a joint committee of Parliament and banks. (Hague, 1908: 365. Italics supplied)

In the period in which portfolio investment was the modal application of private capital, one sees the formation of authentic economic interest groups for the first time. Industry-wide associations began to coordinate price setting, and the notion of the "living profit" which would sustain cartel members emerged.

As combine formation and price fixing became "normal" in the late nineteenth and early twentieth century, industry-wide associations of interests formed.

Bliss has argued that business trade associations in Canada at the turn of the present century acted principally to restrain competition and ensure a "living profit" for established businesses much in the manner of the corporative model. He makes reference to the Dominion Wholesale Grocers' Guild, agreements between Canada's railways to fix rates, and the Canadian Bankers' Association which he says, was founded in 1891 "in response to desires that banks exert more political influence and pull together to limit competition" (1974:36). According to Bliss, the Retail Jewellers' Association went so far as to compile in 1890 a "living profit price list" (1974:37).

Pressure to join such groups was apparently substantial. Bliss writes, for instance:

> Businessmen who stayed out of combines, or, worse still, broke free from arrangements they had been party to, were condemned as commercial mavericks, selfish, unprincipled, and immoral. Price-cutters lacked the courage to 'meet rivals on fair ground and succeed; their business life was 'conceived in selfishness and nurtured by methods the very antithesis of businesslike'. Very probably they were able to cut prices only because they sold inferior goods, exloited their employees, or both. The Retail Merchants' Association never tired of pointing to the low wages and poor working conditions in the department stores and their allied factories. These institutions, it charged, were engaged in 'the vicious process of pauperizing labour' (and were also, according to the *Canadian Pharmaceutical Journal,* 'the supreme personification of egoism, selfishness, and greed') (1974:51).

In the latter part of the period, Clark (1939) showed the Canadian Manufacturers' Association as a general 'umbrella' organization whose impact in the 1930s and previously rested on "its ability to create opinions among the general public" (1939: 39). He concluded that "its really significant influence was exerted through propaganda carried on in the country and lobbying directed by its representatives in the federal and provincial capitals" (1939:39).

However, it is only with the emergence of large-scale direct investment corporate structures that the interest group developed to full flower in the corporatist context. The planning and coordination of government and private interests made necessary because of the threat to all of capricious or ill-conceived government actions has only reached full development in the post-World War II period in Canada. Thus it may be said that the interest group in its present Canadian form is a relatively recent development.

Accounts of interest group activity since the Second World War have been sketchy at best. These accounts include the picture Thorburn has given of a campaign in which business groups undertook to persuade the government to change anti-combines legislation through the "personal influence of prominent business leaders and elaborate briefs prepared by skilled lawyers" (1964: 163). Thorburn concluded that in that instance, the government "gave in to interested parties to such an extent that its more important amendments could not be defended by rational analysis" (1964:174).

Other accounts of interest group activities in the postwar period in Canada are not numerous. Dawson, for example, has given short treatments of the activities of specific interest groups, including the Canadian Federation of Agriculture (1960), and the Consumers' Association of Canada (1963). Kwavnick (1970), Manzer (1969), and the Research Branch of the Library of Parliament (1970) have also provided marginal detail.

Thus, if one thinks of the political integration of private interests in the periods of differing capital structure in Canada, one can say that in the initial case of state sponsored monopoly, there were not interest groups at all. In the second phase of private mercantile empires, interest representation served solely the ends of large owner-operators (in seeking, for instance, massive public investment in public works). In the third period industry-wide groupings emerged to foster 'orderly marketing'; only in this last period have interest groups as institutional entities entered into a close

The Representation of Private Interest in the 1970s

It is important to understand, therefore, the changing format of interest representation in Canada. Close co-ordination of public and private interests, which Mackenzie (1955:146) has called "the new medievalism" and Gonick (1975) has called "friendly fascism", is an interesting example of what some have termed quasi-corporatism, the practice of corporatism without anti-liberal intent. We will show here how the interests of a representative sample of Ontario industrial concerns are maintained, including but not limited to interest group activity, and draw conclusions about the nature of contemporary political integration of private interests in Canada in the 1970s.

In keeping with our initial discussion, it seems most useful to characterize the different means of approaching government in terms of the periods in which they were most useful to private interests. The first of these methods is the direct personal approach to powerful government figures. Alone of the methods currently or previously used, it has retained its utility over time. The efficacy of such appeals, however, may well vary and depend on political circumstances.

One method which seems dated now is appearance before a legislative committee. It reached its highest development in the entrepreneurial mercantile period. In contrast in the succeeding portfolio investment period, cartels and general purpose interest groups, here represented by the Canadian Manufacturers' Association or the Canadian Chamber of Commerce, seem to have risen to prominence, as Clark (1939) suggested. Only in the most recent period, characterized by the rapid concentration of capital and complex direct investment structures, have the authentic sector-wide trade associations and government advisory boards and commissions become fully developed. These now play a coordinating role with governments, often in an institutionalized setting, and may actually have a statutory basis (Lieserson 1942: 160). Presthus sees this as a "delegation of public power through advisory councils and commissions". He further suggests that interests are thus given "the 'legal-rational' authority" which any integral part of government possesses (1974:33).

Boards and commissions in this context come closest to the coordination model of corporatism discussed previously. They are government established groups which are intended to review conditions in industrial sectors and to make suggestions to a minister with respect to new or altered legislation or regulations. Given the semi-official status of such boards, they might fairly be described as quasi-corporatist institutions since they tend to blur the distinction between private capital and government.

We would thus expect to find a drift away from both the legislative committee forum, as indeed Presthus (1974:23) has reported, and from the general interest group as a means of conveying industrial wishes to governments. Direct approaches to government officials constitute a special problem since this type of petitioning is endemic in all periods. One can, however, ask whether such activity is more consistent with the older or newer patterns of interest representation. Recent studies (Ward 1963; Acheson 1972; Rich 1972; Smith and Tepperman 1974; Barkans and Pupo 1974; Clement 1975) suggesting the progressive homogenization of social background characteristics of persons in the upper echelons of Canadian institutional life strongly indicate that the importance of direct contact is increasing.

Method

Data for this study were collected in the course of interviews with the senior executive officers of 176 Ontario industries in 1971 and 1972. Sampling of firms was random and stratified by size of firm (measured by number of employees) and by industrial sector (using the conventional Statistics Canada categories of manufacturing with the addition of mines and utilities). No company employing fewer than 100 persons was included due to our focus on larger firms.

Since a large proportion of industrial employment in Ontario is concentrated in large firms in the Toronto-centered region, and in the adjoining Hamilton-Burlington area, most of the interviews were conducted within a radius of 125 miles from Toronto.

Though one cannot generalize outside of the Ontario context with the data at hand, at the least we are discussing here a major part of Canada's manufacturing complex. The fact that the 176 companies sampled employed about one quarter of a million workers is suggestive of their importance.

Findings

Figure 1 shows the various avenues which companies have available to them in presenting their views to government. We have argued that as the nature of business enterprise has changed, so too has the nature of the relationship between private interests and government, developing progressively into a more institutionalized relationship. Figure 1 shows that the interest group is currently the most used method of approach to government. For instance, 72 per cent of the companies belong to the Canadian Manufacturers' Association and fully 90 per cent belong to at least one trade association. Further, 70 per cent of the firms report using an interest group to approach government. We also see that 61 per cent of the senior executives of the companies hold or have held executive office in an interest group, a position which might be expected to entail the spokesman role. Companies tend, however, to pick a trade association over the Canadian Manufacturers' Association as the most effective conduit to government (63 per cent chose a trade association), an indication of the higher percieved efficacy of the trade associations.

In contrast to the use of interest groups, appearances before a legislative committee are much more limited. Only 27 per cent of the senior executives reported ever appearing in contrast to the situation in the nineteenth century previously described. A substantial level of "regular" direct contact with government officials was, however, reported (33 per cent of the sample) as was membership on a government advisory board or commission. This latter type of activity, which we interpret to be in keeping with an emergent 'quasi-corporatism', was highly prevalent (29 per cent of the senior executives) since the number of such positions are limited.*

Thus in Figure 1, we find evidence that:

1) There is a high level of interest representation by companies in the sample;
2) Trade association use is currently the most prevalent type of interest representation, and apparently the most effective;
3) Appearances before legislative committees are not as prevalent nor as important as they once were;

---

*Forty-six such boards or commissions were mentioned. Examples are the Aircraft Production Board, the national advisory commission on petroleum, and the Canadian Specifications Board.

Figure 1
Use of Different Avenues of Interest
Representation by Companies

(Per Cent of Companies Reporting Incidence)

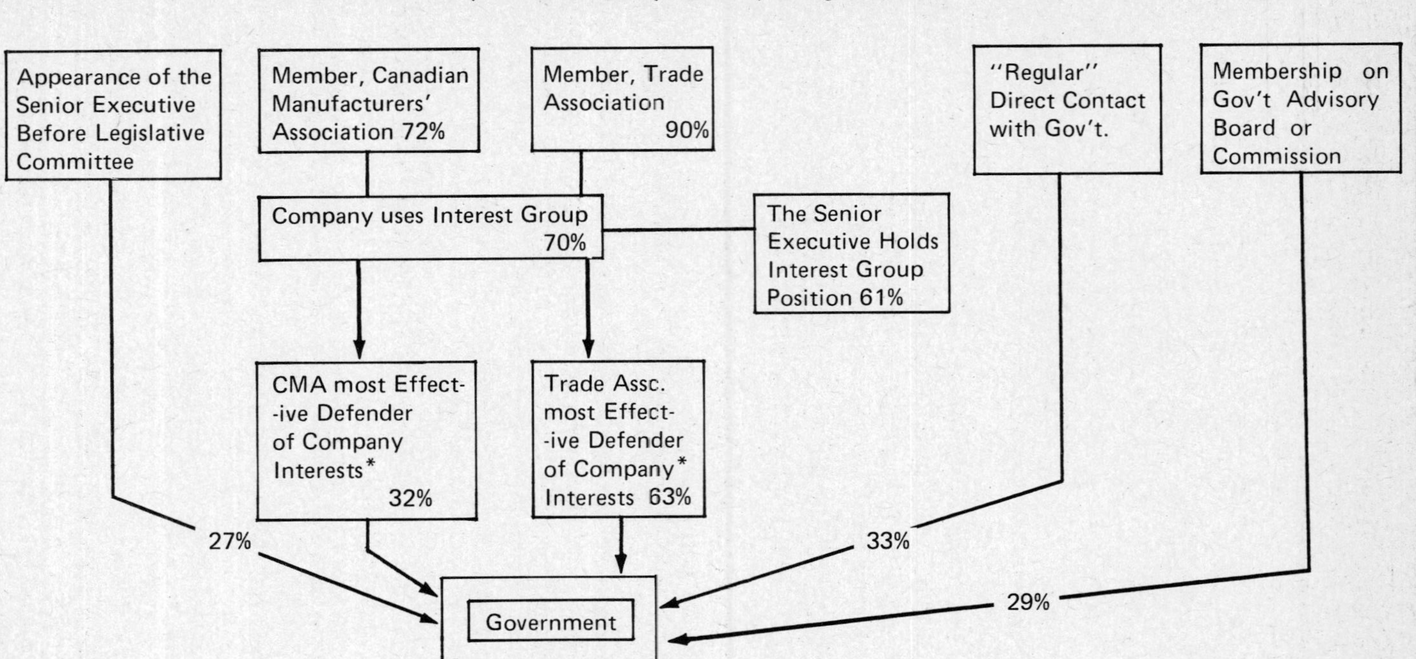

*The remaining 5% was split between the Canadian Chamber of Commerce, other, and 'none'

4) Use of the interest group route is chosen more often than direct contact with officials (but one cannot infer whether direct contact is more closely associated with the declining legislative committee mode or with the rising advisory commission mode); and finally
5) Use of the advisory board or commission avenue is relatively high in the sample.

In order to analyze development over time, we would have to use time series data but these are not now available. Another way of testing the notion of the shift in mode of representation is to compare small and large companies' behaviour. We must make the assumption that the more developed, in terms of size, a company is, the more survival potential that firm has in an environment increasingly characterized by conglomeration, concentration of economic power, and largeness. Thus if we compare the behaviour of small and large firms (as in Figure 2) we can infer the direction in which interest representation is moving, assuming that many small firms will in the future be absorbed by larger companies.

Thus, we hypothesize a trend in which bigger companies, with more economic impact, more employees, and more political importance will behave more like presently large companies than like presently small firms.

Regarding the comparison implied in Figure 2, we note that most forms of interest representation are more prevalent in the large firms. For instance, appearance before legislative committees, which we expected to be a declining form, rises in incidence from 13 per cent in the small firms to 38 per cent in the large firms. This finding may only indicate that this type of activity is now most widely practised among the largest companies. In addition, we do not know when these appearances occurred in the careers of the executives since the question did not specify recent appearances, rather appearances ever. Thus, interpretation of this finding is difficult and the results inconclusive.

More important are the usage patterns in the interest group section of Figure 2. While CMA membership is higher in the large firms (79 per cent compared with 63 per cent in the small companies), use of interest groups is slightly lower, indicating that other forms of interest representation are preferred by large firms. Holding of interest group positions is only marginally higher for senior executives of large firms (64 per cent to 57 per cent), and a somewhat greater proportion of large firms indicate the trade associations are the most effective defenders of their interests (65 per cent to 57 per cent) in preference to the CMA.

But the largest differences between large and small firms are to be found in two types of activity: "regular" direct contact with government (reported by 41 per cent of large companies but only 23 per cent of small firms); and membership on a government advisory board or commission (reported by 40 per cent of large firms and only 15 per cent of small companies).

It is only in the latter two types of activity where bigness clearly counts (and where, if bigness is necessary for survival, the shape of future political integretion of private interests is to be discerned).

There are still problems in the analysis of "regular" direct contact. We have maintained that this strategy is prevalent in all eras and in all political systems. While we know that direct contact and membership on advisory commissions are characteristic forms of activity of large firms today, there still remains the question of whether direct contact is more closely associated with the older style of interest group pressure or the emergent from of institutionalized relationship between business and government on boards and commissions. One way of answering this question lies in the patterns of activity reported by those who expressed a preference for direct contact as opposed to those who preferred to go through interest groups. If we assume that direct approaches are a part of the emergent style, then we should expect to find that

Figure 2
Use of Different Avenues of Interest Representation
By Size of Companies

Small Companies (100-499 Employees) N= 79

(Per Cent of Companies Reporting Incidence)

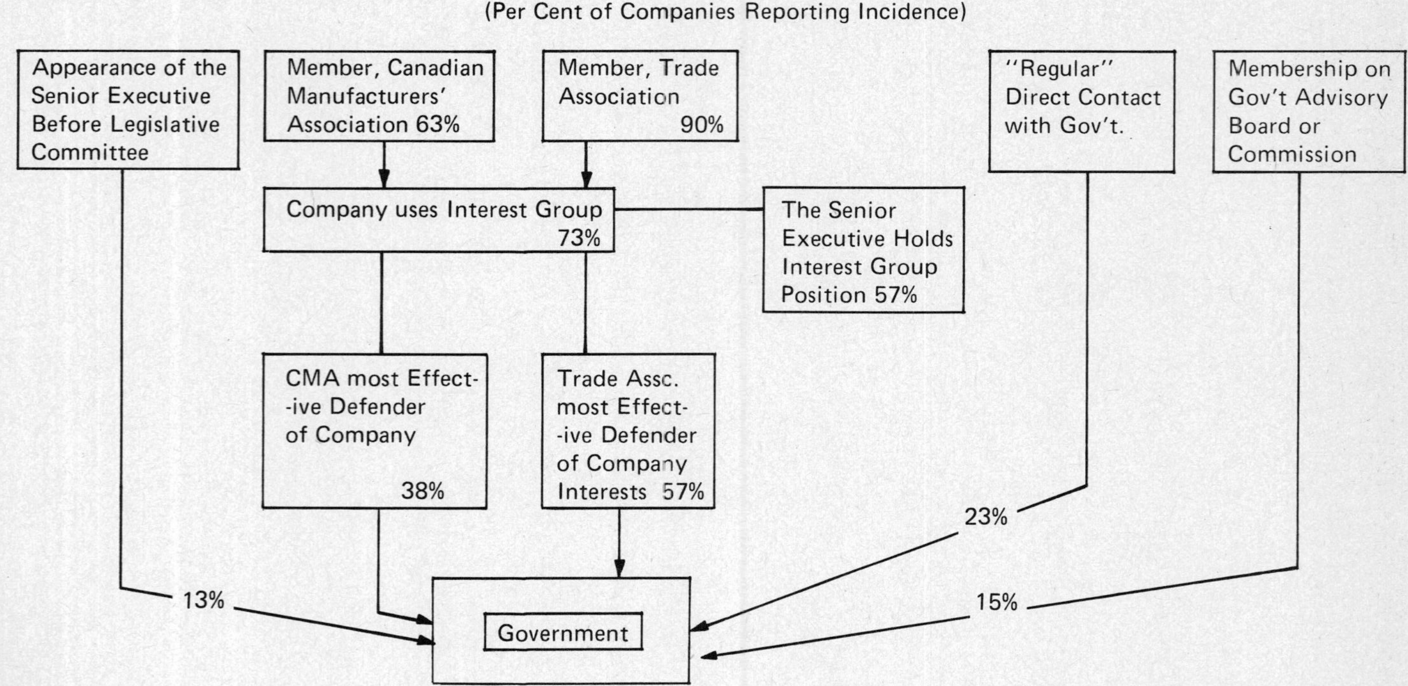

Figure 2 (Continued)

Large Companies (500 + Employees) N=97

(Per Cent of Companies Reporting Incidence)

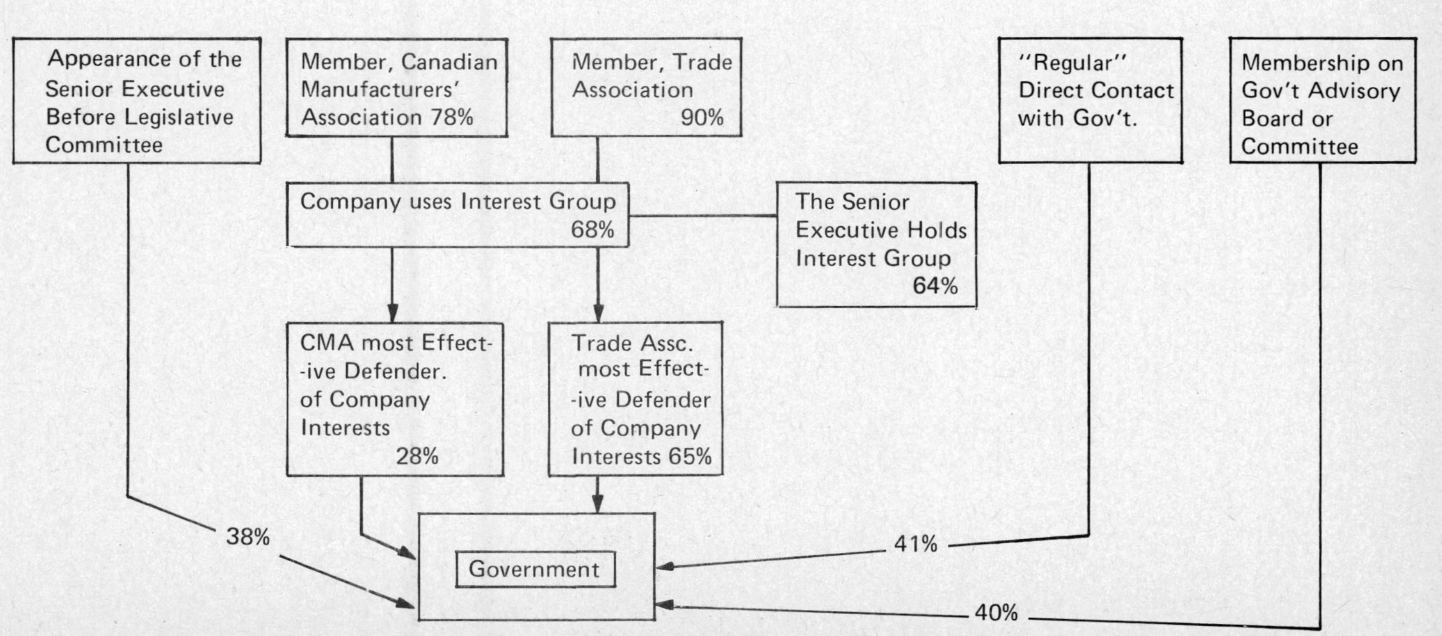

those preferring direct contact with government would now tend to use interest groups less than those who prefer to use organizations. Figure 3 represents such a cross-classification.

Figure 3
Characteristics of Companies, According to Preferred Approach to Government

(Percentages)

Characteristics of Companies	"Do you prefer to go to government directly or through organizations?"	
	To Government Directly (N=51)	Through Organizations (N=102)
Member: Canadian Manufacturers' Association	82%	66%
Trade association	78%	94%
Uses interest group	51%	79%
The senior executive holds an interest group position	53%	61%
Interest group which most effectively defends the interests of the company:		
Canadian Manufacturers' Association	44%	27%
A trade association	54%	66%
The senior executive approaches govern--ment 'regularly' or 'occasionally'	73%	48%

We can see that while those companies which prefer direct contact are more often members of the Canadian Manufacturers' Association (82 per cent to 66 per cent), they belong to a trade association less often (78 per cent to 94 per cent) and, most important, they use an interest group less often (51 per cent to 79 per cent). Those who prefer direct contact also hold offices in interest groups less often (53 per cent to 61 per cent), and are more likely to cite the CMA (a generalist type of interest group of the older type) as the most effective defender of their industry in preference to trade associations. This preference implies little or no use at all since the CMA is not organized to fight for specific industries on specific issues.

Most important, companies which prefer direct contact act consistently with this preference, reporting "regular" or "occasional" approaches to government directly much more often (73 per cent to 48 per cent) than those which prefer the trade association route.

From this pattern we conclude that the higher incidence of direct contact with government reported by large companies in the sample is consistent with a current pattern of reduced use of interest groups. This behaviour is also consistent with the emergent "quasi-corporatist" relationship.

This finding is congruent with the increasing homogeneity of social background characteristics of the corporate elite reported by Clement (1975) and Porter (1965). The increasing homogeneity may parallel both increasing incidence and importance of direct contact between the leaders of private capitalist institutions and their government counterparts.

Discussion and Implications

In a somewhat prophetic passage Robert Brady wrote in 1943:

> So it is that, if the growth in the relative importance of giant corporations is properly termed 'concentration of economic power', expansion of trade association networks means 'mobilization of the entire business community'. If the former is defined as 'trustification', then the latter implies 'unification' or 'synchronization' . . . they are related in time, origin, and processes of growth, in the logic of circumstances which bind them to each other as historical developments, and in the compulsions they exert for an ever and cumulative widening of governmental regulation and control (1943: 8).

As the data presented here show, the development process has largely confirmed Brady's vision. The ultimate conclusion of the process is not yet in sight, however. Just as the multinational conglomerate represents the ultimate in concentration of economic power, so the fully developed corporatist structure may come to represent the couterpart system of political integration of private interests. Whether or not such a development occurs rests in the last analysis on the strength of liberal ideas held by politically important individuals. With the development of corporatist institutions, a peculiar form of contingent liberalism seems to be developing in which freedoms are gained for the powerful, who are protected and fostered by collectivist institutions, while such freedoms are denied the weak and powerless. The inequalities of access to the political process thus produced are in essence, therefore, class-based.

As organizations evolve and companies get larger, more powerful, and more demanding of governments, it seems likely that traditional forms by which interests are represented will decline in favour of corporatist and direct, personal approaches. Together they will form a progressively closer working relationship between private interests and government officials. This will probably lead to lessening differentiation between private and public organizations and a decline in the influence of individuals who are not involved in large corporate entities.

Other types of economic organizations are changing in similar ways. Labour unions, for example, are becoming more centralized and co-ordinated. The proletarianization of the working population, including recently teachers and other public employees, has followed from the difficulty of small groups to contend with industry-wide employer associations. Similarly, senior civil servants are now better educated and more attuned to the function of co-ordination and accordingly have gained more influence in the private sector. As well there is growing homogeneity in social background among persons who occupy senior positions in all institutional realms. These tendencies are fostered by the development of vertical integration in industry, often crossing international boundaries.

The multinational conglomerate corporation now is able to command such vast global resources as to outweigh the power of a single national government. Collectively these corporations wield such formidable power that governments are obliged to seek international ties to preserve a semblance of autonomy. Such links have been discussed under the aegis of the United Nations.

In the light of this process, outraged claims of untold government interference in the private sector may soon come to be regarded as absurd. For the private citizen, the implications are also clear. The possibilities of building small private businesses into mature organizations are decreasing. Instead, the principal route to progress, wealth, and upward social mobility lies through absorption into huge, complex, international corporations. The threats to liberalism, diversity, and individual freedom which follow from the new corporatism are becoming widely evident.

References

Auclair, Gilles A.
1970 "Cultural Differences in Attitudes Toward Industrial Leadership, Their Existence and Impact on Managerial Styles and Organizational Climate in Large Canadian Industrial Organizations." Unpublished paper, University of Montreal.

Acheson, T.W.
1972 "The social Origins of the Canadian Industrial Elite, 1880-1885." In David S. Macmillan, *Canadian Business History.* Toronto: McClelland and Stewart. 144-174.

Barkans, John and Norene Pupo
1974 "The Boards of Governors and the Power Elite: A Case Study of Eight Canadian Universities". *Sociological Focus,* 7:81-98.

Beer, Samuel H.
1957 "The Representation of Interests in British Government: Historical Background." *The American Political Science Review,* 51: 613-650.

Bliss, Michael
1974 *A Living Profit.* Toronto: McClelland and Stewart.

Brady, Robert A.
1943 *Business as a System of Power.* New York: Columbia University Press.

Clark, S.D.
1939 *The Canadian Manufacturers' Association: A study in Collective Bargaining and Political Pressure.* Toronto: University of Toronto History and Economic Series.

Clement, Wallace
1974 "The Changing Structure of the Canadian Economy." In *Aspects of Canadian Society.* Montreal: Canadian Review of Sociology and Anthropology. 3-27.

1975 *The Canadian Corporate Elite.* Toronto: McClelland and Stewart.

Dawson, H.J.
1960 "An Interest Group: The Canadian Federation of Agriculture". *Canadian Public Administration,* 3: 134:149.

1963 "The Consumers' Association of Canada." *Canadian Public Administration,* 6: 92-118.

Eckstein, Harry
1960 *Pressure Group Politics.* London: George Allen and Unwin.

Elbow, Matthew H.
1966 *French Corporative Theory* 1789-1948. New York: Octagon Books.

Gonick, Cy
1975 *Inflation or Despression.* Toronto: James Lorimer.

Hague, George
1908 *Banking and Commerce.* New York: Bankers Publishers.

Innis, Harold
1930 *The Fur Trade in Canada.* New Haven: Yale University Press.

Kwavnick, David
1970 "Pressure Group Demands and the Struggle for Organizational Status: The Case of Organized Labour." *Canadian Journal of Political Science,* 3:56-72.

Lieserson, Avery
1942 *Administration Regulation.* Chicago: University of Chicago Press.

Mackenzie, W.J.M.
1955 "Pressure Groups in British Government." *British Journal of Sociology,* 6: 133-148.

Manzer, Ronald
1969 "Selective Inducements and the Developments of Pressure Groups: The Case of the Canadian Teachers' Association." *Canadian Journal of Political Science.* 2: 103-117.

Nayler, R.T.
1972 "The Rise and Fall of the Third Commercial Empire of the St. Lawrence." in Gary Teeple (ed.), *Capitalism and the National Question in Canada.* Toronto: University of Toronto Press. 1-42.

1975 *The History of Canadian Business, 1867-1914, Volumes I and II.* Toronto: James Lorimer.

Nelles, H.V.
1974 *The Politics of Development.* Toronto: Macmillan of Canada.

Osler, Richard
1976 "Crispo's advise to planners: prepare for big brother". *The Financial Post,* January 3, 1976.

Porter, John
1965 *The Vertical Mosaic.* Toronto: University of Toronto Press.

Presthus, Robert
1973 *Elite Accommodation in Canadian Politics.* Toronto: Macmillan of Canada.

1974 *Elites in the Policy Process.* London: Cambridge University Press.

Research Branch, Library of Parliament
1970 "Pressure Groups in Canada". *Parliamentarian* 51: 11-20.

Rich, Harvey
1972 "A Summary Statement of Survey Date from Higher Civil Servants in Ontario", paper presented at the Annual Meetings of the C.S.A.A., Montreal.

Smith, David and Lorne Tepperman
1974 "Changes in the Canadian Business and Legal Elites". *Canadian Review of Sociology and Anthropology.* 11: 97-109.

Teeple, Gary
1972 Introduction to *Capitalism and the National Question in Canada.* Toronto: University of Toronto Press. x-xv.

Thorburn, H.G.
1964 "Pressure Groups in Canadian Politics: Recent Revisions of the Anti-Combines Legislation." *Canadian Journal of Political Science and Economics* 30.

Vernon, Raymond (ed.)
1974 *Big Business and the State.* Cambridge: Harvard University Press.

Ward, Norman
1963 *The Canadian House of Commons.* Toronto: University of Toronto Press.

Wilkins, Mira
1974 *The Maturing of Multinational Enterprise.* Cambridge: Harvard University Press.

20

Occupational Mobility in Quebec, 1954 and 1964*

Jacques Dofny and Muriel Garon-Audy

The purpose of this article is to measure the mobility of French and English-speaking Canadians[1] in Quebec. The authors are not concerned with the entire population of Quebec. The latter would include 9.6 per cent of New Canadians, a group for which our sampling method does not allow consideration. Working on comparisons of birth and marriage records, we were limited to those people born and married in Canada.[2]

In 1957 Yves de Jocas and Guy Rocher published the results of a study based on a survey of the official registers of birth and marriage certificates in the Demography Service of the province of Quebec for the year of 1954.[3] In this study the occupation of youths who married that year were compared with those of their fathers when the youths were born. Rates of mobility were calculated according to a method set out by Natalie Rogoff in her 1953 study. Rocher and de Jocas concluded that in Francophone Quebec society, mobility was achieved one level at a time. Sons of rural origin entered the industralized work world at the bottom of the occupational scale, at the level of labourer. The sons of labourers in the process of mobility advanced most often to specialized manual jobs, sons of skilled workers to white-collar jobs, and so on up the ladder. In addition the patterns of mobility for French Canadians in Quebec were similar to those observed by Natalie Rogoff[4] in Marion County, Indiana. On the other hand, Anglophone Canadians at a given occupational level seemed to change their positions much faster than their French Québecois counterparts at that level. The former tended to mount the stratification ladder two rungs at a time.

Considering the changes in Quebec society during the last decade, it seems important to look again, ten years later, at the research problem addressed by Rocher and de Jocas. Harold Wilensky[5] has emphasized that there is a great problem in interpreting data on various phenomena if information has been gathered with differing methodologies. With this in mind we decided to conduct a direct replication of the Rocher and de Jocas study, in spite of some obvious limitations in their approach.

Method and Sampling

As in the 1954 sample, one out of every fifteen marriage certificate files was drawn. These records contained the following information: data and place of birth, projected

*Translated by James Curtis and abridged for this volume. The paper first appeared as "Mobilités professionnelles au Québec" in *Sociologie et Sociétés,* 1 (November, 1969), 277-301. By permission of the authors and Les Presses de l'Université de Montréal.

place of residence after marriage, religion, occupation, and ethnic origin. The occupation of the fathers of the newlyweds was not indicated on the marriage certificate, but this could be found on birth certificates also kept by the Bureau of Statistics in each province (a son married in Quebec in 1964 was not necessarily born there) .

The mobility that this study will attempt to measure will be that between two clearly defined points in the life of the subjects studied: birth and marriage. When an individual is born, his status is not random. It is essentially linked and determined by the status of his family, which in turn depends largely on the occupation of the head of the family. The question to be asked here is this: to what extent does the status handed down to an individual at birth indicate the status he will have as an adult?

Table 1 allows us to compare the samples chosen in 1954 and 1964. Since the 1954 sample did not allow for the study of social mobility of sons born before 1926 (it was in 1926 that the Quebec government began to gather information from which our findings are taken), it was decided to consider in 1964 only those sons born after 1935 . . . . If we include only sons born after 1935 in the 1964 sample, this becomes comparable to the 1954 sample with regard to age; we have thus excluded individuals over 28 years of age at marriage.

Table 1

Comparison of Samples

	1954	1964
Basic sample	2,372	2,564
Rejects: Sons born before 1926 (for 1954) or before 1936 (for 1964) or outside Canada	967	836
Final sample		
French Canadian	1,234	1,550
English Canadian	110	120
Others	61	58
Total Marriages	35,516	39,400

As already indicated, the mobility rates used here were developed by Natalie Rogoff in her study in 1953. Essentially these consist of relating the level of occupational achievement of the sons (grouped according to level of origin) to information on the overall structure of occupations in the society. The latter is represented by the total distribution of occupations in the sample.[6]

Rogoff's reasoning is as follows: if, for example, professional and managerial positions occupy 5 per cent of a population then, with equal opportunity for everyone, 5 per cent of the sons, regardless of their origin, should reach this occupational level. If 25 per cent of the sons of professionals stay at this level, they thus enjoy five times greater than chance likelihood of achieving this occupational level. A rate entirely related to chance would thus be equal to 1. Although criticized by certain specialists, these types of rates appear frequently in mobility studies, even in most recent ones.[7] Natalie Rogoff[8] has brought about certain refinements in them, to allow differentiation of the population of a country according to the occupational characteristics of the area from which each group of persons originates. But given the special focus of this article, we will consider only the data bearing on our overall population.[9]

One of the weaknesses of Rogoff's rates lies in their close relation to the importance of given occupations in the overall distribution.[10] The greater the percentage of individuals grouped in the same occupation the lower are the chances that the rate of access to this occupation of sons from a particular social origin much exceeds 1. It is thus that one rarely finds rates of access more than 2 for an occupational category which includes 30 per cent of the population, since such a rate would indicate a concentration of 60 per cent of the individuals of a specific origin in this category. On the other hand, the entry rate into a higher occupational category can easily be more than 5, since this category usually constitutes less than 10 per cent of the total population. Any appreciable variation in the occupational structure thus requires that care be taken in comparing specific rates. Thus, the first question to be posed is: Has the distribution of occupations changed noticeably during the decade being considered?

I. Mobility of French-Speaking Canadians in Quebec

1. *Occupational Structure*

As indicated in Table 2, the occupational structure[11] in the two samples is the same for fathers. With the sons, on the other hand, whereas the percentage of professionals changed little and that of white-collar workers increased slightly, unskilled workers (labourers) dropped from 33.46 per cent to 20.13 per cent. Semi-professionals and the skilled or semi-skilled workers have changed respectively from 5.68 to 15.16 per cent and from 27.31 to 32.32 per cent. The decrease in labourers and the increase of skilled technicians and middle management are the well-known results of technological development.[12] It is interesting to note that this had no real differential effect in the two generations of fathers considered in our samples.

Table 2
Occupational Structure in the Samples of 1954 and 1964

(Percentages)

Occupations	Fathers a		Sons b	
	1954	1964	1954	1964
Professionals and Managers	3.24	2.19	5.84	4.71
Semi-professionals and lower administrators	5.11	5.10	5.68	15.16
White collar	5.24	5.74	11.26	15.80
Skilled and semi-skilled	22.20	22.39	27.31	32.32
Unskilled	27.96	24.13	33.46	20.13
Personal and public service	4.46	5.61	7.54	8.00
Farmers	30.79	34.84	8.91	3.87
Total	(1234)	(1550)	(1234)	(1550)

aΔ = 5.39
bΔ = 19.50

The changes which Table 2 indicated must be kept in mind when reading and interpreting our rates, given their particular influence. It thus becomes mathematically easier to obtain higher rates in the categories of labourers; the opposite is true at the top of the occupational scale.

2. *Growth of Occupational Mobility for the Period, 1954-1964.*

a. *Rate of stability.* It is difficult to approach a mobility study without first evaluating a related phenomenon: the degree of stability, that is, the frequency of transmission to the son of the paternal occupation. A society rigidly stratified in the sense given to this term by O.D. Duncan[13] is a society where privileges are maintained, where there is definite structuring and crystallization of differences. This situation will present high stability rates and a low tendency towards mobility. How does this relate to Quebec, and how does Quebec of 1964 differ from Quebec of 1954?

The rates of stability (Table 3) show that the determining of the son's status at the beginning of his occupational career has become much less dependent upon the status of the father.

A study of the percentage passing on their occupational status (the rates are affected by the growth of the occupational structure) reveals even more interesting results. Whereas about half the sons of the upper stratum (professionals and management) were in this category in 1954, such a situation is true in less than 25 per cent of the cases in 1964. At the other extreme of the social ladder, with the labourers, the rate of inheritance of the father's occupational status went from 43 to 27 per cent of the cases (see Table 3).

Similarly, whereas Rocher and de Jocas stated in 1954 that one quarter of farmers' sons stay on the farm, in 1964 this fraction was no more than one tenth. The only two categories where it was recorded that a greater number of sons follow in the occupational footsteps of their father than in 1954 are: (a) that of semi-professionals (which includes all those persons who received an intermediate professional training between that of skilled workers and office workers, on one hand, and that of university graduates or those who occupy an upper rung in administration, on the other hand); (b) that of personal and public service.

Table 3
Rates of Stability and Percentage Occupational Inheritance

	1954		1964	
	Rate	Percent Inheritance	Rate	Percent Inheritance
Professionals and managers	8.13	47.50	5.00	23.53
Semi-professionals and lower administrators	3.35	19.05	1.92	29.11
White collar	3.00	33.77	1.78	28.09
Skilled and semi-skilled	1.48	40.51	1.10	35.45
Unskilled	2.98	43.48	2.44	26.74
Personal and public service	1.30	5.50	1.33	12.64
Farmers	1.45	26.58	1.58	9.44

b. *Entry rate into different occupational categories.* Given the tendency towards a reduction in occupational "inheritance", it is even more interesting to consider the more frequent case of mobility. Indeed, 78 per cent of sons are now mobile compared to 65 per cent in 1954. But do they move up or down the scale?

An analysis of the specific rates presented in Table 4 indicates a definite increase in upward mobility for 1964 compared to 1954. In contrast, downward mobility is less frequent. Thus, the rates of entry into the professional and managerial category show a noticeable increase for sons of semi-professionals and middle management, of white-collar workers and of skilled or semi-skilled workers. Only the sons of service employees had lower 1964 entry rates at this level.

In the opening up of the semi-professional and middle management category to sons of a lower origin, there is a single marked recession: sons of white-collar workers had relatively less ease of accessibility than in 1954. For all the others, the possibilities of entry are at least as good and often better. This is even more interesting when it is considered that the important increase in size of this occupational category since 1954 has made it more difficult for a higher rate of entry to be obtained.

This tendency towards the acceleration of upward mobility is also shown in access to the category of skilled workers. The slight decrease in access of sons of non-skilled workers is greatly compensated for by the considerable advance that sons of farmers have made at this level.

The outline of downward mobility presents the other side of the picture which has just been drawn for upward mobility. There is in effect an increase in the downward mobility on two levels only: sons of professionals and managers, who remain less often in the occupational stratum of their father, move more often towards the category of semi-professionals and middle management. White-collar workers show a similar pattern of downward mobility. In all other areas downward mobility saw a clear decrease or at least remained stationary.

Table 4
Rates of Stability and Mobility of French - Canadians in Quebec (1964)

Occupation of son	Occupation of Father 1	2	3	4	5	6	7	Rate of Entry
Professionals and Managers	*5.00*	1.61	3.10	1.53	0.40	0.73	0.43	1.30
Semi-professionals and lower admistrators	3.30	*1.92*	1.63	0.99	0.76	1.06	0.78	1.42
White collar	0.74	1.04	*1.78*	1.39	1.07	1.45	0.52	1.04
Skilled and semi-skilled	0.09	0.74	0.56	*1.10*	0.99	0.89	1.13	0.73
Unskilled	0.44	0.69	0.45	0.53	*1.33*	0.80	1.28	0.70
Personal and public service	0.37	1.11	0.70	1.05	1.24	*1.58*	0.79	0.88
Farmers	0.00	0.00	0.00	0.37	0.28	0.00	*2.44*	0.11
Rate of Departure	0.82	0.87	1.07	0.98	0.79	0.82	0.81	
Total	34	79	89	347	374	87	540	

General Rate of Stability: 2.15 -- General Rate of Mobility: 0.88

The overall consequences of these patterns of mobility are summarized in Table 5 through the general rates of entry in each of the occupational categories.

Table 5
General Rates of Entry Ino Each of The Occupational Categories

	1954	1964
Professionals and Managers	1.23	1.30
Semi-professionals and lower administrators	0.95	1.42
White collar	1.31	1.04
Skilled and semi-skilled	0.88	0.73
Unskilled	0.68	0.70
Personal and public service	1.02	0.88
Farmers	0.13	0.11

The accessibility to the two upper occupational categories has noticeably increased. The other categories, except labourers and farmers which remained stationary, realized a clear drop in their recruitment.

c. *Distance covered in the course of mobility.* It is customary in sociology to rank occupations, from the category of professionals and managers to that of labourers, as if they formed a hierarchy. This custom is in fact based on several studies of prestige, the most recent being that of Blau and Duncan.[14] This latter study shows that, in addition to representing a ladder, these occupational levels yield laws of mobility concerning the scope of movement allowed (e.g., passage from the white-collar category to that of semi-professionals and middle management, or to that of professionals and management), and rigidity of boundaries between levels (e.g., between the occupations of white- and blue- collar workers). It then seems appropriate to treat these occupations as levels here and to count the number of levels or stages passed through in the course of mobility. Each level is seen as forming a distinct entity, a step in the climb toward the summit.[15]

The study of mobility of the French-Canadian population of Quebec in terms of the number of rungs climbed is consistent with the observations we made earlier about the increase in mobility for French Canadians[16] (see Table 6).

In 1954, upward mobility was realized by 35.3 per cent of the sample, compared with 51.1 per cent in 1964. In addition, it is no longer possible to say, as did Rocher and de Jocas, that the norm of mobility for French Canadians in Quebec is to climb the occupational scale one level at a time. In 1954 only 14 per cent crossed more than one level, 21.3 per cent a single level. The corresponding percentages for 1964 are 24.4 and 26.9 per cent respectively. The tendency to climb more than one occupational rung is just as common as is ascent one rung at a time.

In general, less stability and downward mobility in 1964 is accompanied by clearly accentuated upward mobility. Such is the tendency observed in the occupational situation of French-speaking Canadians in Quebec. Has this evolution affected the relationship between English Canadians and French Canadians? This will be examined in the second part of this article.

Table 6

Number of Levels Crossed in the Course of Mobility by French-Canadians

(Percentages)

		1954		1964	
Upward		35.3		51.1	
	4 levels		1.4		0.8
	3 levels		3.8		8.1
	2 levels		8.8		15.3
	1 level		21.3		26.9
Stationary		43.7		33.5	
Downward		21.0		15.4	
	I level		13.0		9.9
	2 levels		4.3		3.7
	3 levels		2.9		1.4
	4 levels		0.8		0.4
Total		(728)		(835)	

II. Comparison of Mobility of French-and English-Speaking Canadians

We must limit our observations here to individuals residing in urban counties: the heavy concentration of English Canadians in these counties had already forced Rocher and de Jocas in 1954 to limit their comparisons to French Canadians of these counties (i.e.) to those living in a situation similar to that of English Canadians). A similar concentration in 1964 imposes the same restraints upon us. As in the first part of this article, we shall begin with a comparison of occupations at the two points in time.[17]

1. Occupational Structure

The decade from 1954 to 1964 was marked, at the level of occupational structure, by surprising changes for such a short period of time.

For the French Canadians, the non-manual category increased while that of unskilled labourer declined. The non-manual group among English-speaking also increased, but in this case the services group declined considerably.

Have these changes affected the tendency noted in 1954 by Rocher and de Jocas with regard to the difference which separates the two main ethnic groups in Quebec? In 1954, the changes of the occupational structure from the father's generation to that of their sons clearly indicated the gap between the two groups widened in favour of the English Canadians. This advantage, in the three upper categories, changed from 8.83 to 22.40 per cent (cf. Table 9). The opposite was true for the occupations of skilled workers and labourers where the proportion of French Canadians went on increasing; the split separating them from the English Canadians widened from 26 to 29.30 per cent. Rocher and de Jocas were able to conclude that on the whole "the difference of occupational distribution between French-and English-speaking Canadians is greater for the generation of the sons than it was for their fathers."[18]

What happened in 1964? When one compares in the same way the differences

Table 7

Occupational Structure of Urban French and English Canadians for 1964

(Percentages)

	Fathers [a]		Sons [b]	
	FC	EC	FC	EC
Professionals and managers	3.11	8.93	5.38	9.82
Semi-professionals and lower administrators	6.94	12.50	17.70	28.57
White collar	7.77	16.07	19.73	27.68
Skilled and semi-skilled	25.95	26.79	34.81	21.43
Unskilled	25.95	13.39	13.63	8.04
Public services	4.78	7.14	4.07	3.57
Personal services	2.76	4.47	4.19	0.00
Farmers	22.73	10.71	0.48	0.89
Total	(836)	(112)	(836)	(112)

aΔ = 24.58
bΔ = 23.67

between French and English Canadians for the generation of the fathers and for that of the sons, it seems that the tendency toward distinctions noted in 1954 has slowed down considerably. The differences between French and English Canadians in the category of non-manuals were 19.68 per cent for the generation of the fathers; they are 23.26 per cent for that of the sons. In other respects, if the difference increased noticeably—14.22 per cent for skilled workers, of which the proportion is clearly more important among the French Canadians—this difference was reduced by almost 7 per cent for non-skilled workers, a category which attracts a constantly decreasing proportion of French Canadians.

On the other hand, the service categories, which formerly attracted more English Canadians than French Canadians, show an opposite trend. These categories, however, include only a few persons; they are thus characterized by the least movement. Finally, the disappearance of the difference between French and English Canadians in the category of farmers indicated the almost total disappearance of these jobs in the urban counties.

In summary, the reduction in differences between French- and English-speaking Canadians for the generation of fathers and sons as compared to that observed in 1954 for the same two groups underlines an increase in the amount of mobility of French Canadians. In 1954, in six categories out of eight, the difference grew markedly between the two ethnic groups; in 1964 the opposite holds--the difference lessened in five out of eight categories.

Thus, when one looks not only at the differences between fathers and sons but also those between sons in the two samples (even for an interval of ten years) the slowing down process which has just been observed in the separation between the two ethnic groups seems to continue. The proportional superiority of the English Canadians in the "non-manual" categories is stabilized between 22 and 23 per cent.

Table 8
Changes in the Occupational Structure of Sons
(French and English Canadians Living in Cities)
(Percentages)

	FC		EC	
	1954	1964	1954	1964
Non-Manual	27.60	42.83	50.00	66.07
Skilled and semi-skilled	34.23	34.81	23.64	21.43
Unskilled	25.99	13.63	7.27	8.04
Services	10.21	8.26	18.18	3.57

The surplus of French Canadians over English Canadians in the category of labourers continues to decrease, changing from 18.7 to 5.6 per cent. There are now more French-speaking Canadians in the service occupations.

This lessening of differences between English and French Canadians could result from three factors: (a) the enlargement of the occupational structure at the top, due simply to the increased growth of industry, so that there are no longer enough English Canadians to fill the available positions; (b) proportional withdrawal of English Canadians from the upper categories. This can occur in two ways: (1) the upper positions disappear when certain English-Canadian enterprises are replaced by American and French-Canadian enterprises more willing to employ the French-Canadian group, (2) an emigration of English Canadian personnel occurs and French Canadians take their places, as in the case of the nationalization of Hydro Quebec; (c) the promotion of French Canadians, lessening the chances of the English Canadians. It must be noted, in conclusion, that the lessening of the French-English difference does not eliminate the fact that English Canadians still hold a clear over-representation in the upper occupational categories.

2. *Change of Occupational Mobility for English- and French-Speaking Canadians in Urban Counties*

Do the statements just made about the transformation of structures hold true for the study of stability and mobility of the two groups? (Tables 10 and 11 serve as a basic reference for the paragraphs which follow.)

a. *Rate of stability.* When farmers are excluded,[19] the general rates of stability have hardly changed since 1954 for French Canadians (1.71 vs. 1.67). Stability (or social inheritance) has, on the other hand, noticeably decreased for the English-speaking Canadian group (1.95 vs. 2.39). The rates of the two groups are thus much closer to each other than ten years ago.

Is this pattern true for each occupational category? Rogoff's rates, as noted above, are closely related to the structure of occupations; and as the structure has noticeably evolved during the period (cf. Table 12), comparison of the 1954 rates with those for 1964 is more difficult. Therefore, the change in occupational inheritance will be studied here in percentages.

Table 9

Changes in Differences Between French-and English-Speaking Urban Canadians

(Percentages)

	1954		1964	
	F.C. Fathers minus E.C. Fathers	F.C. Sons minus E.C. Sons	F.C. Fathers minus E.C. Fathers	F.C. Sons minus E.C. Sons
Professionals and Managers } Non-Manual	—8.60	—10.46	—5.82	— 4.44
Semi-professionals and lower administrative } Non-Manual	0.10	— 4.80	—5.56	—10.87
White collar	—0.13	— 7.14	—8.30	— 7.95
Skilled and semi-skilled	1.06	10.59	—0.84	13.38
Unskilled	13.20	18.72	12.56	5.59
Public service	—7.69	— 8.43	—2.36	0.50
Personal service	2.50	0.46	—1.72	4.19
Farmers	—0.44	1.06	12.02	— 0.41

Table 10

Percentage Distribution of the Occupations of Urban French-Canadian Sons in Quebec, Born After 1935, According to Their Father's Occupation, Giving Rates of Stability and Mobility (1964)

Occupation of Son[a]	Occupation of Father						F.C. Total	F.C. and E.C. Total
	1 and 2[b]	3	4	5 and 7[b]	6	8		
1 and 2[b]	50.00[c] *2.01*	35.38 1.42	22.12 0.89	17.50 0.70	12.50 0.50	17.30 0.70	23.08	24.89
3	16.67 0.86	29.23 *1.41*	24.88 1.21	18.33 0.89	32.50 1.57	11.05 0.54	19.73	20.67
4	19.04 0.57	23.08 0.70	36.40 *1.10*	34.58 1.04	32.50 0.98	44.74 1.35	34.81	33.23
5 and 7[b]	13.09 0.79	7.69 0.46	12.44 0.75	25.42 *1.53*	12.50 0.75	21.05 1.26	17.82	16.67
6	1.19 0.30	4.62 1.15	3.69 0.92	4.17 1.04	10.00 *2.50*	4.21 1.05	4.07 0.00	4.01
8	0.00 0.00	0.00 0.00	0.46 0.87	0.00 0.00	0.00 0.00	1.58 *2.98*	0.48	0.53
Total	(84) 10.05	(65) 7.77	(217) 25.95	(240) 28.71	(40) 4.78	(190) 22.73	(836)	(948)

a For the meaning of the numbering see Table 9.

b Combined by Rocher and de Jocas for 1954 because of the small number of individuals in certain categories.

c The first row in each case is a percentage and the second is a rate.

Table 11

Percentage Distribution of the Occupations of Urban English-Canadian Sons in Quebec, Born After 1935, According to Their Father's Occupation, Giving Rates of Stability and Mobility (1964)

Occupation of Son	Occupation of Father [a]						F.C. Total	F.C. and E.C. Total
	1 and 2	3	4	5 and 7	6	8		
1 and 2	66.67 *2.68*	44.44 1.80	26.67 1.07	30.00 1.21	25.00 1.00	25.00 0.94	38.39	24.89
3	20.83 1.01	38.89 *1.88*	33.33 1.60	25.00 1.25	25.00 1.21	16.67 0.86	27.68	20.67
4	8.33 0.25	16.67 0.50	30.00 *0.90*	25.00 0.75	37.75 2.26	16.67 0.50	21.43	33.23
5 and 7	4.17 0.25	0.00 0.00	3.33 0.20	20.00 *1.20*	0.00 0.00	25.00 1.50	8.04	16.67
6	0.00 0.00	0.00 0.00	6.67 0.00	0.00 0.00	12.50 *3.11*	8.33 2.08	3.57	4.01
8	0.00 0.00	0.00 0.00	0.00 0.00	0.00 0.00	0.00 0.00	8.33 15.72	0.89	0.53
Total	(24) 21.43	(18) 16.07	(30) 26.79	(20) 17.86	(8) 7.14	(12) 10.71	(112)	(948)

[a] For the meaning of the measuring see Table 9.

Table 12

Occupational Structure of the Samples for the Urban Areas in the Province of Quebec

	1954	1964[a]
Professionals and Managers	14.52	24.89
Semi-professionals and lower administrators		
White collar	16.77	20.67
Skilled and semi-skilled	32.48	33.23
Unskilled and personal service	28.74	16.67
Public service	5.69	4.01
Farmers	1.80	0.53

aΔ = 15.02

Table 13 clearly shows that the observed general tendency holds for all but one occupational level: that which is at the top of the pyramid. At this level the status of the father appears as a stronger determinant of that of the son than in 1954, and this occurs just as much with English Canadians as with French Canadians.

In all other cases for the French Canadians, the status of the father loses importance in determining that of the son (except for public service personnel, but this influence was insignificant in 1954 and remained so in 1964). This is due to the considerable increase of upward mobility for French-speaking Canadians, as we shall eventually see.

This tendency is less apparent in the English-Canadian group. Paternal influence is reduced at only two levels: for the sons of skilled workers and those in public service occupations. The other cases remain unchanged in relation to 1954

Table 13

Percentage of Sons Who Remain in the Same Occupational Category as their Father, According to Ethnic Origin.

	1954		1964	
	F.C.	E.C.	F.C.	E.C.
Professional and managers	40.82	40.37	50.00	66.67
Semi-professionals and lower administrators				
White collar	34.00	40.00	29.15	38.89
Skilled and semi-skilled	45.10	44.82	36.75	30.00
Unskilled and personal service	43.92	15.00	25.42	20.00
Public service	5.56	25.00	10.00	12.50
Farmers	11.11	5.00	1.58	8.33
Total	36.00	30.00	21.94	33.93

or show a slight increase.

If we now compare within 1954 and 1964, the relative stability of French Canadians and English Canadians within each of the occupational strata, it becomes evident that paternal influence is much stronger for English Canadians than for French Canadians in occupations having a higher socio-economic status (non-manual occupations); the opposite is true for manual occupations.[20] This tendency was also noted in the 1954 data.

Thus, in summary, there is a noticeably reduction in the handing down of occupational status from one generation to the other among French Canadians. In addition, a higher rate of transmitting of manual jobs for French Canadians than for English Canadians continues, and the tendency continues for the English Canadians to hand down non-manual occupations much more frequently than the French Canadians.

b. *Rate of entry into different occupations.* The preponderance of persons of British origin in the upper categories is also seen in rates of accessibility[21] into different occupational categories (i.e., the rates of entry into each category of sons born in another category).

English-speaking Canadians continue to reach the upper levels more easily than the French Canadians, a tendency which is, however, less pronounced than in 1954. Once again the difference between the two groups tends to diminish (cf. Table 14).

c. *Distance covered.* Is the same phenomenon observed concerning differences in speed of ascent? Rocher and de Jocas, as noted above, had stated that English Canadians experienced a definitely more accelerated mobility than French Canadians, and that the English Canadians frequently passed over two levels at a time in their ascent whereas the French Canadians ascended the ladder step by step. From 1954 to 1964 the French-Canadian group covered a large part of the ground which separated them from the group of Anglo-Saxon origin; the relative upward mobility of this latter group seems slowed down. The margin which separates the two language groups has lessened; the French Canadians now climbed two levels at a time almost as often as did English Canadians.

III Conclusion

To interpret the phenomena of mobility which have just been analyzed, it would be necessary to be able to link changes in the occupational structure with changes in economic, political, and social life. Here we cannot show indices of such changes to be directly related to occupations. We can, however, indicate a series of important broad changes (where existing statistics allow) that have taken place between 1954 and 1964 and which seem important in interpreting our findings.

1. Economic and Social Growth

Between the two dates, the population of Quebec increased from 4,388,000 to 5,562,000,[22] an increase of 26.75 per cent. During the period, the natural increase represents about 100,000 people annually and immigrants (mainly from France, Italy, Great Britain, Greece and the United States) an average of about 30,000 people annually.

Table 14

Rates of Entry in Each Occupational Category and Differences Between the Rates of Entry for French Canadians and English Canadians

	1954		Difference	1964		Difference
	F.C.	E.C.	(F.C. - E.C.)	F.C.	E.C.	(F.C.-E.C.)
Professionals and managers	0.99	1.62	−0.63	0.84	1.20	−0.36
Semi-professionals and lower administrators	0.89	1.31	−0.42	1.01	1.19	−0.18
White collar	0.82	0.49	0.33	0.93	8.85	0.08
Skilled and semi-skilled	0.81	0.39	0.42	0.80	0.39	0.41
Unskilled and Personal service	0.82	2.09	−1.27	0.89	0.42	0.47
Public service	0.00	0.00	0.00	0.17	0.00	0.00
Farmers						

During this period the urban concentration increased:

Year	Per cent Urban	Per cent Rural
1951	66.95	33.05
1961	74.27	25.73

In this concentration the Montreal area had a prime role both from a demographic and an industrial point of view. This area contributed 62 per cent of Quebec's personal income assets and 67 per cent of the value for the export of manufactured goods.

A series of indices allows us to show some noteworthy characteristics of the economic underpinnings of the mobility.

(Table A)
Indices of Economic and Social Growth in Quebec 1954 to 1964

Gross National Product (in millions of dollars)			Value of Mineral Production	
1954	6,313		1954	$278,932,718
1964	13,160		1964	$687,666,579
Gross Value of Products of Manufacturing Industries (in thousands of dollars)			**Paper Production (in thousands of tons)**	
1954	5,395,787		1954	3,653
1964	8,773,944		1964	4,473
Income of Labour (in millions of dollars)			**Households with at least one car**	
1955	3,377		1953	332,000 (56%)
1964	6,029		1957	904,000 (70%)
Income (r) and ordinary Expenses (d) in Quebec (in millions of dollars)			**Educational Expenses (in thousands of dollars)**	
1954-	r	d		
1955	335,076	298,422	1954	193,724 (3.1% of GNP)
1964-				
1965	1,227,667	1,188,876	1965	863,192 (6.6% of GNP)

Indexes for Standard of Living in 1964-65:

1) Average income for cases (in Montreal) before tax deductions: $6,342
2) Households with a T.V. set: 1,200,000
3) Households with a telephone: 974,000

In almost all these areas, the period considered between the two surveys is one of exceptional economic and social advancement. There is general growth favourable to an acceleration of mobility.

2. *Accessibility of Post-Secondary Education*

The increased speed of mobility among French-speaking Canadians in the decade

1954-1964 is confirmed by increases in students at both the secondary and university level. From 1956-1969 the number of students in secondary school increased from 130,000 to 262,000. As the Royal Commission report (1964) on education in the province of Quebec indicates, during this short period the proportion of adolescents from 13 to 16 years of age who attended secondary and technical schools increased from 44 to 65 per cent. Statistics from two Montreal universities, one English (McGill), the other French (Montreal), indicate the same trend. From 1950 to 1965, McGill increased its enrolment by 86 per cent and Montreal by 242 per cent. Moreover, at the University of Montreal, the increase in the humanities (traditionally more fully-enrolled) was accompanied this time by just as large an increase in fields more adapted to the growth of industrial society and in areas allowing accessibility to the control of societal development .

The accessibility of post-secondary education for youths from lower socio-economic levels provides another indicator of the degree of openness of the social structure. From 1955 to 1964, the proportion of graduates from a "worker" background went from 22 to 33.5 per cent at the University of Montreal, and from 13.6 to 8.9 per cent for English Protestant Canadians at McGill. It should also be noted that 55.6 and 31.7 per cent of the urban French-Canadian and English-Canadian work force, respectively, is manual. This is equivalent to the rates of accessibility of 0.62 per cent for sons of French-Canadian workers and of 0.31 or 0.39 per cent (depending on whether just English-Canadian Protestants or all students of McGill are considered) for sons of English-Canadian workers.

3. *Tensions of Growth*

a. Results. The results of this increase are apparent in our analysis of mobility. Let us summarize them as follows: as in every society at an advanced level of technology, we see the reduction of agricultural and manual labour, the stability of skilled and semi-skilled workers, and the increase of members in the upper categories.

But, further, there is (a) an increase in the number of individuals with upward mobility and a decrease in those who are downwardly mobile; (b) an acceleration in the crossing of occupational levels: whereas in 1954, only 14 per cent covered two or more levels, in 1964 the percentage goes to 24.4 per cent or one quarter of the labour force; and (c) a change in the means of access into the urbanized industrial society: in 1964 people entered twice as often as skilled workers, whereas in 1954 they entered twice as often as manual labourers. These findings lead in the same direction, that of a lessening of social inheritance, which is the same as saying, a lessening of inherited status and an increase in achieved status.

b. The tensions of values. This "period of recovery" marks the end of the passage from a closed society to an open society, from a society where status and roles are pre-determined, to a society where progressive differentiation in the spheres of religious, political, economic, and social activity isolates the different roles, thereby allowing individuals to attain them separately (at the least cost). Quebec, between 1954 to 1964, was also the battle ground for old and new values--those of the closed hierarchy of inherited status and those of the open hierarchy of achieved status. The advent of this latter mode of stratification called into question those values which are a guarantee of the old mode. Threatened, they seek to grow stronger. "Most of the regions in the development stage emerging from a colonial domination of one kind or another are given to equalitarian ideologies. Since most of these societies have social arrangements of a traditional hierarchical nature, a source of additional tension between the hierarchical and equalitarian principles is introduced by new development."[23]

Table 15 Distribution of Ethnic Groups in Quebec (1961)		
French	4,241,354	80.6%
British	567,057	10.8%
New-Quebec	450,800	9.6%
Source: DBS, Census of 1961		

c. Ethnic tensions . . . . M. Rioux and J. Dofny advanced the idea of "ethnic class" to describe those situations in which an ethnic group occupies a particular class.[24] They have emphasized that while the French-Canadian people form a social entity which has the characteristics of a national collectivity, they occupy, as a people and compared with other ethnic groups, a class position. An analysis made from the 1961 Census seems to confirm this view. At the time of this census, the distribution of the population was as in Table 15.

A classification of all the ethnic groups according to average work income has been carried out by three economists, A. Raynauld, Y. Marion and R. Beland.[25] This classification very clearly shows the economic positions occupied respectively by the English and French group, the former at the top of the scale and the latter at the bottom (cf. Table 16).

Table 16

Average Income of Employed Males in Quebec, According to Ethnic Origin

Ethnic Origin	Income in Dollars	Index
Total	3,469	100.0
British	4,940	142.4
Scandinavian	4,939	142.4
Dutch	4,891	140.9
Jewish	4,851	139.8
Russian	4,828	139.1
German	4,254	122.6
Polish	3,984	114.8
Asian	3,784	107.6
Ukrainian	3,733	107.6
Other Europeans	3,547	102.4
Hungarian	3,537	101.9
French	3,185	91.8
Italian	2,938	84.6
Indian	2,112	60.8

Source: D.B.S., Census of 1961

Here it is useful to recall the conclusions of the second part of this article on a comparison of the mobility of the two groups. The structural movements found for the French Canadians were also shown for English Canadians. With the latter group, it is not, however, the category of unskilled labourers that has a great decrease but that of public and personal service. The reduction of social inheritance is much less pronounced for English Canadians, who form, let us not forget, a much more limited group in each category. Finally, the crossing of mobility levels now shows about equal rates in the two groups, even if the English Canadians continue to move more often to the upper echelons.

Is there an inconsistency between these results and the distribution of income decribed by Raynauld, Marion and Beland? There is none if other distributions are taken into account. For the purpose of this article we have carried out an enumeration of certain professional categories based upon data from the same census . The data were classified in two ways: the first shows the importance of a category in each ethnic group and the second, conversely, the importance of ethnic groups in the occupational category (Table 17).

Table 17

Distribution of Professionals, Managerial, Technical, Skilled and Semi-Skilled Occupations Among French Canadians
and English Canadians in the 1961 Census

(Percentages)

	E.C.	F.C.
Managers Professionals and Technicians	28.4	16.3
Skilled and semi-skilled workers	19.9	32.4
Others	51.7	51.3
Totals	100.0	100.0

	Administrators Professionals Technicians	Skilled Semi-Skilled
E.C.	18.5	7.7
F.C.	68.5	80.9
Others	13.0	11.4
Totals	100.0	100.0

Our two types of statistics, one economic, the other occupational, show the two dimensions of stratification. When we consider ethnic groups, French Canadians are part of an under-privileged group that is largely a majority. It is thus that they constitute what is called an "ethnic class". If, on the contrary, we consider the destinies of French-speaking individuals, there is no doubt that they participate at all levels of stratification and that they are changing their place on the occupational ladder toward a position more and more similar to that of the English Canadians. On the other hand, if we consider the English Canadians as an ethnic group, they form a group definitely privileged on the income scale; their limited number and their privileged position unquestionably give them all the characteristics of a dominant bourgeois class of the colonial type. However, there are English Canadians on all levels of the stratification ladder; 19.9 per cent of them are skilled or semi-skilled workers, and if the 28.4 per cent who are in the upper levels are removed, we see that a majority of them belong to the middle classes.

In such a situation it is very difficult for one group or the other to clearly define its social identity. The existence of a French-Canadian elite makes the interpretation of the situation in terms of classes ambiguous for the entire group. In the same way, the existence of an important percentage of English Canadians in the working class allows this group to reject a class interpretation of itself. Nevertheless, the proportions are there: the overrepresentation of English Canadians in the higher categories with overrepresentation of the French Canadians in the lower categories leave no doubt as to positions of class occupied by the two groups respectively.

However, no simple conclusion can be drawn from this situation. The tensions are multiple between the two ethnic groups considered in this article (recall the methodological limits indicated at the beginning). It is clear that equal attention should be given to relative positions of New Canadians whose preferential choice between the two major language groups will be of decisive importance for the future. The tensions are also great among the French Canadians themselves. Some believe in a continual and accelerated integration into the great North American industrial society, while others believe this development will occur only if the rights of their people are recognized and definitely assured; still others feel that the future will witness a growing socialization of society. In studying the function of the two orders of reality, the ethnic and the social, we must not forget that, if competition between the Negroes and skilled American workers is situated at the bottom of the social scale, in the case studied here, it is rather in the upper middle class that competition and conflict exist. From this example we can establish the orderly and regulated character of this ethnic conflict, which up to this point in time, the majority seem determined to resolve within the parliamentary political process. Social tensions can develop between French-Canadian groups themselves and, with a snowball effect, these conflicts and tensions may pile up and become more intense.

4. *Structural Mobility or the Equalization of Opportunities*

Can the result of this competition in the more or less near future be extrapolated from the conclusions of this article? Whereas French-speaking Canadians kept their ties with rural society and its values for a longer time, the distribution of occupations of the sons in 1964 indicates that these ties have no more than a residual effect since 3.89 per cent of them still have a farmer's job whereas in the generation of their fathers these jobs represented more than one third of the tax-paying population. Because of that, most French Canadians find themselves inside the industrial society like the English Canadians, although they still occupy less favourable positions.

But are the features which marked the growth of this competition between the two ethnic groups during this decade, that is, the tendency for French Canadians to adopt a pattern of mobility closer to that of the English Canadians, of a temporary or permanent sort? This question is raised in order to distinguish the observed mobility that is attributable to factors of social equalization.

By employing a method used by Carlsson and subsequently by Jackson and Crockett.[26] these two aspects of mobility can be considered separately. This method involves the establishing of the maximal stability (maximum possible inheritance of occupations within categories) which a given occupational structure allows, and subtracting from that the "forced" mobility which it necessarily causes, given the limited number of positions available. Certain categories grow narrower and the sons must go elsewhere. Deducting the structural or forced mobility from observed mobility, we obtain figures for pure mobility and its relation to observed mobility. The comparison of English Canadians and French Canadians, following this method, gives the results

Table 18

Relationship Between Expected Observed Mobility Among Urban English and French Canadians in 1954 and 1964

	1954		1964	
	F.C.	E.C.	F.C.	E.C.
Maximum Stability	82.25	74.55	66.14	71.43
Forced Mobility	17.75	25.45	33.86	28.57
Observed Mobility	64.15	70.00	75.12	66.07
Expected Mobility	46.40	44.55	41.26	37.50
Expected Mobility / Observed Mobility	72.33	63.64	54.93	56.76

found in Table 18. This suggests that mobility due to structural changes is much more strongly accentuated for French Canadians than for English Canadians and that the part of pure mobility due to an opening up of strata has considerably lessened. On this latter level, the advantage in pure mobility held by the French Canadians in 1954 appeared to have been lost in 1964.

Will the advancement create for the French (as a group and as individuals) habits and a system of expectations such that a slowing down, a pause, and, still more, a regression of this structural movement would lead them to transform what was a forced mobility into a pure mobility? Modernization, investments, and the political economy will influence the first type of mobility, whereas the second will depend much more on social, linguistic, and educational policies and on the role played in this competition by other ethnic groups.

Notes

1. Throughout this article we use the expressions "English Canadians" and "French Canadians", although only the second term is commonly used. The abbreviations FC and EC are used in the statistical tables.

2. This research was made possible through a grant from the Cultural Affairs Ministry of Quebec.

3. Yves de Jocas and Guy Rocher, "Inter-Generation Occupational Mobility in the Province of Quebec", *The Canadian Journal of Economics and Political Science,* 23 (February, 1957), 58-66.

4. N. Rogoff, *Occupational Mobility* (Free Press, 1953).

5. Harold L. Wilensky, "Measures and Effects of Social Mobility", in N.J. Smelser and S.M. Lipset, eds., *Social Structure and Mobility in Economic Development* (Chicago: Aldine Publishing Co., 1966), 98-140.

6. The 1954 and 1964 samples are not representative of the total population. They only represent the population of those married during those five years. *Cf.* the discussion of this point in Rogoff, *op. cit.,* 34-40.

7. P.M. Blau and O.D. Duncan, *The American Occupational Structure* (New York: John Wiley & Sons Inc., 1964).

8. N. Rogoff Ramsoy, "Changes in Rates and Forms of Mobility", in N.J. Smelser and S.M. Lipset, eds., *Social Structure and Mobility in Economic Development.*

9. In a later publication we shall describe upward mobility and downward mobility according to the degree of development of the different areas of the province.

10. Another weakness arises from the dependence of the rates upon each other.

11. As in the 1954 study, the professional categories are those used by N. Rogoff. When these categories were not detailed enough, we employed the categories used by J.A. Porter and P.C. Pineo in their article, "Occupational Prestige in Canada", *Canadian Review of Sociology and Anthropology,* Vol. 4 No. 1 (February, 1969).

12. These changes might however be explained in part by a number of other factors such as the differential rates of birth and marriage by occupations.

13. O.D. Duncan, "Social Stratification and Mobility", in E.B. Sheldon and W.E. Moore, eds., *Indicators of Social Change* (New York: Russell Sage Foundation, 1968).

14. P.M. Blau and O.D. Duncan, *op. cit.*, 27.

15. The category of farmers (because it often groups farm workers with owners of farmland) and the category of service workers (since it includes groups of unequal prestige; e.g., administrative office workers and public service workers) are placed only with difficulty on the ladder.

16. A.H. Richmond used a similar method to measure mobility in "Social Mobility of Immigrants in Canada", in *Canadian Society,* 3rd ed. (Toronto: Macmillian of Canada, 1968), and in *Post-War Immigrants in Canada* (Toronto: University of Toronto Press, 1967).

17. The reservations that Rocher and de Jocas express in their conclusions, because of the small number of English Canadians in their sample, also apply to our following paragraphs.

18. G. Rocher and Y. de Jocas, *op. cit.*, 65.

19. This exclusion is justified in a population almost entirely urban. We could show, incidentally, a large distortion in the general stability rate of the English Canadians, if the stability rate of farmers is included, but the rate is calculated from a very small number of individuals.

20. One would not be surprised incidentally at the enormous fluctuations of the stability rates in the public service category and especially in farming occupations. An explanation for this may be found in the very small proportions of the sample in these two categories.

21. Here it is completely justified to use Rogoff's rates since it is a question of internal comparisons of the 1954 and 1964 rates.

22. The statistics which follow were taken from the Official Annual Yearbook of Quebec, 1968.

23. N.J. Smelser and S.M. Lipset, eds., *Social Structure and Mobility in Economic Development,* 13; *cf,* also L. Seligman, in *ibid.,* 341.

24. J. Dofny and M. Rioux, "Les classes sociales au Canada français", *Revue francaise de sociologie* (Paris, 1961), 290-300. These situations have not been described – and no doubt for good reason – by either European or American sociologists. The former had great difficulty in explaining the relationships existing in the metropolitan areas or in the colonies between European workers and the numerous labourers of these colonies or of underdeveloped European countries, by adhering to an explanation by class; the latter confined the analysis of these types of relationships to the theory of ethnic relations and never went so far as to explain them in terms of class. Recently an American sociologist, M. Gordon, in his book, *Assimilation in American Life* (New York: Oxford University Press, 1964) used the concept of ethclass in a similar but not identical manner. (Note by J. Dofny.)

25. *Cf.* a publication of this report to the Royal Commission of Enquiry on Bilingualism and Biculturalism (Weekly supplement of *La Presse,* Montreal, October 26, 1968).

26. Y. Carlsson, *Social Mobility and Class Structure* (Lund, Gleerup, 1958): E.F. Jackson and H.J. Crockett Jr., "Occupational Mobility in the United States", *American Sociological Review* (February, 1964).

21

French-Canadian Nationalism and Occupational Dilemmas*

Frederick Elkin

In the early 1960s, Canada experienced what has popularly been called the *Quiet Revolution.* Following the death of 1959 of the premier of the province of Quebec, where the French Canadians make up some 80 per cent of the population, and the election the following year of the Liberal party, there developed a strong neo-nationalistic social movement.[1] The socio-psychological roots lay in the increasing consciousness among French Canadians of their subordinate position compared with the English Canadians and of the lower status of their language and culture. The new Liberal government sought, through a series of striking legislative and administrative acts, to update the province economically and socially and to assert rights of equality with the English Canadians (see Royal Commission 1965, 1967, 1969; Sloan 1965; Desbarats 1965; Guindon 1968; Jones 1967),

One sub-development of the Quiet Revolution was the growth of a movement seeking a politically independent Quebec. In the early 1970s, considerable publicity was given to the FLQ, a militant group of French Canadians who advocated violence as a means of achieving independence. This group, however, was small compared with the much larger group of Separatists, politically organized as the Parti Québecois, which seeks independence by democratic means.[2] And the Separatists in turn are but part of the still larger neo-nationalist social movement, comprising members of all political parties, which seeks more advantages for French Canadians and power for Quebec.

The leaders of this new movement, it has been convincingly argued, do not come from the traditional French-Canadian business and professional elite, the working class, or the rural population; rather they originate from the *new middle class,* that group of relatively well-educated and successful French Canadians ordinarily employed as salaried administrative, professional or white-collar personnel (Brazeau 1963: Guindon 1964). Some members of the new middle class work for French-language institutions, such as French-Canadian business firms, associations, government or quasi-government groups; others are employed in English-Canadian institutions and industries. This paper concerns the latter group.

The neo-nationalist social movement in French Canada was preceded and accompanied by a modernizing socialization process. In years past, the French-Canadian economy had been largely rural; the commerce and industry small; and the professionals, the traditional priests, doctors and lawyers. When the more business oriented and technically advanced outsiders from English Canada, the United States, and Great

*Paper read at the annual meeting of the American Sociological Association, Denver, Colorado, August, 1971. Reprinted by permission of the author and *International Journal of Comparative Sociology,* 13 (March, 1972), where it appeared under the title "Ethnic Revolutions and Occupational Dilemmas".

Britain introduced industry and large-scale commerce, they brought in their own executives and managers, often employing bilingual foremen as intermediaries (Hughes 1943). In the course of this modernizing process, the English-speaking outsiders introduced many new technical and white-collar occupations—one of which was advertising—which were foreign to French-Canadian traditions and ways of thinking.

Over a period of time, the French Canadians, through working with English-speaking personnel, formal course work, and direct experience, acquired the knowledge and skills necessary to handle the more advanced administrative and technical positions. Many in fact learned the knowledge and skills so well that, when the Quiet Revolution came, they felt competent enough to assume major decision-making roles and compete when necessary with English-language personnel.

This dual process of socialization and a developing nationalism has been a familiar pattern in many parts of the world. In one way or another, it has been characteristic of such under-developed nations as India, Egypt, Algeria, and Tanzania, and, in many respects, of such multi-ethnic advanced countries as Belgium and the United States where, in recent years, the increasingly qualified Flemish and Blacks have risen up in protest.[3] In these situations, the outsiders ordinarily are technically more advanced and dominant and the native group economically disadvantaged and subordinate; the language of the outsiders is the language of upper echelon industry and commerce and has higher status; and the language and the popular culture of the outsiders, through the mass media and work world, penetrate and threaten the native culture. This dual process, it is apparent, applies in a general way to bicultural or pluralistic societies; it also applies to particular occupations. The analysis of the former permits certain broad generalizations about ethnic tensions in a society; the analysis of the latter is helpful in bringing out variations within a country and the subtleties of the process.[4]

In this report, in the form of a four-stage model, we analyze the operation of this dual process, in the context of the Quiet Revolution in French Canada, in the new middle class occupation of advertising. The model takes as its starting point the introduction of advertising by the English into Quebec and as its focal divisions, points of crucial decision. The model shows, at each stage, the major path adopted by the mainstream and the paths rejected. The particular path adopted in subsequent years, led to the opening of other limited alternatives. Those who had followed the rejected paths might thereafter forever be outside the mainstream[5] (see Figure 1).

Alternative 1: The Basic Procedure

In introducing advertising into a traditional and relatively stable French Canada that had a distinctive language, the English Canadians had a choice of three patterns: they could advertise in English using the ads already prepared for the English market; they could set up a French-Canadian organization parallel to the English to prepare advertisements in French; or they could translate their English ads into French. Since a high proportion of French Canadians did not know English—and at least the message had to be understood—the first alternative was not considered feasible. The second alternative, the parallel operation, was rejected because the French-Canadian market was not sufficiently large to justify the extra expense and because the French Canadians, in the eyes of the English, did not require this special consideration. This left the third alternative, translation, which was feasible and could be carried out relatively cheaply. It was adopted almost without thought. French and English bilingual personnel, generally French Canadians but including others, were hired to

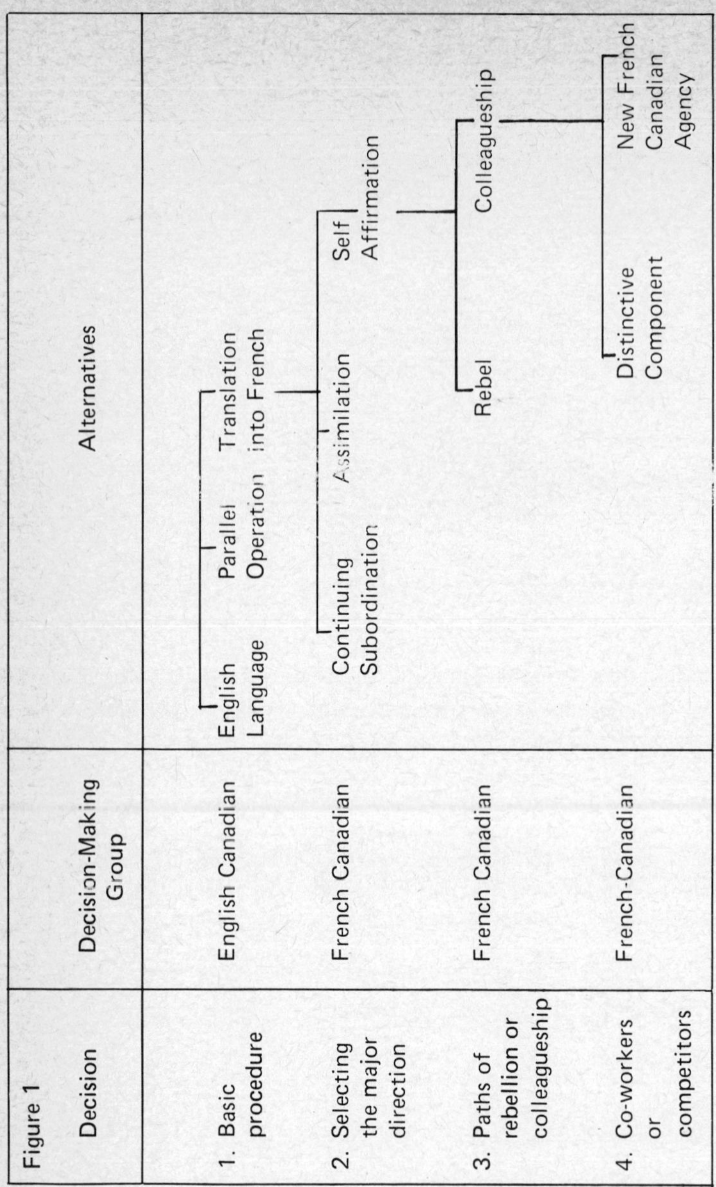

Figure 1

Decision	Decision-Making Group	Alternatives
1. Basic procedure	English Canadian	English Language; Parallel Operation; Translation into French
2. Selecting the major direction	French Canadian	Continuing Subordination; Assimilation; Self Affirmation
3. Paths of rebellion or colleagueship	French Canadian	Rebel; Colleagueship
4. Co-workers or competitors	French-Canadian	Distinctive Component; New French Canadian Agency

translate ads originally prepared in English. These ads, few would deny, were quickly and often poorly done (Elkin 1964).

Alternative 2: Selecting the Major Direction

In the years leading up to the Quiet Revolution, three alternatives were possible for the French Canadian. One was *continuing subordination.* In advertising, the English Canadians were the executives and managers and the French Canadians were translators, secretaries, and clerks. Young English Canadians were given the opportunity to learn the necessary range of skills and move into executive rungs; the French Canadians were not. Thus for the French Canadians, one alternative—if we might call it that—was to accept the ongoing situation.

The second alternative was *assimilation.* In earlier days, hundreds of thousands of French Canadians, for economic reasons, had moved to Western Canada and New England, and, like many immigrant groups, in time lost their original language and cultural distinctiveness (Lamontagne 1960: Theriault 1960). For a few French-Canadian advertising personnel who were perfectly bilingual, ambitious, and acceptable to the English Canadians, this was the path chosen. They were offered and accepted positions in Toronto or Montreal which brought them almost completely into the English-language world. But the great majority of French Canadians chose an altogether different path, *self-affirmation.*

Self-affirmation among advertising personnel, as among many groups in Quebec, began in the 1950s. At first informally and later in memoranda and public addresses the French Canadians in advertising affirmed their many grievances—the low sums spent on French-language advertising, the poor English-imposed translations, the discrimination against French-Canadian personnel, and the lack of understanding and appreciation of the French language and cultural differences. Some French Canadians fought and won the opportunity to do original campaigns in French directed to French Canadians (Elkin 1969 and 1971). In 1959, they formed their own professional association, The Publicité-Club, to assert their rights and fight for French-language advertising. Among their first goals were the publicizing of the French market and a greater recognition for the French-Canadian advertising man in the business world and the community at large (Lacroix 1967). Underlying and accompanying all such activities of the French Canadians was the confidence which came from a successful apprenticeship and an increasing knowledge and skill in the field.

The burgeoning of the Quiet Revolution in Quebec in 1960 gave the French Canadians in advertising a tremendous push forward. It reinforced their feelings as French Canadians, gave a political tinge to their demands, and encouraged them to act firmly and aggressively. It likewise offered them the opportunity to contribute to the new social movement, for within the advertising industry they now had a major voice in decisions on French-language advertising content. Those who had already taken the lead felt reassured and reinforced; those who were hesitant put aside their qualms; and some who were moving towards assimilation returned to their French-Canadian reference group.

Alternative 3: Paths of Rebellion or Colleagueship

French Canadians who chose self-affirmation soon faced another decision. They could become rebels and attack the English dominated advertising structure or strive as best they could within the system to achieve greater influence and power. In the political sphere, those who chose the rebel path were the Separatists, seeking an independent Quebec. In advertising, rebels could only work for small French-Canadian companies or advertising agencies and seek to build up French-Canadian industry.

In general, the French Canadians who chose self-affirmation did not challenge the basic system; they accepted the "fact of life" that the large advertisers and advertising agencies were English-Canadian or American and were likely to remain so for some time. But this led to a dilemma. To follow through on their careers, now a central purpose in their lives, they had to prove their worth in English companies. However, to affirm themselves and support the new social movement, with its anti-English overtones, they had to fight for a greater role in decisions on French-language advertising. They managed to resolve this dilemma by doing both. First they became more direct in their relations with the English—they were more likely to voice their complaints, express their resentment, and affirm their demands. But at the same time, they counter-balanced these more aggressive acts by constructive and solidarity-expressing activities which showed their commitment to advertising and their professional and career orientation. They set high standards for their French-language advertising; in intensive campaigns in French-language media, they affirmed the basic ideology of advertising; and their professional association prepared practical economic reports, organized French-language courses, and established annual awards for French-language advertising. The French Canadians were saying that they were part of the Quiet Revolution and would fight for their ethnic group, but at the same time they accepted the system and believed in advertising as it was practised. Their socialization into the occupation of advertising had not deeply affected their basic sentiments of ethnic group identity, but insofar as it included ideological as well as technical matters, it did make them into authentic advertising men. The French Canadians now asked only to be accepted as worthy and respected French-Canadian colleagues. In part, of course, the success of the revolution stems from the greater flexibility and tolerance of the dominant English-language group which no longer demanded totally conforming colleagues (Cf. Hughes 1952: Ch. 5).

Alternative 4: Co-Workers or Competitors

As the Quiet Revolution continued its forward surge, a further set of alternatives opened up. The French Canadians could work in English-controlled advertising agencies as more or less independent *distinctive components* or they could establish new autonomous agencies of their own.

The Distinctive Component. The primary task of the French Department before the Quiet Revolution was to routinely translate and adapt ads originally prepared in English. It had little decision-making influence and its prestige was low. With the increased consideration given to French-language advertising during the period of self-affirmation, the French Department in advertising agencies became a *distinctive component,* a more or less autonomous and respected unit responsible for French-language advertising. The French-Canadian director exerted almost a veto power over proposed French-language translations and adaptions, his suggestions were always seriously considered, and he was not often overruled.

The New French-Canadian Agency. All French Canadians in advertising recognized the forward step of the distinctive component, but some asserted that this was still not equality. Such equality, they said, required the establishment of French-Canadian controlled advertising agencies, parallel to those of the English. In such agencies, the French Canadians would themselves set policy, hire personnel, seek accounts, take the risks of profit and loss, and work in a French-Canadian milieu.

Beginning in 1963, several such new agencies, reflecting this new spirit of entrepreneurship, were established by experienced, respected, and competent French-Canadian advertising personnel. Besides seeking the French-language accounts of English companies, they hoped to contribute to the Quiet Revolution by giving special help to French-Canadian companies. Ideally, too, as they demonstrated their ability, they would gain English-language accounts and hire English-language personnel. French-Canadians then would have the same opportunities as English Canadians and parity would be achieved.

In theory, for the French Canadians, in both the distinctive components and the new agencies, one ideological problem remained. Since they sought to sell their clients' products, and the leading clients were English-Canadian and American, they were basically helping to reinforce the traditional English-dominated structure—which was hardly the goal of the Quiet Revolution. But this problem was far from the immediate questions of the day and, after all, their chosen path was not that of the rebel.

Conclusion

Our analysis of advertising in French Canada has brought us full circle. Instead of a system of translation or a permanent staff of subordinate French Canadians, instead of an immigrant-type assimilation with the gradual decline of the French language and culture, the trend has been towards what originally seemed to be the least likely alternative, a type of parallel system with relatively independent operations. An instrumental factor was the Quiet Revolution, the unforeseen social movement in which the French Canadians overthrew many of the values of the past; reaffirmed their language and identity; sought to update themselves economically and socially; and fought for greater parity with the dominant English Canadians. The French-Canadian advertising personnel, within their own occupational sphere, contributed to the movement and sought a better place for themselves. As individuals, they experienced a dilemma because their ethnic group sentiments, with its anti-English overtones, ran counter to their prospective career lines. Through a type of dialectic, however, which permitted them to affirm both ethnic group and professional sentiments, the French-Canadian advertising men were able to resolve this dilemma.

Where there are ethnic and occupational struggles, the processes of development are too varied to allow of a single model. The first two stages of our model which link the development of a nationalist social movement with socialization, have wide application. Our third and fourth stages are more limited. Our model assumes an industrializing country in which the subordinate new middle class occupational group members internalize the values of their occupation and come to see their careers as central foci of their lives. In our case, the French-Canadian advertising personnel expressed their grievances, joined the neo-nationalist movement, and were moved to action. But their interest was reform, not the overthrow of the system. Our model permits us to see the paths chosen by the mainstream and the paths rejected; the relationship between the general movement and one particular business and occupational group; the adaptations of dominant and subordinate group members to one another; and dilemmas experienced by particular individuals. The situation in less developed countries, in which the occupational range is narrow and the majority of native members are unskilled, would require a different model.

Notes

1. Writers on the Quiet Revolution have distinguished between *traditional nationalism* of the French Canadians which was characteristic of earlier days and *neo-nationalism* which assumes a modern industralized society with educated and technically skilled French-Canadian personnel (Fortin 1968; Guindon 1968).

2. In the provincial election of 1976, the Parti Québecois was elected to the Quebec National Assembly in a landslide victory. Editors.

3. When a nationalist social movement is successful and the native group has not had adequate socialization, it is likely, as in the Belgian Congo, to experience severe difficulties.

4. A developing nationalism and ethnic socialization, of course, are intertwined. Nationalism itself has its roots in a distinctive socialization and may not become a viable movement until the aspirations of an early socialization process are blocked, and the type of ethnic socialization in turn is likely to determine the limits of a nationalist movement.

5. The material on which this report is based comes from a combination of sources, including a questionnaire to French-Canadian advertising men, over 100 interviews with French- and English-language advertising personnel, and a content analysis of French-language radio and television broadcasts. A monograph with further details is forthcoming.

References

Brazeau, Jacques
1963 "Quebec's Emerging Middle Class", *Canadian Business* 36 (March): 33-40.

Desbarats, Peter
1965 *The State of Quebec.* Toronto: McClelland and Stewart.

Dofny, Jacques and Muriel Garon-Audy
1969 "Mobilités professionnelles au Quebec", *Sociologie et Sociétés* 1 (Novembre): 277-301.

Elkin, Frederick
1964 "Advertising in French Canada; Innovations and Deviations in the Context of a Changing Society", in G. Zollchan and W. Hirsch, eds., *Explorations in Social Change.* New York: Houghton Mifflin.

1969 "Advertising Themes and Quiet Revolutions: Dilemmas in French Canada", *American Journal of Sociology* 75 (July): 112-122.

1971 "Mass Media, Advertising, and the Quiet Revolution", in Richard J. Ossenberg, ed., *Canadian Society: Pluralism, Change, and Conflict.* Scarborough, Ont.: Prentice-Hall.

Fortin, Gérald
1967 "Le Québec: une société globale à la recherche d'elle-meme", *Recherches sociographiques,* 8 (janvier-avril): 7-13.

Guindon, Hubert
1964 "Social Class and Quebec's Bureaucratic Revolution", *Queen's Quarterly* 71 (Summer): 150-162.

1968 "Two Cultures: An Essay on Nationalism, Class and Ethnic Tension", R.H. Leach, ed., *Contemporary Canada.* Toronto: University of Toronto Press.

Hughes, Everett, C.
1943 *French Canada in Transition.* Chicago: University of Chicago Press.

1952 *Where Peoples Meet.* Glencoe, Illinois: Free Press.

Jones, Richard
1967 *Community in Crisis.* Toronto: McClelland and Stewart.

Lacroix, Lucien
1967 "Une nouvelle association professionelle: Le Publicité-Club". Unpublished master's thesis. Université de Montréal.

Lamontagne, Leopold
1960 "Ontario: The Two Races", in Mason Wade, ed., *Canadian Dualism.* Toronto: University of Toronto Press.

Royal Commission on Bilingualism and Biculturalism
1965 *Preliminary Report.* Ottawa: Queen's Printer.

1967 *General Introduction. I. The Official Languages.* Ottawa: Queen's Printer.

1969 *III. The Work World.* Ottawa: Queen's Printer.

Sloan, Thomas
1965 *The Not-so-Quiet Revolution.* Toronto: Ryerson Press.

Theriault, George F.
1960 "The Franco-Americans of New England", in Mason Wade, ed., *Canadian Dualism.* Toronto: University of Toronto Press.

22

Ecological Variations in Black Marginality*

Donald H. Clairmont and Dennis W. Magill

Nova Scotia's Black population is dispersed throughout the province, the single point of concentration being the Halifax-Dartmouth area where, within a radius of twenty miles, approximately fifty per cent of the provincial Black population reside. Our preliminary observations, supported by a few data available[1], indicate that patterns of socio-economic well-being (and life-styles generally) are not coterminous with the distinctions between the Halifax-Dartmouth area and the rest of the province. Some Black communities within the twenty-mile radius of Halifax are much more similar, socio-economically, to the settlements in rural Guysborough County than they are to the urban neighbourhoods. Also, Blacks in Sydney have a life-style more like that of Halifax-Dartmouth Blacks than have Blacks eslewhere in Halifax County. A useful typology to delineate patterns of poverty and life-style is the Dominion Bureau of Statistics categorization of urban, urban fringe, rural, and rural fringe. We follow broadly such an ecological categorization by presenting relevant data for rural non-farm Blacks (rural), a Black urban-fringe community, and Halifax City Blacks. We do not possess, nor are there available, adequate data for precise comparisons.

According to official census data, the Black population of Nova Scotia increased from 6,212 in 1871 to 11,900 in 1961, an increase of 91 per cent.[2] Table 1 was calculated to see whether the population increase had been accompanied by a change in residency patterns over a ninety year time span, from 1871 to 1961. The table shows the percentage of Black population in each of three geographical areas: Halifax-Dartmouth, Cape Breton County, and "Other" Nova Scotia. This classification is not the same as the ideal discussed above, but it represents alternative categorization which differentiates between the commercial-industrial complexes of Halifax-Dartmouth and Sydney, and the rest of Nova Scotia.[3] The Halifax-Dartmouth percentages were calculated because this area has represented historically the major Nova Scotian business, commercial, and industrial complex.[4] The other similar area is the mining-steel complex of Sydney, North Sydney, Sydney Mines, New Waterford, and Glace Bay, concentrated in less than a fifty mile radius.[5] The "Other" Nova Scotia is a residual category; it was used because census data for the ninety year span do not permit more precise classification. Included in this category are Blacks living in three distinct ecological groupings.

1) *Urban Fringe Communities.* These seven Black communities are within a twenty mile radius of the Halifax-Dartmouth urban complex: Beechville, 300; Cherrybrook, 700; Preston North, 1,800; Preston East, 1,200; Cobequid Road, 110; Lucasville Road, 200; and Hammonds Plains, 500. Approximately another

---

*Reprinted with permission of the authors and publisher from Donald H. Clairmont and Dennis W. Magill, 1970. *Nova Scotian Blacks: An Historical and Structural Overview*, Halifax: Institute of Public Affairs, Dalhousie University, 36-67.

130 Blacks live either in Middle Sackville or along the Old Guysborough Road.
2) *Concentrated Black Population of Over 50 in White Communities.*[6] Following the typical population concentration of Blacks throughout most of Nova Scotia, the 2,576 Black residents in these 11 communities live in close proximity to one another:

a) *Amherst* (Population in 1966: 10,558)
Approximately 300 Blacks are concentrated in the "Sand Hill" section of town.

b) *Antigonish* (Population in 1966: 4,856)
The 80 Black residents are settled on the fringe of the town.

c) *Bridgetown* (Population in 1966: 1,060)
The majority of the 140 Black residents are located outside the town, on the Inglewood Road. Others are located in the areas known as "the pasture" and "the tracks".

d) *Digby* (Population in 1966: 2,305)
The 265 Blacks live in a community known as Acadiaville, off the highway at the entrance to the town of Digby.

e) *Liverpool* (Population in 1966: 3,807)
This community has 71 Black residents.

f) *Middleton* (Population in 1966: 1,765)
The 90 Black residents are located within the community, on what is called the "bog".

g) *New Glasgow* (Population in 1966: 10, 489)
The 650 Blacks live in areas known as "the Hill", "the Mountain", and "Parkdale".

h) *Shelburne* (Population in 1966: 2,654)
The 166 Blacks are concentrated in the southern end of town, in the Bell's Cove area.

i) *Springhill* (Population in 1966: 5,380)
The 124 Blacks live principally on three streets.

j) *Truro* (Population in 1966: 13,007)
The 500 Black inhabitants are concentrated in what is known as "the Island" and "the Marsh".

k) *Yarmouth* (Population in 1966: 8,316)
The 190 Blacks are a "fringe" community concentrated mostly on back streets.

3) Rural Inhabitants. The 1961 census[7] reports that 5,316, or 45 per cent of Nova Scotia's Black residents, live in a rural environment. Of these rural Blacks, 8 per cent (382) are farm residents and 92 per cent (4,934) are rural non-farm residents. For the entire province of Nova Scotia, the rural non-farm inhabitants have the lowest total family incomes. For the province, in 1961 the percentage distribution of total incomes for rural non-farm families was: 52 per cent under $2,999; 31 per cent $3,000 to $4,999; and 17 per cent over $5,000.[8] Given these findings, it is possible to estimate that in 1961 the 42 per cent of the 11,900 Blacks (reported by the Dominion Bureau of Statistics) who were rural non-farm residents lived in 'poverty pockets' hardly above the subsistence level. This generalization is supported by a case study (reported below) of three Black rural non-farm communities in Guysborough County, where virtually 100 per cent of the families had total annual incomes under $3,000.

Census publications unfortunately do not supply the data enabling percentage calculations according to the above three groupings. Table 1 does indicate that the percentage in "Other" Nova Scotia has declined over the ninety-year span, and probably

Table 1

Percentage of Black Population in Halifax-Dartmouth, Cape Breton County, and "Other Nova Scotia" at Ten-Year Intervals, 1871-1961[a]

	1871	1881	1891	1901	1911	1921	1931	1941	1951	1961
Halifax-Dartmouth	17%	16%	*	15%	15%	17%	I**	13%	*	19%
Cape Breton County	0.8	0.3	*	0.3	5	5	11	10	*	8
"Other Nova Scotia"	82	83	*	84	80	78	80	77	*	73
Base	(6,212)	(7,062)	(*)	(5,984)	(6,541)	(6,175)	(7,524)	(8,817)	(*)	(11,900)

*Census data are not available for 1891 and 1951.
**Census data on the number of Blacks residing in Dartmouth are not available for 1931.
[a]Due to rounding the percentages by year may not total 100%.
Source: D.B.S., *Census of Canada*

underestimates the extent of this proportionate decline. Unfortunately, it is not possible to determine precisely whether, within the "Other" Nova Scotia category, the Black population has increased or decreased in relation to the three subgroupings. It appears that the Black population in the urban fringe area of Halifax County has increased over the past twenty-five years;[9] over the past decade, there has been an absolute population decline among Blacks living in rural areas and in the White communities enumerated above.

Table 1 indicates also that, from 1871 to 1961, not more than 20 per cent of Nova Scotia's Black population has lived in Halifax-Dartmouth. Our observations and other sources of data (i.e., interviews, and surveys) indicate that in 1969 the percentage in Halifax-Dartmouth would be greater, the increase being due to migration out of "Other" Nova Scotia[10] and to a more accurate estimate of the number of Blacks in the metropolitan area. In view of expected rural-urban migration, it is useful to note that while there has been, over the past century, a steady movement of Blacks from "Other" Nova Scotia to Halifax-Dartmouth, the percentage of Blacks in the latter area has not altered noticeably because of: (a) the steady stream of migration of Blacks from Halifax-Dartmouth to the United States and to Central and Western Canada, and (b) the migration of Blacks in "Other" Nova Scotia to the United States and to Central and Western Canada, as well as to Halifax-Dartmouth.[11] (Not all of the predictable migration from rural to urban areas has been to the Halifax-Dartmouth area.) Since the end of the Second World War, the Halifax-Dartmouth metropolitan area has grown considerably and the population projections indicate that the population may double again by 1985. It is reasonable to predict that, in the immediate future, a much larger percentage of the provincial Black population will be in Halifax County and especially in metropolitan Halifax. Table 1 also indicates that in Cape Breton County the population increase started in 1911 and that from 1921 to 1931 the number of Blacks jumped from 295 to 788. The Black population in this latter area has decreased since the Second World War and will continue to decrease (at least, percentage-wise) if the coal-steel complex should stagnate.

On the whole, Table 1 makes clear that now and in the past most Nova Scotian Blacks have lived outside the major centres of commerce and industry in Nova Scotia. Whitten has observed, "Canadian Maritime Negro communities are characteristically removed from both coastal fishing commercial centers and from inland centers. They are best regarded as grafted on both."[12] Whitten argues that, "with scarcely a store in their communities and with sparse (if any) agricultural or woodlot resources, the Negroes for the most part exist by foraging off the adjacent white communities. Charity trapping and welfare tapping become the dominant subsistence pursuits and networks of individuals exploit what they regard as their resources."[13] Actually Whitten exaggerates the so-called "charity trapping and welfare tapping"; most Black communities are economically marginal, but hard irregular labour, not charity or welfare, is the dominant subsistence pursuit.[14]

We have observed that it would be desirable to analyze, according to ecological pattern, socio-economic conditions and life-styles among the Blacks. Such an analysis presupposes data collected, at the same point in time, on Blacks in urban, urban fringe, and rural non-farm settings. (The number of Blacks classified as farm is small, as noted above.) These kinds of data are not yet available, but we do have data about Halifax mid-city Blacks, Blacks in an urban fringe community, and Blacks in the rural non-farm setting of Guysborough County. These data, although they were not obtained at the same point in time,[15] are fairly representative of the different ecological types and can, with cautious interpretation, yield pertinent comparisons.

Table 2 indicates the age distribution of Blacks in three different ecological settings. Most noticeable is the very large proportion of children and older persons in the rural non-farm area; only 37 per cent of the population is between the ages of 15 and 64. Among Halifax mid-city Blacks, the comparative figure is 52 per cent and, for Halifax as a whole,[16] the corresponding figure is about 66 per cent. These comparisons show the larger dependency ratio among Blacks in rural non-farm and urban-fringe areas. From the point of view of anti-poverty strategies, the implication is that different strategies may be appropriate to the different ecological areas. The age distribution pattern indicates that young adults are leaving the fringe areas and rural areas. Moreover, the larger dependency ratio in rural non-farm and urban fringe communities means that there is a greater strain on family and community resources. In this context it may be that jobs, education, and an end to racism would be insufficient to overcome poverty in the fringe and rural areas. These areas may be fundamentally over-populated and extensive governmental assistance is probably necessary both to facilitate migration and to provide basic community services for those who remain (or for whom migration cannot be an attractive alternative).

Table 3 indicates that households tend to be much larger among rural non-farm Blacks than among either Halifax mid-city or urban fringe Blacks. The latter two have about the same household-size distribution. Here is an instance where the time differential, with reference to data, probably is obscuring a difference; we surmise that large households among mid-city Blacks would be now fewer, proportionately, than in 1959-60. For Halifax as a whole, in 1961, over 70 per cent of the households had between 2 and 5 members; correspondingly, less than 20 per cent of the households had 6 or more residents.[17] The larger household size found among Blacks (in each ecological type over 40 per cent of the households have 6 or more residents) reflects both a higher birth rate and a pronounced tendency for Black households to include "other" relatives and boarders. Table 4 shows that these two tendencies are the more likely to be found among rural non-farm Blacks. They reflect a life-style adapted to both poverty and racism, in that people are packed together for economy reasons.

'Welfare cases'[18] also are incorporated into the household structure and 'unwanted and unplanned' pregnancies are common. Large family size is particularly characteristic of urban fringe and rural non-farm Black communities and adds further disadvantage to their poverty. We have to interpret cautiously the data on average family size among mid-city Blacks; our inference is that the average family size is smaller now than it was in 1959-60.

Table 4 presents additional data on family structure. While rural Black families tend to be larger and their households more complicated, they tend, along with urban fringe families, to be more stable and to have fewer females as heads of household.[19] Almost 30 per cent of the interviewed mid-city families had female heads. For Halifax as a whole, in 1961, some 10 per cent of the families had female heads (in half of these families the female head was widowed).[20]

The structure and size of Black families indicate the need for specific anti-poverty measures. It has been observed repeatedly that large families tend to be less common among people who enjoy higher socio-economic status and when there are adequate opportunities for socio-economic betterment. To argue for birth control programs carries sometimes the implication that people are themselves responsible for their poverty, and that their poverty is due to a personal failing such as ignorance or imprudence. In view of the historical oppression of the Black people in Nova Scotia and the racist character of traditional Nova Scotian society, such an argument is at best naive. It would be naive to suppose that, by itself, effective family planning can obliterate poverty; however, family planning can be an aid and its absence can vitiate the effectiveness of other, more fundamental measures for eradicating poverty.

Table 2

Age Distribution of Mid-City Blacks (1959), The Urban Fringe Community, and Three Rural Non-Farm Communities

Age	Halifax Mid-City	Urban Fringe	Rural Non-Farm
0 - 14	45%	52%	58%
15 - 34	28	22	20
35 - 64	24	22	17
65+	3	4	5
Total	100% (1,227)	100% (328)	100% (618)

Sources: Halifax Mid-City data collected for *The Condition of the Negroes of Halifax City, Nova Scotia* (Halifax, Nova Scotia: Institute of Public Affairs, Dalhousie University, 1962); Urban Fringe data collected for a survey completed by the Nova Scotia Department of Public Welfare, 1967; Rural Non-Farm data from D. Clairmont *et al, A Socio-Economic Study and Recommendations: Sunnyville, Lincoln-Ville, and Upper* Big *Tracadie, Guysborough County, Nova Scotia* (Halifax: Institute of Public Affairs, Dalhousie University, 1965).

Table 3

Household Size among Halifax Mid-City Blacks, The Urban Fringe Community, and Three Rural Non-Farm Communities

Size	Halifax Mid-City	Urban Fringe	Rural Non-Farm
1 person	9%	8%	11%
2 or 3	27	26	17
4 or 5	23	23	12
6 to 9	34	34	38
10 or more	7	9	22
Total	100%(226)	100%(62)	100%(90)

Sources: As listed in Table 2.

Table 4

Family Data for Halifax Mid-City Blacks, The Urban Fringe Community, and Three Rural Non-Farm Communities

	Halifax Mid-City	Urban Fringe	Rural Non-Farm
Total Population Counted	1,227	328	618
Number of Families	248	61	90
Average (mean) Family Size	4.9	5.1	6.6
Number of Families with Female Head	69	7	11
Percentages of Families with Female Head	28%	11%	12%
Percentage in Population with Relation to Family Head of:			
Child	52%	61%	54%
Other Relative	6%	5%	13%
Boarder	6%	5%	12%

Sources: As listed in Table 2.

Table 5

Approximate Distribution of Annual Income Among Male and Female Halifax Mid-City Blacks, The Urban Fringe Community, and Three Rural Non-Farm Communities

Income	Halifax Mid-City			Urban Fringe			Rural Non-Farm		
	Male	Female	Total	Male	Female	Total	Male	Female	Total
Under $1,000	19%	58%	32%	6%	33%	9%	76%	86%	79%
$1000 – $1,999	29	33	31	3	0	3	17	7	15
$2,000 – $2,999	37	8	27	40	67	43	4	0	4
$3,000 – $3,999	13	1	9	37	0	33	2	7	1
$4,000+	2	0	1	14	0	12	1	0	1
	100%	100%	100%	100%	100%	100%	100%	100%	100%
Total Responding	(226)	(118)		(30)	(3)		(92)	(14)	
No Response	(60)	(213)		(18)	(12)		(0)	(0)	

Sources: As listed in Table 2.

The fundamental need is for societal change; that is, change in the distribution of resources, in the structuring of opportunities and in the type of attitudes and behaviour which is tolerated if not legally sanctioned. Given these changes, we can expect reduction in family size and in overcrowding due to the presence of other relatives and boarders. When discrimination lessens and financial resources improve, housing will be available more readily and family planning much easier.[21] Effective anti-poverty approaches will differ according to ecological type. Generally, some form of income maintenance will enable people to live, at least at their present level, without curtailing their family needs or room space by accepting outsiders. In the city, where families tend to be less stable and where there are more female-head households, there will be need for day-care centres and special tax privileges for the single-parent family.

Table 5 presents data on male and female annual income among Blacks in the three ecological settings. The table indicates that only some two per cent of the Blacks in the labour force, in the rural non-farm communities, earn more than $3,000 annually. The extraordinary economic marginality of this population is indicated by the fact that almost 80 per cent earned less than $1,000 in 1964. Over the past four years there have been some economic improvements in the area, but the situation has not changed radically and it is apparent that radical change is necessary.

The urban fringe data, collected in 1967, indicate that some 55 per cent of the respondents earned less than $3,000 annually. Since we did not conduct the survey of this urban fringe community, we do not know how to interpret the large percentage of "no response". We do know, however, that several of the females not responding worked intermittently as domestics and that some of the men not responding were unemployed; consequently, it does not appear that the distribution of reported income exaggerates the extent of poverty in the community.

The Halifax mid-city data on income are inadequate on two counts: they are a decade old, and there is a large percentage of non-response. Current data probably would show that mid-city Blacks are better off than Blacks in urban fringe communities but that about 30 to 40 per cent earn less than $3,000 annually, and that mid-city Blacks are much poorer than the average Haligonian.[22]

Occupationally, Blacks in all three ecological areas are concentrated heavily in the low-skill and poor-pay categories. In the rural non-farm area most men are employed in loading boats or in marginal woods-work, and most employed women are domestics. In the urban fringe community, the same pattern exists, although on a slightly smaller scale, with more men working in higher-status occupations while the bulk of the male labour force is engaged in unskilled work. In the Halifax mid-city Black population, there was, in 1959-60, a wider range of occupational specialization. Nevertheless, the majority of men worked in semiskilled and unskilled employment, and the majority of women worked as domestics or in comparable low-status jobs.[23] The situation has not changed radically for the mid-city Blacks over the past decade, although there has been a tendency for a large number of Blacks to obtain clerical and professional work.

We have indicated earlier that Blacks are ambivalent about the changes in their occupational opportunities. Better education and governmental expansion have created new opportunities, but to some extent these are offset by the sluggish Nova Scotian economy, the decline of some traditional employment opportunities, and the presence of discrimination in some of the service and skilled labour occupations.[24]

Anti-poverty measures to enhance occupational opportunities for Blacks are required in all ecological categories; for instance, payment of a living wage to people engaged in training that they want and need, and the provision of financial and educational resources conducive to establishing a context favourable to the achievement

Table 6

Occupational Classification of Male and Female Halifax Mid-City Blacks, The Urban Fringe Community, and Three Rural Non-Farm Communities

	Halifax Mid-City			Urban Fringe*			Rural Non-Farm		
	Male	Female	Total	Male	Female	Total	Male	Female	Total
Professional	1%	6%	3%	0%	0%	0%	0%	0%	0%
Clerical	4	10	6	8	13	10	1	6	2
Service	1	52	18	3	87	27	0	94	27
Skilled	10	1	7	10	0	7	0	0	0
Semi-skilled	38	4	26	12	0	8	5	0	3
Unskilled	45	26	39	66	0	47	93	0	67
Armed Forces	1	1	1	1	0	1	1	0	1
	100%	100 %	100%	100%	100%	100%	100%	100%	100%
Total Responding	(225)	(130)		(56)	(14)		(81)	(32)	
Non Response	(31)	(201)		(1)	(3)		(0)	(0)	

* In the urban fringe community, the 16 unemployed are classified as unskilled; there are 4 housewifes not employed; and there are 12 pensioners.

Sources: As listed in Table 2.

Table 7

Last School Grade Achieved by Male and Female Halifax Mid-City Blacks, The Urban Fringe Community, and Three Rural Non-Farm Communities

	Halifax Mid-City			Urban Fringe			Rural Non-Farm		
	Male	Female	Total	Male	Female	Total	Male	Female	Total
1 - 3	10	5 %	7%	15%	12%	14%	30%	15%	23%
4 - 6	28	26	27	32	27	29	56	44	52
7 - 9	44	50	48	38	51	45	13	34	22
0 - 12	16	18	17	15	10	12	1	7	3
Over Grade 12	2	1	1	0	0	0	0	0	0
	100%	100%	100%	100%	100%	100%	100%	100%	100%
Total Responding	(234)	(294)		(58)	(63)		(117)	(92)	

Sources: As listed in Table 2.

of occupational aspirations. An anti-poverty approach in the metropolitan areas should include specifically, however, strong efforts to eliminate what appear to be "closed occupations" in some unions as well as in certain service occupations.[25]

Table 7 indicates the educational level, in the different ecological settings, of Blacks who are out of school. Educational achievement declines as one goes from mid-city to urban fringe to rural non-farm populations. Moreover, the difference between mid-city and other sets of data is undoubtedly underestimated, for the former data were collected at an earlier point in time. Most noticeable from these data is that there are few Blacks who have received any senior high school training. Other sources have indicated that this lack of high school training is characteristic of Black communities throughout the province.[26] Educational achievement tends to be lower in Nova Scotia than in many other provinces; for example, a recent study prepared for the Atlantic Development Board indicated that only 24 per cent of the boys and 27 per cent of the girls reach Grade XII while, for British Columbia, the corresponding figures are 64 per cent and 62 per cent.[27] Even within the admittedly poor educational context of Nova Scotia, the Blacks have had poorer opportunities. We have shown this to be the case historically and, even now, school consolidation has not been carried far enough to provide Blacks with equal educational resources.

It is apparent that, with regard to education, certain anti-poverty strategies which are applicable to the province as a whole (i.e., more money for education, and further school consolidation) would benefit, also, the Blacks. We would submit further, however, that the Blacks and the poor should receive not merely equal, but special, educational resources, for the obstacles to effective education imposed by their poverty and oppression are the greater. Thus, specially trained teachers, special tutors, and more community involvement are imperative. An in-depth study of educational values and problems in the Guysborough communities indicated that the Blacks placed a very high value on education, but that most youngsters withdrew from school because they did not believe that many post-school opportunities would be available to them, because it was difficult to study in overcrowded homes among elders who did not relate to their educational experiences, and because the reward system of the schools left them discouraged and disadvantaged. The structure of society and the school system, and the configuration established by historical deprivation, make it natural for many Black children to drop out of school. An unfortunate by-product of this tendency is that, primarily, such inadequate schooling "teaches the schooled the superiority of the better schooled."[28] Education under such circumstances becomes analogous to religion (i.e., part of the official morality) and the dropout feels like a sinner. Having been taught "that those who stay longer (in school) have earned the right to more power, wealth and prestige,"[29] the dropout feels personally inadequate and guilty. Both he and others fail to perceive, and consequently to act upon, the implications of structural and historical factors; thus, personal inadequacy and a second-class-citizen mentality develop. The anguish that often accompanies a "decision" to drop out is something that merits investigation.[30] The seriousness of the situation, even in the city of Halifax, is apparent in the following remarks by Oliver:

> There are 412 Negro students in Junior and Senior high school throughout the Metro area. Over 71 per cent of these students are in grades 7-9, with the mean age being 18. I would speculate that many of these students are potential drop-outs.[31]

Guysborough Blacks: A Case of Extreme Marginality

It has been noted that, for the entire province, the rural non-farm inhabitants have the lowest family incomes. It was observed, also, that almost all rural Blacks are non-farm.

A good example of poverty, and of the problems associated with overcoming poverty, is indicated in the case of the three Guysborough communities of Lincolnville, Sunnyville, and Upper Big Tracadie. It is not known how representative these three communities are of the total rural non-farm Black population. Although we believe that extrapolation is justified for description of income, education, and employment patterns, we are uncertain of extrapolation with regard to anti-poverty strategies.

Reference has been made to the condition of the Guysborough Blacks. It has been pointed out that, in contrast with city and urban-fringe Blacks, who are themselves a poor group, the Guysborough Blacks have a larger dependency ratio, larger household size, bigger families, more complicated household structure, considerably smaller incomes, more unskilled workers, and poorer educational achievement. Guysborough County is, itself, the poorest county in Nova Scotia, and with a per capita income of approximately $600 in 1961. (Inverness County, a better-known poverty pocket in Nova Scotia, by comparison, had a per capita income of $690 in 1961.) The Guysborough Blacks, with a per capita income of $325,[32] can be considered among the poorest of the poor.

The Guysborough Blacks are the descendants of Loyalists, and their roots in the county go back almost two hundred years. Theirs has always been a difficult battle for survival, a battle in which they received very little assistance from either the government or their White neighbours.[33] In 1871, most Guysborough Blacks were attempting to eke out an existence on rocky marginal farms. A large number of women worked as domestics in various White households. A small but significant number of Black males were fishermen or seamen, working out of Guysborough town which, in 1871, was a shipping centre and fishing port.

At the present time, almost one hundred years later, the Black population of Guysborough County is approximately the same in occupational distribution and in size as it was in 1871. A large number of women are still working as domestics in White households, in some instances as far away as Antigonish (30 to 50 miles). Most of the men work as labourers, finding employment at Mulgrave, which is some thirty miles distant, loading boats in the spring and summer, and supplementing their incomes by selling pulp and Christmas trees from their own small woodlots. (Many of these woodlot occupants do not have clear title.) Only slightly greater than one-fifth of the labour force worked more than 40 weeks per year. None of the Guysborough Blacks can be considered a farmer, using Dominion Bureau of Statistics criteria, although some do so identify themselves.[34] Of the total labour force population of 149 in the three Black communities, 115 earned less than $1,000 in 1964.

The Guysborough Blacks are clearly an oppressed people and have been for two hundred years. They are not unaware of their plight. Many have migrated, in search of a better life, to Halifax and to "Upper Canada"; some have narrowed their aspirations and have taken as their reference group the other poor in their communities. Neither of these "solutions" has been adequate (it is, of course, a mark against society that basic goals have been lowered), nor has there been effective collective action towards radical change. People have worked together to support schools and churches, but poverty and other concomitants of a lack of power have limited cooperative efforts. It has been argued that an individual is poor as long as he feels poor, rejected, or alienated from the economic or the cultural mainstream.[35] Certainly the Guysborough Blacks are poor by this definition. Comparative analysis found that the Guysborough Blacks live their lives with feelings of distrust, pessimism, anxiety, and resentment, all characteristics of alienation.[36]

The tendency to look upon poverty as a problem of individual persons has hindered the search for effective anti-poverty strategies. To understand the causes of poverty and to locate sources of change, one must look beyond education and job training to basic structural and cultural factors. These latter would include the historical reality of a racist society which lingers on and structural economic factors that maintain and perpetuate poverty. In discussing structural economic factors, it is important to see the plight of the Guysborough Blacks in the wider context of rural non-farm workers in the Maritimes. It has been noted that one-half the rural wage-earners have annual incomes of less than $2,000.[37] It has been reported elsewhere that, "one of the most striking features of the regional economy is the disproportionately large number of people working in marginal or submarginal activities in the Atlantic Provinces."[38] These rural wage-earners are locked into the countryside by land and home ownership and form a residual group caught in the process of economic change in the primary industries. They earn enough to maintain themselves, but they have no future and little prospect of improving their socio-economic well-being. Moreover, the services and facilities available to them are clearly inferior and inadequate.

We believe that a strong case can be made for the position that rural non-farm workers constitute an exploited class. The term "exploited" is used here with three specific considerations in mind: (a) the poverty of the rural non-farm people is usually highlighted at conferences where federal-provincial equalization grants are requested, but it is questionable how much benefit the rural non-farm people have obtained as a result of large equalization grants; (b) the government has sought hard to attract new industry to the province, but it is questionable how hard they have bargained with such industries on behalf of the workers or how much they have encouraged the development of strong bargaining units; (c) a regional development policy of labour-intensive industries in the manufacturing (secondary) sector depends, if it is to be successful, on a mix of factors, including low wage levels and lack of strong bargaining units.

Notes

1. See, for example, G. Brand, *Survey of Negro Population of Halifax County: A Report to the Interdepartmental Committee on Human Rights*, (Halifax, Nova Scotia: Social Development Division, Nova Scotia Department of Public Welfare, 1964).

2. Census data must be interpreted cautiously. For one thing, the figures in Nova Scotia have always under-represented the Black population. Most knowledgeable authorities put the 1961 census figures as being about 2,000 under the correct count. Moreover, there are often non-random errors in census data on the Blacks, errors which render comparative analysis difficult. For example, the 1921 census makes no reference to Blacks in Guysborough Town, but all other census counts, before and after that date, indicate the presence there of at least 200 Blacks. Moreover, the precise wording of the census' ethnicity has varied over the years. Census Division officials acknowledge (in private correspondence) that 1951 data on Blacks were particularly subject to under-representation because of the wording of instructions to enumerators. See also Daniel G. Hill Junior, "Negroes in Toronto: A Sociological Study of a Minority Group," unpublished Ph.D. thesis, Department of Sociology, University of Toronto, 1960, 48-52. Hill discusses additional problems with census data, including the classification of West Indians (recorded as English in the 1951 census) and the children of mixed marriages.

3. For the value of this distinction see Pierre-Yves Pepin, *Life and Poverty in the Maritimes* (Ottawa: ARDA Project No. 15002, March 1968), 6.

4. In Halifax and Dartmouth the vast majority of Black residents are concentrated in a small number of city blocks. In Halifax, the concentration is on Maynard and Creighton Streets; in Dartmouth, at the extreme end of Crichton Avenue, between the city incinerator and the causeway. See W.P. Oliver, *A Brief Summary of Nova Scotia Negro Communities* (Halifax, Nova Scotia: Adult Education Division, Nova Scotia Department of Education, March, 1964).

5. Census data by ethnic group from 1871 to 1961 are not available for these five communities; thus, the percentages in Table 11 are for Cape Breton County. As few Blacks in Cape Breton County live beyond a fifty mile radius of these communities, the percentages for the County are a close approximation of the Black population in the steel-coal complex.

6. Most of the following population figures were obtained from W.P. Oliver, *op. cit.* These figures are in essential agreement with those given by G. Brand, *op. cit.*, the only exception being those for Amherst, where Oliver's count seems excessively high. In this instance, we took Brand's count as being the more accurate.

7. Dominion Bureau of Statistics, *Census of Canada, 1961*; Vol. I, Part 2 (Ottawa: The Queen's Printer, 1962) Table 36. Some of the Blacks identified as rural by the 1961 census have been included in our categories of 'urban fringe' and 'concentrated populations of more than 50 in White communities'. The number of Blacks living in Nova Scotia, but neither in urban fringe areas, metropolitan areas, nor in the communities listed above, approximates 3,000 (1969).

8. K. Scott Wood, *Profile of Poverty in Nova Scotia* (Halifax, Nova Scotia: Institute of Public Affairs, Dalhousie University, 1965).

9. Compare the population figures in Brookbank, *op. cit.*, and the figures reported in surveys by W.P. Oliver, *op. cit.*, and Brand, *op. cit.*

10. See for example Brand, *op. cit.*, 12, and Clairmont, *op. cit.*, Chapter 5.

11. In the last quarter of the nineteenth century, there was a particularly heavy migration of Blacks to the United States. Elderly people, interviewed during our study of Africville, recalled the "eight-dollar" boat trip to Boston. From the First World War on, a steady stream of Black Nova Scotians went to Upper Canada. See Clairmont and Magill, *op. cit.*

12. Norman Whitten, Jr., "Adaptation and Adaptability as Processes of Microevolutionary Change in the New World Negro Communities", a paper presented at the Annual Meeting, 1967, American Anthropological Association, 8.

13. *Ibid.*

14. Whitten does not appear to be aware of studies such as Brand, *op. cit.* which show that, proportionately, Black welfare recipients are not excessive in number throughout the province. Whitten does not present data to support his view that Blacks are dependent upon "charity trapping and welfare tapping". There are communities, especially near Halifax, where a large percentage of the population draw welfare; in this regard, these are not typical Black communities. In most poor commu-

nities, family allowance, pension, and unemployment insurance benefits are a significant part of family income; however, these are the right of all Canadians, and, in a Canadian context it is misleading to refer to these sources as charity or "welfare".

15. The Halifax mid-city data were collected in 1959-60, under the auspices of the Institute of Public Affairs, Dalhousie University. Data on the urban fringe community and the rural non-farm area were gathered, respectively, in 1967 and 1964-65. Observations in the field indicate that the patterns discovered in the latter two sets of data accurately depict present conditions. The Halifax mid-city data are ten years old, which gives a conservative bias to our comparative analysis; differences between mid-city and other ecological types are not so pronounced in our data as they are in fact.

16. For Halifax figures (1961), see *Population*, Report No. I, City of Halifax, 1965; also, *The Condition of the Negroes of Halifax City, Nova Scotia* (Halifax: Institute of Public Affairs, Dalhousie University, 1962), 5. For the present purpose, the tables of Halifax mid-city Blacks were calculated from the raw data collected in 1959-60.

17. The distribution of household size for Nova Scotia as a whole (1961) was very similar to that for Halifax City; see *Population, op. cit.* The data for Halifax mid-city Blacks are probably representative (apart from the problem of outdated data) of Halifax Blacks as a whole. More middle-class and well-to-do Blacks live outside the mid-city area, but they were counterbalanced by the Africville Blacks, who were poorer than the mid-city Blacks.

18. We allude here to the fact that unadopted Black children, and Black adults needing custodial care, are taken into the household usually for the small payment that the family receives from the welfare department. We are uncertain about the extent of this pattern across the province, but having 'welfare children' is common in Guysborough County area, and caring for unrelated people is not uncommon in the Halifax area.

19. For a discussion of stable family structure in the urban fringe area, see Brookbank, *op. cit.*

20. *Population, op. cit.* Blacks in Halifax appear to have a family structure similar to that found in Black ghettoes in the United States. See Lee Rainwater, "Crucible of Identity", *Daedalus*, Vol. 95, No. 1, Winter 1966.

21. For comparative purposes, it can be noted that in 1961 the average family size in Halifax was 3.6; for Canada it was 3.9. Our argument regarding family planning is that, as the family financial position improves and as opportunities become available, there is more coordinated husband and wife decision-making. It could be argued that among many poor families, husband and wife relations are such that birth control decisions are left to the wife; and given the wife's realization of the hardships entailed by additional pregnancies, there could be a significant reduction in family size merely through the effective communication of family-planning information to the wives.

22. For purposes of comparison it can be noted that, for heads of families in Halifax in 1961, the income distribution indicated that approximately 25 per cent earned less than$3,000. We would expect that the percentage earning $3,000 now would be less than half the 1961 figure. However, one must be cautious in comparing these

figures to the income sets discussed in the text, for household heads are a different population than members of the working force; undoubtedly, the former have higher annual incomes.

23. It is an indicator of historical oppression that about the same percentage of mid-city Blacks in 1960 were in unskilled and semiskilled employment as were classified as labourers and unskilled workers in the 1838 census of Halifax Town Blacks. The occupational distribution of Black males in 1838 showed approximately 80 per cent as labourers and unskilled workers. See Public Archives of Nova Scotia, Vol. 448, Census for the County of Halifax, 1838.

24. See the brief presented by the Black United Front to the Special Senate Committee on Poverty, November 1969, Halifax, Nova Scotia; also, Clairmont and Magill, *op. cit.*

25. There has been apparently, in Nova Scotia, a relationship between Blacks and trade unions analogous to that in the United States. No real effective political co-operation (political in the widest sense) has been forged between Blacks and trade union members.

26. See, for example, the summary analyses of Brand, *op. cit.* and W.P. Oliver, *op. cit.*.

27. Quoted in *The 4th Estate*, Halifax, Nova Scotia, September 18, 1969. In 1961, approximately thirteen per cent of the household heads in the city of Halifax had some university education.

28. Ivan Illich, "Outwitting the Developed Countries", *New York Review of Books*, November 6, 1969.

29. *Ibid.* This treatment of education and the dropout was developed at length by Clairmont (*op. cit.*, Chapter 5) with reference to education among the Guysborough Blacks. Illich develops the theme on a larger basis, dealing with the question of under-development and social consciousness.

30. See, for example, Clairmont, *op. cit.*

31. Jules Oliver, *op. cit.*, 1967-68. It should be noted also that about 50 per cent of the Black students in Halifax high schools in 1969-70 were enrolled in a general course and that the remainder were divided between business education and the academic course. The Director of Instruction, Halifax School Board, explained: "The general course is a three-year course designed for those students who lack the ability, interest or aspiration to complete academic courses with profit and satisfaction, but who desire a general high school level of education for direct entrance into occupations." "Survey What Courses Black Students Taking," *The Mail-Star*, Halifax, Nova Scotia, March 23, 1970, 3.

32. The per capita income of $325 was based on data gathered in 1965; therefore, the poverty of the Blacks is, comparatively, even greater.

33. See Clairmont *et al.*, *op. cit.*

34. A "viable" farmer is one who has a gross income (from his farm) of $5,000 or more.

35. J.S. Reiner and T.A. Reiner, "Urban Poverty", *Journal of the American Institute of Planners* (Washington, D.C.: August, 1965).

36. Clairmont *et al., op. cit.* The comparative analysis was between the residents in three Guysborough Black communities and Whites residing in a sample of non-metropolitan communities in Halifax County.

37. R.A. Jenness, *The Dimensions of Poverty in Canada: Some Preliminary Observations* (Vancouver: University of British Columbia, February 1965), 52-53. Generally "viable" non-farmers are those whose income level is $3,000 or more.

38. R.D. Howland, "Some Regional Aspects of Economic Development in Canada," in *Royal Commission on Canada's Economic Prospects* (Ottawa: Queen's Printer, 1957).

Part III Section B

POLITICS AND CONFLICT

23

Sources of Party Support and the Social Compositio[n] of Canadian Political Parties*

Frederick C. Engelmann and Mildred A. Schwartz

The Meaning of Support

Support can be approached in two distinct ways. On the one hand, we can consider the way in which a given social aggregate distributes its support among the available parties, for example, concentrating on a single party, or at the other extreme, sharing its support equally among all parties. In this case party is treated as the dependent variable, and the emphasis is on the *mobilization* of groups along partisan lines. On the other hand, we can focus on the social makeup of parties, treating parties as independent variables. We will speak of this as the degree to which parties are *polarized* in terms of one or more social characteristics. Our operational measure of mobilization is flexible, and is determined by comparisons among groups. A more precise measure is used for polarization, indicated by a characteristic shared by two-thirds of a party's supporters.

In some respects, an examination of group mobilization will tell us more about social cleavages in the society than about how parties operate.[1] Polarization, in contrast, tells us directly about an attribute of parties. It is the combination of these approaches that gives us the means for better understanding the problems and the processes involved in converting inputs to outputs. Moreover, the consequences of the mobilization of social groups into partisan channels, and the polarization of parties into more or less cohesive forces, can be quite different, as we will see.

---

*Abridged from F.C. Engelmann and M.A. Schwartz, *Canadian Political Parties: Origin[,] Character, Impact*, Scarborough, Prentice-Hall, 1975, Chapter 9, and used by permission of the authors and publisher.

Mobilization of Groups

In general, mobilization results from prolonged interaction, though not necessarily face to face contact. Travel, trade, work experiences that bring people together, the spread of literacy, the distribution of the mass media of communication—all of these contribute to mobilization.[2] Once in contact, information increases, links are forged, and interests clarified. In the process, there is a shift from a category of people sharing some objective qualities to a definable group possessing a subjective awareness of its interests. Mobilization also proceeds as a collectivity organizes for the achievement of its goals.

Whether or not all of the above characteristics are present will not directly concern us. We will simply take as evidence, at least of a minimal level of mobilization, the concentration of a group's votes for a single party.

The major indicator of the existence and continuity of national-local strains is found in the regional distribution of votes. Based on electoral data, and tracing patterns of support as far back as 1908, recent studies have demonstrated the importance of the provincial locus of voters in accounting for national election results.[3] In essence, what this means is that there is no national pattern of support; each province or larger region responds to local problems and the ways these appear to be met by the federal government, making their partisan choices relatively independently of what is done in other provinces. The results are uneven patterns of support, reflected in the extreme variations with which regions give a majority, or even a plurality, of their votes to the governing party (Table 1). For example, in 17 general elections between 1921 and 1974, inclusive, and counting the election of 1925 as a victory for the Liberals, the governing party received at least 50 percent of the popular vote in 7 elections in the Atlantic provinces and in 10 in Quebec. Only in 1972 did support for the government fall below 41 per cent in the Atlantic provinces. In Quebec, characteristically, support for the government has generally been even higher, with two notable exceptions. When the remainder of the country helped elect a Conservative government in 1957 and 1962, Quebec voters gave only grudging support of approximately 30 per cent. While such rejections of the governing party are the exception in Quebec, they are the norm in western Canada. Only once have the prairie provinces contributed a majority of their votes to the government, while British Columbia has come no closer than 49 per cent, both times helping to elect a Conservative government in 1930 and 1958.

Neither support for the governing party, nor lack of it, in themselves tell us if the electors of a particular province are a politically cohesive force. In fact, as we see in Table 2, the presence of support in the case of Quebec is associated with mobilization to the Liberals. Of the Atlantic provinces, Newfoundland had displayed a similar pattern, but since 1968 has moved over to the Conservative Party, and has achieved more even balance in 1974. No other provinces have given consistent and massive support to either of the major parties. It goes without saying that third parties have never approached such levels of support at the federal level.

The consequences of these voting patterns, particularly as they represent the giving or withholding of support for the government, have been crucial to the malintegration of the Canadian political system. On the one hand, they indicate that the governing party fulfills its responsibilities with a mandate only partially reflecting the makeup of the country. On the other hand, provinces in turn, by giving or withholding support, as it were, vary in the way they can make an effective claim on the federal government for the satisfaction of their special interests. The relative power that each province claims within the federal bargaining arena is hence compromised by the support extended by its electors.[4]

Table 1

Support for Governing Party By Region 1921-1974

(Percentage of Votes)

Election	Governing Party	Atlantic	Quebec	Ontario	Prairies	British Columb
1921	Liberal	50.6	70.2	29.8	16.3	29.8
1925	Liberal[a]	42.5	59.3	31.0	30.6	34.7
1926	Liberal	45.6	62.3	38.9	42.1	37.0
1930	Conservative	54.7	44.7	54.4	40.0	49.3
1935	Liberal	54.5	54.4	42.7	35.3	31.8
1940	Liberal	52.5	63.3	50.8	43.1	37.4
1945	Liberal	47.5	50.8	41.1	30.0	27.5
1949	Liberal	55.4	60.4	45.7	41.9	36.7
1953	Liberal	54.9	61.0	46.9	37.5	30.9
1957	Conservative	48.6	31.1	48.8	28.6	32.6
1958	Conservative	54.5	49.6	56.4	56.2	49.4
1962	Conservative	45.4	29.6	39.3	44.9	27.3
1963	Liberal	49.9	45.6	46.3	26.1	32.3
1965	Liberal	47.4	45.6	43.6	25.4	30.0
1968	Liberal	41.4	53.6	46.6	34.8	41.8
1972	Liberal	39.5	49.8	38.4	26.8	29.0
1974[b]	Liberal	44.3	54.1	45.1	27.1	33.3

[a] The election of 1925 resulted in two governments, the first Liberal and the second Conservative.

[b] Supplied in advance of publication by Martin G. Rossignol, Director of Operations, Office of the Chief Electoral Officer.

Regional differences give us one way of encapsulating the national-local lines of cleavage, since they are tied to conflicts between subject and dominant peoples. In the current Canadian experience, this is also manifested through tensions between French and English speaking and between the French and English "charter" groups and those of other origins.[5] The mobilization of these cleavages along partisan lines can be seen in the support patterns of the relevant groups. To begin with, we must acknowledge that the determination of ethnic origin is not a simple matter, and the form of the question used appears to affect responses.[6]

This led us to use two different indicators of ethnicity in order to demonstrate strain between subject and dominant peoples. Support patterns of the French were based on the question, "What language do you speak most often in the home?", asked in the course of a survey taken after the 1965 general election.[7] The distribution of party choices by those who responded to the question on voting was, for the French-speaking, 62 per cent Liberal, 15 per cent Conservative, and about 11 per cent each for the NDP and the Créditistes. This sharply contrasts with the English-speaking, who distributed their votes more equally between the Liberals and Conservatives, 42 and 38 per cent respectively, while there were only 2 instances in the sample of Créditiste voters. We may conclude from these data that the French-speaking have been highly cohesive as a political force, mobilized predominantly for the Liberals. A significant minority support the Créditistes, making the latter a uniquely French-Canadian party.

Table 2

Mobilization of Provinces, 1921-1974

	Number of elections in which at least 50% votes for: Conservatives	Liberals
Newfoundland	1	7
Nova Scotia	6	4
New Brunswick	4	4
Prince Edward Island	7	5
Quebec	–	10
Ontario	4	–
Manitoba	1	–
Saskatchewan	2	1
Alberta	3	–
British Columbia	1	–

Total number of elections = 17
Newfoundland = 10

Using a three-fold division of origin in his 1968 election study, Meisel found 67 per cent of the French-speaking voted Liberal.[8] Mobilization into the Liberal fold was also evident for the French from Canadian Institute of Public Opinion election polls in 1949, 1953, and 1957. These same polls, however, reported a lower level of Liberal voting in the elections of 1965 and 1968 than has been noted here, based on the two national election surveys.[9] These discrepancies may be related to the fact that the Canadian Institute's surveys were pre-election polls, when voting decisions had not yet crystallized, particularly for those still toying with voting for third parties. This is demonstrated by the high level of indecision found in one survey before the 1972 election. Origin in this instance is restricted to language of interview, that is, either English or French. For the French, 18 per cent said they were not sure how they would vote, 11 per cent refused to answer the question of vote intention, and 9 per cent denied that they would vote. Such indifference or uncertainty was expressed by 10 per cent fewer of the English-speaking. But for the remainder of the French, the direction of partisanship remained the same, with 61 per cent indicating they would vote Liberal.[10] The 1972 Gallup pre-election survey, using three categories for language, indicated that 58 per cent of the French intended to vote Liberal.[11]

Approximately one-quarter of the population is neither of French nor British origin, and represents another facet of the subject-dominant strain in Canadian society. We had some difficulty isolating these "other" origins in the 1965 survey, since the question on ancestral birthplace tended to underestimate those, apparently both French and British, whose ancestors had been in Canada for generations. However, close inspection of all possible answers suggests that ancestral birthplace is a reasonable indicator of "other" origins. Of "other" origins with a known party choice in 1965, 45 per cent voted Liberal, 28 per cent Conservative, 20 per cent NDP, and the remainder Social Credit. This compares to a total popular vote of 40.2 per cent for the Liberals, 32.4 for the Conservatives, and 18 for the NDP. The post-1968 national survey showed that "other" origins voted Liberal in 58 per cent of the cases, compared to 24 per cent for the Conservatives.[12] The total popular vote in the 1968 election was 45.5 per cent

Liberal and 31.1 per cent Conservative. The propensity to vote Liberal on the part of those of non-British, non-French origin was thus much clearer in 1968, but we are still hesitant, on the basis of this one election, to conclude that there is a high degree of mobilization in one partisan direction. The subject-dominant strain is most clearly evident in the support patterns of the French-speaking, and in the voting choices encompassed by regional boundaries; to a lesser extent, it can be detected in the voting behaviour of the far from homogeneous grouping termed "other" ethnic groups.

A second component of the local-national dimension of cleavage relates to conflicts over religion.

While the connection between French origin and Catholicism might be assumed to be the major source of correlation between the latter and voting Liberal, it has been shown that religion operates quite independently of ethnicity. That is, Catholics vote Liberal in excess of what would be expected by chance even when they are not of French origin.[13] This degree of political mobilization does not exist for any other religious group, although there is a tendency for Protestants in the largest denominations to adhere to the Conservatives. Fifty-four per cent of the Presbyterians reported voting Conservative in 1965, as did 47 per cent of those in the United Church and 43 per cent of the Anglicans. For those who regard the Anglican Church as the stronghold of British privilege and upper class status, these findings may be surprising. A stronger correlation between United Church and voting Conservative was also found by Jean Laponce for the 1963 general election. Laponce, accepting the previous characterization of Anglicans, was puzzled by this result[14], and we too could speculate on reasons for the behaviour of Anglicans. In any event, these results for the three Protestant denominations give evidence of some partisan mobilization.

The evidence available on support patterns in provincial politics tends to confirm those in federal. The composition of individual provinces is not always, however, representative of the nation as a whole, and these situations alter the general outlines of support. For example, the vast majority of voters in Quebec are of French, Catholic origin. With vigorous party competition at the provincial level, one wonders if there is any variation in the mobilization of origin groups. Not only is the answer yes, but it appears that the Liberal Party in Quebec plays a unique role for the English. In a telephone poll shortly before the 1970 provincial election, Regenstreif found 58 per cent of the English-speaking intending to vote Liberal. A further 24 per cent had not made up their minds, and at least some of these would have ultimately been Liberal voters. At this time only 28 per cent of the French-speaking expected to cast their ballots for the Liberals. Instead, the majority were distributed among the Parti Québécois, Union Nationale, and the Créditistes.[15] These results are due to the special nature of Quebec politics, where the Parti Québécois in particular advocated a course of nationalism antagonistic to the interests of most English-speaking Quebeckers.

Indications of divergence from national support patterns also come from Alberta. During the period of one-party dominance, the governing Social Credit Party could expect to obtain support from a broad spectrum of the electorate. In a 1969 survey of the electorate, we find not only 60 per cent of the Protestants voting for Social Credit, but also 41 per cent of the Catholics. The weak Liberal Party could expect only 9 per cent of the Protestants to select their candidates. For the Catholics, however, 28 per cent indicated Liberal support.[16] One-party dominance, while weakening customary patterns of mobilization, did not completely erode these.

With the NDP and Social Credit replacing the major parties in British Columbia, that province's support patterns are even more divergent than those elsewhere. In a telephone survey conducted before the 1972 provincial election, 42 per cent of the Lutherans and 49 per cent of unidentified, other Protestants (but not the higher prestige Anglicans or United Church), planned to vote Social Credit. Altogether, 35 per cent of the Protestants favoured Social Credit, compared to 28 per cent of Catholics. Thirty-three per cent of the Catholics planned to vote for the NDP, and 30 per cent for the Liberals. The British Columbia survey permitted a category of atheists, agnostics, and non-church affiliates, and of these, 57 per cent inclined to the NDP.[17] Particularly noteworthy was the nature of Protestant support for Social Credit, the attraction of Catholics to the NDP, but still their greater support for the Liberals, exceeding Protestants by 10 per cent.

Strains of Industrial Development

The second principal dimension of cleavage underlying party formation is that stemming from the strains of industrial development. The tensions generated by the opposing demands of primary and secondary types of economic organization have been a concommitant of national-local strains. They were manifested in regional cleavages and in regional differences in support patterns. In addition, we have another perspective on their current operation through the support patterns of related occupational groups. We cannot treat here those occupations associated with the secondary sector, since they include owners, managers, other white collar workers, and blue collar workers. In other words, the occupations covered include much more salient interests than those confined to secondary industry. The primary sector also has some of these characteristics, with "farmer" including owners, tenants, and workers. However, in this instance there is an expectation that the problems of farmers, regardless of landowning status, will provide sufficient shared experience to generate some common outlook. This contention would appear to be supported with data from the 1965 survey, where, of respondents in households headed by someone employed in primary industry who also revealed their past vote, 51 per cent supported the Conservatives. While one-third voted Liberal, we still find these results evidence of considerable political cohesiveness on the part of those in primary industries, since the Conservatives in total received only 32.4 per cent of the popular vote. Results were less conclusive in 1968, but even so, 44 per cent of the farmers voted Conservative, compared to a popular vote of 31.4 per cent.[18] In Regenstreif's sample prior to the 1972 election, farmers were few in number, but taking that into account, his data show considerable mobilization to the Conservatives (41 per cent with a known party preference, and much more if we extrapolate to probable vote). Similarly, 44 per cent with a known party preference in the Canadian Institute of Public Opinion pre-election poll in 1972 reported that they would vote Conservative.[19]

The more "modern" form of economic strain is related to conflicts between owners and managers on the one hand, and workers on the other. The manifestation of such tensions in Canada have been obscured by other forms of cleavage. While primary-secondary strains have been the basis for the formation of most third parties, worker-employer strains have led to more localized and more short-lived parties. In a comparative study of class-based voting in Britain, Australia, the United States and Canada, Alford found Canada at the bottom of a class voting scale. Between 1952 and 1962, the index of class voting was 40 in Britain, 33 in Australia, 16 in the United States, but only 8 in Canada.[20] A follow-up study of these countries found the same rank order, and no increase in class voting in Canada.[21] The class-based voting that does occur emerges in particular provinces, being strongest in Ontario and then British Columbia. In contrast, Quebec and the prairie provinces are almost invariably low. Later studies confirm these patterns and show little evidence of increased class voting.[22]

The sucess of working class parties, whether as governing parties or as national political forces, is tied to their success in mobilizing their natural constituency, the working class. Industrial development creates a large working class whose mobilization is then partially dependent on the growth of identification in class terms. Currently, the NDP is seen as the special defender of working class interests and its fortunes are tied to the extent of support it can generate from among the working class. While we have already indicated that class-based voting is relatively low in Canada, it is worthwhile to pursue this further, in order to examine in detail the nature of support patterns, in a way similar to that which we followed for social aggregates tied to other cleavages. Using again data supplied by the 1965 survey, we can examine support in terms of gross class divisions. That is, dividing non-farm households into white collar and blue collar, we look for evidence of partisanship within each group. To the extent that it is evident, it is clearer for the white collar, of whom 52 per cent said they voted for the Liberals. The Liberals received 40 per cent of the popular vote in the 1965 election, and the support patterns of the white collar are then indicative of some mobilization. But blue collar households turn out to be quite similar, with 49 per cent voting Liberal. The difference in choice is somewhat greater between blue and white collar who vote Conservative, and the slack produced in this way goes from blue collar workers to the NDP and the Créditistes. Subjective awareness of class position shows even less distinctiveness among working class identifiers—31 per cent reported voting Conservative, compared to 25 per cent of the objectively blue collar. Among the middle class, however, the tendency to mobilization as Liberal supporters remained evident for 53 per cent.

If neither objective class position nor subjective awareness of this contributed to the political cohesiveness of the working class, we may still wonder about that segment of the working class organized into trade unions. Again we find that, in general, those in union households have not been concentrated as CCF/NDP supporters, although they do have some preference in that direction.[23] There is some evidence that the combination of skilled labour, trade union membership, and British origin contributed to a greater propensity to vote CCF in 1953, and similarly, NDP in 1963, but these were far from overwhelming trends.[24]

On the national scene, the NDP, and the CCF before it, were not able to supplant one of the older parties in a manner similar to the British Labour Party, nor were they successful in forging workers into a stable electoral force, as has occurred in most continental European systems. Whatever the reasons for their limited fortunes, these are not the result of the absence of a large industrial labour force, nor of class consciousness. There are classes in Canada, and these are associated with special interests and problems of inequality. The lack of class-based voting, as it affects the working class, is tied to failures of mobilization. This means that the working class has not found a single partisan channel for the expression of its interests, interests which moreover are probably quite diverse, if only because of the primacy of the other cleavages we have described.

In summary, support patterns give an additional perspective on the cleavage structure of Canadian society, in which the strains associated with an imperfect process of nation-building have taken shape in the partisan responses of voters. Not all population groups associated with lines of cleavage have been mobilized, but those which have—the French-speaking, Catholics, farmers, and to some extent the middle class and high status Protestant denominations, in all cases affected and at times reinforced by regional boundaries—have helped perpetuate a society in which systematic strains are ever ready for political expression.

Polarization of Parties

Class and Status. Summaries of the characteristics on which parties are polarized are presented in Table 3. The basis for these generalizations are two national surveys of the electorate conducted after the 1965 and the 1968 general elections, Canadian Institute of Public Opinion pre-election polls in 1963, 1965, 1968, and 1972,[25] and an unpublished study prior to the 1972 election by Peter Regenstreif.[26]

In the time spanned, and with no evidence of contrary trends either before, or in the immediate future, the Conservatives, NDP, and Social Credit are polarized as Protestant, English-speaking parties. One possible source of exception to the characterization of the NDP as a Protestant-supported party comes from the 1965 election survey, in which 57 per cent of NDP were Protestants, fewer than our criterion for polarization. A closer examination of these data indicates that there was, at that time at least, some modest support from Catholics in Ontario and Quebec. The early years of the CCF, the predecessor of the NDP, were constrained by opposition from the Catholic Church, inhibiting those with close ties to the religious community from voting along class lines. Apparently there has been some decline in negative class voting as indicated by Alford's findings comparing Catholic workers in Ontario and Quebec, and also Wilson's, in a survey in Waterloo-South.[27] Studies of voters in Ontario provincial elections also suggest a greater place for Catholics in the NDP, compared to the Conservatives.[28] None of this seriously challenges the major outlines of ethnic-religious polarization in the three parties mentioned.

The obverse form of polarization was found in the Ralliement des Créditistes, which was a uniquely French, Catholic party. While this is not clearly shown in the data presented by Meisel and Laponce, since the small samples of Social Credit and Créditiste voters have been combined, we should have no hesitation in accepting our characterization. With the Créditistes restricted to Quebec, they could hardly be other than French-speaking and Catholic; this is confirmed by the study of the party's emergence and support by Maurice Pinard.[29]

With the exception of the Créditistes, we present no other party in Table 3 as polarized on class lines. To some extent, this is a matter of interpretation, tied to the criteria of polarization used, particularly the two-thirds requirement. Rose and Urwin suggest that when a less concentrated measure seems appropriate, there should be over 50 per cent[30] homogeneity, with the national average exceeded by 17 per cent. On this basis we can consider data in Table 4, where instead of using the national distribution of blue collar households, we consider the composition of the Liberals. It is evident that there is greater polarization in the NDP, particularly in 1968, but it still does not resemble European working class parties. The relative looseness of the NDP's class character is, in one sense, a measure of its success in appealing to middle class voters.

Given the regional character of Canadian existence, and the persistence of regional ties reinforced by a federal system of government, it can be hypothesized that territorial factors are more important for the functioning of political parties and the persistence of voter alignments than are potentially cross-cutting functional-economic factors.[31] One of the results could be that social class plays a greater role in provincial politics than on the national scene, particularly in the more highly industrialized provinces. Some signs of this are already evident from the greater indications of class-based voting in Ontario during federal elections. This seems to be the case as well in Ontario provincial elections,[32] and those in British Columbia[33] and Saskatchewan.[34] In none of these instances, however, is the evidence overwhelming, nor do we have sufficient data for testing polarization in the way we have done for federal elections. Conversely, class voting has been distinctly low in Alberta during the period of Social Credit dominance,[35] as it has been in Quebec, at least since the 1930s[36]. The demonstration of a high level of working class support for the Union Nationale was not, according to Pinard, the result of "false consciousness," but primarily its availability as a party of protest.

> . . . the workers did not turn to the National Union because of its ideology—although it was reformist in the early phases—but rather because it was a movement well suited for the mobilization of social unrest born from serious economic adversities.[37]

His thesis is also of relevance to working class support for Social Credit in Alberta. Alberta, in its own way, has also represented a unique regional culture characterized by one-party dominance. The parties available to voters, most strikingly in such situations, are ones that acquire their ideologies from the guiding elites, not from the interests of supporters.

> If the culture of the elites represents a highly monolithic and closed system and if little dissension is tolerated among the elites, it is very likely that the organizations of the lower classes will be controlled by typical members of the elites and imbued with middle-class and elite values; a great amount of redirection of class sentiments will tend to take place.[38]

Regional factors permit the expression of greater political polarization along class lines where urbanization and industrialization accompany a strong, competitive party system. Where there is a weakness of competition, and a social system that emphasizes a unified, territorially-defined definition of interests, such polarization will be minimized. These conclusions should be understood as consistent with our earlier discussion of the conditions making for mobilization. Mobilization was tied to the existence of common problems and interests, creating a group's objective life chances.

Table 3.

Polarization of Parties on Origin and Class

Characteristic of Polarization	Liberal	Conservative	NDP	Social Credit	
Religion	—	Protestant	Protestant	Protestant	Catholic
Language	—	English	English	English	French
Class	—	—	—	—	(blue collar)

Criteria of polarization include having party supporters with two-thirds of a given characteristic. For further details, see text and Rose and Urwin, 1969.

We also indicated that a second component of mobilization was the recognition by group members of their common interests, leading to the emergence of a group identity. We may ask, then, whether the relatively low level of polarization on class, particularly for the NDP, is tied to imperfections in class consciousness. This certainly appears to have been the case when the post-1965 election survey was conducted. At that time the NDP was made up of 49 per cent working class identifiers, compared to 58 per cent of Social Credit and 59 per cent of le Ralliement des Créditistes. Ontario again showed the greatest consistency in class voting, with 64 per cent of NDP voters made up of those with working class self-identifications.[39] Similarly, in a study of provincial voting in 1967, Wilson and Hoffman found the appropriate kind of class consciousness among 68 per cent of those identifying with the NDP. Yet we must

Findings more consistent with the image of the NDP as a working class party were reported by Meisel in his study of the 1968 election, where 68 per cent were appropriately class conscious.[42] However, Regenstreif's 1972 election study reported only 53 per cent of prospective NDP voters gave a working class identification.[43]

The fluctuations reported could be due to sampling error, differences in question wording, and other vagaries of survey research.[44] But although we may want to treat them on methodological grounds, they have a clear sociological meaning. Class consciousness exists, but as an ambiguous concept in Canada. It does not have a uniform meaning for all people—for example, English-speaking Protestants are more likely to correctly identify themselves in class terms with respect to their socio-economic status than are French-speaking Catholics.[45] If its expression is affected by factors of origin, so important to Canadians, it can hardly be expected to have a a unidirectional relationship with party politics. As Pinard observes in discussing the Créditistes:

> We contend that in the absence of (1) a well-developed class-consciousness, and (2) class organizations which go beyond the economic problems to encompass the social and political life of the working class, this unincorporated class is as likely to support a conservative movement as a progressive one, whichever is most available, when their conditions lead them to revolt.[46]

Since neither objective life chances nor subjective identifications contribute strongly to polarization, we may consider yet a third factor, that provided by social organization. In the case of polarization on class lines, we anticipate a critical role for the organization of workers into trade unions. In other words, this should be manifested through a New Democratic Party made up predominantly of trade unionists and their families. If this were the case, however, this party would always be relegated to a minor role in Canadian politics, since less than 30 per cent of all households have at least one union member. In reviewing data since 1953 in Table 5, the largest concentration of those affiliated with unions occurred in 1958, 1968, and 1972.[47] On these three occasions, 44 per cent of the NDP's electoral party was made up of those who were themselves members of a trade union or living in households where someone else was. There is a suggestion, then, in some tendencies in the direction of polarization. Reasons for the lack of overwhelming support by trade unionists for the NDP may be found in the structural sources of weak working class parties in Canada. These may well be augmented by personal feelings of animosity toward trade union involvement in partisan politics, as Pinard reports for Quebec voters.[48]

Percent of Liberal and NDP Supporters Who Live in Trade Union Households, Federal Elections, 1953-72

		NDP	Liberal	% Difference
1965	(Schwartz, "Canadian Voting Behaviour")	54	44	10
1968	(Meisel, *Working Papers)*	59	47	12
1972	(CIPO, based on households where the head is in the labour force)	5	47	8

Table 5

Percent of Liberal and NDP Supporters Who Live In Trade Unions Households, Federal Elections 1953-72

	CCF/NDP	Liberal	% Difference
1953	39	26	13
1958	44	31	13
1963	40	22	18
1963-65 (combined)	41	23	18
1968	44	33	11
1972	44	26	18

Source: Canadian Institute of Public opinion pre-election surveys.

With this we leave the issue of a moderate level of class polarization in the NDP. We have examined sufficient material and enough varied sources to let the matter rest. Whatever ideological rationale can be given for considering the NDP as a working clsss party needs to be evaluated in conjunction with the character of its support. Yet even if it is not sharply polarized along lines of class, the NDP is far from a heterogeneous, broad-based party. Along with all other parties except the Liberal, it too has a restricted social base. This generalization is based on support patterns for federal parties, but it has also been apparent for provincial parties, except in those few instances of one-party dominance, as with Social Credit in Alberta, where the dominating role is associated with a broad base.

Provincial Divisions. From the first federal election contested in 1935 until 1949, Social Credit was overwhelmingly an Alberta party. With growing strength at the provincial level in British Columbia, supporters became about evenly divided by the time of the 1953 election, with 45 per cent from Alberta and 40 per cent from British Columbia. The two provinces accounted for 70 per cent of all support in 1957 and 83 per cent in 1958. Following this, Social Credit assumed new vigour in Quebec, with that province making up more than 60 per cent of the electoral party in 1962 and 1963. Such dominance contributed to breaking away of the Quebec wing, resuming its provincial title of le Ralliement des Créditistes. That change permitted the weight of the party to move back to the west, first divided between the the two westernmost provinces in 1965, and overwhelmingly in British Columbia in 1968. The 1972 election saw the complete rout of the party in the west, despite a far greater number of candidates than in 1968, so that now it is almost totally a Quebec party.[49]

No other party in recent years has displayed such polarization. While the Progressives were not uniformly distributed across the country, their concentrations of support were never much more than 40 per cent, and that in most heavily populated Ontario.

For the remaining parties we can only see tendencies to regional concentrations. For example, from its beginnings until the 1958 election, the CCF had more than 50 per cent of its supporters from western Canada. The creation of the NDP was accompanied by a shift in regional balance, declining in favour in the prairie provinces though not in British Columbia, and now with concentrations of over 40 per cent of its supporters in Ontario.

The major parties do not display even this degree of cohesiveness. The Conservatives, with a history of low support from Quebec, cannot be considered polarized in the direction of non-Quebec. Even the consistency of support from Quebec for the

Liberals does not make that party a Quebec party. The closest this came to being true was in the election of 1921, when wartime grievances were still fresh. At that time, the Liberals were, as an electoral body, made up of 44 per cent Quebeckers. For comparative purposes, we note that Quebec voters were then 25 per cent of the voting public.

Polarization is a feature of all parties except the Liberal when support patterns of major origin groups are considered. Class is a weaker factor, and was most prominent in le Ralliement des Créditistes and to a lesser extent in the CCF/NDP. Le Ralliement as well as Social Credit, were the only ones to display sharp regional polarization. We have demonstrated the broadest base for the Liberals. As Laponce concludes after his analysis of cleavages:

> They show the least social class identification and are the only party to have been systematically associated over the past twenty years (and obviously longer) with the second province, the second language, and the second religion: an illustration of how to be second in order to be first.[50]

Notes

1. For a relevant and provocative discussion, see John Meisel, "Cleavages, Parties, and Values in Canada," paper presented to the Ninth World Congress, International Political Science Association, Montreal, August, 1973.

2. Karl Deutsch, "Social Mobilization and Political Development," *American Political Science Review* 55 (September, 1961), 493-415.

3. Donald E. Blake, "The Measurement of Regionalism in Canadian Voting Patterns," *Canadian Journal of Political Science* 5 (March, 1972), 55-81; Mildred A. Schwartz, *Politics and Territory* (Montreal: McGill-Queen's University Press, 1974), 53-63; Robert W. Jackman, "Political Parties, Voting and National Integration," *Comparative Politics* (July, 1972), 511-536.

4. This argument on relative power is elaborated in Schwartz, *Politics and Territory,* Chapter 3.

5. See John Porter, *The Vertical Mosaic* (Toronto: University of Toronto Press, 1965); *Report of the Royal Commission on Bilingualism and Biculturalism*, I-IV (Ottawa: Queen's Printer, 1967-1969); Mildred A Schwartz, "Politics: The Issue of Citizenship," in *Issues in Canadian Society,* Dennis Forcese and Stephen Richer (Scarborough: Prentice-Hall, 1975).

6. For a discussion, with examples, see Mildred A. Schwartz, "Canadian Voting Behaviour," in Richard Rose, ed., *Electoral Behavior, A Comparative Handbook*; (New York: Free Press, 1974).

7. This study was done by Philip E. Converse, John Meisel, Maurice Pinard, Peter Regenstreif, and Mildred A. Schwartz, funded by the Canada Council and the Committee on Election Expenses. Tabulations presented here were made possible by grants from the National Science Foundation and the Graduate College Research Board of the University of Illinois at Chicago Circle to Mildred Schwartz. Sample sizes refer to weighted case bases. For details, see Schwartz, *Politics and Territory,* 84-85.

8. John Meilse, *Working Papers on Canadian Politics* (Montreal: McGill-Queen's University Press, 1972), Table II.

9. J.A. Laponce, "Post-Dicting Electoral Cleavages in Canadian Federal Elections, 1949-1968: Material for a Footnote," *Canadian Journal of Political Science* 5 (June, 1972), 271.

10. Data on the 1972 election were generously supplied by Professor Peter Regenstreif from his national pre-election survey for the *Toronto Star.*

11. Canadian Institute of Public Opinion, Gallup Poll release, November 18, 1972.

12. Meisel, *Working Papers*, Table II.

13. Robert R. Alford, *Party and Society.* (Chicago: Rand-McNally. 1963): Robert R. Alford. "The Social Bases of Political Cleavage in 1962," in John Meisel, ed., *Papers on the 1962 Election*, (Toronto: University of Toronto Press, 1964), 215; Grace M. Anderson, "Voting Behaviour and the Ethnic-Religious Variable: A study of a Federal Election in Hamilton, Ontario", *Canadian Journal of Economics and Political Science* 32 (February, 1966) 27-37; Meisel, "Cleavages, Parties and Values," 10-11; John C.. Terry and Richard J. Schultz, "Canadian Electoral Behaviour: A Propositional Inventory," in Orest Kruhlak, Richard Schultz, Sidney Pobihushchy, eds., *The Canadian Political Process*, 2nd ed. (Toronto: Holt, Rinehart and Winston, 1973), 260-262. This does not deny, of course, that there is some interaction between ethnic origin and religion which may affect the consistency of Catholic mobilization, and this is also true of the interaction between religion and region. *Ibid.*, 262-264. Yet, in Terry and Schultz's inventory, the interactive effects of religion with ethnicity and region were treated as both less reliable and valid than those of the religious variable alone. *Ibid.*, 281.

14. Laponce, "Ethnicity, Religion, and Politics in Canada," 213-214.

15. These data, supplied by Peter Regenstreif, were also collected for a series of articles for the *Toronto Star*. Earlier confirmations of the mobilization of English speaking voters to the Liberals is contained in the two mimeographed reports of the Groupe de Recherche Sociale, *Les électeurs québécois; attitudes et opinions à la veille de l'élection de 1960* (Montreal: 1960); and *Les préférences politiques des électeurs québécois en 1962* (Montreal: 1964).

16. J.A. Long and F.Q. Quo, "Alberta, One Party Dominance." In Martin Robin, ed., *Canadian Provincial Politics* (Scarborough: Prentice-Hall, 1972), 18.

17. Data are from a survey conducted for the Vancouver *Province*, in which a random sample of 50 eligible voters was selected in each of the 48 provincial ridings. Tabulations were generously provided by Professor Jean Laponce and Mrs. Pamela Smortchevsky of the University of British Columbia data library, 197, 202-203.

18. Meisel, *Working Papers*, Table II.

19. The 1972 CIPO data have been computed by Wendy Thompson at York University's Institute for Behavioural Research. Some independent support for the mobi-

lization of farmers to the Conservatives also comes from studies comparing urban-rural party preferences, See Terry and Schultz, "Canadian Electoral Behaviour," 270.

20. Alford, *Party and Society*, 102. Alford combines votes for the Liberals and NDP as representing left voting. The Liberals, however, are not a clearly left-wing party. But since his technique is primarily a comparison of the party choices of manual and non-manual workers (and not of parties themselves), it still does not vitiate his conclusion that class-based voting is low in Canada.

21. Robert R. Alford, "Class Voting in the Anglo-American Political Systems," in S.M. Lipset and Stein Rokkan, eds., *Party Systems and Voter Alignments* (New York: Free Press, 1967) 85. Here Alford differentiates between Liberal and NDP votes.

22. Schwartz, "Canadian Voting Behaviour", 585-588; Meisel, *Working Papers*, 3-5. A review of constituency studies by Terry and Schultz failed to confirm the proposition that "Working class voters tend to prefer the NDP, middle and upper class voters the Liberals or Conservatives," and led them to attribute low validity and medium to low reliability to the findings. Terry and Schultz, "Canadian Electoral Behaviour," 253-281.

23. This is based on evidence from 1953 to 1972, Peter Regenstreif, *The Diefenbaker Interlude* (Toronto: Longmans, 1965), 14, 33, 37, 38; Laponce, "Post-Dicting Electoral Cleavages", 279, unpublished data from Regenstreif's 1972 election study; Canadian Institute of Public Opinion Gallup Poll, Nov. 11, 1972.

24. Regenstreif, *The Diefenbaker Interlude*, 101-2.

25. Data have been recomputed from those presented in Jean Laponce, *People vs Politics* (Toronto: University of Toronto Press, 1969).

26. Wendy Thompson of York University supplied the special tabulation of the 1972 Gallup data. A national sample of 1262, weighted to 1997, were interviewed for a series of pre-election articles, published in the *Toronto Star*. We are grateful to Professor Regenstreif's generosity in making these unpublished data available.

27. Robert R. Alford, *Party and Society*, 272; John Wilson, "Politics and Social Class in Canada: The Case of Waterloo South," *Canadian Journal of Political Science* 1 (September, 1968), 288-309. See also Wallace Gagne and Peter Regenstreif, "Some Aspects of New Democratic Party Support in 1965," *Canadian Journal of Economics and Political Science* 33 (November, 1967), 537.

28. John Wilson and David Hoffman, "Ontario, A Three-Party System in Transition," in Martin Robin, ed., *Canadian Provincial Politics* (Scarborough: Prentice-Hall of Canada, 1972), 198-239; Peter Regenstreif, unpublished data collected for a series of articles for the *Toronto Star* prior to the 1971 election.

29. Maurice Pinard, *The Rise of a Third Party* (Englewood Cliffs: Prentice-Hall, 1971).

30. Rose and Urwin, "Social Cohesion, Political Parties and Strains in Regimes," 11.

31. Schwartz, *Politics and Territory*, 281-308.

32. John Wilson and David Hoffman, "Ontario, a Three-Party System in Transition," 234-235.

33. Martin Robin, "The Politics of Class Conflict," in Robin, *Canadian Provincial Politics*, 67; data for Vancouver *Province* study supplied by Laponce.

34. John C. Courtney and David E. Smith, "Saskatchewan, Parties in a Politically Competitive Province," in Robin, *Canadian Provincial Politics*, 316 and sources cited on 317.

35. Evidence based on data recomputed from J.A. Long and F.Q. Quo, "Alberta, One Party Dominance," in Robin, *Canadian Provincial Politics*, 20.

36. Kenneth H. McRoberts, "Contrasts in French-Canadian Nationalism: The Impact of Industrialization upon the Electoral Role of French Canadian Nationalism." Unpublished M.A. thesis, Department of Political Science, University of Chicago, 1966; Le Groupe de Recherche Sociale, *Les électeurs québecois;* Le Groupe de Recherche Sociale, *Les préférences politiques en 1962*; Maurice Pinard, "Classes sociales et comportement électoral," in Vincent Lemieux, ed., *Quatre élections provinciales au Québec, 1956-1966* (Québec: Les presses de l'Université Laval, 1969), 141-178; Maurice Pinard, "Working Class Politics: An interpretation of the Quebec Case," *Canadian Review of Sociology and Anthropology* 7 (May, 1970), 87-109.

37. Pinard's "Working Class Politics". Reprinted from the *Canadian Review of Sociology and Anthropology* 7:12, 106.

38. *Ibid.*, 106.

39. Schwartz, *Politics and Territory*, 135.

40. Wilson and Hoffman, "Ontario, A Three-Party System in Transition," 220. We note that the authors use identification with a party as their measure of partisanship.

41. Respondents in both the Regenstreif and Wilson and Hoffman studies could choose from three categories of class.The Regenstreif results come from a province-wide survey prior to the 1971 election, done for the *Toronto Star.*

42. Meisel, *Working Papers*, 7.

43. In this study as well, Regenstreif permitted respondents three categories of response, compared to five in the 1965 and 1968 studies.

44. For example, a study of occupational prestige in 1965, and using the same question as the election study, found more self-reported middle class and fewer working class. P.C. Pineo and John C. Goyder, "Social Class Identification of National Sub-Groups," in James E. Curtis and William G. Scott, *Social Stratification in Canada* (Scarborough: Prentice-Hall of Canada, 1973), 18.

45. *Ibid.*, 189-195.

46. Pinard, *The Rise of a Third Party*, 95.

47. The 1972 data come from special tabulations of the Canadian Institute of Public Opinion pre-election study, while the earlier results come from Gallup Poll pre-election surveys reported in Regenstreif, *The Diefenbaker Interlude*, 104, or derived from Laponce, *People vs Politics.*

48. Pinard, *The Rise of a Third Party,* 98, see Chapter 2.

49. The Social Credit Party in B.C. returned to power with a strong majority in 1975. Editors.

50. Laponce, "Post-Dicting Electoral Cleavages", 204.

24

The Evolution of French Unilingualism in Urban Quebec*

Pierre Roberge

Since the mid-sixties linguistic issues—*la question linguistique*—have acquired an unprecedented centrality in Canadian political life. In less than a decade the leaders of all federal parties have developed firm support for institutional bilingualism in the federal civil service and related organizations. By contrast, in Quebec, the only bilingual province, there has been extensive division in public opinion and among political parties on both the goals and means of a linguistic policy. There is in this a striking break from those alignments which history has made familiar. Up until now unanimity on linguistic matters had been primarily a characteristic of the French, while resistance to bilingualism normally has come from English-speaking quarters.

Debates on linguistic issues have nourished—and fed on—a literature that has become considerable. Among the scientific contributions to this literature one must note, in addition to the score of studies begun by the Laurendeau-Dunton and the Gendron Commissions, the independent work of Henripin[1], Joy[2], Lieberson[3] and Maheu[4]. Using different methods and indexes, all these studies nevertheless tend to establish two facts of some political and ideological importance. The first of these facts is the very significant increase, since the turn of this century, in linguistic assimilation among Canadians of French origin residing outside Quebec. The second fact is the predominance of English at various levels and in various sectors of social and economic life in Quebec itself. Some of these studies insist on a third fact of even greater import, the breakdown of the system of demographic forces that gave Quebec a remarkable linguistic stability over the past century. This system was a simple one involving two countervailing forces: immigration flows that strengthened Quebec's English-speaking population, on the one hand, and a higher francophone birthrate that offset these pressures, on the other. These facts are well known and established.

Given these facts, it is tempting to explain the increased intensity of linguistic confrontations in Quebec by the growing precariousness of the status of the French language in this region. There are, indeed, countless francophones, especially in Mon-

---

*This is a revised and expanded version of a paper published first in *Le Devoir* on December 16, 1974. It appears here in the author's translation with his permission and that of *Le Devoir.*

treal, who put forward the following argument: history has shown that French-speaking communities outside Quebec are not viable; in Quebec itself the decline of the French birthrate, the anglophilia of the immigrants, and the collapse of traditional defences against assimilation in the face of urbanization and secularization, all combine to threaten the already inferior status of the French language. In consequence, strong protective measures are necessary. This argument is so widespread and so powerful that even those who do not share the linguistic radicalism of some groups can understand their concern.

I want to offer some slightly dissonant evidence pertaining to the historical evolution of the predominance of the English language in Quebec society. A large segment of public opinion holds that the ascendancy of English is asserting itself anew. I submit that, on the contrary, the predominance of English is decreasing considerably, and where it counts most, that is, in urban Quebec.

The best data we have to establish the relevant facts are to be found in the various censuses of Canada. The 1971 census contained no less than four distinct ethno-linguistic questions. The first question dealt with the ethnic origin of the respondent, that is, the cultural affiliation of his or her first male ancestor to come to America, a census question asked since 1851. The second question was on the knowledge of the official languages, the respondent's ability to speak French, English, both, or neither of those languages; these data have been available since 1901. The third question was on mother tongue, that is, the first language learned and still understood by the respondent; it was introduced in 1921. Finally a new question was asked on the respondent's habitual language, that is, the language most frequently used at home.

Responses to these questions pertain to distinct yet cognate phenomena. In fact, all our measures and indices of assimilation, inequality, and asymmetry are cross-tabulations of answers to these various questions. For instance, someone whose mother tongue is English and whose ethnic origin is French will be said to be assimilated. Bilingualism will be said to be asymmetrical if its incidence is much higher in one mother-tongue than the other. We must, of course, remind ourselves of the many problems of validity and reliability involved in the use of these data. In addition there are numerous more strictly technical problems involved in the construction of time series: the wording of the questions changes over time; breakdowns published in one census report will not be available in previous or subsequent ones; the boundaries of reporting areas are not stable over time, etc. Yet, provided one is willing to pay the price of some simplification, it is possible to capture the broad evolution of the phenomenon that interests us here.

In a situation in which many linguistic groups co-exist, one can measure the ascendancy of any one group by its ability to impose its language on the others, either through pure and simple assimilation or through the asymmetry of bilingualism. The ascendancy will depend on demographic variables, for instance the number and relative sizes of the groups involved, as well as on institutional factors, such as control over the school system. Moreover, it will not be felt everywhere to the same extent nor in the same manner. One pattern has been especially frequent in the history of linguistic contacts.[5] In this situation we find two groups distinguished by language size, geographic location and power: a linguistic minority who enjoy a dominant position in the economic and/or the political system and whose influence, linguistic or otherwise, is mostly felt in the urban areas; and a numerical majority who, even though dominated and turned into a sociological minority, are nevertheless isolated to a large degree in the rural areas. The linguistic ascendancy of the dominant minority is first and foremost an urban phenomenon.

With this in mind, let us come to the Quebec case and begin our observations in the middle of the nineteenth century when the population was small and mostly rural.

Table 1

Persons of French Origin (FO), of French mother tongue (FMT), and French unilinguals (FU) in agglomerations of 30,000 inhabitants or more, Quebec, 1851, 1901-1971.

	I French Origin (FO)	II French Mother Tongue (FMT)	III French Unilinguals (FU)	IV Total Population	V FO as % of Total Population	VI FU as % of Total Population	VII FU as % of FO
1851	50,526	—	—	99,767	50.6	—	—
1901	260,244	—	139,650	394,015	66.0	35.4	53.6
1911	359,311	—	—	549,878	65.3	—	—
1921	485,027	—	252,909	730,700	65.6	34.2	52.1
1931	698,808	—	357,148	1,045,366	66.8	34.1	51.1
1941	950,411	961,037	546,187	1,401,597	67.8	39.0	57.5
1951	1,285,385	1,294,299	779,595	1,810,237	71.0	43.0	60.6
1961	2,164,830	2,181,416	1,445,296	2,977,375	72.2	48.5	66.7
1971	2,943,020	3,022,210	2,071,695	4,026,195	73.0	51.4	70.3

In 1951, Montreal and Quebec City, the only two urban centres of any consequence, contained just under 11 per cent of the total population of the province. The urban and the rural worlds had few organic relationships. Agriculture tended more towards self-sufficiency than towards the production of cash crops. The economic activity of the cities revolved around the trading of staples, in the production of which the rural populations were marginally involved. But especially, from the point of view of our current problem, the ethnic composition of the urban population was not at all comparable to that of today. For instance, Quebeckers of French origin, who counted for 75.2 per cent of the total population, only represented 50.6 per cent of the combined populations of Montreal and Quebec City.

The 1851 census does not report strictly linguistic data. One must wait for the 1901 census to obtain data on the incidence of bilingualism among the major ethnic groups. By 1901, the cities had increased their share of the total population: the citizens of Montreal and Quebec City now counted for close to a quarter of the total population. The ethnic composition of these urban populations had been modified; persons of French origin, although still under-represented, had increased their proportion of the total. Yet, the ascendancy of the English language was very strong among these urban dwellers of French origin; almost half, 46.4 per cent are recorded as bilingual in the 1901 census. As far as they are concerned, one can speak of mass bilingualism. But, more important, the under-urbanization of the French and the linguistic adaptability of those French who were urbanized combined to create a situation in which there was a minority of French unilinguals in urban Quebec, 35.4 per cent of the total urban population. These French unilinguals were mostly to be found in the inactive population of children, women, and retired persons. Thus, at the beginning of this century, urban Quebec could and probably did, operate in English in essential activities.

Whatever became of the mass bilingualism that was a trait of the urban dwellers of French origin at the beginning of this century? The last column of Table I shows that the incidence of bilingualism remained stable and even increased a little from 1901 to the beginning of the thirties, and then began to decrease with remarkable speed and regularity. This increase in French unilingualism, combined with an ongoing increase in the proportion of urban residents of French origin, led to the recent emergence of an actual majority of French unilinguals in urban Quebec.

As is perhaps too often the case, to use only the data on ethnic origin or on mother tongue to assess the linguistic status of a group may well have prevented the making of some crucial observations. Thus, far from resulting, as one could have expected, in an increase or at least a maintenance of the incidence of bilingualism among persons of French origin, the urbanization of the last generation has been accompanied by an unexpected decrease in bilingualism and, undoubtedly, by a profound, if subterranean and obscure, transformation in the balance between Quebec's major linguistic groups. The urban Quebec of the seventies is "français" to a degree unimaginable in the first three decades of this century, an era during which many of the images that still haunt the nationalist mind were born.

This transformation—and this is a basic point—is far more a result of changes that have taken place in the *behaviour* of the population than in the *composition* of that population. To put it differently, urban Quebec is now more French than it used to be, not because it contains a larger proportion of persons of French origin but because these persons, for reasons yet to be explored, are less likely to learn English than their parents and grandparents were.

This is not obvious upon inspection of Table 1. In fact, Table 1 does suggest, on the contrary, that the increase of French unilingualism is concomitant with a change in the ethnic composition of the population towards an increased proportion of persons

Table 2

Persons of French Origin (FO), of French mother tongue (FMT), and French unilinguals (FU)
Quebec City and Quebec Metropolitan Census Area
1851, 1901-1971*

	I French Origin (FO)	II French Mother Tongue (FMT)	III French Unilinguals (FU)	IV Total Population	V FO as % of Total Population	VI FU as % of Total Population	VII FU as % of FO
1851	24,506			42,052	58.2		
1901	57,016		34,873	68,840	82.8	50.6	61.1
1911	58,080			78,710	86.4		
1921	85,350		55,190	95,193	88.6	57.9	64.6
1931	119.292		78,832	130,594	91.5	60.3	66.0
1941	138,923	140,791	102,336	150,757	92.1	67.8	73.6
1951	259,467	262,284	198,671	274,827	94.4	72.2	76.5
1961	336,832	341,197	265,227	357,368	84.2	74.1	78.7
1971	448,395	458,435	358,075	480,500	93.3	74.5	79.8

* Beginning in 1951, data pertain to the Quebec metropolitan census area. The same trends holds for Quebec City proper.

Table 3

Persons of French origin (FO), of French mother tongue (FMT), and French unilinguals (FO)*
Montreal 1851, 1901-1971

	I French Origin (FO)	II French Mother Tongue (FMT)	III French Unilinguals (FU)	IV Total Population	V FO as % of Total Population	VI FU as % of Total Population	VII FU as % of FO
1851	26,020			57,715	45.0		
1901	203,228		104,777	325,175	62.4	32.2	51.5
1911	291,231			471,168	61.8		
1921	399,677		197,719	643,507	62.1	30.7	49.4
1931	546,340		254,899	879,322	62.1	28.9	46.6
1941	713,522	720,963	383,806	1,139,921	62.5	33.6	53.7
1951	900,825	905,948	501,649	1,395,400	64.5	35.9	55.6
1961	1,353,480	1,366,357	826,333	2,019,509	67.0	40.9	60.4
1971	1,762,690	2,819,640	1,163,330	2,743,235	64.2	42.4	65.9

* For 1901 and 1911, Hochelaga, Maisonneuve, Montreal Sainte-Anne, Saint-Antoine, Saint-Jacques, Saint-Laurent and Sainte-Marie; for 1921 and 1931, cities of Montreal and Verdun; beginning in 1941, Montreal metropolitan census area. The same trends hold for the city and the island of Montreal.

of French origin. But a comparison of Tables 2 and 3 dispels this impression. Thus if for the city and then the census metropolitan area of Quebec both curves (Columns V and VII) run roughly parallel, such is not the case in Montreal where French unilingualism increases while the ethnic composition of the population remains stable, at least insofar as the proportion of persons of French origin is concerned.

What factors, then explain the decrease of bilingualism among the francophones? One might think that this is the result of the decrease of the pressures towards bilingualism exerted on the labour market. The growth of an employment sector in which management and ownership are French and the upward drift of the hierarchical level at which English becomes necessary in the sector of the economy that is controlled by anglophones are two well-known trends that would tend to decrease the demand for bilingualism. But, well-known as they are, these trends are poorly measured and the only hard data I could come across flatly contradict the impression just stated.

Data first produced by Lieberson for the 1939-1964 period[6] and updated to 1971 by the research staff of the Gendron Commission[7] indicate, on the contrary, that bilingualism is fast becoming a pre-requisite to employment on the Montreal labour market. Thus, the proportion of job offers requiring from applicants the knowledge of both official languages was, according to *La Presse*: 13 per cent in 1939, 25 per cent in 1964 and 59 per cent in 1971. The requirements for bilingualism according to the *Montreal Star* were 15 per cent in 1939, 19 per cent in 1964, and 54 per cent in 1971.

Should this trend toward the generalization of bilingualism as a prerequisite for employment be as powerful as these data suggest, the current wave of linguistic agitation could be seen as proceeding from rapid and opposite evolution in the supply and demand of bilinguals. For, as I have shown, there is a very real decrease in the supply of bilinguals. This sheds some unusual light on the nature and intensity of linguistic tensions now experienced in Quebec, but contributes little to the explanation of the decrease of bilingualism among the francophones. Nor does it explain the apparent and puzzling absence of links between the supply and demand of bilinguals.

We may advance two hypotheses about this phenomenon. The first pertains to education. The autonomy of the school system and of the economic system, their traditional, mutual impermeability, which is denounced by businessmen throughout the Western World and re-inforced in Quebec by what has historically been the ethnic division of labour in that province, may contribute to an explanation of the seemingly absurd absence of links between the supply of and demand for bilinguals. We may formulate the hypothesis that the spread of formal education and the lengthening of the period of school attendance have, paradoxically, favoured the increase of unilingualism in Quebec.

In a school system like that of Quebec growing cohorts of individuals will, for longer and longer periods, be more firmly oriented toward the language of the school in a linguistically homogeneous environment. As a result, the average age at which the first real-life contact with a second language will take place will tend to be postponed. When this contact takes place the structures of the mother tongue and, more important, the communication habits associated with it, will be more firmly anchored than was the case among previous less formally educated generations. That bilingualism should be a less frequent result of this contact should not come as a surprise.

But this is not all. Someone once said of the linguistic homogenization of the United States that it resulted as much from the movie house as from the classroom. The learning of a second language is not exclusively, nor perhaps even mostly, a school-related phenomenon. A historical study of the publics or clienteles and of the control of newspapers, theatres, cinemas and later of radio and television stations, especially in the Montreal area, would most likely yield interesting results. Such a study would likely show a decline in the anglophone control over the means of diffusion of popular or mass culture. For instance, industry sources[8] listed less than 10 per cent of all Quebec cinemas as showing films exclusively in French in 1949. By 1970, this proportion had risen to 60 per cent. In Montreal, less than 6 per cent of the cinemas showed films exclusively in the French language in 1950, but in 1970 36 per cent did. Indeed, given the elitist orientation of French-Canadian producers of culture and the clerical influence in matters of cultural diffusion in the late nineteenth and early twentieth centuries, it is conceivable that for the first few generations of francophone urban dwellers mass culture available in their language was totally without interest when compared to what was available, generally more cheaply, from anglophone sources and in the English language. If one thinks of the Quebec linguistic situation as diglossic, one should remember that the language of sin is very attractive.

One would, of course, have to test these hypotheses, or formulate alternative or supplementary ones. This obviously cannot be done here. I will simply say that the key to the solution of that problem is likely to be found in events not of the sixties but of the thirties, when the trend to the increase of unilingualism among francophones started. I might add, on a different level, that at the root of current linguistic conflict in Quebec lies not only the fact that francophones are a threatened majority but also that they form, at long last, an emergent one.

Notes

1. Henripin, Jacques, "Quebec and the Demographic Dilemma of French Canadian Society" in Dale C. Thomson, ed., *Quebec: Society and Politics*. Toronto: McClelland and Stewart, 1973, 155-166.

2. Joy, Richard J., *Languages in Conflict.* Toronto: McClelland and Stewart, 1972.

3. Lieberson, Stanley, *Language and Ethnic Relations in Canada.* New York: Wiley, 1970.

4. Maheu, Robert, *Les francophones du Canada: 1941-1991.* Ottawa: Parti-Pris, 1970.

5. On this point, see especially, Deutsch, Karl W., *Nationalism and Social Communication.* Cambridge: The M.I.T. Press, 2nd ed., 1966, Chapters 5 and 6.

6. Lieberson, Stanley, *op. cit.*, 138-175.

7. Laporte, Pierre E., *L'usage des langues dans la vie économique au Québec: situation actuelle et possibilités de changement.* Québec: Editeur officiel du Québec, 1974, 91.

8. See Hye Bossin, ed., *Year Book of the Canadian Motion Picture Industry*, Toronto: Film Publications of Canada, 1951; and E. Hocura, ed., *1970-71 Year Book Canadian Entertainment Industry*, Toronto: Film Publications of Canada, 1971.

25

A Good Blanket Has Four Corners: A Comparison of Aboriginal Administration in Canada and the United States*

Don Whiteside (sin a paw)

There are signs that a new Indian era has been born in North America. For example, while most people in 1972 were enjoying their Thanksgiving dinners aboriginals across the United States were busily protesting. One group assaulted the Mayflower II and burned its Union Jack on Plymouth Rock.[1] This flurry of activity took place on the heels of the occupation and looting of the headquarters of the Bureau of Indian Affairs in Washington.[2] Then there was the armed occupation of Wounded Knee in 1973.

Growing militancy among aboriginal people in the United States is evident in other acts of resistance. Alcatraz was occupied for nineteen months, military bases in various states were occupied for shorter periods of time, as were the sacred grounds in the Black Hills of South Dakota.[3] Aboriginals "eliminated" Hogansburg, N.Y., and marched 1,000 strong in Gordon, Nebraska, to protest the lack of an inquest into the death of one of our people. Repeatedly, aboriginals have invaded anthropologists' laboratories to demand that the bones of our ancestors be reburied.[4]

Signs of this new awakening are also present in Canada. There was the sit-in at Lac La Biche, the dispute over control of the Blue Quills elementary school, and protest marches in Kenora, Winnipeg, and Edmonton.[5] Further, there was the six-month sit-in over conditions at Cold Lake, Alberta, the burning of an all-white school in Restigouche, Quebec, and other acts of resistance such as demands for justice at Loon Island, Cornwall, Sudbury, The Pas, Brandon, and in the Fred Quilt case at William's Lake, B.C.[6] There was also the vigorous protest a few years ago over the colonial government's proposal to officially terminate aboriginal rights and treaties, as well as the many legal disputes over hunting and fishing rights and northern development.[7] In spite of all these acts of overt resistance in Canada, however, it is clear that aboriginals in the United States have tended to be more forceful in their protest.

There are a number of possible explanations for the variation in the level of protest. One might argue that in Canada the aboriginal population is smaller. This could be further compounded by the fact that in Canada the aboriginal population is split into two factions of almost equal size due to federal government regulations which define part of the population as "Status-Indians" and part as "Métis" or "non-status-Indians". Another possible explanation might be that in Canada there are very

*This paper by Dr. Whiteside, Research Officer of the National Indian Brotherhood, Ottawa, was revised for this volume. It is based on an address to the annual meeting of the Western Association of Sociology and Anthropology in Calgary, December, 1972.

few large concentrations of aboriginals; they tend to be scattered into small isolated groupings, whereas in the United States there are a fair number of heavily populated reservations. It is also possible that because two of the three large concentrations of aboriginals in Canada, the Six Nations and the Sioux, were refugees from the United States, they may have had a mediating influence on the level of protest.

A more common explanation for the difference in the level of protest by aboriginals in the United States and Canada is the popular belief that the treatment accorded our people in Canada was, and is, more humane.[8] This popular belief is based upon two major assumptions. First, there is the assumption that while Indian Wars raged throughout the history of the United States there were few such wars in Canada. The second assumption is that unlike the United States, treaties were strictly adhered to in Canada; thus, legitimate dissatisfaction was reduced to a minimum. In addition to questioning these two assumptions, there are a number of disquieting facts that should force us to re-examine the validity of this popular belief.

One disquieting fact is that in Canada there is little demand for social justice for our people. The Europeans are not as concerned about our state of deprivation as are Europeans in the United States.

Another fact which is disquieting is that in Canada there are few aboriginal voluntary associations which exist without explicit governmental approval. For example, among the aboriginal population in the United States of approximately 792,000 in 1970, it is estimated that there were over 3,000 voluntary associations, most of which are not funded by any level of government. In Canada, on the other hand, among the approximately 550,000 aboriginals in 1972, there were only about 150 voluntary associations, almost all of which received direct funding from various levels of government.

It is my contention that these facts indicate that the European government in Canada has been, and is, more repressive than the European government in the United States. The purpose of this paper will be to explore the two patterns of social control.[9]

It is important to briefly note some of the more striking similarities in the basic aboriginal policies followed by both Canada and the United States. First, in both countries the major original colonial power was Great Britain. The policy of this power toward aboriginal people in North America remained unchanged after the United States gained its independence in 1783 and after Canada attained Confederation status in 1867. Second, while the European colonial governments of both countries continually expressed a strong desire for peaceful relations with the various Indian Nations, this peace was always enforced on European terms. Third, in both countries the European invaders exhibited an insatiable hunger for Indian land, a hunger which is still not satisfied. Fourth, the European governments of both countries made a host of treaties with the various Indian Nations and in both countries the spirit of the treaties was violated. It should also be noted that these treaties were far from "just" and in some of the early treaties of "Peace and Friendship" the European powers demanded aboriginal hostages as security.[10] Fifth, since the European governments of both countries viewed the Indian Nations as remnants of a passing historical period the only acceptable alternatives were physical or cultural genocide. It is a matter of public record that physical genocide was practised in both countries. In Canada and the United States our people were massacred, monetary rewards were offered for Indian scalps, and smallpox was deliberately introduced in order to eliminate the "problem".[11] While the United States government tended to pursue openly a policy of physical genocide, both countries for many years neglected the medical needs of our people to a degree which almost insured the death of the Indian Nations. It is also a matter of public record that both countries actively pursued the goal of cultural genocide. Native religions were outlawed; children were kidnapped from their homes and sent to boarding schools where our culture was forceably discouraged; and European forms of religion, politics and education were imposed. Finally, in both countries there is no difference in the low social and low economic standing of the aboriginal people, although the educational level of our people in the United States is slightly higher than in Canada.

From these comments on the differences and similarities between the situation of aboriginals in Canada and the United States, it may be seen that I believe that any explanation for the differential behaviour between aboriginals on either side of the border is more likely to be found in the manner in which the policies were administered rather than in differences in basic policies. For example, we have noted that it was the policy of both governments to acquire Indian land. In the United States this tended to be accomplished in the following manner. First, Europeans intruded upon Indian land. Inevitably these intrusions led to retaliation by the aboriginals. Then colonial military forces entered the disputed area to establish "peace" and a new treaty was "negotiated" which gave the Europeans the land and relocated the aboriginals to more remote areas of the country. Then the process would be repeated. In Canada, the European government paid their Indian Commissioner 10 per cent of the monies collected from the sale of Indian lands.[12] In order not to starve, the commissioners had to be very skilful land agents.

It is important to note from this example that the end result was the same: the land base of the Indian Nations continued to shrink. Most people would argue that it is more humane to buy land (even at an unreasonably low price) than to kill off the owners. But the issue was not that clear. In both cases the land was stolen, in one instance by force, in the other by fraud and guile. In point of fact, it may be psychologically worse to discover that you have lost your brithright by fraud than if superior military strength forced the land from your hands. In the latter case the enemy is clearly defined, as are the power tactics needed to win the struggle. In Canada, while the same bitterness and anger exists, the enemy is blurred by the fact that the aboriginals were smothered by guile and it is not clear as to the type of tactics needed to insure success.[13]

The most significant variation I have observed between Canada and the United States in regards to aboriginal affairs is in the amount of control exercised by the administrators. While both countries tried to exercise complete control over their "wards", Canadian control was more comprehensive and in many ways more successful.

One of the most important reasons for the success of the control system in Canada was the stability of the Europeans who were most intimately connected with aboriginal affairs, that is, the fur traders, the churchmen, the federal police (NWMP), and the Indian agents. It is my hypothesis that these four classes of Europeans remained in positions of authority and power for longer periods of time in Canada than did their counterparts in the United States. These four classes of Europeans encompassed the economic, religious, political, social, and legal aspects of the aboriginal world and formed a comprehensive system of control, a four-cornered "blanket" which covered the Indian Nations.

Rather than present a test of this hypothesis the remainder of this paper will be devoted to a general discussion of it. It is public knowledge that the fur traders and their trading posts lasted for a longer period in Canada than in the United States. While trading posts such as those of the Hudson's Bay Company are now unkown in the United States, they are still important in the economic life of many northern Canadian communities. Further, from what little information is available on the relations between these traders and the European government, it is clear that they were part of the colonial power structure. One must remember that the Hudson's Bay Company was chartered by Great Britain and the traders were licensed by the colonial government. Thus, it is not unreasonable to suppose that they provided the colonial government with widely dispersed bases of power which were used to control and unify the economic life of the widely scattered Indian Nations.[14]

Various denominations of Christian churchmen followed the fur traders. In Canada, missions were quickly established throughout the Indian Nations. Many of these churchmen, especially those of the Roman Catholic faith, saw their tasks as being life-long and they learned the language and the ways of our people and became crucial links between our people and the European government. In the United States, on the other hand, most churchmen apparently did not see their Indian missions as vineyards which required their personal devotion for life. Another difference is that in Canada the colonial government and the various churches saw their interests as being compatible, and in most areas the church became an extension of the government. This pattern was especially true in the field of education where the colonial government transferred this vital function to the various churches.

It is a matter of public record that churchmen on both sides of the border did all in their power to destroy the aboriginal religion and our way of life. It seems logical that where the churchmen were stable over time and acted with the authority of the European government, as its agent, a greater degree of control over aboriginal culture and life-style would result.[15] It is significant that the Ghost Dance which spread amongst aboriginals in the United States did not make deep inroads among the aboriginals in Canada. This implies that in Canada the churchmen had greater influence and control over the aboriginal people than did their counterparts in the United States.

The third point of our four-cornered "blanket" is the North West Mounted Police (now the Royal Canadian Mounted Police). Their vital role in the settlement of western Canada has been documented in other sources. We can note, however, that there was no comparable para-military force in the United States. Control over aboriginal affairs in the United States was left in the hands of Indian agents and the army. Thus, when an agent had more trouble than he could handle his only recourse was to define the problem as an "uprising" and call in the army. This constant threat of "overkill" was deeply resented and often insured armed conflict. In Canada, on the other hand, the agent could call upon the Mounted Police and the situation could be controlled without having to be defined as an "uprising", As a result, most disputes in Canada were easily defused. It is also significant that for many years the major role of the North West Mounted Police was the supervision of the aboriginal population and in many instances they acted as Indian agents in distributing supplies and dealing with land disputes. Because of this role they were able to develop cooperative working relations with the traders, the churchmen, and the Indian agents to manipulate the aboriginal people to conform to the wishes of the federal government.[16]

While the preceeding classes of Europeans contributed their fair share to the suppression of the aboriginal people, the Indian agent and his superiors were the crucial link in the fourth corner of the "blanket" which was used to cover the Indian Nations. Few studies exist in Canada on the actions of Indian agents and their superiors. In the United States there are many studies about these people. The reason for this difference is understandable. In the United States the Indian agent was a political appointee, which implied that the agent would receive additional income from the illegal sale of supplies that should have gone to the aboriginal people. The activities of agents made good newspaper copy in the never-ending public political dogfights that occur in the United States. Rarely do we hear of corrupt agents in Canada, although undoubtedly there were some. The basic reason for this is that in Canada the agent was usually not a political appointee in the usual sense of the term but more akin to a civil servant. He had a career in the federal service. In addition, the opportunities for widespread corruption were reduced in Canada by the federal government's requirements for fastidious records. Also, because of the career orientation of the agents in Canada they acted to insure that every facet of Indian life was under control. Unforseen events might cause the abrupt end of a career. In the United States, on the other hand, the agent had to make the most of a temporary appointment and tended to avoid too much involvement with the aboriginals so long as relative tranquility was preserved.

Of particular interest to students of social control are the different strategies the agents and their superiors used to insure subordination of the aboriginal people in Canada. For many years the colonial powers maintained that they wanted the aboriginal people to become sedentary and take up farming. Yet in 1896 when aboriginals requested the federal government to provide machinery to enhance their agricultural capability it was refused on the grounds that with machinery the aboriginals would be able to compete favourably with European farmers.[17] Although the equipment was refused and the government formally abandoned the objective of making aboriginals efficient farmers, the Europeans continued to give lip service to this objective and criticized the aboriginals for failing to become farmers.

Another example of a conflict between stated objectives and racist actions concerns the formation of voluntary associations. After the submission of the Indian Nations in Canada our people were dispersed to widely scattered reserves in order to insure the white mans' peace. The dispersal was accompanied by concerted attempts to destroy all forms of tribal government and organization. Further, the colonial government acted to insure that meaningful contact between the isolated reserves would not occur. No Indian was permitted to leave the reserve without a signed pass from the agent which stated the duration and purpose of the trip. Without this pass, which was used into the 1940s, Indians were subject to arrest by the Royal Canadian Mounted Police.[18] In addition to direct control of the movements of aboriginal people, band funds could not be used for trips to other reserves for the purpose of organizing to deal more effectively with the federal government.[19] Thus, for well over seventy years the various reserves were forceably kept apart while the European government continued to give lip service to the objective of self-determination. The role of the RCMP in this effort is particulary instructive.[20]

In short, the aboriginals in Canada lived under the ever watchful eyes of the Indian agent and his superiors. Even marriages, in some cases, were subject to the approval of the district office.[21] The Indian agent not only had almost absolute control over the lives of his "wards"; he fully exercised his power. With the aid of the traders, the churchmen, and the Mounted Police, the "blanket" covered the Indian Nations and there were few, if any, avenues of redress. In point of fact, after the churches sold their services to the European government there were no non-governmental personnel in close contact with the aboriginal people.

In the face of so much power to suppress our people in Canada it is easy to understand why aboriginals in the United States tend to be more aggressive. In the United States the four corners of the "blanket" either never existed or were never interwoven well enough to be used effectively. The blanket never protected us, nor did it smother our desire for freedom. The traders, the churchmen, the military, and the Indian agents were but shadows that quickly passed across our faces, the sun reappearing once again to warm the desire for freedom. Now in Canada, however, the strands of webbing which connected the four corners of this "blanket" and blocked out the sunlight are being systematically shattered by a variety of forces, many of which are beyond our control. With the sunlight to warm the desire for freedom, institutionalized racism is coming to an end and a new era for the Indian Nations is being born.

Notes

1. "Union Jack Burned at Plymouth Rock," *Vancouver Sun,* November 24, 1972.

2. "U.S. Indians End Occupation after Seizing Documents," *The Globe and Mail*, November 9, 1972.

3. "Indians Lose Hold on Alcatraz", *Ottawa Citizen*, June 14, 1971; Jack D. Forbes, "Alcatraz: What its Seizure Means to Indian People". *The Warpath* (San Francisco), 1970, 2:5; Walter M. Morrison, "Old Coast Guard Station Occupied by Militants", *Milwaukee Journal*, August 14, 1971; "35 Indians Evicted from Naval Station: Sioux Treaty Cited", *The New York Times*, May 22, 1971; "60 Indians Occupy Mt. Rushmore Peak to Push Demands", *The New York Times*, June 7, 1971.

4. "Indians 'Eliminate' Hogansburg", *Ottawa Citizen*, May 17, 1971; "1000 Indians Invade Town in Nebraska", *The Globe and Mail*, March 8, 1972; Roger Billottee, "Prof. and Students Arrested: American Indians Protest Anthro Studies", *Akwesasne Notes* (Roosevelt, N.Y.), Autumn, 1971.

5. Marilyn I. Assheton-Smith and W. Bruce Handley, *The Lac La Biche Native Sit-In*, Lac La Biche, Alberta, New Start, October 1970, 12 pp.; "Native Sit-In at New Start", *The Native People* (Edmonton) January, 1970, 2:1-2; "Blue Quills Taken Over by Indians", *The Native People* (Edmonton August, 1970, 3:2; "Indians March for Freedom", *The New Nation* (Winnipeg) October, 1972, 1(5):1; Fred Favel, "Wabasca . . . A Lesson in Politics", Edmonton, unpublished manuscript, October, 1967. "Indians, Métis Stage March", *Edmonton Journal*, July 30, 1966; "Kenora Indians Stage Protest", *The Winnipeg Tribune*, November 23, 1965.

6. "Chretien Signs Cold Lake Agreement: Alberta Indians Get Their School, End Six-month Sit-in", *The Globe and Mail* April 22, 1972; "All-White School Burned", (Restigouche, Quebec), *Montreal Star*, September 30, 1971; "Submissions to Kenora Town Council, re: Indian-non-Indian Relations", Kenora, unpublished manuscript, November 22, 1965; "Aid Kenora Indians' Brief", *Canadian Labour*, January, 1966; "Indians-Métis Demand C.F.I. Employment Rights", *The Pas Herald*, September 30, 1970; Michael Posluns, "Conflict at Akwesasne", *Canadian Welfare*, March-April 1971; "Press Release: re: Judge Collins of Sudbury, Ontario", Ottawa, Native Council of Canada, April 21, 1972; *The Case of Fred Quilt*, William's Lake, British Columbia, The Fred Quilt Committee, 1972; "Indian Group Quits Brandon Inquiry", *Winnipeg Tribune*, February 22, 1972.

7. Harold Cardinal, *The Unjust Society: The Tragedy of Canada's Indians,* (Edmonton: M.G. Hurtig, 1969); "Indian Leaders Attack Government Over New Indian Policy", Indian-Eskimo Association of Canada Bulletin, July, 1969; *Citizens Plus*, A Presentation by the Indian Chiefs of Alberta to the Government of Canada, June, 1970; *A Declaration of Indian Rights: the B.C. Indian Position Paper,* The Union of British Columbia Indian Chiefs, November, 1970; *Wahbung: Our Tomorrows*, The

Indian Tribes of Manitoba, October, 1971; *The Association of Iroquois and Allied Indians*, Position Paper, November, 1971; Boyce Richardson, *James Bay: The Plot to Drown the North Woods* (Clarke-Irwin, 1972); Boyce Richardson, "Angry Crees Burn Hundreds of James Bay Ecology Reports: Protest Against Hydro Project Mounting", *The Montreal Star*, February 24, 1972.

8. For example, see "Canada's Treatment of Indians", *Canadian Gazette*, December 22, 1890; "Our Indian Wards", *Toronto Mail*, April 20, 1890; and "An Object Lesson for the States, Canadian Redskins To Go To World's Fair", *The Globe*, June, 1893.

9. One must remember, however, that aboriginals in the United States also have a greater degree of freedom from direct governmental control in their internal affairs. For example, the Indian Nations in the United States are considered to be "domestic dependent nations" (*Cherokee Nation v. Georgia*, 1831) and, as a result, the tribal governments were left intact but with much reduced powers. In Canada, on the other hand, tribal government was all but rendered useless by systematic undermining.

10. "And we do in like manner further promise and engage that for the more effectual securing of the due performance of this Treaty and every part thereof, a certain number, which shall not be less than three from each of the aforesaid Tribes, shall from and after the ratification hereof constantly reside in Fort Frederick at St. Johns or at such other place or places within the Province, as shall be appointed for that purpose by His Majesty's Governors of the said Province, as Hostages, which Hostages shall be exchanged for a like number of others of the said Tribe when requested." *Treaty of Peace and Friendship concluded with the delegates of the St. Johns and Passamaquody Tribes of Indians at Halifax*, February, 1760.

11. See Sir Jeffery Amherst correspondence with Colonel Bourquet: "Might we not try to spread smallpox among the Indians? We must in this occasion make use of every devise to reduce them" he wrote. "I will try," answered Bourquet, "to introduce smallpox by means of blankets, which we will cause to fall into their hands." "You will do well," he wrote again, "to try to spread smallpox by means of blankets, and by every other means which might help to exterminate that abominable race." Emile Lauvriere, *La Tragedie d'un Peuple*, Paris, 1922, quoted in Dudley J. LeBlanc, *Acadian Miracle* (LaFayette, La.: Evangeline Press, 1966) 275. See also Karl H. Schlesier, *The Indians in the United States: An Essay on Cultural Resistance*, Wichita, Kansas, Wichita State University Bulletin, November, 1969.

On scalping: "We do hereby promise a reward of thirty pounds ($150) for every male Indian prisoner above the age of sixteen years brought in alive or for the scalp for each male Indian: twenth-five pounds for every Indian woman or child brought in alive." *Proclamation*, May 14, 1756.

On massacres see James P. Howley, *The Beothuks or Red Indians, the Aboriginal Inhabitants of Newfoundland* (Cambridge University Press, 1915); and Frank G. Speck, *Beothuk and Micmac,* Museum of the American Indian, Heye Foundation, 1922.

12. "I have the honor to inform you that, by an Order in Council on the 18th Inst., you have been appointed, under the provisions of Act 31 Victoria, Capter 21, Agent for Indian Affairs in the Province of Nova Scotia with an allowance of ten per cent on all money collected by you in that capacity." Letter, Hector L. Langevin, Secretary of State, to Samuel P. Fairbanks, Halifax, N.S., September 28, 1868.

13. For a brief analysis of how this affects such basic problems as membership see my paper, "The Lavell Case: Another Indian Tragedy or an Opportunity for the Possible Return to the Traditional Judicial Authority of the Tribal and Band Councils?", *Indian Voice* (Vancouver), February, 1973, and *The Forgotten People* (Ottawa), January, 1973.

14. "There are other interesting byproducts of the study which may be indicated briefly. Canada has had no serious problems with her native peoples since the fur trade depended primarily on these races. In the United States no point of contact of such magnitude was at hand and troubles with the Indians were a result." Harold A. Innis, *The Fur Trade in Canada*, 1930 (University of Toronto Press, 1970), 392. See also Walter M. Hlady, "Power Structure in a Métis Community", unpublished manuscript, Centre for Community Studies, University of Saskatchewan, April, 1960.

15. See, for example, Robert J.W. Garthson, *The imperial process of attempted de-Indianization in British-Upper Canada to the year 1860: Protestant missionary-government cooperation in the destruction of the material bases of Indian culture, and Indian response*, P.H.M. dissertation, University of Waterloo, 1970; and Jacqueline J. Kennedy, *Qu'Appelle Industrial School: "Rites" for the Indians of the Old North West*, master's thesis, Carleton University, 1970.

16. The amount of cooperation between the Mounted Police and the colonial government can be seen in the following reference to the strategy of Major Walsh of the North West Mounted Police in dealing with the threat of Sitting Bull to attack U.S. soldiers camped south of the border. "It was still possible that the old chief could rally enough hotheads about him to make good his threat even though Walsh had for some time been undermining his influence. Now he consulted with level-headed Spotted Eagle on matters that only a short while ago would have been settled by Sitting Bull. Only in this way, Walsh felt, could the warlike intentions of the Sioux be crushed. It was far better to have the Sioux divided, rather than under the influence of such a chief as Sitting Bull who still held power, particularly with his own large band of Hunkpapas." Iris Allen, *White Sioux: Major Walsh of the Mounted Police* (Grays Publishing Co., 1969), 150. See also Jerry T. Gambill, "Sitting Bull: Canada's Indian Hero", Ottawa, unpublished manuscript, May 26, 1968.

17. Letter dated August 29, 1896, Deputy Minister Reed to Mr. Forget, Indian Commission, Indian Affairs, Ottawa.

18. For a copy of this type of pass see *The Native People* (Edmonton), January, 1972.

19. See "An Act to Amend the Indian Act", assented to March 31, 1927, 15 George V, Chapter 23, Section 6.

20. See, for example, Jerry T. Gambill, "The Thunder Water Movement: An Anthropological Examination of the Indian Affairs Branch Reaction to Stress", *Akwesasne Notes* (Roosevelt, N.Y.), Autumn, 1971.

21. "Marriage between pupils and outsiders who have not had the advantage of training at one of our Institutions should receive no encouragement, and in no case

should a marriage be allowed to take place without consent being first obtained from this office." Circular, Red Group 10, Volume 1135, Office of the Commissioner of Indian Affairs, Regina, January 14, 1895.

Part III Section C

EDUCATION AND SOCIALIZATION

26

Teachers and Students: A Preliminary Analysis of Collective Reciprocity*

Alan J.C. King and Reginald A. Ripton

Over the past few years many educational innovations have been introduced into Canadian secondary schools. Some of these have been validated as educationally sound, in a semi-clinical way, but very few of them have had a lasting impact on the secondary schools. Most of the current innovations have been conceived in the rhetoric of an ideology directed toward the individualization and liberalization of the educational experience. "Creativity", "self-actualization", "student-centred", "student responsibility", are representative of the kinds of terms that have been used as testimonials to the worth of proposed innovations.

This paper is an outgrowth from an evaluation study of Ontario secondary schools undergoing major educational innovation. The preliminary findings indicated that, in spite of the large-scale organizational changes, there appeared to be very little change in the nature of the student-teacher relationship. It was felt that an explanation for the rejection of many innovations might lie in the basic character of this relationship.

A Tentative Model

The model which follows has been designed to explain the behaviour and underlying motivations of teachers and students in secondary school classrooms. It is a model based on a system of complex elements or components directly or indirectly related i a causal network, such that each component has some stability over a particular peric of time. Patched-up or modified versions of the bureaucratic model, as well as traditional role theory, have been rejected in place of a model that offers an explanation for social exchange in terms of relations among groups.[1] Rather than a consensus definition of teacher and student roles that has long-term stability, the character of t student-teacher relationship is seen as dynamic, producing tacit contracts as the prod ucts of continued collective negotiations. The ultimate aim of such collective recipro cities is the maximizing of both short-term and long-term rewards for students and

*Abridged from *The Canadian Review of Sociology and Anthropology*, 7:1 (1970), 35-48. By permission of the authors and the Canadian Sociology and Anthropology Association.

teachers. If educationally sound innovations are rejected, then they must not be congruent with rewards sought by students and teachers. This does not mean that need-priorities of students and teachers, and objectives currently maintained by educators are mutually exclusive, nor does it mean that individual social transactions, based on the exchange of attitudes, sentiments, and activities,[2] do not take place. But, the model is based on the premise that relationships exist between students and teachers that are collectively reinforced, and these collective reciprocities are characterized by transactions and implicit contracts that mitigate against the meeting of certain educational objectives. A collective reciprocity is seen as the product of the interaction, mediation, and resolution of a set of forces which affect teachers and students in their interaction in secondary school classrooms.

In presenting the model, attention is first directed at the forces influencing teachers and students which determine the general content of the interaction process, in order to test the viability of the forces as operational constructs. The character of the major reciprocity is described and its role as a dependent variable is briefly considered in terms of the relative influence of the forces.

Teachers

Teachers can be seen as operating in the classroom under the pressures of four major influences. Firstly, under the supervision of department heads, principals, Boards of Education, and the Departments of Education, teachers are the vested agents of legal authority. Within carefully prescribed limitations, they have the responsibility of defining those activities which take place in their classrooms. Teachers, in responding to this function, do so within a framework of expectations and regulations reinforced by administrators and which include: (1) covering the required curricula; (2) maintaining a quiet, industrious-appearing classroom; and (3) joining with other staff and administrators to represent a unified policy on curriculum and discipline.

Secondly, teachers maintain an ideology of teaching. This ideology is a product of their socio-economic background and their educational and social experiences. It usually features many of the egalitarian tenets of North American society transcribed into educational objectives that stress individualization, creativity, independence, and self-actualization.

Thirdly, teachers maintain some form of career orientation, an orientation that is rarely defined in specific terms, but one which rejects a long-term career perspective as "just a teacher". For male teachers in particular, this orientation virtually prohibits a non-mobile conception of career. The typical male career perspective is directed toward educational administration or consultation, and predisposes the aspirant to the control "ethos" characterized and rewarded by the efficiency-conscious educational bureaucracy.[3] For female teachers, it often includes a realization of the goals of marriage and motherhood. Since classroom teaching in itself is not usually defined as a career, teachers anticipate, in general terms, the fulfilment of some other role.

The fourth influence on teachers is effected through their desire for autonomy in their teaching. Most professionals seek a position where they can control the definition of their work. Within certain limitations, teachers are able to meet an entire array of their own personal needs in the confines of their own classrooms. They can shape their work experience in such a way that they meet needs for power, affection, etc.

Students

The circumstances surrounding the student in secondary school can be seen in terms of the responses to two basic questions: (1) Why should I stay in school? and (2) To what extent can I control the educational environment? There are four main forces that generate these questions. Firstly, an ethic of personal achievement, derived from the competitive North American milieu, links education to status acquisition. Consequently, educational activities are defined in terms of their importance in assigning status to the participants as an end product and not for the intrinsic value of the educational experience. Education is thus seen by students as being instrumental in obtaining post-school status.[4] Although it is conceded that the peer group plays a fundamental role in supplying the modes of identification so critical to adolescents, the primary differentiation role is played by teachers and school administrators. They are empowered with the legal authority to differentiate among students. By assigning marks differentially, teachers not only allocate status within the school, but also determine who will have access to post-secondary educational institutions. Since the students have virtually no control over the socialization and differentiation processes of the secondary school, they generate their own counter-structure by rewarding forms of behaviour other than those indicative of academic competence or socialized docility. This counter-structure, with its own norms, values, sanctions, and argot allows students to determine their own criteria of status within the school. It is not surprising that this counter-structure can effectively mitigate the influence of the teacher.[5]

Secondly, students are influenced by societal pressure to remain in school. This influence is reinforced, in part, by legal restrictions on age of school-leaving as well as a generalized stigmatization of the school dropout. While this pressure reinforces the instrumental conception of education, it also provides students with a rationalization for their day-to-day attendance.

Thirdly, although students are to some extent prisoners within the social system of the school, they have the power of reacting individually or collectively in various ways to the services provided. In fact, throughout North America we are seeing more and more examples of collective student reaction to real or imagined educational problems. The extent to which the students are willing to react to the learning environment has considerable implication for the way in which this environment is defined by teachers. Successful students can develop high tolerance for subjects which they often feel are irrelevant but which ascribe status to them. Since education is instrumental in allocating status, secondary schools usually take the form of a class system based on the vocational implications of the programs in which students are enrolled. Broadly speaking, there are two main groups of students: the university-bound and the non-university-bound. A degree of stigma is attached to those students who have been effectively blocked off from university by failing grades or program selection. A large proportion of this latter group of students have low tolerance for a system that has defined them as unsuccessful. It is this latter group of students that produces the greater challenge to classroom control for teachers. For these students, education at the secondary school level becomes a "cooling out" process.[6]

And fourthly, students are beginning to react against the apparent dehumanization of educational systems and the contradictions that exist in adult life. This influence is reinforced by college student activism directed at politics, business, and higher education throughout the world. Whereas the students who are being "cooled-out" because status access is being effectively denied tend to react with indifference and lethargy, the students who detect the lack of congruency between educational ideology and educational programs tend to actively engage in criticisms of the educational system. Although at the present time, activism among high school students is not widespread, it is a growing force.

The Climate

In industry, it is usually possible to measure in very specific terms the productivity of the system as well as the efficiency of its human components. However, the widely varying and inconsistent expectations of educational productivity held by teachers, students, parents, post-secondary institutions, and potential employers create a very imprecise atmosphere that provides the operational flexibility for the negotiations to take place between students and teachers. Failure rates have become routinized, but the criteria against which failure in a subject is determined are rarely stated in behavioural terms. School marks as a currency of exchange become an arbitrary combination of achievement and social behaviour and as such are the basic criteria of productivity.

The Reciprocity

Although a number of reciprocal agreements exist between various sub-groups of students and teachers, there is only one that is truly pervasive in its implications. This reciprocity is premised on the reality that formalized status allocation is the primary function of the secondary school and that the often poorly-stated aims of creativity, responsibility, and flexibility are rarely made operational. The cornerston of this reciprocity is the near congruency of teachers' career needs and students' conception of education as an instrumental process. While the other forces we have discussed are present and, under certain conditions, have considerable visibility, priorities in classroom behaviour can be effectively explained on the basis of the primary motivations of career for teachers, and what is equivalent to career for students.

Since students define the educational experience as instrumental, it becomes a fundamental requirement and the classroom in which status is allocated is rationalized and routinized. Students require a clear definition of the expectations held of them by teachers, and the nature of the evaluation procedures associated with this expectation. For teachers to effectively minister to these needs, they must first demonstrate competence in their subject fields. From the point of view of teachers, a classroom environment characterized by quiet, industrious student performance, and a set of failure rates consistent with administrative expectations provides the basis for career mobility. In effect, we have a fortuitous meeting of the needs of administration-oriented teachers and university-bound students.

The ideological goals of creativity, responsibility, citizenship, self-actualization, and the consequent disorganization of the classroom that they imply, are anathema to career considerations. Most creative or individualized learning experiences, while ideologically sound, tend to threaten teacher control and weaken evaluation procedures because students undergo widely different educational experiences, but must be evaluated against similar criteria. However, for a small number of teachers in the forefront of change, innovation can be effectively linked with ideological objectives. Innovative programs can be sustained by the excitement generated among students over a new methodology of curriculum and the extra effort required by a teacher to introduce it. And, of course, for many teachers it can be a stepping-stone to an administrative post. But, teachers in the second wave of change do not have the same support structures to sustain them. They cannot justify the extra work to themselves and for students the novelty effect soon wears off.

The Research Methodology

In this paper, the viability of all aspects of the model is not tested. Attention is focused on three main considerations. Firstly, an attempt is made to determine the validity as operational constructs, of: (a) teachers' career perspectives; (b) a consensual ideology of education; and (c) students' instrumental orientation to education. Secondly, the following postulate derived from the model is tested: teachers maintain an ideology of education that is functionally contradictory to their operational definition of teaching. And thirdly, the basic character of the reciprocal relationship from the perspectives of students and teachers is analysed.

The subjects of the study were 240 teachers on the staffs of three secondary schools in a medium-sized Ontario metropolitan area, 230 students randomly selected from the same three secondary schools, and 187 students enrolled in an Ontario teacher preparation institution. All 240 teachers were surveyed by a 54 item questionnaire and a 40 item attitude instrument. One hundred and ten of the teachers were interviewed, employing a structured interview schedule with provision for probing (30 minutes). The prospective teachers were surveyed by a brief questionnaire.

The Findings

Teachers and the Ideology of Education

As expected, teachers stated that the major purpose of a high school is to provide a liberal education (88 per cent), that the most helpful student experiences are creative in nature (84 per cent) and that the function of the school is to encourage all students to aim at the highest academic goals (65 per cent). Also, 78 per cent of the teachers from the interview sample responded with statements couched in the ideological idiom of creativity, freedom, responsibility, and student-centredness.

The following quotations serve to illustrate this emphasis on liberal ideology: "The major aim of education, to my way of thinking, is to set the person free from his own narrow perspectives." "I suppose to try and teach the children in such a way that they will be perhaps better people for it with broader horizons." "To provide a fertile culture in which they can grow." "Well it is certainly not to learn the facts because the facts are forgotten in the next week. I think one of the biggest things that can happen in high school is when the child becomes more mature."

In order to test the postulate that teachers maintain an operational definition of the act of teaching that is, in part, contradictory to their ideological statements regarding the purpose of education, the teachers from the interview sample were asked, "Who is the good teacher?" Pretesting indicated that teachers respond to this item in a manner that reflects their perceptions of the day-to-day work activities of the effective teacher.

Over 75 per cent of the teachers stated that the good teacher was the one who could transfer information effectively and who knew his subject well. In responding to this item, less than 5 per cent of the teachers employed similar terms to those they employed in describing the purpose of education. The following excerpts are indicative of the kinds of responses: "The teacher who can make the students get information, either from him, or from books, or from anything." "One who really knows his subject and who can get it across." "The teacher who manages to get the students to go away at the end of the year with a few facts in their heads." If the teachers had derived their instructional procedures from their ideological statements, then descriptions of the good teacher would probably have included statements such as the following: "The one who can provide the most creative experiences and who produces responsible behaviour among his students." But statements of this genre were not found.

It appears that teachers do in fact maintain an ideological conception of the purposes of education that is far removed from their operational definition of the act of teaching. Curricula derived from their ideological statements would be substantially different from those assumed in their descriptions of the good teacher.

Teachers and Career

The model assumes that teachers' classroom behaviour is influenced by their career aspirations. To determine whether teachers perceive themselves in some role other than teaching in the future, a sample of 187 secondary school teaching candidates from a college of education were asked, "What do you expect to be doing fifteen years from now?" and teachers in the survey sample were asked, "Thinking realistically, what is the highest administrative level you are likely to achieve?" and "Of how much importance to you is it that you become a school administrator?"

Table 1 indicates that only 14 per cent of male student teachers and 7 per cent of female student teachers perceive themselves as teachers fifteen years after commencing teaching. More than 80 per cent of the male student teachers foresee themselves in an occupational category of higher status than high school teaching. The large "undecided" category of female student teachers is undoubtedly a function of their anticipation of marriage as career realization.

Table 1

Career Expectations of Prospective Secondary School Teachers

	Male (per cent)	Female (per cent)
High school administration	55	3
University teaching	11	5
Research	2	20
Consultation	16	8
Married	—	13
Teaching	14	7
Undecided	2	44
Total	100 (*n*=101)	100 (*n*=86)

Over 80 per cent of the teachers in the three secondary schools indicated that they expected to attain an administrative level higher than their present one. Approximately one-half of the respondents who indicated that it was of no importance to them to become a school administrator (37.7 per cent of the total) were at an age (over 50) when the likelihood of promotion was substantially reduced. It is quite evident that not only practising teachers, but also teachers in training tend to define their educational careers as moving to administrative or consultative roles outside the classroom.

To determine whether teachers perceived significant differences in the personal characteristics required to be a good teacher and those required to get ahead in a career sense, they were asked on the questionnaire, "What two factors are most important in moving up the administrative ladder in education?" and, "What are the two most important characteristics of a good teacher?" Their responses are summarized in Table 2. Whereas the ability to transfer knowledge effectively ranks first among the qualities required of a good teacher, it ranks only fourth when it comes to being promoted. Ability to get along well with colleagues, good personality, and having a sound educational background predominate when it comes to getting ahead.

To exhibit some of the visible characteristics of promotable teachers, it appears necessary that teachers reorder their priorities.

Education as Instrumental

The model postulates that students perceive education as a series of hurdles that must be overcome to reach occupational goals, that is, education is instrumental in allocating status to them.

The data dealing with the students' perceptions of the purpose of education were obtained by interviews which asked, "Why are you in school? " Over 90 per cent of the respondents gave answers indicative of a definition of education as instrumental. The following excerpts are representative of the students' responses: "To get an education. *Why get an education?* You gotta have an education today if you want to be anything." "If I leave school now, I'd have no place to work, except maybe as a delivery boy or something." "Oh, to get a good job, to earn lots of money, buy whatever I want." Education as an intrinsically satisfying experience was suggested only incidentally and by less than 3 per cent of the student respondents.

All students interviewed described the experience in which they made their choice of secondary school program as one which was based almost in its entirety on the conception of education as instrumental.

Characteristics of the Reciprocity

The model presents a view of personal interaction based on the social transactions of collective entities (students and teachers) within the constraints of the social system of the secondary school. The product of this interaction and exchange is a dynamic reciprocity varying in terms of the strengths of the motives of the participants and the influence of the larger system. At this stage of the research, variations in the strengths of the motives and system pressures as they relate to the reciprocity are not considered.

If students view education as an instrumental activity, then they are likely to define the good teacher as one who presents a competitive educational environment characterized by humane control, clearly defined expectations, and impartial evaluation procedures. Data bearing on this postulate were derived from student interview responses to the questions, "What are the qualities of a good teacher?" and "Why do we have rules and regulations in schools?" and subsequent probing.

More than 80 per cent of the students from the interview sample incorporated at least two of the following four characteristics in their responses to the "good teacher" item: ability to maintain control; ability to transfer knowledge effectively; a good sense of humour; and impartiality. This is quite compatible with the definition of the good teacher held by teachers.

It is quite noticeable that whereas students universally define education as instrumental, they do not manifest concern for the relevancy of curricula as they relate to this process of acquiring credentials. When given the opportunity to criticize their own programs of study, less than 6 per cent of the students in the interview sample indicated some concern about the relevancy of subjects. Even if curricula are irrelevant, as long as they are presented interestingly and impartially evaluated, the instru-

Table 2

Characteristics Required of the "Good Teacher" and for Promotion*

	Teacher promotion			Good Teacher	
	Choice	*Per Cent*	*Rank+*	*Per Cent*	*Rank +*
Ability to maintain good discipline	1st	11	5	8	5
	2nd	7		9	
Ability to transfer knowledge effectively	1st	10	4	47	1
	2nd	11		25	
Ability to get along well with colleagues	1st	27	1	0	8
	2nd	24		1	
Ability to get along well with students	1st	1	8	9	3
	2nd	6		18	
Creativity	1st	6	6	12	4
	2nd	8		13	
Good personality	1st	17	2	6	6
	2nd	21		7	
Knowing the subject matter	lst	5	7	14	2
	2nd	8		21	
Sound educational background	1st	23	2	4	7
	2nd	15		6	
		(*n*=228)		(*n*=213)	

* Response to Staff Questionnaire Items: "What two factors are most important in moving up the administrative ladder in education?" and "What are the two most important characteristics of a good teacher?"
+ Ranks are based on a composite of first and second choices.

mental conception of education is maintained. However, it is also true that all students cannot directly benefit from this form of reciprocity. For some students, access to desirable occupations is being denied by the secondary school and its vested agents, the teachers. A reciprocity of a different character, almost a counter-structure, is anticipated from the model in this instance. It is hoped that this aspect will be developed in a further paper.

Students appear to define themselves as collectively irresponsible, as asocial, and requiring "control" for socialization. Although the students were critical of some of the rules and regulations in their schools, they agreed that certain rules were necessary. The definition of the student as socially irresponsible, although perhaps not originally engendered by teachers, is certainly reinforced by teachers and accepted by students.

The model implies that teachers cannot control the learning environment merely by recourse to their legal authority. Control must be vested in methodological expertise and knowledge of the subject field. Both teachers and students tend to define the optimum classroom environment in such a way that it is mutually advantageous to their general career perspectives.

Discussion

On the basis of a preliminary analysis of data, it appears that further development and testing of the model is warranted. Although there is evidence that a reciprocity based on the priority influences of the career aspirations of teachers, and the instrumental orientation of students exists it is quite apparent that there are students who would not benefit by being part of such a collective reciprocal agreement. The very nature of the competitive process in education requires that some students be unsuccessful in attaining their occupational goals. A counter-structure also based on reciprocal relationships appears appropriate as a device for analysis of the interaction between teachers and this latter group of students.

Since the data were obtained by survey procedures and represent the perceptions of students and teachers regarding attitudes and events, in the next phase of the research it is clearly necessary to investigate directly the dynamics of the interaction process by systematic observation in order to test effectively the viability of the proposed model.

Notes

1. Krohn (1963) employs the reciprocal relationship and the corporate group to theorize how bureaucracies are formed and how they influence the behaviour that occurs within them. The perspective is essentially that of social behaviourism.

2. Blau's extension of Homan's social exchange theory provides us with a matrix of interrelated factors concept of change which constitutes a more secure basis for a theory of collective reciprocity than does the reductionist stance. For a pertinent discussion, see Walter Buckley (1967).

3. Callahan (1962) documents the influence that principles of scientific management have had on attitudes of school administrators in the United States.

4. Bidwell (1968) notes that schooling in modern societies contains contradictory tendencies toward the "impractical and instrumental", but he does not develop fully the important role many "impractical" courses play in determining which students

will gain access to universities.

5. Coleman (1961) has shown that the values of the student sub-culture depress the utilization of academic abilities. However, Friesen states that although the athletic and popularity areas are important, they are not as overpowering as Coleman suggests. Friesen (1968, 39-52) feels that they are now "inexorably at variance" with the goals of the school.

6. Clark's (1960, 569-576) development of this concept with regard to California's Community Colleges can be paralleled with the situation in Ontario secondary schools.

References

Bidwell, Charles E.
1968 "Youth in Modern Society", in Talcott Parsons ed., *American Sociology.* New York: Basic Books. 244-257.

Buckley, Walter
1967 *Sociology and Modern Systems Theory.* Englewood Cliffs, N.J.: Prentice-Hall.

Callahan, Raymond E.
1962 *Education and the Cult of Efficiency.* Chicago: University of Chicago Press.

Clark, Burton
1960 "The 'Cooling-Out' Function in Higher Education", *American Journal of Sociology* 65: 569-576.

Coleman, J.A.
1961 *The Adolescent Society.* New York: The Free Press.

Friesen, D.
1968 "Academic-Athletic Popularity Syndrome in the Canadian High School Society (1967)", *Adolescence* 3, 9:39-52.

Krohn, Roger G.
1963 "The Reciprocal Relationships, the Corporate Groups, and the Concept of Bureaucracy". A paper presented at the Meetings of the Learned Societies of Canada, Sessions of the Chapter for Sociology and Anthropology of the Canadian Political Science Association."

27

Backgrounds and Educational Plans of Canadian Students*

Raymond Breton

Several characteristics of the student's background are basic to understanding his educational plans. These include: region and size of the community in which he resides; his level of mental ability; the socio-economic status of his family; and the linguistic group to which he belongs. They are basic because they correspond to distributions of different structural and cultural factors in the population.

Province and Size of Community

Table 1 presents the educational plans of secondary school boys and girls for each of the provinces. Although the percentage planning to complete high school is relatively high in all provinces, some are higher than others. In considering post-secondary plans the range of variation is even greater.

If the provinces are ordered in terms of these percentages and then compared with the various indices of socio-economic development, there is a similarity with secondary plans, but comparatively little with post-secondary. One major exception is Newfoundland, which occupies a much higher rank in the percentage of students planning to finish high school than on the indices of development. Ontario is another exception, occupying a much lower rank for both secondary and post-secondary plans than its economic development would indicate. Finally, Quebec demonstrates a rank higher than expected and British Columbia is a rank lower than expected with respect to post-secondary plans.

Several studies indicate that adolescents from smaller communities have lower educational aspirations, or experience less upward mobility, than those from larger.[1] It has also been found that educational plans are more strongly related to community size among boys than girls. Table 2 shows a similar pattern of results: whereas 85 per cent of the boys and 87 per cent of the girls living in large urban centres plan to finish high school, only 69 per cent of the boys and 75 per cent of the girls from small communities plan to do so (a 16 per cent difference for boys and a 12 per cent difference for

---

*Abridged from Raymond Breton, with the collaboration of John McDonald and Stephen Richer. 1972. *Social and Academic Factors in the Career Decisions of Canadian Youth.* Ottawa: Department of Manpower and Immigration, Chapter III-2. Data for this study were collected from 373 publicly operated secondary schools within all ten provinces, small and large, rural and urban, and of different types—academic, technical and vocational, commercial, and composite. Approximately 150,000 secondary school students drawn from all grade levels were included in the sample. By permission of Information Canada.

Table 1

Educational Plans of Secondary School Students, Canada and the Provinces

(Percentages)

	Planning to finish high school		Planning to attend post-secondary school	
Province	Boys	Girls	Boys	Girls
Nfld.	80.9	83.4	51.6	50.6
P.E.I.	70.0	77.2	61.6	62.4
N.S.	70.7	75.3	64.4	71.2
N.B.	78.2	81.7	60.9	64.2
Que.	77.5	77.0	73.7	67.6
Ont.	76.7	77.4	61.3	57.0
Man.	78.7	81.3	67.7	65.2
Sask.	74.3	83.6	64.5	70.7
Alta.	81.3	86.6	66.9	61.3
B.C.	86.9	88.4	63.4	59.5

Table 2

Educational Plans, by Size of Community

(Percentages)

	Planning to finish high school		Planning to attend post-secondary school	
Size of community	Boys	Girls	Boys	Girls
250,000 or more	85	87	71	61
10,000-249,999	80	83	67	62
Less than 10,000	69	75	59	63

girls). Furthermore, of the boys who plan to finish high school and who live in small communities, 59 per cent plan to continue to post-secondary school; by contrast, the figure is 71 per cent for those living in large communities (a 12 per cent difference). Among girls who plan to finish, the difference between large and small communities in the proportion to go beyond high school is negative and extremely small (−2 per cent.

Measured Mental Ability

It is reasonable to expect that students who rank high in intelligence are more likely to want to go further in school than those who rank low. The percentage of those who are definite about finishing high school confirms this: there is a 21 per cent difference with boys and 23 per cent difference with girls between those in the top three deciles and those in the bottom three deciles of the distribution of mental ability scores. Similarly with post-secondary plans, the above-average in intelligence are much more likely to want to continue formal education after high school on a full-time basis than the less intelligent: a 26 per cent difference with boys and a 28 per cent difference for girls (Table 3).

Table 3

Educational Plans, by Mental Ability Rank

(Percentages)

	Planning to finish high school		Planning to attend post-secondary school	
Mental Ability Rank	Boys	Girls	Boys	Girls
High	89	92	80	76
Medium	79	83	64	62
Low	68	69	54	48

It may be argued that the bright—but unambitious—student will set low educational goals, thus bringing the likelihood of wanting to attend post-secondary school closer to those who are less bright and unambitious. Alternatively, a high level of ambition can compensate for a relatively low level of ability. Consequently, the difference in educational aspirations between the more and the less intelligent who are ambitious would be relatively small. Finally, it could be argued that both these processes—or neither—actually occur, and that no interaction effect takes place; that is, that both factors have an independent effect.

Two measures of ambition were used to test these possibilities: the attitudinal measure of the desire to succeed and the weekly time spent studying. Our data support the second interpretation: that the effect of mental ability is smaller among the very ambitious, regardless of whether ambition is defined as an attitude or as an investment of time in school work. In other words, to the ambitious, the rank he occupies in intelligence is of less significance to his educational plans than it is to his unambitious counterpart.

Socio-Economic Origin

The existence of a relationship between socio-economic background and educational intentions is strong and well established in research literature. A correlation between these two variables is consistently evident with samples of different sizes, with those drawn from culturally different populations or using various measures of socio-economic background, and with a different formulation of questions about educational plans. This study presents no exception to this general pattern: about 14 per cent more students from high socio-economic status, compared with those of low status, intend to complete high school. In addition, of those who intend to finish, about 12 per cent more from high- rather than low-status families plan to continue to post-secondary school (Table 4).

We analyzed the relationship between socio-economic background and educational plans, controlling for mental ability rank. Both those factors have an effect on educational plans; however, the impact of mental ability—particularly on post-secondary plans—is greater than socio-economic background. These results conceal an interesting interaction regarding post-secondary plans: social class has a greater effect among more

Table 4

Educational Plans by Occupational Status of Father

(Percentages)

	Planning to finish high school		Planning to attend post-secondary school	
Occupational status of father	Boys	Girls	Boys	Girls
High	86	88	73	69
Medium	81	83	66	61
Low	73	74	60	59

intelligent students for both boys and girls. The less intelligent are not as likely to plan to attend post secondary school, regardless of their social class. It is a definite advantage, however, if the brighter boy belongs to a high social class family. Similar results were also obtained by Pavalko and Bishop[2] in their study of college plans among high school students in a small Canadian city.

Social Class and Attitudes Towards Work and the Future

Several years ago, Hyman concluded his study of the value systems of different classes by observing that "the data presented show clearly that there is reduced striving for success among the lower classes, an awareness of lack of opportunity, and a lack of valuation of education."[3] He also reports that middle-class people, when choosing life's work, attach importance to "the congeniality of the career pattern to the individual's personality, interests, and individual qualifications. Lower-class people, on the other hand, are more likely to pay attention to economic considerations such as security, wages or subsidiary economic benefits."

Kahl found that occupational primacy, or the importance of occupational success relative to other areas of endeavour, was related in a curvilinear pattern to occupational status in both a Massachusetts and a Brazilian sample[4] : occupational primacy tends to be low among people who are either high or low in occupational status, and high among those in the middle. Social classes also differ in their awareness of opportunities and in their views concerning the means for achieving success. In this regard, Katz[5] found that children of manual workers are more likely to consider "luck" and "influence" than those with middle-class parents.

Finally, several studies indicate a relationship between social class and level of aspiration or the achievement motive. Rosen discovered a positive correlation between class level and the need for achievement.[6] However, Keller and Zevalloni[7] indicated the possibility that the correlation between social class and ambition is partly the result of a "middle-class bias" in the way ambition is measured. Studies by Guest and Chinoy[8] suggest that "getting ahead" is perhaps as highly valued among workers as among the middle-class, but that it neither means the same thing nor is achieved in the same way by people who start out in different positions in the stratification system.

Tables 5 and 6 present this study's findings on a number of these attitudes and evaluations. The items are classified into six groups: self-evaluations; sense of control over future events; anxiety about finding a job; evaluation of chances of success in

Table 5

Attitudes Towards Self and the Future, by Occupational Status of Father

(Percentages)

	Occupational Status of Father					
	Boys			Girls		
	High	Medium	Low	High	Medium	Low
A. "If I could change, I would be someone different from myself."	27	27	27	27	28	28
B. Feel above average in intelligence	48	43	33	38	33	28
C. "Even with a good education, a person like me will have a tough time getting the job he wants."	25	26	29	17	20	24
D. High sense of control over events	50	48	38	61	55	46
E. Very anxious about finding a job	16	20	22	19	22	29
F. High degree of vocational competence	32	29	23	40	36	30
G. Above average chances of success in post-secondary school, given one's ability	32	33	28	26	24	25
H. Above average chances of getting a good job, compared to classmates	34	34	27	26	21	21
I. High ambition to succeed	36	42	44	24	28	38
J. Spends 12 or more hours studying each week	34	31	33	51	51	51
	(1,284-1,376)	(2,271-2,334)	(1,243-1,288)	(1,132-1,182)	(1,946-1,999)	(1,279 1,318)

a The base for the percentages in the column varies between the numbers given in parentheses.

the future; ambition to succeed; and values concerning work and occupation.

Social class affiliation is associated with several—but not all—of these attitudes; for example, it is not strongly correlated with the student's self-evaluation. Part A of Table 5 shows there is no difference between the classes on two of the three self-evaluation items. Furthermore, the difference on the subjective mental ability rank is partly a product of the actual level of mental ability rather than socio-economic origin. Indeed, if mental ability rank is controlled for, the class difference in subjective ability is reduced by a third among boys (from 15 to 10 per cent) and by about two thirds among girls (from 11 to 4 per cent). [Editor's Note: The table showing the relationship between socio-economic origin and subjective mental ability rank, controlling for rank on mental ability test, is not presented here.] Nevertheless, a social-class difference remains in the evaluation of an individual's ability: lower-class students consider themselves less intelligent than those from more advantaged families; this is particularly true of boys.

Secondly—and predictably—students from high-status families are more likely than others to have a high sense of personal control over their future; they are less worried about finding a job and more inclined to demonstrate competence in deciding their careers. Students from white-collar families are also somewhat more optimistic about their chances of getting a good job, although the differences are not very large. Part of the effect of social class origin on the evaluation of the chances of success is confounded by the language factor: French-speaking students are much *more* likely to evaluate their chances as above average than their English-speaking associates. This somewhat puzzling result is discussed in the next section of this chapter. Within the present context it suggests that language should be controlled for, in which case the difference between social classes among English-speaking students is about 10 per cent among boys and girls for both success in post-secondary school and in finding a job. Among French-speaking students there is no social class difference on the evaluation of chances of success.

The data show a correlation between social class and the level of ambition, but in a reverse direction to that expected: lower class students show a higher desire to succeed than those from high-status families. The introduction of language into the analysis is necessary before this unexpected result may be interpreted, and this is particularly important in view of the fact that French-speaking students, who frequently have a lower socio-economic origin, show a much *higher* level of ambition than those who are English-speaking. Controlling for language reduces the effect of social class on ambition to an almost negligible magnitude: 4 per cent for boys and 3 per cent for girls. But the effect, although small, remains in the same negative direction.

The findings concerning the other measure of ambition—namely, the investment of time in academic work—show a similar pattern. There is no difference between students of different social classes in the time they spend studying each week and controlling for language does not affect this result.

These findings lend some support to the suspicions of Keller and Zavalloni who consider that the relationship between social class and ambition observed in several studies is the result of a measurement artifact, that is, of defining ambition in terms of goals peculiar to certain social classes. Students of various classes apparently have internalized the goal of success in life to the same degree, and any differences probably would be in the specific goals selected and/or in the means used for reaching them.

Table 6 presents data concerning occupational success as a goal and the valuation of different aspects of a job. Lower-class students, both boys and girls, attach more importance to occupational success (occupational primacy) than those from more-advantaged families. In considering work itself, students from white-collar families tend to look more for intrinsically interesting activity than for monetary rewards, but

Table 6

Values Concerning Work, by Occupational Status of Father

(Percentages)

	Occupational Status of Father					
	Boys			Girls		
	High	Medium	Low	High	Medium	Low
A. High degree of occupational primacy	24	28	33	15	20	27
B. Interesting work valued over high income in a job	48	45	43	64	61	59
C. Prestige valued over money in a job	25	24	28	50	47	48
D. Opportunity to get ahead valued in a job	63	63	63	41	46	47
E. Chance to help others valued in a job	49	51	54	65	66	72
F. Freedom of action valued in a job	51	49	49	37	33	34
G. Chance to do what you believe is valued in a job	86	85	86	91	87	85
	(1,136-1,376)*	(1,948-2,331)	(1,096-1,287)	(1,019-1,179)	(1,699-2,000)	(1,157-1,318)

* *See* footnote to Table 5.

the class difference is small.

Results show that both socio-economic background and the attitudinal variables influence educational plans; in addition, the effect of the first is not significantly reduced when the attitudes are controlled. It is also interesting to note that the student's evaluation of his own abilities and his chances of success, either in post-secondary studies or in getting a good job, have more impact on educational plan, particularly secondary, than socio-economic background.

Similar results are obtained when other attitudes are introduced, such as: the sense of relevance of school work for an individual's future status; the desire to succeed measured in terms of time spent studying; the values of occupational primacy and whether work is considered intrinsically rewarding or valued because of the chances it offers for getting ahead, helping others, and for prestige or monetary gain; and the feeling that the chances of success in life vary with relative social origins. In other words, these findings indicate that several of the variables frequently used to explain how social class affects the aspirations of adolescents—ambition, sense of relevance of present activity for future status, and values attached to work—apparently do not provide an explanation for the observed relationship between it and educational plans. These variables are influential, but they do not reveal the process whereby social class is related to aspirations.

It has been shown that students of different social classes do not differ significantly on a number of values concerning work; however, if a student has decided upon certain values, social origin has an effect on whether education is the route used to reach that goal. This is almost exclusively true for a boy. For example, if he is seeking interesting work in a job, his social class influences his high school plans less than when he is striving for a position with high monetary gain. In other words, the boy who values money in a job and is from a low-status family is 23 per cent less likely to plan to finish high school than if he has similar values but has a high-status family. On the other hand, if he values interesting work, the probability of his wanting to finish is only about 12 per cent lower.

Language

One relatively common opinion about the educational plans of the country's two major linguistic groups is that French-speaking Canadians value education less than their English-speaking counterparts. Statistics on school retention rates and educational achievement also show that Quebec, particularly its French-speaking population, is significantly below the national average (53). The 1961 Canadian census also showed a substantial discrepancy in educational attainment between the two groups. The present data, collected only a few years later (1965), *do not*—except in one instance (Table 7)—reveal the expected differences between French-speaking and English-speaking students. About the same proportion of French-speaking (77 per cent) and English-speaking (80 per cent) boys are definite about finishing high school. The results are more predictable, however, with girls: a corresponding 83 per cent for English-speaking girls, compared with only 74 per cent for French-speaking girls, who definitely intend to finish high school. These differences follow the expected direction but perhaps do not show the expected magnitude.

With post-secondary plans the differences are opposite to the direction expected: French-speaking students show higher aspirations than English-speaking students. Among boys the difference is 10 per cent; with girls, 6 per cent.

These results are somewhat puzzling, particularly as English-speaking students are more likely to come from white-collar families and rank higher in measured mental ability than French-speaking students.

Table 7
Educational Plans, by Language
(Percentages)

	Planning to finish high school		Planning to attend post-secondary school	
	Boys	Girls	Boys	Girls
English	80	83	64	61
French	77	74	74	67

Socio-economic origin and mental ability rank were introduced into the analysis of post-secondary plans to establish if this pattern of differences held in each of the social class and mental ability categories. Apparently it does not: there is no English-French difference between students in the top deciles of the mental ability distribution, but a large one in favour of the French-speaking in the other two categories (among boys 16 and 20 per cent, respectively; with girls, the corresponding differences are 10 and 18 per cent). Similarly, when controlling for class origin, there is no difference among white-collar students, a large one among upper blue-collar (14 per cent for boys and 12 per cent for girls), and a still larger one among lower blue-collar boys (21 per cent) but not girls (6 per cent only). It is also interesting to note that mental ability rank has a greater influence on the post-secondary plans of English-speaking students (33 per cent among boys and 34 per cent among girls) than French-speaking (17 per cent among boys and 15 per cent among girls). Furthermore, while the likelihood of planning to attend a post-secondary school varies widely with the social class of English-speaking boys (21 per cent), it does not among French (1 per cent).

The pattern of English-French differences for post-secondary plans is attributable to the fact that the aspirations of French-speaking students with relatively low mental ability and social status are not as low as their position on these variables would indicate.

The results of other studies suggest that these findings might be a "subordinate group phenomenon", or the product of the interaction between subordinate status and class position. Sherif and Sherif[9] found the level of personal goals of Negro youth to be strikingly high; and for the education and occupation desire, the "responses of the Negro youth resembled those of students at the high rank school". Coleman *et al*[10] discovered that in the United States as a whole, the percentage "desiring to finish college" is about the same among five different ethnic groups as it is in the white majority. Gist and Bennett[11] sampled students in a mid-west urban high school and concluded that Negroes have higher educational and mobility aspirations than whites.

An interesting paper on this question by Antonovsky and Lerner[12] discusses their own findings as well as those of other studies dealing with the high aspirations of lower-class Negro youth. Together with other authors they also found that this particular group has higher occupational and educational aspirations than lower-class white youth—among both boys and girls. They observed that differences between Negroes and whites were even more striking in the lower class than in the lower middle-class; this study found a similar result.

Antonovsky and Lerner's paper suggests one interesting interpretation for their findings: the critical influence upon Negro youth "is the existence of what we would call 'models of dissociation'." They point out that this is "very distinct from the notion of the absence of role models". It is the process of treating a group as a negative reference and of choosing models "as clear examples of what not to be like." The aspirations reflect a radical rejection of the inferior status of an individual's parents and quite probably of his or her ethnic group, a rejection which is frequently encouraged by the parents themselves. The phrase "I don't want you to lead the life I led," or some other variant, is likely used in the lower class Negro families as widely as it is among immigrant groups.

The fear-of-failure hypothesis[13] bears a strong relationship to the theory regarding dissociation to avoid a feeling of inferiority; indeed, the experience of failure probably influences an individual's self-esteem.

Within the present context, it can be argued that membership in a disadvantaged group in society—a linguistic group—has a tendency to create feelings of inferiority and/or a fear of failure. These feelings, in turn, probably prompt the individual to formulate either very low or very high goals to avoid competition or to dissociate himself from a possible source of his sense of inadequacy.

The aspirations of a number of French-speaking students may be a response to a situation of comparative disadvantage. This is suggested by the relatively high frequency of those from the lower ranks of mental ability who aspire to post-secondary education—presumably a group which is the least likely to succeed in this regard. Although the level of ambition to succeed is much higher among French-speaking than English-speaking students, the number of hours spent studying each week is the same for both groups. Consequently, there appears to be an underlying mechanism resulting in a high degree of ambition and the intention to enter post-secondary school without a correspondingly high expenditure of effort in academic work.

The data show that the French-speaking students are more susceptible to worry and feel less competent in making career decisions. (The differences between the two language groups are around 14 per cent, depending on the variable and on the student's sex.) Again, with these two variables, the differences between French- and English-speaking students are maintained when controlling for their socio-economic origin.

French-English differences in post-secondary plans for each attitudinal variable, controlling for socio-economic background tend to be greater among students who feel inadequate than among those who do not; and larger among those who are correspondingly more anxious about the future. This tendency, however, occurs mostly with students from middle and lower socio-economic backgrounds. The French-English differences appear smaller and less consistent with white-collar students than with those from blue-collar categories.

The Curvilinearity Hypothesis

The theory of the effect of the fear of failure and the sense of inferiority and inefficacy on goal-setting concludes that the relationship is curvilinear; that anxiety, for example, stimulates the setting of *both* very low and overly high goals. Its application to the present data would result in French-speaking students not only being more likely to want to continue their education beyond high school, but more susceptible to dropping out of it. If the hypothesis and the argument presented on the previous pages are valid, then the predictable pattern should be found mostly among those who are disadvantaged in terms of class origin and mental ability, as well as those who feel inadequate, are anxious and fatalistic about the future, and who feel below average in their chances of success.

The findings support the theory, but they are more consistent for boys than for girls. The English-French differences in educational plans tend to be small among students who are from white-collar familes; are in the top ranks of mental ability; disagree with the statement, "Even with a good education, a person like me will have a tough time getting the job he wants"; feel they have some control over future events; and are not too worried about finding a job. The language difference is reversed however, with students who feel above average in their chances of success in post-secondary school: English-speaking students are more likely to plan to continue beyond high school.

On the other hand, French-speaking students, in contrast with their English-speaking associates, are more likely to set both very high and very low educational goals for themselves if they score negatively on the above variables. The curvilinear pattern—especially with boys—is clearly evident if a student is disadvantaged in terms of socio-economic background and mental ability, and if there is a feeling of inadequacy, inferiority, fatalism, and anxiety about the future. If a condition of social and psychological disadvantage is shown, then the subordinate group student is more likely to approach the extremes in goal-setting than the member of a group occupying a dominant position in society.

As a conclusion to this section on the analysis, it should be pointed out that there is a possibility that the "social awakening" that has occurred among French-speaking Canadians, particularly in Quebec, since the early 1960s may have contributed to the above results. It does not in itself appear to provide an adequate explanation for the goal-setting behaviour which has been observed, however, and its role has been to trigger or accentuate processes associated with a low rank in the ethnic stratification system. It is worth remembering that similar results were evident in the United States as early as 1936.[14]

Although no argument based on empirical data is possible, it seems invalid to attempt an explanation of goal-setting behaviour uniquely in terms of current events, at least without reference to the basic characteristics of the social structure and the position people occupy in it.

Notes

1. G.H. Elder, "Achievement Orientations and Career Patterns of Rural Youth", *Sociology of Education*, 37 (1963), 30-58; C.M. Grigg and R. Middleton, "Community of Orientation and Occupational Aspirations of Ninth Grade Students", *Social Forces*, 38 (1960), 303-308; S.M. Lipset and R. Bendix, *Social Mobility in Industrial Society* (University of California Press, 1959); S.M. Lipset, "Social Mobility and Urbanization", *Rural Sociology*, 20 (1955), 220-228; and W.H. Sewell, "Community of Residence and College Plans", *American Sociological Review*, 29 (1964), 24-37.

2. R.M. Pavalko and D.R. Bishop, "Socioeconomic Status and College Plans: A Study of Canadian High School Students", *Sociology of Education*, 39 (1966), 288-298.

3. H.H. Hyman, "The Value Systems of Different Classes", 426-442 in R. Bendix and S.M. Lipset, eds., *Class, Status and Power* (1953).

4. J.A. Kahl, "Some Measurements of Achievement Orientation", *American Journal of Sociology*, 70 (1965), 669-681.

5. F. M. Katz, "The Meaning of Success: Some Differences in Value Systems of Social Classes", *Journal of Social Psychology*, 62 (1964), 141-148.

6. B.C. Rosen, "The Achievement Syndrome", *American Sociological Review*, 21 (1956), 203-211.

7. S. Keller and M. Zavalloni, "Ambition and Social Class: A Respecification", *Social Forces*, 43 (1964), 58-70.

8. R.H. Guest, "Work Careers and Aspirations of Automobile Workers", *American Sociological Review*, 19 (1954), 155-163; E. Chinoy, *Automobile Workers and the American Dream* (Garden City, N.Y.: Doubleday and Co., 1955).

9. M. Sherif and C.W. Sherif, *Reference Groups* (New York: Harper and Row, 1964), 211.

10. J.S. Coleman *et al.*, *Equality of Educational Opportunity*, U.S. Office of Education, 1966.

11. N.P. Gist and W.S. Bennett Jr., "Aspirations of Negro and White Students", *Social Forces*, 42 (1963), 40-48.

12. A. Antonovsky and M.J. Lerner, "Occupational Aspirations of Lower Class Negro and White Youth", *Social Problems*, 7 (1959), 132-138.

13. C.H. Mahone, "Fear of Failure and Unrealistic Vocational Aspirations", *Journal of Abnormal, Social Psychology*, 60 (1960), 253-261; E. Burnstein, "Fear of Failure, Achievement Motivation, and Aspiring to Prestigeful Occupations", *Journal of Abnormal Clinical Psychology*, 67 (1963), 189-193; R.L. Isaacson, "Relation between N Achievement, Test Anxiety, and Curricular Choices", *Journal of Abnormal, Social Psychology*, 68 (1964), 447-452; J.W. Atkinson, "The Mainsprings of Achievement-Oriented Activity", in J.D. Krumboltz, ed., *Learning and the Education Process* (Chicago: Rand McNally, 1965).

14. See references in Antonovsky and Lerner, *op. cit.*

28

Young Canadians Learn About Violence*

Judy Torrance

1. Introduction

Knowledge forms that part of our mental baggage which provides us with models or analogies in our efforts to understand the world around us. From it we can obtain suggestions about how we should interpret events and guides to appropriate behaviour in response to them. As such, knowledge can be idiosyncratic, that is, drawn from the unique experience of an individual, or cultural, that is derived from the recorded experience of the collectivity. For the latter we can use Berger and Luckmann's term, the social stock of knowledge, which they define as the selective accumulation of experience transmitted from generation to generation.[1] This paper is concerned with the social stock of knowledge Canadians might draw upon in their dealings with violence.

As Berger and Luckman's definition makes clear, knowledge is not equivalent to experience. It is based on selected experiences. We do not remember everything that has happened to us; nor does oral or written history record all that has befallen a society. Citizens of a country may turn their backs on violent traditions for one reason or another and, by letting incidents drop from the collective memory, end up with little retained knowledge of violence. The amount of violence experienced, then, can be only a rough indicator of the amount of knowledge retained.

Two factors in particular seem to determine the extent to which violence is remembered. The first is the importance of the past incident. An individual may remember because of his close involvement with violence: he may have fought on one side or the other, he may have had his house burned down, or he may have been thrust into political office as a result of it. For the incident to pass into the social stock of knowledge, its political consequences must have been serious. Tilly remarks on how quickly violence can be forgotten and suggests as one reason for this the tendency for history to be written "from the top", so that "the only protests which matter are those which produce some rearrangement of power."[2] Unless the regime has been toppled or some other substantial dent been made in the political structures, the violence will tend to sink into oblivion.

The second factor affecting the remembrance of violence is the labelling process by which an incident is regarded as good or bad. It seems that we tend to remember what we regard with favour and to repress the memory of unpleasant events.[3] A

---

*An original paper adapted by the editors from Judy Torrance, "Cultural Factors and the Response of Governments to Violence: The Case of Canada", unpublished Ph.D. dissertation, Department of Political Science, York University, 1975, Chapter 8. With the permission of the author.

country which proudly traces its origins to a revolution or a national struggle for liberation may place a high value on such events and so enshrine their memory in word and song. In contrast, a country which has experienced no incident which has been defined as creative or progressive has no fond memories of violence and in all likelihood will retain only a hazy notion of such violence as has occurred in its past.

Canadians do not have in their collective memory a positive model of violence. McNaught refers to the assumption "widely held by Canadian historians, ... that our history has been largely free from the violence and extremism in action that have scarred American history".[4]

To ascertain the content of Canadian knowledge about violence, the reports of violent incidents contained in history textbooks will be analysed. There are a number of reasons for this choice of approach. Historians are in a sense the keepers of a nation's traditions. To a large extent, they decide what is important about the past and what consequently is worth remembering. Once this choice is made, they reduce the complexity of events to an orderly progression of paragraphs, put an incident in context, suggest causes and consequences, and make judgments on its necessity, usefulness, propriety, and so on. The incident thus moulded then passes into the realm of knowledge. According to Hodgetts, "Canadian history is the main academic subject through which political socialization is meant to take place. . . . Civic education in Canada, it seems, has been delegated primarily to the history teacher."[5]

The plan of research is simple. Five incidents of violence were selected, and the treatment accorded them by the various texts was studied with the following questions in mind:

—In the author's opinion, what are the causes of violence?

—What does he have to say on the question of who engages in violence?

—What does he suggest to be the cure for violence?

—What consequences of violence does he point to?

—Does he imply that violence can be a useful or morally justifiable tactic?

We will consider 24 texts published between 1920 and 1970 and authorized by the Ontario Department of Education for use in the province's schools.[6] Table 1 lists these school books. I have chosen 1920 as a starting point, first, because prior to this date there were relatively few books with a Canadian, as opposed to a British or imperial focus and, second, because I wished to give the authors a chance to discuss some incidents besides the two Riel rebellions. There is no reason for believing that the books used in Ontario are atypical; according to Hodgetts, "Canadian history courses from coast to coast present virtually identical material", with the one obvious exception of the French-speaking Catholic school system of Quebec.[7]

Only references to domestic violence are considered. In other words, violence that took place outside our boundaries when Canada was at war is excluded. A second limitation is that only the Canadian recorded experience with violence since Confederation is dealt with. Thus no reference is made to the 1837 rebellions, for example.

The five incidents to be analysed are:

1. The Red River rebellion, 1869-1870;
2. The Northwest rebellion, 1885;
3. The anti-draft riots, Quebec City, 1918;
4. The riots between strikers and police during the Winnipeg general strike, 1919; and
5. The riot between unemployed and police, Regina, 1935.

These incidents struck me as the most serious challenges to the authority of the Canadian government. Once the conflict became violent, the issues and emotions were critical enough to push the violence to increasing lengths and the ability of the government to deal with the situation was a crucial variable in determining how far the violence spread.

Table 1
Canadian History Texts Used in Ontario Schools (arranged by year of publication)

Author	Title	Last year of authorized use	Cited in text as:
Wrong, G.M.	*Ontario Public School History of Canada.* Toronto: Ryerson, 1921, 2nd edn.	1927	Wrong
Grant, W.L.	*Ontario High School History of Canada.* Toronto: Ryerson, 1922, 2nd edn.	1929	Grant
Wallace, W.S.	*A First Book of Canadian History.* Toronto: Macmillan, 1928.	1950	Wallace (1928)
Wallace, W.S.	*A History of the Canadian People.* Toronto: Copp Clark, 1930.	1946	Wallace (1930)
Brown, G.W.	*Building the Canadian Nation.* Toronto: Dent, 1942.	1959	Brown
Chafe, J.W. & A.R.M. Lower	*Canada: A New Nation and How It Came to Be.* New York: Longmans, Green, 1948.	1959	C & L
Brown, G., E. Harman & M. Jeanneret	*The Story of Canada.* Toronto: Copp Clark, 1950	1960*	B,H & J
Deyell, E.	*Canada: The New Nation.* Toronto: Gage, 1958.	current	Deyell
Hardy, W.G.	*From Sea unto Sea: The Road to Nationhood, 1850-1910.* Toronto: Doubleday, 1959.	current	Hardy
Hodgetts, A.B.	*Decisive Decades: A History of the Twentieth Century for Canadians.* Toronto: Nelson, 1960.	current	Hodgetts
Lambert, R.S.	*The Twentieth Century: Canada, Britain, U.S.A.* Toronto: Grant, 1960.	current	Lambert

Table 1 (continued)

Author	Title	Last year of authorized use	Cited in text as:
Ricker, J., J. Saywell & E. Rose	*The Modern Era.* Toronto: Clarke, Irwin, 1960.	current	R,S & R
Allen, R.	*Ordeal by Fire: Canada 1910-1945.* Toronto: Doubleday, 1961.	current	Allen
Garland, A.	*Canada: Our Country.* Toronto: Macmillan, 1961.	current	Garland
Peart, H.W. & J. Schaffter	*The Winds of Change: A History of Canada and the Canadians in the Twentieth Century.* Toronto: Ryerson, 1961.	current	P & S
Frère Charles & Frère Leon	*La Confédération.* Toronto: Nelson, 1962.	current	C & Léon
Field, J.L. & L.A. Dennis	*From Sea to Sea.* Toronto: Grant, 1962.	current	F & D
Nicholson, G.W. L., H.H. Boyd, R.J. Rannie, & A.E. Hobbs	*Three Nations: Canada, Great Britain, the United States of American in the Twentieth Century.* Toronto: McClelland and Stewart, 1962.	current	N,B,R&H
Tait, G.E.	*One Dominion: The Story of Canada from 1800 to 1900.* Toronto: Ryerson, 1962.	current	Tait
Brault, L.	*Le Canada au XXe siècle.* Toronto: Nelson, 1965.	current	Brault
Roger, S.J., D.F. Harris & J.T. Saywell	*Nation of the North* Toronto: Clarke, Irwin, 1967.	current	R, H & S
Herstein, H.H., L.J. Hughes & R.C. Kirbyson	*Challenge and Survival: The History of Canada.* Scarborough: Prentice-Hall, 1970.	current	H,H, & K

Table 1 (continued)

Author	Title	Last year of authorized use	Cited in text as:
Moir, J.S. & R.E. Saunders	*Northern Destiny: A History of Canada.* Toronto: Dent, 1970.	current	M & S
Willows, D.G., & S. Richmond	*Canada: Colony to Centennial.* Toronto: McGraw Hill, 1970.	current	W & R

* The text of this book made several appearances. Translated by C. Bilodeau, it became *Notre Historie* (Toronto: Copp Clark, 1952), and with some modification it reappeared as *Canada in North America* (Toronto: Copp Clark, 1961).

The Riel Rebellions

To obtain an indication of what the various authors consider to be the relative significance of the five incidents, the number of sentences used to describe them were counted, on the assumption that the more space devoted to an incident, the more important it was taken to be. By this method of reckoning the two Riel rebellions are the premier violent events in Canadian history. The school authors take on average 59 sentences to cover the Red River rebellion and 72 for the Northwest rebellion. None of the other three incidents is dealt with at remotely similar length: the Quebec City riots are described on average in two sentences, the Winnipeg general strike in eighteen, and the Regina riot in six.

The school texts all tell essentially the same story about the Riel rebellions. Admittedly they differ in their selection of details, the illustrations they use to make a point, and the amount of emphasis they place on various events. But despite such differences, the texts are largely in agreement on the basic questions of concern to us: What causes violence? Who engages in violence? What, from the government's point of view, is the cure for violence and what are its consequences? Is violence a proper or useful tactic?

Three causes of violence are identified. In the first place, both rebellions are presented as the collision of two different ways of life. In all the books, the Métis and Indians are presented as reacting in defence of their culture and economy in the face of an influx of English-speaking farmers. While this collision of cultures is seen as an inescapable tragedy, that it should be productive of violence is not regarded as inevitable. Other factors must also be present.

Of these other conditions, the one taken as central has to do with the relations between governed and government. A breakdown in communications between the two is unanimously ranked as among the foremost causes of the two rebellions. The Red River incident is ascribed to the failure of the government to consult with and inform the inhabitants of its intentions. The Northwest Rebellion is attributed to the government's neglect and tardiness in dealing with Métis and Indian grievances. In both incidents the moral of the story is that rebellions are largely caused by governments which fail to maintain communications with the citizen body.

The third cause noted for the rebellions is that violence occurs in the absence of authority, meaning both the absence of respected leaders and the lack of police or military forces. This cause does not figure as prominently as the previous two; only eight of the books refer to it specifically. The absence of respected leaders is linked to the Red River incident as mention is made of the sickness of Governor Mactavish, Bishop Taché's presence in Rome, and McDougall's proclamation which seemingly left the colony without any legal form of government. For both incidents, the absence of military forces and the difficulties of bringing an expeditionary force from the east are noted by all authors. However, only a minority point to this factor as a cause of the violence.

Turning to the question of who engages in violence, the answer which the authors give is, in brief, the insane, the simple-minded, the savage, and the alien. Riel's insanity is referred to in each book. Some authors choose to demonstrate Riel's insanity by reference to his violence or counselling of violence:

Wrong: 333 – Riel's madness increased, and at last his cry was: "We want blood; it is a war of extermination."

Deyell: 411 – Doctors who examined him said he was insane; they sent him to a mental hospital where it often took three men to keep him quiet.

Hardy: 346 – From this point forward the signs of Riel's dementia are clear. What Riel had decided upon was to repeat the tactics of 1869-70.

Tait: 377 – By March, 1885, Riel, confused and embittered, . . . decided to repeat the tactics of 1869-70.

H, H & K: 269 – Reflecting the mental imbalance that had grown worse with the years, . . . Riel established a provisional government.

Riel's Métis followers are described both as fearless fighters and as simple-minded, credulous primitives, unable to comprehend the changes in the world around them. Only two authors attempt to counteract the general impression of Métis simplicity. Wallace (1929) points out that Riel's provisional government of 1869-70 "was not the government of uneducated half-breeds it has sometimes been described as being", while Garland speaks of the same government as having "capable men". However, Wallace somewhat mitigates his point by only citing in support of it the presence in the government of an educated man from Ontario. No Métis, other than Riel himself, is described by Wallace or any other historian as well-educated.

Also identified as involved in the violence of 1885 are the Indians. This group is by and large simply branded as savages. Even though there is no evidence that the Indians who took part in the rebellion conducted themselves in any manner substantially different from other combatants, discriminatory language is persistently used to describe them. While the engagement at Duck Lake, involving Métis for the most part, is described as resulting in "killing", the Indians, the terms concerning the fate of the settlers at Frog Lake were "murder", "massacre" and "slaughter". Of the 13 books referring to attacks by Indians on the settlers, only two, Deyell and Garland, restrict themselves to the verb "to kill". Unlike the Métis, the Indians are not driven to arms to secure their rights; they 'go on the warpath' (Wallace [1928], Hardy, Deyell, Garland, R & H).

If the combatants were, broadly speaking, insane, primitive or savage, the subtle message to the reader is that normal people would not engage in rebellious activities. This message is reinforced by another attribute ascribed to the Métis and Indians: their strangeness or alienness. Simply by emphasizing the collision-of-cultures aspect of the rebellions, the authors point to the differences separating the inhabitants of the prairies from the rest of Canada. The we/they distinction is buttressed by other, perhaps unconscious, slips of the pen. Thus the troops sent west are sometimes referred to as "our men" (Grant; F&D). Decisions on how to handle the rebellions or public reactions to them are made by "Canada", as if the rebel territory were not part of the country. This, of course, was actually the case in 1869-70, and thus description of the Red River affair in terms of Canada versus non-Canada need arouse no comment. However the practice is continued for 1885, as if the rebellion were a foreign, not a domestic incident.

The strangeness of the Métis and Indians is made more pointed by the authors' habit of overlooking the role played in the two rebellions by whites and English-speaking half-breeds. Only Wallace (1928) points out that Riel's provisional government of 1870 contained non-Métis members. The decision to invite Riel back to Canada in 1884 was in fact taken at the Lindsay School House meeting of whites and half-breeds of both tongues, and the four-man deputation sent down to Montana included an English-speaking half-breed as well as Métis. However, of the 15 books which specify the composition of the Lindsay meeting or of the delegation, 12 mention only Métis participation. Again, in discussing the ultimate fate of the rebels at Regina, only Riel, the Métis and Indians are referred to in 15 of the 17 books. That Riel's chief English-speaking associate, W.H. Jackson, also stood trial but was found not guilty by reason of insanity is noted only by Hardy and R & H. That another white, Thomas Scott, was also tried but discharged, is mentioned by Hardy alone. Some authors explicitly make the point that whites would have nothing to do with violence.

Broadly speaking, the government is thus seen as having on its hands rebellions caused to some extent by its own negligence and manned by primitive, savage aliens under the leadership of a man of unbalanced mind. What countering action should it have taken to bring the episodes to a speedy and painless conclusion? On this point the school books give us relatively little information. For the most part, they ignore the difficulties faced by governments—or for that matter, by rebel leaders—in making decisions, reacting to popular pressures and maintaining prestige. Indeed, in the case of the 1885 incident, ten of the 17 books simply report without discussion a single decision made by the federal government during the course of the affair: to send troops to put down the rebellion or to prevent a general Indian uprising. Nevertheless, it is possible to extract a few maxims of prudence from the authors' discussion.

From the earlier incident, nine of the books make the point that, in dealing with violent challenges to its authority, a government should never forget that it is venturing out on the thin ice of the art of the possible. In particular, it should never command that to which it cannot compel obedience, lest it risk seeing that fragile edifice—the dignity and authority of the state—disintegrate in ridicule. This point is made by reference to the exploits of McDougall. The authors regard McDougall's actions as evidence of political imbecility and have no sympathy for the uncertainties, aggravations, and misinformation with which the man had to deal.

A second maxim of prudence for governments, again extracted from the discussion of the Red River affair, is that, if violence is caused by a breakdown of communications between citizens and government, then an obvious remedial step is to open lines of communication as soon as possible. Thirteen of the books remark on one or both of the sending of the Canadian commissioners to Red River and the arrival in Ottawa of delegates from the colony to negotiate a settlement of the affair. Deyell (388-390), perhaps, makes the clearest statement of the efficacy of negotiation:

> Someone had blundered. Sir John A. took steps to put things right. He asked Bishop Taché . . . to hurry home from Rome to talk to the Métis. He asked Donald Smith . . . to hurry to Fort Garry too. . . . Smith told Canada's side of the story . . . [As a result] by mid-February the committee had drawn up a "Bill of Rights" and started to make plans to take it to Ottawa.
>
> At Ottawa the Government began to breathe more easily. It had remedied its errors by calmly discussing the problems for a solution.

Most of the authors argue that the government' persistent efforts to establish a dialogue with the colonists were a major element in bringing the rebellion to a close. By and large they agree that the government's initiatives would have brought the affair to a speedy conclusion, but for the political furore created in Canada by the death of Thomas Scott. To cite Deyell (389) again, "It was Riel who spoiled the happy ending to the Red River story."

While the authors with a few exceptions make allowances for Scott's obstreperous behaviour, his death is explicitly or implicitly regarded as a blunder on Riel's part. It was a blunder because, as a result of the ensuing outcry, it made the government's task of negotiating with the Red River colonists far more difficult. The cautionary maxim that might be extracted from the sorry tale of Scott is that a Canadian government can no longer act as a free agent, as it were, once the country's basic cultural cleavage has been opened up by an incident. There may be little the government can do to prevent an inflamed popular opinion dividing on ethnic or religious grounds. It must simply recognize that its freedom of choice is limited by the possible consequences of its actions on national unity. All the books comment on the division of opinion in the country in 1870, although only four (Hardy; F & D; Tait; and M & S) explicitly refer to the resulting pressures on the government. The bitter debate over the ultimate fate of Riel in 1885 is discussed in similar terms: all the authors remark on the division of the country and some explicitly link this to the delicacy of the government's position (cf. Wallace [1928]: 190; Hardy: 387; and Garland: 332).

One solution discussed is to combine sternness with leniency in the hope of pacifying both sections of popular opinion. Wolseley's expedition to the Red River is described by six authors as a sop to Ontario opinion, while at the same time mention is made of the Manitoba Act with its linguistic and religious safeguards. After discussing the pressures on the cabinet, Tait, for example, writes (355-356):

> The Dominion government, in order to play safe, decided on action that displayed both sympathy and sternness toward the rebels. A new province would be established within the Dominion, but troops would be dispatched to ensure law and order.

The carrot-and-stick approach is favoured by some not simply as a means of mollifying public opinion, but also as a useful ploy in dealing with the rebels themselves or with potential rebels. The quotation from Tait, immediately above, is somewhat ambiguous as it is not altogether clear from the context whether the government is seeking 'to play safe' in respect to popular opinion or to the rebel colony. However, four other books (Deyell; Hardy; Garland; and R, H & S) refer to the government's action in 1885 of sending script to the Métis and food supplies to the Indians, in addition to the outfitting of an armed expedition, as a means of localizing the revolt.

So far, our authors have not been very helpful to the future cabinet ministers sitting at the school desks of Ontario. Apart from the general counsel against over-extending authority and for the opening of negotiations, they provide at best a few scattered hints on handling public opinion and dealing with rebellious citizenry. On the question of the use of armed force, they offer only confusion. All the books mention that the government sent military expeditions in 1870 and 1885, but what object the government hoped to secure is largely ignored for the later incident and treated inconsistently for the earlier one. A primary function of the military is evidently seen to be police-type violence—to forcibly remove the rebels from power and hand them over to the judicial process. Military-type violence—the destruction of the rebels—is not mentioned. Beyond this, however, armed forces can serve several purposes. Reminiscent of the belief that the absence of authority is a cause of violence are the roles of deterring future trouble or potential rebels by their presence, facilitating the establishment of a new government, and providing law and order. A military expedition can also be a sop to public opinion and a demonstration to a foreign power of national sovereignty. Apart from four references to costs, there is no mention of disadvantage in the use of armed forces.

The consequences of violence for a government are universally regarded as serious. Riel's actions and his fate, we are told, "stirred deep passions", "rent Canada in twain", had "disastrous" aftereffects, "left an aftermath of bitterness which did not soon die out", had "a tragic effect on our country", "tore open old wounds", "had a lasting effect on the relations between French and English Canada", "threatened to split the union wide open", "divisa les Canadiens pendant de nombreuses années", "revived old race hatreds . . . that carried over into the twentieth century", "crystallized all the divisive forces that challenged Canadian unity and provided them with a rallying cry", and so on. Some authors also note one result of the agitation in Quebec of practical interest to the government: the rise of Mercier (Hardy; R, S & R; and H, H & K) and the beginning of the end of Conservative party dominance in that province (Wrong; Hardy; C & L; Deyell; and F & D).

The authors agree that the punishment of rebels is a delicate business for governments. Tait (357) notes that Riel's departure before the arrival of the Wolseley expedition in 1870 "relieved the Dominion government of the difficult duty of deciding on a suitable punishment." Wallace (1930: 226-267) adds that "it was a sign of the embarrassment of the government that, although Riel was outlawed, no attempt was made to arrest him". C & L (348) reproduce the famous Bengough cartoon, "A Case of *Riel* Distress", showing Macdonald clad as a policeman pretending mightily to search for Riel, and Deyell (412) observes that Riel was paid to stay out of the country "in the hope of avoiding trouble." On the question of amnesty, Hardy (244) comments that passions were such that "John A. could only hem and haw". Concerning the events of 1885, Wallace (1930: 288-289) remarks that "the problem of what should be done with Riel . . . was destined to prove a source of great embarrassment to the government". M & S (330) note that "the punishment of Riel was not so easily settled" as the restoration of order.

While pointing to the government's dilemma, the authors do not suggest that Riel should not have been hanged. The one possible exception is the book by C & Léon (245), who cite Laurier's accusation: "On dit qu'il a eu un procès équitable. Je le nie fortement." Most of the authors give the arguments raised in Riel's defence, but the general attitude seems to be that the law must take its course. Indeed, some of the statements are particularly blunt on this point (cf. Garland below), perhaps as a warning to future rebels at the school desks of Ontario:

> Wrong: 334 – Following the rebellion came the demands of justice. . . . even insane people are responsible for their actions.
>
> Wallace (1928): 167, 190 – the penalty that unsuccessful rebels pay – the penalty of death. . . . But in the end Sir John Macdonald decided that the law must take its course. . . . Riel paid the price of his mad career on the scaffold.
>
> Garland: 322 – Rebellion is treason. The punishment for treason is death.

What the authors have to say on the justification for the violence can be surmised from the discussion. The general viewpoint is that the rebels had genuine grievances which the government ignored, and that in 1869-1870 their actions brought satisfaction to most of their demands in the form of the Manitoba Act. The 1885 rebellion is treated as a failure except for the minor achievements of hastening the granting of script and land titles for the Métis. However, both incidents are regarded as retrograde, as tragedies which any thinking man would strive hard to avoid repeating, if only because of their divisive effects on the country as a whole. In the best of all possible worlds, grievances would not go unnoticed and no blood would be shed.

Even the heavily qualified justification the authors accord the incidents, however, refers to what emerges from their description as rather tame, anaemic affairs. There is no question of regarding blood-spattered, melodramatic events as understandable, if regrettable. Indeed, many authors doubt whether 1869 in fact amounted to rebellion. Four books (B, H & J; Deyell; C & Léon; and R,H & S)simply avoid the use of the term rebellion or revolt, preferring less colourful words, such as disturbance, agitation, or resistance. Wallace (1930) and H, H & K speak of rebellion, but only in quotation marks. Others are more explicit in their choice of terminology:

> Wallace (1928): 165 – the Métis were merely trying to safeguard their rights as British subjects against what they regarded as an illegal invasion. To describe them as rebels against the Queen is perhaps wrong.
>
> C & L: 348 fn. – Most authorities now agree that the Riel movement was not actually a rebellion.
>
> Garland: 289 – it is not fair to describe them as rebels.

Grant and Tait, despite using the word rebellion, both add that no real disloyalty was intended.

From the various accounts, the Red River affair emerges as even more bloodless than it actually was. Thirteen books give the impression that Scott was the only person to lose his life. Only Hardy, C & L, and H, H & K mention the deaths resulting from the clash between the Portage men and the Métis; only Hardy and W & R mention the bloodshed after Wolseley's arrival at Fort Garry. Scott's execution is nevertheless regarded as an inky blot on Riel's record. It was this one act of violence that raises doubts as to the justification for the rebellion:

> Grant: 278 – So far, Riel had done little more than fight for his rights, but in March, 1870, he put himself forever in the wrong by the execution.
>
> C & L: 347 – If he had gone no further, Riel might today be regarded as the champion of the rights of a minority.

Deyell (416) and Garland (293) echo the sentiment of the latter quotation.

Concerning the events of 1885, doubts over status vanish: 15 of the 17 books label it a rebellion. However, the bloodiness of the affair is again downplayed. Apart from the deaths on the gallows of Regina, only three authors (Grant; Hardy; and W & R) indicate that the blood of non-whites as well as whites flowed in the Northwest (and about half fail to mention that anyone else but Riel went to the scaffold at Regina). While one author (Wrong) speaks of the rebellion costing "the lives of probably 200 men on the loyal side" and another (Hardy) of 91 deaths among the settlers, NWMP and soldiers, none of the other writers cites a figure above 30. Indeed, two authors (C & L; and C & Léon) manage to describe the whole affair as if Riel were the only person to come out of it with less than a whole skin.

The 1885 rebellion is also minimized in another way by about half the authors. They emphasize the restricted nature of the uprising by pointing out that Riel never managed to mobilize all his potential followers. I have already noted references to the reluctance of the white settlers to join Riel's banner, but in a number of books the same point is made in reference to the Métis and Indians. For example:

> M & S: 329 – Only one thousand rebels took up arms. Most Indians followed the advice of . . . Father Lacombe to remain peaceful, while most Métis and white settlers refused to support an uprising led by the half-mad religious fanatic.
>
> H, H & K: 270 – A few Indian tribes had joined the Métis . . . , but neither showed much will to fight.
>
> Tait: 384 – It should be remembered that many Métis and the vast majority of the Indians took no part in the North-West rebellion.

Grant, Wallace (1928) and Garland attribute the limited Indian participation to the fact that the Hudson's Bay Company and the Mounted Police had previously treated the Indians with consideration. Garland (322) puts it, "Canada now reaped the reward for this fair treatment, for the wiser chiefs held their bands back from war."

A number of expressions of peaceable kingdom sentiments cropped up. The authors in effect say that violence, which we find understandable, if regrettable, was exceptional and did not amount to very much when put in a comparative perspective.

Quebec, Winnipeg, and Regina

If we count the number of sentences used in the 17 books to describe the violence that took place at Quebec City, Winnipeg, and Regina during the inter-war period, it is evident that the authors consider these incidents to be of a totally different order of magnitude to the Riel rebellions. Instead of the numerous pages devoted to the two nineteenth century affairs, we find the Quebec City riots not even mentioned in ten of the 17 books and the average reference only 1.7 sentences in length. Winnipeg is not mentioned in four books, and a further three, while referring to the general strike, give no description of the violence which occurred. On average the authors take 17.6 sentences to cover the strike, but give only one sentence to the violence. The On-to-Ottawa trek is ignored in five of the 13 books published after the event took place, while another two mention the trek but not the Regina riot. On average six sentences are devoted to the general context of the violence and 1.2 to the riot itself. For the three incidents, then, there are 47 possible descriptions of violence (17 + 17 + 13),[8] but only 23 references (7 + 10 + 6) are in fact made.

The twentieth century incidents are more difficult to analyse than the Riel rebellions in determining what knowledge Ontario school children might gain concerning violence. For one thing, the references are so short that it is difficult to comment on them intelligently. It is, for example, not easy to make much of the four books which cover the Quebec City riots in a single sentence each. For another thing, the books agree less often in their interpretations. This is particularly true for the Winnipeg general strike.

The largest measure of agreement does concern an important issue: the general causes of violence. However cursory the reference to an incident, it is placed within the wider context of the conscription crisis, the post-war economic upheavals, or the depression. The incidents are treated either as a climax of a crisis or as illustrations of the general tension of the time. A number of authors emphasize that the incident was but one crest among many in a stormy sea by referring to other outbursts of violence or protest within the same period of unrest.

The three incidents, in other words, differ from the Riel rebellions in that they are not *sui generis*, but part and parcel of the general discontent of the times. They arise out of grievances; indeed, they are a vocalization of these grievances, a means of protest against the indifference of government and country to the wishes or special needs of a particular section of the population. Implicitly, then, the authors return to the interpretation offered for the nineteenth century incidents in placing the blame for the violence on the inability of an aggrieved group to make its voice heard in the councils of the realm. This point is made explicitly by books in relation to conscription and the Quebec City violence:

> C & L: 427 – [The conscription crisis is a reminder to Canadians] that their country exists only upon compromise . . . neither race can force its unlimited will upon the other.
>
> P & S: 159 – Canada learned a hard lesson from the conscription crisis. . . . [the need for the] principle of compromise.

A second and more immediate cause of violence named by some but not all authors is the provocation of the discontented by the use of governmental force against them. C & L and P & S claim the Quebec violence arose out of the government's attempt to enforce the conscription act. Brault (124) blames the "rigueur excessive" with which the law was applied for the original outbreak, and the presence of heavily armed troops for the final incident: "On poste des mitrailleuses ça et là et la cavalerie patrouille les rues de la ville. Cette provocation fait éclater la bagarre." Four books (Lambert; Allen; M & S; and W & R) argue that the arrest of the strike leaders touched off the June 21 riot in Winnipeg. Two others (R, S & R; P & S) claim that the violence was actually started by the authorities. With Regina also, three books (Brault; N, B, R & K; and H, H & K) blame the riot on the intervention of the police. Of the 23 accounts of violence, then, 12 refer to the provocative behaviour of the authorities.

A third cause mentioned by a few authors is the incitement of agitators. It is not raised in connection with Quebec, and only Allen (236) refers to the leader of the On-to-Ottawa trek being "bent on inciting a riot" at Regina. The role of agitators in the Winnipeg general strike, and thus indirectly in the accompanying violence, is noted rather more often. Three authors (P & S; Hodgetts; and Brault) speak of the strike taking place "according to plan" or as a result of agitation. The agitators referred to are the delegates to the Calgary convention of March, 1919. Of the five books mentioning the convention in the context of the Winnipeg strike, all comment on its radicalism. Allen (174) labels the delegates "these revolutionaries – Canada's first true revolutionaries, as distinct from its rebels", while Hodgetts (269) calls the convention "the first important sign of revolutionary activity—there seems no other word for it". Presumably the use of the word "revolutionary" designates at least a deliberate attempt at agitation.

This impression is strengthened by the comment that the delegates broke up "spoiling for a fight/battle" (Allen: 178; M & S: 178). Hodgetts, P & S, and Allen note that the strike leaders were charged with seditious conspiracy. Wallace (217) also refers to the labour movement taking on "a revolutionary character" at Winnipeg, and six authors mention that the strike leaders called themselves the Winnipeg Soviet. Rather more than half the books, then, allow some role for agitation at Winnipeg. Only H, H & K (322) take space to deny the existence of a conspiracy, although R, S & R (174) describe the strike as resulting from the decision of the "entire working force", and W & R (340) speak of it as arising from the decision of individual unions.

The presence of agitators serves as an answer both to the question of what causes violence and to that of who engages in violence. On the latter question little further information is given. Of the 23 descriptions of violence, six give no clue to the participants and a further nine simply name the obvious participants, such as strikers or marchers. This leaves eight references of further interest. In five of the eight, the violent are described as a mob or a crowd, terms which imply a measure of irrationality and destructiveness absent from the more colourless references to strikers or marchers. Two further references, Brault's "milliers de grevistes" and N, B, R & H's "transients milling around in a troublesome mood", carry some of the same connotation. Three of the eight references refer as well to the youthfulness of the participants, again implying an element of irresponsibility. Such descriptions are nevertheless very much in a minority.

Government actions to counter the crises are dealt with fairly widely. Four of seven books dealing with Quebec mention some governmental response, as do 11 of the 13 books covering the Winnipeg general strike and all six books dealing with the Regina riot. The four relating to Quebec City simply note the sending of troops, with P & S (158-159) adding: "the government passed an Order-in-Council that anyone preventing the enforcement of the Military Service Act would be considered as drafted." Only Brault is critical of the government's military coercion, which he considers to have been provocative.

With regard to the Winnipeg general strike, the federal government's actions in relation to the strike must be distinguished from its actions in relation to the violence. On the latter we are told very little beyond the fact that troops as well as police were involved. R, S & R (174) and Allen (180), however, mention that the government had quietly sent military reinforcements into the city prior to the violence. The authors have more to say on the government's response to the strike as a whole.

The following actions are attributed to the federal authorities:

—arrest of strike leaders: Hodgetts; Lambert; R, S & R; Allen; P & S; Brault; H, H & K; M & S; W & R. (9 mentions)

—section 98: C & L; P & S; N, B, R & H; M & S. (4 mentions)

—streets patrolled by NWMP and troops: Allen; P & S; H, H & K; R, S & R. (4 mentions)

—ordered own employees back to work: R, S & R; Allen. (2 mentions)

—two cabinet ministers come to city to tell "populace to stand firm": Allen

—labour newspaper suppressed, meetings and parades banned: P & S

—attempt to pin strike on foreign agitators: H, H & K.

All these actions are repressive in nature. There is no suggestion in any of the books that the government tried to negotiate with the strikers or to remedy their grievances.

Practically all the books criticize the government's actions. As noted above, four books argue that the arrest of the strike leaders triggered off violence, one of them (W & R) specifically calling the arrests a blunder. Three other books (Hodgetts; Brault; and H, H & K) remark on the protests that greeted the arrests. Section 98, the criminal code amendment dealing with "unlawful associations", is invariably described as being "rushed" through Parliament and as being an affront to Canadian civil liberties. In addition, R, S & R are scornful of the government's imposition of "yellow-dog" contracts on its employees, and H, H & K cite J.S. Woodsworth being contemptuous of the government's attempt to find foreign Bolsheviks under the Winnipeg bed. M & S describe the government as acting in a panic. Allen generally finds the federal government hesitant and dilatory. The books, in short, have very little good to say of the federal government's handling of the strike. What counsel they offer, however, is mainly of a negative nature, with the arrest of the strike leaders being particularly condemned.

With the Regina riot as well, three (Brault; N, B, R & H; and H, H & K) of the six books treat the attempted arrest of the march leaders as a blunder which touched off the rioting. While C & L do not mention the Regina incident specifically, they note (442) that "when armies of unemployed went on 'hunger marches', they were, on some occasions, handled with severity by the R.C.M.P." This, the authors argue, gave radical elements "all the glory of martyrdom without its disadvantages." N, B, R & H (233) also contend that incidents such as Regina offered Communists "added propaganda about what they advertised as the brutal oppression of the working class." Allen, Brault and M & S note that the government, while ordering the marchers to halt at Regina (why at Regina is not explained), invited a delegation to come east and meet with the prime minister. The issuing of the invitation is not commented upon; the failure of the ensuing discussion to achieve anything is simply noted.

All in all, the books offer little positive advice to a government confronted with violence. One can only extract from the texts as a whole a weak admonition to think twice before using troops or making arrests. As with the treatment of the Riel rebellions, the authors ignore the pressures and uncertainty amid which a government must work. In addition, they fail to mention the complications resulting from federal-provincial-municipal relations. While occasionally bringing the mayor or provincial premier into the picture, the authors usually leave these characters in the background. They seem to assume that an outburst of violence is automatically a problem for Ottawa to solve and that the other levels of government will fall meekly into line. In fact, especially with Regina, relations between the federal and provincial governments could have become very strained.

The consequences attributed to the incidents are various. One consequence noted by a number of authors (C & L; Lambert; P & S; Brault; and M & S) is an exacerbation of inter-group relations. On the one hand, the rioters are left with bitter memories of governmental repression; on the other, to non-rioters, the rioters seem more distant than ever. Such costs, moreover, are not balanced by benefits. Conscription did not end with the Quebec riot; most authors agree that the Winnipeg general strike collapsed without accomplishing its major goals; the On-to-Ottawa marchers did not find employment.´ The consequences of rioting, apparently, are mainly negative. Positive aspects are mentioned only in respect to Winnipeg: three books (Hodgetts, R, S & R; and H, H & K) note that the leaders of the Winnipeg protest came to political prominence as a result of their roles in the strike. In addition, Allen, H, H & K, W & R, and perhaps Lambert, speak of Winnipeg as opening the curtain on a new age of industrial and social relations. However, all these positive references are to the strike rather than to the violence. In short, while the authors' sympathies often lie with the Québécois, the strikers and the marchers, the resort to violence, although perhaps understandable if it was provoked by the authorities, is not regarded as justifiable in terms of what it achieved.

Like the commentaries on the Riel rebellion, references to violence downplay bloodiness. Most authors ignore violent incidents during the Quebec riots and the Winnipeg general strike. The Quebec City affair included at least four separate outbursts—separate in the sense that the violence had died down and then flared up again. Only Brault of the seven authors describing Quebec mentions this number of outbursts. During the Winnipeg general strike there were two riots (June 16 and June 21) as well as a number of lesser incidents. Of the ten books, only Allen and M & S refer to more than one riot, while R, S & R mention one riot and one of the lesser incidents.

Three of the seven books mentioning the Quebec riots give no figures for deaths or wounded. Only two of the ten Winnipeg references fail to mention at least one death, but on the other hand only half refer to less serious injuries. Of the six books dealing with the Regina riot, three refer to deaths and two to injuries. Roughly half, then, of the references to violence are made without drawing attention to the full extent of the casualties.

In labelling violence, too, the authors for the most part simply choose a noun without colouring adjectives. Riot(s) or rioting is the most popular choice, but other similar words also appear: disturbance, outburst, melee, and clash. On six occassions nouns are given some adornment: the violence is characterized as "serious" twice, "bloody" twice, and "wild" and "tragic" once each. In addition, Hodgetts and Brault, for reasons best known to themselves, describe the Quebec riots as civil war. Such references are exceptions, however; the great majority of books do not dramatically label the incidents.

In the case of Winnipeg and, to a lesser extent, Regina, a number of authors downplay violence in other ways as well. Some simply remark on the absence of violence in the country or the general peacefulness of the strike. Others treat the strike as anomalous. Still others view the period as highly tense and volatile, the breeding ground for explosions of violence. In comparison, the actual outbreaks are made to appear restrained and limited. Two reasons are offered for this restraint: the wisdom of the strike leaders and the refusal of "ordinary" citizens (that is, non-strikers) to panic. Calmness in the face of an emergency is elevated to the level of a national characteristic. Notions of Canada as a peaceable kingdom appear as the authors compare Canadians with their neighbours to the south.

Notes

1. *The Social Construction of Reality*, 41.

2. "Collective violence in European perspective", 7-8.

3. C. Hovland *et al., Communication and Persuasion,* 250.

4. "Violence in Canadian history", 68.

5. *What Culture? What Heritage?*, 18.

6. Many more than these 24 texts have been authorized for use in Ontario schools.

7. *What Culture? What Heritage?*, 18.

8. There are only 13 possible references to the Regina riot instead of 17 because four books were published before 1935.

Part III Section D

CONTROL AND DEVIANCE

29

Socialization in Prison*

W.E. Mann

The focus of this article is on the process whereby offenders sent to a medium-security reformatory in Central Canada are socialized to accept and support its inmate subculture and value system. An examination is made of the inmates' culture, the stages by which the new inmate is introduced to it, the means used to induce him to accept and internalize the norms and values that compose it, and some of the changes in self-image and role which occur, as well as the difficulties faced by inmate culture-bearers in socializing the new inmates fully.

The reformatory in question is given here the name of Jointville because prisoners call it "the joint". It has a population of 950 to 1,000 inmates, ranging in age from 16 to over 70. Sentences range from three months to a possible maximum of six years less four days, with the average term served being five to six months. In deference to the principle of segregation of offenders, Jointville screens out the better risk first offenders that reach its doors and sends them to a nearby minimum-security institution, and does not admit any second offenders over the age of 20. The result is that, in 1961, 66.5 per cent of its inmates were under the age of 21, and of the total population 14.5 per cent were first offenders, 28 per cent second offenders, and 26 per cent third offenders; fourth offenders and over comprised 31 per cent. Roughly half the men are confined to individual cells and half to dormitories.

To ensure the custody of the inmates a staff of 270 guards was employed in 1961, along with some other administrative and rehabilitative personnel. Prisoner counts to ensure against escapes are conducted a dozen times in the average day. Punishment devices include twelve solitary cells in the basement, which chaplains are not allowed to visit and in which food and living conditions are rigorously spartan.

The general structure of what Goffman in *Asylums* has called the totalitarian system prevails at Jointville, with a military type of organization of officials enforcing

---

*Abridged from *The Canadian Review of Sociology and Anthropology,* 1:3 (August 1964), 138-155. A complete version appears in W.E. Mann, *Society Behind Bars,* Toronto: Social Science Publishers, 1967. By permission of the author and the Canadian Sociology and Anthropology Association.

a large body of regulations. After three weeks in reception, inmates are assigned to work gangs which run a farm, maintain elaborate grounds, shift sand from place to place, make uniforms, prepare meals, can food and construct park benches. About fifty inmates are learning trades, although skills attained were in 1961 not acceptable by unions for apprenticeship purposes.

The research for this study was based on three methods of investigation. First, certain simple and basic observations were made as the writer acted for a year as a voluntary unpaid chaplain to Anglican inmates. The second major line of investigation consisted of interviews with former inmates a few days or weeks after their release, and some participation in their leisure activities. The third line of investigation was an examination of the annual published reports of the provincial department that runs Jointville.

As in other penal institutions, the inmates at Jointville have created a distinctive cultural and moral system which meets many of the basic social, sexual, and escape needs of its participants. Jointville's inmate culture has several main components. It has an economy using scarce, administratively illegal items called contraband—tobacco and pills, as well as money—as media of economic exchange. It has a stratification system with five "classes", an upper level of wheels, an upper-middle-class grouping called "wheelers and dealers" who itch for upper status and work hard at contraband merchandising and contact making, a middle class called solid types, an amorphous, unintegrated collection of prisoners labelled "goofs" (few of whom, naturally, admit such status) who are but partially socialized to criminal values, and finally the "scum" of Jointville. the "rats", men who are detached from the inmate codes to the point where they occasionally assist officials with "inside" information. As in other prisons, there is in addition a politician's group, called at Jointville the "fifth floor men", who by virtue of white-collar jobs can wring concessions from the authorities by fraud, ruse, or deceit, and who are aligned, ambivalently, with the "wheels".

There is also a pro-con ideology and moral system, concentrated in the prisoner's code and enforced mainly by wheels and solid types, which enjoins inmates to avoid fraternizing with guards or giving aid or information to the administration, to avoid hard work, to dress and operate smartly, to be tough, and to stick by friends.[1] The subculture has recreational institutions focused around some admistratively supervised items like boxing and such inmate interests as teasing and gambling and escapes as means of releasing tensions; barbiturates, home-made brews, naphtha gas, and contrband imported liquor are used illicitly. It also includes many mechanisms for getting around official restrictions and norms, sometimes called conniving, and a system of mutual obligations and reciprocities, making for a loose kind of social integration.[2]

The emergence of an inmate subculture and its acceptance by many prisoners is intimately related to a selection process whereby the population of Jointville tends to be composed mainly of lower-class or working-class males. The successful socialization of new inmates (fish) to the inmate subculture and much of the form that it takes is dependent to a high degree upon their prior internalization of, or exposure to, a lower-working-class or lower-class value system. This, Cohen has noted, emphasizes values of violence, personal autonomy, and impulse gratification.[3] Departmental records indicate that over 77.8 per cent of the inmates admit to unskilled or semi-skilled occupations, such as trucking and labouring, and that over 54 per cent have a grade 8 education or less; [4] these figures suggest a predominantly lower-class and working-class background for the inmate group. Interviews and random contacts with scores of ex-inmates also indicate that well over 50 per cent have resided in urban or rural slum or lower-working-class areas.[5] It may be expected, then, that a substantial number of the inmates have been exposed to techniques of petty crime, to certain basic anti-social norms and values common to the lower class and the criminal culture[6] and to significant defensive and neutralizing rationalizations about police, social workers, clergy, and psychiatrists. The fact that a great majority of Jointville's prisoners were convicted of at least two illegal offences before incarceration also indicates some significant degree of acquintance with anti-social or delinquent values.[7] B and E (break and enter) "artists", thieves, and assault offenders, who make up over 75 per cent of Jointville's members are more likely to have such acquaintance than those convicted of white-collar crimes or simple (joy ride) car thefts.

The length of term and number of terms served also affect the degree of socialization attained. Interviews indicate that repeaters, especially those serving a third or fourth term, have internalized a great proportion of the subculture and its values. It is these who teach the newer prisoners, acting in a way as parent surrogates. Long termers serving twelve to twenty-four months likewise tend, other things being equal, to identify strongly with the inmate subculture. But even first timers serving short terms of five or six months usually move significantly towards the inmate norm and value system. Usually, only those serving the very short three-month term can avoid the impact of the inmate society and its socializing agents. Apart from class factors, age and marital status are significant. Men over 30 and those with strong home ties are more resistant to the socializing pressures. The influence of a stable domestic life and settled habits block rapid and sweeping changes in norms and self-image.

Analysis of the process of socialization must begin by an examination of certain common pre-Jointville experiences that facilitate acceptance of the standards and ways of the inmate community. First, a majority of inmates have a history of membership in cliques, "partnerships", or small gangs in which lying, stealing, drinking, and concealment devices designed to fool the police and other representatives of the community are common. Though not necessarily participants in the type of gang characteristic of the depression, the majority of inmates have experienced, usually before the age of 12, some personal ties with one or more such formative primary groups. Secondly, from 30 to 40 per cent of the fish coming to Jointville have previously spend up to a year in juvenile correctional institutions.[8] Even before arriving at such institutions juveniles are often held for a week or more in detention homes where they may associate with a ready-made primary group whose subterranean code favour lying, conniving, and anti-authority attitudes.

At the provincial juvenile institution for those 13 and older, inmates often learn certain basic aspects of the criminal subculture, including techniques of thieving, conning the guards, conniving, and avoiding imposed work. They also may develop an interest in some criminal values and a certain psychological immunity to such normally disturbing experiences as brutal beatings and homosexuality. One informant told how he learned at a juvenile institution that the correct way to handle anyone who rats to the police is to "smash" him at the earliest opportunity.

When "graduates" of juvenile institutions first enter Jointville they already know quite a few prisoners and, what is equally useful, have some know-how by which to discriminate among the various types. As one such prisoner intimated, finding old "buddies" at Jointville can be really useful: "A guy is away ahead if he goes in and knows somebody already there. This guy briefs you on what smocks and boots are worth, gives you the score on gambling and makes it so you won't get pushed around." Thus, prior experience in a correctional institution helps in avoiding some of the penalties of being a novice, and may accelerate identification with the inmate subculture and value system.

Incarceration in a county jail may have similar results. Thus, the experience of being locked up in the county "bucket", as it is called, and faced with trial and a possible sentence turns the prisoner's thoughts to how he will get along, if sentenced, in Jointville. Because many young lower-class youths are caught with the evidence and do not seek a lawyer they tend to expect a term of imprisonment when first in the county jail. One inmate noted, "From the time you get sentenced you begin thinking of what you will do in the institution. Your mind wanders to Jointville till you get there." Many fish in this situation, surrounded by a great assortment of jail recidivists, will turn to jail inmates of more experience and higher status for advice on or the "scoop" about Jointville. Again owing to the minimum or re-creational facilities provided—cards and checkers—and the prisoner's disinterest in the offerings of the library much of their day is spend in conversation, which revolves around such topics as sex, crime, tricks of fooling the police and magistrates, and the merits and demerits of the province's main correctional institutions. Besides hearing how to pull "good scores" neophytes may rub shoulders with rounders and members of the underworld, men who uphold anti-social, anti-police, and anti-bourgeois attitudes and values. One young fellow elaborates:

I met him in the county jail—he had been there before—and he told me a few things I didn't know, like what to do when you pull a score or when you get snaffled (picked up by the police). I was never to sign a statement or never to plead guilty when arrested and he told me different things to do to get out on bail.

Practical warnings like "Don't talk to anybody in a crowd unless you really them," and "Watch out for the finks or they'll turn you in before you've had a chance to think," are common. In addition, one young inmate confided, "The older men, they usually kid you along and try to make you real scared." But the older men will also give useful advice to the fish.

Further initiation into Jointville's life is provided when the prisoner is handcuffed and shipped down with other prisoners in the bus. A busload or "chain" usually consists of twenty-five to thirty prisoners. The bus ride, depending on the location of the county jail, the weather, and the route, may be short or may last several days. Handcuffed in pairs, the bus riders are drawn together by their common fate and fears, and some new friendships are begun. Conversation revolves around the institution, its rules and restrictions, on who might be there, and on devices for "making out", that is, adjusting. Formal rules and regulations are discussed and memorized. The same groups goes through three weeks of classification procedures together and its members , particularly the first-timers, may hang together for their first month or two and jointly accept increasing amounts of the inmate sub-culture, thus reinforcing its impact.

A succession of experiences in the first few weeks impress upon the rookie that he has entered a new and distinctive community and that if he fails to observe the formal regulations of the authorities and the norms of the inmate group serious trouble awaits him. In the Superintendent's speech of "welcome" he is warned not only that he is now in a prison and not a "boy scout camp", but also that he has to watch out for other inmates, and eschew their schemes. Yet it is quickly apparent that not all the prison's rules and penalties are covered in the issue rule sheet and that to find out what is legitimate and illegitimate one has to depend upon other inmates.

Like recuits in the army, newcomers at Jointville learn to watch and copy others. As one man put it: "When you first go in, the thing to do is to do exactly as the man beside you and as the man in front of you does. Always follow the man in front." In self protection, new inmates stick close to those with whom they came in, or to acquaintances from their home town, or to members of their racial group. Indeed they soon discover that they need some friends not only for protection but for comfortable survival as well. Early apprised by guards that inmates in reception are occasionally conned out of their new issue cigarette lighters, rookies become aware of their vulnerability and eager for tips on what to watch out for from fellow inmates or officials. Hence, an urgent need for orientation and reassurance drives them to seek acquaintance with one or two experienced inmates and sonsciously or unconsciously to fall in with some of the existing norms and practices for getting along.

Various official reception procedures, which begin on the first day, prepare the fish to accept prison life.[9] Among other things, he is given a short haircut, known as the "Whiffle", which takes about three weeks to grow out and identifies newcomers to guards and inmates alike.[10] It has several useful functions: one ex-inmate explained, "On two occasions I became lost in the institution, and if it hadn't been for my high haircut I might have been charged with being in an unauthorized place." This ready identification helps to unify newcomers as a group and may assist them in learning how to deal with the con lines and exploitative manoeuvres of more seasoned prisoners.

Certain reception procedures involve a thorough-going humiliation, both symbolic and physical, of new inmates. Already degraded and stigmatized by the trial and incarceration in the county jail, they are stripped, searched, finger-printed, manhandled, and deprived of almost all personal possessions. At the same time they find themselves shouted at and ordered around by the guards and generally treated as untrustworthy. Freedom to choose their clothing, toilet articles, food, or work is gone. The daily regime, corseted by a host of rules and regulations, many of which seem senseless, also reminds them that their total round of life is now beyond their own control. Though such humiliation will affect men differently, for many it strengthens feelings of inferiority and hostility to authority. For many it also leads to a search for "angles" and ways around the many rules. The rookie is on his way to discovering that almost everyone resorts to lying and evasions when possible.[11] In general, the totalitarian regimentation arouses an interest in the patterned ways of escaping from the work, the hated PT, and the custodial supervision which are available and well-developed in the inmate subculture. Thus, this early and repeated experience of ego derogation and hostility to rules and officials propels the new inmate in the direction of some of the central attitudes and values of the inmate society.

Reception over, new inmates not sent to the nearly minimum-security institution of Hopeville are plunged fully into the Jointville routine, going either to a cell or to a dorm and, after a Work Board, participating in the daily work program. Sending good reform risks to Hopeville means concentrating the more uncooperative and less educable persons at Jointville. Though aiding rehabilitation of the Hopeville inmates, the classification process also helps to consolidate the Jointville inmates into a homogeneous community.

The rookie's adjustment to the role-playing and beliefs characteristic of the prison is aided by his segregation from the law-abiding society outside. Such segregation includes the physical isolation of prisoners, their wearing of a special uniform, and their demeaning treatment as convicts. They are allowed a minimum of contact with the outside world.[12] Permitted to write one weekly one-page letter, which is then censored, they find it difficult to maintain a correspondence with more than two or three relatives or friends.[13] (This regulation is evaded by some who send out illegal notes called "kites" through cooperative guards.) Many inmates keep in touch with only one person, some with none, and their communications, though perhaps maintaining a friendship, rarely touch on or initiate important social norms or activities characteristic of the "street", Again, inmate chats with visitors are usually so short and infrequent that outside interests and realities easily grow dim.

The lack of female companionship, besides cutting the men off from a significant comformist element in the outside world, also leads to homosexual activity. The new inmate soon hears considerable homosexual talk and banter and learns that most of the anti-homosexual stigma found outside is reduced or waived at Jointville. Among a proportion of the prisoners, homosexual references are smart. In addition, a specific social relationship called lugging promotes varying degrees of homosexual behaviour. In this relationship an older inmate befriends a young and attractive boy, giving him tobacco and other gifts (such as a cross and chain) and protecting him in return for personal or sexual favours. From twenty to forty men, usually inmates of some status, are lugging someone at Jointville. Lugging introduces the new inmates into a network of reciprocities, mainly illicit. At first, the neophyte is happy to have found a strong friend and seldom sees where the new relationship is likely to lead.

A veteran summed up the attractions of being lugged: "I guess it affects his jail (prison) status. The sweet kid being lugged gets better than average clothes, etc., and shares somewhat in the solid status of his partner." The older man confirms his status by lugging a "sweet kid", who may, however, consider himself privileged and later on, if he does a second term, try to lug someone. Through such attachments the younger fish inevitably is introduced to numerous items in the prisoners' code and to central values of the inmate culture. One detached observer of the Jointville scene who spent six months there on a white-collar conviction summed up, "Of all the influence toward criminalization, this (lugging) is the most powerful." The extent of overt homosexuality is not great and many involve fifty to seventy-five inmates at a given time. However, segregation of those caught in the act fails to eradicate the pattern which guards and prisoners alike regard indifferently or accept facetiously.

Though administrative regulations and policies effectively cut off most inmates from regular means of identification with beliefs, standards, groups, and persons who uphold conventional anti-criminal norms and goals, placing young inmates in work groups of various kinds exposes them to the norms and goals of experienced prisoners, repeaters, and older men.[14] Each work group has its own work standard and methods of stalling, its own peculiar privileges or opportunities for conniving or stealing, and its own place within the status hierarchy of good or poor "Joes". This is, of course, not unlike a department in a large corporation. The difference is that the official heads of Jointville work gangs, the guards, have few incentives to offer—and none of them financial—to secure the worker-inmates' compliance with the goals of production or responsible labour.[15]

Some gangs by virtue of their method of functioning and type of membership or both generate among their members relatively little pressure to accept criminal mores. For instance, farm and teamster gangs are small units functioning far from the main body of prisoners and their daily isolation from the exercise yard and the main inmate group tends to weaken the pull of the prisoner subculture. Jobs in the tailor shop, where prison garments are made, are considered women's work and accorded the lowest status in the inmate ranking system. Few, if any, inmate leaders or aggressive "solid type" bearers of the inmate culture are found in the shop and, because great care is exercised by the administration to prevent stealing, inmates are usually unable to take out shop valuables for contraband sale. On the other hand, work gangs high in status, in solid-type membership, and in opportunities for stealing and for wheeling and dealing, are significant in orienting prisoners to the inmate culture and value system. Two of these are the kitchen, which may employ up to forty men, and the buller or main work party which often numbers over a hundred. "The kitchen is the control centre for all foods and favours, the cookies, and the ice cream and the oranges, etc. . . . A job in the kitchen gives you a great deal of control and a great deal of opportunity to buy favours and to wield influence." On the buller, the inmates' sense of belonging to a tough "solid" bunch managed by the real wheels explains much of its influential socializing role. Only physically strong prisoners can hold their own in heavy work and a certain kind of prisoner therefore finds his way into this gang which develops practices and standards highly integrated with inmate patterns of conniving, fighting, and self-promotion. Contraband is passed around, rules are broken, and malingering and conniving are common. Most of the other work gangs, such as the cannery or sheet metal shop, play no specially influential role in inmate socialization. In contrast to the buller, whose members tend to hang together a good deal in off hours, members of most other gangs disperse in the evenings into other social groups.

In a dorm the average fish has little choice but to adjust his ways to the group already there. "You've got a kinda fit into their pattern. They are used to doing things in a certain order." In such a small group refusal to accept norms on dress, language, and behaviour can hardly go unnoticed. New inmates are also put through a series of testing experiences, both verbal and physical, designed to discover their courage and fighting ability, shrewdness, social skills, and loyalty to the prisoners' code. Failures can lead to psychological or physical punishments, while success guarantees fuller acceptance.[16] It seems to be the solid types who usually enforce conformity through such techniques as ridiculing, teasing, or occasionally beating up the non-conformists. Others, of course, often join in. The power of the solid types lies partially in the fact, that, because they are not afraid of losing parole or good remission time through fighting, their threats of beatings are more meaningful than the threats of those interested in getting an early release.

The dorm, through its heirarchy and possibility of friendship, offers positive inducements to conformity, in particular some elevation of status. A rookie member may be forced to take on more than his share of sweeping and also have to act "six" (call out six, meaning nix, when a guard is seen coming), which can be both tiresome and risky. However, by conformity he may earn some status, avoid these "Joe" jobs, and perhaps get "cut in" on a profitable contraband "deal" being promoted by dorm associates.

Because legal dorm recreation is confined to reading, checkers, and chess, much free time is devoted to conversation, and inmates spin endless stories about illegal exploits, imaginary and actual. The concentration on crime in these stories reflects the fact that the only significant behaviour pattern all inmates share is illegal activity. Such conversation may seduce listeners into exaggerating their criminal experience, fighting successes, physical toughness, or loyalty to the prisoners' code. A dorm thus exposes the new inmate to a wide range of information and tricks about crime which may well excite his imagination and interest.

The process of conforming to the inmate value system typically begins with the learning and use of the prison argot. Although not as extensive as in the "Big House" (provincial penitentiary) the prison argot at Jointville includes dozens of words identical or nearly identical with those in use in other North American institutions. It is usually the younger prisoners who pick up and use the argot with enjoyment and facility while some of the older men "tend to keep to themselves a bit and loathe the way they (the main body of prisoners) like to talk."

Plunged into work gang and dormitory, after three weeks in the joint and beginning to learn the argot, the newcomer also has to pick up certain details of the economy and its operation. He learns how much various items of contraband costs in cash or "bales" of tobacco, how he can convert eight bales for $1.00, and the going price of such items as a cross and chain. His eyes are opened to ways of gambling with bales of tobacco, to places to hide extra bales, and to ways of carrying around money hidden on various parts of the body. Learning the various tricks of fooling the administration is part of "learning the ropes", that is, of making an initial adjustment to the ways of the subculture. The typical fish, owing to his low status, inexperience, and vulnerability, usually accepts the apparently inevitable and fits in at least superficially with much of the system. His adjustment occurs much faster than the usual adjustment of a stranger to a new community. "You catch on fast at Jointville or else," inmates agree. "For instance, when I first went in there, they took me for twenty-seven bales (of tobacco) in gambling and I didn't even know what was going on. Finally I got onto it, it took time, but I got on to it."[17] A fifth-floor man amplified the rigours of the learning process: "When the new men come in the wheels take them for everything that they got, which isn't much, such as tobacco, razor blades, etc. They haven't got much choice because if they don't give it to them, they just take if off them anyway, the hard way." Usually when someone is threatened only his buddy, if he has one, comes to his aid. Thus, the first timer is often one man against the crowd.

Prolonged incarceration whether in cell or dorm produces changes in self-image which are significant for socialization to the inmate culture. Certain things are clear. First, the self-image of the average offender, especially the first timer, has been shaken by the events of arrest, conviction, imprisonment, loss of liberty, and status derogation. Segregation in prison also involves the absence of such social supports as family and peer group which previously buttressed his self-image. Psychological vulnerability implies an openness to defensive rationalizations and behaviour patterns which are conveniently available in the prisoners' culture .

Though threats and acts of physical violence are common and undoubtedly exert a powerful influence, the more subtle sanctions are probably equally effective.[18] For example, in a dorm, the inmate who violates an important norm may be put on the dummy (no one will take to him) for a day or two, or be subjected to ridicule, teasing or "suckering" (being hit when he is not looking). The sanction system includes penalties severe enough to lead an inmate to seek administrative protection in the PC (protective custody) cells which are the equivalent of excommunication from the inmate community. At any given time there may be thiry to fifty inmates in such cells in Jointville. A dorm's solid types may also make a member's life so unpleasant, without actual physical violence, that in desperation he will seek from the administrators a change to another dorm.

Acceptance, at least outwardly, of the prisoner's code is also strongly pressed upon the new inmate by the ideology promoted by the experienced prisoners and seldom criticized openly. The ideology supports the value system. Key items in it are affirmations such as "We've gotta stick together," "Help the underdog," "Never trust the guards or the administration," "Don't let the guards put anything over on you," and "Working is for dopes." New inmates discover that disregarding these articles of faith brings penalties. A man may be labelled a rat of a Square John or a goof. Ratting is often dealt with by physical sanctions. Being friendly with guards—unless one is a wheel—usually leads to verbal criticism or "centring out", being singled out by a number of prisoners for derogatory or humiliating remarks. Among the solid types other basic dogmas include "Don't let anyone push you around," and "Have heart (courage)" and "Always back up your pals when they're in trouble." To gain full acceptance by this class of inmate the new inmate must in due course demonstrate loyalty to these stiffer injunctions.

The significant thing at Jointville and most other North American prisons is that the inmate group dominates the socializing process, while the administration, in the absence of clear-cut reform policies and adequate qualified staff, carries on at best a rearguard, defensive action. This is not to say that the large majority of inmates become unequivocally socialized to the norms of the rounders. Some find it most expedient "to play it cool". When one three-timer ex-inmate was asked how he would advise a rookie to steer clear of criminal influences, he answered, "I'd tell him to just use his head and not to be taken in by all these guys. Play it cool. There's a time and a place for everything." As Goffman defines it, playing it cool "involves a somewhat opportunistic combination of secondary adjustment, conversion, colonization and loyalty to the inmate group, so that the inmate will have a maximum chance in the particular circumstances of eventually getting out physically and psychologically undamaged."[19] He elaborates, "Typically, when an inmate is with fellow inmates he will support the counter mores and conceal from them how tractably he acts when alone with staff. Such two-facedness is very commonly found in total institutions. Those who play it cool tend to subordinate contacts with their fellows to the higher goal of 'keeping out of touble' ".[20]

At Jointville, probably a fifth or more of the inmates remain goofs and Square Johns, but a large number accept segments of the inmate value system, and a sizable percentage identify with it more or less completely. The major social influences are one-directional; the prison administration is completely powerless to eliminate the basic criminalizing forces so long as present policies and institutional conditions are maintained.

Notes

1. Sykes and Messenger succinctly itemize the main items of the code as follows: "don't interfere with inmate interests; never rat on a con; don't be nosey, don't put a guy on a spot, play it cool, don't exploit inmates, don't welsh on debts; don't weaken, don't cop out, don't suck around, and don't be a sucker." Richard A. Cloward *et al., Theoretical Studies in Social Organization of the Prison* (New York, 1960), 6-8.

2. Goffman calls these secondary adjustments.

3. Albert K. Cohen, *Deliquent Boys: The Culture of the Gang* (Glencoe, Ill., 1955). Miller and others have described other central values of this group.

4. This figure is slightly lower than that given in the records because the Department's base figure includes Hopeville inmates, a higher proportion of whom reached high school.

5. See W.E. Mann, "Social System of a Slum", in S.D. Clark, ed., *Urbanism in the Changing Canadian Society* (Toronto, 1962).

6. See Howard S. Becker, *The Other Side* (Glencoe, Ill., 1964).

7. Most teenagers in the province where Jointville is located are given probation nowadays on their first offence and are sent to the reformatory only after a second.

8. The percentage of first offenders with such experience varies from year to year and it is not readily obtained from the Department of Reform Institutions.

9. Reception procedures are encountered by those doing terms of six months or over, first offenders, and those under 21; the others go at once to dormitories. They include a battery of physical and psychological tests and an interview with the psychologist.

10. Repeaters may be able to persaude the barber to give them a regular haircut.

11. Talking out of the side of the mouth at meals, where talking is forbidden, and forging excuse slips to get out of compulsory calisthenics are two simple examples.

12. "There is often a weakening of such relationships as may have been previously built up in family, job, or community". A.M. Kirkpatrick, *Prisons and their Products,* Publication of the Ontario John Howard Society, Toronto, 5.

13. In cases of emergency this regulation is stretched.

14. Kirkpatrick summarizes as follows: "There is exposure to a social and anti-social behaviour". *Prisons and their Products,* 5.

15. Although it has been discussed by officials, there is no system of pay for work at Jointville.

16. Cressey notes, "The new man was gradually admitted into the mysteries of the inmate tribe as he bore its tests without violating its norms." Cressey, *The Prison,* 166.

17. "A young fool pays to learn", in Donald Clemmer, *The Prison Community* (Boston, 1950), 241.

18. Clemmer, *The Prison Community,* 102.

19. Cressey, *The Prison,* 60.

20. *Ibid.,* 61.

30

Social Class and Bar Behaviour During the Calgary Stampede*

Richard J. Ossenberg

Very little seems to be known about who actually participates in "community" festivals. Social scientists as well as laymen apparently assume that people generally, regardless of status in the community, more or less participate in and benefit from such festivals. In discussing crowds in general, for example, Davis states: "The individuals who constitute any particular crowd are together by accident. Having no organization and being ephemeral, the crowd does not select its participants. Necessarily, the members are drawn from all walks of life and are present in the situation only because, in pursuing their private ends, they have to make use of common conveniences."[1] And in their view of "conventional crowds" (including institutionalized festivals), Killian and Turner state that these "function in facilitating the resolution of cultural conflict,"[2] thereby implying that community solidarity is temporarily restored.

It must be obvious from daily observations, however, that such views, while democratic, are anything but accurate. Every community has its distinctive geographical and social boundary lines between rich and poor and between majority and minority ethnic groups. Certainly these lines are not absolute; but there is bound to be disproportionate representation of the various status groups in the crowds that gather for different community activities, whether for nocturnal recreation or Saturday shopping or something else. The "red-light district" thus attracts a rather different clientele than more exclusive entertainment areas, and "hock-shops" and second-hand stores are not frequented by the same persons who patronize exclusive specialty and department stores.

Certain social groups also are known to be more likely than others to participate in relatively uncontrolled forms of collective behaviour such as lynchings, race riots, and political separatist movements.[3] On the other hand, it is argued that community festivals (such as the Calgary Stampede discussed here) function specifically to enhance community solidarity through generalized participation in tension-release behaviour.[4] An historical example was the "King-of-Fools" festival of the Middle Ages which was subsidized by the aristocracy who actively participated in the fun and games, but which featured a temporary inversion of the class structure. The annual Japanese village festivals also appear to have the same purpose and consist of extremely unorthodox behaviour as well as inversion of the class structure and other

---

*Abridged from *Human Organization*, Vol. 28, No. 1 (Spring 1969) 29-34, by permission of the author and publishers. The author acknowledges the assistance of Geoffrey Caldwell, a graduate student in Sociology at The University of Calgary, in preparing this paper.

releases from everyday constrictions.[5] Similar ceremonies in urbanized societies have not received, to my knowledge, as much attention from social scientists. As a result, we lack adequate studies of the Oktober-Fest of Germany, the Mardi Gras of New Orleans, the Winter Carnival of Quebec, and the Calgary Stampede of Alberta, not to mention thousands of other community festivals in the United States, Canada, and Western Europe.

Both the paucity of analyzed cases and the implicit acceptance by many sociologists and anthropologists of a functionalist view of the integrating effect of community ritual suggested the present study of selective participation. It is based on observations made during a systematic "pub-crawl" on two evenings of the week-long Stampede which is held every July in Calgary, Alberta. The study was prompted by curiosity about the role of social stratification in encouraging or discouraging participation in this type of collective behaviour, which would be designated by Davis as a "planned expressive group" and by Turner and Killian as a "conventional crowd".[6] From a theoretical point of view, it was assumed that variations in the social class structure of communities largely determine differentiated participation in planned community festivals. In *Gemeinschaft* communities where "mechanical solidarity" within a small and homogeneous population prevails, generalized participation in festival occasions is probably usual. In urban *Gesellschaft* communities, however, social class structure seems too complex to expect the same general response.

In Canada and the United States we have considerable evidence pertaining to the "life-styles" of the different socio-economic classes. In general, for example, it can be said that middle-class attitudes abound with inhibitions and taboos against progressive and deviant behaviour, while people in lower socio-economic class positions are more concerned with immediate gratifications that sometimes explode into temporary violence. On the other hand, members of the middle class are more sensitive to legal and other restrictive norms and consequently may be more responsive to the relaxation of social controls represented by the relatively lax enforcement of those norms during community festivals like the Stampede.

It is therefore hypothesized that participation in the Calgary Stampede (as measured by bar behaviour) will be high among middle-class people and low among lower-class people. More specifically, patrons of middle-class drinking establishments during the Calgary Stampede will exhibit more festival-related aggressive/expressive behaviour than patrons of lower-class drinking establishments.

Background and Methods

The annual Calgary Stampede features a rodeo and related "cowboy" themes as central attractions. There is also the usual carnival midway (larger than most), and street dancing is common. In addition, there is a general relaxation of formal social controls, with fewer arrests than usual of ambitious tipplers, "car-cowboys", women of ill repute, and the like.

The Stampede is actively promoted in local and national mass media and has become reasonably well known throughout most of North America. As a result, it attracts a generous influx of tourists from the western United States. Since its founding in 1912, it has undergone the usual transition from agricultural fair and exhibition to urban commercial carnival which has accompanied the rapid growth of cities. The population of Calgary has increased from about 20,000 in 1912 to around 350,000 in 1966. Symbolic of this transition was the new "salute to petroleum" theme in 1966, which brought a large and expensive petroleum exhibit to the Stampede grounds. The Western Cowboy and farm themes are still present, but they are somewhat obscured by the many diverse features of the contemporary festival. In 1966, attendance exceeded 600,000 establishing a record.

In order to study one important aspect of the festival behaviour, nine beer parlours and cocktail lounges[7]—representing a cross-section of social-class-related drinking establishments in Calgary—were visited on two separate evenings during Stampede Week. I had gained some knowledge previously of the social class characteristics and behavioural patterns of customers usually found in these establishments through periodic visits in the year prior to the Stampede festival. During this year I had casually observed behaviour in all of these bars in the process of searching for a "shorthand" method of discovering social class structure in Calgary. That is, as other researchers have suggested, bars are an effective informal index of the social structure in which they exist.[8] In this connection, each of the drinking establishments was visited on at least three different occasions, including both weekdays and Saturdays.

The establishments selected for study are located in the central business district, as well as the surrounding fringe area, or "Zone-in-transition", which contains the cheaper hotels and entertainment areas found in most medium-to-large cities in North America. This fringe area, which includes Calgary's priority urban renewal project, is populated by economically-deprived people. Unlike many older industrial cities, Calgary's ecological pattern also includes deprived areas in what would normally be "affluent" sectors of other cities. Thus, in areas equidistant from the city centre can be found *nouveau riche* suburbs as well as deprived and ramshackle neighbourhoods. The two types are, of course, separated, and the annexation by the city of Calgary of formerly rural and presently deprived communities largely accounts for this ecological anomaly.

The bars that were visited were chosen both because of my knowledge of their usual social composition and activities and because of their proximity to the Stampede Grounds, thus assuring a maximum sample of celebrants. The sample was then divided into "class" groups as follows: two upper-class, three middle-class; and four lower-class. The definition of the social class identity of the bars is admittedly subjective and informal but, I believe, valid.

The upper-class establishments are usually patronized by the elite oil and ranching group as well as the *nouveau riche* and the occasional white-collar couple celebrating an anniversary. The middle-class bars are patronized by clerical workers, small businessmen, and generally middle-range employees of the larger local firms, with occasional labourers drifting in. The lower-class bars are the clearest in definition. They are patronized by service personnel, labourers, winos, and deprived Indians as well as by members of newly-arrived immigrant groups. The class distribution of bars in the sample was "biased" toward the lower-status groups. Calgary has a higher proportion of white-collar and professional workers than most cities and if the choice of bars had been based on this consideration, only two or three lower-class bars would have been included. My knowledge of composition and activities of the lower-class bars, however, was greater than that of the middle- and upper-class bars and the choice was made accordingly.

Being rather conservative with respect to confirming our hypothesis, we selected two evenings in which cross-class interaction could reasonably be expected to be maximized: namely, the first night of Stampede week, and the night before the final day of festivities. We reasoned that these evenings, unlike the "in-between" nights, would reveal the most frantic collective search for gratifications and, if only accidentally, result in cross-class contacts. The anticipation of festivities is so great in Calgary during the few days prior to the Stampede that the first "green light" day witnesses the greatest crowds, both at the rodeo grounds and in the bars. The last day is perceived as the "last chance"; it was assumed that celebrants would then attempt to "let loose" one last time.

We chose drinking establishments rather than other sites of festival activity for the following reasons:

(1) We felt that participant observation would be more easily facilitated in bars than "on the streets" or at the Stampede Rodeo grounds;
(2) It was reasonable to assume that inhibitions concerning cross-class interaction are more easily dissolved with the aid of alcoholic beverages;
(3) We theorized that excessive drinking represents a form of deviant behaviour which becomes "normal" and even goal-directed during many community festivals; and
(4) We enjoy beer.

Within the bars, we concentrated on:

(1) The apparent social class composition of patrons;
(2) The wearing of costumes suitable to the "Western cowboy theme" of the Calgary Stampede;
(3) the noise level (including the spontaneity and intent of expressive vocalization); and
(4) Physical and social interaction, including evidences of aggression and general themes of conversation.

Findings

Lower-Class Establishments. In three of the four beer parlours visited, activities could be described as "business as usual". Beer parlours in general are lower class, and the patrons appeared to be the same as those who frequent these establishments throughout the year. Most of the customers were dressed in their normal work clothes or service-trade uniforms. If anything, there were fewer patrons than usual.

Beer parlours normally abound in service personnel, labourers, marginal drifters, and members of economically-depressed minority groups, most of whom live within walking distance. Conversations generally consist of work problems, family problems, sex exploits, cars, dialogue with self (the drifters), and general backslapping and spontaneous camaraderie. Sex distinctions are maintained by segregating the men's parlour from "ladies and escorts", and fights between patrons erupt about once an hour. Police patrols outside of these bars are conspicuous at most times of the year.

During the evenings of observation only about one out of ten of the tipplers wore Western cowboy costume, and most of those who did were completely ignored by other patrons. The noise level was lower than usual. There were virtually no "yippees" or "yahoos" or other shouts of the sort commonly associated with rodeos. Social interaction was quite normal, and there were fewer than the usual number of fights between patrons. None of the conversation overheard dealt even remotely with the Calgary Stampede. Two patrons whom we questioned specifically about the Stampede indicated that they "couldn't care less", and that the Stampede was "a big fraud". One of these, a loner wearing the service-personnel uniform of a local firm, suggested that if he had his way, he would abolish the Stampede because it interfered with his usual drinking activities by "draining" the number of friends he usually found at the bar. When questioned specifically about this, he responded that during Stampede, "they just stay home". The other patron, a travelling resident of a neighbouring province, exclaimed that all he wanted was peace and quiet and he just wished he "had all the money that is spent on the phony Stampede".

The most interesting pattern was the maintenance of sex segregation. In Calgary, as in some other Canadian cities, beer parlours are divided by license into rooms for "men" and for "ladies and escorts". During the Stampede the legal ban against an "open" drinking establishment was lifted. However, patrons of three of the four lower-class establishments sampled continued their usual segregated drinking. In fact, several of us were specifically barred from entering the "ladies and escorts' " sections of these bars; and we observed that at least eight of every ten males were in the "men's" section, leaving a more than usual surplus of females in the "ladies and escorts' " section.

The only evidence of unusual behaviour was the greater than usual number of "streetwalker" prostitutes in all four of the beer parlours. During a usual evening about one in ten females in these pubs is a prostitute, whereas one in five appeared to be a prostitute during the evenings under study. We concluded that these girls were present for two reasons: (1) some may have anticipated that there would be more "tricks" in the lower-class pubs on the assumption that "slumming" parties would gravitate toward lower-class areas; and (2) some may have been excluded from middle-class establishments by bouncers hired for the occasion, or may have been discouraged by the general confusion of such places at Stampede time.

In the fourth beer parlour, patterns of behaviour deviated more from the usual daily routine. About half of the customers were in the Stampede "spirit". This included appropriate costumes, spontaneous "yippees" and "yahoos", physical interstimulation (e.g., backslapping), cross-sex interaction in the form of indiscriminate necking, and conversations characterized by expressive pleasure-seeking themes such as "sex in the office", "I'll get that bastard (boss)", "let's really rip tonight", "how's about a gang-bang", and the like. The other half of the customers behaved like the patrons of the other three lower-class establishments, but there was very little evidence of any cross-class interaction between them and patrons of different status backgrounds. Apparently the fourth beer parlour differed from the others because of its proximity to the central "high-class" entertainment core of Calgary and to the Rodeo Grounds. Accidental "drifting" seemed to account for the disruption of normal business. Certainly, this conclusion is reasonable in the light of the following observations of middle-class drinking places.

Middle-Class Establishments. Two of the three middle-class drinking establishments were cocktail lounges and the other was a beer parlour in a relatively plush hotel. Since the legal requirements for a lounge generally distinguish the "haves" from the "have nots" in Canada, it is not surprising that the majority of customers at Stampede time were apparently middle class. Nevertheless, the middle class constituted a higher percentage than usual at these places. Many of the patrons were frequent and accepted visitors. But some were out-of-towners whose class identification depended on affluent costuming and the spontaneity with which they related to and were accepted by the "regulars". Absent was the usual smattering of blue-collar workers who tend to drift into these bars and are tolerated so long as they "behave themselves".

At least 90 per cent of the patrons in these establishments wore cowboy and Western costumes. It is interesting to note that we were consistently ridiculed for not being dressed in similar costumes (hopefully, this will increase our research sophistication in the future although we still may not be able to afford cowboy outfits). The noise level in these middle-class establishments was almost intolerable. There were dozens of spontaneous "yippees" and "yahoos" competing with each other; and verbal and physical stimulation such as males clapping each other on shoulders and couples necking indiscriminately was virtually universal. From the conversations we overheard, we gathered that the collective search for sensate gratifications was extensive. Most of the customers were obviously well along the continuum from sobriety to inebriation. The majority of the table groupings seemed to consist of people who worked in the same office, with executive types freely interacting with secretaries and sundry female assistants. In spite of this clustering, however, there was considerable table-hopping; and tourists were quickly assimilated by locals who seemed ebullient about showing them a good time. For example, a rather lost looking "out-of-towner" who wandered into one of the bars wearing expensive cowboy garb was invited by one of the local celebrants to "come join us, pardner". He was immediately introduced to a newly-acquired "harem" of girls sitting at the table. In another case, a jubilant couple from a neighbouring province invited themselves to a table and were immediately accepted as friends. In this latter case, all of the celebrants, including the visitors, whipped off to a party together. Even in the one middle-class beer parlour there was absolutely no sex segregation and customers took full advantage of the temporary freedom of cross-sex interaction in contrast to the more highly segregated patterns observed in the lower-class establishments.

The prostitutes at the middle-class bars were of the more sophisticated call-girl type. Streetwalkers and lower-class revellers generally were barred from entering these establishments by guards and bouncers stationed at all entrances. The few street-walkers who wandered in seemed confused by the chaos and shortly departed without seriously attempting to solicit "tricks". We concluded that even during community festivals middle-class people tend to be endogamous in their deviant behaviour.

Upper-Middle-class Establishments. The two cocktail lounges visited are located in Calgary's most plush and reputable hotels. We had not formulated hypotheses about expected behaviour patterns of patrons in these lounges but did expect that emotional expressive release encouraged during Stampede week would not so directly affect relatively elite members of the community. Actually, the two cocktail lounges throughout the year cater to both upper-middle-class and upper-class customers who for various reasons are not drinking in their private clubs. Our expectation was based on the premise that upper-class people, similar in some ways to members of the lower class in terms of assured status and spontaneity, manage to minimize inhibitions against deviant behaviour in everyday life, and consequently generally engage more in tension-release behaviour.

Our speculation was largely confirmed. Although there was a higher proportion of costumed patrons than in the lower-class beer parlours (about 25 per cent), there was very little noise or celebration. Again, it was generally a picture of "business as usual". The costumed customers who were attempting to stimulate behaviour more in keeping with the festival soon became discouraged by the lack of spontaneous emotional contagion and wandered out to seek more gratifying places. We overheard one member of such a group exclaim (with disappointment and disgust), "Let's blow this joint—it's like a graveyard." He was a member of a group of three, all of whom were elaborately costumed and obviously disappointed by the lack of conviviality. He specifically pointed to me as I was jotting down notes and exclaimed, "Jesus, he's working at a time like this!"

Conclusion

Observations of behaviour in drinking establishments during the Calgary Stampede confirmed our initial hypothesis. Middle-class customers were obviously engaging in more spontaneous expressive behaviour than either lower- or upper-class patrons. The

Stampede week therefore seems more "functional" for people who tend to be inhibited in their daily lives and look forward to the "green light" of tolerated deviance during a community festival.

We cannot, of course, conclude that our findings suggest similar selective factors relating to participation in all community festivals. As we suggested earlier, the appeal of a festival probably depends on variations in the nature of social class structure of various communities. More specifically, festival participation may depend on the rigidity of the class structure and the extent to which ventilation of frustrations is inhibited and punished through formal social control. For example, we would expect that members of a lower social class group or a minority group who are systematically exploited and punished for deviant behaviour, would participate in "legitimate" community festivals to a much greater extent than found in the present study. We suggest that such situations might include the separate Negro parade and festivities during the Mardi Gras of New Orleans and the widespread "peasant" participation in Rio de Janeiro's "Carnival".

The findings suggest that community festivals held in cities such as Calgary reflect social class structure but do not "function" to reinforce social solidarity of members of different social class status groups. The Calgary Stampede, according to our observations, is a middle-class "binge", suggesting that even socially-approved deviant behaviour is endogamous. In a sense, the Calgary Stampede does serve to partially invert social class structure by allowing middle-class celebrants to indulge in the spontaneous and aggressive behaviour permitted to members of the lower class throughout the year. Members of the lower class, if our sample is any indication, view the contrived Stampede as frivolous and phony and apparently attempt to avoid being contaminated by the festivities.

Notes

1. Kingsley Davis, *Human Society* (New York: The Macmillan Co., 1949) 350.

2. Ralph H. Turner and Lewis Killian, *Collective Behavior* (Englewood Cliffs, N.J.: Prentice-Hall, 1957), 155.

3. See, for example, Durward Pruden, "A Sociological Study of a Texas Lynching", *Studies in Sociology*, Vol. 1, No. 1 (1963) 3-9; Howard Odum, *Folk, Region and Society: Selected Papers of Howard W. Odum*, Catherine Jocher, *et al.,* editors and arrangers (Chapel Hill: The University of North Carolina Press, 1964), 37-38; E.V. Essien-Udom, *Black Nationalism,* (Chicago: University of Chicago Press, 1962); and R.J. Ossenberg, "The Conquest Revisited: Another Look at Canadian Dualism", *The Canadian Review of Sociology and Anthropology,* Vol. 4, No. 4, (November, 1967), 201-218.

4. Turner and Killian, *op. cit.*, 153-154.

5. William Caudill, "Observations on the Cultural Context of Japanese Psychiatry", in Marvin K. Opler, ed., *Culture and Mental Health* (New York: The Macmillan Company, 1959), 218-219.

6. Davis, *op. cit.*, 355; Turner and Killian, *op cit.*, 153.

7. Distinctions are made in Calgary between "beer parlours", which may only serve beer, and "licensed lounges", which may serve an alcoholic beverage, including beer.

8. See, for example, John Dollard, "Drinking Mores of the Social Classes", in *Alcohol Studies and Society* (Yale University, Center of Alcohol Studies, 1954), esp. 96, and Marshall B. Clinard, *Sociology of Deviant Behavior* (New York: Holt, Rinehart and Winston, 1963), 331-332.

31

Marital Murder

Peter D. Chimbos

The Problem

Despite the ubiquitous nature of the family institution, much has still to be learned about the social psychology of family interaction. In particular, research on intra-family conflicts serious enough to create violence is almost nonexistent.[1] But intra-family violence is much more common than the paucity of literature would lead one to expect. This selective inattention to intrafamily violence is mainly due to the depiction of the family as a group wherein the individual finds love, cooperation, and affectionate care, and thus where his sociopsychological needs are met. Such an idealized picture of family life in western nations has been described by Steinmetz and Straus (1974) as a social myth and also as a crucial ideology which encourages people to get and stay married.

Data contradicting the idealized scenario of marital bliss are difficult to obtain, and often are not well received.[2] Intrafamilial stress lies in the secretive and private nature of family life, and relevant facts are closely guarded not only by participants but by social workers and medical doctors who respect the onus of confidentiality. In other words, intra-familial relationships, whether harmonious or violent, are considered private affairs by all concerned and resist the scrutiny of social scientists.

Intrafamily homicide, the intentional killing of one family member by another, constitutes the extreme case of intrafamily violence. The criminological literature on homicide provides us with some information about the incidence of lethal violence within the family. American data, show, for example, that 40 to 50 per cent of all homicides are carried out within the family group (Goode 1971: 631). Just over half of these homicides involved one spouse killing the other. According to Statistics Canada, at least 40 per cent of Canadian murder victims are closely related to their slayer; the majority (57 per cent) being husband or wife of the slayer. (Thus, about 20 per cent of all Canadians murdered are murdered by their spouse.) Other types of intrafamily violence[3] are far more common but they are rarely brought to the attention of public agencies such as police, family court, and social welfare institutions.

Most of the sociological information on intrafamily homicides has been obtained from general studies on homicidal behaviour. The existing studies are primarily concerned with descriptive data such as patterns (place of occurrence, methods or weapons used to inflict death) in interspouse homicide, and how the traditional

---

*Abridged and revised from the article by Peter D. Chimbos. "Marital Violence: A Study of Interspouse Homicide", in K. Ishwaran, ed., 1976, *The Canadian Family,* rev. edn. Toronto: Holt, Rinehart and Winston. By permission of the author and publisher. The author wishes to thank Mr. Randal Montgomery for reading the manuscript and providing useful suggestions.

variables of age and sex are related to such violent behaviour (Wolfgang 1958: Pokorny 1965; Voss and Hepburn 1966; Bourdouris 1971). However, there is limited research on the social processes or circumstances that lead the spouses to terminate their marriages through a lethal act.[4] Interspouse homicide is probably the most personalized of all types of homicides. Therefore, such behaviour cannot be adequately understood without considering the dynamics of interaction between the actors involved.

The present study is confined to the intentional killing of one spouse by another.[5] Our analysis is thus much less complicated than one involving other types of intrafamily homicides (e.g., infanticide, matricide) requiring different explanatory perspectives. For example, in infanticide the helpless infant plays no self-conscious role in precipitating the act, whereas in interspouse homicide the victim is usually fully aware of his or her contribution to the phenomenon.

The aim of this study was to go beyond existing explanations (patterns, age, and sex variations) and seek to determine more precisely other social conditions and processes under which interspouse homicide is likely to occur. Our methodology promises relevant information not only on violent behaviour, but also on the influence of various social and sociopsychological factors on family behaviour. This being the first "in-depth" sociological study of husband-wife homicide in Canada, it must to some extent be considered exploratory.

Toward a Value-Added Perspective of Interspouse Homicide

While violence between spouses may be related to certain variables (e.g. lower socioeconomic class, violent subculture, etc.) any comprehensive examination of interspouse homicide must do more than indicate statistical relationships between these variables. It also requires the specification of social processes and sequences of events that lead to lethal acts.We must consider then the "situational" elements which may, or may not, operate together with "historical" elements to produce the homicidal act.[6] According to Sutherland and Cressey (1970: 74-75) "the situational approach is important to criminality in that it provides an opportunity for a criminal act. However, the events in the personal situation complex at the time the crime occurs cannot be separated from the prior experience of the criminal."

Gibbons (1971) indicates that social scientists have over-emphasized the importance of early socialization and suggests that more attention should be given to situational pressures as they interact with other factors. He has suggested a "value added" orientation to homicide which examines the individual's early life experiences and the situational influences that grow out of the events closely tied to location and time of the homicidal act. A "value-added" perspective refers to a multitude of factors accumulating consecutively over the person's lifetime without which the deviant behaviour could not be elicited. Gibbons (1971: 274) writes:

> A "value added" conception of homicide would assert that the experience of growing up in a subcultural setting where violence is a common theme is a precondition for violent acts, but the specific instances of aggression and homicide do not occur until other events transpire, such as a marital dispute while drinking.

The exploration of situational elements involved in interspouse homicide is the primary concern of this inquiry. But scientific conclusions drawn from such perspectives would be limited unless we determine to what degree "historical" elements have accounted for a predisposition to violence. Historical elements would comprise the offender's early life experiences which form a potentially violent person. Such experiences include one or more of the following: (1) parents' marital conflicts including physical violence, (2) severe physical punishment or rejection by parents or guardians, and (3) involvement in physical violence as a means of solving personal disputes.[7]

Situational factors in this study are meant to apply also to the conflicting events and processes which occur during marital life. Our contention is that interspouse homicide is not "explosive" in nature; it is constructed within a situation through the process of dyadic interaction. The act itself is preceded by previous experience with violence, unresolved marital conflicts (convert or overt) related to identity threats and perpetuated by a state of psychological encapsulation and its facilitative agents or circumstances. These processes have been suggested by Lofland (1969) from an interactionist perspective.

Lofland distinguishes between adventurous and defensive deviant acts. The latter type have three phases: threat (to the actor), encapsulation (becoming immersed so deeply in the situation that the actor cannot transcend it), and closure (seizing upon a deviant solution). This sequential process, according to Lofland, may be facilitated by certain places, hardware, other persons, and by certain characteristics of the actor. For example, the risk of a violent outcome in a threatening situation is highest in a private place (or a place where violence is condoned), where weapons are present, where actively-intervening others are absent, and where the actor possesses relatively little in the way of knowledge, non-violent skills, commitment to convention, self-control, and resistance to disorientation.

Data and Methods

The data were obtained by means of personal interviews with 34 offenders (29 husbands and 5 wives) who were serving time in penal institutions of Ontario and in the Oak Ridge (criminally insane) section of the Penetanguishene Mental Health Centre. Four of the 34 subjects had been recently released from prison and were under the care of social agencies. Seventeen of the interspouse homicides in this study took place in common-law marriages, as described by legal authorities and the offenders. The other 17 marriages were legal and many were performed with religious ceremonies. In certain ways the 34 couples were much alike. They had lived as nuclear families (some with young children), and in none of them did parents or grandparents reside in the same household.

In this study we are dealing with an availability sample of adults who had recently killed their spouses on purpose. We have mainly relied on the criminal justice system to define a case of intentional killing (homicide). It should be noted that there are certain feasible limitations this inquiry has encountered. For example, our sample does not include slayers who had been acquitted or, of course, those slayers who committed suicide after killing their spouses. Some difficulties in making contacts with slayers were also experienced by the investigator. For example, a few offenders (in penal institutions) refused to be interviewed.

The cases of interspouse homicide which have been examined cannot be treated as representative of interspouse homicides in Canada or other cultures. The facts and conclusions drawn from the findings are meant to apply only to these cases. However, hypotheses and interpretations developed in this work could have general relevance.

The semistructured interview was the method chosen to gather data on family dynamics, history, and socioeconomic aspects of interspouse homicide. The first part of the interview schedule dealt with qualitative information on the subject's early childhood experiences and marital life. The subject was also asked to give a personal account of the social pressures that led him or her to the homicidal act. The questions were designed so as to specifically ascertain (a) early family background (parents' relationship, subject's relationship to parents, physical punishment), (b) conflicts, separations or divorces, (c) involvement in previous violence with spouse or others,

(d) whether the slayer felt his or her self-image was threatened by the victim's remarks or actions, (e) the degree of involvement by friends, relatives or counsellors and (f) the structuring of the homicidal act.

The interviews were conducted over a twelve month period. This unexpectedly long time was due chiefly to delays on the part of the institutions arranging the interviews. For most subjects, at least a year had elapsed between the homicide and the interview. The average span was three years.

The investigator was aware of the difficulties in getting valid information from personal interview with the offenders. Some subjects were reluctant to answer or expand on delicate questions but efforts to establish a sympathetic and confidential relationship minimized difficulties.[8]

Findings

The mean age of the respondents at the time they committed the homicidal act was 35.0 and the median age was 33.0. Not surprisingly, there were more men than women.[9] The majority of the respondents had relatively low academic achievement and came mainly from unskilled or semiskilled occupations. An examination of the offenders' employment status and financial difficulties prior to the act suggests that economic pressures were not relevant factors in producing lethal violence. For example, 26 (74 per cent) of the respondents stated that they had no financial difficulties during the six months prior to the homicidal act. Even the 8 (26 per cent) of the respondents who were unemployed, working part time, or irregularly employed reported that their financial difficulties were minor and not directly related to their marital conflicts.

The length of marriage at the time of the offense has also been considered. The data suggest that common-law marriages are more likely to terminate earlier than legal marriages through lethal violence.Specifically, 53 per cent of the common-law marriages had existed less than four years when the homicide occurred, compared to 29 per cent of the official marriages. Only 17 per cent of the common-law marriages had lasted over ten years compared to 41 per cent of the official marriages. The majority of families had children, but contact between parents and children (especially children of divorced couples) was minimal.

The demographic attributes cited above could be considered as predispositions in the aggregate sense that they identify high risk groups, but they have little validity for individuals. Millions of couples may have high-risk attributes without being involved in interspouse homicide. In the following pages we trace specific individual and familial events which carried the spouse along the path to homicide.

Actor's Early Life Experiences

Previous studies based on learning theory have revealed some relevant information regarding particular socialization patterns (e.g., physical punishment, parental rejection) as being preconditions to homicidal behaviour in later life (Gold 1958; Palmer 1960). A more recent inquiry by Straus (1971: 658-663) has shown that the use of much physical punishment tends to produce a child who is high on aggression, lacks internalized direction, and hence is more amenable to external controls. Owens and Straus (1973) verified the hypothesis that the more a person experiences violence as a child (e.g., being a victim of violence, committing, or observing violence) the more likely he is, as an adult, to approve of violence as a means of social control. Early life experiences have deep seated and lasting effects on attitudes toward violence (Owens and Straus 1973: 5). The learning process, however, takes place within primary groups, especially the family of orientation. In other words, family violence is learned in early childhood. Thus, when husbands and wives are involved in violent interaction they are both acting out models of behaviour learned in childhood from significant adults, and supplying the same role models for their own offspring.

In this inquiry the respondents were asked to give an account of their early family experiences by indicating how their parents got along. Respondents were probed concerning any severe quarrels, assaults, separations and divorces that might have occurred. Further probing was used to obtain information regarding the respondents' childhood relationships with parents, siblings, and peers.

Respondents seemed to have no difficulty recalling traumatic experiences of childhood such as severe punishment and serious conflicts between parents. Incidents of brutal beatings by parents or guardians were related in considerable detail by respondents who were victims.

A majority of the respondents had experienced a rather unhappy early family life. Approximately 65 per cent had seen their parents embroiled in serious arguments or assaults. Thirteen (35 per cent) stated their parents had been divorced or separated at least once. The respondents who had practised common-law unions were more likely to come from unstable families.

An attempt was made to explore the interviewees' direct experiences with violence throughout their lives. As Table 1 indicates, 23 (approximately 68 per cent) ot the respondents had experienced physical violence in early life, mainly at the hands of parents or guardians. Nine (26 per cent) did not experience physical violence in their early family life but had been involved in physical fights at least once after the age of 16. Only two of the respondents had never experienced (or at least could not recall) physical violence in their lives. These results tend to confirm the assumption that early exposure to violence is a precondition for later violence. However, they do not unequivocally confirm this assumption insofar as two respondents reported no childhood violence.

Table 1

Experience with Violence in Early Family Life and Involvement in Violence after the Age of 16 and prior to the Homicidal Act

Experience with violence	Frequency	Percentage
Experienced violence in early family life and after the age of 16	20	58.8
Did not experience violence in early family life but experienced violence after the age of 16	9	26.5
Experienced violence in early family life but not after the age of 16	3	9.1
No previous experience with violence	2	5.6
Total	34	100

Beatings and beltings were the most common methods used by parents to control the child's behaviour. At least twenty (59 per cent) of the respondents described physical punishment by parents as severe. For some the punishment can only be described as brutal as it caused physical harm (e.g., broken ribs, cuts in the head, black eyes). The following quotations are typical examples of physical punishment described by many respondents.

> I remember three serious beatings I got from my father. One time he beat me up so bad I had to go to hospital for broken ribs. He used to beat all of us children senselessly. I always felt that my father hated me. I had nothing else but fear of him. He was a dirty, sick old man.

> I was really mistreated by my foster parents when I was about fourteen. I got many good beatings from them, especially black eyes. I just couldn't stand them and many times I ran away from home. Later on I had many good fights with other children at school, and even with my teachers.

Early family life experience, especially relationships between the respondents and their parents, can be characterized as being physically punitive, distant, conflicting and, for some, psychologically traumatic. Thus, growing up in a familial setting where physical punishment, parental resentment, and conflicts are common tends to be at least an inadequate preparation for future social adjustments.

Marital Relationships and Conflicts

What happens from the time couples enter conjugal union is just as important to our analysis as early socialization. The lethal act is built upon previous events of significance to the spouses.

One of the most important single findings is that the lethal act was rarely "sudden, explosive, and unexpected". In 85 per cent of the cases (29) it was the end result of a long-standing series of conflicts over sexual refusals or extramarital affairs. Nine per cent (3) cited ongoing quarrels over excessive drinking of alcohol. Only six per cent reported no serious chronic conflicts in the marriage, but these two respondents were mentally ill.

Twenty-two (65 per cent) of the killers stated that they had been temporarily separated from their spouses at least once. At least 43 per cent of the respondents mentioned that threats to kill (on the part of the offender, victim, or both) had been made previous to the final act. These threats were usually made during marital squabbles over sexual fidelity, sexual refusal, or, much less often, drinking. Thirteen of the offenders had previously received death threats from their spouses during arguments.

An attempt was also made to find out the extent to which marital quarrels involved physical violence. The following question was asked: "Had you ever been involved in physical violence—fights—with your wife (husband)?" No less than 23 (70 per cent of the respondents replied in the affirmative. In fact, for 19 of these couples (83 per cent of the 23), the homicide occurred within four months of a previous fight. Of the couples who had fought at least once, over half (13 or 56 per cent) had fought three or more times. Stated another way, almost 40 per cent of the total sample of couples had engaged in violent fights three or more times prior to the homicide.

Only 11 respondents claimed that there had been no fights prior to the fatal deed. Of these 11 respondents, six admitted physical fights with others at least once after the age of 16. Therefore, the vast majority (85 per cent) of the respondents had been participants in previous violent interaction with spouses or others after the age of 16. The five respondents who were not involved in physical fights after the age of sixteen declared their early family life as frustrating. For example, two of them had received severe beatings from parents and older siblings, while others felt they had been denied proper love and affection. Four of these five respondents were classified as mentally ill.

The finding regarding previous marital quarrels and violence is extremely important in that it could be useful to police and social workers in preventing interspouse homicide. It also destroys the claims of certain psychiatrists who hold that marital homicide is an unpredictable outburst by someone who has made no complaints. Again the discrepancy between such contentions and our own findings is due to the fact that psychiatrists generalize from their clinical observations of mentally disturbed patients. Such findings, while valid, do not apply to the majority of husband or wife slayers (who are not labelled insane).

Our results concur, however, with the contentions of others who have propounded that homicidal behaviour is learned and built upon previous physical violence (Wolfgang, 1958; Wolfgang and Ferrauti, 1967; and Hartung, 1966).

The Structuring of the Homicidal Act

The specific act of killing does not occur without the presence of situational factors, that is, a diathesis or proneness instilled by early experience is a necessary but insufficient factor. The immediate situation is itself a key variable in determining whether murder will be committed. Therefore we must consider the conditions or processes upon which the phenomenon of spouse killing is built. In other words, our analysis must examine the transactions that occurred between the actors just prior to homicide.

Lofland's (1969) discussion of defensive deviant acts also recommends exploring the conditions which facilitate the occurrence of violent interaction. The process must first involve an event or events which the actor defines as being a threat to his or her identity. Toch (1969), in analyzing chronic assaulters, found that humiliating remarks and threats to reputation were the major precipitants of violence. Hepburn (1973: 423) concurred that "It is the perception of threat that transforms a harmonious nonidentity-directed interaction into a hostile, identity-directed encounter."

In this inquiry the following question was asked in order to find out whether the respondents had experienced social threats by their spouses: "Did your wife (husband) ever do or say anything to you that really hurt your feelings, or humiliated you before others? If yes, what did he (she) say or do to you, and how did you feel about it?" This question enabled the researcher to determine the presence of identity threats perceived by the actor (slayer) as destructive to his personal pride and self-esteem. According to the respondents the ego-threats presented by their spouses prior to the lethal act ranged from verbal insults (e.g., humiliating and vulgar remarks) to deviant acts (e.g., extra-marital affairs). In many instances both verbal insults and extra-marital affairs operated jointly to instigate serious conflicts or assaults between the spouses.

Our data show that identity threats presented to the offender by the victim were primarily based on deviations from socio-moral (rather than peculiarly individualistic) expectations. At least 82 per cent of the respondents mentioned social threats associated with sexual matters and deviant love affairs. Even two of the five slayers who were classified as mentally ill had experienced marital conflicts based on sexual behaviour.

The following comments made by respondents are illustrative:

> The love affairs she had with another man and making nasty comments about my sexual performance really hurt me. I felt that everything was drained out of me. The other fact was that my car, home, truck, was in her name. She wanted everything in her name.

She would humiliate me in front of others on purpose. She knew I wouldn't argue in front of others and she said nasty things to hurt me. At times she tried to belittle me about my sexual performance. She did not enjoy sex with me, but I never had any complaints from other women. I started to believe that I was impotent. I tried to talk to her about our problem but she would ignore me.

Since there is little difference between the type of immediate threats made and the source of chronic quarrels it is concluded that most of the victims contributed to their own demise over a period of years. By continually and repeatedly threatening the offender, by withholding sex, having affairs, or insulting the offender's sexual skills, the victims unwittingly set the stage for their own murder.

Serious threats played an important role in building up hostilities between the marital partners prior to the homicidal act. At least 76 per cent of the respondents had received threats from the victims the same day. Sixteen (47 per cent mentioned that their quarrels immediately before the homicidal act were based on threats related to extramarital affairs and sexual refusals. The comments below describe final quarrels based primarily on sexual and extramarital matters.

You see, we were always arguing about her extramarital affairs. That day was something more than that. I came home from work and as soon as I entered the house I picked up my little daughter and held her in my arms. Then my wife turned around and said to me: 'you are so damned stupid that you don't even know she is someone else's child and not yours.' I was shocked! I became so mad, I took the rifle and shot her.

We were quarrelling about her extramarital affairs. To be more specific we had an argument about her dancing with another man in the bar that night. I told her to be careful with him. Then she said to me: 'Don't be a fool. You are not the first person I have been to bed with.' Then I returned to my car, took a knife and came back and stabbed her.

Although 13 (38 per cent) of the respondents blamed these last quarrels on excessive drinking or said they could not remember the nature of the quarrels because of "black out", their previous marital quarrels were also based on the same kind of threatening events.

During their final quarrels, ten of the victims engaged or attempted to engage in physical assaults against the slayer. Various weapons, especially knives and bottles, were used. It is difficult, however, to determine in these cases whether the lethal act would have occurred without the victim's assaults. Such "protective reaction" violence was a common occurrence between violent spouses studied by Gelles (1973: 114-117). His findings indicate that wives are more likely to initiate protective reaction strikes against their threatening husbands. All four female respondents in our sample had experienced severe physical beatings by their husbands (victims). Three of these women committed the lethal act soon after they were physically assaulted by their husbands.

Despite the importance of the threat to self esteem, Lofland (1969) has argued that such threats are not in and of themselves sufficient for the occurrence of a violent act. To be more specific, "encapsulation in response to threat heightens Actor's sensitivity to, and proclivity to engage in acts that are short-term or quick, simple and close at hand or proximate" (Lofland, 1969: 53).

Two additional conditions which facilitate encapsulation must also be considered: the absence of actively-intervening others and intoxication from alcohol or other drugs. Following Lofland (1969: 55), the author contends that during the encapsulation period if others are not present to physically intervene, remind the actor of the long term consequences of his possibly violent act, or provide him with meaningful alternatives, the likelihood of encapsulation and its violent climax is heightened.

To what degree did respondents receive active social support from others prior to or at the time of the homicidal? Since most respondents had experienced marital problems they were asked by the investigator if they had ever been advised by anyone in coping with such difficulties. None of the respondents reported that much advice had been received. Eighteen per cent said that some advice was received, and 82 per cent reported that no advice whatsoever was received. An attempt was made to probe for possible reasons for the absence of active intervention by others. It seemed that since most of the marital problems involved moral and "personal" issues (e.g., extramarital affairs and humiliating insults), the actors felt too proud or ashamed to seek advice. The following comments are typical examples:

> I never asked anyone for advice because of my pride. I was only separated from my legal husband and did not want people to know that I now had a common law marriage. My common law husband was also separated from his legal wife. We were also completely isolated from our relatives. And our friends were alcoholics, so they couldn't help us.

> Well, my parole officer could advise me but I was afraid that he might tell me to leave her. And more than that I was ashamed to tell anyone about my common law wife. She'd been charged with prostitution three times! I could not see my explaining my wife's behaviour to anyone.

Since some marital conflicts were not only based on marital issues but also on a holism or heavy drinking on the part of one or both spouses, problem-solving was eve more difficult. Even those who tried to seek advice from others were not successful because of lack of cooperation by the spouse. The following instance is an example o such circumstances:

> My wife and I went for psychiatric help once, but we did not keep it up. The wife did not want to continue the treatment. You see the wife and I could not agree on anything so we decided to separate from each other. But I found my life very difficult without a family. My family was all that I had in this world.

The lack of involvement by others in marital conflicts is not surprising since the offenders and their spouses had been socially isolated from close relatives. The respondents were asked how well they got along with relatives during the six months prior to the homicide. Thirty-two (93 per cent) described their relationships with relatives as "cool" and "distant". Few friends were available, or able to assist the respondents. The friends were either non-existent, rarely seen, or handicapped by their own marital or alcohol problems. This finding concurs with Gelles' (1973: 241) conclusion that "violent families are characterized by isolation from their neighbours".

Encapsulation can also be facilitated when others are not present to actively intervene at the time when the lethal act is committed. Each respondent was asked if any relative or friend was present at the time of the lethal attack. If so, what did he do? Did he try to talk the actor (offender) out of it? Did he remind the offender of the consequences, or advise him to use other nonviolent alternatives to deal with the spouse? In only 20 per cent of the cases (7) was someone present at the time of the homicide, and in these cases the "others" were either too young or too drunk to help. Thus, in no case was anyone present who could effectively intervene.

The additional fact that 32 (94 per cent) of the homicides were committed in private residences suggests that the site of occurrence contributed to the tragedy insofar as the "his home is his castle" ethic prevails. The home, as Lofland (1969: 63) reminds us, is the most protected of places, wherein potentially interfering others are excluded by reason of physical barriers (walls and doors) or by virtue of legal rules regarding entry.

Intoxicants such as alcohol and drugs are also facilitants of encapsulation. The impact of alcohol upon the actor who is confronted with identity threats has been discussed by Hepburn (1973: 425). An attempt was made to find out whether intoxicants were involved in the homicidal act. The following question was asked: "Were alcohol or drugs involved in the homicidal act? If yes, who was under the influence (you, your spouse or both?)" In the majority of the incidents (at least 70 per cent) the slayers were under the influence of alcohol. In 53 per cent of the incidents both the slayer and the victim were under the influence of alcohol. As indicated earlier, nine of the slayers reported that they had been drinking so heavily that they developed "black outs" and thus could not remember the incident.

Conclusion

Firstly, early life experiences could predispose individuals to violent behaviour in their marriages. The two most important experiences were an unsatisfactory or frustrating relationship with parents and the learning of violent reactions. The data tend to substantiate theories which maintain that violence is a learned response. The findings regarding early family experiences of violent offenders concur with those of Palmer (1969), Owen and Straus (1973) and Steinmetz and Straus (1974). These studies have emphasized the social learning and role modelling of violence witnessed in childhood.

The second major focus of this study was on marital relationships and conflicts. In the vast majority of cases the murder was the end-point of (a) a series of bitter quarrels over extramarital affairs or sexual refusals, and (b) heavy alcoholic drinking patterns of slayers and victims, especially intoxication at the time of the fatal act. The culmination of the above incidents in homicide (and to a lesser extent the lack of appeals for help) means that the marital partners were incapable of solving their problems.

The findings and conceptual frame have distinguished between the ongoing conflicts of the marriages, and the particular incident which triggered the homicide. The slayer felt acutely threatened by the spouse's activities (e.g., extramarital affairs) or by specific remarks the spouse had made (e.g., insulting the slayer, especially in his or her "sensitive zone"). At this point the threatened spouse entered a mental state which Lofland calls encapsulation. Restraint and future-oriented thoughts are replaced by a seizing upon simple, immediate, often violent "solutions".

Certain conditions facilitate encapsulation, according to Lofland, and these facilitators were present at the time of the homicide. One condition was intoxication. The second condition was the absence of persons with intervening capability, such as police, social workers, clerics, respected friends, concerned relatives, and neighbours.

Notes

1. O'Brien (1971: 692), for example, indicates that in the *Journal of Marriage and the Family* (the standard reference for scientific family research) not one article on intrafamily violence has appeared in the thirty year history of the journal.

2. Recent examples are the Bakan (1971) study on child beating, thwarted attempts by others to pursue investigations of this taboo topic, and resistance to the new legal concept of Children's Rights.

3. Intrafamily violence may be "legitimate" when used in situations approved by the norms of the society (e.g., spanking the child). "Illegitimate" intrafamily violence on the other hand refers to such acts as beating a disobedient wife in contemporary American society (Straus *et al.*, 1973: 6). In certain societies, however, lethal intrafamily violence (e.g., the killing of one family member by another) has been considered a socially and legally sanctioned human interaction. Examples of such sanctioned violent acts include female infanticide among peoples of Tibet, geronticide among the Eskimos and the killing of a child or even a wife by the early Roman father who possessed strong patriarchal powers. In such cultural settings, the actor's violent act against a member of his own family is neither "pathological" nor guilt-laden.

4. On the other hand psychiatric inquiries on interspouse homicide have been primarily concerned with personality, characteristics of offenders (e.g., "pathological jealousies," "catastrophic attitudes," "unconscious furies" and "sadomasochistic complexes"). Such inquiries however, convey little of the dynamics of personal interaction and the circumstances that lead to the killings of a spouse (see for example, the works of Kurland *et al.*, 1955; Guttmacher 1955; and Cormier 1961).

5. Legally the present sample includes both homicides and manslaughters but we have not made this distinction in our analysis as we feel that the same social dynamics apply to both legal categories.

6. "Historical" elements refer to factors found in the early life experiences (e.g., severe physical punishment or rejection by parents) of the individual to which his lethal assault against his spouse can be linked. "Situational" elements refer to factors (e.g., physical assaults, and threatening acts by the victim) operating prior to or at the time of the violent event.

7. Although many of such physical fights occurred in adolescence and adult life, we consider them as "historical" in order to see the continuance of such personal experiences.

8. The number of interspouse homicides in Canada in recent years is given in Murder Statistics, 1973, cat. No. 85-209 published by Statistics Canada, Ottawa.

9. This is partly because the author was unable to interview several women, but mainly because there are many more wife-slayers than husband-slayers in Canada as elsewhere.

References

Bakan, David
1971 *Slaughter of the Innocents: A Study of the Battered Child Phenomenon.* Boston: Beacon Press.

Bourdouris, James
1971 "Homicide in the Family", *Journal of Marriage and the Family* 33: 667-67

Burgess, Ernest W. and Leonard S. Cottrell
1939 *Predicting Success or Failure in Marriage,* Englewood Cliffs, N.J.: Prentice Hall.

Cormier, Bruno M.

1961 "Psychodynamics of Homicide Committed in a Marital Relationship". Paper read at the Third World Congress of Psychiatry, Montreal.

Gelles, Richart J.

1973 *The Other Side of the Family: Conjugal Violence.* Durham: University of New Hampshire, unpublished Ph.D. dissertation.

Gibbons, Don C.

1971 "Observations on the Study of Crime Causation", *American Journal of Sociology* 77: 262-278.

Gold, Martin

1958 "Suicide, Homicide and Socialization of Aggression", *American Journal of Sociology* 63: 651-661.

Goode, William J.

1969 "Violence Among Intimates". In Muvihill, Donald J. *et al.* (ed.), *Crimes of Violence.* Washington: United States Government Printing Office.

1971 "Force and Violence in the Family", *Journal of Marriage and the Family* 33: 624-635.

Guttmacher, Manfred S.

1955 "Criminal Responsibility in Certain Homicide Cases Involving Family Members". In Hoch, Paul H. and Joseph Zubin (eds), *Psychiatry and the Law.* New York: Grune and Stratton.

Hepburn, John

1973 "Violent Behaviour in Interpersonal Relationships", *The Sociological Quarterly* 14: 419-429.

Kurland, Albert A. *et al.*

1955 "A Comparative Study of Wife Murderers Admitted to State Psychiatric Hospital", *The Journal of Social Therapy* 1: 7-15.

Lofland, John

1969 *Deviance and Identity.* Englewood Cliffs, N.J.: Prentice-Hall.

O'Brien, John E.

1971 "Violence in Divorce-Prone Families", *The Journal of Marriage and the Family* 33: 692-698.

Owens, David and Murray M. Strauss

1973 "Childhood Violence and Adult Approval of Violence". Paper presented at the 1973 meeting of the American Orthopsychiatric Association.

Palmer, Stuart *rt*

1960 *A Study of Murder.* New York: Thomas Y. Crowell

Pokorny, Alex D.

1965 "A Comparison of Homicides in Two Cities", *Journal of Criminal Law, Criminology and Police Science* 26: 479-487.

Smelser, Neil J.
1963 *Theory of Collective Behavior.* New York: Free Press.

Steinmetz, Susanne K. and Murray A. Straus, eds.
1974 *Violence in the Family.* New York: Dodd, Mead.

Straus, Murray A.
1971 "Some Social Antecedents of Physical Punishment: A Linkage Theory Interpretation", *Journal of Marriage and the Family* 33: 658-663.

Strauss, Murray A. *et al.* ,
1973 "Theories, Methods and Controversies in the Study of Violence Between Family Members". Paper presented at the 1973 meeting of the American Sociological Association.

Sutherland, Edwin and Donald Cressey
1970 *Principles of Criminology.* Philadelphia: J.B. Lippincott.

Toch, Hans
1969 *Violent Men.* Chicago: Aldine.

Voss, Harwin L. and John R. Hepburn
1968 "Patterns in Criminal Homicide in Chicago". *Journal of Criminal Law, Criminology and Police Science* 59: 499-508.

Wolfgang, Marvin E.
1958 *Patterns in Criminal Homicide.* Philadelphia: University of Pennsylvania Press.

Wolfgang, Marvin E. and Francio Ferracuti
1967 *The Subculture of Violence.* London: Tavistock.

Part III Section E

THE CITY AND URBANIZATION

32

Role Differentiation in Urban Networks*

Norman Shulman

At long last, the old rural-urban debate is running out of steam. While a few shots are still being fired, many recent studies have redirected attention to more detailed investigations of social relations and their variations in urban society. One focus of some of these studies has been the differentiations within primary relationships. In this paper, studies of such role differentiation conducted in Britain, the United States, Hungary, and Israel are examined in relation to comparable data from a Canadian sample. These latter data allow for an extension of some conclusions offered in earlier studies.

Social Relationships in Urban-Industrial Society

The so-called rural-urban debate, begun by the early statements of such eminent sociologists as Simmel (1950), Park (1925) and Wirth (1938), suggest the demise of traditional forms of social organization and particularly of primary group relationships. To this was added the view that in modern urban society, the nuclear family was isolated from the extended kin unit. Since then several writers have challenged that view by providing evidence of contact and exchange of aid among kin (Sharpe and Axelrod, 1956; Sussman, 1953, 1959, 1965). Similar, though somewhat less compelling evidence of neighbouring interaction has been offered (Gans, 1962, 1967; Keller, 1968; Tomeh, 1964), as has evidence of continuing friendships (Axelrod, 1956; Babchuk and Bates, 1963; Laumann, 1973; Secord and Backman, 1964).

The cumulative evidence eventually modified the widespread view of the city as a cold, unfriendly environment, but has never completely dissipated that view. At the same time, refuting arguments (Parsons, 1965; Guterman, 1969) have pointed out that

*Reprinted from *Sociological Focus* 9:2 (April) 1976), 149-158, with the permission of the author and publisher. The research reported here was supported in part by a grant from the Clarke Institute of Psychiatry, University of Toronto. Several people made valuable contributions to the research and/or earlier versions of the paper. In particular, the contributions of D.B. Coates, A.A. Hunter, William Michelson, S.A. Moyer, Peter C. Pineo, Charles Tilly and Barry Wellman are gratefully acknowledged.

the original statements on social relations in the city were relativistic and therefore can be challenged only by comparative data. Such data are hard to come by in a society almost completely under the sway of expanding urban centres. A new focus on urban social relations in more detailed form, has been one response. (Adams, 1968; Gans, 1962; Litwak and Szelenyi, 1969; Michelson, 1970; Pahl, 1968.)

Recent studies conducted in several countries have examined different kinds of primary relationships and have reported distinctions among roles such as kin and neighbours. In a study conducted in England, Firth et al. found evidence that kin and friends "fulfilled separate functions; . . . for the most part the two categories were kept distinct, each with its own special quality" (1970: 116).

Similar differentiations among the roles of kin, neighbours, and friends were reported by Rieger-Shlonsky (1969) using data collected from 90 interviews conducted in Israel. While considerable overlap in these roles was found, there was also noticeable specialization. The data indicated that kin were seen as providers of material benefits while neighbours were seen as most likely to be involved in social responses. Friends were higher on psychological responses such as emotional support but also provided material support. Respondents tended to report commitment as a requirement in kin relationships, likeness as the important requirement for friendships, and manners and other behaviour characteristics for neighbours.

Two studies conducted in the U.S.A. also provide evidence of specialization in the content of relationships and in their basis. Litwak and Szelenyi (1969) indicate that under contemporary social conditions the traditional types of primary group relationships–kin, neighbours, and friends–continue to function but in modified ways. They present evidence to support their hypotheses that kin sustain long term ties in spite of separation; that neighbours visit and exchange aid in spite of rapid turnover; and that friendships continue in spite of both separation and mobility. They suggest that each of these categories of relationship specializes in particular kinds of exchange. Kin are utilized for long term aid and for career and attitude formation. Neighbours, they argue, utilize proximity and face to face contact to provide aid of an immediate nature as well as in tasks based on common territorial interests, and matters of daily routine. Friends, since they are chosen on the basis of shared interests, are seen as most readily involved in shifting social concerns which are related to life status. Litwak and Szeleny (1969: 472) also present "some initial evidence" from data collected in Detroit and in Hungary which suggest support for the hypotheses, indicating that neighbours are seen as more helpful in short term (one day) aid situations while kin are perceived as more helpful for long term (three month) needs.

Adams (1967) examined the categories of primary relationships which make up the social networks of urban residents and reported two factors which seem to account for interaction: (a) affection and perceived "likeness" which he terms *consensus*, and (b) mutual need and obligation which he terms *concern*. Focusing on two categories of relationship, kin and non-kin, Adams suggested that consensus is the major factor in friendship, while concern is salient in kin relations. While his data cannot directly test this proposition (1967: 71), he does provide data to indirectly support its validity. He also found a slight preference among his young adult respondents for interaction with friends rather than kin, but kin relations were more persistent and more likely to involve open communication and discussion of confidential matters. Adams concludes that in most cases "a clear distinction was drawn between close friends . . . and . . . kin" (1967: 75). He also notes, as do Litwak and Szelenyi, that these primary relationships are sustained without on-going face to face contact.

Based on fidings reported in these earlier studies we expected our respondents to report continuation of primary relationships with kin, neighbours and friends, despite separation and rapid change; and distinction among role categories, especially between kin and non-kin.

Research Design

Data were collected by interviewing 198 residents of an inner city suburb of a large Canadian metropolis. Respondents were asked to name and provide information about their closest relationships. From the list of persons named as "intimates," 149 were selected and interviewed. The total sample then, includes 347 cases.[1]

In studying the "primary group" relationships of our respondents, we conceptualized them not as a group of relationships, but as a network. The network is seen as "a specific set of linkages with the additional property that the characteristics of these linkages as a whole may be used to interpret the social behaviour of the persons involved" (Mitchell, 1969: 2). The network, we argue, is a more accurate and appropriate conception of the set of social relationships than is the group. Many authors, including Litwak and Szelenyi (1969: 466) note that these sets of relationships are not really groups, yet they often continue to use the group concept rather than the network.

By using the network as our structural framework we are able to focus on kin, friends, and neighbours and determine their relative importance, as well as any variations in the basis or content of these relationships. We begin by identifying the composition of the personal networks of our respondents and the relative intensity of the relationships. By examining the stability of the relationships we are able to test assumptions about the effects of mobility. We then go on to examine frequency of contact, forms of exchange and the bases of exchange and the bases of relationships in the personal network.

Personal Networks of Primary Relationships

Evidence of enduring primary relationships in contemporary society is abundant. The existence of kin relationships (Adams, 1968; Firth et al., 1970; Litwak, 1959; Pineo, 1968; Sussman, 1953, 1959, 1965), of neighbour relations (Bracey, 1964; Fava, 1958; Gans, 1962, 1967; Keller, 1968, Pfeil, 1968; Shulman, 1967; Tomeh, 1964) and of friendship relations (Babchuk and Bates, 1963; Cohen, 1961; Katz, 1966; Laumann, 1973) have been established in several western societies including Canada and the United States. Our focus in this study was not any single role category but the set of closest relationships as perceived by the respondent. Respondents were asked to name, in order of closeness, the people outside the household to whom they felt closest. Those named were categorized on the basis of kinship, or of living within several blocks of the respondent. Those who were neither kin nor neighbours were labelled friends.

Most respondents named six intimates, the maximum allowed.[2] Kin accounted for 41 per cent of persons named as close, neighbours for 14 per cent, and 45 per cent were friends. The large proportion of friends is not unexpected given the relatively large field of eligibles available from which to recruit.[3]

In ranking "intimates" in terms of closeness, respondents typically placed kin—especially close kin such as parents and offspring—at the top of the list, and neighbours near the bottom. This would seem to reflect closer feelings and greater familiarity between kin than exists between neighbours.

Most of the people named were long term acquaintances. This is self-apparent in the case of kin but was found to hold for friends and neighbours also. Overall, 57 per cent of the friends and neighbours named had been known by the respondents for more than ten years and an additional 20 per cent of these relationships were between 6 and 10 years in duration. This may indicate that the rapid turnover suggested by Litwak and Szelenyi may not be widespread or that Canadian-American differences exist in this phenomenon. The reported stability of relationships suggests that it may be only over a considerable period of time that very close relationships develop. This stability exists, in some cases, in spite of an absence of regular face to face contact.

In general, most respondents saw people in their networks between three and ten times a month. This is consistent with findings of weekly contact reported in the literature (Sussman, 1959; Sharpe and Axelrod, 1956). About 20 per cent of intimates are not seen in the course of a typical month. That they continue to be perceived as close indicates, as Litwak and Szelenyi suggest, that primary relationships can be sustained without face to face contact. In many of these cases, periodic visits, regular telephone conversations, and letters are exchanged and these presumably help sustain the relationships. Relationships in which both regular visits and telephone contact were absent were reported in less than 8 per cent of the cases.

To explore the content of relationships in the personal network we questioned respondents about exchange of goods and of service. We found that lending and borrowing was reported for 26 per cent of the relationships. The most usual items exchanged were tools and equipment (23 per cent), household goods (18 per cent), and money (15 per cent). While 26 per cent seemed a rather small proportion, it proved useful to view such exchange in the context of the *network* rather than individual *relationships*. Doing so, we found that over two-thirds of the networks involved some exchange of goods. It appears then, that people require only a few sources in their total set of relationships from which to borrow to satisfy their needs. Borrowing from every person in the network would be redundant.

When asked about exchange of service and other aspects of the content of relationship, respondents usually replied that they and their intimates provided each other with a general support and companionship. Other, more specific replies were less frequent and included advice-giving on a wide range of topics (from careers to child rearing) companionship, assistance with repairs. Respondents appeared to find it difficult to specify such exchange, especially for the very closest relationships. This suggests that people find it difficult or distasteful to see close relationships in an instrumental way.

Differentiation in Relationships

The data presented to this point have indicated the existence of close relationships and the exchange of goods and services in many of these relationships. When refined, the data also show significant variation by category of relationship and by degree of closeness (these two being interrelated as noted above).

One measure of relationships is the frequency with which the parties interact. Though this may be influenced by imposed proximity at home or at work, it has been seen as a basic element of primary relationships (Cooley, 1955; Homans, 1961). Our data show that considerable variation in contact by category of relationship and degree of closeness does exist. They also indicate that, as suggested by Litwak and Szelenyi, at least some kin "learn to communicate and exchange services in other than face-to-face situations" (1969: 466). As seen in Table 1, persons named as the very closest are likely to be seen most frequently. Since those named first are often (51 per cent) kin, we find too that contact with kin is quite frequent. Usually, frequency of contact with kin is equivalent to weekly meetings. However, more than 21 per cent of kin named to the network are not seen during a typical month. This suggests that despite the absence of face-to-face contact, their relationship continues to be seen as close. Most frequent contact is with neighbours, the result, no doubt, of physical proximity. While almost 20 per cent of friends are seen very frequently, a slightly larger number are not seen at all during the month, again suggesting that methods other than face-to-face contact do sustain relationships. The major difference in contact found here is between those who are in the immediate daily environment—neighbours and work friends—and those who are not.

Table 1

Number of Contracts Per Month by Category of Relationship

No. of Contacts	Kin		Neighbours		Friends		Total
	N	%	N	%	N	%	
none	131	21.3	14	8.0	166	22.2	311
1 or 2	151	24.5	32	18.4	248	34.2	431
3 to 10	250	40.7	50	28.7	189	25.3	489
over 10	83	13.5	78	44.9	144	19.3	305
Total	615	100.0	174	100.0	747	100.0	1536

$x^2 = 120.775$ df = 6 $p < .001$

* The number of cases (1536) results from each of our 347 respondents reporting on up to 6 relationships.

Table 2

Exchange of Aid by Category of Relationship
(Percentages)

	Kin		Neighbour		Friend	
	Yes	No	Yes	No	Yes	No
Lend	25.6	74.4	45.4	54.6	23.7	76.3
Borrow	24.4	75.6	43.7	56.3	22.1	77.9
Give Help	25.9	74.1	24.7	75.3	20.2	79.8
Receive Help	15.5	84.5	18.4	81.6	15.0	85.0
					(N = 1536)	

More important than frequency of contact is the question of what people do for and with the people in their network. Earlier studies (for example, Sussman, 1959) and the high ranking of kin by our respondents, led us to expect that kin would be the most involved in exchange of goods and services. Our data support this expectation only in part. As shown in Table 2, kin are slightly more likely to provide aid in the form of services but neighbours are the most likely by far to exchange goods. Considering the most frequently exchanged items (tools, equipment, household goods) it is plausible that they most conveniently borrowed from neighbours who are located close at hand.

Table 3

Exchange of Aid by Category of Relationship
(Percentages)

Type of Aid	Kin	Neighbours	Friends	No. of Cases
General Support	58.4	46.8	69.3	408
Advice on Family & Personal Matters	8.6	6.3	1.0	33
Advice on Career, Social & Related Matters	2.4	5.1	6.9	31
Short-term Service	2.1	13.9	2.1	23
Long-term or Repeated Service	9.3	5.1	2.4	38
Social/Recreation Companionship	12.7	13.9	14.1	89
Other	6.5	8.9	4.1	38
	N =291	N =79	N =290	660
		no exchange reported		876
				1536

While kin and friends are more involved in providing general support, they appear to specialize in specific forms of aid, with kin more likely to provide advice on family related and "life" decisions (Table 3). In close accord with Litwak and Szelenyi, our data show that kin specialize in services which are required regularly or those which involve long periods of time. In contrast, neighbours, while they too provide some general support and advice are the most likely to provide short term services and to lend things. Friend relationships can be characterized as providing general support and are the most likely category to provide advice on matters of career, and various other matters related to social life, such as companionship. While the number of cases in many of the cells are too small to be conclusive, our data suggest a pattern of specialized functions similar to those indicated by Litwak and Szelenyi.

Table 4

Reasons for Maintaining Contact by Category of Relationship

	Very Important		Somewhat Important		Not Important		Total	
	N	%	N	%	N	%	N	%
(A) Obligation								
Kin	193	31.80	112	18.45	302	49.75	607	100.00
Non Kin	145	15.73	190	20.61	587	63.66	922	100.00
	$x^2 = 55.8139$		d.f. = 2		$p < .001$		1529	
(B) Their Need								
Kin	50	8.20	105	17.21	455	74.59	610	100.00
Non-Kin	54	5.82	208	22.41	666	71.77	928	100.00
	$x^2 = 8.3722$		d.f. = 2		$p < .02$		1538	
(C) Own Need								
Kin	76	12.48	129	21.18	404	66.34	609	
Non-Kin	64	6.96	199	21.65	656	71.38	919	
	$x^2 = 13.5446$		d.f. = 2		$p < .01$		1528	
(D) Enjoyment								
Kin	548	90.13	54	8.88	6	0.99	608	100.00
Non-Kin	776	83.44	137	14.73	17	1.83	930	100.00
	$x^2 = 13.7946$		d.f. = 2		$p < .01$		1538	

We pursued Adams' suggestion 1967; 1968: 195-210) that concern and consensus are the major factors in kin and non-kin relationships respectively. As shown in Table 4, our data suggest that for all categories enjoyment is the most usual reason reported for sustaining relationships. When responses are refined by category of relationship we find that obligation is given as a reason for kin relationships twice as frequently as for non-kin relationships. Need is also more frequently reported for kin relationships. These data suggest support for Adams' contention that concern factors are more salient for kin relationships.

In an attempt to further explore this kind of differentiation, we utilized two sociometric questions. First, we asked our respondents to indicate which of their intimates they would choose to help out if only one could be helped, and to give the reason for their choice. We found that choice followed rank very closely, with 55 per cent of choices coming from those named first. A large majority (62 per cent) of these were kin. Indeed many respondents (28 per cent) gave as their reason for choosing the person, the fact that it was a relative. Neighbours were the least likely to be chosen (13 per cent) while friends were chosen in 25 per cent of the cases. Here too we see the salience of concern in kin relationships.

When asked which person they would choose as a companion for a social activity, 43 per cent of the respondents indicated a friend, 31 per cent chose a relative and 26 per cent a neighbour. The differences in the two types of choices reflect a degree of differentiation by category. Kin are seen in terms of an obligation to help and concern for their welfare to a more pronounced extent than are other non-kin categories. For social purposes, however, friends are the preferred category due to the greater similarity and shared interests which characterize friend relationships.

Conclusion

When the set of primary relationships of individuals is conceptualized as a personal network, the relative importance attached to the different categories of relationships can be determined. Kin, who comprised 41 per cent of the personal networks, were typically seen as the closest intimates in the network, followed by friends. Neighbours are distinctly less important according to their numbers and the perceived closeness attached to them by respondents. The network perspective also allows us to note the availability of various forms of aid as seen by the fact that while only a minority of *relationships* involve lending, a majority of *networks* provide such aid.

It appears that primary relationships with kin, friends, and to a lesser degree, neighbours, are sustained despite the separation which occurs in some cases. As an alternative to regular face-to-face contact, telephone calls, letters, and periodic visits are used to sustain relationships. While these findings corroborate the contentions of Litwak and Szelenyi, they indicate less pervasive separation and mobility. Indeed, the relatively few neighbours in the network, and most friends, show long term relationships rather than short-term turnovers. This may point to some systematic difference between Canada and the U.S.A. in this respect.

Our data also corroborate the suggested specialization among categories of relationships. Kin tend to specialize in long term assistance, involvement in family related decisions and concerns. Since kin tend to be seen as the closest and best known intimates, reliance on them for more major forms of assistance seems appropriate. Neighbours, in contrast, are used for short-term and immediate needs, such as borrowing tools, equipment or the like, and they tend to be perceived as the least close category of intimates. Their "specialties" are based on the convenience of their proximate location. Friends specialize in a variety of things such as companionship and their variety of "specialties" can be seen as related to the heterogeneity of the category.

The specialization found in our Canadian sample is closely in line with that suggested by Litwak and Szelenyi and parallels the differentiations suggested by Adams. The predominance of *concern* is reflected in the bases reported for the sustaining of relationships and the strong inclination of respondents to make kin their primary choice for any requested assistance. Friends, on the other hand, are chosen for companionship and friendships are based largely on enjoyment, reflecting the salience of what Adams has called *consensus*. To these two types of bases we add a third: *convenience*, which is a key feature of neighbour relationships.

The differentiation and specialization which occur in primary relationships reflect changes, such as mobility, which characterize modern industrial society. When the set of primary relationships is viewed as a network, it is no longer necessary to force these relationships into a context of primary *groups*. The more appropriate network context allows us to view a variety of categories of relationships, recruited from various "primary groups" and consequently note the relative importance and intensity assigned to each type. By viewing them in this way we can also note the specializations and the ways in which these "fit" together to provide a full array of sources for many social needs of the individual. The network thus provides a useful perspective for furthering the study of social relations.

Notes

1. The 198 respondents represent a stratified random sample based on age and a personality score (which is not relevant for the matters under discussion) selected from a sampling pool of 845 adults who had been interviewed for a related study one year earlier. We sampled 71 of these 198 cases, using a stratified random procedure based

on age. We then attempted to interview as many as possible of those named by the 71 as "intimates." An average of 2.1 intimates per case were successfully interviewed, for a total of 149.

2. This arbitrary maximum was imposed for reasons: first to maintain comparability with an earlier and related study, and second to limit the named "intimates" to a manageable number since the study pursued the network to the extent of interviewing other members of some of the networks.

3. In fact, friends were often recruited from work-mates, school-mates, and persons met through relatives and other friends.

References

Adams, B.N.

1967 "Interaction theory and the social network" *Sociometry* 30: 64-78.

1968 Kinship in an Urban Setting. Chicago: Markham Publishing.

Axelrod, M.

1956 "Urban structure and social participation." *American Sociological Review* 21: 13-18.

Babchuk, N and A. Bates

1963 "The primary relations of middle class couples: A study in male dominance." *American Sociological Review* 28: 377-384.

Bracey, H.

1964 *Neighbours, Subdivision Life in England and the United States.* Baton Rouge: Louisiana State University Press.

Cohen, Y.A.

1961 "Patterns of friendship." In Y. Cohen (ed.), *Social Structure and Personality.* New York: Holt Rinehart and Winston.

Cooley, C.H.

1909 *Social Organization.* N.Y.: Scribner.

1958 "Contrasts in neighbouring." In W. Dobriner (ed.), *The Surburban Community.* New York: Putman.

Firth, R., J. Hubert and A. Forge

1970 *Families and their Relations.* London: Routledge & Kegan Paul.

Gans, H.J.

1962 *The Urban Villagers.* New York: Free Press.

1962 *The Levittowners.* New York: Pantheon.

Guterman, S.

1969 "In defense of Wirth's 'Urbanism as a way of life'." *American Journal of Sociology* 74: 492-499.

Homas, G.C.
1961 *Social Behaviour: Its Elementary Forms.* New York: Harcourt, Brace and World.

Katz, F.
1966 "Social participation and social structure." *Social Forces* 45: 199-210.

Keller, S.
1968 *The Urban Neighborhood.* New York: Random House.

Laumann, E.
1973 *Bonds of Pluralism: The Form and Substance of Urban Social Networks.* New York: John Wiley & Sons.

Litwak, E.
1959 "The uses of extended family groups in the achievement of social goals." *Social Problems* 7:177-187.

Litwak, E. and I. Szelenyi
1969 "Primary group structures and their functions." *American Sociological Review* 34: 465-481.

Michelson, W.
1970 *Man and His Urban Environment.* New York: Addison Wesley.

Mitchell, J.C.
1969 "The concept and use of social networks." In J.C. Mitchell (ed.) *Social Networks in Urban Situations.* Manchester: University of Manchester Press.

Pahl, R.
1968 "A perspective on urban sociology." In R. Pahl (ed.), *Readings in Urban Sociology.* Oxford: Pergamon.

Park, R. E.
1925 *The City.* Chicago: University of Chicago Press.

Parsons, T.
1965 "The normal American family." In S.M. Farber, *et al.* (eds.), *Man and Civilization.* New York: McGraw-Hill.

Pfeil, E.
1968 "The patterns of neighbouring relations in Dortmund-Nordstadt." In R. Pahl (ed.), *Readings in Urban Sociology.* Oxford: Pergamon.

Pineo, P.C.
1968 "The extended family in a working class area of Hamilton." In B. Blishen. *et al.* (eds.), *Canadian Society.* Toronto: Macmillan.

Rieger-Shlonsky, H.
1969 "The conceptualization of the roles of a relative, a friend and a neighbour." *Human Relations* 22:355-369.

Secord, P. and C. Backman
1964 "Interpersonal congruency, perceived similarity and friendship." *Sociometry* 27.

Sharpe, H. and M. Axelrod
1956 "Mutal aid among relatives in an urban population." In R. Freedman, et al. (eds.), *Principles of Sociology.* New York: Holt.

Shulman, N.
1967 "Mutual aid and neighbouring patterns: The lower town study." *Anthropologica* 9: 51-60.

Simmel, G.
1950 "The metropolis and mental life." In K. Wolff (trans.), *The Sociology of Georg Simmel.* New York: Free Press.

Sussman, M.B.
1953 "The help pattern in the middle class family." *American Sociological Review* 18:22-28.

1959 "The isolated nuclear family: fact or fiction?" *Social Problems 6: 333-340.*

1965 "Relationships of adult children with their parents in the United States." In E. Shanas and G. Streib (eds.), *Social Structure and the Family.* Englewood Cliffs, N.J.: Prentice-Hall.

Tomeh, A.
1964 Informal group participation and residential patterns." *American Journal of Sociology* 70: 28-35.

Wirth, L.
1938 "Urbanism as a way of life." *American Journal of Sociology* 44: 1-24.

33

Small Harbour*

Ralph Matthews

The people of two communities in Notre Dame Bay have said point-blank that they will stay where they are. The following is a text of a telegram sent to the minister responsible for the resettlement programme.

> The people of Ship Harbour and Small Harbour are shocked over the recent statement by the Member of Parliament. It is hard to believe that our government could have so little regard for human beings and reach such a deplorable decision. This decision by our government to strip us of our birthright and deny us of our freedom of choice is only the same as the Russians did in Czechoslovakia in 1968. Since 98 per cent of the people of our community are opposed to the centralization programme we are proud to announce that we are here to stay. Therefore it is time for the government to abandon their attempt to force the people to move by denying them public services, and make a speedy decision to give our community the public services we are requesting but have long been denied.

News Item,
CJON Radio Network, May 12, 1969

"We are proud to announce that we are here to stay"

In many ways the statement quoted above inaugurated this study. On May 12, 1969 I was driving across Newfoundland after spending three days with a rural development field worker. I had been totally involved in the problems of small rural communities as they attempted to organize regional development councils. Almost everyone we talked with seemed convinced that such organizations were essential if communities like theirs were ever to develop. Yet it was readily apparent that inter-community co-operation was not easy to achieve and that organizational skills were sadly lacking. Most of the communities I visited would be easy prey for those wishing resettlement rather than redevelopment.

---

*Abridged from *There's No Better Place Than Here*, Toronto: Peter Martin Associates, 1976, Chapter III, with permission of the author and publisher. The author expresses his to Robert Chanteloup for insightful comments on a draft of this chapter.
Dr. Chanteloup lived in Small Harbour for several months as part of his study of religious conversion in rural Newfoundland.

As I turned these experiences over in my mind, the car radio carried the news that two small communities on an isolated island 200 miles away had, through a community council acting on their behalf, declared that they would not be moved. To my knowledge they were (and still are) the only communities in Newfoundland to issue a statement publicly opposing the resettlement programme. Clearly they were unique, and I resolved to find out why. In August, 1970 I took a coastal boat to Small Harbour.

Small Harbour lies on the southwest shore of Centre Island, a nine-by-four-mile promontory off Newfoundland's northeast coast. Its 192 residents share this island with the 350 inhabitants of Ship Harbour, a community located almost directly across the island along the shores of Pleasant Arm. The island itself is at the outer edge of a small archipelago which stretches some twenty miles into the centre of Notre Dame Bay.

Small Harbour in 1971 was a community bustling with activity. No sooner had our ship entered the harbour than one could hear the raucous staccato of chain saws over the continuous grind of heavy tractors. Workmen were building a road from Small Harbour to Ship Harbour, and were upgrading the village paths to the point where they could take motor vehicles. There were signs of other recent changes. A throbbing diesel generating station, located in a large, galvanized metal building in the heart of the community, now provided electricity to homes all over the island.

The credit for these accomplishments was directly linked, at least in the minds of community respondents to their "proclamation" of 1969, and to the formation in November, 1967, of the combined community council representing all island communities. Why Small Harbour and her sister community came to form a community council is not completely clear. One community leader suggested that it was formed largely out of frustration with government inaction.

> It was here in Small Harbour and in Ship Harbour as well. We get together and have a chat, you know, and talk about what you think should be done. We tried on different occasions to get a road; but we didn't seem to be heard owing to we had no local government or anything.

Little seems to have happened for fifteen months after the community council was formed. Then a Small Harbour representative resigned and was replaced by the main shopkeeper in Small Harbour in a subsequent by-election. He was not its formal leader, but his presence seems to have spurred the council to action.

> So we started right off the bat then. It's been eighteen months now and you can see what we've accomplished. We got $200,000 worth of electricity last year, and we got a beginning on the road. We're guaranteed a $24,000 post office this fall, and we're guaranteed the telephones this fall. I'll say we've accomplished more in fifteen months than any other council that ever was founded.

These accomplishments may not have been solely the result of action by the community council, but the result of a major tactical error by the federal government.

In the course of their efforts the community council petitioned the federal government for a new central post office to serve both island communities. In his reply the minister responsible apparently indicated that he could not seriously consider their request because both Small Harbour and Ship Harbour were on a provincial government list of communities which were to be resettled. The provincian government had long maintained that there was no list of communities "slated for resettlement", and had argued that the decision to resettle was always a local decision. The federal disclosure therefore caused them considerable embarrassment and it was quickly turned into a *cause célèbre* with far-reaching repercussions.

In some way the news director of CJON radio and television learned of the affair. Just how this happened is unclear, but he may well have been contacted by members of Small Harbour's community council. In any case he sent a telegram to the main shopkeeper in Small Harbour (who was now also the key figure in council affairs), asking him for his views on the subject. In co-operation with some other council members, the shopkeeper immediately drafted the proclamation of protest which was heard on radio throughout Newfoundland. Although the statement was purportedly issued by the community council on behalf of the people, most residents learned of it only after it was made public. Those who were instrumental in drafting it justified their action by claiming that they had "been dealing with the people long enough to know what their wishes were".

The (Progressive Conservative) member of parliament for the area immediately demanded that the (Liberal) provincial and federal governments "prove" that Centre Island was not about to be resettled.

> So this is where the dirt was stirred up. . . . [the MP], he got on our side. He told the provincial government, "If it's not true . . . get out and prove it then. Give them the lights."

Holding this political firecracker, both governments rushed to shower Centre Island with amenities. Lights, a road and even the promise of a new post office were thrust upon them. It is no wonder that members of the community council used hyperbole in describing their accomplishments, even though some of their good fortune may have resulted from circumstances over which they had little influence.

The actual process by which Small Harbour obtained improvements has implications for our study. I originally became interested in Small Harbour because it and Ship Harbour were the only communities in all of Newfoundland which had both formed a community council and rejected the pressures to resettle. This seemed to suggest that some form of intercommunity co-operation and formal organization operated in the community, enabling the residents to make and carry out decisions which would affect their future. But most people had no prior knowledge of their public proclamation. This supposedly collective sentiment had actually been drafted by a few community leaders. there was also little to suggest that any strong spirit of community co-operation had ever existed. Historically the community had been divided by religious cleavages as the numerous churches and one-room schools bore witness. Although the formation of a community council seemed to indicate a new spirit of co-operation, a closer look at its origins and mode of operation revealed the existence of an elite organization, rather than a wide base of social co-operation.

What were the true "wishes of the majority of the people"? Were most residents of Small Harbour really "proud to announce that they were there to stay", or was this the decision which the traditional leaders hoped that they would make? Moreover, did the provision of services really ensure that they would stay? To answer these questions we must examine more closely the pattern of life in Small Harbour and the attitudes and values of the residents.

"There's a lot of people went out of it"

Is Small Harbour a community in decline? A major indicator of community decline is population decline and the population of Small Harbour has decreased some 18 per cent from its peak during the early 1950s. The high rate of out-migration was obvious from our survey sample. From the post office list of 40 household heads, 30 members of the general population and three merchants who appeared to be potential communaity leaders were selected. Although the list was only two years old, fully 19 of the 33 householders were not in the community: nine had moved away (they had either taken their families with them, or were single men with little to tie them to the community); seven other men were away working, but had wives and families remaining in the community; one household head was away in hospital; two others had died. Those who had moved away had travelled to Labrador, Ontario or to nearby communities. Of the six families in nearby communities, four were in "mainland" communities with road access to the outside world, while two others had moved to a nearby island community which is, despite its isolation, a centre of economic activity within the region. The seven persons from our sample who were still residents of Small Harbour but who were away working, were employed either in some aspect of the fishery (e.g. fish inspector), as crew members of trading boats, or as construction workers. This extensive out-migration meant that only 14 formal interviews were completed.

Movement from Small Harbour is by no means a new phenomenon. Every household head whom we interviewed reported that he had a sibling living elsewhere.[1] In the traditional marriage pattern there is a greater tendency for women to move than men. Thus the husbands in our sample had a total of thirty-one sisters living in other communities and only ten still in Small Harbour. Brothers were evenly divided, with eleven living in Small Harbour and eleven living elsewhere. There is every sign that migration from the community is accelerating among the younger generation. The respondents had thirty children aged eighteen and over. Of these, only five lived in Small Harbour.[2] Ten of the respondents themselves had worked elsewhere for various periods of time. Most of these had been engaged as loggers or employed in the Labrador fishery. However only three of our respondents had worked away from the community in the preceding five years.

In sum, the community has seen at least two generations of accelerating out-migration. One-third of the present household heads work elsewhere, separated from their families for long periods of the year either because they are unable to afford the cost of relocating their family, or because they wish to remain in Small Harbour.

With the exception of two people over 75 years old, the sample was generally middle-aged, with an average (mean) age of 46.7 years. Although poorly educated by most standards, two of our sample had completed grade ten and another six had completed at least grade seven, which is somewhat higher than normal for that age group in most rural Newfoundland communities. Of the 14 household heads interviewed, twelve were born in Small Harbour, while the remaining two were born less than five miles away. Eight of the twelve who were married had chosen wives from outside their birthplace, but all of the wives were Newfoundland-born.

Despite the long period of out-migration and the slow decline in population in recent years, one could argue that only the excess population has left. There are, for example, no abandoned homesites, and most residents do not consider Small Harbour a declining community. Few are even aware of the extent of emigration. Most estimated that only three or four families had left in the preceding five years.

> There've been about three moved out. But then somebody got married and keeped the number up.

Only the aged appeared to reflect on the overall trend. One elderly gentleman rattled off a list of 15 families who had moved, while another announced that "twenty-two families are moved out of this in my time". Both persons were referring to a period of 70 years.

Residents denied that out-migration had affected community life in any substantial way. Many indicated that those who left had been drains on the community and society, and implied that the place was better without them.

> They were people living on social assistance or welfare. They're not turning in anything to the government. They're only an expense.

> Two of them was old age pensioners and I don't see where that would make much difference to the place.

Still others emphasized that accomplishments had been achieved without them:

> Well, we got the lights since the two of them went, and we got the road since they went.

The implication is that those who had moved had given up on the community prematurely.

Part of the reason for such low estimates of migration is that few *families* migrate. Most of those who move are young people who drift away to a variety of initially temporary, if ultimately permanent jobs and their departure is not as obvious as the premeditated move of a whole family. Even though most of the residents of Small Harbour spoke positively about the community, they encourage their own children to leave. Most felt that there was simply nothing on the island for young people to do.

> I don't think there's anything here on this island for them. They can't make a living here anyway.

Only three respondents disagreed. One offered insights into the dilemma facing young people:

> If they'd stay here they could make the community a better place, but I don't know if they could make a living here or not. Those fellows going to university, it must be hard for them to settle down here.

Only one man suggested an alternative means of livelihood for those who might wish to remain.

> Well, if you got an education there's no way to use it here. . . . But there is ways that several more families could make a living on this island. Say there's room here for a farmer, maybe two. Then there's a poultry farm. There's a lot of chicken and eggs eat around this bay. And a sawmill. There's 20,000 cord of wood on this island.

Ironically, his own children had left the island years before.

It seems safe to conclude that the normal process whereby excess population emigrates had become transformed, in the case of Small Harbour, into a process of general community decline. Not only was the community unable to provide sustaining employment for its existing adult population, but it encouraged its children to move away. Nevertheless at the time of the study, many residents were beginning to think that the "tide had turned" and the community was beginning to develop again.

"She's just picking up again"

> We're just started here and we're fifteen years behind. It's only now two years since the council's been formed, and now we're getting ahead. We never had nothing before. . . . She was going down for eight years or so, and now she's just picking up again.

Such was the hopeful sentiment of most of the residents of Small Harbour. After several decades of out-migration and decline, things did indeed seem to be "picking up again". The road and electricity were seen as the main indicators of a revival, but there were also other encouraging changes. The most important of these in the minds of the community members and in the effect it was having, was the appearance of a new religious group in the community.

Religion had always been an important factor in the life of Small Harbour, but there had been great difficulties in attracting a resident clergyman. Frustration led many community members to abandon their traditional faith for another denomination which could satisfy their spiritual and social needs more directly. The Salvation Army, which proselytized the community between the 1920s and the 1950s, gained the followers that other denominations lost. Their church stands almost next door to that of the United Church, but when this study was conducted, it had been months since a clergyman had preached in either church. Like the Church of England and the United Church before them, the Salvationists found it almost impossible to staff some of their churches. Their last resident officer in Small Harbour was a single woman who left the community after only two months. Both the Salvation Army and United Church buildings in Small Harbour remained locked, as abandoned and desolate as the nearby graveyards.

Across the harbour, however, hammers were at work putting the finishing touches on a third church for the community: Small Harbour was in the midst of a religious conversion. For nearly a year a Pentecostal pastor had been stationed in the community. This man had grown up on a nearby island, had been sent to Ontario for training and had served in other parts of Newfoundland before arriving in Small Harbour. According to the pastor, the decision to station him in Small Harbour was made after an expedition to the area by one of the church officials. According to the people, he had been sent to Small Harbour in response to a petition from local residents. The man responsible for this petition provided this account:

> I went up to Robert's Arm on Sunday to see the pastor up there, and told him we wanted a pastor on Centre Island, wanted the gospel preached, I said. He said, "Why? Where's your Lieutenant to? What about the Salvation Army?" I said, "Sir, as far as I'm concerned the Army is gone to the wall. Down there all the day there's no Sunday school for the children." I said, "We wants a church there." "Well," he said, "if you can get eight names, we'll come in Small Harbour and build you a church!" So I got seventeen names and carried them up to him. And after that they just started coming here.

For the first few months the Pentecostal pastor held services in the United Church building. After four months the United Church minister of a neighbouring island, whose charge also included Small Harbour, came at the request of some United Church members and "drove the pastor out of the United Church". The pastor set about constructing his own church. His long hours of hard work, during which he almost single-handedly built both a church and a house for himself and his wife, earned him the respect of most community members. His acceptance was eased even more because he was from salvationist stock and his services were generally familiar to local residents, and because his wife was a teacher who began to teach in one of the schools. The latter was important since there was considerable danger that some classrooms might be closed for lack of students. The presence of his wife ensured that there would be a teacher even if this should happen.

This does not mean that there was no opposition to his coming. The traditional community leaders were aligned with the older religious denominations and none was among the petitioners for the new church. As the new church began to dominate community affairs it threatened to upset the traditional class balance within the community. The tensions and conflicts which arose cut across traditionally harmonious relationships, even to the extent of splitting families.

Despite the tensions his arrival created the Pentecostal pastor had filled an important spiritual and social need during the year he had been in the community. Even if no Salvation Army or United Church clergy were available, there were still people to be married, children to be baptized and the dead to be buried. His Sunday services and twice-weekly prayer meetings had both a spiritual and a social function, providing a focus for the daily lives of many residents. It was just like the old days. For the first time in several years there was some place to go.

By the time we left the community, several residents had been converted to the new faith, and the new church was rapidly becoming the centre of social and spiritual life in the community.

"We're still in the dark ages as far as schools are concerned"

Most residents of Small Harbour were eager to claim that things in their community were "picking up". Certainly, if one were to go by the level of activity in the community, this seemed to be true. Yet in spite of their assertions that life in their community was changing for the better, one fundamental worry continued to bother them—the school system. Their concern originated with the provincial government's decision several years before to build a central high school to serve all the communities in the district. This was subsequently built in a community on the nearby mainland, some 20 miles by sea from Small Harbour.

For most communities in the region the school was a remarkable step forward. No longer must their children be satisfied with an inadequate high school education in a one-room school. They could be bussed daily to a modern school where they would be taught by well-qualified teachers. But for Small Harbour this new school created a major dilemma. Local children were unable to commute to school because the island community was cut off from the mainland by ice and high seas for much of the winter. Instead, when they reached the high school age of 14 or 15, Small Harbour children had to leave home and live in boarding houses near the school. They were able to journey home for an occasional weekend during the autumn, but there were months on end during which they could not see their families.

Any parent might be unhappy with a situation in which his children were separated from their family at such an early age, but it was particularly distasteful to many Small Harbour parents. Formal education has not been highly valued in rural Newfoundland until very recently. Most children left school early and learned the skills of fishing and homemaking from their parents. In addition most Newfoundlanders maintain extensive kin ties and great emphasis is placed on family life. To have children carried away at such an early age not only placed massive strains on the children, but it also undermined their parents' conception of themselves and their worth.

There was also general dissatisfaction with the quality of education in the junior schools remaining in the community. Approximately two-thirds of our sample indicated that the "chances for [their] children to get an education in Small Harbour are poor". They felt that there were too many one-room schools and not enough teachers with university degrees.

The problems of commuting and of poor primary education worried Small Harbour parents, but the most ominous threat of all was that declining school enrollment jeopardized existing facilities. The Newfoundland Department of Education regulations require that there be a minimum number of students per classroom. If numbers fall below a certain level, they simply eliminate the salary available for one of the teachers. In Small Harbour this would mean that they would eliminate a one-room school.

During the time we were in Small Harbour it became doubtful that there would be enough pupils to open one of the schools. Most residents considered this a major catastrophe. Ultimately the school was able to open, but as one school board member explained:

> If we'd have lost one more pupil this year, we'd have lost a room. So if one big family went, the schooling would be bad enough right there we'd have to move.

"We didn't know what to do, go or stay"

To most outsiders, life in an outport such as Small Harbour seems tranquil and unchanging. But to those who live there, every day brings new promises and hopes, despair and fears. In recent years roads, lights and a new church have all come to Small Harbour; during that same time people have left and the schools, in most people's eyes, have "gone down". Such changes would affect any community, but in Small Harbour, where people are aware that they live on the brink of abandonment as a community, even the smallest change may have major implications.

How then do the people of Small Harbour regard their community and evaluate its future? Their proclamation indicated that they were deeply committed to the community, but is this really the sentiment of the majority of residents? Each of the families interviewed were asked whether they thought life in Small Harbour had improved or declined in the past 15 or 20 years. Somewhat surprisingly, given recent developments, less than half of the respondents felt that their community had improved. Those who did pointed to the new amenities. But the majority of household heads felt that the community had declined because of extensive out-migration and the failing fishing economy.

> There's a lot of people went out of it. A lot of homes went out. A lot of merchants left. This was a flourishing community in the 1930s in regards of labour. A lot of merchants here owned their own vessels. I would say it has declined in the last fifteen years, and the reason for that is that the Premier said, "Haul up your boats and let them rot, there'll be two jobs for every man." People thought that was going to be a reality and it proved to be a fake. Everyone did away with their schooners. There used to be fifteen schooners here one time fishing, and 200 men going fishing, coming here and getting berths.

As the above quote indicates, there was a tendency to foreshorten history. The prosperous fishery was destroyed by the Depression of the 1930s, and most fishing schooners had disappeared long before the 1950s when Premier Smallwood was reputed to have encouraged people to burn their boats.

The attitude of Small Harbour residents toward their community became clearer when the subject of resettlement was raised. Although the residents had heard of resettlement, all denied that they intended to move. This is a common pattern: many people deny any desire to leave right up to the moment of doing so. They could hardly do otherwise without being branded as traitors, for their departure makes life harder for those who remain and likely hastens the day when they, too, might be forced out. But in Small Harbour half of the respondents, including all those who might be considered community leaders, were willing to admit that they had considered moving at one time. Their comments revealed a wide range of reasons for *not* going.

> We've talked about it, but I don't know where to go to better myself. I can't do nothing beside fish.

> Well I did a few years ago, yes. . . . I had a small business and I was getting tired of it after twenty years.

> If I could get a job. . . .

> We thought we might better ourself. We didn't know what to do; go or stay. So I decided I'd stay.

If resettlement had provided an attractive alternative, the residents would have moved. However most Small Harbour men have been to the nearby relocation centres and many have even worked there. In their opinion these centres offer no possibility of lasting employment. They have chosen not to move simply because resettlement does not hold out a better alternative. From their perspective, it would *not* be a sensible decision.

This became quite clear when they were asked to compare their way of life with that of nearby communities, specifically, Robert's Arm and Springdale. Both are likely "reception centres" and some former residents of Small Harbour already live in them. Robert's Arm is a small village like Small Harbour, but it is located on the mainland and linked to the rest of the province by road. Its primary disadvantage is that it is too far up the bay to sustain a viable fishery. Springdale is a regional supply centre of approximately 3,000 people located on the mainland some 20 miles from Small Harbour.

No one spoke favourably of Robert's Arm: Small Harbour people thought it was a more expensive place in which to live, and that the employment prospects were scarce. We received several gloomy pictures of people struggling to find work or languishing on welfare.

> It's cheaper to live here. If I go into Robert's Arm to live, I got a lot of things to pay.

> If I go to Robert's Arm, I'd starve to death—I think I would. Most of them may have a job, but for me to go there would be the finish.

> You don't see so many lying around the government wharf here as you do in Robert's Arm or Springdale. You can go up there when you like and the wharf is lined with people with nothing to do, only lie around. You don't see nothing like that here. Only a few youngsters out there swimming. Everybody's occupied at something here.

Springdale also offered little attraction. Although two people did mention that it was cheaper to buy food in the supermarkets there, and another three indicated that school and hospital facilities were better, others felt that there would be no permanent jobs for them there.

In fact, most respondents ignored both communities when they attempted to explain their decision to remain in Small Harbour. Most emphasized that it was cheaper for them to live on the island than anywhere else because they owned their own houses and had few other expenses. Others noted that it was possible to fish from Small Harbour, that they were self-sufficient, and that the people just seemed "more contented" there.

Given these attitudes, it is nor surprising that resettlement officials have had little success in getting people to move, even though reportedly they have visited the community at least twice.

Most of those with whom we talked seemed content to remain as long as the schools and transportation improved. We were told frequently that the island needed a causeway linking it to the mainland. The most realistic admitted that they would settle for a regular ferry service and in fact this service was provided some six months later. It operates daily throughout the nine months of the year that the bay is free of ice and travels to several of the nearby islands, linking them to one another as well as to the nearby mainland. When regular ferry service was established, the isolation of Centre Island was greatly reduced. Since it allowed children to return home from school on weekends, it also helped to alleviate the problem of family breakups.

But even though this service cuts some of the isolation and privation, Small Harbour still has one major problem: there is nothing for local residents to do. When questioned about this, most of our respondents suggested many ways of giving the island an economic base. Some elderly men, recalling the old days, felt that the government should provide for a new schooner fishery; middle-aged men argued for assistance to build longliners; others proposed saw mills, logging operations, chicken ranches and farms.

All of these suggestions came in reply to our question concerning how the government might assist people to earn a better living. When we asked how the people might better themselves, our queries were met with stony silence. A few vaguely recognized the need to "pull together", because "there's not five people on the island got the one mind". But only two respondents were able to propose anything that local residents could initiate without government assistance. Both were on the community council and were community leaders. One suggested that, if they could form a producers' co-operative, it might be possible to obtain loans for economic development that are not available to individual residents. But he saw lack of management experience as a major obstacle to success.

Lack of imagination, lack of organizational skill, lack of capital, lack of markets and isolation are still obstacles to the economic development of Small Harbour. Until these difficulties are overcome and new jobs are created, the people of Small Harbour will have to leave to find work. Many who do will not come back.

Commentary

Today every house in Small Harbour has electricity and there are roads and a new ferry. Television, radio and the community's radio-telephone provide communication with the outside world. In time of emergency help is usually available in minutes by sea-plane or helicopter. The days of discomfort and isolation are over and, in this respect, the people of Small Harbour have never had it so good.

Yet Small Harbour today may be on the verge of extinction. There is little for her people to do either for employment or amusement. While radio and television provide some entertainment, they also tell of opportunities for work and personal development elsewhere. Under such circumstances it is likely that the young will continue to leave Small Harbour and the population will continue to decline. At the very time when life in Small Harbour can at last be said to have a modicum of comfort and ease, many of her residents are tempted to abandon the community. Such is the irony of modernization.

Small Harbour is almost totally dependent on the outside world for survival and has very little control over its own fate. The extent of this dependency can be seen in the community's efforts to obtain modern facilities. It is unlikely that the community council would have been effective in getting facilities had it not been for the bureaucratic bumbling of government officials. The community's lack of control over its own fate is also obvious in the sphere of religion. Small Harbour has been unable to attract a resident clergyman for any of its traditional churches. Although some residents were apparently instrumental in attracting a new religions group to the community, there is no guarantee that the new church will survive. Other churches to which the residents have given their allegiance and their souls in the past have been forced to close their doors. Thus the real situation of the community contrasts vividly with the romanticized picture of the small rural community as the one remaining self-sufficient entity in this fragmented, urbanized society.

The people of Small Harbour are in a double bind. They are at the mercy of outside bureaucrats on one hand and at the mercy of their own neighbours on the other. Should one or more large families leave, schoolrooms will be closed and other families will feel compelled to leave. One community leader, who does manage to obtain an adequate living on the island, dubbed this process "the tyranny of the weak". It is but another aspect of the dependence of the people of Small Harbour.

Small Harbour has been left behind in the process of modernization. But, while it is largely the *victim of modernization*, it continues to exist only because it has become the *client of modernization.* My argument here is a modification of Alvin Gouldner's analysis of the role of the welfare state in his book *The Coming Crisis in Western Sociology* (1970).

Gouldner contends that the modern developed state is a welfare state which values people primarily in terms of their utility (61-76). But in the modern welfare state many people are rendered "useless" to society by the process of modernization. A central problem for the modern welfare state is, therefore, a treatment of these "useless" people.

I would argue that rural people, particularly those living in a traditional environment like that of Small Harbour, are regarded as peripheral and essentially "useless" by the planners of modernization. Some planners freely admitted that resettlement was likely to be to the detriment of many adults, but that it would ultimately be of benefit to their children. Even many of those who agreed to be resettled did so with full knowledge that there was little employment for them in their chosen growth centre. They, too, had come to regard themselves as "useless", and had moved so that their children might have a future in an urbanized society.

But the modern nation state is a welfare state. It does not simply define people as useless. It is committed to the process of rehabilitating them as useful members of society. Thus, although Small Harbour has outlived its usefulness, it continues to exist largely because of the welfare and rehabilitation programmes of modern society. Many people in Small Harbour have adopted a welfare-oriented strategy: they are able to remain in the community because they are supported by various forms of social assistance. Others derive a large portion of their income from the rehabilitation programmes themselves. At least one "fisherman" supports himself by attending Fisheries College in St. John's each year. In addition to his board and lodging, he is paid a salary which helps support his family through the rest of the year. As a result, he has not needed to fish for several years. Other residents take advantage of similar "upgrading" programmes available from trades schools across the province. They learn to be carpenters, plumbers or heavy equipment operators—skills which are of little use to them in Small Harbour. While such courses obviously are intended to rehabilitate them for useful employment outside, the salaries that they pay to students allow many Small Harbour men to remain where they are a little while longer. In this way they have been able to transform outside forces normally beyond their control into programmes in line with their own goals and values. But even with these new skills, their dependence on outside forces is so great that most were unable to suggest any local initiatives which could increase the number of jobs available on the island. Almost everyone looked directly to the government to plan and provide for his future.

The type of development that most concerns centralized government is the *top-down* variety which focuses on general strategies and rarely reaches the level of the small community. These development plans are directed towards major industrial complexes which provide large numbers of jobs quickly. In contrast *bottom-up* planning focuses on assisting community members, helping them design feasible projects, and training them in the managerial skills necessary to carry them out. It also provides the usually modest funds which make such local operations successful.

Top-down planners seem inclined to focus on economic and industrial development, ignoring the consequences of their actions on social and cultural values. In contrast, those who orient their planning towards community development are more likely to focus on the effect that planning is having on the existing pattern of life.

At the time of this study there was no bottom-up planning taking place in Small Harbour. Although the community council had been formed and perhaps had the potential to develop managerial skills, it was simply a means to plead for favours in the name of the community. Until recently the only government plans which in any way affected the community were those related to industrialization and resettlement. These were directed towards phasing out the community, not developing it. Even though the government had made major efforts to improve the quality of living in Small Harbour, there was really no evidence to indicate that it was concerned with developing the community's employment prospects. Until that happens the people of Small Harbour will still have to go away to work. Those residents who think otherwise are only deluding themselves by mistaking improvements in quality of living for change in the community's ability to sustain life.

Many residents of Small Harbour and communities like her are so committed to their way of life that they would prefer to commute to work for much of the year rather than move. They are willing to delude themselves into thinking that changes in the cosmetics of community life are really changes in its fundamental economic structure. If we are to resolve this discrepancy, we must begin to investigate the criteria from which these conflicting attitudes arise. We must begin to develop a framework of concepts and tools whereby we can judge the viability of rural life.

I would argue that such a framework must start with a distinction between the criteria of *economic viability* and those which I will call *social vitality*. Most regional and community planning is based almost solely on economic criteria. Obviously a strong case can be made for the primacy of economic considerations in economic and regional development. Only when people have satisfied their basic needs for food, clothing and shelter can they begin to think in terms of human excellence. I do not argue that we should neglect economic concerns, or that economic disparity should not be a central consideration in any strategy of regional planning. My concern is that most regional planners seem to focus almost exclusively on economic considerations and that they neglect to consider the social structure, culture and values of the people for whom they are planning.

The social vitality of a community operates on two levels. The institutions and organizations which formalize on-going daily activity and which structure social life constitute the *formal level of community social vitality*. These include the institutions of socialization and social control (Martindale 1962, 1963, 1966). In a small rural community the institutions of socialization are usually represented by the organizations of the family, the school and the church. The institutions of social control include everything from informal gossip to a formalized community council. These two institutional areas complement the economic institutions of a community or society and are integrated with them.

Underlying the formal institutional level there is an *informal level of community social vitality*. Here the focus is on the *attitudes and values* of the community members and on their *involvement and commitment* to community life. It is impossible to overestimate the importance of these factors in community life. Without the involvement and commitment of its members, the institutions of a community could and would not function. In a community such as Small Harbour where economic viability has all but disappeared, it is often only the commitment of the community members which maintains the community. Furthermore, this focus on commitment and involvement provides an insight into two other important dimensions of community life; *the pattern of leadership* and the *extent of community co-operation*. Both are reflections of the commitment and involvement of community members, and both are important measures of the social vitality of a community.

Even though it was the one community in all of Newfoundland to proclaim that it was "here to stay", Small Harbour is faced with an uncertain future. In the economic sphere it has declined to the point that there is now virtually no employment base. The community is so small that the emigration of a few families would probably result in the evacuation of the community. Even if it should remain, its survival beyond the present adult generation is in doubt. The main signs of revival are in the sphere of formal social vitality. The new council and new church have the potential to rebuild Small Harbour's social and economic life, but this requires a whole new approach to leadership and a new spirit of co-operation.

Notes

1. In all but one case these siblings previously had lived in Small Harbour.

2. There were an additional 48 children under age 18, of whom 30 were less than ten years old. Only three of this total group were living outside the community; two as students and a third as a domestic servant.

References

Gouldner, Alvin W.
1970 *The Coming Crisis of Western Sociology.* New York: Basic Books.

Martindale, Don
1962 *Social Life and Cultural Change.* Princeton: Van Nostrand.

1963 "The Formation and Destruction of Communities." In G.K. Zollschan and W. Hirsch, eds. *Explorations in Social Change.* Boston: Houghton Mifflin.

1966 *Institutions, Organizations, and Mass Society.* Boston: Houghton, Mifflin.

34

Policies for the Urban Future*

N.H. Lithwick

a. An Appraisal of the Unconstrained Future

Our analysis of the unconstrained future reveals that major transformations in Canadian urban society will take place. They will result from the further development of processes already under way, particularly the increased specialization and growing scale of modern economic activity. We have not dwelt on the many social ramifications of these forecasts that have come to engage the attention of futurists, such as the impact on family relations, the growing importance of leisure time and leisure activity.

From our narrower structural approach we have been able to indicate broad national urban trends in the unconstrained future: the growing polarization of economic activity in the major metropolitan areas, the shift towards labour-intensive service activity, the rapid population expansion to meet these demands, the increasing importance of in-migration as a source of this population and the consequent draining of rural and small urban areas, and the growing importance of inter-urban links which will reinforce the dominance of the largest elements in the macro-system.

This emerging urban pattern is most important, because our analysis has revealed that there are inherent contradictions in the process that are not sufficiently appreciated. On the one hand, there will be apparently great economic benefits associated with this expansion. Real incomes will rise from 50 to 100 per cent per capita, providing individuals with a greatly increased potential for acquiring an extremely wide range of goods and services. Greater productivity and higher incomes will permit more leisure activity. Much higher levels of education will prevail, shaping the tastes of society in new and different ways. Access to more and different jobs and markets will be enhanced by improved transit and communications systems. All these developments will provide the individual with an enormous potential range of choice, not only of commodities, but of life-styles, permitting the attainment of individual and collective welfare beyond any level conceivable at present.

But this promise of greater individuality and real welfare is not unencumbered; attached to it are the inherent costs of the process of unconstrained development. These costs will certainly diminish the promised gains, and may in the end totally eliminate them. The growing polarization of urban society will impose an enormous burden on urban man.

---

*Abridged from "Urban Canada: Problems and Prospects", a report by N.H. Lithwick for the Minister of State for Urban Affairs, Government of Canada, and published by Central Mortgage and Housing Corporation, Ottawa, December, 1970. By permission of the author and corporation.

(1) Land will continue to become so costly as to preclude all but extremely dense residential development within reasonable distance from the core.
(2) Families with children seeking single-family homes will have to commute for several hours per day.
(3) Downtown areas will be congested, polluted, and noisy.
(4) The drain on public funds to service the increasingly sprawled suburban areas and the increasingly intractable problems of the core will lead to higher taxes and yet higher land costs.
(5) Industries will flee to the suburbs leaving the poor without access to jobs, and the inner city without a tax base.
(6) Skilled workers will move increasingly to the suburbs with the jobs, reducing the quality of resident leadership in the core.
(7) The growing number of firms necessarily located in the core will require white-collar, technologically sophisticated service employees. Their space needs will squeeze the urban poor even further.
(8) The need to transport service workers to the core will add to the pressure on core space.
(9) The steady erosion of stable neighbourhoods, the growing economic uncertainty facing core dwellers, and the deteriorating quality of their environment will create an increasingly explosive situation.
(10) The increased segregation of economic classes in the city because of land costs will serve to fragment the community at a time when divisiveness is of great concern to the nation.

Thus, the cost of urbanization will rise along with the benefits. While the benefits will likely grow at a steady rate, the costs will grow exponentially because of the interdependency of urban problems and their sensitivity to growth pressures which we have forecast to be extremely great.

We have suggested that current policy instruments could relieve parts of the problem areas. But this would entail essentially a continuation of the present approach, which attacks symptoms, not causes. The approach will fail because the exponentiality inherent in the costs of growth will lead to a steadily increasing need for public assistance which in the extreme will eliminate the potential gains from urban development. Thus, the apparent welfare gains will be illusory, for real income will be watered down by the inflationary pressures latent in the accelerating costs of the urban system, and chopped into by the taxes requred to deal with the growing problems.

Because of the interconnectedness of the national urban system, these costs will not be restricted to individual urbanites in a particular problem area; they will get built into the whole range of exports and imports of the various centres. Because of the economic dominance of the largest centres, which of necessity also have the greatest urban problems, their high-level costs will be transmitted throughout the national economy. Such costs include the increasing cost of land, growing transport costs in the face of congestion as well as that part of the rising property tax burden that can be passed on to consumers, and the rising cost of labour for housing, that can be passed on by the metropolitan firms in the form of higher prices. In a highly competitive economy, these results could be offset. High costs would drive firms to cheaper locations. But the Canadian economy is far from competitive, particularly in the manufacture of urban goods. Tariffs and locational advantages have given firms, especially in the Montreal-Toronto corridor, a strong monopoly position. As a result, they do not have to adjust to rising costs, and indeed can easily pass them on. With further urban polarization, these monopolistic advantages will increase, so that the ability to impose the costs of urbanization on the rest of the nation will grow.

The implication is that unconstrained growth ultimately will not provide greater welfare through greater resources, but will require either an increasing share of those resources to deal with the costs of that type of growth or a reduction of the potential benefits of urbanization. The promises are thus not those of greater welfare and individuality, but of wasted resources and a growing oppressiveness of the urban system on individuals.

The major alternative is to reject the central assumption that the future is inevitable—that we must, as a nation, passively adjust to its demands upon us. Rather, we must consider how we might possibly shape the future urban system so that it can serve our objectives, rather than thwart them.

This is not an easy task, and we do not pretend to have a complete answer. The major problem is that we do not really know what our future objectives will be. However, it is possible to extrapolate into the future from present trends, although here we have much less faith in our estimates. Thus, we shall merely list the major anticipated tendencies with no attempt to quantify them or to be exhaustive.

(1) Higher incomes will lead to a greater increase in the variety of goods and services sought.

(2) More education and more leisure time will reinforce the trend to services and white-collar employment.

(3) Since an increasing variety of services are best provided in large markets, polarization in large metropolitan areas will be reinforced.

(4) Higher incomes will permit greater mobility and therefore more choice between jobs as well as markets.

(5) New technology of transport will make *inter-urban* access particularly easy.

(6) Communications technology will further reinforce the cultural dominance of the cities by promoting the urban ideology throughout the nation. It will also reinforce the links between the major urban nodes, and accelerate their growth.

These all point to the central feature of the future—*the increasing potential for and preference for choice*. But because of the inherent problems of the unconstrained urban future, the potential for expanding choice will be severely limited. This applies not only to the increasingly numerous aged and socially or physically handicapped, but to the average urbanite as well. Land costs will augment the flight to the suburbs, and leisure time will be spent commuting. The greater potential for access will be eroded through escalating congestion. Higher incomes will be diminished by higher taxes and higher costs of urban goods and services.

The urban system appears to be necessarily destructive of quality when it is left to follow its own course. It pollutes rather than cleanses; it congests rather than flows smoothly; it sprawls rather than expands in an orderly fashion; it penalizes the weakest rather than giving them preferred status; and it creates tension and violence rather than relaxation and safety.

Many of these problems are urban reflections of societal ills. But our analysis convinces us that an important dimension is uniquely urban. While we do not presume to have a cure for social problems, there are reasons for believing that the urban institutions can be reformed, that it is neither necessary nor optimal to take the urban system as given. If so, then the question is how can we begin to engage in reform, and what should be the objective of that reform? The second point is paramount: without direction, reform is pointless.

b. Policy Options in the Constrained Future

Perhaps the optimal strategy is to devise techniques for ensuring that the urban system is continually responsive to the changing needs of urbanites, and that it maximizes the range of choice open to them. The prospects for doing this effectively appear to be quite good. The scope of future changes in the urban system are such that the *increment* in urban population over the next thirty years will be almost twice as great as the current urban population. The associated additions to the urban system in terms of housing, transport systems, infra-structure, and so forth far outweigh in scale what we now have. If to this we add the needs for replacement as a result of the obsolescence through aging of our current facilities, that proportion of the urban system in the year 2001 over which we do and shall have discretionary power is dominant. We thus have the potential to shape the urban system of the future to meet our desires.

How then can we design the urban system to be responsive to changing needs and to maximize choice? We propose a new institutional structure for framing relevant urban policy: a National Urban Council, an Urban Research Institute, and an Urban Planning Body. These institutions are even more important in the context of the designed future, where it is essential that urban policy should serve society's evolving needs effectively.

As we have seen, these institutional reforms are meant to achieve interest aggregation and constraint recognition. The actual delivery system requires a clearly defined strategy, and the one we propose emerges from our preceding analysis. We have found that the unconstrained urbanization process appears incapable of providing an urban future based on expanded choice. The alternative is to control that process —*to optimize urban growth.*

c. Limiting Urban Growth

A key source of urban demographic growth has been immigration. By shutting off most in-migration, we can effectively slow down the rate of urban growth. This is not a difficult strategy since our immigration policy is a highly flexible one, responding at present to short-term labour requirements. Thus, the means for effectively controlling one important dimension of urban growth is already available, and it is clearly in the federal government's hands.

As a side effect of this strategy, migration to the cities from backward areas within Canada will be encouraged. If it is felt that the priority objective is to eliminate regional disparities, this might well prove to be an effective scheme, although it would do nothing towards solving the urban problem. If we truly want to limit urban growth, then we shall have to engage in policies to fix the rural population; higher income support programs via unemployment insurance, higher minimum wages, or a guaranteed annual income, all would likely reduce the current high levels of internal migration by making the alternative of moving less attractive. This urban policy option will have to be carried out in conjunction with other national policies—regional development, *immigration*, and manpower—with a clear consensus on priorities, if it is to be fully effective.

This option is controversial because it is almost universally assumed that immigration is "good". Two benefits are claimed: one, that rapid population growth is good; the other, that immigrants improve the quality of our labour force. The latter is true, although this benefit must be evaluated in the light of its cost (the primary one being the urban cost). The former is difficult to prove or disprove. Although Canada will be bigger in the future, current international political realities will hardly be affected by even major increases in our population size. A rapidly growing population will increase the rate of return to capital and resources, but at the expense of lowering the wage rate of Canadian labour. In addition, to the extent that the capital is foreign owned, there is a strong argument against this sort of growth. If the profits are reinvested, and if the economy grows faster, there may be a future-improvement argument, but higher rates of saving by labour (forced or otherwise) can yield equivalent rates of accumulation and growth. Other arguments for large size, such as populating an empty country, are essentially trivial in an era of metropolitan dominance.

To summarize this option, there are apparent urban advantages to lowering the rate of population growth by reducing rates of immigration and internal migration. This would conflict with other national objectives, such as growth and regional balance, and may therefore be politically unacceptable.

d. The Preferred Urban Future

The second option attempts a synthesis by preserving the benefits of growth while reducing the costs. The difficulty with the first approach is that slowing urban growth reduces benefits as well as costs. The benefits accrue from the agglomeration economies inherent in urban areas—the fact that there is maximum access to primary inputs, other firms, and final markets in dense clusters of population. The costs arise because scarce land raises a barrier to access; the direct and social costs of urbanization, which we have termed the urban problem, make access continually more difficult. Improving access within our existing urban areas ultimately has been self-defeating because it has led to more sprawl, more congestion, and so forth.

An additional disadvantage of the first approach is that it tends to condemn those not now in an urban environment to continual public assistance. It forecloses the very important option of acquiring an increasingly indispensable life-style, that of urban living. It may be argued quite appropriately that current urban centres have little to offer in terms of this option; there are very few real choices to be made in our largest cities. To choose them is to choose a cluster of urban problems which are only aggravated if that choice is made. The choice is being made because the private benefits exceed the private costs. The social accounting result, which is difficult to measure, may reveal a reverse net benefit. If we accept as a national objective the right of individuals to choose where and how to live, then our present urban system makes this right not a fully realizable one; but the policy option which limits growth would terminate that right.

Our synthesis thus has two aims: to make the right of individuals to choose when and how to live an effective one, and to separate the urban mechnisms providing benefits from those creating costs. To achieve them we must channel further expansion in a specific way. The economic dynamic of presently large centres must not be destroyed; the labour force and markets must remain accessible. Thus, future expansion must be fully integrated into the urban system. At the same time, it must not add to the land-use problems of the large metropolitan areas. This requires the siting of new development beyond the urbanized area. These two superficially conflicting requirements—of integration yet spatial divorce—leads to only one solution: the sequential development of new communities.

A policy of new community development requires at least the following supporting programs:

(1) limiting sprawl at the pressure points;
(2) assisting growth where viable;
(3) developing new communities.

Some powerful techniques for limiting growth are now available to the federal government. They include assistance in the provision of services, the use of mortgages for approved land use plans, and the land assembly program (although this latter appears to be a costly procedure). With provincial and municipal planning and zoning cooperation, the strategy would be fully effective.

This strategy would be aimed at building an urban infra-structure already in place in relatively small areas closely linked to the main urban system. Policies would be required which would avoid increasing the costs of urbanization and would better link these areas into the metropolitan system without adding to metropolitan problems. Of necessity, most of these steps would be provincial and local, but the coordinated provision of housing under the NHA and assistance for transit in particular, as well as the location of new federal buildings, could lead to a more positive federal role in these communities.

The main element of this option is the development of fully planned new communities. To meet our twin objectives of integration with spatial divorce these communities will have to be connected to the metropolitan system by new high-speed mass transit systems. Concurrent policies will be required that ensure that the automobile will provide no realistic alternative. This will break the links connecting greater distance, more cars, more congestion, more core pollution, more wasted core space, and so on; and it will also ensure high rates of transit utilization and an end to the vicious circle of transit subsidy, fare increase, and passenger decline.

In the new communities, public acquisition of land will yield to the public authorities all incremental land values. Pre-planning can reserve rights of way for infra-structure, provide enormous economies of on-site factories for construction of utilities, structures, and roadways, as well as housing. Even such innovations as central heating (nuclear?) and cooling systems can be attempted, reducing pollution and providing low-cost services.

The concept is not new, although the program when applied elsewhere has been generally limited as a result of the failure to integrate it into the full urban system and its dynamic processes. The one attempt that comes closest to our concept has been the Vallingby-Stockholm model. The linearity of the Canadian urban system would seem to make it extremely relevant.

We have noted that the *increase* in metropolitan population will amount to somewhere between 10 million and 16 million by 2001. Much of this (one-half) will take place in the major metropolitan centres of Montreal and Toronto. Consequently, our policy must be geared primarily towards solving the problems of these centres. If we are to stabilize the growth of their respective populations, some six to seven million persons will have to be accommodated in the Montreal-Toronto corridor over the next thirty years. A good proportion can be accommodated in the rapidly growing communities presently in the corridor, particularly if these are well conceived. But several million at least will require the facilities that our new communities can best provide. Let us assume a minimum of two and one-half million, to be domiciled in three new communities of about 800,000 each. To achieve this size, each community must grow by about 120,000 in the first decade, and double the rate of increase (7 per cent per year) each decade thereafter. The initial rate of increase of 12,000 per year, on the average, is feasible. Toronto grows by six or seven times this amount every year, but that growth is essentially unplanned. Our new program will require a huge planning effort on a scale not undertaken before. We believe this is not a serious constraint.

Part III Section F

RELIGION AND SOCIAL CHANGE

35

Some Problematic Aspects of Religion in Canada*

Stewart Crysdale

The kindling of interest among sociologists and other social scientists in recent years in the place of religion in Canadian society has two broad implications. To begin with, it represents a renewal of the classical notion that a knowledge of religious beliefs and practices is necessary for an understanding of the historical and cultural roots of a society. Religion contributes in important ways to the formation, maintenance, and modification of the distinctive values and norms, collective sentiments, and structures, both formal and informal, that characterize a society (Weber 1905, 1922; Durkheim 1912; Berger and Luckmann 1966; Berger 1967; Luckmann 1967). Again, increased enquiry indicates that religion, both institutional and individual, which in the middle decades of the 20th century was largely taken for granted by detached observers, is now seen to be greatly varied, having complex interrelations with other social institutions and holding different meanings for various groups. In short, it is recognized as problematic and therefore needs to be explained.

For one thing, traditional forms in church orders and courts, in worship, in teaching, and in theology are being widely challenged and alternative forms have appeared and are gaining limited acceptance, both within churches, and in the less permanent sects and cults. More profoundly, conventional or orthodox beliefs and practices have been questioned by large numbers of persons, resulting in the erosion of accustomed observances such as frequent church attendance, in the privatizing of faith, and in the decline in the influence of formal religion in other spheres such as politics, economics, education, the arts, entertainment, and family life. Finally, religion is problematic in the sense that alternative ideologies have gained ground in the search for meaning and direction in a secular, urbanized, pluralistic, and pragmatic age.

The rise of other ideologies has led to the reconsideration of the definition of religion. Until very recently in North America, "religion" meant for most people, including social scientists, a system of practices, beliefs, and attitudes relating to sacred ends and objects which brought together a group of persons who thought of themselves as believers or members of a religious body in distinction from others whose

*Reprinted from *Sociological Focus* (April) 1976, 137-148, with the permission of the author and publisher. This paper draws heavily on Stewart Crysdale and Les Wheatcroft (eds.), *Religion in Canadian Society* (Toronto: Macmillan of Canada), 1976.

practices, beliefs, and attitudes were different. Now, some scholars reason that religion is whatever an individual may consider to be of ultimate worth in his or her hierarchy of values or life goals (Tillich 1951: 211 ff; Glock and Stark 1965: Ch. 1; Bellah 1970: Ch. 2). Others argue that it is whatever set of values and beliefs that permits a person to unify all of life's experiences in a meaningful framework (Fallding 1974). Thus, it is claimed that for some persons religion may be dedication to Mao's teachings, to benevolent humanitarianism, Fascism, Anarchism, hedonism (the pleasure principle) or to pragmatic realism or rationalism. In this paper, religion is viewed in a more conventional western sense, connoting a system of practices, beliefs, and attitudes which joins believers in relation to the supranatural and which typically affects both the empirical and nonempirical aspects of life (*cf.* van der Leeuw 1933; Wach 1944; Geertz 1966; Berger 1974).

The paper deals with two main aspects of the problematic nature of religion in Canada: the shape and impact of religion in broad outline, and the principal directions which sociological enquiry into religion is now taking.

The Shape and Impact of Religion

It is clear that formal or institutional religion in Canada in the past twenty years has lost much of its direct influence in other realms of social action, such as politics, education, and family life. But its impact was powerful in the early days of exploration and settlement, during the time of agrarian development, and more recently in the formative days of industrial growth. It still provides the most integrative basis for voluntary association in every community, and, apart from ethnicity and socio-economic status, religion is the principal social and cultural attribute which distinguishes each major part of the population from the others. In some important respects, religion has more influence than ethnicity and socio-economic status, as in party preference in elections.

Religion was a unifying and stabilizing force in Quebec during the era of French exploration and settlement and before the British conquest in 1760. Nearly all the French-speaking population were Roman Catholic, and clergy were powerful leaders in governing councils, schools, and hospitals. The church was the largest land owner and was entitled to a tithe or tax on crops. But the provision of an adequate number of clergy was made possible only by grants from the French crown, both in funds and in land (Falardeau 1952). With the conquest and subsequent efforts by the British to unite French-speaking, Catholic, Lower Canada with English-speaking, Protestant, Upper Canada, religion became a divisive force in the northern British colonies. However, religious conflict was largely contained geographically because Roman Catholicism was concentrated in French-speaking Quebec while Protestantism dominated in English-speaking Upper Canada (later Ontario) and in the Atlantic colonies. With Confederation in 1867, compromises were worked out whereby the Catholic Church in Quebec continued to have strong status and to dominate many areas of life until the 1960s. The Protestant churches for their part exercised considerable influence in English-speaking parts of Canada, but, because of their view that the church's role is distinct from that of the state, because of their emphasis on individual rather than communal responsibility, and because they were divided, their power never equalled that of the Catholic Church in Quebec (Walsh 1956; Moir 1959; French 1962). Thus, as a consequence of the duality of cultures and of religious affiliation for the vast majority of the population in the later decades of the 19th century—French-Catholic and British-Protestant—a middle-of-the-road position has characterized the relations between church and state. This may best be called cooperation, in contrast to establishment as in Britain and in some European countries and to explicit separation as in the case of the United States.

Another historical feature has strengthened the close though unofficial linkage between church and state. This is the tendency toward centralism in Canadian political structures. While the British North America Act of 1867 gave important constitutional rights to the provinces, including the control of natural resources, education, and the administration of justice within their boundaries, the crucial matters of finance, taxation of income, communication, criminal justice, and defence were reserved to the federal government. Centralized control was deemed essential for the cohesive development of a vast, diverse, and thinly populated domain and the preservation of sovereignty in the shadow of its mighty and rapidly expanding neighbour. Proneness to centralism, for similar reasons, has characterized the development of religious bodies (Clark 1948; Walsh 1956). Although the first truly national church did not emerge until 1925 with the formation of the United Church of Canada, which brought together three denominations with different backgrounds under a strong national administration, movements in the direction of merger and regional association were common among the major denominations since the 1860s. Thus, the establishment of new congregations, hospitals, and schools in western, northern, and low-income "mission" areas has typically been undertaken by central church authorities rather than by individual religious entrepreneurs. While there are, of course, many independent congregations, some of them churches and others sects or cults, they are for the most part very small. The more successful among them, significantly, are intimately linked with sponsoring bodies and leaders in the United States.

The affiliations of the population by major denominations in 1921, 1941, and 1971 are shown in Table 1. Changes in the size of denominations are the result chiefly of variations in birth rate and immigration. For example, the proportion of Catholics among the native-born has remained relatively constant since 1951, but the proportion of Catholics among the foreign-born increased from 28 to 42 per cent between 1951 and 1971. If this trend continues Canada may have a Catholic majority by the time of the 1981 census (Kalbach and McVey 1976). The national figures, however, obscure the high degree of religious and ethnic homogeneity which exists in many areas and also the extent of diversity between areas.

Gross figures to church attendance likewise hide important variations in behaviour between groups. In Table 2 we see that for the national sample, attendance at church or synagogue declined from 61 per cent in 1956 to 55 per cent in 1965 and to 39 per cent in 1974. Catholics still attend in larger proportion than Protestants, but Catholic attendance since 1965 has fallen as steeply as among Protestants. Further cross-tabulations not shown here reveal that there is no systematic relation between level of education or occupation, on the one hand, and attendance, on the other. However, church attendance among English-speaking Protestants is highest in the Atlantic provinces and on the Prairies, somewhat lower in Ontario, and lowest of all in British Columbia. Regional variations are less marked among French-speaking Catholics, but Catholics living in Quebec and Ontario tend more to go to church than those living elsewhere. Regional variations remind us of the importance of historical and cultural factors in social behaviour with respect to religion as well as other social institutions.

Variations in attendance *between* denominations may be explained to a large degree by differences in theology or belief concerning the meaning of faith and the fuctions of the church in the processes of salvation and sanctification. But variations in attendance *within* denominations call for historical and, sometimes, social psychological explanations. J.J. Mol (1976a, 1976b) proposes that when a religious group has minority status and feels that it must fight for survival, its members will stress attend-

Table 1

Religious Affiliation of Population of Canada, 1921, 1941, 1971*
by Major Denominations

(In percentages)

	1921	1941	1971
Catholic	40.6	44.6	48.8
Roman Catholic	38.7	41.8	46.2
Greek Orthodox	1.9	1.2	1.5
Ukrainian Catholic	—a	1.6	1.1
Protestant	54.7	51.1	42.1
United	0.1	19.2	17.5
Anglican	16.1	15.2	11.8
Presbyterian	16.1	7.2[b]	4.0
Lutheran	3.3	3.5	3.3
Baptist	4.8	4.2	3.1
Mennonite	0.7	1.0	0.8
Methodist	13.2[c]	—c	—c
Pentecostal	0.1	0.5	1.0
Salvation Army	0.3	0.3	0.6
Jewish	1.4	1.5	1.3
Other	3.4	2.8	3.6
No Religion	0.002	0.0016	4.3[d]
Totals	100.1[e]	100.0	100.1[e]

*Computed From Statistics Canada, Sept. 1973: *1971 Census of Canada.* "Population: Religious Denominations", Cat. 92-724, Vol. 1- pt. 3 (Bull 1.3-3). Ottawa.

Notes:

a. In 1921, Ukrainian Catholic not shown separately.

b. Decrease in Presbyterian from 1921 to 1941 is largely accounted for by the formation in 1925 of the United Church of Canada, which included a majority of Presbyterians. In 1931 continuing Presbyterians were 8.4% of the population.

c. Since 1925, Methodists were absorbed into the United Church, except for a small number of Free Methodists.

d. Increase in "No religion" in 1971 is probably due partly to method of reporting, by mail, as well as to decline in affiliation.

e. Totals other than 100.0% are due to rounding.

Table 2

Church Attendance in Canada From Gallup Polls, 1956, 1965, and May 1974*

(In percentages)

	1956	1965	1974
Roman Catholics	87	83	59
Protestants	43	32	27
National Totals	61	55	39

* Responses were to this question: "Did you, yourself, happen to attend church or synagogue in the last seven days?" By permission of the Canadian Institute of Public Opinion.

ance in order to strengthen their social cohesion and emphasize their identity. Hence, the six million French-speaking residents of Quebec, fearing absorption by nearly three times as many Canadians whose language for the most part is English and whose religion is Protestant, and resisting the cultural pressures of the Protestant Anglo-American multitudes to the south, emphasize the Catholic religion as a means of reinforcing and legitimating their distinctiveness. Religious observance, including attendance at mass, is also much stronger in Quebec than in other industrialized, predominantly Catholic countries such as France and Italy where culture and religion are not so fragmented as in North America and therefore not so problematic (*cf.* Herberg 1955; Lenski 1961; Greeley 1972).

At the same time, other broad factors, such as urbanization, are at work in Canada, as elsewhere, to modify and usually attenuate religious belief and practices. In a study of the impact of urbanism as a style of life on beliefs and behaviour of a national sample of United Church members and adherents, Crysdale (1965; *cf.* Wirth, 1938) found that high urbanism was consistently related with high liberalism in beliefs, with tolerance of minority groups, and with approval of centralized public controls over economic activity. This basic relationship persisted regardless of region, size of community, age, education, occupation, or income. The findings of this study complement Mol's in that individuals who have been socialized into a heterogeneous, mobile, universalistic style of life—attributes of urbanism—feel less constrained than others to conform with traditional and distinctive patterns of belief and practice. At the same time they are apt to be uncertain of their faith and thus less sure of their identity as believers.

Colette Moreux (1976) reached similar conclusions in a study of female Catholics in the village parish of "Saint-Pierre," near metropolitan Montreal. As urbanism and secularism spread, the traditional beliefs of Catholic Christianity diminish. Most women, especially the young and old and to a less extent the young adults, still profess themselves as believers and attend mass with moderate regularity. But their reasons for doing so are more social and expedient than religious. They know little of Catholic dogma and experience little or no emotional attachment to the faith of the Church.

The problematic condition of religion today appears also in Evelyn Kallen's (1976) analysis of how religious revival and ethnic identity interact for members of three synagogues in Toronto. Because of the more recent Jewish immigration into Canada in comparison with the United States, second generation Canadian Jews are less assimilated or acculturated by the dominant culture than their American counterparts. Following the Nazi holocaust, the realization that discrimination persists in

North America, and the galvanizing birth of the New Israel, authenticated by the Seven Days War, the majority of Canadian Jews have tended toward positive ethnic identity. Kallen concludes that the "religious revival" among North American Jews really represents an ethnic revival a shift from negative to positive ethnic identification.

Numerous researchers have observed that the most persistent variable which affects party preference in voting is religious affiliation. The latter is at least as strong as or stronger than social class or ethnicity in its impact on party preference. Meisel (1956, 1962, 1964), examining data on the 1953 federal and 1955 provincial elections in an eastern Ontario riding (electoral district), found that members of the Anglican and United churches were apt to vote Progressive Conservative while Catholics supported the Liberal party (see also Alford 1963). Anderson (1966) found that in Hamilton, Ontario, while the basic pattern documented in earlier studies prevailed, the younger age groups were less inclined than older people to vote according to their religious tradition. She also learned that the New Democratic Party was supported chiefly by young, male Protestant, non-church-goers. Alford (1964) showed that the prevalent pattern of relations between party preference and religious affiliation varied in degree from one province to another. In a few rare instances the pattern was reversed, as Perlin (1964) documented in his study of St. John's, Newfoundland, where Protestants voted Liberal and Catholics voted Conservative.

Attempting to explain denominational voting preferences, McDonald (1969) found that in the 1968 federal election in Ontario, specific issues such as support for the Catholic separate school system and attitudes on the welfare state, made no measurable difference in party preference. Neither did the religion of candidates. What did make a difference in the degree of party preference was social involvement in the religious community.

The rise to power in the western province of Saskatchewan in 1944 of the socialist CCF (later NDP) party presents special problems for sociological enquiry. Silverstein (1968), reviewing returns for provincial elections from 1948 to 1964, found that Roman Catholics were consistently opposed to the CCF and loyal to the Liberals, while United Church members consistently supported the CCF. Laskin and Baird (1970) revealed that in Saskatchewan, contrary to experience elsewhere, Anglican voting preferences were more similar to those of Roman Catholics than to those of United Church people, and variations by religion did not overturn variations by social class.

The support of socialist principles and parties by a significant minority of Protestants, particularly in the early decades of the 20th century by Methodists, and in recent decades by some United Church people, originated with the development of Christian socialism in Britain and later with the rise of the Social Gospel movement in North America. The disruption which followed from large-scale immigration in the second decade was compounded by widespread unemployment, the exploitation of unorganized labour, and blatant profiteering which accompanied early industrialization. Then came the horrors and heroism of the First World War, evoking in response a wave of social idealism. This led to efforts to "build the Kingdom of God on earth."

In 1906 the General Conference of the Methodist Church strongly criticized the existing competitive order and stated that the work of the church is to set up "a social order founded on the principles of the Gospel, the Golden Rule, and the Sermon on the Mount—and made possible through the regeneration of men's lives" (Methodist Church 1906: 274-276). A national council which included representatives of major Protestant churches and the Trades and Labour Congress of Canada was formed in 1907 as an instrument in the struggle for social justice. This was expanded in 1914 into the Social Service Council of Canada, including such agrarian groups as the

Dominion Grange and Farmers' Association and the Canadian Council of Agriculture (Crysdale 1961: Ch. 2).

In 1918 the far-reaching reforms sought by Christian socialists were stated explicitly in the annual report of the Methodist Committee on Social Service and Evangelism. It condemned special privilege not based on useful service to the community, called for labour to have a voice in management and a share in the profits and risks of business, and disparaged all autocratic organization of business. It recommended Old Age Insurance on a national scale, in which the annuity should be based on the average earnings of the country. And it argued for the nationalization of natural resources, such as mines, water power, fisheries, forests, means of communication, transportation, and public utilities on which all the people depend (Methodist Church 1918: 341-342).

As a social movement with coherent goals, program, leadership, and organization, the Social Gospel in Canada had reached a peak by 1928 and was beginning to fragment (Allen 1971). Its direct impact, however, continued for some years, for example, in the work of the Fellowship for a Christian Social Order (Scott and Vlastos 1936).

The Social Gospel bore political fruit in Saskatchewan with the election in 1944 of a CCF government because of its convergence with other dynamic forces of an economic, political, and social nature. The world-wide economic collapse and successive failures of the wheat crop in that province, combined with ineptitude and corruption in the old parties and the rise of strong agrarian populist movements, led to the CCF victory (Crysdale 1976). It was not coincidence that the national founder of the new party of reform was a former United Church minister, J.S. Woodsworth, and the first CCF premier of Saskatchewan was a Baptist minister, T.C. Douglas, who later became the national leader.

The upheaval of the Second World War involved the churches in new ministries and presented different problems for ethics and theology. The excesses of both Fascism and Communism cooled social and political idealism, and the necessity for reconstruction and expansion led to emphases on pastoral ministry and moderate, pragmatic, ethical concerns. The radical reform elements in the churches gave way in the 1950s and 1960s to those more interested in civil rights and peace movements and in adapting the Gospel to the needs of a secular age. The threats of environmental disaster, of the drug "culture." and of inner city blight, and the awakening of interest among some youth in the simple old-time religion and among others in eastern mysticism present alternative opportunities for religious action.

The Principal Areas of Sociological Enquiry

The growth of interest in religion by Canadian social scientists has led to an annotated inventory of studies done over the past 25 years (Crysdale and Montimy 1974). Over one-half of the 173 French-language and 143 English-language studies included were dated from 1965 on—a further indication that studies have proliferated as problems have become more apparent. In both cultures over one-half of the works were directed by sociologists, followed by anthropologists. In English the third most numerous enquiries were in the area of political sociology, no doubt reflecting the close but ambiguous relations between religion and public policy and voting discussed above. In French the third most numerous studies were in the field of social psychology, indicating a strong interest in the adaptive patterns of laity, especially children and youth, of members of orders, and clergy, in a secularizing culture.

The breadth of recent and current work is evident from a brief sketch of selections from the English and French-language literature. Studies using the historical perspective and method, although not the approach most frequent in Anglophone Canada, have been the most influential. Examining the pre-industrial period, Falardeau (1952) traces the homogeneity and integration of beliefs, practices and social structures of the parish in Quebec, continuing from the 17th to the 19th century. This stand in sharp contrast to the relatively rapid changes which occured in religious organization and behaviour in Protestant-British areas of settlement in the Atlantic region and Upper Canada (Clark 1948; Moir 1959). Clark adapts the church-sect typological appraoch to historical dynamics as he shows that formal structures and theology were not flexible enough to meet the needs of pioneers and, later, workers in industralizing cities. But as some sects became established they, too, took on more formal structures and tended to become church-like, for example, the Salvation Army. Sects which did not adapt usually disappeared, to be succeeded by new groups and movements. W.E. Mann (1955) applied the typological-historical appraoch in his study of sects, cults, and churches in Alberta during the depression years.

The pressures of widespread social change, such as invasion of the territory of indigenous peoples by whites and the impact of industrialization, urbanization, and secularization in settled areas are the subject of numerous studies from the viewpoint of historical sociology and cultural anthropology. Bock (1966), Vallée (1967), Shimpo (1976), and Warburton (1976) are among those who have traced the dislocating effects of invasion on the religious life of native peoples. Miner (1939), Hughes (1943, 1976), Falardeau (1949), Guindon (1960), Kernaghan (1966), and Milner (1973) show how religious bodies at first resist social change and later sometimes adapt more or less and at other times undergo extensive changes in the process (Grant 1972); Crysdale 1961, 1965, 1976).

A large number of studies have been conducted on the basis of community form and process. Bennett (1969), for example, describes how Hutterites withdraw as much as possible by creating their own farming communities. Lucas (1970) shows how social conflicts which typify single-industry towns are reflected and also generated in competing churches and sect. Driedger (1968, 1972) finds that less than one-half of Mennonites live in cities, but that those who do adapt to urban contexts in several ways. The rural church has not been widely studied by sociologists (Whyte 1966, Settle 1971), although there are numerous parish and diocesan studies which were designed for administrative purposes.

Another category of studies deals chiefly with interaction within religious bodies and with their interface with society. Westhues (1976) examines the flexibility of Roman Catholic Church as it encounters different structures and value patterns. In Quebec, where the Roman Catholic Church enjoys majority status, it assumes one stance, but in those provinces where it is in a minority situation it assumes a different stance. Parenton (1948) shows that the Catholic Church in South Louisiana, because of its minority position, ethnic heterogeneity, and rivalry between orders, never gained the power that it had in Quebec. Bird and Reimer (1976) examine the differences in structures, goals, and practices of contemporary sects and cults in Montreal, while O'Toole (1976) shows that applying the analytical framework of sect to small, radical political groups helps to explain their persistence in spite of failure to win converts or to achieve explicit goals.

Some studies examine the behaviour of kinds of religious persons. Johnson and Cornell (1972) learned that Canadian clergy were more theologically conservative than U.S. clergy, their own laity, and U.S. laity. But Canadian clergy were conspicuously more tolerant than the rest with regard to the behaviour of others. Crysdale (1965) found that ministers of the United Church of Canada were more reformist than lay people in attitudes towards social issues. Stryckman and Gaudet (1971) observed that Roman Catholic clergy preferred ideally to stress their prophetic and pastoral functions but that the demands of parish structures emphasized priestly and administrative functions. Younger clergy felt that priests should be permitted to be married. Bibby and Brinkerhoff (1973) discovered that the large majority of "converts" into evangelical sects are the children of members or recruits from similar groups.

A number of recent studies have investigated religious socialization and commitment among youth. Sévigny (1969) found that French-speaking Roman Catholic youth in their late teens express faith in individual rather than church-oriented terms. Lachance (1955) reported that the internalization of beliefs by five and six-year-olds depends on differences in their cognition and perception. Currie (1976) learned in a cross-sectional survey of youth in Calgary that those who were most apt to retain strong identification in religious faith and practice had been socialized into strong commitment during childhood, regardless of denomination. While loss of commitment was greatest among Roman Catholic youth, they were most apt to continue in membership. Differences in rates of belonging were related not only to early socialization, but also to the meaning of religion and the church in different traditions.

The largest proportion of scientific studies of religion in Canada have to do with its functions in meeting social and personal needs, following Durkheim's methods but usually without accepting either his positivism or reductionism. More recently some investigators have raised questions regarding the place of religion in dealing with the elemental problems of meaning, with far-reaching implications for individual and social behaviour. This direction of enquiry promises well for a renewal of the theoretically fruitful emphases which have always characterized the sociology of religion at its best.

References

Alford, Robert

1963 *Party and Society.* Chicago: Rand-McNally.

1964 "The social bases of political cleavage in 1962." In John Meisel, 1964.

Allen, Richard

1971 *The Social Passion: Religion and Social Reform in Canada, 1914-28.* Toronto: University of Toronto Press.

Anderson, Grace M.

1966 "Voting behaviour and the ethnic religious variable." *Canadian Journal of Economics and Political Science* 32: 27-37.

Bellah, Robert

1970 *Beyond Belief.* New York: Harper and Row.

Bennett, John W.

1976 "The Hutterites: A communal sect." In Crysdale and Wheatcroft (1976). From *Plains People*, Chicago: Aldine, 1969.

Berger, Peter L.

1967 *The Sacred Canopy.* Garden City, N.Y.: Doubleday.

1974 "Some thoughts on defining religion." *Journal for the Scientific Study of Religion* 13.

Berger, Peter L., and Thomas Luckmann
1966 *The Social Construction of Reality.* Garden City, N.Y.: Doubleday.

Bibby, Reginald W., and Merlin B. Brinkerhoff
1973 "The circulation of the saints." *Journal for the Scientific Study of Religion* 12. Reprinted in Crysdale and Wheatcroft, 1976.

Bird, Frederick and William Reimer
1976 "New religious and para-religious movements in Montreal." In Crysdale and Wheatcroft, 1976.

Bock, Philip K.
1966 *The Micmac Indians of Restigouche.* Ottawa: National Museum of Canada, Bulletin 213. Selection in Crysdale and Wheatcroft, 1976.

Clark, S.D.
1948 *Church and Sect in Canada.* Toronto: University of Toront Press.

Crysdale, Stewart
1961 *The Industrial Struggle and Protestant Ethics in Canada.* Toronto: Ryerson.

1965 *The Changing Church in Canada: National Survey of the United Church in Canadian Society.* Toronto: United Church of Canada.

Crysdale, Stewart, and J.P. Montminy, with L. Wheatcroft and H. Urbano
1974 *La Religion au Canada/Religion in Canada: Annotated Inventory of Scientific Studies of Religion, 1945-1972.* Downsview, Ont.: York University.

Crysdale, Stewart, and L. Wheatcroft
1976 *Religion in Canadian Society: A Text-Reader.* Toronto: Macmillan of Canada.

Currie, Raymond F.
1976 "Belonging, commitment, and early socialization." In Crysdale and Wheatcroft, 1976.

Driedger, Leo
1968 "A perspective on Canadian Mennonite urbanization." *Mennonite Life* 23: 147-51.

1972 Urbanization of Mennonites in Canada." In H. Poettcker and R. Regehr (eds.), *Call to Faithfulness.* Altona, Man.: D.W. Friesen.

Durkheim, Emile
1915 *The Elementary Forms of the Religious Life,* trans. J. Swain. London: George Allen and Unwin.

Falardeau, Jean-Charles
1949 "The parish as an institutional type." *Canadian Journal of Economics and Political Science* 15.

1962 "Les recherches religieuses au Canada français." *Recherches Sociographiques* 3.

1964 "The role and importance of the Church in French Canada." In M. Rioux and Y. Martin (eds.), *French Canadian Society*, Vol. 1. Toronto: McClelland and Stewart. First published in 1954.

1976 "The seventeenth-century parish in French Canada." In Crysdale and Wheatcroft, 1976. From M. Rioux and Y. Martin, eds. *French Canadian Society*, Vol. 1, Toronto: McClelland and Stewart, 1964.

Fallding, Harold
1974 *The Sociology of Religion.* Toronto: McGraw-Hill Ryerson.

French, Goldwyn
1962 *Parsons and Politics.* Toronto: Ryerson.

Geertz, Clifford
1966 "Religion as a cultural system." In M. Banton (ed.), *Anthropological Approaches to the Study of Religion.* London: Tavistock.

Glock, Charles Y., and Rodney Stark
1965 *Religion and Society in Tension.* Chicago: Rand-McNally.

Grant, John Webster
1972 *The Church in the Canadian Era.* Toronto: McGraw-Hill Ryerson. Selection in Crysdale and Wheatcroft, 1976.

Greeley, Andrew M.
1972 *The Denominational Society.* Glenview, Ill.: Scott, Foresman.

Guindon, Hubert
1960 "The social evolution of Quebec reconsidered." *Canadian Journal of Economics and Political Science* 26.

Herberg, Will
1955 *Protestant, Catholic, Jew.* New York: Doubleday.

Hughes, Everett C.
1943 *French Canada in Transition.* Chicago: University of Chicago Press.

1976 "Action Catholique and nationalism: A memorandum on the Church and society in French Canada, 1942." In Crysdale and Wheatcroft, 1976.

Johnson, Douglas, and George Cornell
1972 *Punctured Preconceptions.* New York: Friendship Press.

Kalbach, Warren E., and Wayne W. McVey, Jr.
1971 *The Demographic Bases of Canadian Society.* Toronto: McGraw-Hill. Revised in Crysdale and Wheatcroft, 1976.

Kernaghan, W.D.K.
1966 "Freedom of Religion in Quebec, with Particular Reference to the Jews, Jehovah's Witnesses, and Church-State Relations." Unpublished Ph.D. dissertation, Duke University.

Kallen, Evelyn
1976 "Synagogues in transition: Religious revival or ethnic survival?" In Crysdale and Wheatcroft.

Lachance, Jean Marie
1966 "Etude sur l'enseignement du catéchisme d'après les théories de Jean Piaget." Unpublished thesis, University of Montreal.

Laskin, Richard, and Peter Baird
1970 "Factors in voter turnout and party preference in a Saskatchewan town." *Canadian Journal of Political Science* 3: 450-62.

Lucas, Rex
1971 *Minetown, Milltown, Railtown.* Toronto: University of Toronto Press. Selection in Crysdale and Wheatcroft, 1976.

Luckmann, Thomas
1967 *The Invisible Religion.* New York: Macmillan.

Mann, W.E.
1955 *Sect, Cult, and Church in Alberta.* Toronto: University of Toronto Press.

McDonald, Lynn
1966 "Religion and voting: The 1968 federal election in Ontario." *Canadian Review of Sociology and Anthropology* 3: 129-44. Reprinted in Crysdale and Wheatcroft, 1976.

Meisel, John
1956 "Religious affiliation and voting behaviour." *Canadian Journal of Economics and Political Science* 22: 481-96.

1962 *The Canadian Federal Election of 1957.* Toronto: University of Toronto Press.

1964 *Papers on the 1962 Election.* Toronto: University of Toronto Press.

Methodist Church of Canada
1906 Journal of Proceedings, 7th General Conference. Toronto.

1918 Report of the Committee on Social Service and Evangelism. Toronto.

Milner, Sheilagh H., and Henry Milner
1973 *The Decolonization of Quebec.* Toronto: McClelland and Stewart. Selection in Crysdale and Wheatcroft, 1976.

Miner, Horace
1939 *St. Denis: A French-Canadian Parish.* Chicago: University of Chicago Press.

Moir, John S.
1959 *Church and State in Canada West.* Toronto: University of Toronto Press. Selections in Crysdale and Wheatcroft, 1976.

Mol, J.J.
1976a "Major correlates of church-going in Canada." In Crysdale and Wheatcroft.

1976b *Identify and the Sacred.* Agincourt, Ont.: Book Society.

Moreux, Colette
1976 "The end of a religion?" In Crysdale and Wheatcroft. From *Fin d'une religion?* Montréal: Les Presses de l'Université Laval, 1969.

O'Toole, Roger
1976 "Sectarianism in politics: The Internationalists and the Socialist Labour Party." In Crysdale and Wheatcroft.

Parenton, Vernon J.
1948 "The Rural French-Speaking People of Quebec and South Louisiana: A comparative Study of the Social Structure and Organization with Emphasis on the Role of the Catholic Church." Unpublished Ph.D. dissertation, Harvard University.

Perlin, George
1964 "St. John's West." In Meisel, 1964.

Porter, John
1965 *The Vertical Mosaic.* Toronto: University of Toronto Press.

Scott, R.B.Y., and Gregory Vlastos (eds.)
1936 *Towards the Christian Revolution.* Chicago: Willett, Clarke.

Settle, Lester M.
1971 "The Functional Community and Parish Organizations: West Colchester Research Project." Toronto: Division of Outreach, United Church of Canada.

Sévigny, Robert
1976 "Conceptions of religion among Quebec youth." In Crysdale and Wheatcroft. From "La conception de l'expérience religieuse". *Sociologie et Sociétés* 1:1 (mai) 1969, 7-21.

Shimpo, Mitsuru
1976 "Native religion in socio-cultural change: The Cree and Saulteaux in southern Saskatchewan, 1830-1900." In Crysdale and Wheatcroft, 1976.

Silverstein, Sandford
1968 "Occupational class and voting behaviour: Electoral tendencies of a left-wing protest movement in a period of prosperity." In S.M. Lipset, *Agrarian Socialism.* Garden City, N.Y.: Doubleday Anchor.

Stryckman, Paul, and Robert Gaudet
1976 "Priests under stress" In Crysdale and Wheatcrof. From *Priests in Canada.* Québec: Centre de Recherche en Sociologie Religiéuse l'Universite Laval.

Tillich, Paul
1951 *Systematic Theology*, vol. 1. Chicago: Univeristy of Chicago Press.

Vallee, Frank G.
1976. "Religion among the Kabloona and Eskimo." In Crysdale and Wheatcroft. First pub. 1967.

van der Leeuw, G.
1967 *Religion in Essence and Manifestation,* 2 vols., trans J.E. Turner. Gloucester, Mass.: Peter Smith. First published in German, 1933.

Wach, Joachim
1944 *The Sociology of Religion.* Chicago: University of Chicago Press.

Walsh, H.H.
1956 *The Christian Church in Canada.* Toronto: Ryerson.

Warburton, Rennie
1976 "Religion and the control of native people." In Crysdale and Wheatcroft.

Weber, Max
1958 *The Protestant Ethic and the Spirit of Capitalism,* trans T. Parsons. New York: Scribner's. First published in German 1904.

1963 *The Sociology of Religion,* trans. E. Fischoff. Boston: Beacon Press. First published in German, 1922.

Westhues, Kenneth
1976 "The adaptation of the Roman Catholic Church to Canadian society." In Crysdale and Wheatcroft.

Whyte, Donald
1966 "Religion and the rural church." In M.A. Tremblay and W.J. Anderson (eds.), *Rural Canada in Transition.* Ottawa: Agricultural Economics Research Council of Canada.

Wirth, Louis
1938 "Urbanism as a way of life." *American Journal of Sociology* 44: 1-24.

36

Religious Experience Among Quebec Youth*

Robert Sévigny

This article is taken from a larger study of religious experience and the psychological process of self-actualization.[1] Within this perspective, religious experiences are analyzed by taking into account some fundamental concepts related at the same time to the notion of the "religious" and to the theory of self-actualization, as proposed by Carl Rogers. The analysis of religious experiences is based upon such questions as these: Are these experiences emotional or rational? Are they individual or collective? Are they experiences in personal or impersonal relationships? What are the values related to these experiences, and, more specifically, are they experiences of autonomy or of constraint? How is the process of integration of various experiences or of different regions of the psychological field carried out?

Interviews were conducted with students in Montreal in classical college (Philosophy 1)[2] and in the scientific section of the twelfth grade in secondary public school. Afterwards, a questionnaire of the Q-Sort type was prepared from the answers given in the interviews and this was distributed to a second sample drawn from the same settings: 50 students in Philosophy 1 and 50 students in the scientific section.[3]

In the first part of this questionnaire, the informant indicated on a scale with nine ranks whether each statement described "very little" or "very well" the image he had of his own religious experiences. In the second part, he indicated on a scale of the same type what was for him the ideal religious experience.

The form of the questionnaire implied the notion of degree rather than the notion of type. Moreover, when gathering the data, the nine-rank scale raised few technical problems and approximated quite closely the informants' way of thinking. We have regrouped these ranks to arrive at three categories made up of the first three, the last three, and the three middle ranks of the scale. Since each item was usually situated on one or several bipolar dimensions, we can consider that the first and the last third constitute two opposite poles.

The reader will find in an appendix the results of the responses to this questionnaire. It describes the proportion of the answers situated in the first and the last third. These answers also deal with the image of the actual experience and the image of the ideal experience. They allow the exploration of the following aspects of religious experience: the general feeling of religiosity, God and Christ, the Church and the priest, practices in worship, and morality.

---

*Translated by Louise Gervais-Barker and abridged from "La conception de l'expérience religieuse", *Sociologie et Sociétés*, 1: 1 (mai, 1969), 7-21. By permission of the author and publisher.

1. The General Feeling of Religiosity

The items of the questionnaire expressing a general feeling of religiosity show that at least half of the students are placed at the "religious" pole: 49.5 per cent consider that the phrase, "I don't have a religious feeling" (item 1), describe them very little; 47.5 per cent judge that "religion has an important place in [their] life" (item 10); 55.7 per cent say that they like to "discuss religion" (item 31); 76.3 per cent feel they are very well described by item 22 which asserts, "In my religious life, I try as much as possible to clarify my thinking."[4] Yet, this percentage falls to 40.1 per cent for an adequate understanding of religion. For item 37, "I have not yet really understood what religion is," the informants distribute themselves in an approximately equal way at the two poles of the scale (35.1 per cent and 40.1 per cent).

If one puts the question in terms of the evolution of religious attitudes, a smaller number of informants place themselves at the "religious" pole. Thus, item 25: "I am less religious than before" is judged by 45.4 per cent as describing them very well.

On the whole, nearly half of the informants define themselves as having a religious feeling, but a still larger proportion define themselves as being less religious than in the past and as not having a very great understanding of religious matters.

Considering the ideal self, the proportion of those at the "religious" pole is much larger, and this holds for all the items (1, 10, 22, 25, and 37). Between 56.4 per cent and 75.3 per cent define themselves as having very religious ideals.

2. God and Christ

Let us look first at the items which express an emotional attitude towards a divine world. Seventy-seven per cent judge they are very well described by item 4: "God appears to me as an understanding person with whom you can get in touch." Nearly 58 per cent are situated at the "religious" pole for item 40: "I often think about the salvation of my soul." But 46.3 per cent have "the impression of not knowing much about Christ" (item 13); in fact, for this last item, only 26.8 per cent are placed at the "religious" pole.

The most significant result is perhaps the gap between the item on God and the one on Christ. The notion of God is much more important for the informants than the notion of Christ. We will see that this result corresponds to their conception of the Church and the priest.

If we look now at items 7, 16, and 28 which measure more explicitly the rational attitude towards religious beliefs, we see that the informants place themselves at this "rational" pole which, in the scale, is opposed to the religious pole.

Nearly 62 per cent of the informants say they distinguish in their belief in God, "that which comes from [their] individual reflection and that which comes from faith." Personal reflection plays an important part for them. Responses indicate a certain tension between the domain of emotion and that of rationality.

This tendency is still more evident in the answers to item 16: "I try to arrive at intellectual certainty in relation to the problem of eternity and the soul." Nearly 59 per cent of informants think that this statement describes them very well while only 20.6 per cent consider that it describes them very little. Thus, there is quite a clear tendency to adopt a rational attitude towards religious belief. This is what we also find for item 28: nearly half of the informants (47.4 per cent) approach a belief in Christ from a logical or historical perspective.

Let us consider now the students' images of ideal religious beliefs. For each item, the proportion of those who situate themselves at the "religious" pole is greater in the case of the ideal image than in the case of the actual image. On the whole, the informants believe they should be more religious than they are now. But it is significant to see that the largest gap between these two images is found in item 13 which deals with knowledge of Christ. While only 26.8 per cent think they have quite good knowledge of Christ, 53.6 per cent judge that ideally they should have.

3. The Church and the Priest

The Church as a Religious Institution. In response to item 43 ("I think that the Church is more a human institution than a religious institution"), a large number (40.2 per cent) said that this statement describes their view very well. Even at the level of their ideal image of religion, 32.0 per cent of the informants answered in the same way. This is the modal response, for the other informants are equally distributed between the two remaining categories. We may conclude that at least 40 per cent of the informants do not see in the Church an institution which primarily symbolizes the existence of God. The Church does not have an essential relationship with their religious experience. However, a third of the informants take a more traditionally "religious" view of the nature of the Church.

Individual or Collective Experience. If this tendency not to see in the Church the existence of divine reality does come through with certainty, we should also find a large proportion of informants for whom religious experience is individual and not collective. If we examine the answers to items 6, 15, 36, and 42, we do reach this conclusion.

For item 6: "I believe that my religious life would not have any meaning out of the Church," an equal proportion of the informants are placed at each of the two poles of the scale (38.1 per cent). Even at the level of their ideal religion, 36.1 per cent judge that this statement does not describe them well; however, a majority think that this statement well describes their ideal (47.5 per cent).

For item 15, 44.3 per cent agree with this statement: "I place less importance on worship organized by the Church than on the prayers I offer by myself."

Item 36 takes up again the fundamental question but in a positive form: "I place more importance on collective prayers (in the church, family, etc. . . .) than on prayers I offer by myself." Only 8.3 per cent informants think that this statement describes them well, whereas 68.0 per cent judge that it describes them poorly. Again we see a rejection of religious experience which would take a collective form. We find the same tendency in additional answers.

Interestingly, 73.2 per cent of the informants think that item 42 ("For me, religion is above all a personal dialogue between God and me") describes well their conception of religion. This proportion goes up to 87.6 per cent for the ideal image of religion.

Therefore, on the whole, the Church is an institution that is not highly valued by the informants. They tend more towards a private religious experience, oriented towards personal communication between themselves and their God. This orientation has an influence on their attitudes towards the dogmas of the Church.

The Teachings. From the point of view of this research, the teachings are rules proposed by the Church to its members. These rules deal as much with basic beliefs (e.g., God in Three Persons) as with norms prescribing certain practices or elements of Catholic worship (e.g., rules related to mass or to various sacraments). Insofar as the Church is little valued by many informants, we can presume that the beliefs proposed by the Church do not constitute an important element of their religious experience. This does not necessarily mean that the informants do not hold any religious beliefs, or that the beliefs they hold are not beliefs proposed by the Church. It may mean that the informants have a tendency to choose between the various dogmas proposed by the Church and that this choice is a function of the personal conception that each one has of religious experience. The fact that a dogma is proposed by the Church does not ensure the adherence of the students.

Item 19 deals explicitly with teachings. It is not surprising to find that only 16.4 per cent of the informants think that "in [their] religious life, the teachings are the most important thing." The modal tendency is situated at the other extremity of the continuum, since 50.4 per cent believe that this statement describes their attitude very pooly. Item 41 deals with beliefs relative to mass: "Going to mass often brings me to think about the teachings concerning the mass, the Eucharist, etc." We find here the same tendency: only 27.8 per cent of the informants think that this item describes them very well while 46.3 per cent judge the contrary.

Item 20 ("I find that a weekday mass has as much value as a Sunday mass") relates to the definition of Sunday as the Lord's Day and as the commemorative day of Christ's Resurrection. Again, 67.0 per cent of the informants agree with the statement and thus move away from the official position of the Church.

The Priest. Only one question deals directly with the conception of the priesthood, item 34: "In my own religious life, the priest is more a man like any other than a representative of Christ." The proportion of the informants who find that this statement describes them well is larger than the proportion of the informants that reject it (43.3 per cent as against 28.9 per cent). This tendency, as we see it, is logically in agreement with their conception of the Church. This does not signify that the priest is perceived or defined as a person not at all symbolizing a religious value. But the value of the priest is related to his capacity to enter into a profound human relation with the layman.

4. The Practices of Worship

We refer here especially to public worship, that is, to the practices proposed by the Church and implying collective participation.

Worship in General. The response to item 5 shows that 52.6 per cent of the informants think "that religious worship (mass, confession, etc.) is the least important aspect of religion," while only 26.7 per cent reject this statement. The modal tendency is not to attach a very great value to formal worship. As high school is a time of evolution, we measured the same attitude in terms of change. Item 35 reads: "Religious worship has for me less and less meaning." An approximately equal proportion of informants accept or reject this statement (41.2 per cent and 37.0 per cent). If we take into account these two statements, we may conclude that among those who concede relatively minor importance to worship, for at least 10 per cent (52.6 per cent less 41.2 per cent) this attitude has been established for some time.

Worship and Beliefs. For most believers, the mass is the symbol and expression of certain religious beliefs like the death and the resurrection of Christ or of the teachings about the communion of the saints. The minor importance of the mass in the view of many students may reflect their view that it is not symbolically associated to the world of religious beliefs.

The Mass: Individual Experience of Dialogue. The affective value of the mass, however, may be explained by the feeling that the mass is a privileged moment that allows one to be in touch with God. This feeling of being in the presence of God assumes a belief in God. But the fundamental point here is not so much the relation between the different expressive movements which characterize the mass (prayer, consecration, etc.) and the beliefs relative to God. It is rather the fact that the mass is the occasion of a personal contact between the individual and God.

The notion of a dialogue expresses well, in the minds of the informants, the experience we are describing here. Responding to item 14 ("For me, Sunday mass is a way to continue a dialogue with God") an approximately equal proportion of informants accept and reject the statement—about 40 per cent. But, again here, there is a very large gap between these answers and the ones relating to the ideal image of religion. While only 39.2 per cent of the informants believe that this statement describes their position very well, 67.0 per cent judge that it describes very well their religious ideal. Thus we can logically presume that a good part of the negative attitudes towards mass corresponds to an absence of a feeling of dialogue during the formal ritual.

There is a relation between this tendency to conceive the mass as a privileged moment of dialogue between God and the individual and the tendency to favour the weekday mass as much as the Sunday mass. To the extent that the mass is defined as a means of personal dialogue between God and the individual, it matters little whether it takes place on a Sunday or on a weekday. The same reasoning is valid for item 21 which deals with the choice between confession to the priest and direct confession to God.[5]

Importance of Personal Motivations. Our analysis so far has shown a widespread tendency to place more value on beliefs or practices which concern personal experience. Students tend, for example, to reject the practices which do not conform with their personal beliefs. They tend to place some value on the mass insofar as it is an occasion for dialogue with God. They tend to retain beliefs which have integrated with their personal system of beliefs and they do not accept a belief merely because it is proposed by the Church. The analysis of items 9 and 24 will permit us to test this interpretation.

Item 9 reads: "I say to myself that the more I pray, the more I have merit." Only 10.3 per cent of the informants believe that this statement describes them very well and 72.2 per cent say the contrary.

Item 24 states: "I perefer (or I would prefer) sometimes not to go to mass on Sunday rather than going without it meaning anything to me." The modal tendency goes in the same direction as the preceding item: 57.8 per cent of the informants think that this statement describes their attitude very well. Thus we may say that students seem to place importance on the intent or the individual motivation as a source of merit.[6]

We can summarize in a few propositions the tendencies relative to worship: Worship tends to be less valued in relation to the other dimensions of religious experience. But at the level of the ideal conception of religion, the informants in much greater proportions take positions at the "religious" pole, that is, they place more value on the practice of worship. Worship is one of the areas in which there is a large gap between the actual image and the ideal image: this corresponds with the tendency to value more the personal rather than collective contacts with God. Religious practices, and especially the mass, are not indispensable for a religious experience. This attitude is related to the tendency that some informants have to reject experiences the meaning and value of which they do not perceive.

5. Morality

We will analyze at first one item dealing with the general attitude towards morality. Afterwards, we will distinguish general morality from specific morals.

a. Morality as a Whole. The following item permits us to give a general judgment about morality. Concerning the statement: "I rarely think about the problems of religious morality (sexual morals, political morals, etc.)," 23.7 per cent accept the position and 50.4 per cent reject it. Thus, half of the informants are situated at the pole supporting a religious morality. We will ask now what generalizations are possible based on these findings.

The modal tendency is to conceive of religion as related to a system of moral norms or values. The fact of defining it as religious should normally have some repercussions for human relations and behaviour (studies, work, relations with family and friends, etc.). On the whole, students accept the general principle of such a relation between religion and morality, as proposed by the Church. But they seem to accept to a lesser degree specific moral norms put forward by the Church.

b. General Morality or Specific Morals? Four items deal with general morality, that is, essentially, with the idea that religious beliefs serve or must serve as the basis of a system of values encompassing all human experience. From this perspective religious values establish the criteria of good and bad for all the main areas of life.

This general statement deals with this idea: "Religion must influence my whole existence." The theme reappears in items 2, 32, 38, and 44.

Item	Statement	Self-Image Religion	Image of Ideal Religion
2	My religious ideal really influences my everday life.	24.8%	70.1%
32	What I do in my family, in my work (or my studies), etc. is done for God.	19.6%	61.9%
38	The fact of going to mass does not change the different areas of my life very much.	14.5%	60.5%
44	The things to which I attach the most value in my life are not related to my religious ideal.	35.1%	56.4%

At the level of self-image a low proportion of informants are situated at the pole of the integration of moral values: 24.8 per cent for item 2, 19.6 per cent for item 32, 14.5 per cent for item 38, and 35.1 per cent for item 44. Overall, few informants believe that their religious experience "really influences [their] everyday life."

However, in expressing their ideals, the young people are generally situated at the pole of the integration of moral and religious values: 70.1 per cent for item 2, 61.9 per cent for item 32, 60.5 per cent for item 38, and 56.4 per cent for item 44. The modal tendency is to consider religious values as being related in one way or another to the whole range of activities. A religious belief or a practice in worship has value in their eyes on the condition that their everyday life prolongs or actualizes it. This modal tendency implies that religion provides a moral direction in life: it does not necessarily imply adherence to a series of specific moral norms.

This finding indicates that students feel that there should not be a barrier between religion and other aspects of psychological behaviour. The concrete manifestation of morality remains necessarily the responsibility of each person. Before interpreting these results more generally, we will look at answers to items dealing with specific moral rules.

Specific Morals. Some religious norms specify certain practices of worship or prescribe proper behaviour in a wide variety of situations in everyday life. The most striking example—and one which the informants would talk about willingly—is sexual morals.

In most interviews, informants recalled that in the name of religion, various agents of religious socialization (clergy and family, for the most part) proposed (and often imposed) very strict sexual morals. Item 3 ("I have some difficulty in not equating sexuality with sin") bears directly on this state of mind. Altough only 26.8 per cent thought that this statement described their position very well, most would agree that this attitude was proposed to them and that they held it at one time or another. A large number have the feeling of being freed from religious sanctions regarding sexual behaviour and some believe that the norms of the Church are changing in this matter.

Another area is work and studies. This area is the one judged most often to be related with religion. Indeed, 72.2 per cent accept the following statement: "For me, to be honest and competent in my work (or my studies) is a way to respect catholic morals" (item 27).

c. Modal Tendencies

Rejection of Institutionalized Morals. The rejection of specific norms, as in the case of norms related to sexuality, probably constitutes a rejection of what appears in the eyes of informants to be excessive institutionalization of religious experience. They accept the general framework proposed by the Church for religion and morals but they deny that the Church can define solely how general principles must be applied.

Morals and Authentication. The acceptance of the general morality related to religious experience also appears as a form of authentication. Religious experience would not have a profound meaning if it were isolated from general human experiences. Taking into account religious values in everyday experiences satisfies a need for coherence and authenticity. The morality of a person becomes the most concrete sign of his religiosity. Responsible behaviour indicates that adherence to belief is not superficial and is authentic.

Relation between Religion and Morals. It is possible, on one hand, to conceive of religion and morals as being related to each other but differentiated in tension, and on the other hand, it is possible to conceive of this relation in terms of identity and integration. For most of the students in our sample, it does not seem that either mode has priority. This is what emerges from answers to item 12: "I think that if I relaxed my

Catholic morals, I would come to abandon all my religious life." While 44.3 per cent of the students think that this statement describes them very well and they do not differentiate sharply between morals and religion, almost as large a proportion (34.1 per cent) think that this statement does not describe them very well.

There is no support, however, for an inference that the majority of the students, in establishing a relation between religion and morals, necessarily reject the existence of other foundations for a system of morals. No item dealt with the existence of morals which would not have religion as their foundation. Nevertheless, the analysis of the answers shows that a large number of informants accept the notion of human or natural morals. This is not necessarily a contradiction or an inconsistency. On the one hand, the students can recognize the existence of a multiple foundation for morals. On the other hand, they consider that religion must express itself in moral concern without going so far as to assert that all morals must have a religious base.

Notes

1. Robert Sévigny, *L'expérience religieuse et l'actualisation de soi*, doctoral dissertation, Université Laval.

2. In Quebec, the classical college was a private college. The class "Philosophy 1" was equivalent to third year college [or secondary school].

3. The questionnaire was distributed in 1964.

4. This item was meant to measure the rational attitude towards religion, but it is most probable that those who agreed with this phrase generally expressed their tendency to consider religion as a serious matter.

5. For Item 21, 56.4 per cent declare that they would prefer to confess directly to God rather than to a priest. The answers to this item can be explained by many aspects of the confession experience, for example, the relation with a priest who would not symbolize God, the recognition of our sins, etc. But it is plausible that the answers were also indluenced by an orientation towards individual religious experience.

6. The lack of congruence between response to items 9 and 24 reveals a certain confusion, reflecting the ambiguity of what is proposed by the Church. The content of these two items also expresses this ambiguity.

Appendix
Answers to the Questionnaire of the Q-Sort Type Dealing with the Conception of Students' Religion and of the Ideal Religion (N=97)[d]

Item	Statement	Describes *my* religion		Describes my ideal religion	
		very little 1st third %	very well 3rd third %	very little 1st third %	very well 3rd third %
1.	I do not have a religious feeling.	49.5	26.8	59.8	19.6
2.	My religious ideal really influences my everyday life.	39.9	24.8	14.5	70.1
3.	I have difficulty in not equating sexuality with sin.	50.6	26.8	14.9	18.6
4.	God appears to me as an understanding person with whom one can get in touch.	13.4	77.0	10.3	80.5
5.	I consider that religious worship (mass, confession, etc.) is the least important aspect of religion.	26.7	52.6	38.1	30.9
6.	I believe that my religious life would not have any meaning out of the church.	38.1	38.1	36.1	47.5
7.	In my belief in God, I distinguish what comes from my individual reflections and what comes from my faith.	11.3	61.9	6.2	75.3
9.	I say to myself that the more I pray the more I have merit.	72.2	10.3	60.7	22.7

Item	Statement	Describes *my* religion		Describes my ideal religion	
		very little 1st third %	very well 3rd third %	very little 1st third %	very well 3rd third %
10.	The religious question has an important place in my whole life.	19.9	47.5	7.2	75.3
11.	For me, one of the best ways to live one's religion is to be a member of associations or social movements.	54.6	28.9	40.2	36.0
12.	I think that if I relaxed my Catholic morals, I would come to abandon all my religious life.	34.1	44.3	36.2	48.5
13.	I have the impression of not knowing much about Christ.	26.8	46.3	53.6	25.8
14.	For me, Sunday mass is a way to continue a dialogue with God.	41.2	39.2	18.6	67.0
15.	I place less importance on worship organized by the church than on the prayers I do by myself.	22.6	44.3	25.8	44.3
16.	I try to arrive at intellectual certainty in relation to the problem of eternity of the soul.	20.6	58.8	9.3	76.3

19. The teachings are the most important thing in my religious life.	50.4	16.4	48.4	25.8
20. I find that a weekday mass has as much value as a Sunday mass.	18.6	67.0	11.3	68.1
21. I would prefer (or I prefer) to confess myself directly to God rather than to a priest.	28.8	56.4	22.7	54.7
22. In my religious life, I try as much as possible to reason out my thinking.	6.2	76.3	7.2	79.4
24. I prefer (or I would prefer) sometimes not to go to mass on Sunday rather than going without it meaning anything to me.	30.0	57.8	26.8	69.3
25. I am less religious than before.	35.0	45.4	69.0	16.5
26. I feel that my religious ideal enables me or could enable me to participate in politics.	65.9	15.5	54.7	23.6
27. For me to be honest and competent in my work (or my studies) is a way to respect Catholic morals.	12.4	72.2	11.4	73.3
28. I ask myself logically and historically if the belief in Christ has a meaning or not.	35.0	47.4	30.0	40.1

Item Statement	Describes *my* religion		Describes my ideal religion	
	very little 1st third %	very well 3rd third %	very little 1st third %	very well 3rd third %
31. I like to discuss religion.	11.3	55.7	7.2	74.2
32. What I do in my family, in my work (or my studies), etc. is done for God.	42.2	19.6	22.7	61.9
33. I think that fundamentally, political honesty has nothing to do with religion.	47.4	36.0	56.7	23.8
34. In my own religious life, the priest is more a man like any other than a representative of Christ.	28.9	43.3	37.0	41.3
35. Religious worship has for me less and less meaning.	37.0	41.2	57.7	26.8
36. I place more importance on collective prayers (in the church, family, etc.) than on prayer I can do by myself.	68.0	8.3	48.4	15.5
37. I have not yet really understood what religion is.	40.1	35.1	19.5	56.4
38. The fact of going to mass does not change the different areas of my life very much.	14.5	55.7	60.5	29.9

39. I rarely think about the problems of religious morality (sexual morals, political morals, etc.)	50.4	23.7	62.9	20.7
40. I often think of the salvation of my soul.	14.4	57.7	14.4	70.2
41. Going to mass often brings me to think about the teachings concerning the mass, the Eucharist, etc.	46.3	27.8	36.1	47.5
42. For me, my religion is above all a personal dialogue between God and me.	5.2	73.2	4.1	87.6
43. I think that the Church is more a human institution than a religious institution.	30.9	40.2	41.3	32.0
44. The things to which I attach the most value in my life are not related to my religious ideal.	35.1	42.2	56.4	31.9

37

Religiosity in Canada: A National Survey*

Reginald W. Bibby

Although religion has had an important place in North American culture since the settling of the New World, little empirical data exists pertaining to religious commitment. The approach of most social scientists has been theoretical, historical, and impressionistic and empirical research on personal commitment has been limited in scope. For example, with respect to church attendance in Canada, Mol (1976: 241) has commented that "church attendance figures either are confined to specific localities or regions or are restricted to one denomination. If they are national, they do not provide for crucial cross-tabulations."

Not until the mid-1960s was a comprehensive empirical study of religious commitment undertaken in the United States (Stark and Glock 1968). Further, enquiry into new forms of religious consciousness among Americans has been attempted only in recent years (Glock and Bellah 1976).

This paper presents some of the findings of the first comprehensive national survey of religious belief and behaviour to be conducted in Canada. It examines commitment not only to the dominant Judaic-Christian tradition but to other belief systems as well.

Between May and November of 1975 the author conducted a national mail survey entitled "Project Canada" from York University in Toronto. Some 2,000 randomly selected Canadians in 30 size-stratified communities filled out the 11-page, 303-item questionnaire, representing a return rate of 52 per cent.[1]

In addition to social problems and intergroup relations, the study gave considerable attention to religion. A large number of items were drawn from Glock and Stark's 1963 examination of religion in the United States, along with Glock's more recent work on religious consciousness. Because of the large number of social background variables included, the data permit detailed analyses in three directions: (a) the *nature* of religiosity in Canada, (b) the social and psychological *sources* of religiosity, and (c) the correlates or *consequences* of being religious (e.g., the relationship between religiosity and compassion, prejudice, mental health, economics, politics, family life, sex roles, values).[2]

This paper will examine commitment to Judaic-Christian beliefs and practices and also explore religiosity more generally.

---

*An original paper prepared for this volume.

Methodology

Following Stark and Glock (1968), it appears that Judaic-Christian commitment has four major dimensions. Those committed to such a tradition are expected to (a) adhere to a number of theological precepts ("belief"), (b) engage in public and private religious activities ("practice"), (c) be familiar with the main idea of the faith ("knowledge"), and (d) encounter the supernatural ("experience"). This paper utilizes items pertaining to all four of these dimensions. The specific items which will be used are as follows:

Belief

God "Which of the following statements comes closest to expressing what you believe about God?"
1. I know God exists, and I have no doubts about it.
2. While I have doubts, I feel that I do believe in God.
3. I find myself believing in God some of the time, but not at other times.
4. I don't believe in a personal God, but I do believe in a higher power of some kind.
5. I don't know whether there is a God, and I don't believe there is any way to find out.
6. I don't believe in God.
7. Other.

Jesus "Which of the following statements comes closest to expressing what you believe about Jesus?"
1. Jesus is the Divine Son of God and I have no doubts about it.
2. While I have some doubts, I basically feel that Jesus is Divine.
3. I feel that Jesus was a great man and very holy, but I don't feel Him to be the Son of God.
4. I think Jesus was only a man, although an extraordinary one.
5. Frankly, I'm not entirely sure there really was such a person as Jesus.
6. Other.

Death "Do you believe there is a life after death?
1. Yes 2. No 3. Uncertain

Practice

Church Attendance "Thinking specifically of religious services, how often do you attend them?"
1. Never
2. Less than once a year
3. About once a year
4. Several times a year
5. About once a month.
6. Two or three times a month
7. Nearly every week
8. Every week
9. Several times a week

Prayer "How often do you pray privately?"
1. I never pray, or only in religious services
2. Only on special occasions
3. Sometimes but not regularly
4. Regularly once a week
5. Regularly many times a week
6. Regularly once a day or more.

Bible Reading "How often do you read the Bible privately?"
1. Never or rarely
2. Only on special occasions
3. Sometimes but not regularly
4. Regularly once a week
5. Regularly many times a week
6. Regularly once a day or more.

Experience

God "Have you ever had . . . a feeling that you were somehow in the presence of God?"
1. Yes, I'm sure I have 2. Yes, I think I have 3. No

Devil "Have you ever had . . . a feeling that you were somehow in the presence of the Devil?"
1. Yes, I'm sure I have 2. Yes, I think I have 3. No

Knowledge

Peter's Denial "Do you happen to know which of Christ's disciples denied him three times?"
1. Thomas
2. Paul
3. Judas
4. Peter
5. John
6. Jacob
7. No, I don't know

Biblical Prophets "Can you pick out the Old Testament prophets from the following?"
Deuteronomy, Jeremiah, Leviticus, Ezekiel
1. Is 2. Is Not 3. Don't Know

In assessing religiosity beyond the Judaic-Christian tradition, the extent to which Canadians reflect upon the so-called "ultimate questions" will also be examined, along with other possible systems of meaning which people use to interpret life. The following items are used:

Ultimate Questions

"To what extent would you say you think about the following questions?"
a. What is the purpose of life?
b. How did the world come into being?
c. Why is there suffering in the world?
d. What happens after death?

1. Often 2. Sometimes 3. No Longer 4. Never Have

Other Orientations[3]

Transcendental Meditation "How interested or opposed are you with respect to transcendental meditation?"
1. Strongly Interested
2. Mildly Interested
3. Not Very Interested
4. Strongly Opposed
5. Never Heard of the Group

Yoga "How interested or opposed are you with respect to yoga?"
1. Strongly Interested
2. Mildly Interested
3. Not Very Interested
4. Strongly Opposed
5. Never Heard of the Group

Astrology "People who believe in astrology claim that the stars, the planets, and our birthdays have a lot to do with our destiny in life. What do you think about this?"

1. A Firm Believer
2. Perhaps Possible
3. Very Doubtful
4. Firm Disbeliever

Certainty "How sure are you that you have found the answer to the meaning of life?"

1. Very Certain
2. Quite Certain
3. Rather Uncertain
4. I don't think there is an answer to such a question

Personal Religiosity "Would you say that you have tended to regard yourself as:"

1. Very Religious
2. Somewhat Religious
3. Not Very Religious

Finally, religious commitment is examined according to seven independent variables: region, community size, age, sex, education, income and religious affiliation.

Findings

The totals column of Table 1 summarizes the national responses on each of the religiosity items. Slightly less than 50 per cent of Canadians assert "unwavering" belief in God, the Divinity of Jesus, and life after death. While less than one in ten read the Bible privately once a week or oftener, one in three attend religious services on a weekly basis and close to the same number claim to engage in daily private prayer. Almost one-quarter are sure that they have experienced the reality of God (another 24 per cent think they may have); but only 3 per cent say the same for the Devil. One in two can identify Peter as having denied Jesus, while less than one in five can differentiate certain Old Testament prophets from books.

With respect to religious consciousness beyond the Judaic-Christian tradition, one in three appear to be concerned about the "ultimate questions" of meaning and purpose, suffering and death. Some 20 per cent say they are interested in transcendental meditation—almost 30 per cent indicate interest in yoga. One-half maintain that the claims of astrology are plausible. Over one-half are certain either that they have found the answer to life's meaning or that there is no answer to be found. Only 17 per cent see themselves as "Very Religious"; however, another 47 per cent view themselves as "Somewhat Religious".

These data indicate that the late twentieth century Canadians are highly religious people. Approximately one-half or more of the people in this country (1) have *no doubts* about the existence of a Supernatural Being,[4] (2) believe He has made Himself known in a person, (3) feel they have experienced such a Supernatural reality, (4) take time to converse with Him,[5] and (5) say they regard themselves as religious. Further, one in three of Canadians meet each week to worship the Deity; less than one in five (17 per cent) *never* do so. The alleged impact of secularization notwithstanding, Canadians in the last quarter of this century still have ideas and practices which suggest continued respect for "something beyond themselves".

Such data should caution observers (a) to be skeptical of "experts" on secularization who often generalize from their own biographies to the whole scene and (b) to avoid equating the decline of organized religion with the demise of religious commitment generally. The day that Canadians "see the Heavens as empty" has not yet come.

Further, while of considerable importance, alternative meaning systems need to

Table 1
Religiosity by Region (In Percentages)

Religiosity Indicators		Region					
		B.C. (122)	Prairies (197)	Ontario (430)	Quebec (336)	Atlantic (110)	TOTALS (1195)
Belief	God ("No doubts")	38	44	38	62	58	47
	Jesus ("No doubts")	35	50	39	50	64	44
	Immortality ("Yes")	42	52	41	52	63	47
Practice	Attendance (Weekly)[a]	18	28	27	35	52	31
	Prayer (Regularly)[b]	13	25	23	32	43	26
	Bible (Regularly)[c]	7	11	8	5	8	7
Experience	God ("I'm sure")	23	27	19	19	34	21
	The Devil ("I'm sure")	2	5	3	3	5	3
Knowledge	Peter (Correct)	43	51	47	59	61	50
	Prophets (All Correct)	11	12	13	27	17	17
Ultimate Questions	"Often" Raise Two or More	23	27	31	40	29	32
Other Systems	TM (Interested)	28	20	18	25	13	20
	Yoga (Interested)	37	29	23	34	23	26
	Astrology (Receptive)[d]	54	46	52	46	45	49
Certainty	Non-ambivalent[e]	56	56	54	53	56	54
Self-Rating	"Very Religious"	9	11	10	31	22	17

[a] "Nearly every week" or more

[b] "Regularly once a day or more"

[c] "Regularly once a week" or more

[d] "A firm believer" or "Perhaps possible"

[e] "Very certain" or "I don't think there is an answer to such a question"

be kept in numerical perspective relative to the dominant Judaic-Christian tradition. The findings show that TM, yoga, and astrology are being noticed by a sizable number of Canadians. However, their significance as *unique* meaning systems appears to be slight. No more than 5 per cent of the people have indicated a "strong" interest in either TM or yoga, while only 5 per cent they are "firm believers" in astrology. Moreover, it remains to be seen to what extent such systems have a substitutionary versus complementary function relative to traditional religion. We will return to this question shortly.

Table 2
Religiosity by Community Size* (In Percentages)

Religiosity Indicators		Community Size		
		Large Cities (661)	Small Cities (221)	Small Towns (314)
Belief	God	41	48	62
	Jesus	36	53	61
	Immortality	42	45	62
Practice	Attendance	26	33	39
	Prayer	21	34	34
	Bible	7	8	7
Experience	God	20	21	28
	Devil	4	1	4
Knowledge	Peter	53	52	49
	Prophets	18	14	16
Ultimate Questions	"Often" Raise Two or More	28	35	38
Other Systems	TM	23	24	15
	Yoga	31	25	24
	Astrology	52	43	47
Certainty	Non-ambivalent	59	53	46
Self-Rating	"Very Religious"	14	17	24

*"Large Cities" = 100,000 metropolitan area or larger; "Small Cities" = 15,000 – 99,000, "Small Towns" = under 15,000, including rural areas.

Region

As Table 1 indicates, Judaic-Christian commitment is highest in the Atlantic provinces, followed by Quebec and then the Prairies. People from Ontario and British Columbia consistently rank lower than the rest of Canada on all four dimensions of religious commitment.

British Columbians show the greatest interest in TM, yoga, and astrology, but the "system alternative" thesis is confounded by the finding that interest in TM and yoga is also relatively high in Quebec. While the inclination to raise "ultimate questions" is highest in Quebec, there is little difference between regions with respect to the feeling that the issue of life's meaning has been resolved. Overall, people from Quebec and the Atlantic provinces are considerably more likely than others to see themselves as "very religious".

Community Size

Canadians from smaller communities are consistently more inclined to score higher on all dimensions of religious commitment with the exception of *knowledge*, where the relationship is slightly negative (Table 2). While large city and small city residents show a greater interest in transcendental meditation, yoga, and astrology, the relationship is neither strong nor consistent: interest in astrology, for example, seems relatively high in the small towns. People from the smaller communities are somewhat more likely to raise ultimate questions and to regard themselves as "very religious", but they are not as unequivocal as others concerning understanding life's meaning.

Age

A fairly consistent direct relationship exists between age and Judaic-Christian commitment, but there is no relationship between age and belief in immortality, the Devil, and in knowledge (Table 3). At the same time, people under 30 appear to be highly concerned about ultimate questions. The 30 to 39 cohort seemingly has become at least temporarily preoccupied with other things, the 40 to 59 cohort has begun to

Table 3.
Religiosity by Age (In Percentages)

Religiosity Indicators		Age Cohort 18-29 (311)	30-39 (213)	40-49 (221)	50-59 (196)	60+ (219)
Belief	God	37	40	52	46	63
	Jesus	36	41	46	46	61
	Immortality	45	42	54	48	46
Practice	Attendance	14	27	35	37	47
	Prayer	14	19	19	36	47
	Bible	2	6	3	12	14
Experience	God	14	17	20	26	38
	Devil	4	5	1	4	1
Knowledge	Peter	51	51	48	51	59
	Prophets	15	23	18	13	17
Ultimate Questions	"Often" Raise Two or More	38	24	32	36	31
Other Systems	TM	33	23	17	16	12
	Yoga	45	33	20	24	13
	Astrology	63	53	39	44	38
Certainty	Non-ambivalent	51	52	53	59	62
Self-Rating	"Very Religious"	7	17	15	20	31

re-raise such questions, and those over 60 are more inclined to feel that they have resolved them (see "Certainty" responses). Interest in TM, yoga, and astrology is highest among those under 30 and generally wanes progressively with age. The overall perception of oneself as strongly religious increases sharply with age.

The non-traditional meaning systems do seem to be of some interest to young Canadians, and again it is tempting to apply the "system alternative" thesis. However, the data suggest that such an application may be premature. For example, the percentage of those under 30 who said they are "strongly interested" was 7 per cent and 9 per cent for TM and yoga respectively, while only 2 per cent said they are "firm believers" in astrology. By comparison, almost 40 per cent of those under 30 asserted unequivocal belief in both God and the divinity of Jesus, and 14 per cent said they attend religious services every week. Given "syncretistic" overlap, the case for new forms supplanting the old faith is not yet a convincing one. Nevertheless, the interest of young people in "eastern religion" is an interesting aspect of religious behaviour.

Sex

Canadian women tend to be more religious than men (Table 4). A larger proportion of women are more strongly committed to the general Judaic-Christian tradition, raise

Table 4.
Religiosity by Sex (In Percentages)

Religiosity Indicators		Sex	
		Male (598)	Female (597)
Belief	God	45	50
	Jesus	43	49
	Immortaility	45	51
Practice	Attendance	32	30
	Prayer	23	30
	Bible	7	8
Experience	God	16	28
	Devil	4	3
Knowledge	Peter	47	57
	Prophets	15	19
Ultimate Questions	"Often" Raise Two or More	29	35
Other Systems	TM	19	23
	Yoga	22	35
	Astrology	41	57
Certainty	Non-ambivalent	53	56
Self-Rating	"Very Religious"	15	19

ultimate questions, take an interest in transcendental meditation, yoga, and astrology, and further see themselves as "very religious." Men, however, are just as likely to a attend religious services weekly and to feel that they have resolved the question of life's meaning.

The North American differences by sex have traditionally been seen by social scientists as a result of social deprivation brought about by social inequality. Consequently, it logically holds that one correlate of sexual equality in our society will be the dissipation of differences in religiosity between men and women. This already appears to have been realized with church attendance, a development which may have vital consequences for Judaic-Christian differences in the relatively near future. What isn't so clear is why women—notably younger women—show a greater interest than men in "the newer" meaning systems—TM, yoga and astrology.

Table 5
Religiosity by Education (In Percentages)

Religiosity Indicators		Educational Level		
		High School or Less (707)	Some Post-Secondary (258)	A Degree* or More (190)
Belief	God	53	47	29
	Jesus	52	43	27
	Immortaility	49	49	43
Practice	Attendance	31	33	28
	Prayer	29	27	16
	Bible	8	6	6
Experience	God	25	23	11
	Devil	3	5	1
Knowledge	Peter	45	66	59
	Prophets	12	25	26
Ultimate Questions	"Often" Raise Two or More	35	32	24
Other Systems	TM	16	23	37
	Yoga	22	34	44
	Astrology	51	51	39
Certainty	Non-ambivalent	58	54	44
Self-Rating	"Very Religious"	20	15	12

*Considerable difficulty has been experienced both in assessing the precise educational level of respondents and comparing the sample to the Canadian population. It is the author's assertion that the sample is slightly overrepresented with the higher educated, yet our findings with respect to other social background variables have not led to the conclusion that the difference is either so clear or large as to warrant a weighting correction.

Education

As Table 5 shows, for the population as a whole higher education is associated with lower levels in the *belief*, private *practice* (prayer), and *experiential* dimensions of religious commitment. However, higher education is not related to lower attendance and it is conducive to religious knowledge. Close to an equal proportion of people with different levels of education appear to be active in religious institutions. Their much-publicized absence would seem largely to reflect the failure of observers to think in terms of proportional representation rather than absolute numerical representation (university graduates currently make up only about 6 per cent of the Canadian population).[6]

Thus those with more formal education are proportionately represented in religious groups, yet seemingly are characterized by both a "tentative," non-dogmatic posture toward belief-experience and a theologically-reshaped faith. Such a stance is further reflected in the responses of the "better-educated" to questions pertaining to certainty of life's meaning and self-perceived religiosity.

People with higher levels of education do not indicate as much concern with ultimate questions, perhaps reflecting a tendency to focus rather upon the world as it is. They do show a greater interest than others in TM and yoga, but—in the case of university graduates—less interest in astrology.

Income

As would be expected in view of the previous findings pertaining to religiosity, age, and education, commitment to the Judaic-Christian tradition generally declines with an increase in family income (Table 6). However, this inverse relationship is halted and slightly reversed in the case of people making over $20,000.

Given the pervasiveness of this pattern along all four dimensions of religious commitment, such a finding may reflect (1) an older age structure among upper income people and (2) the proclivity of this social stratum toward organizational involvement generally.

While those with the highest incomes do not claim to be as concerned with ultimate questions—again, in part a function of age—no clear pattern is evident regarding interest in TM, yoga, and astrology, although the highest income stratum shows the least interest in astrology. In general, people at the lower income levels are inclined to see themselves as "very religious" while individuals with a family income over $10,000 are somewhat more likely to feel they have resolved the question of life's meaning.

Religious Affiliation

Table 7 summarizes the religiosity measures by religious affiliation. Catholics consistently score higher than Protestants on all dimensions except *experience* (and Bible-reading within the practice dimension), while Jews[7] and those claiming no religious affiliation follow far behind. Catholics along with Jews are more likely than Protestants and "Nones" to raise ultimate questions, yet Jews are far more inclined to be unequivocal about having dealt with the issue of life's meaning. The "nones" show the most interest in the new religious forms, yet a substantial percentage of Protestants, Catholics, and Jews also indicate interest. Catholics are the most likely to regard themselves as "very religious."

Table 6

Religiosity by Income (In Percentages)

Religiosity Indicators		Income Level				
		$5,000 (176)	$5,000-9,999 (326)	$10,000-14,999 (239)	$15,000-19,999 (201)	$20,000+ (184)
Belief	God	63	53	40	37	40
	Jesus	64	50	38	33	40
	Immortality	63	51	40	39	45
Practice	Attendance	44	28	25	26	32
	Prayer	52	27	18	16	22
	Bible	15	6	7	4	5
Experience	God	48	19	16	15	18
	Devil	8	3	3	2	1
Knowledge	Peter	57	54	46	51	51
	Prophets	13	21	13	16	24
Ultimate Questions	"Often" Raise Two or More	34	34	36	36	21
Other Systems	TM	16	19	26	18	25
	Yoga	25	31	30	26	31
	Astrology	49	56	51	46	33
Certainty	Non-ambivalent	51	48	57	62	54
Self-Rating	"Very Religious"	38	18	13	8	10

Within Protestant ranks the Baptists and other Evangelicals[8] score the highest on all Judaic-Christian religiosity measures. These two groupings are also the least ambivalent about life's meaning and are the most inclined to see themselves as strongly religious. On other items, similar proportions of people within each denomination raise ultimate questions and, with the exception of Evangelicals, show an interest in transcendental meditation, yoga and astrology. On the surface, at least, no one denomination seems to be particularly susceptible to these non-traditional meaning systems.

Such findings suggest that considerable variation in commitment exists both between and within the major religious groups in Canada. These data would seem to have important implications for commonality, again on both inter-group and intra-group levels. For example, with respect to ideas and practice, people with United Church and Anglican affiliations appear to have a great deal in common, in contrast to Presbyterians and Baptists. However, at the same time—once more on an ideational and practice level—clearly some Presbyterians would have more in common with some Baptists and some Catholics than with many people within their own Presbyterian

Table 7

Religiosity by Religious Affiliation*

(In Percentages)

Religiosity Indicators		Presby-terian (62)	United Church (443)	Lutheran (69)	Anglican (280)	Baptist (90)	Evangel-ical (75)	Prot. (534)	Cath. (486)	Jew** (23)	None (96)
		Religious Affiliation									
BELIEF Belief	God	30	36	37	39	60	79	41	66	31	2
	Jesus	27	39	38	41	67	84	44	59	—	5
	Immortality	30	42	44	49	75	88	47	56	12	19
Practice	Attendance	20	25	24	20	42	62	26	45	10	0
	Prayer	21	22	23	19	40	54	27	33	1	1
	Bible	2	7	9	9	32	48	11	5	1	0
EXPERIENC Experience	God	18	19	22	16	41	63	24	23	11	4
	Devil	1	1	1	5	9	17	3	3	0	5
KNOWLEDG Knowledge	Peter	46	47	55	49	66	77	50	62	—	29
	Prophets	13	14	15	11	38	34	14	20	40	11
Ultimate Questions	"Often" Raise "Two or More	26	22	26	23	26	20	26	39	48	31
Other Systems	TM	17	22	17	21	23	11	17	20	4	43
	Yoga	27	30	26	24	28	22	27	25	16	50
	Astrology	52	50	49	51	47	26	51	44	52	62
Certainty	"Non-ambivalent	56	59	53	47	65	64	56	52	83	54
Self-Rating	"Very Religious"	2	5	12	10	24	25	11	28	1	3

*These denominational percentages are based upon the original number of respondents (1917), weighted only for sex, in order that the maximum number of denominational "representatives" could be utilized.

**This category has been included for heuristic value, even though the size of the sample of Jews clearly results in unstable per-

ranks. Following Glock and Stark (1965), this stratification of commitment *within denominations* may represent an important new form of religious differentiation, replacing that which formerly was found primarily *between* religious groups.

Conclusion

These data indicate that as Canada moves into the last part of the twentieth century, its people demonstrate a high level of religious interest, belief, and activity. As yet we are not a nation which, in Freud's (1961: 82) words, has discarded religion in favour of reason, leaving "Heaven to the angels and the sparrows".

At the same time, there is good reason to believe that religious commitment and interest may be in the process of gradual dissipation. While the present findings indicate a pervasive commitment to some aspects of the Judaic-Christian tradition, they also show that institutional involvement is declining. An examination of the paths to involvement in organized religion leads to the conclusion that a declining trend is unlikely to reverse itself in the forseeable future (Bibby 1976a). From a sociological point of view, ideas and practices of any kind require social sustenance—they are socially instilled and maintained. Without future socialization by religious institutions, it is highly doubtful that a majority of Canadians will continue for long to be religious within the Judaic-Christian tradition.

One might object that group participation is not necessary for religion to be influential and that religious groups may exert influence through the media. Apart from the questions of whether the media can have an influence comparable to group membership and participation and the source of funds for such media efforts, the viability of religious socialization through media is highly suspect. The people who give attention to religious programming are precisely the people most highly involved in religious groups. Further, the suggestion that informal groupings and institutions such as the school and the family will take over religious functions suffers from a basic flaw: it minimizes the importance of organized religion in providing the chief impetus for religious thought and behaviour within schools and families.

In short, without the sustaining influence of organized religion, commitment to the Judaic-Christian tradition is destined to diminish.

Some will argue that new systems of meaning will arise, reflecting the prophecy of Durkheim (1964: 475-476) as he surveyed the religious scene in Europe almost a century ago:

> . . . the old gods are growing old or already dead, and others are not yet born. . . . There are no gospels which are immortal, but neither is there any reason for believing that humanity is incapable of inventing new ones.

This may be the case. Yet despite the publicity they have received, meaning forms such as transcendental meditation, yoga, and astrology appear to be taken seriously by a very small minority. Further, as Table 8 shows, many churchgoers are also involved in new forms of belief and practice.

Durkheim commented that he did not know what new forms religion might take. My somewhat narrower concept of religion as a "meaning system," along with the data at my disposal, tempt me to be somewhat more bold. It is apparent that people in Canada are currently continuing to raise ultimate questions; only around 10 per cent say they never have reflected upon such subjects. However, while Canadians raise these questions, substantial numbers seem to be content with their unanswerability.

Table 8

General Religiosity by Church Attendance (In Percentages)

Religiosity Indicators		Attendance Level				
		Never (205)	Yearly (243)	Sev. Times Per Year (251)	Monthly (118)	Weekly (362)
Ultimate Questions	"Often" Raise Two or More	31	30	37	30	31
Other	TM	31	25	18	22	15
	Yoga	37	34	27	22	23
	Astrology	51	57	57	51	37
Certainty	Non-ambivalent	68	54	51	51	52
Self-Rating	"Very Religious"	5	3	6	10	44

Specifically, while they ask, "What is the purpose of life?" close to one-half (43 per cent) say, "I don't think there is an answer to such a question." Although they raise the question, "Why is there suffering in the world?" 87 per cent agree that "Suffering is simply a fact of life, experienced by virtually all of us in the course of a lifetime." And while they ask, "What happens after death?" two in ten conclude nothing happens while another three in ten are uncertain that there is any continuation of life. While some people (17 per cent) express fear concerning death, a full 40 per cent have either "no particular feeling" (22 per cent) or a feeling of "sorrow" (18 per cent), the latter seemingly reflecting regret over the passing of one's life.

In the light of such findings, it seems that Canadians will continue to raise questions of meaning. However, given the dominance of science with its focus upon the empirical world, Canadians will increasingly be content with the proposition that such questions—while interesting and worthy of reflection—cannot be answered. Thus empiricism—whereby reality is limited to the perceivable—and the correlate of materialism—whereby the empirical world becomes the object of one's commitment—may form the dominant system of meaning. "Deviant" meaning systems will continue to exist, but will have salience only for relatively small numbers of people.

The key to variation from this prospect would seem to lie in old or new forms of organized religion being able to embrace the population generally and thus inculcate a rival system of meaning. As Canada concludes the twentieth century, the likelihood of this happening does not seem high.

Notes

1. In order to compensate for differences between the sample and total population with regard to province, community size, and sex, the sample has been weighted and compressed into 1,200 cases. The result is a sample highly representative of the Canadian population, with the percentages on almost all items accurate within about 5 per cent of the population figures 95 per cent of the time. Obviously percentages computed for categories within the population are subject to a higher level of error.

2. For related papers pertaining to these areas, see Reginald W. Bibby, "The Decline of Institutional Religion in Canada," presented at the annual meeting of the Canadian Sociology and Anthropology Association, Quebec City, May, 1976, and "Sources and Correlates of Religious Involvement," presented at the annual meeting of the Society for the Scientific Study of Religion, Philadelphia, October, 1976.

3. Respondents were asked to indicate their level of interest in Children of God, Krishna, Zen, Yoga, Satanism, Hassid, Guru, Transcendental Meditation, and Astrology. The greatest interest was shown in three: TM, yoga, and astrology; hence their use here.

4. Only 2 per cent say, "I don't believe in God."

5. Some 37 per cent claim to pray regularly weekly or more; another 33 per cent say they pray "sometimes but not regularly." Only 18 per cent maintain they "never pray, or only in religious services."

6. An exception to this pattern are French-speaking Roman Catholics with low education who score high on traditional measures of religiosity, which affects the gross national figures. Yet as Mol (1976) showed, people with high education among Protestants in particular attend church more often than those with low education. – *Editors.*

7. As noted, the small number of Jews obviously makes percentages and generalizations very unreliable. Nonetheless, Jews are included for the purpose of information and the encouragement of thought and further research.

8. While there are people in all religious groupings who see themselves as "evangelicals," this term is used here to refer to hose who list the following as their denominational affiliations: Brethren, Christian, Christian and Missionary Alliance, Christian Reformed, Church of Christ, Church of God, Evangelical, Full Gospel, Mennonite, Nazarene, Non-denominational, Pentecostal, Quaker, and Salvation Army.

References

Bibby, Reginald W.
1976a "The Decline of Institutional Religion in Canada." Presented at the annual meeting of *The Canadian Sociology and Anthropology Association*, Quebec City, May.

1976b "Sources and Correlates of Religious Involvement." Presented at the annual meeting of *The Society for the Scientific Study of Religion*, Philadelphia, October.

Durkheim, Emile
1964 *The Elementary Forms of Religious Life.* Glencoe, Illinois: Free Press.

Freud, Sigmund
1961 *The Future of An Illusion.* New York: Doubleday.

Glock, Charles and Robert Bellah (eds.)
1976 *The New Religious Consciousness.* Berkeley: University of California Press.

Glock, Charles and Rodney Stark
1965 *Religion and Society in Tension.* Chicago: Rand-McNally.

Mol, Hans
1976 "Major Correlates of Churchgoing in Canada," in Stewart Crysdale and Les Wheatcroft (eds.). *Religion in Canadian Society.* Toronto: Macmillan.

Stark, Rodney and Charles Glock
1968 *American Piety: The Nature of Religious Commitment.* Berkeley: University of California Press.

38

Social Movements and Social Change in Contemporary Canada*

J. Paul Grayson and Linda M. Grayson

Introduction

One can scarcely walk down major avenues of large Canadian urban centres, or pick up a daily newspaper, without noticing the existence of contemporary social movements in Canadian society. The Hare Krishna, a religious movement, for example, with members clad in unconventional costumes and with shaved heads, actively solicits adherents to the chant of "Hare Krishna." Indeed, their appeal was not long ago expressed in a song written by a former Beatle and reached millions over European and North American airwaves. Further evidence of current social movements is provided by the "Why Not?" slogan of International Women's Year (1975), the current demands of native peoples' groups with respect to treaty lands and rights, movements like the Waffle and the Committee for an Independent Canada that are concerned with "Americanization" of the Canadian economy and culture, and Quebec separatists.

These movements, and many others, have one thing in common. They are consciously attempting to either bring about or resist social change. In fact, the defining characteristic of all social movements anywhere, anytime, is an attempt on the part of a group of people to bring about or resist social change.

The Hare Krishna, for example, can be thought of as attempting to change peoples' attitudes and behaviour with respect to religion and its relationship to everyday activity. The so-called women's liberation movement hopes to introduce sexual equality into major spheres of activity (institutions) in our society, like education, work, and so on. Native peoples' groups are attempting to ensure that Indians and Inuit finally get their rightful due. Likewise, Quebec separatists, in general, feel that the French-speaking sector of our population has not benefited from Confederation; consequently, they are currently concerned with bringing about a dissociation of the province of Quebec from the rest of Canada. Other movements, like the Waffle movement, the Canadian Liberation Movement, and the Committee for an Independent Canada, can be thought of as both resisting social change and at the same time trying to bring it about. All three groups are attempting to *resist* American encroachment in the economy, polity, and in the cultural realm, and at the same time are concerned with *introducing changes* in Canadian institutions that would make these institutions more compatible with Canadian needs.

This short description by no means exhausts the number of social movements evident on the current Canadian scene—movements concerned with preserving the environment, attending to the needs of the underprivileged, homosexual liberation,

---

*From *The Quarterly of Canadian Studies* 4:1, 1975, 50-57, by permission of the author and publisher.

and so on; all qualify under the definition of social movements employed here. The intent, however, is not simply to enumerate the number of contemporary social movements in Canadian society—the reader can do this for himself or herself. Our aim is to show that social movements *per se* have been a permanent feature of twentieth century Canadian society and that they demonstrate dissatisfaction on the part of certain groups of Canadians with the type of society they have encountered. In addition, it will be shown that certain aspects of Canadian society have remained constant sources of irritation for some sectors of society and have therefore spawned or sustained particular social movements. Other social movements have been generated by more immediate and short-term developments in Canadian society. However, despite their persistence and the factors leading to their formation, it will be shown that Canadian social movements, in the twentieth century, have seldom completely realized their objectives.

Requisites of Social Movements

Central to the study of any social movement is the notion that people will only attempt to either promote or resist social change when they perceive that major social institutions like the economy or polity, are not operating as they should. To use a contemporary example, in the late sixties, individuals who founded the Committee for an Independent Canada, came to the conclusion that current government policies with respect to the economy, the mass media, and so on, were not sufficient to prevent an eventual erosion of Canadian sovereignty and complete domination by the United States. Consequently, this group came together in an attempt to both educate the public as to what was happening and to exert pressure on government leaders to introduce legislation to guarantee Canadian autonomy.

Implicit in the activities of this movement, as in all others, is a *goal.* In this particular case, the goal of the movement happens to be the preservation of Canadian autonomy. Also evident is a set of ideas or an *ideology* as to what is happening in society and what action has to be taken in order to achieve the goals of the movement. Again, to use the example of the Committee for an Independent Canada, it can be argued that its ideology contains ideas regarding the fact that Canadian business, universities, magazines, and so on, are increasingly being controlled by non-Canadians, particularly Americans, and that the government should legislate policy to prevent this type of development. In order for a movement to disseminate its ideology it should be clear that it requires forceful and articulate *leaders* and access to *means of communication.* The latter can be provided by the formal media or through less obvious sources, such as an attentive audience that might be provided by a businessmen's luncheon, a trade union meeting, a lecture in a school or university, or a talk to a church or community group. Where movements have prior attachments to groups such as the above, we can think of them as having an *organizational base* through which they can *mobilize* people in support of their goal. An organizational base is one of the most important factors in the success of a social movement.

With respect to the last four mentioned factors, the Committee for an Independent Canada is well endowed. Its leadership includes able individuals like Walter Gordon, a former Liberal Cabinet Minister, and Jack McClelland of the McClelland and Stewart publishing company. The media connections of individuals like McClelland and fellow publisher Mel Hurtig would be an obvious asset in the dissemination of the ideology of the Committee. Equally important are the more informal affiliations of various members with other groups in Canadian society that could serve as avenues for the dissemination of communication. Again, it must be stressed that in order to successfully realize its goals, a movement must have the characteristics noted above.

Having these characteristics, however, does not automatically guarantee success. In any one case of a social movement, sucess or failure results from a plethora of interrelated historical and social contingencies that are too numerous to elaborate here.

Suffice it to say that in general, social movements are most likely to arise in societies characterized by a high degree of what social scientists refer to as *social segmentation.* This term refers to the presence of social divisions in a society whereby it is split into two or more groups (like English and French Canadians), among whom there is little effective communication, few co-operative relationships, and, in many cases, overt hostility. The segments in a segmented society often have cultural characterists of their own, and almost always have a "we group" feeling that social scientists call *group consciousness.* People are aware of belonging to a certain group, and they believe that their personal goals or interests depend upon the attainments of that group as a whole. The more social cleavage that exists in a society, the greater the potential for the emergence of social movements. It stands to reason that where group consciousness exists, people will be aware of their group needs and the degree to which these needs are being met by existing institutions. This point will perhaps be more evident after a discussion of segmentation in Canadian society.

Social Segmentation

At the societal level, long-term lines of cleavage that have continued to give rise to social movements in twentieth century Canada include the English-French cleavage, the East-West division, and the difference between employers and employees in industrial and service establishments. Differences in law *etc.,* regarding the status of females as compared to males have also led to the generation of movements on different occasions. In the years around World War One, Canadian women were actively involved in a movement seeking votes for women. Currently, women are concerned with the introduction of sexual equality in other realms of our society. Despite these women's movements, however, given the definition of social segmentation offered earlier, the notion of "cleavage" between men and women would seem inappropriate in these cases. This is not true with respect to other movements.

Cleavages between English and French Canadians gave rise, in this century, to movements dating from Henri Bourassa and the Nationalist League to René Levesque and the separatists. It must be stressed that earlier movements, like Bourassa's, did not advocate separatism. They were more concerned with, among other things, the degree to which Canadian ties to Britain were becoming too strong. Although a number of French-Canadians have advocated separtism since the time of Confederation, it has only become a mass movement in the last dozen years.

The historical division that has existed between East and West in Canada clearly underlaid the support received by the federal Progressive Party (1921) in the western provinces, the provincial United Farmers of Alberta (1921), the Social Credit movement in Alberta (1935), and, to a certain extent, the Saskatchewan Co-operative Commonwealth Federation (1944). In each case, whether at the federal or provincial level, there was a feeling that the traditional parties – Liberals and/or Conservatives – were not meeting the needs of western farmers. While in recent years there have been no significant new movements spawned in the West, Westerners remain very sensitive to regional issues that affect their lives. In the federal election of 1974, for example, federal policies on oil tariffs and freight rates were important for prairie residents.

In addition to ethnic and geographical cleavages, divisions between employers an employees have continued to have important consequences in recent years. The entire labour movement may be viewed as a response to objective divisions that exist between employers and employees. Within the labour movement, increasing numbers of workers are beginning to believe that their affiliations with American unions do not work to their advantage. Hence, many are "breaking-away" from American unions and forming autonomous Canadian ones. Even more important, as an indication of the degree of division between employers and employees, is the growing militancy of white-collar and blue-collar workers, especially in the province of Quebec. It is obvious, then, that not only do cleavages persist between workers and employers, but also, increasing numbers of workers are questioning the usefulness of affiliation with American unions in achieving their goals. Consequently, there is an impetus to the formation of autonomous Canadian unions.

In addition to movements based on well-defined lines of cleavage, a number of social movements have emerged that have not coincided with major social divisions in Canadian society. Such movements have been generated by immediate short-term Canadian developments. Moreover, in recent years, a new moverment — the native peoples' movement — has emerged that is based on very obvious ethnic divisions in society. Previously, however, despite historical confrontations between Indians and other Canadians, these cleavages did not spawn social movements in the sense that we have been dealing with them.

Examples of movements not based on permanent lines of cleavage are the temperance and youth movements: the former came to full strength in the World War One years and attempted to abolish the sale of liquor; the latter reached its climax in the late sixties and, due to its manifestations in university "sit ins" and so on, is no doubt familiar to many readers. While such movements may appeal to specific groups within society, the memberships of these movements have cut across the significant lines of cleavage in Canadian society. The temperance movement, for example, drafted members from all classes and all regions of Canada. Although a disproportionate number of middle-class adolescents may have been attracted to the youth movement, its scope was generally wide. By way of contrast, the separatist movement in Quebec reflects clear and persistent divisions and appeals to a distinct group, culturally and geographically separated from the rest of the society.

Organizational Bases

As examination of movements that have arisen from persistent cleavages in Canadian society reveals that the organizational base for at least some of the movements has remained the same over a long period of time. For others, it has changed. Early in the century, for example, the plight of the English-Canadian working class was championed by both the emerging trade unions and the churches in the wider community. Both served as organizational bases for workers *vis à vis* management. By the middle twenties, however, the Protestant churches, and their associated "missions" no longer served as an organizational base for labour. In Quebec, though, the Roman Catholic church continued its involvement in the concerns of labour. Today, in all parts of Canada, the primary organizational base for the extension of labour union activities is the trade union itself.

The organizational base of the Quebec nationalist movement has likewise changed. In the early years of the century, the church was prominent in the dissemination and preservation of nationalist ideas regarding the ideal French-Canadian way of life. The church, for example, encouraged the formation of Quebec unions to offset the influence of American "internationals". It also sponsored youth groups and other community activities. In recent years, however, the organizational base of Quebec nationalist movements—especially the separatist movement – has become more secular. The current nationalist movements are grounded in the trade unions, the colleges and universities, and the Parti-Québécois – organizations that are relatively free of religious influence. For some years the provincial Union Nationale Party, under Maurice Duplessis also considered itself a "nationalist" party. In retrospect, however, its affiliations with Anglo-American business, affiliations which contributed to outside control of the province, makes this a somewhat suspect claim.

The organizational base of the current women's movement also differs from that of the World War One suffrage movement. For the latter, there was a great deal of overlap with the social gospel movement that was concerned with using the Protestant churches to develop a humane Christian society, and with the temperance movement. To this extent, some Protestant churches, as well as organizations more specifically oriented to the suffrage cause, were particularly important in the movement. Currently, universities and colleges, and some trade unions, are more important as organizational bases for the women's movement.

With respect to movements based on the East-West cleavage, organizational bases were perhaps more consistent over time than for the other movements we have discussed. Farmers' organizations were most important in disseminating ideologies and in providing needed leadership for the western Progressives, the United Farmers' movements, and the Co-operative Commonwealth Federation. For the Social Credit, the religious organization established by William Aberhart, its foremost exponent, was also important. Given the similarity in the life circumstances of Western farmers, and the institutions needed to cope with their way of life, it is not surprising that the organizational base of Western social movements remained more or less the same for a number of these movements.

Attainment of Goals

It is safe to argue, that with the partial exception of the suffrage movement and co-operative movements in the West, that assisted farmers in the purchase and sale of commodities, no Canadian social movements in the twentieth century has fully achieved all its original goals. The social gospel movement, for example, may have influenced certain legislation, but it did not achieve the "Christian society" that its more optimistic adherents had hoped for. Likewise, although the Progressives were able to influence legislation of special interest to farmers, it is impossible to argue that the movement *per se* was successful: the Progressives themselves were uncertain as to their overall goals. Later in the century the Social Credit movement was able to win office in the province of Alberta but was unable to implement certain [fiscal] policies as they violated the British North America Act.

It is more difficult to assess the success of the Co-operative Commonwealth Federation (C.C.F.), the New Democratic Party (N.D.P.), various trade union movements, and the Quebec nationalist movements. The goals of the C.C.F. and its successors, the N.D.P., have changed over the years. The radical socialist goals of the C.C.F. at its founding convention in 1932 are clearly not those of the N.D.P.. Trade union movements have usually been successful only in a limited sense. The formation of a break-away union may mean the realization of one goal, but it leaves unanswered the question of whether it will attain the long term goals for which it was established, *i.e.,* to better serve the needs of Canadian workers. Labour history in

Canada is full of examples of disappointed trade unionists. Similarly, even if the most recent manifestation of Quebec nationalism – the separatist movement – were to achieve its principle goal, it is difficult to predict the extent to which this success would contribute to the maintenance of French-Canadian cultural and linguistic integrity. That prior nationalist movements accomplished relatively little in this respect is evident. And it is not yet possible to comment on the success of the women's movement, the native peoples' movement, and others which are still in their formative stages.

The Social Legacy

It must be stressed that although movements may have been, in the course of their development, compelled to modify goals – or to abandon them completely as was the case with the temperance movement – they have left their imprint on the Canadian social fabric. In some cases the legacy has taken the form of federal or provincial legislation. In other cases, the legacy is an addition to Canadian culture. Ideas that were anathema before their adoption by a movement became more legitimate to certain sections of the population. For example, many of the arguments of the Social Gospel movement or the early C.C.F. regarding the responsibility of society to provide for its less priviledged members are now accepted by most Canadians. Arguments made by early French-Canadian nationalists are now implicit in recent language policies enacted in Quebec. Most recently as a result of disclosures made by groups such as the Committee for an Independent Canada or the Waffle, regarding the Americanization of our economy and culture. English-Canadian nationalism now enjoys more public approval than it did in the early sixties.

Conclusion

In conclusion, we can say that it is essential that we accord social movements a proper place in the study of Canadian society. They are not mere aberrations. They call attention to the lack of consensus in this society. It cannot be argued that Canada is a country in which all residents share a similar perception regarding the extent to which major social institutions have been realizing desired goals. To the employer, the economy may be working just fine. To the worker, things may not seem quite as satisfactory. Equally important, when Canadians have considered existing institutions inadequate, there has not necessarily been consensus regarding the way in which change should be implemented. Some solutions have been conservative, some radical. In general, at different times and in different parts of the country, groups have reacted in different ways to perceived problems within Canadian society. In the majority of cases, their efforts at effecting change have not yielded anticipated results. Nonetheless, their activities have had important consequences for the changing nature of Canadian society.

PART IV

SOCIOLOGY AND CANADIAN SOCIETY

INTRODUCTION

With Part IV we have come full circle. We began this volume in Part I with articles discussing the broad values, structures, and dilemmas of Canadian society. Then in Part II we examined the social experiences of individuals through the life cycle. In Part III we returned to a broad perspective and considered the major systems and processes which make up the macrostructures of our society. Now in Part IV we attempt to unify the individual and social aspects of experience by focussing on the role of the sociologist and the place his or her discipline has in society as a whole. Ronald Lambert and James Curtis treat one issue which has arisen in recent years through a comparison of the interests and status of sociologists working in Canada who come from American and Canadian backgrounds.

In a concluding article which has become a classic for its insight into the most crucial issue for Canada, that of our dual culture, Guy Rocher summarizes the possibilities and limitations of sociology, both as a science and as an agent of change. He challenges English-speaking sociologists to become involved in the global issues of society, as their francophone counterparts have been, and invites the latter to increase their influence through scholarly work, after the anglophone tradition. He appeals to both for intensified efforts toward bridging the two socio-cultural worlds which comprise our country.

39

Comparison of Canadian and American Sociologists Working in Canada*

Ronald D. Lambert and James Curtis

Recently there has been inquiry into Canada's economically and politically dependent and interdependent relations with the United States.[1] In addition, educators from various disciplines have provided discussions on the sociology of knowledge aspects of national linkages and national differences in the analysis of Canada's cultural interdependence with the U.S. For example, several persons have claimed through the years that despite many similarities there remain theoretically-and empirically-significant differences between how Americans and Canadians regard social reality (Horowitz 1966, Berger 1970, and Lambert 1970. *Cf.* also Lipset 1964, and Truman 1971). Such claims have perhaps received their sharpest and most vigorous expression in recent years in the writings of Mathews and Steele and others who have participated in the debates concerning the extent and function of the "Americanization" of Canadian higher education by this country's heavy recruitment of American citizens to teach and research in universities (Mathews and Steele 1969, Mathews 1972, Repo 1970).

We present some new data of the sort that should serve as a logical starting point in what has been to date a highly speculative and conjectural side of the literature. Our purpose is to examine, in some detail, C.S.A.A. survey data on differences in characteristics and activities of English-Canadian and American sociologists.

Some Conventional Wisdoms and Working Hypotheses

We address ourselves to certain common wisdoms or assumptions (phrased here as working hypotheses) from the debate about the contribution of American academics to Canadian higher education. The assumptions which inform much of this debate, and around which much disagreement occurs, may be summarized in the following way. The initial point of contention is how citizenship may best be operationalized when studying its effect on academic activitiy. In the absence of evidence bearing directly on an academic's citizenship, the claim has been made that country of first degree is an acceptable surrogate within reasonable bounds of error.

---

*Abridged from "Nationality and Professional Activity Correlates Among Social Scientists", *The Canadian Review of Sociology and Anthropology* 10:1 (February) 1973. By permission of the authors and publisher. The survey data presented here were made available by the Canadian Sociology and Anthropology Association. The authors thank Desmond Connor and Richard Salisbury for providing details on the survey and Bruce Kappel and Cathy Atack for processing the data.

It is further argued that higher education in Canada has, historically, been founded on a model quite different from that which prevails in the U.S. Canadian universities, rooted in the British tradition, have been far less likely to regard the Ph.D. as necessary evidence for understanding or wisdom, and have not (at least, until quite recently) built the doctorate firmly into their recruitment and promotion practices. This is quite unlike the U.S. system of higher education which, it is said, has long built the German innovation of the doctorate into its accreditation process. As the Canadian universities shifted their criteria for admission of students in the 1960s to a less exclusive basis, the markedly increased need for teaching staff opened the way for the hiring of numerous academics who were different in professional background and activity characteristics from those previously in the Canadian system. It has also been contended that, in a period of heavy foreign recruiting, Canadian universities have not attracted the most qualified researchers and teachers from the American system.

Many American teachers continue to orient themselves to the labour market in the U.S. and presumably some are merely waiting for the most propitious moment to return to it. This being the case, they tend not to concern themselves with Canadian history or thought, nor to orient themselves to the value system which an evolved in this country. Their continuing orientation to American society (and influential earlier professional socialization) is reflected at the intellectual level by the use of American models of analysis and at the level of citizenship by their reluctance to assume Canadian citizenship. An example of American loyalty to American models is to be found in the application of propositions from the Congressional system to Canadian political institutions or in the overemphasis on individualism in a more collectivist Canadian milieu which concedes the claims for autonomy of several cultural groupings (Ishwaran 1971, 3ff). Citizenship is taken to be a critical variable because it represents one of the strongest testimonies of commitment which an individual can make to a society. Some argue that until American academics renounce what they may regard as the most important citizenship in the world they should not enjoy the full fruits of the Canadian system. Running through the whole Americanization discussion, then, is a conception of stewardship; that the proper exercise of stewardship requires a firm commitment to an assumption of the continuing existence and importance of the Canadian community.

Finally, a further set of assumptions has to do with discrimination against Canadian applicants for academic employment. Americans tend to hire "their own kind". This assertion is offered ordinarily not as the product of machiavellian intent or of conspiratoral design, but as the normal workings of an imperial cultural system. It is said that academics from the U.S. tend to look for new faculty in the higher educational system they know best, the system through which they have moved and whose values they have absorbed. The "old boy" network is an informal system for recruitment which has the effect of discriminating against Canadian graduates who are not party to the peculiar socialization trajectory characteristic of American academics. Discrimination is most likely to occur where the majority of a department is American, where the chairman or senior faculty are American, and where senior university officials are indifferent to the issue of nationality. It is alleged that Canadian academics are not earnestly advertised for, and where they are, there is the suspicion that this is *pro forma* and does not indicate an earnest search for qualified Canadian citizens and Canadian trained persons.

These are a few of the recurring suppositions, briefly stated, in the continuing debate on Americanization. The debate has yielded little research and is least clear on how the heavy U.S. recruitment pattern manifests itself in specific American-

Canadian differences in research and teaching in specific fields. But, presumably, American academics in sociology, for example, would more frequently have completed Ph.D. degree requirements, be more oriented to the discipline in the U.S. (for example, to American professional associations), more frequently apply "American models and perspectives" in their work, perhaps be less likely to do research on Canadian problems and from a "Canadian perspective", have less knowledge of Canadian geographic and cultural areas, and perhaps differ from Canadian sociologists in their areas of specialization and competence, their primary work functions, and other characteristics. All such assertions are acknowledged to be empirical, and should, therefore, be susceptible to empirical study, at least in principle. The exigencies of the data source drawn on in the present discussion leave something to be desired in that information was not afforded on all the issues just noted, nor did the study yield some sensitive pieces of information perhaps more suitable for operationalizing our concepts. But data are available which touch in one way or another on a number of the assertions just described.

Data and Procedures

Our data are taken from the Canadian Sociology and Anthropology Association's (C.S.A.A.) recent survey of persons in the two disciplines in Canada. In order to up-date their 1968 directory of sociologists and anthropologists, the C.S.A.A. mailed questionnaires (in French and English) early in 1970 to lists of names compiled in a procedure similar to that used for the 1968 edition of the directory. Over 1200 questionnaires were sent to those in the previous directory, to other current and past C.S.A.A. members with Canadian addresses (this included all students) and to all other individuals thought to be teaching in sociology or anthropology departments of universities and colleges or working in the two fields in government agencies in this country. One follow-up mailing to non-respondents was carried out and by September 1970, 420 completed questionnaires had been received along with over 200 letters which either did not reach the addressees or were returned by them as not applicable (that is, the recipients were not in sociology or anthropology). The total returns represent a response rate of 41 per cent of all questionnaires delivered (answered or unreturned in two mailings).

The population referred to includes respondents identifying themselves as sociologists who had English as their first language, professional training beyond the B.A. and full-time employment in this country. A total of 154 respondents met these criteria. Our conservative estimate of the response rate for persons in this group is 50 to 55 per cent. From this population we have isolated working samples of anglophone Canadians and Americans who gave information on (1) place of birth, (2) citizenship, and (3) university of their B.A. and highest degree. These provide data for our analysis by "nationality".

We emphasize that the data reported here must be interpreted with some caution, given the response rate. It is likely that individuals who were most interested in C.S.A.A. activities and those wanting to be listed in the forthcoming directory were most likely to reply. No significant selection of respondents by geographical area could be found. There was probably a higher response rate for persons in academic positions and for those who had been in Canada for a while than for persons with other employment and for new arrivals in this country. The same selection factors probably operated in the compilation of the mailing lists. Such selection should work against the hypotheses that we consider here. The case is weighted against American-Canadian differences obtaining when persons least like, and most alienated from, the English-Canadian disciplinary community are less likely to have responded. Any differences that we do find are likely to be more marked in samples more representative of Americans and other new immigrant groups in the discipline.

Findings and Interpretations

Findings are derived from the basic sample of 154 English mother-tongue respondents taken from an overall sample of 213 sociologists who completed questionnaires (anthropologists, 59 French-speaking sociologists, and sociologists with other first languages are excluded from the analysis). It is to this group of 154 sociologists, variously reduced for analytic purposes, that the question of correlates of national status is put. Quite simple, whether being American or being Canadian "makes a difference" will be examined using a number of different operational definitions of national status, and considering an array of characteristics and behaviours which might be affected.

Three sets of characteristics were examined as correlates. The first consists of "background" attributes which are not uniquely pertinent to an interest in the activity of social scientists. Those examined were sex, birthplace, age, citizenship, and second-language skills. "Professional" characteristics, the second descriptive set, included degree status, national origins of first and highest degrees, specialty of highest degree, first and second areas of professional competence, area knowledge, and number of nationality of professional association memberships. These attributes have to do primarily with the professional socialization of social scientists, in terms of the interests and competence presumably conferred by their training. The third set of attributes has to do with the present work setting. These represent still a third set of forces impinging on social scientists, affecting their work, and possibly interacting with other attributes (such as national status). Included among these attributes were location and type of employment, rank, major work function and employment competence, nature, quantity, and funding of research activity, and salary. It should be acknowledged that the three categories of attributes described here are not "clean". There is some obvious overlap or room for disagreement about where a characteristic "properly" belongs. But it should be remembered that what these categories should really tap are three kinds of forces impinging on the social scientist, perhaps manifesting themselves in the attributes indicated.

A number of empirical indicators recommend themselves for the identification of national status. None of the indicators is entirely satisfactory, but each has been used at one time or other in speculation about the (alleged) national determination of academic practice. We examined four indicators, taken singly and in various combinations: country of birth, citizenship, country of first degree, and country of highest degree beyond the bachelors degree. Two "pure types" were also constructed for heuristic purposes. One set of comparisons employs three criteria simultaneously, so that a "pure" Canadian is defined as a person who was born in Canada, is a Canadian citizen, and obtained a Canadian first degree. There were 71 of these "pure" Canadians. In contrast, there were 54 "pure" Americans, people who were born in the U.S., were still American citizens at the time of the study, and obtained their B.A.s in their homeland. A more restrictive set of comparisons added the criterion of national origin of graduate degree (masters or doctorate) to the previous three criteria. This definition of national status yielded 29 Canadians and 51 Americans, the smallest frequencies to be considered here. We also employed a third composite index consisting of two indicators, country of birth and possession of the Ph.D. regardless of its national origin. This index afforded comparisons between 43 Canadians and 49 Americans. Unfortunately, it was not feasible to employ national origin of the doctorate as the fourth criterion for the four-way pure comparisons, because only 14 per cent of Canadians (by birth or citizenship) obtained their doctorates in Canada. The doctorate criterion, then, unlike the other criteria, does not refer to degrees of Canadian origin. We consider it, however, because it allows us to examine what Canadian-American differences, if any, remain when degree status is controlled. If the Ph.D. constitutes a significant set of professionalization experiences, differences between those Canadian born and those American born should diminish in comparisons controlling for highest degree completed, given the approximately three-quarters of Canadians who went to the U.S. for their Ph.D.s.

Background Characteristics

The composition of American sociologists coming to Canada tends overwhelmingly to be male. Americans tend to predominate in the 35 to 39 age category in all comparisons. In all but the comparison between respondents possessing doctorates, Canadians tend to predominate in the youngest age category, up to and including age 29. Among sociologists with a Ph.D., however, the distribution of Canadians and Americans over the two youngest age groups (up to age 34) is very similar. Among the doctorates, in addition to the greater numbers of Americans in the 35-39 age category, Canadians are more likely to be age 40 or above. The figures for Canadians and Americans in this age grouping are 47 and 28 per cent, respectively. It would appear that there is a wave of modest proportions of Americans following somewhat older Canadians. Behind the two oldest categories in which marked disparities exist, Canadians and Americans seem to be present in fairly equal proportions. In addition to the relative equality in the youngest age groups, however, there remains a preponderance of Canadians among those lacking the Ph.D. As the greater number of Canadians still working on their Ph.D.s complete their studies, and so move from the two "pure" columns to the doctorate column, the proportion of younger Canadians in the latter comparisons should increase (barring differential hiring of Americans under age 35 in the near future).

The data suggest that we would be correct more than 95 per cent of the time were we to infer Canadian citizenship from a Canadian B.A. Though less accurate, we would still be correct more than 90 per cent of the time inferring American citizenship from an American B.A. Given the kinds of validity which sociologists ordinarily have to settle for in their measurements, we must be reasonably impressed with the level of accuracy obtained using the bachelors degree as a measurement of citizenship.

Respondents were also asked about any second language skills they might possess. In all cases, Canadians exceed their American colleagues in mastery of French. Approximately 80 per cent and more of any of the Canadian groups offer French, compared to generally less than 50 per cent of the Americans. Though most of the Canadians went to the U.S. for their Ph.D.s, nearly 90 per cent claim French as a second language. If the American sociologists had planned for some time to move to Canada, there is no substantial evidence of language preparation among them; about half offer French. However, about a third of Americans, by any measure of national status, brought non-French second language skills to Canada. No more than 7 per cent of any Canadian group possesses facility with a language other than French as a second language. There are, of course, at least two ways in which one may regard the distribution of language skills among immigrant Americans. On the other hand, Americans can be seen as bringing to Canada a complementary foreign language resource which Canadians evidently do not possess. On the other hand, their relative ignorance of French will not help narrow the gulf between the two Canadian professional communities when both a degree of bilingualism and exchange of ideas may be desirable.

Professional Characteristics

The four-way pure comparisons indicate that 90 per cent of the Americans have completed their doctoral studies, compared to about 20 per cent of the Canadians. It has been proposed that there are two traditions of higher education in conflict in Anglo-Canada, one British, the other American. It is said that the first, or British, tradition does not demand the doctorate as evidence of satisfactory preparation for an academic career. The second, or American tradition, generally requires the Ph.D. for licensing purposes. We note that about 25 per cent of the Canadians in the four-way column report a masters degree, while another 50 per cent are still working on a doctorate. If the latter are interpreted as having opted for the second, or American, tradition; then it appears that Canadians are less well prepared academically than Americans, using the standards of preparation for which they themselves have opted. Consistent with this interpretation, approximately three-quarters of Canadians in possession of the Ph.D. earned it from American institutions. Only 14 per cent were awarded the degree in Canada.

Respondents were asked about the sociological area of specialization of their highest degree (responses for the M.A. degree were coded for those who had not completed their doctoral studies). Consistent with previous findings reported by Harp and Curtis (1971), Americans are marginally (less than 10 per cent difference) more likely to specialize in social psychological approaches, a difference which diminishes when current work activities are considered. In other words, there may be a licensing effect, whereby Americans are more likely to elect social psychology in graduate school. There is the suggestion, too, that Americans may be more specialized in demography and methods combined, at least among the three-way pure sociologists and among those who have completed the Ph.D. Only among the latter is there any indication that Canadian doctorates may be more trained in areas of institutional and social organizational analysis.

A related question concerned the "specialties in which respondents have the most competence." Two tendencies are suggested from the data reporting on first specialties. Methods and demography combined, which some view as highly "scientific", "quantitative", and "empirical", specialties, are favoured more by Americans than Canadians in every comparison. Even among the doctorates, 14 per cent of the Americans claim one of these two areas as their first spectialty, while only 2 per cent of the Canadians, most of whom received their advanced training in the U.S., mentioned one of these two areas. There is also an uneven tendency for Canadians to exceed Americans in claimed competence in institutional and social organizational analysis. The only other difference of note, among respondents defined by national origins of their highest degrees, is in social problems. About 23 per cent of the Canadians and 10 per cent of the Americans cited this speciality.

Strong nationality differences are found for "area knowledge", that is, areas with which persons consider themselves professionally familiar "on the basis of research or residence". As one might expect, Canadians were more likely to mention Canada. However, only half as many Canadians with doctorates as four-criteria Canadians report professional knowledge of Canada. This difference is not explained away by the slightly higher percentage of Canadian Ph.D.s who mention both Canada and the U.S. We are struck by the findings that 41 per cent of Americans with doctorates believe they are professionally knowledgeable about both countries. It is tempting to hypothesize that Americans who come to Canada are (at least initially) relatively devoid of knowledge of this country, but are inclined to assume that they "know" Canada on the basis of certain striking similarities which quickly manifest themselves after they take up residence in Canada. The implications of these differences may touch a particularly sore point among Canadian nationalists. In addition, approximately 10 per cent of three-way and four-way Americans, and Americans with doctorates, report that their knowledge is limited to the U.S. Finally, it is of some interest to observe that about one-quarter of each group of sociologists, regardless of definition of national status, did not answer this question. This failure may reflect a fairly common assumption that sociological knowledge is somehow not culture-or nation-bound. Such an assumption has also been a cause for some concern among Canadian nationalists.

Respondents were also asked about their participation in professional associations. Nearly 20 per cent of the three-way and four-way Americans, and Americans with doctorates, belong exclusively to American professional bodies. For a sizeable proportion of American sociologists, then, their orientation is "continentalist" in nature in that their principal loyalties remain with their native American professional organizations. This finding also contains some significance for the adequacy of the sample of sociologists reported on here. The nearly 20 per cent pure-Americans who reported membership limited to American association would not have been picked up by polling the membership of the C.S.A.A. In other words, the techniques employed by the C.S.A.A. in recruiting the sample has, to this extent, permitted us to reach into that pool of hyper-Americans who would otherwise have been beyond reach. We cannot say, unfortunately, how many more hyper-Americans the C.S.A.A. failed to recruit into the sample. The estimate of 20 per cent may be taken as a lower estimate of these people and provide, to that extent, conservative tests of Canadian-American differences.

Employment Characteristics

American sociologists are to be found in all but two of the Canadian provinces: Prince Edward Island and Manitoba. Among three- and four-way pure sociologists, Americans are twice as prevalent as Canadians in Alberta. Twenty-two per cent of Americans with doctorates are employed in Alberta, compared to 7 per cent of Canadians with doctorates. Canadians are consistently more prevalent in Ontario, a difference which is not diminished among sociologists with doctorates. In the latter case, 65 per cent of the Canadians and 43 per cent of the Americans are located in Ontario. Sociologists continue to be creatures of the public sector. None was totally self-employed or employed in private industry. About 95 per cent of the three- and four-way Americans are employed in academe, compared to 85 per cent of the three-way and 76 per cent of the four-way Canadians. Among the pure types, Canadians are more likely to be employed in research institutes and governmental agencies, settings where perhaps citizenship is a requirement and the doctorate less likely required. National differences disappear among sociologists possessing a Ph.D. In this case, the percentage of Canadians employed in universities increases to 94 per cent, almost identical with the Americans. Americans are disproportionately represented in the associate professor rank, a finding which seems consistent with their greater numbers in the age bracket 35 to 39; and consistent with the greater likelihood of three- and four-way Canadians to be employed outside the academic setting. It is noteworthy that 30 percent of Canadians with doctorates are ranked as full professors. This contrasts with 18 per cent of Americans with doctorates.

Reported earlier were data concerning specialty of highest graduate degree and current specialty competences. Respondents were also asked about the "one specialty most closely related to (their) present principal employment." Canadians are again somewhat more likely to indicate a special interest in institutional and social organization analysis, though this difference fails to occur in comparisons for the graduate degree criterion of national status and for the four-way pure respondents. Fourteen per cent more Canadians with doctorates than Americans report this specialty. Canadians defined by nationality of highest degree and four-way pure Canadians also favour social problems; three times as many, in the latter case. Taken together, these differences may indicate a greater attention on the part of Canadian sociologists to systemic problems in Canadian society.

A number of questions were asked about research activity. About 85 per cent of each of the four three- and four-way pure groups responded that they are presently engaged in research. Interesting differences did emerge, however, when they were asked about the number of projects on which they were designated principal investigator. Both pure type comparisons indicate that Canadians are more likely to be in charge of one project, and Americans more likely to be in charge of two. These differences disappear, however, among sociologists possessing the Ph.D.

Finally, respondents were asked to indicate their professional salary. Fifty-two per cent of the three-way and 69 per cent of the four-way Canadians reported salaries ranging up to and including $12,000. These figures compare with 24 per cent of the Americans in each comparison. Americans were much more likely to fall in the $13,000 to $18,000 bracket. These differences diminish among those with the Ph.D., at least among the lower income bracket. Forty-four per cent of the Canadians and 63 per cent of the Americans fall into the 'middle' income bracket. The difference between the two groups of Ph.D.s above $18,000 is only 5 per cent, but this time favouring the Canadians. Seven per cent of the Canadian Ph.D.s failed to answer this question, while none of the Americans failed to do so.

Conclusions

The following composite picture may be constructed from the observed differences between Canadian and American respondents. American sociologists are more likely to be male, somewhat older, of higher rank (though not disproportionately full professors or chairmen), and better financially remunerated than Canadians. They are more likely to have completed their graduate training to the level of the doctorate, are more tied into the academic work setting, and are more likely to be engaged in research as principal investigators of several projects. Although there are few differences in reports on areas of professional specialization, Americans are somewhat more often trained in social psychology; they may be more inclined to favour the heavily quantitative specialties of demography and methodology; and they are less likely to cite expertise in areas of institutional and social organizational analysis and social problems. Some proportion of Americans remain oriented professionally to the U.S. in their exclusively American associational memberships. They are more likely than Canadians to feel professionally knowledgeable about both Canada and the United States. Two of the 57 American-born sociologists had assumed Canadian citizenship at the time of the study. At least 13 of the 57 were eligible for citizenship at that time, judging from information given on time of entry into this country.

The above is a profile drawn mainly from the two national groups by varying definitions. However, since the Canadian and American groups differ considerably in some aspects of professional background, it is difficult to attribute observed differences as effects of nationality. Therefore, without diminishing the validity or importance of that profile, it is of interest to consider the pattern of findings controlling for level of formal training. The picture is changed in the following ways when only sociologists reporting a Ph.D. are compared.

The distribution of background characteristics changes to the extent that the sex difference is reduced and the proportions of Canadians and Americans in the two youngest age categories (less than age 35) are equalized. Presumably the barriers of sex to the attainment of the Ph.D. exist in more or less the same degree in both countries. Thus, the remaining 12 per cent difference among doctorates might be attributable to a disproportionate tendency for male academics to emigrate from the U.S. or for men to be offered jobs in Canada. Americans continue to be over-represented in the over-40 age group. Differences in command of French as a second language remain relatively unchanged. This probably reflects a greater tendency on the part of Canadians to obtain some familiarity with that language in high school.

Most of the differences in professional characteristics remain relatively unchanged. In particular, differences having to do with area knowledge, first and second specialties, and professional associational memberships persist. The differing tendencies of four-way respondents to belong exclusively to Canadian associations is reduced, however. This appears to be due to an increase in the proportion of Canadians who, once they have obtained their advanced training (mainly) in the U.S., expand their association affiliations to include non-Canadian ones.

There are three notable and perhaps related disappearances of national differences in terms of employment characteristics. Discrepancies in non-academic employment, non-professorial positions, and interest in social problems are lost in comparisons for those with doctorates. In every case, however, the changes are due to the tendency for Canadians to come to resemble their American colleagues. An interesting addition of a difference between Canadian and American Ph.D.s occurs in the greater proportion of Canadians who hold the rank of full professor. This finding is consistent with the greater proportion of Canadians over age 40 which appeared when the doctorate control was introduced for analysis of background characteristics. For the most part, the other differences already identified for the pure comparisons persist when level of professional preparation is controlled.

Our results favour the tentative conclusion that there are some differences of interest and of possible consequence between Canadian and American sociologists currently practising in Canada. Controlling the effect of doctoral training leaves these differences intact, suggesting that they are not to be easily discounted. In fact, the pattern of differences and what happens to them when the control is introduced is suggestive. Differences seem to persist primarily where the activity of Americans is most relevant to their roles in the American professional community. Those differences which disappear seem to be due largely to a kind of homogenization imposed by the doctorate, so that Canadians with high degrees come to resemble Americans in several areas of activity relevant to the career trajectory of Ph.D. holders.

We are now able to return to the folk-assumptions mentioned earlier. Practically speaking, country of first degre appears to be a reasonable substitute for data on citizenship where the latter are missing. There is little evidence for a British *cum* Canadian as opposed to an American professional socialization career. If there was once such a model, it is scarcely in evidence today. Half of the four-way pure Canadians were embarked on studies beyond the M.A.; another 20 per cent of that group already possess Ph.D.s; and three-quarters of Canadian-born doctorates obtained that degree from American institutions. About 25 per cent of the four-way pure Canadians reported a masters degree, perhaps signifying that they had terminated their studies at that level.

The data afford no evidence to permit a test of the assumption that "our" Americans are somehow less competent than "their" Americans. There are grounds to believe that a sizeable proportion of Americans continue to orient themselves to the United States professionally. This is suggested by their continuing exclusive membership in American professional associations, area knowledge, and citizenship status. The kind of data considered here do not permit us to affirm one way or the other in the matter of discrimination in favour of Americans in hiring. But the data concerning degree status should give pause to the occasional allegation that less qualified predoctorate Americans are given preference since only 10 per cent of the four-way Americans reported they were still engaged in doctoral studies. Nevertheless, caution is recommended, because of the distinct possibility that pre-doctoral Americans may be under-represented in the sample. One has the impression from the pattern of the present data of three waves of sociologists: the first, senior Canadians, whose modest numbers permitted them to represent sociology in a slowly expanding system of higher education; the second, a wave of Americans who migrated during a burst in student enrolments in Canadian instititutions in the 1960s; and the third, a wave of Canadians and Americans, many of the former returning from American graduate schools, with the two groups competing for vacancies in a system whose growth is slowing down.

We may conclude with the overworked observation that further research in the area is called for. This is an apt conclusion, however, granted the theoretical and practical import attending the issue of "Americanization" of Canadian intellectual life. Theoretically, the Canadian case will provide an intriguing chapter in the sociological history of the social sciences and an example in the phenomenon of "intellectual imperialism". Practically, there are potential policy implications flowing from any substantive demonstration of the essential Mathews and Steele thesis. The findings reported here offer both some reason for caution in sometimes over-drawn statements of the thesis, and they may provide some basis for concern in respect to the nature of American participation in Canadian higher education. The findings suggest further questions. One has to do with the possible homogenizing effect of doctoral training, especially with regard to career expectancies and perhaps even in terms of sex and age composition of the discipline. Also still at issue is the capacity of the discipline to deal with peculiarly Canadian concerns and interests from Canadian value positions. Another related question has to do with "area knowledge", that is, the relevance of national boundaries for a truly comparative or international sociology. It is our impression that sociologists have too long shunned this question and have yet to offer convincing evidence that knowledge of a given industrialized metropolitan nation can gratuitously be extrapolated in most of its specifics and in its implied value assumptions to other less metropolitan nations. These are questions which our own data are unsuitable to answer, though they may contribute to the clarification of these issues.

Note

1. Important and influential in this regard have been works by Safarian (1966), Watkins (1968), Grant (1969), and Levitt (1970) among others.

References

Berger C.
1970 *The Sense of Power.* Toronto: University of Toronto Press.

Blishen, B.R.
1970 "Social Class and Opportunity in Canada", *Canadian Review of Sociology and Anthropology* 7: 110-127.

Clark, S.D.
1950 "The Canadian Community", in G.W. Brown, ed., *Canada.* Toronto: University of Toronto Press.

Connor, D.M. and J.E. Curtis
1970 *Directory of Sociologists and Anthropologists in Canada.* Montreal: C.S.A.A.

Grant, G.
1969 *Technology and Empire.* Toronto: House of Anansi.

Harp J. and J. Curtis
1971 "Linguistic Communities and Sociology: Data from the Canadian Case", in J. Gallagher and R. Lambert eds., *Social Process and Institution.* Toronto: Holt, Rinehart and Winston.

Horowitz, G.
1966 "Conservatism, Liberalism, and Socialism in Canada: An Interpretation", *Canadian Journal of Economics and Political Science* 32: 144-171.

Hughes, E.C.
1964 "A Sociologist's View", in J.S. Dickey, ed., *The United States and Canada.* Englewood Cliffs, N.J.: Prentice-Hall.

Ishwaran, K.
1971 "The Canadian Family: An Overview", in K. Ishwaran, ed., *The Canadian Family.* Toronto: Holt, Rinehart and Winston.

Lambert, W.E.
1970 "What are They Like, These Canadians? A Social Psychological Analysis", *The Canadian Psychologist* 11: 313-333.

Levitt, K.
1970 *Silent Surrender.* Toronto: Macmillan.

Lipset, S.M.
1964 "Canada and the United States—A Comparative View", *Canadian Review of Sociology and Anthropology* 1: 179-184.

Mathews, R.
1972 "Charles D.G. Roberts and the Destruction of the Canadian Imagination", *Journal of Canadian Fiction* 1:47-56.

Mathews, R. and J. Steele
1969 *The Struggle for Canadian Universities.* Toronto: New Press.

Naegele, K.
1964 "Canadian Society: Some Reflections", in B.R. Blishen *et al.*, eds., *Canadian Society: Sociological Perspectives.* Toronto: Macmillian.

Porter, J.
1965 *The Vertical Mosaic.* Toronto: University of Toronto Press.

Repo, M.
1970 *I'm a Ph.D. Who Needs the Ph.D.?* Toronto: Graduate Students' Union, University of Toronto.

Safarian, A.E.
1965 "Foreign Ownership and Control of Canadian Industry", in A. Rotstein, ed., *The Prospect of Change.* Toronto: McGraw-Hill.

Truman, T.
1971 "A Critique of S.M. Lipset's Article, Value Differences, Absolute or Relative: the English-Speaking Democracies", *Canadian Journal of Political Science* 4: 497-525.

Watkins, M.
1968 "Foreign Ownership and the Structure of Canadian Industry", Report of the Task Force on the Structure of Canadian Industry. Ottawa: Queen's Printer.

Wrong, D.
1950 *American and Canadian Viewpoints.* Washington: American Council on Education.

40

The Future of Sociology in Canada*

Guy Rocher

Three problems are likely, in my opinion, to be of great consequence to the future of sociology in Canada as well as in many other countries. These problems are: the relationship between sociology and values; the role of the sociologist in social change; and the practice of sociology in a bicultural and bilingual environment.

Sociology and Values in French Canada

From the vantage point of the sociology of knowledge, French Canada is an extremely interesting case for the study of the relationships between the practice of sociology and the values of a given society. Consequently, I begin with a brief analysis of this case in order to raise general considerations, which could be relevant to a discussion of the future of Canadian sociology.

One could contend that the debate which arose several years ago about the presence and role of values in sociological theory and research is much more emotional among English-language persons because in the English-Protestant tradition there have been sharp distinctions between science and religion and between social philosophy and sociological research. This last distinction seems so well established that one would not have thought it could be questioned. It can be understood, then, that the champions of a critical and radical sociology, who denounce the distinction between science and values as the screen for a moral and intellectual hypocrisy, are instigating a profound disturbance in a world of thought which seemed solidly established.

In Catholic circles, where the distinction between social thought and social science has never been so sharply drawn, the process has been quite different. Catholicism retained from the middles ages a unitary conception of life and the universe which resists differentiating fully among various sectors of reality and areas of activity. For instance, Catholics everywhere maintain private, denominational institutions (hospitals, schools, economic institutions, voluntary associations) which serve to transmit religious values into every aspect of the life of members of the community. Thus, for the faithful of the church, there is one universe where they find themselves among their own kind, and where all their activities can maintain an internal coherence. Again, this global attitude leads them to expect, more or less consciously, that science will support and confirm religious doctrine rather than

*Abstracted from a paper presented to the plenary session on "The Future of Sociology", annual meeting of the Canadian Sociology and Anthropology Association, Winnipeg, May, 1970. Translated from the French by Judith Beattie and Pierre Roberge. By permission of the author and the Association.

call it into question and that social science will be a branch of a social philosophy. These expectations about social science explain why the question of the relations between sociology and values is much more recent in Catholic than in Protestant society. In any case, the debate has a long tradition in French Canada, while it started in English Canada only a short time ago.

When sociology, defined as a scientific discipline, made its first appearance in higher education in Quebec during the 1930s, it encountered the resistance which was typical at that time in Catholic circles. It was not resistance to sociology as such, but to sociology of a positivist and Durkheimian inspiration. What was objected to was less scientific orientation than an anti-religious philosophy. In Catholic eyes, sociology was tied to that school of thought which maintained that religion had no foundation in the objective reality of the supernatural world, and that God was nothing more than a symbol of humanity or society. Sociology then, carried the stigma of the positivist and atheistic philosophy of Auguste Comte and Emile Durkheim.

As an alternative, a sociology founded on what was called "sound Christian doctrine" was proposed. It was hoped that a sociology inspired by a conception of man, life, and ultimate values, founded on Christian theology and philosophy, could be developed. Traces of this current of thought are evident in French Canada. For example, the first social science faculties, created at the Université de Montréal in the 1920s by Monsieur Edouard Montpetit and at the Université Laval in the 1930s by Père Georges - Henri Lévesque, were directly inspired by similar institutions in Catholic faculties in France. In both it was proposed to teach and develop social science in the light and spirit of Christian doctrine. This Christian social science hopefully would form an effective counter-balance to atheistic and positivist social science and finally would open the way to the creation of a new Christian civilization.

It is curious to note that, in this context, economics did not seem to pose as great a problem as sociology. Sociology was perceived to touch more intimately on the fundamental values of society and to contribute to secularization, while economics left, or made a pretense of leaving, values outside their field of exploration. Sociology, then, became the target of those who mistrusted the invasion of positivist social sciences in Quebec. In fact, as a result of the Second World War in 1939, Père Lévesque's early students at the Université Laval, who wanted to pursue advanced studies in social science, could not go to French Catholic faculties. They had to turn to the American universities and, as an indication of an evolution already in progress, they did not generally enrol in the Catholic universities but rather at Chicago, Harvard, Columbia, or Cornell. On their return, they posed in new terms the problem of the relations between social science and social philosophy.

In the ensuing debate one must accord a special place to the role played by Père Lévesque.[1] Speaking both as theologian and as social science expert, he maintained that the complementary nature of social science and social philosophy was founded on a clear distinction between the two. He proposed that what he called normative thought and positive research should not be confused. They follow pathways and proceed along courses that are totally different. Normative thought has its source in philosophic reflection, and its course is essentially deductive; positive research obeys the canons of science and its course is principally inductive. Normative thought could sustain itself on the fruit of scientific research, to the extent that the latter had proceeded independent of the preestablished norms and values of the researcher. Père Lévesque required that philosophy and theology not be replaced by science, which allowed him to keep his distance from Comtian positivism, but he demanded also that theology and philosophy respect the peculiar course of science, which permitted him to keep his distance from those who proclaimed a Catholic sociology.

On this point, as on many others, Père Lévesque was the butt of various attacks and trials, which echoed and sometimes ended in Rome. He was accused of destroying the foundations of the Christian social doctrine. His right to teach in a Catholic university was questioned. And it was feared that he was corrupting a generation of young people.

It was under Père Lévesque's auspices that sociology made its appearance in Quebec higher education. His students discovered and circulated the work of the French-Canadian sociologist, Léon Gérin, who for forty years had carried on research in Quebec, following the school of LePlay, without once questioning the relations between sociology and religion. Université Laval, a Catholic institution, directed exclusively by members of the clergy, became one of the primary university centres teaching sociology and conducting research in the 1940s. The opposition of traditional Catholic groups was weakened as they were unable to obtain from Rome or from Quebec bishops an explicit condemnation of positivist social science.

The presence of social science, and notably of sociology, in Quebec promoted the evolution of social meanings and social structures since the end of World War II. As Jean-Charles Falardeau (1964: 57-58) wrote:

> By its very existence and activities, social science has contributed to the disintegration of what had been universal in the French-Canadian collective conscience; through the research and works that it has inspired it has broadcast some of the factors and some of the results of the process of diversification and pluralization of our social universe. It also, by the rigorous and continuous use of positivist discussion appropriate to it, stimulated a rationality, that is, at the same time, a secularization of thought about social realities. This evolution is evident not only at the level of university teaching; it can be observed also, to a lesser degree it is true, in many fields of thought. In the Quebec of 1964, problems are no longer posed in the same way as twenty or thirty years ago. Whether it concerns commercial, political, scholarly, or religious questions, there are few who do not now aim at being "objective" in presenting the problem.

It is striking and paradoxical to see sociology criticized and called once again into question today precisely because of what has been called its "false objectivity". The latter is said to have served until now to cover up essentially conservative ideologies, so that sociology and sociologists have been closely allied with the dominant classes and elites in modern industrial societies. Sociologists even find themselves accused of being among the main props of power, suspected of supplying powerful instruments of cultural and social manipulation. Sociologists are invited to rethink sociological theory and their own role in a new way in the face of this prostitution to power. It is not easy to disengage the main threads of the new perspective proposed to sociology, but it seems to me that it is principally dominated by the idea that society can be seen as a power struggle, a game of force, and that sociology cannot remain outside this power play but must abandon a pseudo-objectivity and squarely take a position against the forces of exploitation and domination.

It would be futile on my part to attempt here to treat in depth the epistemological and ethical problem posed to sociology in various but allied terms, by the champions of Catholic sociology and those of radical sociology. I would simply like to present three brief considerations.

First, the example from French Canada that we have used as a special case sheds light on the relativity of relations between sociology and values. A few years ago in Quebec, sociology was considered a dangerous innovation questioning the primacy of

Christian philosophic thought. At the same time sociology and sociologists were suspected of being accomplices in social revolution, egalitarian ideology, and reforms of a socialist inspiration. Today one more frequently hears the opposite complaint: sociology is suspected of being inspired by a conservative ideology, and sociologists of being supporters of the *status quo* and of the ruling power. We can draw some important conclusions from this paradox. It indicates one aspect of the relations between sociology and values that has been illuminated until now; namely the role of the circumstances and context in which these relations take place. Let changes be brought about in a society, let new ideologies appear there, and sociology which up until then was defined as dangerously revolutionary would suddenly appear to be terribly conservative. This conditioning by circumstances is an important source of insecurity in sociology as a scientific discipline and is a permanent basis for tensions between sociologists with respect to the nature and functions of sociological theory and research.

In the second place, questions raised by critical sociology do not lack relevance. They shed light on a number of ambiguities in sociology as a scientific discipline and in the status of the sociologists in modern industrial society. But I find that this critical and radical sociology has not been critical enough of its own ideological positions. For it, too, rests on *a priori* assumptions. It implicitly invokes an objectivity which it too easily suggests is its monopoly. And it is founded on implicit conceptions of man, of the meaning of life, and of history. Finally, it also entertains relations with other powers.

One of the most important social functions of sociology is to debunk and demystify all ideologies and powers, whether they be of the right or the left, tied to or excluded from power and authority. If "official" sociology has let itself be taken in through its relations with those in control of power and is too submissive to dominant ideologies, critical sociology for its part has not kept distant enough from Marxist ideology, of which it has finally become the all too ready interpreter and to which it confers a scientific authority which one may call into question. The influence of critical sociology would be much greater if it were as lucid and critical toward Marxist ideologies as it is toward established sociology.

Lastly, the problem of relations between sociology and values is far from being definitely settled; we will live with this problem for a long time. If this is the case it is because, as I have already explained elsewhere (Rocher 1972) sociology is a science-in-situation, that is, it is immersed in history and is part of what it studies, from which it always tries by every means to disengage itself in order to take a view at once objective and subjective, external to the object and internal to subject-objects. This is what I call the "historicism of sociology", and this historicism poses a greater problem in the case of sociology than in other social sciences because our science studies in a more immediate way even the world of values. Sociology cannot, like economics, put the world of values between brackets or, like psychology, accept it as an external given fact. On the contrary, sociology examines this world of values precisely in order to comprehend its structure, evolution, and relations with other sectors of society or of the social system. Consequently, the sociologist is always in the peculiar position of questioning himself and seeing himself questioned by others on the values from which he perceives, understands, and assesses the values of the society of which he is a member, or of another society in which he is interested.

Again, the object of the study of sociology is an unfinished object. Societies always continue to invent their history, and this is an unlimited process which is an essential part of the social system, whether it be conceived of as a system of action or, in the Marxian manner, as a system of conflict. The invention and pursuit of goals form a vital part of the texture of the social system. Sociology, then, searches endlessly to understand an object which always, in part, is of the future. The new knowledge which the sociologist brings to contemporary society is another element to feed the historic action of collectivities. Thus, the sociologist contributes indirectly to nourish a history which he tries at the same time to understand. Thus, the relations of sociology and values are characterized by perpetual tension between knowledge and historic action, objectivity and subjectivity, participation by the subject-object in life and detachment from the object of study.

Sociologists: Agents of Social Change

The preceding considerations, based on a brief history of sociology in French Canada, pose the problem of the role of the sociologist in social change. Whether he wants to or not and whether he is conscious of it or not, the sociologist is increasingly an agent of historical change, and, in the future, he is destined to play an even more active and important role. Parsons (1968: 101) writes: "Our science may well be destined to play a major role, not only in its primary task of understanding the social and cultural world we live in as object of its investigations, but, in ways which cannot be foreseen, in actually shaping the world."

The sociologist may fill this social function in different ways, according to his personality, his conception of his calling, and also according to the expectations directed at the sociologist to which he responds more or less consciously. One should apply an interaction model because for the sociologist, society is not only his object of study, it is also an *alter* on which he imposes or perceives expectations, which he attempts to reply to or tries to change. These expectations crystallize around three principal modes of social interaction.

Through his research, first of all, the sociologist produces an ever less approximate knowledge of social reality, and this knowledge is capable of being used to manipulate situations, to exercise power or influence. In post-industrial society, knowledge is a new form of "capital", or it may be considered analogous to capital. It is one of the factors of production and of the motivations of historic action (Touraine 1969). Consequently, if he does not himself use his knowledge for direct action, the sociologist brings to those who possess or influence authority an element of power. In this way the sociologist acquires influence which he can decide to use immediately, put in reserve, or save.

More and more, a second form of social intervention is sought by the sociologist: his empirical analysis of the global society or of large social institutions. Talcott Parsons noted several years ago that American sociologists were not in the habit of making general analyses which might exceed the rigorous limits imposed by the canons of scientific research. He emphasized that C. Wright Mills was one exception and one could add that Parsons (1957) was himself another exception. A growing number of sociologists are attempting this type of global analysis, even on contentions and hot issues such as revolution, student movements, poverty, and war.

There is a third type of intervention. Through his activity in bureaucratic organizations, public and private, in voluntary associations, social movements, or by various forms of participation in public debates, the sociologist is destined to perform an occasionally ambiguous action but one whose impact is certain: an action in which he finds himself playing at the same time the role of expert, consultant, and intellectual leader. In the sense in which Bales (1950) uses these expressions, the sociologist is called on to furnish information, to provide orientation, and to answer questions. The type of knowledge which he furnishes has the effect of setting apart, of making his contribution conspicuous, and consequently, of imputing his leadership with a greater weight of influence than is the case for other participants.

If one looks at the Canadian situation in the light of the above thoughts a clear distinction may be drawn between the Francophone and the Anglophone parts of the discipline. In the Anglophone setting, it is more through their research that sociologists have provided leadership whether for the benefit of governments, certain businesses, or for different associations. In the Francophone setting, on the other hand, it is more through their global analysis and their direct participation in political life and public debates that sociologists have had an influence. Imitating, perhaps, their colleagues in France, but also responding to the particular expectations of their setting, Quebec sociologists have been led or invited to take a position on the evolution and options of their national community; they participated in different organizations which were instrumental in what is called, more or less justifiably, the "quiet revolution" in Quebec. In general, the equivalent of such direct action is not found in English-speaking Canada.

In looking into the future, one can speculate on how Canadian sociologists will act as agents of social change. I do not question whether or not they will be agents of social change; I am convinced they will be. In any case, for me it is an essential working hypothesis. It remains, therefore, to know in what way this action will be carried out.

I hope that in the future Anglophone sociologists exercise more influence by their global analysis and by their participation in movements and organizations. Conversely, I hope that Francophone sociologists will exert more influence, not only inside but also outside Quebec, through the quality, quantity, and extent of their research. The former are not, perhaps, well enough known as citizens able to intervene in historical action as well as to study it. The latter have not sufficiently established themselves as researchers, able to clarify the questions and options on which they make pronouncements as citizens.

Sociology in a Bilingual and Bicultural Context

If the sociologist can be an agent of social change, then we must also ask whether we can seriously hope that sociology will be able to cross the language barrier which divides this country. Will Canadian sociologists of today be ready to communicate in French and English, to participate in common sessions, to undertake joint research projects, to be aware of each other's research, to cite one another, independently of the language in which they write?

It must be recognized that among many differences, Canadian sociology separates clearly into two major categories: French-language sociology and English-language sociology. They are almost airtight entities. Two almost impermeable worlds live side by side in almost total, mutual ignorance.

Except for a few individuals who try to communicate with the other world, usually in a sporadic and rather superficial way, the vast majority of Canadian sociologists stick closely to their own linguistic world. An examination of the program of the annual meetings of the Canadian Sociology and Anthropology Association shows barely a symbolic presence of French-language sociology. One or two Francophone professors from Quebec are invited to preside over a session and one or two others present addresses. This participation bears no relation to the number of French-language sociologists in Quebec, the research they pursue, and what they could contribute.

In the *Canadian Review of Sociology and Anthropology* French-language sociology is almost wholly absent. In the total issues to date, does one dare count the number of articles signed by Canadian sociologists of the French language? Instead, Quebec Francophone sociologists have created their own journals, *Recherches Sociographiques* and *Sociologie et Société*.

Doubtless, the Canadian Association has always tried to have French-language sociologists represented in the executive committee and all the subcommittees. An alternating principle has also been practised in the presidency of the Association; a French-language president always succeeds an English-language president. But that takes on the appearance of a symbolic gesture, for it is striking that the real activity of the society, that is, the scientific activity itself, contradicts the official image that the Association tries to present.

Actually, the problem is beyond us. This description of Canadian sociology corresponds closely to the Canadian duality. To construct a sociology of science and knowledge here, one must recognize that the linguistic division within Canadian sociology reflects the "two solitudes" which continue to live together in the immense Canadian country. One could not say that there are two schools of sociology; rather there are two socio-cultural worlds of sociology. Between these two worlds, many attitudes are different; the writers, ideas, and problems are different; moreover, each world has its social structure, its scale of prestige, its sanctions and rewards, its controls and fellowships, its channels of communication, its rites and its ceremonies. So there are two social systems as well as two cultures of Canadian sociology.

The insularity of these two systems is reinforced by the fact that each can find an international market of ideas so that no strong urge is felt to lower the barriers. Of course, the linguistic barrier within Canada is just the continuation of the wall which, in the modern world, separates two sociologies, one of the English language, the other of the French. Nearly all sociology texts used in American colleges and universities are notable for the total exclusion of French sociology. Durkheim generally is given a primary place but, by all appearances, only the part of Durkheim's work which has been translated into English is referred to, ignoring everything not yet translated. In the eyes of the student who studies these texts sociology is reduced to American sociology. Very few American sociologists know anything of contemporary French sociology. Even the few French sociologists who have been translated into English, such as Raymond Aron and Georges Friedmann, are little known and rarely cited.

From the point of view of French-language sociology, the conclusions are scarcely more satisfactory. Certainly, French-language sociology cannot ignore English-language sociology to the same degree that the latter ignores French-language sociology. The weight of the American sociological production is too over-powering to allow total isolation. In spite of that, it is astonishing to observe how much of English-language sociology is only partially known by French-language sociologists and how little it is cited. If one looks more closely, one realizes that French sociologists almost always refer to the same American sociologists that they in some ways have adopted, and, who by chance it turns out, have had a part of their work translated into French. This is the case, for example, with C. Wright Mills, who is still very popular in France, with Robert K. Merton who is known mainly through the translation of a few of his articles, and with Talcott Parsons who is prudently alluded to without being quoted, referring always to his first works of 1940 or 1950 which are known thanks to a French resumé made by François Bourricault (Parsons 1955).

Coexistence of French and English cultures in Canada has not been strongly enough established yet to serve as the footings for a bridge between French-language and English-language sociologies. What should have been originally a case of interpenetration more closely resembles, in the end, a divorce, supposing there was ever a marriage! The question now is whether sociology will be able to transcend the linguistic and cultural barriers that divide Canada and form a real scientific community. In the shrinking of the planet that we hear so much about, especially with the advent of mass communications, science has been an important factor in bringing people together across many frontiers.

The social sciences, however, have not yet succeeded in creating an international scientific community. In my opinion, sociology in this regard lags behind other disciplines such as linguistics, economics, psychology, and anthropology.

That sociology is slower than the other social science disciplines in creating a scientific community may be an indication of a lack of maturity. But one can also see in this a science which, by its very nature, is attached more than any other to a specific socio-cultural setting, of which it is at least partially a reflection of a mirror. Besides, for my part, I cannot help but see in these two socio-cultural worlds of sociology the confirmation of the "two nation theory" which the Canadian government and most Canadian people persist in denying. Beyond regional differences, beyond divisions of the Canadian population according to ethnic origin, religion, class, and life-style, there is this cleavage between two worlds of language and thought. And this cleavage is so deep that it separates two cultures and two societies. Apart from political considerations and the uncertainty which hovers over the future of Canada and Quebec, in the interest of the future of sociology and, perhaps, in the interest of international understanding, Canadian sociologists of the French and English tongues must make a special effort to break down or at least lower the wall of silence which separates them. I propose for this purpose:

(1) That Canadian sociologists begin by recognizing clearly and without finding fault the separation which in fact isolates their two linguistic communities;

(2) That all Canadian sociologists come to read fluently in the other official language. It is not enough to know how to read the other language. The necessary motivation and interest must also be found to make meaningful contact with the work done by colleagues of the other language;

(3) That common and comparative research be undertaken by teams of French-language and English-language sociologists. Research of this nature would profit from the different perspectives brought by the sociologists of the two socio-cultural worlds;

(4) Sociologists of both languages should search out fields of social concern and action in which to make a common front, for example, against war, against pollution, against segregation, for the freedom of scientific research, and for the reform of university structures.

Conclusion

Jean-Paul Sartre (1963: 167-168) writes: "within this living universe, man occupies, *for us,* a privileged place. First, because he is able to be historical; that is, he can continually define himself by his own *praxis* by means of changes suffered or provoked and their internalization, and then by the very surpassing of the internalized relations. Second, because he is characterized as the *existent (being) which we are.* In this case, the questioner finds himself to be precisely the questioned." Pursuing Sartre's idea, sociology occupies a privileged place for us. As a science of subject-objects, it is also historical because it is worked out, structured, and modified by the particular *praxis* which characterizes it, that is, the work done on reality, by which this reality is changed at the same time that it is understood. As a result, it is not surprising that the sociologist, who thinks of himself first as a questioner, sees himself suddenly as the questioned: those who submit to his questions feel the need to know where he himself stands, and to ask him to state who he is and where he places himself.

Perhaps in the past we have had too great a tendency to ignore the interaction between the sociologist-researcher and the society of which he was a part or those that he studied. In my opinion that is the main aspect of the status of the sociologist and of sociology which will be changed in the future. Tomorrow's sociologist will have to be very sensitive to society's expectations of him, to the modifications he wants to or must bring to these expectations, to the changes that his activity as researcher and other connected activities can bring to society, and to the consequences which could result from his research. Consequently, tomorrow's sociologist will have to be very clear and constantly critical of the values which inspire him, motivate him, and influence his research and interventions.

The future will require of the sociologist a more acute perception of the exigencies of his intervention in society and of the epistemological and ethical consequences of this intervention for him as well as for society.

Note

1. An indefatigable builder, Père Georges-Henri Lévesque unfortunately wrote very little. It is mainly by his initiatives, his public conferences, and even more by the teaching that he conducted for twenty-five years that he exercised a profound influence in Quebec.

References

Bales, Robert
1950 *Interaction Process Analysis.* Cambridge: Addison-Wesley.

Falardeau, Jean-Charles
1964 *L'essor des Sciences sociales au Canada français.* Québec: Ministère des Affaires culturelles. 57-58.

Parson, Talcott
1955 *Eléments pour une sociologie de l'action.* Translated with an introduction by François Bourricault. Paris: Plon.

1957 "The Distribution of Power in American Society", *World Politics* 10 (October) –: 123-143.

1968 "Evaluation and Objectivity in Social Science: An Interpretation of Max Weber's Contributions", in *Sociological Theory and Modern Society.* New York: Free Press. 101.

Rocher, Guy
1972 *A General Introduction to Sociology: A Theoretical Perspective.* Translated from the French by Peta Sheriff. Toronto: Macmillan Co. of Canada.

Sartre, Jean-Paul
1960 *Critique de la raison dialectique.* Paris: Gallimard. 103-104.

Touraine, Alain
1969 *La société post-industrielle.* Paris: Denoël.